MW00818189

Chinese History and Culture

VOLUME 1

MASTERS OF CHINESE STUDIES

Chinese History and Culture

❖

VOLUME 1

SIXTH CENTURY B.C.E. TO
SEVENTEENTH CENTURY

Ying-shih Yü

With the editorial assistance of

Josephine Chiu-Duke and Michael S. Duke

COLUMBIA UNIVERSITY PRESS

NEW YORK

Columbia University Press wishes to express its appreciation for assistance
given by the Chiang Ching-kuo Foundation for International Scholarly Exchange
and Council for Cultural Affairs in the publication of this book.

Columbia University Press
Publishers Since 1893
New York   Chichester, West Sussex
cup.columbia.edu

Library of Congress Cataloging-in-Publication Data

Names: Yü, Ying-shih, author.
Title: Chinese history and culture : sixth century B.C.E. to seventeenth century /
Ying-shih Yü; with the editorial assistance of Josephine Chiu-Duke and Michael S. Duke.
Description: New York : Columbia University Press, 2016. | Series: Masters of
Chinese studies | Includes bibliographical references and index.
Identifiers: LCCN 2015040772 (print) | LCCN 2015049874 (ebook) | ISBN 9780231178587
(vol. 1 : cloth : alk. paper) | ISBN 9780231542012 (electronic) | ISBN 9780231178600
(vol. 2 : cloth : alk. paper) | ISBN 9780231542005 (electronic : vol. 2)
Subjects: LCSH: China—History. | China—Civilization.
Classification: LCC DS736 .Y867 2016 (print) | LCC DS736 (ebook) | DDC 951—dc23
LC record available at https://lccn.loc.gov/2015040772

Columbia University Press books are printed on permanent and durable acid-free paper.
Printed in the United States of America

COVER DESIGN: CHANG JAE LEE

Dedicated to Monica Shu-ping Chen Yü

CONTENTS

AUTHOR'S PREFACE

Collected in these two volumes are essays published during the past five decades, on various aspects of Chinese cultural and intellectual traditions and their modern transformations. Written on different occasions and in different times, they are scattered in a great variety of publications, some obscure and out of print. However, since all of them possess, to a greater or lesser degree, a unity of theme regarding the Chinese tradition in its historical changes, I consider it desirable to make them accessible to the general reading public by way of reprinting in a collected form.

It is my extraordinary fortune that two of my highly esteemed colleagues, Professors Josephine Chiu-Duke and Michael S. Duke, agreed to serve as editors of my two volumes. They have edited each and every one of my essays with meticulous and diligent care, resulting in the elimination of a great deal of imperfections in the original versions. I am particularly grateful to both of them for providing, in the "Editorial Note," a lucid account of my views discussed in these essays. It is also remarkable that instead of taking my views in the English essays as a self-contained category, they have made every effort to understand them in the context of my published oeuvre as a whole and specifically emphasized their interrelatedness to my Chinese writings.

In this connection, a word may be said about my bilingual historical writings. Generally speaking, since the 1970s, it has been an established practice on my part to write book-length monographical studies in Chinese and present these findings in a more concise format in English as articles in journals, periodicals, or symposia. The difference is more than between a longer and a shorter version, however; it also has something to do with two different ways of historical representation. Full documentation is often emphasized in Chinese historical writings—traditional and modern—as a positive feature. As a result, direct quotation of original sources has been established as a common historical method. On the other hand, I deeply appreciate the Western style of argumentation in historical studies that, more often than not, refrains from extensive quotation of sources. Thus, in writing bilingually, I often secretly wished that my two versions might somehow strengthen and supplement, as well as complement, each other.

I wish to take this opportunity to express my deep gratitude to Professor David Der-wei Wang for his kindness and, indeed, patience in including these two volumes of mine in a series of books he has specifically designed for Columbia University Press. I also wish to thank all of the various presses for generously granting their respective permissions to reprint my essays, Mr. Jeff S. Heller of Princeton's East Asian Studies Department for conveying materials back and forth to the editors, and Ms. Su Hue Kim for her years of preparing my many drafts into typed form.

I dedicate these two volumes to my wife, Monica Shu-ping Chen Yü, whose abiding love and support have sustained me throughout my career.

Ying-shih Yü
September 2, 2015

EDITORIAL NOTE

Professor Ying-shih Yü is a leading scholar in the field of Chinese studies. He was awarded the John W. Kluge Prize in 2006 for achievement in the Study of Humanity, and in September 2014, he also received the first Tang Prize international award in Sinology. As an eminent historian and a conscientious intellectual, Professor Yü has dedicated more than sixty years of his life to the study of Chinese history, thought, politics, and culture,[1] crossing "many disciplines, time periods and issues, examining in a profound way major questions and deeper truths about human nature."[2] Through this comprehensive and integrative lifetime study, Professor Yü has published some thirty books, forty-one monographs, and more than five hundred articles and essays.[3] At the same time, he has redefined the Chinese intellectual and cultural tradition, excavated the meaning of and instilled new life into that tradition, and, above all, has persistently put his intellectual convictions into practice without worrying about acting "against the current." Such actions are evident in his scholarly articles analyzing, for example, the problematic nature of a "new wave of Chinese nationalism," and of "the study of history" based on Chinese official orthodoxy of "the Marxist-Stalinist five-stage formulation."[4] They are also apparent in his "outspoken criticism" of the Chinese government's suppression of the peaceful 1989 Tiananmen demonstration, his support for many scholars, young students, and liberal-minded intellectuals who left China after 1989, and his ongoing regular commentary on China's social, intellectual, and political phenomena for Radio Free Asia.[5]

Professor Yü exerted himself to complete a major revision of the article on Wang Yangming (1472–1529) in late 2014, but his health has prevented him from writing an introduction to these two volumes, and his deep modesty would also not permit us to use his address on receiving the Kluge Prize and his Tang Prize in Sinology acceptance speech as a comprehensive introduction. Thus, at the risk of not doing full justice to the breadth and depth of his creative contribution to the field of Chinese studies, we feel it necessary to offer a few initial observations on the primary concerns that have emerged in his research on China's cultural and intellectual tradition, while also explaining the structure of this book of essays.

Since Professor Yü left China in the beginning of 1950 and enrolled in the first class of the then newly established New Asia College in Hong Kong, two questions have always dominated his intellectual consciousness: As an ancient civilization, what was China's essential value system that had sustained the life of its culture through ages of tumultuous political changes? Furthermore, would this system survive its modern revolutionary overhaul and find its way to secure itself as a culture that has historically displayed "a great deal of overlapping consensus in basic values" with the mainstream of Western culture?[6] In a way, these two questions are tied to his overall concern about where China would go after the radical transformation of its 1949 revolution. The rich body of his decades of research that started during his college days in Hong Kong and continued throughout his academic life at the universities of Michigan, Harvard, Yale, and Princeton, and especially the work he carried out during the time after he retired from Princeton in 2001, reflects his examinations of and responses to these key questions.

In the summer of 1971, when he revisited his alma mater and took his first trip to the major research institutes in Japan and Taipei, Professor Yü discovered that almost all of the China specialists there had never read his book or articles published in English. At the time, he began to think that if he wanted to play a role in bringing about meaningful communication between the Western and East Asian intellectual communities, he probably should try to make his research available in the Chinese-language world. Later, between 1973 and 1975, he took a leave from Harvard and returned to Hong Kong to serve as president of the New Asia College, and concurrently as the pro-vice-chancellor of the Chinese University of Hong Kong. Due to the demands of his daily work, Chinese became the most natural and reasonable medium for his writing. It was then that he decided he would resume writing large and detailed research articles and books in Chinese, and would present similar topics on a smaller scale and in a more concise format in English.[7]

As a result of that decision, his works in English constitute only a small part of his vast publication record, but the thirty-three scholarly articles collected in these two volumes nevertheless represent the essence of his fundamental concerns about and systematic interpretations of Chinese culture and history ranging over a time span of more than two thousand years. They demonstrate how his extraordinary knowledge about a wide variety of primary sources enabled him to investigate the crucial changes in Chinese cultural and intellectual traditions during the major transitions of China's history. They also show how he has always explored and approached a series of questions and issues centering on his concerns from both diachronic and synchronic perspectives while never failing to compare important aspects of Chinese culture with relevant historical phenomena in Western or other Asian cultures. More important, they reveal the complex changes crisscrossing with the unbroken line of the foundational values that have connected China's past and present, and probably its future as well. We should also note that several of Professor Yü's Chinese books, especially his magnum opus on the historical world of Zhu Xi (1130–1200) 朱熹 的歷史世界: 宋代士大夫政治文化的研究 (*Zhu Xi de lishi shijie: Songdai shidafu zhengzhi wenhua de yanjiu* [The Historical World of Zhu Xi: A Study of the Political Culture of Song Intellectuals]) (Taipei: Yunchen, 2003; Beijing: Sanlian, 2011), and his most recent breakthrough study, 論天人之際: 中國古代思想起源 試探 (*Lun tianren zhiji: Zhongguo gudai sixiang qiyuan shi tan* [Between Heaven and Man: An Exploration of the Origin of Ancient Chinese Thought]) (Taipei: Linking Publishing, 2014), have developed from some of the articles presented here.[8]

The earliest article in these two volumes was published in 1965 and the most recent one was completed near the end of 2014. For the present volumes, these articles are not arranged by their publication dates, but rather in chronological sequence by Chinese dynasties and with respect to their interconnected nature. In this manner, the central theme of continuity and transformation that links these articles together in relation to Professor Yü's overall investigation and interpretation of Chinese civilization may unfold in accordance with its own inner logic.

In his 2006 John W. Kluge Prize acceptance speech, Professor Yü asserts, "the *Dao*, or the Way, and history constitute the inside and outside of Chinese civilization."[9] Indeed, unraveling the unique dynamics between Chinese intellectuals' discourse on the *Dao* 道 and their criticism of contemporary reality in different periods of time throughout China's historical trajectory has always been ingrained in Professor Yü's intellectual efforts. This endeavor is explicitly manifest in his earlier studies of the tension-fraught ruler-minister relationship embedded in Chinese political tradition. These studies had a strong, "wide and enduring" influence, and like many of his later works, have since become classic essays for students of Chinese history and culture in Taiwan, Hong Kong, and even in China after Mao.[10] Professor Yü's endeavor is equally discernible in his nonpareil study of the post-1949 inner landscape of the late historian Chen Yinque (1890–1969).[11] Its impact has been and continues to be far-reaching. It caused quite a bit of consternation to the Chinese official academic leadership, and gave rise to an extensive trend of studying Chen Yinque's works among different generations of Chinese scholars during the past three decades.[12]

Likewise, one can also detect Professor Yü's efforts in the above-mentioned trailblazing masterpieces on Zhu Xi and *Between Heaven and Man* centering on the formation and development of China's reflexive system of knowledge and thought on the *Dao*, or if one may, the transcendentally rooted set of moral principles for a symbolized ideal world order, throughout what Karl Jaspers called the "Axial Age."

We believe that the articles made available here on the intellectual and cultural changes from ancient times down to the late nineteenth century can help illustrate just exactly how and why the *Dao*, according to Professor Yü, became the defining characteristic of Chinese culture during the "Axial Age," and how it was upheld by some of the finest Chinese intellectuals throughout traditional Chinese history as a critical standard in their striving for an ideal world order vis-à-vis their harsh political reality. These works should also serve to reveal just how the *Dao* was reformulated, expanded, defended, and preserved by these intellectuals generation after generation so that the lifeline of Chinese culture could continue on even though the individual political regimes perished in the flow of Chinese history. It is the *Dao*, then, as Professor Yü argues, that ultimately sustained these intellectuals to keep their faith in their cultural tradition and to take a stand during the dark moments of Chinese history.

The noble efforts of these intellectuals undoubtedly command our respect, but on a closer reading of Professor Yü's work, one may find that they actually impel us further to see how the Chinese intellectual striving for the realization of the *Dao* never actually secured an environment in which their struggles would no longer be vulnerable to the abuses of arbitrary power. Thus, one will also find that this tragic side of the Chinese intellectual tradition comprises another underlying theme that is embodied in Professor Yü's articles and is even more prominent and prevalent in his comprehensive lifelong project on that tradition. In this light, one may be justified in viewing this portrayal of the parallel yet crisscrossing relations between these two themes not only as a major vehicle to illustrate the crucial continuity and changes that surfaced in China's own tradition, but also as reflecting the critical tension between the *daotong* 道統, or the tradition of the *Dao*, and the *zhengtong* 政統, or the tradition of political power, throughout Chinese history. This tension is clearly notable in Professor Yü's perceptive analysis of Wang Yangming's "reorientation" and his Confucian efforts to enlighten the ordinary Chinese people, specifically including the traditionally denigrated merchant class, so that they could realize the *Dao* in their daily lives. Although this "reorientation" was an innovative reinterpretation and expansion of the *Dao*, the tragic side of the Confucian intellectual tradition remained unchanged.

It is from that perspective, we believe, that Professor Yü has, since 1951, and distinctly since the 1989 Tiananmen demonstrations, persistently discussed why it is necessary for China to resume its nineteenth-century path toward the establishment of constitutional democracy so that the century-long intellectual struggle for a free, just, and civilized China will have a real chance to take root in Chinese soil. Discussion of these issues, with China's tortuous path to modernity as a presupposed historical background, is one of the main focuses of the second volume.

On one reading, these two volumes can be viewed as a complex tapestry into which all of the articles weave together the penetrative explorations and insights that shape Professor Yü's portrait of China as a coherent whole. On the other hand, they can also be seen as two independent units, with one focusing on the continuities and ruptures in China's traditional intellectual and cultural history, and one concentrating on the transformations of Chinese traditions in modern times. As Professor Yü's articles illustrate, however, tradition always finds its way back into modernity in a dialectically entangled manner, whether in Chinese intellectuals' narrative search to delineate China's place in the modern world, or in their new conceptualization of how to write Chinese history.

One perhaps may question how Han Chinese ideas of the afterlife and their food or elite seating orders, or even the fictional world of China's greatest Qing dynasty novel, *Honglou meng* (Dream of the Red Chamber), are related to the central themes of Professor Yü's two volumes. When one reads these articles, one is likely to marvel that China's age-old practice of linking the seating order with a person's seniority, or his or her social, political, and economic status, can, in fact, trace its roots at least to as early as the third century B.C.E., but it is even more pertinent to note that this seemingly innocuous cultural practice of seating orders actually played a decisive role in the subsequent development of Chinese imperial history in its initial stage. In short, a certain cultural custom may be just as important as historical contingency in shaping the direction of one's destiny, be it for an individual, or for an empire.

At the same time, the way that Han Chinese transformed their indigenous culinary arts by creatively incorporating foreign foods and cooking methods into their own cuisine certainly demonstrates the adaptability, as well as the tenacity, of Chinese tradition. The enduring nature of Chinese tradition is also obvious in Professor Yü's article on the afterlife. It shows that the Han Chinese perception of the worlds between the living and the dead were quite similar to the earlier Chinese conceptualization of the relationship between the transcendental or the ideal world symbolized by the *Dao* and the earthly reality in the sense that the two worlds were never perceived as two mutually exclusive realms, nor were they seen as two identical ones either. Furthermore, it also shows that the Han Chinese concepts of life and death were an "extension" of their integrative worldview of the human, Heaven, and Earth as comprising an inseparable unity that was sustained by the ever-so-close yet ever-so-distant *Dao*.[13]

The same thing can be said about the article on the *Dream of the Red Chamber* in volume 2. The difference is that Professor Yü's discussion of the two interconnected worlds in this Qing novel, the ideal world and the world of reality, and the irreversible collapse of the ideal world did not evoke too much of a lament for this lost paradise. It did, however, lead us to place this article after the one that gives an intricate synopsis of Qing Confucianism as a whole. The collapse of a fictional world thus serves as a symbolic parallel to the final disintegration of the traditional Chinese imperial order and foreshadows the coming "radicalization of China in the twentieth century."

All these articles were originally selected by Professor Yü and sent to Ms. Leslie Kriesel at Columbia University Press some years ago. They were intended for an important project on distinguished scholars of Chinese studies organized by Professor David Der-wei Wang. Ms. Kriesel had them formatted as Word files, proofread them, and sent them to Professor Yü for review, but he was unable to attend to them due to his medical condition. In October 2014, when Professor Wang asked us whether we could help complete the editorial work, we had no doubt that this meaningful project should be completed.

During the complicated process of reformatting, many passages and sections in the original articles, as well as all the Chinese characters, were lost. We have, where possible, retrieved the original English versions in books or from journals, located Chinese originals of essays translated into English and Chinese translations of English versions, restored the missing passages and sections, and changed all of the Wade-Giles romanizations of Chinese names and terms to contemporary Pinyin romanization.[14] In the process, Chinese characters were reentered and additional Chinese characters were supplied for clarity in several essays.

Meanwhile, English translations of most Chinese book titles mentioned in the text (but not in the endnotes) are also provided. At first mention in the main text, for example, we have *Yijing* 易經 (Classic of Changes), but only *Yijing* in the endnotes. Our other editorial tasks included standardizing the endnoting format, entering new notes for several published speeches that were not endnoted, adding notes to citations not referenced in some places, and shortening all notes by means of abbreviations of frequently cited titles. Names well known in the English-speaking world or used by Chinese scholars active in English are given in their familiar way, such as Chiang Kai-shek, Fung Yu-lan, Hu Shih, Lien-sheng Yang, Sun Yat-sen, and Ying-shih Yü. In Chinese references, however, such names are given as Feng Youlan, Hu Shi, Yang Liansheng, Yü Ying-shih, etc. As an example: Ying-shih Yü, *Trade and Expansion in Han China* (Berkeley: University of California Press, 1967), but Yü Ying-shih 余英時, *Lishi yu sixiang* 歷史與思想 (Taipei: Lianjing, 1976).

With Professor Yü's permission, we made a few minor changes in some of the Chinese-to-English translations and changed a small number of other wordings. Professor Yü's two scholarly prize acceptance speeches mentioned above are in an appendix per his insistence, but we suggest that one read them as an introduction to his multifaceted and multilayered but integrated narrative world. In these speeches, one finds that while his narratives explore the unique characteristics of Chinese culture, they simultaneously illustrate how this uniqueness is inherently universal in its honoring of "common humanity and human dignity" as the core values of Chinese culture.

To understand Professor Yü's lifetime contribution to the Chinese intellectual and cultural tradition, one of course has to become familiar with his entire oeuvre, above all, his extensive publications in Chinese. However, editing these articles has made us increasingly aware of why and how Professor Yü has been "hailed as the greatest Chinese intellectual historian of his generation," "a paradigm for [Chinese] humanism," and "the epitome of a traditional Chinese *shi*-intellectual"[15] who never gives up his efforts to ameliorate social ills and improve public well-being, whether through words or actions. That various "Yü Ying-shih fan clubs" (*Yü Ying-shih fensi tuan* 余英時粉絲團) have emerged among the general reading public in the Chinese-language world no doubt provides further endorsement of the above tributes to him, and they may just further serve to indicate the unusual nature of both his work and his actions.[16] These "fans" among the reading public most likely also hold what they learn from Professor Yü's works to represent what the Chinese cultural and intellectual tradition genuinely stands for, and thus would likely agree that his contribution is not only significant for the field of Chinese studies but is also relevant to anyone who believes in the shared values of the best humane traditions, be they Chinese or Western, in today's world community.

In conclusion to this note, we would like to thank Professor David Der-wei Wang for arranging this editorial work. At Columbia University Press, we also thank Ms. Leslie Kriesel for all her preliminary work on these essays, editorial assistant Jonathan Fiedler, and the final copyeditors, Sue Sakai and John Donohue of Westchester Publishing Services. Further thanks are due to Professor Chin-shing Huang, director of the Institute of History and Philology of the Academia Sinica in Taiwan, and his able assistant Ms. Yaling Lee for providing Professor Yü's revised and expanded article on Wang Yangming. We also wish to express our gratitude to Dr. Jiu-jung Lo of the Institute of Modern History of the Academia Sinica and Ms. Liu Jing of the Asian Library at the University of British Columbia, who helped us locate information on old journal articles.

Last, but most important, we want to thank Professor Yü for trusting us with this worthy project and for assisting us throughout. Our deep gratitude goes equally to Mrs. Monica Yü, or Chen Shuping, for her encouragement and support. Without Professor Yü's warm and kind understanding, which helped our work proceed smoothly, and his providing us with some hard-to-find documents, we could not possibly have brought this project to its completion within the intended time limit. It goes without saying that any errors that may have occurred in the process are ours alone.

Josephine Chiu-Duke and Michael S. Duke

NOTES

1. On June 20, 2014, when the Tang Prize Award Committee announced that Professor Yü was the winner, their statement acknowledged Professor Yü's work in these areas. See http://www.tang-prize.org/ENG/Publish.aspx?CNID=300.

2. These are the remarks Librarian of Congress Dr. James H. Billington made on Professor Yü's research. See Library of Congress, http://www.loc.gov/today/pr/2006/06–214.html.

3. Part of Professor Yü's bibliography can be found on the Academia Sinica website at http://www2.ihp.sinica.edu.tw/en/staffProfilePrint.php?TM=3&M=1&uid=84. For a more complete bibliography, see "Yü Ying-shih jiaoshou zhuzuo mulu" 余英時教授著作目錄, compiled by Che Hsing-chien 車行健, in *Wenhua yu lishi de zhuisuo: Yü Ying-shih jiaoshou bazhi shouqing lunwen ji* 文化與歷史的追索: 余英時教授八秩壽慶論文集, ed. Hoyt Tillman (Taipei: Lianjing, 2009), 917–960.

4. These articles are included in the second volume of this book.

5. Dr. Billington's remarks on awarding Professor Yü the Kluge Prize noted his support for China's democracy movement. See Library of Congress, http://www.loc.gov/today/pr/2006/06-214.html. Professor Yü's critical discussion of the 1989 suppression can be found in his *Lishi renwu yu wenhua weiji* 歷史人物與文化危機 (Taipei: Dongda tushu, 1997), esp. pp. 151–173. Professor Yü's regular commentary is available at http://www.rfa.org/mandarin/.

6. See "Address of Yü Ying-shih on the Occasion of Receiving the John W. Kluge Prize at the Library of Congress," December 5, 2006, at http://www.loc.gov/today/pr/2006/06-A07.html. For more details, see Chen Zhi 陳致, *Wo zou guo de lu: Yü Ying-shih fangtan lu* 我走過的路: 余英時訪談錄 (Taipei: Lianjing, 2012), 3–15, esp. p. 11.

7. See how Professor Yü recently discussed this decision in his "*Lishi yu sixiang* sanshiba nian" 《歷史與思想》三十八年, published by *Pingguo ribao* 蘋果日報 on April 27, 2014. See also http://hk.apple.nextmedia.com/supplement/apple/art/20140427/18701478.

8. See the articles "Between the Heavenly and the Human" and "Morality and Knowledge in Zhu Xi's Philosophical System" in volume 1.

9. "Address of Yü Ying-shih," p. 2.

10. These studies include "Fanzhi lun yu Zhongguo zhengzhi chuantong—lun Ru, Dao, Fa sanjia zhengzhi sixiang de fenye yu huiliu" 反智論與中國政治傳統—論儒, 道, 法三家政治思想的分野與匯流 and "'Jun zun chen bei' xia de junquan yu xiangquan—'Fanzhi lun yu Zhongguo zhengzhi chuantong' yulun" '君尊臣卑' 下的君權與相權—'反智論與中國政治傳統' 餘論. They are included in Yü Ying-shih, *Lishi yu sixiang* 歷史與思想 (Taipei: Lianjing, 1976), 1–75. For their influence, see his discussion of *Lishi yu sixiang* in "*Lishi yu sixiang* sanshiba nian." See also how Chen Zhengguo 陳正國 and Lu Yang 陸揚 discuss the impact of Professor Yü's work on his readers in Taiwan and China, respectively, in Chen's "Taiwan shixue zhong de Yü Ying-shih shenying" 台灣史學中的余英時身影, *Dangdai* 當代, no. 232 (December 1, 2006): 34–51, esp. p. 39, and Lu's article in the same issue of *Dangdai*, "Cong ta-nei dao tawai—Tan Yü Ying-shih xiansheng de renwenxue yanjiu yu Keluge jiang de yiyi" 從塔內到塔外—-談余英時先生的人文學研究與克魯格獎的意義, 52–59, esp. pp. 54–57.

11. See Yü Ying-shih, *Chen Yinque wannian shiwen shizheng* 陳寅恪晚年詩文釋證 (Taipei: Shibao wenhua, 1984), the expanded edition published in 1986 by the same publisher, and the third expanded edition published in 2004 (Taipei: Dongda tushu). The second new edition was also published by Dongda tushu in 2011.

12. The impact of Professor Yü's study of Chen Yinque itself had a complex development. The consternation of the Chinese official academic leadership occurred twice and lasted quite a while each time. The first refers to the reaction of the then official leadership to Professor Yü's 1958 study of Chen Yinque's work on *Zaisheng yuan* 再生緣, an eighteenth-century *Tanci* ballad (*Tanci* is a popular form of singing accompanied by instrumental music), and it involved the top security official Kang Sheng 康生 and scholars such as Guo Moruo 郭沫若, serving at the time as the head of the Chinese Academy of Sciences. The second refers to Chinese official responses to a series of Professor Yü's articles discussing Chen Yinque's inner landscape published in 1983 and 1984 (later reworked into his 1984 book on Chen). This time, Hu Qiaomu 胡喬木, the head of the Chinese Academy of Social Sciences was involved. For this development, see Yü Ying-shih, "Chen Yinque yanjiu de fansi he zhanwang" 陳寅恪研究的反思和展望, in *Chen Yinque yanjiu* 陳寅恪研究, ed. Zhou Yan 周言 (Beijing: Jiuzhou chubanshe, 2013), 1–19, esp. pp. 4–6, 11–15; see also Zhang Qiuhui 張求會, "*Xia Nai riji* li de 'Chen Yinque huati'" 《夏鼐日記》里的 "陳寅恪話題," and Xu Qingquan 徐慶全, "Chen Yinque *Lun Zaisheng yuan* chuban fengbo" 陳寅恪《論再生緣》出版風波. Both articles are included in Zhou Yan's book; see 48–61, esp. pp. 57–58, and 195–208, esp. pp. 205–207. These three articles and some other essays in Zhou Yan's book, including Zhou Yan's own editorial comments (4–5), all demonstrate the impact of Professor Yü's works on the rise of this extensive trend.

13. For further explanation of this view, see Yü Ying-shih, "Cong jiazhi xitong kan Zhongguo wenhua de xiandai yiyi" 從價值系統看中國文化的現代意義, in his *Zhongguo sixiang chuantong de xiandai quanshi* 中國思想傳統的現代詮釋 (Taipei: Lianjing, 1987), 46–48.

14. *Renwen yu lixing de Zhongguo* 人文與理性的中國, by Yü Ying-shih, ed. and trans. (from English to Chinese) Cheng Nensheng 程嫩生, Luo Qun 羅群, and He Jun 何俊 (Taipei: Lianjing, 2008), was very useful for us in completing the endnotes in spite of the few errors and omissions it contained.

15. The first citation is provided in Dr. Billington's remarks on awarding Professor Yü the Kluge Prize in 2006 and also quoted by the Tang Prize Award Committee made in late June 2014. See http://www.tang-prize.org/ENG/Publish.aspx?CNID=300.

  The second quote is from the title of a scholarly article by Li Xianyu 李顯裕, "Renwen zhuyi de dianfan—Yü Ying-shih de xueshu jingshen chutan" 人文主義的典範—余英時的學術精神初探, *Tongshi jiaoyu yu jingcha xueshu yantaohui lunwenji* 通識教育與警察學術研討會論文集 (2007): 131–137. See http://gec.cpu.edu.tw/ezfiles/91/1091/img/388/196741845.pdf.

  The third citation is by the late Professor Anthony C. Yü (Yu Guofan 余國藩, 1938–2015) in his "Yü Ying-shih jiaoshou de xueshu chengjiu yu shixue gongxian" 余英時教授的學術成就與史學貢獻, *Dangdai*, no. 232 (2006): 29–33, esp. p. 33. It was also cited by one of the members of the Tang Prize Award Committee. See "Yü Ying-shih huo ban

'Tang jiang' Hanxue jiang" 余英時獲頒 '唐獎' 漢學獎, Radio Free Asia (Mandarin branch), June 20, 2014, http://www.rfa.org/mandarin/yataibaodao/gangtai/al-06202014095122 .html.

Hao Chang (Zhang Hao 張灝) made a similar comment describing Professor Yü as a "public intellectual" for the Hong Kong television documentary series on "Jiechu Huaren 傑出華人," or "outstanding Chinese." The program on Professor Yü was produced by the late Mr. Weng Zhiyu (1968–2015) 翁志羽 and aired on January 6, 2008. See http://app1.rthk.org.hk/php/tvarchivecatalog/episode.php?progid=554&tvcat=2.

16. It is interesting to note that *fensi*, the Chinese word for fan (supporter, admirer, etc.), is a kind of noodle made from meng bean flour. It sticks together in a ball (*tuan*) and is difficult to separate; thus, *fensi tuan* also symbolizes the solidarity of such fans. We have found from 16,800 to 85,200 results when we googled "Yü Ying-shih fensi tuan" in Chinese several times in July 2015.

ABBREVIATIONS

AM	*Asia Major*
BPZ	*Baopuzi* 抱朴子
CASS	Chinese Academy of Social Science 中國社會科學院
CBETA	Chinese Buddhist Electronic Text Association
Chan, *SB*	Wing-tsit Chan, *A Source Book in Chinese Philosophy* (Princeton: Princeton University Press, 1963)
CSJC	*Congshu jicheng* 叢書集成
CUHK	Chinese University of Hong Kong 香港中文大學
DNP	*Dai Dongyuan xiansheng nianpu* 戴東原先生年譜
DWJ	*Dai Zhen wenji* 戴震文集
GXCK	*Guoxue congkan* 國學叢刊
GXJB	*Guoxue jiben congshu jianbian* 國學基本叢書簡編
GXJBCS	*Guoxue jiben congshu* 國學基本叢書
HHS	*Hou Hanshu* 後漢書
HJAS	*Harvard Journal of Asiatic Studies*
HKU	Hong Kong University 香港大學
HS	*Hanshu* 漢書

JAOS	*Journal of the American Oriental Society*
JAS	*Journal of Asian Studies*
JTS	*Jiu Tangshu* 舊唐書
KG	*Kao Gu* 考古
LHJJ	*Lunheng jijie* 論衡集解
LSCQJS	*Lüshi chunqiu jishi* 呂氏春秋集釋
LSYJ	*Lishi yanjiu* 歷史研究
MRXA	*Mingru xue-an* 明儒學案
MZS	*Mengzi ziyi shuzheng* 孟子字義疏證
QHHW	*Quan Hou Han wen* 全後漢文
QSW	*Quan shanggu sandai Qin Han Sanguo Liuchao wen* 全上古三代秦漢三國六朝文
QTW	*Quan Tang wen* 全唐文
SBBY	Sibu beiyao 四部備要
SBCK	Sibu congkan 四部叢刊
SBE	Max Müller, ed., *The Sacred Books of the East* (Oxford, UK: Clarendon Press, 1879–1910)
SGZ	*Sanguo zhi* 三國志
Shangwu	Commercial Press
SJ	*Shiji* 史記
SKQS	Siku quanshu 四庫全書
SMZY	*Sanmin zhuyi* 三民主義
SYXA	*Song-Yuan xue-an* 宋元學案
TP	*T'oung P'ao*
TPJHJ	*Taipingjing hejiao* 太平經合校
WSTY	*Wenshi tongyi* 文史通義
WW	*Wenwu* 文物
WWCKZL	*Wenwu cankao ziliao* 文物參考資料
WYWK	Wanyou wenku 萬有文庫
XTS	*Xin Tangshu* 新唐書
Zhonghua	Zhonghua shuju 中華書局
ZJS	*Zhuangzi jishi* 莊子集釋
ZJSNXS	*Zhonguo jin sanbai nian xueshu shi* 中國近三百年學術史
ZLQS	*Zongli quanshu* (孫中山) 總理全書
ZSCS	*Zhongshan congshu* (孫) 中山叢書
ZYL	*Zhuzi yulei* 朱子語類
ZYYY	*Zhongyang yanjiuyuan lishi yuyan yanjiusuo jikan* 中央研究院歷史語言研究所集刊
ZZ	*Zuozhuan* 左傳
ZZTJ	*Zizhi tongjian* 資治通鑑

CHRONOLOGY OF DYNASTIES

Xia	2000?–1600? B.C.E.
Shang	1600?–1027? B.C.E.
Zhou	1027?–256 B.C.E.
Western	1027?–771 B.C.E.
Eastern	771–256 B.C.E.
Spring and Autumn Period	771–481 B.C.E.
Warring States Period	481–221 B.C.E.
Qin	221–206 B.C.E.
Former (Western) Han	202 B.C.E.–8 C.E.
Xin (Wang Mang)	9–23 C.E.
Later (Eastern) Han	25–220 C.E.
Three Kingdoms	220–280
Wei	220–265
Shu	221–263
Wu	222–280
Western Jin	265–316
Sixteen Kingdoms	301–439
North-South Dynasties	317–589
Eastern Jin	317–420
Northern (Tuoba) Wei	386–535
Sui	581–618

Tang	618–907
Five Dynasties and Ten Kingdoms	907–960
Song	960–1127
Northern	960–1127
Southern	1127–1276
Mongol Yuan	1271–1368
Ming	1368–1644
Manchu Qing	1636–1911
Republican Era	1911–present

Chinese History and Culture

VOLUME 1

1. Between the Heavenly and the Human

The idea of the "unity of Heaven and man" (*tian ren heyi* 天人合一) has been generally regarded as a feature uniquely characteristic of Chinese religious and philosophical imagination. The *tian-ren* polarity as a category of thinking was already essential to Chinese philosophical analysis in classical antiquity. Thus, in the *Zhuangzi*, the question of where the fine line is to be drawn between "the heavenly" and "the human" is often asked. Zhuangzi's emphasis on the notion of *tian* was later sharply criticized by Xunzi (ca. 312–230 B.C.E.) as being blinded by the heavenly and insensitive to the human. For his own part, however, Xunzi also insisted that true knowledge of the world must begin with a clear recognition of the distinction between the two realms.

By the second century B.C.E. at the latest, the *tian-ren* category had been firmly established as a basic way of thinking due, in no small measure, to the pervasive influence of the *yin-yang* 陰陽 cosmology in general and Dong Zhongshu (ca. 179–ca. 104 B.C.E.) in particular. Throughout the Han dynasty (206 B.C.E.–220 C.E.), belief in the mutual interaction between the Way of Heaven (*tiandao* 天道) and human affairs in both elite and popular cultures was nearly universal. It was in such a climate of opinion that Sima Qian (145–90? B.C.E.), the Grand Historian of China, devoted his entire life to the writing of his monumental *Shiji* 史記 (Records of the Grand Historian), which was intended, in his own words, "to examine all that concerns Heaven and man." Thus, he set an example for historians of later centuries to follow. It is by no means a mere coincidence that Liu

Zhiji 劉知幾 (661–721), the great Tang official historiographer, was praised by his contemporaries as a man "whose learning joined together the realms of Heaven and man." In the eighteenth century, Zhang Xuecheng 章學誠 (1738–1801), arguably the most philosophically minded of all historians in the Chinese tradition, also took great pride in the purpose he set for his work, which was "to show the interrelatedness of the heavenly to the human, thereby throwing light on the Great Way." In both cases, the allusion to Sima Qian 司馬遷 is unmistakable.

The *tian-ren* polarity also figured prominently in both Wei-Jin Neo-Daoism and Song-Ming Neo-Confucianism. He Yan 何晏 (?–249) and Wang Bi 王弼 (226–249) enjoyed each other's company because they could always discuss "matters concerning the interrelationships between Heaven and man" with perfect understanding. Needless to say, complex metaphysical issues arising from the basic distinction between the "Heavenly principle" (*tianli* 天理) and "human desires" (*renyu* 人欲) constituted the very core of Neo-Confucian discourse. The story is too familiar to require further elaboration here.

The notion of "unity of Heaven and man" proved to be so surprisingly resilient that it continues to haunt the Chinese mind in the twentieth century. During the early 1940s, Chin Yueh-lin (Jin Yuelin 金岳霖, 1895–1984), a leading Chinese metaphysician thoroughly trained in Western philosophy, and Fung Yu-lan (Feng Youlan 馮友蘭) made a concerted philosophical effort to develop the idea of *tian ren heyi* each in his own way, with the explicit purpose of exploring the possibility of its relevance to the modern world. In a comparativist context, Chin singled out *tian ren heyi* as the "most distinguishing characteristic" of Chinese philosophy. Fully aware of the comprehensiveness and complexity of the thesis, he nevertheless tended to interpret it in terms of the "unity of nature and man" and contrasted it to the dominant Western idea of "conquest of nature."[1] On the other hand, Fung applied this thesis to what he called "the transcendent sphere of living," the highest ideal in his philosophy of life. In his own words, "the highest achievement of the man living in this sphere is the identification of himself with the universe, and in this identification, he also transcends the intellect."[2]

Since the early 1990s, a great controversy has flared up in the Chinese intellectual world around the notion of *tian ren heyi*. In this ongoing debate, many questions have been raised regarding the exact meanings of this classic thesis. Some are continuous with Chin's interpretation but focus more sharply on the dilemma of how to achieve oneness with nature and simultaneously accommodate science and technology in Chinese culture. Others echo Fung's metaphysical, ethical, or religious concerns but go beyond him by drawing modern, and even postmodern, implications from this thesis for Chinese spirituality. The details of this current debate need not concern us here. I mention it only to show that *tian ren heyi* is by no means a fossilized idea of merely historical interest.

Instead, it remains a central component of the Chinese frame of mind to this very day. Indeed, it may hold the key to one of the doors leading to the World of Chinese spirituality.

As a historian, however, I do not feel at ease with pure speculation. In what follows, I propose first to offer an account of the genesis and development of this idea and then to endeavor to explain how it eventually evolved into one of the defining features of Chinese mentality. My approach is essentially historical.

To begin with, let me introduce the ancient myth of the "Separation of Heaven and Earth" (*Jue di tian tong* 絕地天通). Briefly, the myth runs as follows: In high antiquity, humans and deities did not intermingle. Humans, for their part, held the gods in reverence and kept themselves in their assigned places in the cosmic order. On the other hand, deities also descended among them from time to time through the intermediaries of shamans (*wu* 巫). As a consequence, the spheres of the divine and the profane were kept distinct. The deities sent down blessings on the people and accepted from them their offerings. There were no natural calamities. Then came the age of decay, in which humans and deities became intermingled, with each household indiscriminately performing for itself the religious observances that had hitherto been conducted by the shamans. As a result, the people lost their reverence for the deities, the gods violated the rules of the human world, and calamities arose. It was at this point that the sage-ruler Zhuanxu 顓頊 (traditionally dated to the twenty-fifth century B.C.E.) intervened, presumably with the approval of the God-on-High (Shang Di 上帝); he rearranged the cosmic order by cutting the communication between Heaven and Earth.[3]

This myth is very rich with meanings and can be interpreted in a variety of ways. In the present context, I wish to make only a simple historical observation: it may have served as a justification for the fact that in ancient China, only the universal king had direct access to Heaven. According to tradition, under the Three Dynasties of Xia 夏, Shang 商, and Zhou 周, making sacrificial offerings to Heaven was a prerogative exclusively reserved for the king. The local feudal lords were entitled to communicate with the earthly deities through sacrificial rites within their domains but not with the celestial ones. In other words, the "unity between the Heavenly and the human" was strictly confined to the Son of Heaven, who, as one modern interpretation suggests, was also the head shaman.

Here, however, a difficulty inevitably arises: the idea of the "unity between the heavenly and the human" mentioned in the beginning of this chapter is built on an assumption diametrically opposed to the myth of the "Separation of Heaven and Earth"; it presupposes that every individual person on earth is, in principle, able to communicate with Heaven. Admittedly, the exact meanings of the concept "Heaven" are quite different in these two theses. Nevertheless, structurally speaking, the two must be viewed as each other's negation. The very notion that everyone can communicate with Heaven without the assistance even of a shaman clearly implies that access to Heaven is no longer a royal monopoly. Since, as we shall see, the beginning of an individualistic version of *tian ren heyi* can be traced to no earlier than the sixth century B.C.E., we may assume that it was developed, at least partly, as a conscious response to the ancient myth of "separation" that had dominated the Chinese mind for many centuries. It is to this important development of Chinese spirituality that I must now turn.

The author of the last chapter of the *Zhuangzi*—perhaps a latter-day follower of the Master—describes with a profound sense of sadness the "breakup" of the primeval oneness of *Dao* 道. He linked this "breakup" to the rise of the "Hundred Schools" of philosophy in China. Each of the schools, he said, comprehended but a singular aspect of the original whole. It is like the case of the ear, eye, nose, and mouth, each having a particular sense, without being able to function interchangeably. As a result, the purity of Heaven and Earth and the wholeness of *Dao* have been forever lost.[4] In this earliest account of the first philosophical movement in Chinese classical antiquity, our writer historicizes an original allegory suggested by Zhuangzi 莊子 himself. It runs as follows:

> The God of the South Sea was called Shu 儵 [Swift], the God of the North Sea was called Hu 忽 [Sudden], and the God of the central region was called Hundun 渾沌 [Chaos]. Shu and Hu from time to time came together for a meeting in the territory of Hundun, and Hundun treated them very generously. Shu and Hu discussed how they could repay his kindness. "All men," they said, "have seven openings so they can see, hear, eat, and breathe. But Hundun alone doesn't have any. Let's try boring him some."
>
> Every day they bored another hole, and on the seventh day Hundun died. (97)

I am quite convinced that the latter-day follower's historical account is a truthful reading of the Master's original allegory. The analogy of sensory apertures in both cases makes it clear that Zhuangzi's Chaos (Hundun) is the symbol of the primordial wholeness of *Dao*. In making use of this famous allegory about the death of Chaos, Zhuangzi must have had in mind what historians today see as a "swift" (Shu) and "sudden" (Hu) beginning of spiritual enlightenment in ancient China. Laozi 老子, Confucius, and Mo Di (or Mozi) 墨翟—to mention only three of the greatest names in the history of Chinese philosophy—all appeared in the sixth and fifth centuries B.C.E.

Now the question is, how are we to understand this sudden spiritual enlightenment and relate it to the distinction between the heavenly and the human? In this connection, I would like to begin by placing the question in a comparative perspective, because China was not the only civilization in the ancient world that experienced this enlightenment. It took place in other civilizations as well. Some four decades ago, Karl Jaspers called our attention to the most fascinating fact that in the first millennium B.C.E., which he called the Axial Period, a spiritual "breakthrough" occurred in several high cultures, including China, India, Persia, Israel, and Greece. It took the form of either philosophical reasoning or postmythical religious imagination, or a mixed type of moral-philosophic-religious consciousness, as in the case of China. Apparently, the breakthroughs in the Axial Period all took place independently of one another and no mutual influences can be established. The most we can say about them is probably that when civilizations or cultures developed to a certain stage, they would undergo a common experience of spiritual awakening of some kind. Jaspers further suggested that the ultimate importance of this Axial breakthrough lies in the fact that it tended to exert a defining and formative influence on the character of the civilizations involved.[5] In the past decades, much has been discussed about Jaspers's concept of "breakthrough," and there is a general consensus that the great transformation of the Chinese mind in the time of Confucius can be more sensibly understood as one of the major breakthroughs during the Axial Period. It is therefore all the more remarkable that Zhuangzi and his followers had already grasped the historical significance of the very intellectual movement that they themselves were promoting. "Death of Chaos" or "breakup of the primeval *Dao*" has indeed captured the essential meaning of the idea of "Axial breakthrough."

There are many ways of characterizing the Axial breakthrough. For the purpose of my discussion here, I prefer to see it as China's first spiritual awakening, involving centrally an original transcendence. It is "transcendence" in the sense of, as Benjamin I. Schwartz has suggested, "a kind of critical, reflective questioning of the actual and a new vision of what lies beyond."[6] The transcendence is "original" in the sense that it has ever since remained, by and large, a central defining feature of the Chinese mentality throughout the traditional period.

Scholars are also in basic agreement that the Axial breakthrough led directly to the emergence of the dichotomy between the actual world and the world beyond. This is essentially what transcendence is all about: the actual world is transcended but not negated. On the other hand, however, the exact shape, empirical content, and historical process of transcendence varied from civilization to civilization as each had taken place on a pre-breakthrough foundation uniquely its own. In what immediately follows, I shall try to say something about the uniqueness of Chinese transcendence. Some Western scholars have already noticed that in contrast to other Axial breakthroughs, China's appears to have been a "least radical"[7] or "most conservative"[8] one. I think this judgment is well grounded and reasonable. There are many different ways to argue for the case. One would be the Chinese emphasis on historical continuity during and since the Axial Period. The "breakthrough" did occur, but it was not a complete break with the pre-breakthrough tradition. Another way is to look into the relationship between the actual world and the world beyond.

In the Chinese breakthrough, the two worlds, actual and transcendental, do not appear to have been sharply divided. There is nothing in the early Chinese philosophical visions that suggests Plato's conception of an unseen eternal world of which the actual world is only a pale copy. In the religious tradition, the sharp dichotomy of a Christian type between the world of God and the world of humans is also absent. Nor do we find in classical Chinese thought in all its varieties anything that closely resembles the radical negativity of early Buddhism, with its insistence on the unrealness and worthlessness of this world. In the case of China during the Axial Period, the idea of *Dao* emerged as a symbol of the transcendental world in contrast to the actual world of everyday life. This was equally true of the Confucians and the Daoists. In either case, however, *Dao* was never perceived as very far from everyday life. Confucius said: "The *Dao* is not far from man. When a man pursues the *Dao* and remains away from man, his course cannot be considered the *Dao*."[9] "Zhongyong" 中庸 (Doctrine of the Mean) also stressed the point that the *Dao* functions everywhere and yet is hidden. Men and women of simple intelligence can share its knowledge or practice it, and yet in its utmost reaches, there is something that even the sage does not know or is unable to put into practice. Both Laozi and Zhuangzi took *Dao* to be a "higher realm" of existence as opposed to the actual world. Generally speaking, the distinction between "this world" and "other world" is more sharply drawn in Daoism than in Confucianism. Nevertheless, the Daoists' two worlds are not neatly separate either. Thus, when Zhuangzi was asked, "This thing called the *Dao*—where does it exist?" The Master's answer is, "There is no place it doesn't exist." As he further explained to the questioner, "You must not expect to find the *Dao* in any particular place—there is no thing that escapes its presence!" (240–241). Zhuangzi's admirer once described him in the following way: "He came and went alone with the pure spirit of Heaven and earth, yet he did not view the ten thousand things with arrogant eyes. He did not scold over "right" and "wrong," but lived with the age and its vulgarity. . . . Above, he wandered with the Creator; below, he made friends with those who have gotten outside of life and death, who know nothing of beginning or end" (373). In other words, Zhuangzi lived in "this world," but at the same time, his spirit wandered in the "other world."

Up to this point, what I have been trying to show is that as a result of the Axial breakthrough, China also developed its own duality of the transcendental and actual worlds. However, this Chinese duality differed from that in other civilizations by being not as sharply differentiated. The typical Chinese description of the relationship between these two worlds is "neither identical nor separate" (*buji buli* 不即不離). This description may be hard to comprehend for those who are accustomed to dichotomist thinking, but it does constitute a central feature of Chinese transcendence. The title of this chapter, "Between the

Heavenly and the Human," is also chosen to convey this unique Chinese imagination. To take a step further, I now propose to interpret the Chinese case as "inward transcendence" (*neixiang chaoyue* 内向超越).

The inwardness of Chinese transcendence cannot be understood without a brief discussion of the historical process of the Axial breakthrough in early China. It has been suggested that the Axial breakthrough took place in Greece against the background of the world of Homeric gods, in Israel against the background of the early books of the Bible and the story of Moses, and in India against the background of the long Vedic tradition. What, then, was the Chinese background against which the breakthrough occurred? My straightforward answer is: the long ritual tradition of the Three Dynasties (Xia-Shang-Zhou). By "ritual tradition," I refer to both *li* 禮 (rites) and *yue* 樂 (music), which had been embodied in the way of life of the ruling elite since the Xia dynasty. Confucius's famous characterization of the Xia-Shang-Zhou ritual tradition as a continuous but ever-renovating system (*Lunyu* [Analects], 11.23) seems to have been validated by every major advance in archaeology as far as the last two dynasties are concerned. By the time of Confucius, however, this ritual order was already on the brink of total breakdown, due largely to the widespread transgressions and violations of rites by the ruling elite. Here we have a classic example of breakdowns preceding breakthroughs in history.

Next, we must try to establish the historical link between the Axial breakthrough and the ritual breakdown in terms of transcendence. In the interest of brevity, it suffices to point out that the ritual tradition was indeed the point of departure of Chinese transcendence resulting directly from the Axial breakthrough. One of Confucius's central visions consisted in transcending the existing ritual practice by searching for the "basis of rites." His new search ended, as we all know, in the reinterpretation of *ren* 仁 (in this case, "human-heartedness") as the spiritual kernel of *li*. Thus, he departed from the traditional view that *li* originated in human imitation of the divine models provided by Heaven and Earth (*Zuozhuan* 左傳, or Zuo Commentary to the Spring and Autumn Annals, Duke Zhao, twenty-fifth year). Instead of looking outwardly toward Heaven and Earth, he now turned inwardly toward the human heart, for the "basis of rites." Similarly, both the Mohist and the Daoist breakthroughs, which came after Confucius's, also took the ritual tradition to serious task. Mozi not only viewed the ever-growing complexity and elaborateness of *li* through the ages as steadily but irreversibly falling into decay but also severely criticized Confucius's reform for its failure to eradicate all the existing ritual practices developed during the Zhou Period—hence, his advocacy of a return to the simplicity of the original Xia ritual system. As for the Daoists, theirs may be described as the most radical of all the breakthroughs among the pre-Qin schools of thought. This is the case because it alone drew a distinction between the actual world and the world beyond, one that was sharper than in any other school. Zhuangzi, in particular, has been the main source of the strain of otherworldliness in the Chinese spiritual tradition. It must be emphatically pointed out, however, that the Daoists also took the ritual tradition as the starting point of their transcendence. As clearly stated in the *Daodejing* 道德經 (or the *Laozi*, chapter 38), "rites" are "the beginning of disorder," meaning that the spirit of original *Dao* has degenerated, step by step, to its lowest point. On the other hand, Zhuangzi tried to show us how to return to *Dao* by transcending the actual world, also step by step, beginning with the "rites" (90).[10] Thus, the process of "fall," so to speak, in the *Daodejing* is reversed to become the process of "salvation" in the *Zhuangzi*. Rejecting all the current ritual practices as artificial nonsense, Zhuangzi nevertheless did not go so far as to propose discarding the very notion of *li* itself; he continued to speak of the "meaning of rites" (*liyi* 禮意). In his conception, obviously, "pounding on a tub and singing" in the presence of his wife's corpse is a more meaningful funeral rite than weeping (191–192).

In the above three cases, it is significant that the founders of Confucianism, Mohism, and Daoism all "philosophically reinterpreted the existing religious practice rather than directly withdrawing themselves from it," a fact Max Weber considered to be "of fundamental importance."[11] I would venture to suggest that reinterpretation instead of withdrawal may help explain to a large extent why, of all the Axial breakthroughs, China's turned out to be the "least radical" or "most conservative."

Lastly, let us examine "inward transcendence" in relation to the changing conception of the "unity of Heaven and man." It may be recalled that during the time when the myth of the "Separation of Heaven and Earth" was generally accepted, only the king could directly communicate with Heaven with the assistance of *wu*-shamans. As a result, the "unity of Heaven and man" became a prerogative exclusively reserved for the king, who, theoretically, was decreed by Heaven as the sole representative of all the humans on earth as a collectivity. In an important sense, it was against this royal monopoly of the access to Heaven that the Chinese Axial breakthrough began as a spiritual revolt.

In his further characterizations of the Axial breakthrough, Jaspers particularly called our attention to two of its distinguishing features. First, the breakthrough is the spiritual awakening and liberation of humans as *individuals*; for the first time, they "dared to rely on themselves as individuals," to embark on a spiritual journey beyond not only their own selves but the actual world as well. Second, with the breakthrough, the spiritually awakened and liberated individual appears to have been in need of relating his or her own existence in this world meaningfully to "the whole of Being."

This general characterization, it seems to me, throws a comparativist light on the individualistic turn of the *tian ren heyi* thesis during China's Axial breakthrough. Take the idea of *tianming* 天命 ("Mandate or Decree of Heaven"), for example. Confucius said, "at fifty, I understood the Decree of Heaven" (*Analects*, 2.4) and the gentleman "is in awe of the Decree of Heaven" (16.8). As D. C. Lau rightly points out in his translator's introduction to the *Analects*, "The only development by Confucius' time was that the Decree of Heaven was no longer confined to the Emperor. Every man was subject to the Decree of Heaven which enjoined him to be moral and it was his duty to live up to the demands of that Decree."[12] Onozawa Seiichi also made a similar observation in 1978. By associating the concept of *tianming* with *xin* ("heart") and *de* 德 ("virtue," also with a "heart" component) in a bronze inscription, he came to the conclusion that during Confucius's time, the idea of *tianming* underwent a subtle shift from something in support of dynastic politics to that which is to be conferred on the individuals and, ultimately, to be seated in their hearts.[13] Thus, with *tianming* being conferred on every individual, the direct line of communication between Heaven and individual humans was reestablished after a long period of "separation of Heaven and Earth." As a result, Confucius often spoke as if he were constantly in personal contact with Heaven: "Heaven is author of the virtue that is in me" (*Analects*, 7.23) or "If I am understood at all, it is, perhaps, by Heaven" (*Analects*, 14.35). Statements like these clearly suggest that Confucius as an individual was capable of communicating with Heaven directly. It is also fascinating that Zhuangzi once put the following words into the mouth of Yan Hui 顏回, Confucius's favorite disciple: "By being inwardly straight, I can be the companion of Heaven. Being a companion of Heaven, I know that the Son of Heaven and I are equally the sons of Heaven" (56).[14] Here, in his unique way, Zhuangzi tried to convey the radical Daoist idea that every individual person, by being "inwardly straight"—a reference to "virtue" in the heart—could be a son of Heaven. With this twist, Zhuangzi demolished the claim of the king that he alone is the Son of Heaven. Needless to say, as sons of Heaven, all individual humans can directly communicate with Heaven so long as they are able to keep their hearts "straight."

Up to this point, we have seen how the individual's turn of *tian ren heyi* led to the reopening of the direct line of communication between Heaven, on the one hand, and the spiritually awakened and liberated individual humans, on the other. Moreover, as both Onozawa's study and the passage quoted from the *Zhuangzi* indicate, the center of communication seems to have been located in the heart. The time has now arrived for us to move on to the question of "inward transcendence."

Communication between Heaven and Humanity was at the very center of the whole concept of *tian ren heyi*. Therefore, we must first ask: How did the universal king communicate with Heaven during the entire pre-Axial period? This question brings us to the communicative function of the ritual (*li*) practice. As already mentioned earlier, the king had all along relied on the assistance of *wu*-shamans to communicate with Heaven. As the king's trusted religious functionaries, *wu*-shamans claimed that they alone had access to Heaven: they either ascended to Heaven to seek instructions from the God-on-High, deities, and royal ancestral spirits on behalf of the reigning king or made celestial deities and spirits descend to the human world. To do so, however, they had to perform certain rituals with the help of a great variety of ritual paraphernalia.

To a considerable extent, the Axial breakthrough was directed against the shamanistic component of the ritual system. Confucius's reinterpretation of the ritual practice may well be understood in this light. As a spiritually awakened and liberated thinker, Confucius needed no *wu*-shamans to serve as intermediaries in his direct communication with Heaven. Thus, the enormous communicative power previously believed to be the monopoly of *wu*-shamans was now assigned to *ren* 仁, the spiritual kernel of *li* 禮, which could only be located in the human heart.

This inward turn took a giant step forward in the fourth century B.C.E. with the emergence of the new cosmology of *qi* 氣 (vital energy). According to this new theory, the *qi* permeates the entire cosmos. It is in constant movement and, when differentiated and individuated, all things in the world are formed. However, this *qi* is vastly varied in consistency, ranging from the most refined to the grossest. Generally speaking, two types may be distinguished: the pure *qi* (*qing qi* 清氣), being light, is associated with Heaven, whereas the gross *qi* (*zhuoqi* 濁氣), being heavy, is associated with Earth. The human person is a mixture of both, with his body being made up of the grosser *qi* and his heart being the seat of the refined *qi*.

With this cosmology of *qi*, the idea of *tian ren heyi* entered into a completely new age. As a consequence, thinkers of various persuasions began to develop their new versions of *tian ren heyi* with a view to displacing the earlier *wu*-shamanistic interpretation. When Mencius talked about his concept of *haoran zhi qi* 浩然之氣 ("floodlike *qi*"), he was actually presenting his individualist view of the "unity of Heaven and man." Only by turning inward to nourish the most refined *qi* in the heart can one hope to attain oneness with the cosmos (*Mencius*, 2A.2). Elsewhere he also said, "A gentleman transforms where he passes, and works wonders where he abides. He is in the same stream as Heaven above and Earth below" (6A.13).[15] In this new conception of *tian ren heyi*, the communicative function was assumed, according to him, by the most refined *qi* seated in the innermost part—heart—of every individual human person.

A similar development may also be found in the *Zhuangzi*. In discussing the possibility of an individual person's attainment of oneness with the transcendent *Dao*, the Daoist philosopher offered his famous theory of "fasting of the heart" (*xinzhai* 心齋). According to this theory, the heart must be, on the one hand, emptied of everything else, and on the other hand, filled with *qi* of the purest kind so that *Dao* may find it hospitable. Like Mencius, he also emphasized the utmost importance of cultivation of *qi*, which alone can sharpen one's sensitivity and ability to the highest degree in order to monitor the rhythm of the infinitely ongoing cosmic transformation (57–58). Thus, the cases of Confucius, Mencius, and Zhuangzi provide us with three concrete and vivid examples of what I propose to call "inward transcendence," which distinguishes the Chinese Axial breakthrough from the rest in a fundamental way.

The historical process, reconstructed above, is intended as an explanation of how the Chinese Axial breakthrough led to an "inward transcendence" and why. As shown in my brief discussion of the idea of *tianming*, Axial thinkers, as spiritually awakened and liberated individuals, made a subtle strategic move to break the royal monopoly of access to Heaven by transferring the center of communication from the ritual system dominated by *wu*-shamanism to the heart of every individual human. Here we have a concrete example illustrative of the breakthrough taking place right in the center of the Xia-Shang-Zhou ritual tradition. It also shows that the Heaven–human relationship took a decidedly new turn as China moved from the pre-Axial to the Axial Period, which was individualist and inward in the same breath. Between the pre-Axial ritual tradition and the philosophic breakthrough, a qualitative leap in Chinese spirituality occurred. Having transcended the ritual tradition, the Chinese mind raised itself to a new level of articulation and conceptualization.

At this juncture, however, a further question calls for our critical attention. I have suggested above that all the three major schools of thought—Confucianism, Mohism, and Daoism—reinterpreted the idea of *li* each in its own way, and none arrived at a complete break with the ritual tradition. This less-than-complete break with the pre-Axial tradition seems to bear significantly, as I have hinted above, "on the fact that the Chinese Axial breakthrough did not give rise to a transcendental world setting itself in explicit opposition to the actual." Such being the case, an account, however brief, of the continuity between tradition and breakthrough seems very much in order. Let me now return to the *tian ren heyi* thesis, with special reference to the concept of the Decree of Heaven.

To begin with, the whole notion of *tian ren heyi* itself was directly continuous from tradition to breakthrough; it was only interpreted differently. During Shang-Zhou times, the king and the ruling elite looked up to Heaven as the ultimate source of wisdom and power of the highest kind, to which the shaman-dominated ritual system alone provided access. During the Axial Period, spiritually awakened individuals also needed to keep themselves in daily contact with the sources of spiritual power. As shown in the cases of Mencius and Zhuangzi, they relied on the cultivation of the most refined *qi* in their hearts to accomplish this delicate task. Thus, the "heart" became the only medium through which the line of communication between the individual human and Heaven, or *Dao*, was kept open. Vast differences in content of thought aside, the continuity of the new version of *tian ren heyi* with its pre-Axial ritual archetype is clearly recognizable.

The concept of the Decree of Heaven stood at the very center of the pre-Axial *tian ren heyi* thesis. The term *tianming* is generally believed to be of western Zhou origin, but it has also been suggested that a functional equivalent without this term may have already been available to the Shang king for legitimation of his political authority. At any rate, it can be safely assumed that the necessity of renewing his *tianming* from time to time must have been among the most important reasons for the king to communicate with Heaven through performance of certain rituals aided by a wide range of paraphernalia. According to Zhou theory, a reigning dynasty is qualified for *tianming* only when the king and the ruling elite are in possession of certain "brilliant virtues" (*mingde* 明德) such as "fearful reverence of Heaven," "loving care for the people," "conscientious attention to administration," "practice of frugality," and so on.[16] Later, when Mencius summed up his discussion of this notion, he quoted a saying from a lost chapter of the *Shujing* (Book of History) as follows: "Heaven sees with the eyes of its people. Heaven hears with the ears of its people" (*Mencius*, 5A.5). This is clearly the Chinese version of *vox populi, vox Dei*. Modern classicists are well grounded when they suggest that the concept of the Decree of Heaven, understood in this way, constituted the very essence of the *tian ren heyi* thesis in western Zhou times.[17]

I would like to suggest several lines of continuity between tradition and breakthrough. First, we have seen how Confucius used the term *tianming* to describe his personal relationship with Heaven. According to the *Zuozhuan*, Duke Zhao, seventh year, a nobleman of Lu, made this remark about Confucius: "If a sagely man of brilliant virtue (*mingde*) does not become distinguished in his time, among his posterity there is sure to be someone of vast intelligence." It is important to note that the term *mingde*, which was the precondition for the king and his dynasty to receive the Decree of Heaven, also began to be applied to the individual, in this case, the descendants of Confucius. Thus, we see that the whole notion of *tianming* continued well into the Axial Period despite its shift of emphasis from a collectivistic to an individualistic sense.

Second, Confucius's famous "rule of virtue" (*wei zheng yi de* 為政以德; *Analects*, 2.1) must also be understood as a continuation of the western Zhou conception of government based on "brilliant virtues," even though in the latter case the power of *de* may have been conceived of as associated with ritual communication under shamanistic influences. For Confucius, however, the power of "virtue" was generated by the heart through "cultivation" (*Analects*, 7.3). This line of political thinking later culminated in Mencius's idea of "benevolent government" (*renzheng* 仁政), with particular emphasis on the importance of "a heart sensitive to the suffering of others" on the part of the king (*Mencius*, 2A.6). Indeed, the thread of "rule of virtue" ran continuously from early Zhou through Confucius to Mencius, while turning ever-increasingly inward.

Last but not least, the inward turn of the idea of *tianming* itself had its beginning earlier than the time of Confucius. The *Zuozhuan*, Duke Xuan, third year, reports a well-known event of 605 B.C.E., which may be summed up as follows. The Lord of Chu asked a court official of the eastern Zhou about the size and weight of the Nine Tripods, which were the ritual symbol of *tianming* for the

Zhou. He meant to carry them back so that the Chu could replace the Zhou house as the new recipient of the Decree of Heaven. The Zhou official replied by saying: "The size and weight are not in the tripods but in virtue. . . . Though the virtue of Zhou is decayed, the Decree of Heaven is not yet changed." This is the earliest evidence, as far as I know, of the inward turn of *tianming* with specific reference to *de* as inner virtue or power vis-à-vis the Nine Tripods as sacred ritual symbols. This anecdote suggests that the Lord of Chu probably still subscribed to the traditional belief that whoever possessed the Nine Tripods also possessed the Decree of Heaven. However, the eastern Zhou official's reply clearly indicates that a new belief had come into being according to which the *tianming* was linked primarily to *de* as inner spiritual virtue, not the external ritual paraphernalia such as the Nine Tripods.

In this connection, I may briefly mention that the character *de* 德 itself also underwent a similar change toward inwardness. Its earlier written form is composed of two parts: "action" (*chi* 彳) and "straight" (*zhi* 直). Then in some of the later Zhou bronze inscriptions, a third element, "heart" (*xin* 心), is added. It has been suggested lately that the meaning of *de* may have changed from something descriptive of external human behavior to that of inner human qualities. It may be significant that in the newly discovered Daoist and Confucian texts on bamboo slips from Guodian tentatively dated around 300 B.C.E., the character *de* is invariably written in the form of "straight" plus "heart." The inward turn of the *tian ren heyi* thesis may well have begun before the process of Axial breakthrough was fully activated.

With *tian ren heyi* as a central thread, I have outlined a historical account of the genesis and evolution of "inward transcendence" from the pre-Axial ritual tradition to Axial breakthrough. The continuity of the notion of *tian ren heyi*, in particular, strongly suggests that its earliest archetype may have been provided by the ritual communication between Heaven and humans under the influence of *wu*-shamanism. As the "Separation" myth shows, *wu*-shamans played a pivotal role as intermediaries in this celestial communication. It is true that Axial thinkers beginning with Confucius eventually transcended the ritual tradition, which resulted in an epoch-making philosophic breakthrough, but they did this by way of "reinterpretation" of, not "complete withdrawal" from, the original ritual system. As a result, "Heaven" was reinterpreted in a variety of senses, including *Dao*; the medium of communication changed from "*wu*-shaman" to "heart"; and ritual performance was also replaced by spiritual cultivation. Nevertheless, the archetypal structure remained intact: the spiritually awakened individual human continued to long for "unity" or "oneness" with the realm beyond, where the deepest sources of wisdom and power were supposedly to be found. Because the center of communication was now located in the human heart (*xin*, also "mind"), however, the search for the realm beyond must of necessity begin by turning inward. This is beautifully expressed by D. C. Lau in the introduction to his translation of the *Mencius*:

Acting in accordance with Heaven's Decree is something one can do joyfully by looking inwards and finding the roots of morality within one's own spiritual make-up. In this way, Mencius broke down the barrier between Heaven and Man and between Decree and human nature. There is a secret passage leading from the innermost part of a man's person to Heaven, and what pertains to Heaven, instead of being external to man, turns out to pertain to his truest nature.[18]

This is a perfect example of what I mean by "inward transcendence."

Understood in this sense, the notion of *tianren heyi* must not be misread as a "theory" with specific contents of thought. Instead, it is only a mode of thinking manifesting itself in practically all aspects of Chinese culture such as art, literature, philosophy, religion, political thought, social relations, and so on, which cannot be pursued here. This also explains why "inward transcendence" has become a defining feature of Chinese mentality since the time of Confucius. In what follows, I outline, in a highly sketchy manner, some of its expressions in the post-Axial Chinese mentality.

I would like to begin with the negative side as a contrast to the external transcendence of the West. The Chinese transcendental world is not systematically externalized, formalized, or objectivized, especially when compared to its Western counterpart. After the Axial breakthrough, Chinese thinkers tended not to apply their imaginative powers to the nature, shape, characteristics, and so on of the world beyond, whether Heaven or *Dao*, even though they apparently had deep feelings about it. As best expressed by Zhuangzi, "As to what lies beyond the universe, the sage admits its existence but does not theorize" (44). This Chinese attitude contrasts sharply with the Western predilection to imagine, often vividly and profusely, about the world beyond with the aid of speculative reason.

As a matter of fact, the absence of theology in the Chinese tradition is something that no intellectual historian can possibly fail to notice. Chinese speculations on heaven or the cosmos from the third century B.C.E. on led only to the rise of the *yin-yang* cosmology, not theology. Buddhism introduced to China not only a host of ever-compassionate deities in the form of bodhisattvas but also a hierarchy of heavens and hells. In imitation, religious Daoists brought forth a class of transcendent beings called *tianzun* (天尊, venerable celestial deities). These imported beliefs, though appealing to popular imagination, were never taken seriously by the thinking elite. Zhu Xi 朱熹 (1130–1200), for example, dismissed the Daoist *tianzun* as thoughtless imitations. Unlike for Plato or Kant, neither the regular movement of heavenly bodies nor moral principles in the mind/heart could convince Zhu Xi of the existence of God.

By contrast, theology as a systematic knowledge of God began in the West with Plato's metaphysics and continued with Aristotle as one of the three "theoretical sciences." In medieval Europe, Christian theology prevailed over Greek thought. As Jaroslav Pelikan points out, however, "the victory of orthodox Christian doctrine over classical thought was, to some extent a Pyrrhic victory, for the theology that triumphed over Greek philosophy has continued to be shaped ever since by the language and the thought of classical metaphysics."[19] Thus, the absence of theology in the Chinese tradition on the one hand and its full flowering in the West on the other may well be taken as an illustrative example of the contrast between inward transcendence and external transcendence. Hegel once criticized the sharp separation between the clergy and the laity in medieval Christianity as follows: "Here arises *ipso facto* a separation between those who possess this blessing and those who have to receive it from others—between the *Clergy* and *the Laity*. The laity as such are alien to the Divine. This is the absolute schism in which the Church in the Middle Ages was involved; it arose from the recognition of the Holy as something external."[20] Thus, Hegel has confirmed my point about the externalization of Western transcendence in no uncertain terms.

Note further what the great Chan (Zen) Master Huineng 惠能 (or 慧能) had to say about the very same problem in the *Liuzu Tanjing* (Platform Sutra of the Sixth Patriarch) (section 36):

> Good friends, if you wish to practice, it is all right to do so as
>   laymen; you don't have to be in a temple.
> Again,
> From the outset the Dharma has been in the world;
> Being in the world, it transcends the world.
> Hence do not seek the transcendental world outside,
> By discarding the present world itself. [21]

Clearly, the two worlds, actual and transcendental, are linked together by the purified mind/heart in a way that is "neither identical nor separate." In this Chinese version of Buddhism, we find a quintessential expression of inward transcendence.

Turning to the positive side, I would like to point out emphatically that the overwhelming concentration on the nature and function of the "mind/ heart" (*xin* 心) in Confucian, Daoist, and Buddhist discourses has given rise to the unique Chinese "Learning of the Mind and Heart" (*xinxue* 心學), which can be equated neither with "psychology" nor with philosophy of mind in the West. Thus, we find in *Mencius*, "penetrating one's own mind and knowing one's own nature in order to know Heaven"; in *Zhuangzi*, "fasting of the heart" for attainment of oneness with *Dao*; and in Chan Buddhism, "point directly, to the human mind" and "see one's nature and become a Buddha." The greatest contribution to the Learning of the Mind and Heart comes, needless to say, from Neo-Confucianism. In spite of the central importance of "principle" (*li* 理) in his philosophical system, Zhu Xi nevertheless held that "principles," though obtained from Heaven, are ultimately embodied in the mind. In his own words, "Without the mind, principles would have nothing in which to inhere."[22] But, after all, it was Wang Yangming who developed the *xinxue* to its full maturity. The following conversation between Wang and his friend will serve our purpose well. The friend pointed to flowering trees on a cliff and said:

> "You say there is nothing under heaven external to the mind. These
>   flowering trees on the high mountain blossom and drop their blossoms
>   of themselves. What have they to do with my mind?"
> Wang replied:
> "Before you look at these flowers, they and your mind are in a state of silent
>   vacancy. As you come to look at them, their colors at once show up
>   clearly. From this you can know that these flowers are not external to
>   your mind."[23]

What Wang is saying is not that the "flowers" as a thing do not exist in the external world, but that what makes a flower a "flower" to a human observer is the contribution of the mind. These include all its qualities, relations to other things, and the very fact that it is called a "flower." He identified this mind as *liangzhi* 良知, "innate knowledge." Obviously, here Wang is talking about the sources and structure of values and meanings, not the external world and our objective knowledge of it. According to his way of thinking, we may say that values and meanings are provided by the mind or innate knowledge, which, being a unity of the Heavenly and the human, radiates a legislative power much broader than does Kant's practical reason. It may not be too much of an exaggeration to suggest that in Wang Yangming's philosophy, the spirit of inward transcendence has found its fullest and highest expression.

To sum up, I have tried to establish the uniqueness of Chinese religious and philosophical imagination in a comparativist perspective by taking three interpretive steps. First, I used the idea of "inward transcendence" as an overall characterization of the Chinese mentality. Historically, it first took shape during the Axial breakthrough, and then over the centuries, has become deeply entrenched in Chinese spirituality, as shown in the three major traditions of Confucianism, Daoism, and Buddhism. Second, I further discussed inward transcendence in terms of the relationship between the transcendental and actual worlds, and suggested that it may best be described as "neither identical nor separate." Third, the recognition of the sacred as something internal led necessarily to a great deal of imagination about the wondrous function of the mind, in whose mediation alone lies the hope of a harmonious union of the Heavenly and the human.

In conclusion, I would like to mention one specific point, namely, the possible relevance of inward transcendence to our modern world. In her penetrating analysis of the human condition in the modern age, Hannah Arendt made an important point about the reversal of the hierarchical order between the *vita contemplativa* and the *vita activa*. As a result, action has dominated our modern life while contemplation has been reduced to nonexistence. According to Arendt, however, modern people did not gain this world when they lost the other world.[24] More recently, Charles Taylor has also struggled with the same problem but from a different perspective and in different terms. As he sees it, the modern identity of the West consists very largely in what he calls the affirmation of ordinary life. Still, not unlike Arendt, who is concerned about the "thoughtlessness" of modern persons, Taylor also shows considerable anxiety about a tendency in Western culture "to stifle the spirit." In the end, he only sees "a hope implicit in Judeo-Christian theism and in its central promise of a divine affirmation of the human."[25] As far as I can see, this is a spiritual crisis rooted in the external transcendence of Western culture.

It is interesting to note that we find a central element in the Chinese imagination that seems to be speaking precisely to this kind of crisis. There was a common saying among Chinese Chan Buddhists: "In carrying water and chopping firewood: therein lies the wonderful *Dao*."[26] Wang Yangming once described the *Dao* in this way: "It is not divorced from daily ordinary activities, yet it goes straight to what antedated Heaven."[27] What both statements seem to suggest is that there is a possibility that contemplation and action or ordinary life and spiritual edification may be united without either being wholly abandoned. Above, I used the words "speaking to" advisedly because I am not at all sure whether this line of Chinese thinking can really "provide solutions" to the modern crisis. Nevertheless, since the Chinese spiritual tradition has been centrally concerned with the question of how to live a life combining this-worldliness with other-worldliness, we have reason to believe that it may contain ideas worthy of reexamination. After all, this line of thinking is not wholly alien to the West. As is generally known, the idea of combining practical sense and cool utilitarianism with an otherworldly aim was developed by Calvinism long ago.

NOTES

1. Yueh-lin Chin, "Chinese Philosophy," *Social Sciences in China* 1, no. 1 (March 1980): 83–93.

2. Fung Yu-lan, *A Short History of Chinese Philosophy* (New York: Macmillan, 1948), 339–340.

3. See Derk Bodde, "Myths of Ancient China," in his *Essays on Chinese Civilization* (Princeton: Princeton University Press, 1981), 65–70. On *wu*-shamans, see K. C. Chang, "Shang Shamans," in *The Power of Culture: Studies in Chinese Cultural History*, ed. Willard J. Peterson, Andrew H. Plaks, and Ying-shih Yü (Hong Kong: Chinese University Press, 1994), 10–36.

4. "The 'art of the Way (*daoshu* 道術)' in time came to be rent and torn apart by the world." Burton Watson, trans., *The Complete Works of Chuang Tzu* (New York: Columbia University Press, 1968), 364. I have translated the Chinese character *lie* 裂 as "breakup" instead of following Watson's "to be rent and torn apart." Further quotations to the *Zhuangzi* are noted by Watson's page numbers in parentheses.

5. Karl Jaspers, "The Axial Period," in *The Origin and Goal of History*, trans. Michael Bullock (New Haven: Yale University Press, 1953), 1–21.

6. Benjamin I. Schwartz, "The Age of Transcendence," *Daedalus* 104, no. 2 (Spring 1975): 3.

7. Talcott Parsons, "'The Intellectual': A Social Role Category," in *On Intellectuals*, ed. Philip Rieff (Garden City, N.Y.: Doubleday Anchor, 1970), 7.

8. Benjamin I. Schwartz, "Transcendence in Ancient China," *Daedalus* 104, no. 2 (Spring 1975): 60.

9. "Zhongyong," chap. 13.

10. I am following the text of the *Huainanzi*, where the transcending process begins with "rites and music." SBCK, chap. 12, p. 88. The textual problem is too technical to be discussed here.

11. Max Weber, *Economy and Society* (Berkeley: University of California Press, 1978), 502–503.

12. D. C. Lau, trans., *Confucius: The Analects* (Harmondsworth, UK: Penguin, 1979), 20.

13. Onozawa Seiichi 小野澤精, Mitsuji Fukunaga 福永光司, and Yû Yamanoi山井湧, eds., *Ki no shisô* 氣の思想 (Tokyo: Tokyo University Press, 1978).

14. Here I have changed Watson's "inwardly direct" to "inwardly straight." The original term is *neizhi* 內直. In this instance, Zhuangzi is playing with the character *de* 德 (virtue), which in his time was composed of two parts: "heart" (*xin* 心) and "straight" (*zhi* 直). "Straight" seems closer to the meaning of *zhi*. For the written form of *de*, see the most recently discovered texts in *Guodian Chumu zhujian* 郭店楚墓竹簡 (Beijing: Wenwu, 1998).

15. D. C. Lau, trans., *Mencius* (Harmondsworth, UK: Penguin, 1970), 184.

16. Fu Sinian 傅斯年, "Xingming guxun bianzheng" 性命古訓辨證, in Fu, *Sinian quanji* 傅斯年全集 (Taipei: Lianjing, 1980), 2:279–292.

17. Zeng Yunqian 曾運乾, *Shangshu zhengdu* 尚書正讀 (Beijing: Zhonghua, 1964), 35–36.

18. Lau, *Mencius*, 15.

19. Jaroslav Pelikan, *The Christian Tradition: A History of the Development of Doctrine*, vol. 1, *The Emergence of the Catholic Tradition (100–600)* (Chicago: University of Chicago Press, 1971), 44.

20. Georg Wilhelm Friedrich Hegel, *The Philosophy of History*, trans. J. Sibree (New York: Dover, 1956), 378.

21. Philip B. Yampolsky, *The Platform Sutra of the Sixth Patriarch* (the Text of the Tun-Huang Manuscript with Translation, Introduction, and Notes) (New York: Columbia University Press, 1967), 159, 161.

22. Translated in Wm. Theodore De Bary and Irene Bloom, eds., *Sources of the Chinese Tradition*, 2nd ed. (New York: Columbia University Press, 1999), 1:708.

23. Wang Yangming 王陽明, *Chuanxi lu xia* 傳習録下 (Taipei: Shangwu, 1967), 234. Translation from Wang Yang-ming, *Instructions for Practical Living and Other Neo-Confucian Writings*, trans. Wing-tsit Chan (New York: Columbia University Press, 1963), 222.

24. Hannah Arendt, *The Human Condition* (Chicago: University of Chicago Press, 1958).

25. Charles Taylor, *Sources of the Self: The Making of the Modern Identity* (Cambridge, Mass.: Harvard University Press, 1989), 521.

26. *Chuandeng lu* 傳燈録 8.263, CBETA, vol. 51, no. 2076; Fung Yu-lan, *A History of Chinese Philosophy*, trans. Derk Bodde (Princeton: Princeton University Press, 1953), 2:403.

27. See Wang Yangming's poem entitled "Bie zhu sheng 別諸生" (Departing from My Students), in *Wang Yangming quanji* 王陽明全集 (Shanghai: Shanghai guji, 1992), 1279.

2. Life and Immortality in the Mind of Han China

Confucius once said, "While you do not know life, how can you know about death?"[1] Life and death are among the basic problems with which the traditional Chinese mind has been grappling unceasingly ever since the time of Confucius, and to which various kinds of answers have been given. Especially during the Han Period, these two problems were discussed with even greater enthusiasm, not only because of scholars' intellectual interest but also because of the existential necessity of the common people.

As the above familiar saying of Confucius suggests, however, in Chinese intellectual history, the emphasis seems to have been laid much more on the problem of life than on that of death. Sometimes one may even find that the latter is important, not because it is a problem as such, but because it is, in the last analysis, a prolongation of the former. "For," as a Western philosopher has best expressed it, "humanly speaking, death is the last thing of all, and, humanly speaking, there is hope only so long as there is life."[2] It is hoped that the case study of the views on life and immortality in the intellectual history of the Han Period presented below will, to a certain extent, support this generalization.

THE IMPORTANCE OF LIFE

The idea of life occupied a uniquely prominent place in the mind of ancient China. This point is amply borne out by the fact that the term "life" (*sheng* 生) appears very frequently in pre-Qin literature from bronze inscriptions to philosophical writings.[3] One may say that, as an idea, "life" was a point of departure for most of the Chinese philosophical systems at their founding stage. It may even be further suggested that these philosophical systems varied from one another primarily because their original builders viewed life from different angles and, accordingly, interpreted it in different ways.

Of the leading pre-Qin philosophical schools, Confucianism stressed the idea of life with special emphasis on the worldly aspect. It therefore taught people to cultivate worldly virtues while leaving to fate such matters as happiness or misfortune and length of life.[4] Mohism, on the other hand, paid more attention to death than did other schools because it alone laid emphasis on the existence of spirits. As for life, the Mohist view is one of unbearable harshness and has been criticized ever since its appearance as a thorough denial of all the pleasures of human life. It is Daoism that established its philosophy centering on the idea of life. Moreover, unlike the Confucians, the Daoists conceived of life not merely in terms of a vast vital force that pervades the entire universe, but also in terms of the concrete individual life. Thus, both Laozi and Zhuangzi show a deep concern for man's life and death, and discuss the cultivation and prolongation of life. Therefore, we see that from about the end of the Warring States Period (481–221 B.C.E.) to early Han (Western Han, 202 B.C.E.–8 C.E.) times, the idea of life developed along two general lines. One is the Confucian-Daoist view, which took life as a productive cosmic force. The other is a Daoist conception, which emphasized the importance of individual life. Let us now examine these two aspects of the idea of life in more detail.

In the *Laozi* (or *Daodejing*), we find that *Dao* 道 (the Way) and *De* 德 (Virtue), the two most important concepts in Daoist philosophy, are described as forces that produce and nourish life, respectively.[5] In the "Xici" (Commentary on the Appended Phrases) to the *Yijing* (Classic of Changes), probably a Confucian work of the early Han tinged with much Daoist flavor, the idea of life takes on two basic meanings. First, life is regarded as the paramount virtue of Heaven and Earth.[6] Second, it is also an infinite process of production and reproduction.[7] Such an idea of life, as will be shown below, was not only accepted but also greatly elaborated upon in popular thought of the Later Han (25–220 C.E.) Period, as is attested by some of the earliest Daoist canons.

A further distinction between a hedonistic and naturalistic view of life may be made with regard to the individual aspect of life as developed by the early Daoists.[8] According to the hedonists, the meaning of life lies in the pursuit of pleasures, with special emphasis on satisfaction of sensual desires. For instance,

Tuo Xiao 它囂 and Wei Mou 魏牟, who are criticized by Xunzi for advocating a theory of self-indulgence in sensual pleasure, may be taken as hedonists.[9] This hedonism was generally known as the doctrine of *quansheng* 全生 (perfecting the individual life).[10] In the eyes of the moralists, this doctrine was inimical to social order. "If the doctrine of perfecting the individual life prevails," one criticism states, "then integrity and shame will not stand."[11] Whether the hedonists ever went so far as to put the importance of individual life above that of social order, we have no way of knowing. Nevertheless, they did value the enjoyment of life much more than its prolongation. In their opinion, suppression of free will as well as of basic desires would make for a life so miserable as to be worse than death.[12]

The naturalistic view of life takes individual life as an end rather than a means. According to it, the individual life is more honorable than an imperial throne and more valuable than the total wealth of the world.[13] It does not reject pleasure as an ideal of life but argues that unless one lives long, he will not be able to enjoy life.[14] Thus, longevity is desirable, and for its attainment, the cultivation of life becomes necessary. To obtain longevity through cultivation of life, according to this view, is fully in accord with rather than against nature, because it is believed that man's life is naturally long. The fact that all people cannot live out their natural span of life is a result of the unrestrained pursuit of sensual pleasure. The *Lüshi chunqiu* 呂氏春秋 (Annals of Lü Buwei) states: "Longevity is the nature of man. Since [this nature] is being disturbed by things, man cannot live long. It is things that are to nourish [man's] nature; [it is] not [man's] nature to nourish things."[15] According to the commentary of Gao You 高誘 (fl. 205–212 C.E.), the "things" in this passage refer to the material objects of wealth, and the criticism is directed at the fact that most people give unlimited rein to their material desires. Cultivation of life is, therefore, nothing more than bringing life back to its natural course.[16]

LIFE AS A COSMIC FORCE

With this general historical background of the idea of life, we can now examine the manifestation of the idea in the popular thought of the Han Period. More will be said on the individual aspect of life below. In this section, we shall examine the idea of life as a cosmic productive force.

First there is a general stress on the importance of life. A Daoist canon of about the second century C.E.,[17] the *Taipingjing* 太平經 (Scripture of Great Peace), following the Confucian-Daoist tradition, regards life as the paramount virtue of Heaven and Earth. The idea that Heaven produces life and Earth nourishes it is emphatically repeated there.[18] And since *Dao* and *De* are equated with Heaven and Earth, respectively, it is the attribute of *Dao* to produce life and of *De* to nourish it. Therefore, as the argument goes, all things come to life when *Dao* flourishes, and all things, including human beings, are well nourished when *De* flourishes.[19] In the *Laozi Xiang-er zhu* 老子想爾注 (Xiang-er Commentary to Laozi), a Daoist work of the late second century C.E. discovered at Dunhuang,[20] the importance of life is given still greater emphasis. There the idea of life is enhanced to something equivalent to *Dao* itself. "Life is a different substance of *Dao*," it states,[21] and in some places the commentator does not hesitate to emend the character "king" (*wang* 王) in the original text to "life" (*sheng* 生) to support this new conception of life.[22]

Another aspect of the idea of life that is elaborately developed in popular thought is its reproductiveness. The *Scripture of Great Peace* says: "Now what Heaven stresses and values is the succession of life. Therefore, the four seasons, following the teachings of the Heavenly Way, carry on and help to complete the development of life in an endless process so that all kinds of things can grow. So Heaven is known as Father, the Life Producer, and Earth is known as Mother, the Life Fosterer."[23] At another juncture, the work further stresses the necessity of reproduction: "*Dao* produces life. When *Dao* ceases [to exist], all things will cease to live. When all things cease to live, there will be no species of life left in the world and nothing to pass on [to later generations]. When all things cease to reproduce and propagate their species, there will be destruction."[24] The same idea is also discernible in the *Xiang-er Commentary*. On one occasion, for instance, it says: "What *Dao* stresses is the succession of [ancestral] worship. [It is, therefore, necessary that the human] species must not perish."[25] This is precisely one of the theoretical bases on which female infanticide is denounced by the *Scripture of Great Peace*:

Man is to carry on the tradition of Heaven, and woman, the tradition of Earth. Now people cut off the tradition of Earth and thus make reproduction of life impossible. So people [who exercise female infanticide] are mostly deprived of their offspring. How heavy is the sin they commit! These people should all have offspring to propagate their species from generation to generation. But on account of their having cut off the tradition of Earth and destroyed human beings, as a punishment, Heaven takes away from them their posterity forever.[26]

It is still more interesting to note that even chastity is repudiated on the same ground:

A chaste man is one who does not disseminate [seeds] and a chaste woman is one who refuses to transform [seeds into life]. If females and males had no intercourse, all species of life would perish. Thus, being covetous of the fictitious and artificial name [of chastity], two persons together cut off the tradition of Heaven and Earth, and on that account, suffer an actual loss by being deprived of offspring. These are certainly a great evil in the world.[27]

The emphasis so lavishly laid on the importance of life, as will become clear, throws much light on our understanding of many of the ideas in the *Scripture of Great Peace*. It may be legitimately argued that this idea of life must be taken as a point of departure for the study of the ideological system of early Daoist religion.

LONGEVITY AND IMMORTALITY

It is only natural that the general emphasis on life should finally lead to a particular stress on individual human life. In this connection, we must examine two time-honored ideas: longevity and immortality. The idea of longevity is a very old one originating in time immemorial. In Zhou bronze inscriptions, *shou* 壽 (longevity) is found to be by far the most popular term in prayers for blessing.[28] It was a general practice of the Zhou people to pray to their ancestors, and sometimes also to Heaven, for prolongation of life.[29] Longevity, therefore, may be said to be one of the most ancient and universal worldly desires of the Chinese people.[30]

The idea of immortality, on the other hand, came into existence rather late. Not until the early Eastern Zhou Period (eighth century B.C.E.) was there, either in literary references or in bronze inscriptions, any trace of the idea that man could preserve his physical body permanently. From the eighth century on, however, such terms as *nanlao* 難老 (retarding old age) and *wusi* 毋死 (no death) abound in prayers for blessing in bronze inscriptions.[31] The use of these terms marks the beginning of the idea of physical immortality.

Before we discuss immortality more fully, a few important points must be clarified. First, the Chinese concept of immortality contains some subtle differences that its English equivalent fails to convey. Under the general label of immortality, a number of terms, such as *changsheng* 長生 (long life), *busi* 不死 (no death), *baoshen* 保身 (preservation of the body),[32] *dushi* 度世 (transcending the world), *dengxiu* 登遐 (ascending to the distant place),[33] *chengxian* 成仙 (becoming an immortal), etc., may be grouped together as unit-ideas.[34] Although they may all be rendered as immortality, they refer to immortality on different levels. The first three probably developed out of the traditional worldly desire for longevity because the early stage of that development is still evident in bronze inscriptions and in literature, especially in the *Shijing* (Classic of Poetry). In general, during the Western Zhou Period (1027?–771 B.C.E.), people only prayed for limited longevity and natural death. But during the Spring and Autumn (Chunqiu) Period (771–481 B.C.E.), people became more avid and began to pray for escape from old age as well as for "no death."[35] Thus, the idea of immortality may very well be regarded as a result of the intensification of the worldly desire for longevity and need not be interpreted wholly in terms of exotic impact.[36]

The last three terms, however, indicate immortality of a different kind and probably of a different origin as well. This is the immortality of the immortality cult. Modern scholars are divided in their opinions on the origin of this cult, but their theories may be roughly classified into two groups: one regarding the cult as a purely native product[37] and the other holding the view that it arose under the influence of imported ideas.[38] We are not concerned here with which theory is better. The only point to be stressed is the fact that toward the end of the Warring States Period, there emerged a new conception of immortality that differed considerably from its traditional counterpart. To achieve this new immortality was not to live permanently on Earth as a man but rather to leave this world as a *xian* 仙, or immortal.[39] Terms like *dushi* and *xiaju* 退居, which are used in literature in association with *xian*, indicate unmistakably that the achievement of *xian* immortality necessarily involves departure from this human world. The new conception of immortality is, therefore, essentially otherworldly in nature. For convenience we shall hereafter call the traditional immortality that developed out of the ancient worldly desire for longevity "worldly immortality" and the later *xian* immortality "otherworldly immortality." It goes without saying that the two kinds are not always easy to distinguish because of their mutual influence or cross-fertilization. Moreover, it is also true that in later Han times, as we shall see, the two streams tended to merge into one. Nevertheless, the distinction between a worldly immortality and an otherworldly one is, on the whole, not only clear but very useful in tracing the development of the idea of immortality.

In the case of worldly immortality, we have seen how intensification of the desire for longevity gradually led to the idea of "no death." Because of the lords' or princes' interest in longevity, this idea became particularly widespread toward the end of the Warring States Period. As early as 522 B.C.E., Duke Jing of Qi 齊景公 is reported to have expressed his longing for longevity thus: "How happy it would be if there had been no death since ancient times!"[40] It is evident from this report that even during the Chunqiu Period, the idea of "no death" was already deeply imprinted in men's minds. Down to the late Warring States Period (481–221 B.C.E.), princes of various states pursued worldly immortality with even greater enthusiasm at the instigation of *fangshi* 方士 (necromancers). For instance, according to *Hanfeizi*, a sort of "drug of no death" (*busi zhi yao* 不死之藥) was once presented to the Prince of Jing 荊 (i.e., Chu 楚)[41] and a certain guest taught the Prince of Yan 燕 how to cultivate the "way of no death" (*busi zhi dao* 不死之道).[42] Sima Qian has assured us that since the time of King Wei 威 (358–320 B.C.E.) and King Xuan 宣 (319–301 B.C.E.) of Qi and King Zhao 昭 of Yan (311–279 B.C.E.),[43] people had been sent to sea in quest of *xian*, or immortals and "drugs of no death," which all the princes desired.[44] This kind of search for "drugs of no death" by later princes culminated in the efforts of Qin Shi Huang (the First Emperor of the Qin) and Han Wudi (the Martial Emperor of Han, 140–87 B.C.E.), which will be discussed below.

The idea of "no death" became so popular at the time that it was used lavishly to name many things, such as "no death people,"[45] "no death country,"[46] "no death mountain,"[47] "no death tree,"[48] and "no death water."[49]

It is interesting to note, however, that prior to the time of Qin Shi Huang, the idea of "no death" was only indirectly related to *xian*; the kind of immortality sought by the princes was still within the tradition of the worldly desire for longevity. There is no evidence, not even the above-mentioned rather ambiguous passage in Sima Qian's *Shiji* (Records of the Grand Historian), that any prince before Qin Shi Huang ever sought to become immortal in the sense of *xian*. The princes probably wanted only the "drugs of no death," to which the *xian* of the Three Divine Mountains (*san shenshan* 三神山) in the sea alone had access. It is unlikely that the pre-Qin princes aspired to become *xian* themselves, as did Qin Shi Huang and Han Wu-di in later days.

We do not know exactly when the otherworldly *xian* immortality first appeared, although the consensus of opinion among modern scholars dates its rise late in the fourth century B.C.E.[50] The otherworldliness of the *xian* can best be seen in the descriptions of them in pre-Qin and early Han literature. The earliest such description is in the *Zhuangzi*. In the first chapter, we read: "Far away on the mountain of Gu Ye 姑射 there lived a spiritual man 神人. His flesh and skin were like ice and snow. His manner was elegant and graceful as that of a maiden. He did not eat any of the five grains, but inhaled the wind and drank the dew. He rode on clouds, drove along the flying dragons, and thus rambled beyond the four seas."[51] "Yuanyou" 遠遊 (Distant Excursions), traditionally attributed to Qu Yuan but considered by modern scholars to be a product of early Han times,[52] is one of the finest descriptions of the *xian*.[53] It also characterizes the immortals in purely otherworldly terms. Throughout the whole poem runs the central theme of an immortal's flight through space.[54] It is probably in this poem that we first see the term *dushi* (transcending this world) used in connection with the *xian*.

The transformation of Chi Songzi 赤松子 and Wang Qiao 王喬 from men of longevity to *xian* is a concrete illustration of the otherworldliness of the *xian*. In pre-Qin times, these two were regarded only as men of longevity. For instance, the *Zhanguoce* (Intrigues of the Warring States) once mentions the "longevity of [Wang] Qiao and [Chi] Song [zi]," but does not regard them as *xian*.[55] In the "Distant Excursions," however, both Chi Song and Wang Qiao are represented as transmundane *xian* wandering in the sky in a leisurely manner. As early as the second century B.C.E., Zhang Liang 張良, one of the greatest ministers of the Former Han dynasty (202 B.C.E.–8 C.E.), expressed a wish to retire by saying that he wanted to leave worldly affairs behind and wander with Chi Songzi.[56] This again makes clear that, as a *xian*, Chi Songzi was in no way tied to the human world. In the *Huainanzi,* both Wang Qiao and Chi Songzi are depicted as having kept away from the dust of the world as well as having avoided the complications of worldly troubles.[57] Wang Bao 王褒, in his "Shengzhu de xianchen song" 聖主得賢臣頌 (Eulogy on Obtainment of Worthy Ministers by the Sacred Emperor), written during the reign of Emperor Xuandi (73–49 B.C.E.), criticizes those who follow in the footsteps of such *xian* as Wang and Chi for having cut off worldly ties (*jueshi lisu* 絕世離俗).[58] Thus, the case of these two men shows clearly that the *xian,* by definition, assumed an otherworldly and seclusive character.

The nature of the *xian,* or immortality cult, at the beginning of the Former Han is illustrated by a highly illuminating passage from Lu Jia's 陸賈 *Xinyu* 新語 (New Sayings):

> [If a man] treats his body bitterly and harshly and goes deep into the mountains in search of *xian* immortality, [if he] leaves behind his parents, casts aside his kindred, abstains from the five grains, gives up classical learning, thus running counter to what is cherished by Heaven and Earth in quest of the way of "no death," then he is in no way to communicate with this world or to prevent what is not right from happening (*fei suoyi tongshi fangfei ye* 非所以通世防非也).[59]

Lu Jia seems to be of the opinion that only the worldly, Confucian *Dao* is the true *Dao,* whereas the otherworldly *Dao* followed by the *xian* immortals is not the right path for man. In this passage, two interesting points may be observed. First, during early Former Han times, the cult of immortality as here described was still thoroughly otherworldly in character. Only by cutting off all worldly bonds could one expect to become a *xian.* This early cult of immortality, as we shall see, differed greatly from the same cult in the Later Han Period. Second, otherworldly *xian* immortality is identified with the "way of no death," which, as our preceding analysis has shown, is an outgrowth of the ancient worldly desire for longevity. Here we already see the confluence of the streams of worldly and otherworldly immortality, a historical trend that became readily discernible, if it did not originate, in Qin Shi Huang's quest for immortality, to which we now turn.

WORLDLY TRANSFORMATION OF THE IMMORTALITY CULT

As has been pointed out, in pre-Qin times, it was already a general practice among the princes of various states to seek immortality drugs for the prolongation of life. With the unification of China under Qin Shi Huang in 221 B.C.E., the imperial quest for immortality drugs was intensified and undertaken on a much larger scale, probably the result, at least in part, of the fact that now the *fangshi* 方士 (necromancers) had only a single emperor to work for rather than a number of princes. In 219 B.C.E., only two years after unification, the *fangshi* from the coastal region of Qi flocked to the court, offering the emperor their services in seeking "drugs of no death" out in the sea.[60] According to Sima Qian, after Qin Shi Huang achieved unification, numerous immortals talked to him about the *xian* and "drugs of no death."[61] A first-century-B.C.E. source relates that as soon as Qin Shi Huang sent men to sea in search of *xian* and drugs, the people of Yan and Qi contended with one another in talking about *xian* immortality. Thousands of *fangshi* rushed to the capital, Xianyang, saying that by taking elixirs of gold and pearls, *xian* could live as long as Heaven and Earth.[62]

With the popularization of the immortality cult came its vulgarization as well. Thus, the otherworldly and seclusive *xian* immortality gradually underwent an Earthly transformation. With Qin Shi Huang, we encounter for the first time the conflict of worldly with otherworldly immortality. Since "no death" was now identifiable with *xian* immortality, to achieve the former was to become a *xian*. This fact explains why Qin Shi Huang preferred to call himself "True Man" (*zhenren* 真人), another name for *xian*, rather than the more dignified and honorable *zhen* 朕, the royal "we."[63]

In spite of the emperor's efforts to make himself a *xian*, however, the gap between worldly and otherworldly immortality could not be so easily bridged. What the emperor was really after was longevity or immortality. Obviously, it was the *xian*'s reputation for knowing the best way to gain these ends that attracted the emperor to the cult. No Earthly person such as he could have been interested in the otherworldly life of the *xian* as described in such literary passages as those mentioned above. From the scanty sources at our disposal, it is evident that his quest for immortality must be understood in terms of the traditional worldly desire for longevity or "no death."

His real position is best reflected in his attitude toward death. Near the end of his life, he disliked death so much that no one dared mention it in his presence.[64] This fact reveals the worldly considerations that motivated his interest in the cult, however incompatible with the idea of the *xian* this motive may have been. One of the *fangshi* blamed the failure to obtain immortality drugs on the fact that the emperor was ruling the empire and therefore not practicing that quietism which was a necessary condition for attaining immortality. The *fangshi* then suggested that the emperor live a solitary and secluded life, always keeping his whereabouts secret—advice that he followed. The emperor's greed for power, which made him unworthy of immortality drugs, is one of the reasons given for the departure of many *fangshi* from the court.[65] It may well be that they used the emperor's worldly life as a convenient excuse for their failure to procure the promised drugs; nevertheless, we can discern here a difference

between the ideas of worldly and otherworldly immortality that even the ingenious *fangshi* found difficult to reconcile.

Intensification of the emperor's quest for immortality furthered the popularization as well as the transformation of *xian* immortality, both as a cult and
as an idea. The rapid development of the cult during the reign of Han Wudi
was such a striking and well-known phenomenon that it startled his contemporaries as much as it amuses us. Sima Qian repeatedly tells us that since Wudi
became involved in the pursuit of immortality and honored some *fangshi* with
noble titles and generous gifts, *fangshi* from Yan and Qi contended with one
another in making lavish claims to secret recipes for immortality and communications with *xian*.[66] In the latter part of the first century B.C.E., Gu Yong 谷永
succinctly summarized the efforts of these two rulers and their *fangshi*:

> When Qin Shi Huang first unified the empire, he indulged in the cult of
> *xian* immortality. Thereupon, he sent people like Xu Fu 徐福 and Han
> Zhong 韓終 to sea, with unmarried boys and girls, in search of *xian* as
> well as drugs. But [these people] took the opportunity to run away and
> never came back. Such efforts aroused the resentment and hatred of all
> under Heaven. With the rise of Han, Xinyuan Ping 新垣平 of Zhao (in
> the reign of Wendi, 179–157 B.C.E.), Shaoweng 少翁, Gongsun Qing 公孫卿,
> Luan Da 欒大, and others of Qi,[67] all received honors and favors from Em-
> peror Wudi on account of their [claimed magical powers, such as] ac-
> quaintanceship with *xian*, alchemy, sacrificial offerings, serving and
> controlling spirits, and going to sea to search for *xian* and drugs. Gifts
> bestowed on them amounted to thousands of measures of gold. [Luan] Da
> was particularly honored, and even married a princess. Titles and posi-
> tions were heaped on him to such an extent that all within the seas were
> shocked. Therefore, during the *yuanding* and *yuanfeng* periods [116–103
> B.C.E.], there were thousands of *fangshi* in the areas of Yan and Qi who
> protruded their eyes and clasped their hands, saying that they knew such
> arts as those of achieving *xian* immortality, of sacrificial offerings, and of
> obtaining blessings.[68]

Furthermore, in the year 31 B.C.E., according to a joint memorial of Kuang Heng
匡衡 and Zhang Tan 張譚 to Emperor Chengdi, 683 sacrificial halls were
erected throughout the empire for the purpose of meeting gods or *xian* and
were placed in the care of *fangshi*.[69] This fact, together with Gu Yong's statement, indicates beyond a doubt how popular the cult of *xian* immortality had
become since the time of Qin Shi Huang, and especially Han Wudi.

The unprecedented intensity with which the cult was practiced under the
latter's reign is discernible in at least two important ways. First, according to
tradition, there were two mythical residences for *xian* immortals: one in the

extreme east in the sea and the other in the extreme west on the summit of Mount Kunlun, the supposed residence of the well-known Xi Wangmu 西王母 (Western Queen Mother).[70] Prior to Han Wudi, however, royal seekers of immortality, such as the princes of Qi and Yan and the First Emperor, sent envoys beyond the sea to the east in hopes of communicating with immortals. Probably because of the limited geographical knowledge of the time, none of them seems to have made any attempt to reach immortals on Mount Kunlun in the west. Even Han Wudi's quest was, in his early years, still directed mainly toward the sea. The opening of the western region by Zhang Qian in the second half of the second century B.C.E., however, diverted the attention of the emperor and the Daoist immortals more and more to the west.[71] The failure to obtain immortality drugs from the sea helped kindle the emperor's imagination in other directions and intensified his expectation of procuring them from the Western Queen Mother. According to Wen Ying 文穎, a commentator on the *Hanshu* (History of the Former Han Dynasty), he actually expressed his desire to ascend Mount Kunlun and become a *xian*.[72] Thus, during Han times, following on the increase in geographical knowledge, the imperial quest for *xian* immortality ranged geographically wider than ever before.

Second, although previous royal seekers of *xian* immortality had all been so concerned with means of prolonging their lives, they were rational enough not to let these personal longings interfere with the public undertakings of their states to any serious degree. With Han Wudi, however, the case was somewhat different. In his quest for *xian* immortality, he went a step further by sometimes allowing this personal concern to affect the foreign relations of the empire. That the emperor's opening up of the western region was motivated not only by military and diplomatic considerations but also by his personal craving for foreign rare products, such as the well-known "Heavenly Horses" of Ferghana (Dawan or Dayuan 大宛), is a fact that has been observed by almost every historian dealing with the period.[73] It has further been suggested that the widespread belief in the Western Queen Mother of Mount Kunlun may also have somewhat accentuated the emperor's interest in westward expansion. And in his official trip to Central Asia, Zhang Qian was probably also entrusted with the additional imperial mission of learning the exact whereabouts of the Western Queen Mother.[74] Even behind the emperor's curiosity about rare foreign products, one may again find at work the eager quest for *xian* immortality. The "Heavenly Horses" of Ferghana are a case in point. As one highly suggestive study has ably shown, Han Wudi's conquest of Ferghana was, to a great extent, precipitated by his preoccupation with *xian* immortality. It seems that Han Wudi's rather excessive fondness for the "Heavenly Horses" cannot be explained to our full satisfaction by the practical consideration of getting horses of good stock for war purposes. Still less can it be simply taken as a peculiar obsession with horses as such. Rather, a deeper reason is to be found in the emperor's staunch belief in the "Heavenly Horses" as a medium of communication between the world of man and that of the *xian* immortals. Somewhat disappointed by the failure to find immortality in the seas to the east but not yet quite emancipated from the ingenious deception of the Daoist immortals, the emperor now believed that the "Heavenly Horses" of Ferghana were of the same family as the dragons and would eventually carry him to meet the Western Queen Mother on Mount Kunlun. This is, as we shall see later, simply a slightly revised version of the Yellow Emperor's ascension to Heaven on a dragon's back. It was probably this belief that made Han Wudi so determined to get the "Heavenly Horses," even at the cost of aggressive wars.[75]

The further worldly transformation of the idea of immortality needs more elaboration. Generally speaking, it may be seen in the fact that in almost all of Han Wudi's efforts in connection with the cult of *xian* immortality, his worldly desire for longevity or immortality can always be discerned. In the case of the famous *fangshi* named Li Shaojun 李少君, we see very clearly that Emperor Wudi was much more concerned with achieving longevity or immortality than with transcending this human world to become a seclusive *xian*. It is possible that Li won so much of the emperor's confidence primarily because he was particularly known to be versed, among other magical arts, in the method of "avoiding old age" (*quelao* 郤老). It is true that Li also promised that the emperor would meet the *xian* of Penglai 蓬萊, one of the three divine mountains in the sea. This does not mean, however, that the emperor would join the *xian* on Penglai. Rather, it reflects the belief that seeing the *xian* would lead to the result of "no death," and thus accounts for Emperor Wudi's enthusiasm for the cult of *xian* immortality.[76]

Wudi's worldly desire for longevity is also instanced by his revival of the sacrificial offerings to spirits of the dead (*gui* 鬼) in Nan Yue 南越 (modern Guangdong, Guangxi, and part of Vietnam). After the pacification of Nan Yue in the year 111 B.C.E., the emperor was told that formerly a king there had lived one hundred and sixty years because he had made sacrificial offerings to spirits of the dead. But later, people failed to follow the king's example, which resulted in the population becoming much weakened and exhausted. Upon learning this, the emperor ordered the shamans of Yue to make sacrificial offerings not only to Heavenly gods but also to all kinds of spirits as well.[77] Since this sort of sacrificial offering was originally unrelated to the cult of *xian* immortality, Emperor Wudi, in reviving the traditional practices of the former long-lived king of Yue, was obviously motivated by the worldly desire for prolongation of life. By illustration, we may cite still another example. At the suggestion of the famous *fangshi* Gongsun Qing, Emperor Wudi ordered the erection of two halls at Changan, then the capital, and another at Ganquan 甘泉, one hundred *li* from the capital, for the accommodation of *xian*. The latter was named Yiyanshou 益延壽, which may be rendered as "longevity."[78] Such a name seems to be highly indicative of the true intention of the emperor: he was anxious to meet the *xian* in order to prolong his own life.

Lastly, Han Wudi's worldly desire for longevity or "no death" may also be seen in the famous *feng* and *shan* sacrifices. To be sure, the problem of the *feng* and *shan* sacrifices is too complicated to be discussed extensively here.[79] Roughly speaking, during the period of the Qin and Han dynasties, there existed side by side two different interpretations of the *feng* and *shan* sacrifices. One was the political interpretation held by the Confucians and the other was what may be called the quasi-religious interpretation held by the *fangshi*. According to the former, the function of the *feng* and *shan* sacrifices, which were to be performed on Mount Tai and the adjacent hill called Liangfu 梁父, respectively, was to announce the accomplishment of general peace by a new dynasty as a result of receiving the Mandate of Heaven.[80] According to the latter, performance of the *feng* and *shan* sacrifices was to bring immortality ("no death") to the emperor.[81] As most modern scholars agree, however, the *feng* and *shan* sacrifices made by Qin Shi Huang, and particularly Han Wudi, were intended primarily to secure prolongation of life or avoidance of death. It is true that the "Fengshan shu" (Treatise on the *Feng* and *Shan* Sacrifices) in the *Records of the Grand Historian* does not explicitly relate Qin Shi Huang's performance of the *feng* and *shan* sacrifices to the quest for immortality. In view of the fact that he did not let the Confucian scholars arrange the sacrifices,[82] however, it may be that he used some *fangshi* as his advisers. Moreover, the well-known "posthumous edict of Qin Shi Huang" counterfeited by Zhao Gao 趙高, the notorious chief eunuch, begins with the following sentence: "I have made an imperial tour throughout the whole empire and performed sacrifices to various gods of famous mountains in the hope of prolonging my life."[83] In spite of its being a forgery, this sentence may still contain some truth as far as the emperor's intention is concerned. Otherwise, it would hardly be able to serve the purpose of fabrication. Needless to say, Mount Tai must have been included in the "famous mountains." Thus understood, it seems beyond doubt that Qin Shi Huang's performance of the *feng* and *shan* sacrifices was also motivated by his worldly desire for longevity.[84]

Like Qin Shi Huang, Han Wudi, too, made no use of the Confucians in the *fengshan* arrangements.[85] In Han Wudi's *fengshan* performance, however, the influence of *fangshi* was much stronger and the emperor's worldly desire for longevity or "no death" had also become more intense.[86] What makes the *fengshan* of Han Wudi different from that of Qin Shi Huang,[87] it seems to me, is the fact that in performing the sacrifices, the former aspired not only to prolongation of life in this world, but also, paradoxically enough, to ascend to Heaven to become a *xian*, which Huangdi (the Yellow Emperor) was then believed to have achieved. Han Wudi is even reported to have said that he would not hesitate to leave behind his wives and children if only he could follow the example of the Yellow Emperor and ascend to Heaven as a *xian*.[88] At first sight, it would seem that in Han Wudi's case, the distinction between otherworldly and worldly immortality that we have been trying to make does not make much sense. Yet on closer examination, one finds that in the time of Han Wudi, obviously due to the ingenious elaborations of the *fangshi*, the idea of *xian* was already beginning to take on a more or less worldly character. In the case of Qin Shi Huang, we have seen the conflict of the two kinds of immortality, a conflict of which the *fangshi* must have been well aware. For the *fangshi*, there were only two ways in which this conflict could be avoided: give up the cult of *xian* immortality, which by then had already become their profession, or transform the traditional otherworldly idea of *xian* into a worldly one so that it would match the worldly desire of the worldly ruler. Naturally, the *fangshi* chose the latter alternative.

The worldly transformation of *xian* may best be illustrated by a statement by Sima Xiangru, the best-known *fu* writer of Wudi's time: "The *xian* take their residence in mountains or swamps and look rather emaciated. But this is not what the emperor means by *xian*."[89] Even such a simple statement reveals two relevant facts: *xian* were traditionally conceived as being seclusive and otherworldly, and worldly emperors were not interested in this kind of *xian*. To determine what kind of *xian* Wudi was interested in becoming leads us to reexamine the legendary sage-king, Huangdi (the Yellow Emperor), whom the *fangshi* made a model of emperor-turned-*xian* for Wudi to follow.

In pre-Qin literature, the Yellow Emperor did not occupy as prominent a position as did other legendary sage-kings such as Yao, Shun, and Yu. The earliest reference to him is found in a bronze inscription of the state of Qi dated about 375 B.C.E., in which the Yellow Emperor is called by the King of Qi a "remote ancestor" (*gaozu* 高祖).[90] In this inscription, the Yellow Emperor is obviously considered a mortal man and is in no way related to the cult of *xian* immortality. We have good reason to believe with Sima Qian that he is found not in the orthodox Confucian classics but in the works of the "Hundred Schools," whose language is rather loose.[91]

Sima Xiangru's statement also indicates when the transformation of *xian* took place. The Grand Historian mentions the Yellow Emperor only as the first ruler in the "Annals of the Five Emperors." It is only in the "Treatise on the Feng and Shan Sacrifices" that he is presented as a *xian* in connection with *fangshi*, showing that the change took place at a late date. Among pre-Qin philosophers, Zou Yan 鄒衍 of Qi (305–340 B.C.E.) is probably one of the earliest, if not the earliest, to mention the Yellow Emperor in conjunction with the theory of the cycle of five virtues,[92] an indication that the legend of the Yellow Emperor is particularly related to the state of Qi, the home of the *fangshi*.[93] On the other hand, the ideas of "no death" and *xian* immortality also seem to have originated in Qi,[94] and it is here that we first see the flourishing of Huang-Lao 黄老 Daoism. In the fourth and third centuries B.C.E., a great number of the well-known Jixia 稷下 scholars of Qi were Huang-Lao Daoists.[95] From the late Warring States Period through early Han times, almost all Huang-Lao scholars are found to be either natives of Qi or associated with that state.[96] It is therefore justifiable to conjecture that Huang-Lao Daoism had its origin in Qi toward the end of the Warring States Period.[97] This fact may explain why the cult of *xian* immortality took the name of Huang-Lao Daoism during the Later Han Period.[98]

To what extent Huang-Lao Daoism and *xian* immortality were related to each other is hard to determine, but there is no doubt the two were already associated by the middle of the second century B.C.E.[99] For instance, the famous Anqi Sheng 安期生 of the third and second centuries B.C.E., originally known as one of the early masters of Huang-Lao Daoism,[100] was made a *xian* in Han Wudi's time by the *fangshi* of Qi.[101] According to a modern scholar, he himself was probably a *fangshi* of Qi, one who was also versed in Huang-Lao philosophy.[102] The *fangshi* of Qi at Wudi's court were also responsible for the transformation of the Yellow Emperor from a legendary sage-king to a *xian* immortal.[103] The idea was probably first suggested by Li Shaojun, who indicated to Wudi that the Yellow Emperor had achieved "no death" after having seen the *xian* on Peng-lai and having performed the *feng* and *shan* sacrifices.[104] Further elaborations by Gongsun Qing and other *fangshi* made the Yellow Emperor actually become a *xian* and ascend to Heaven on a dragon's back. What is even more revealing of the worldly character of the idea of immortality is the fact that he was said to have ascended to Heaven with his whole suite, including a harem of over seventy.[105] This type of *xian*, gregarious and still pursuing worldly pleasures, is in sharp contradistinction to the traditional concept of a secluded and ascetic *xian*, and it probably explains why Sima Xiangru insisted that the traditional seclusive *xian* did not appeal to the emperors at all. Ascension to Heaven in the manner of the Yellow Emperor is actually a transplantation of the imperial life from this world to another, and to one in which human desires probably would be better gratified than annihilated.[106]

The invention of the story of the Yellow Emperor's ascension to Heaven with his whole suite is the first step taken by the *fangshi* to transform the idea of *xian* to suit the worldly taste of immortality seekers. As time went on, the same theme received further elaboration. Moreover, its application was no longer limited to the emperor, but extended to nobles and commoners as well. The following two instances will suffice as illustrations. The first is the case of the Prince of Huainan named Liu An 劉安 (d. 122 B.C.E.), the reputed author of *Huainanzi*, which has been widely known ever since Han times. He was a great patron of *fangshi* as well as of scholars and was forced to commit suicide after planning sedition against Emperor Wudi.[107] After his death, however, there arose a legend in which the prince did not really die but ascended to Heaven as a *xian*. This story is imbued with even more earthly flavor than the Yellow Emperor's, because not only his whole household but even his dogs and cocks are said to have followed him to Heaven as a result of taking immortality drugs.[108] A Later Han scholar explained this story as an expedient used by the *fangshi* to gloss over the actual reason for the death of the prince.[109] This might

well have been the case, but in view of the fact that the *fangshi* had first suggested the idea in its prototype to Emperor Wudi, we may conjecture that the
gospel of ascension to Heaven with one's entire household might already have
been preached to Prince Liu An by the *fangshi* to induce him to embark on the
search for *xian* immortality. Since immortality seekers from the ruling class
were all motivated by worldly considerations, this was a most persuasive gospel
and one most likely to touch their hearts. Although there is no reason to doubt
the sincerity of people like Han Wudi and Liu An in seeking immortality, it is
certainly beyond anyone's comprehension why they should be interested in becoming traditional *xian* at the cost of all their earthly pleasures.

The idea of ascension to Heaven with one's family, however, also found its
way among the common people. Our second instance, although less well
known to students of Daoism, is of considerable importance to our understanding of the worldly transformation of the idea of *xian* in Han times. This story,
taken from a Han stone inscription dedicated to a *xian* immortal named Tang
Gongfang, relates that in 7 B.C.E., Tang Gongfang 唐公房 served as a petty official in the provincial government of his native place, Hanzhong 漢中. By luck
he met and won the favor of a "True Man," who took him as a disciple and gave
him immortality drugs. Thus, Tang himself became a *xian* while still in government service. Later he offended the governor by failing to teach him the
Dao as the governor wished. Enraged, the latter ordered his subordinates to ar-
rest Tang's wife and children. When Tang learned of this and went to his master for help, the True Man made his wife and children take some drugs, saying,
"Now is the time to go." But the wife and children were reluctant to leave their
home. "Do you wish your whole household to go too?" asked the True Man. "Yes,
that is exactly what we want," they answered. Thereupon, he daubed the house
with drugs and, at the same time, gave drugs to all the domestic animals. There
immediately rose a great wind and a dark cloud to carry away Tang Gongfang and
his family. Their house as well as their animals disappeared. The inscription
goes on to make the following remark: "Formerly people like Wang Ziqiao and Ji
Songzi all became *xian* singly, but Tang Gongfang was translated into another
existence with his whole family. It is indeed remarkable."[110]

This story is rich in hidden meanings, but a few points directly related to our
discussion may be emphasized here. First, it shows that by this time, the cult of
xian immortality had already acquired a wider social basis and was no longer
an exclusive affair between *fangshi* and the ruling class, for the hero of the story
was only a petty official in a provincial government. Second, it shows the popular belief in drugs as the best, or rather the easiest, way to achieve immortality.
Third, the growing worldliness of the *xian* concept is reflected in the entire
household's removal from Earth to Heaven. In pre-Qin times, man ascended as a
xian only singly. With the Yellow Emperor, ascension to Heaven included his
harem and some of his ministers. With the Prince of Huainan, not only his
whole family but also his dogs and cocks were added, and in the case of Tang

Gongfang, in addition to his family and his domestic animals, even his house was translated to Heaven. This transition to worldliness suits Han times particularly well, for at that time, family ties were becoming more close-knit under the influence of Confucian teachings.

In light of the above discussion, we can now better understand Ban Gu's general criticism of the cult of *xian* immortality: "The *xian* immortal is one who preserves his life truly and yet seeks to transcend [life]. He clarifies his intention and pacifies his mind, so that he has no fear in his heart. But since there are people who make [the art of *xian* immortality] their special profession, literature of a deceptive and strange nature increases unceasingly. This is not what the sage-kings intended to teach [us]."[111] This criticism was undoubtedly directed at the vulgarization of the cult that we have been tracing. Therefore, in Later Han times, the idea of *xian* became almost identical with longevity and "no death,"[112] and otherworldly terms, such as "transcending this world," and earthly ones, such as "no death," were used indiscriminately by writers to mean physical immortality.[113]

THE IDEA OF IMMORTALITY IN POPULAR THOUGHT

Before turning to popular thought, let us first glance at the literati's attitude toward the cult of *xian* immortality. The literati's general view may be conveniently characterized as a rationalistic and naturalistic one. Although most of that class considered longevity desirable and worth seeking, they generally ruled out physical immortality as something humanly impossible to attain. For instance, Yang Xiong (53 B.C.E.–18 C.E.) vigorously rejected the doctrine of immortality through magical techniques by saying that immortality is nonexistent and death is inevitable.[114] A contemporary thinker, Huan Tan 桓譚, was also of the opinion that the doctrine that immortality may be obtained through learning was but the empty words of the *fangshi*.[115] Wang Chong, the greatest critical philosopher of the first century C.E., devoted a whole chapter of his *Lunheng* 論衡 (Balanced Inquiries) to the refutation, point by point, of the possibility of achieving immortality.[116] According to Ying Shao of the second century C.E., a common saying among the literati stated, "gold cannot be transmuted [from other materials] and *xian* immortality cannot be achieved [by man]."[117]

In spite of the literati's skepticism, the idea of physical immortality struck deep roots in popular thought. From Wang Chong's criticism of the prevailing ideas of the time, we know that people generally believed in various ways of achieving physical immortality. For instance, they believed in ascension to Heaven by performing *feng* and *shan* sacrifices, as in the case of the Yellow Emperor; by taking immortality drugs, as in the case of the Prince of Huainan (both of which we have discussed above); or by drinking an elixir of gold and gems and eating the flowers of the purple boletus, which, it was said, would make the body light, as in the case of a certain Lu Ao 盧敖.[118] There were also people who believed that physical immortality could be achieved by following Laozi's teaching of quietism and dispassionateness,[119] by abstaining from eating cereals,[120] by regulating the breath as well as cultivating nature,[121] or, even more strangely, by metamorphosing the human body into the shape of a bird.[122]

Wang Chong's report has the merit of providing us with a general picture of the widespread belief in physical immortality. Moreover, the fact that he used such terms as *dushi* (transcending this world), *busi* (no death), *shengtian* (ascending to Heaven), *xian* (becoming an immortal), *changsheng* (long life), and *shou* (longevity) indiscriminately to denote physical immortality indicates that the demarcation line between otherworldly and worldly immortality had become increasingly blurred.[123] His occasional use of the word *shou* (longevity) as a synonym for physical immortality also shows that people of his time probably regarded immortality and longevity as belonging more or less to the same category.[124] The fact that there were long-lived people much strengthened the popular belief in the possibility of achieving immortality. In Wang Chong's own words: "There are no instances of anyone having obtained *Dao*, but there have been very long-lived persons. People remarking that these persons, while studying *Dao* and the art of immortality, become over one hundred years old without dying, call them immortals."[125] When immortality and longevity were thus made out to be identical, a further step was taken to divert the traditional otherworldly immortality in the direction of this-worldliness.

Some details concerning the popular belief in physical immortality as criticized by Wang Chong can still be found in the *Scripture of Great Peace*. According to this work, not only can physical immortality be achieved but it constitutes one of man's most important objectives. This is, of course, only a logical extension of its general emphasis on life, as discussed above: "Among all things in the universe, longevity excels the rest in virtue. . . . Heaven is greatly greedy of longevity, of everlasting life. The immortals (*xianren*) are also greedy of longevity as well as of life. Those who are greedy of life dare not do evil, because each of them has to take into consideration the preservation of his person."[126] The only novel, and religious, element in the *Scripture of Great Peace* concerning immortality would seem to be the theory that one's life span can be extended or shortened according to one's deeds. If one leads a virtuous life, one can, on that very account, achieve immortality. For instance, ascension to Heaven in the daytime is mentioned several times in the work as something definitely capable of accomplishment, but only on the basis of virtuous deeds:

There are instances in which people did ascend to Heaven in broad daylight. Those who ascended in broad daylight behaved in such a way that their natures were good, their hearts full of light, their wills never wavered, to goods and profit they paid no attention at all, and their clothes

were coarse and barely enough to cover their bodies. Heaven, appreciat-
ing their virtuous deeds, therefore appointed virtuous deities to keep
them company as well as for their protection, so that they might not be
led astray [by demons]. With the love and care of the celestial deities, they
thus accomplished the feat [of ascension to Heaven]. After all, it is the
fashion in which they led their lives that produced this result. Trusting
that their filial piety was true and sincere, and their conduct free from
fault, Heaven therefore often receives them in broad daylight. There have
been such cases that were witnessed by many people. [Heaven] helped
them to bring about the accomplishment in order to show people the result of being virtuous. It must be pointed out, however, that not even one
out of a million people could expect to get [access to Heaven] in broad
daylight. One could do so only under the protection and with the trust of
the great celestial deities.[127]

To be sure, this theory of retribution was itself not at all novel. Indeed, it was
deeply rooted and widely diffused in Chinese thought,[128] but was particularly
in keeping with the climate of opinion of Han times among intellectuals as
well as common people.[129]

To return to the idea of ascension to Heaven, in the previous section we
traced the worldly transformation of this idea in the Former Han Period. The
frequency with which it is mentioned in the *Scripture of Great Peace* indicates
that the idea was still regarded favorably by Later Han immortals. The idea that
ascension to Heaven may be achieved through virtuous deeds in addition to, or
even instead of, taking drugs throws further light on the worldly character of
xian, because cultivation of virtue is by definition humanistic and therefore
worldly in nature.

We can even find grounds—although no historical evidence—in Later Han
times for the statement in the *Scripture of Great Peace* that people had witnessed
immortals ascending to Heaven in broad daylight. According to the *Hou
Hanshu* (History of the Later Han Dynasty), a native of Mixian in Henan,
Shangcheng Gong 上成公 by name, returned after a long absence to tell his
family that he had become an immortal and bade them farewell. His family
then saw him go up to Heaven step by step until he was out of sight. The story
also says that Chen Shi 陳寔 and Han Shao 韓韶, both well-known literati of the
period,[130] happened to witness the scene.[131] This story, unhistorical as it is,
must have had a fairly wide circulation at the time because Zhongchang Tong
仲長統, the famous political philosopher of the second century C.E., is said to
have told a slightly different version of it, in which the name of the hero is
changed to Bu Cheng卜成 (*bu* 卜 presumably being a corruption of Shang 上)
and the witnesses are not Chen and Han, but their fathers and grandfathers.[132]
From this instance, we know that the belief in the possibility of ascension to

Heaven was also shared by some of the Han literati, which probably accounts for the severe criticism by Wang Chong.

Apart from ascension to Heaven, the highest form of physical immortality, such related matters as immortality recipes and immortality drugs are also discussed at some length in the *Scripture of Great Peace*; it is very positive about the existence of such things, but explains the extremely restricted access to them by referring to the theory of retribution. In answering the True Man (*zhenren* 真人) as to whether immortality recipes are obtainable, the Heavenly Teacher (*Tianshi* 天師) says:

> Yes, they are obtainable. The number of immortality drugs stored in Heaven may be compared to that of grain stored in the imperial granaries; the number of immortals' clothes to that of government cloth; and the number of houses of the immortals to that of official buildings. . . . Heaven is by no means sparing of the immortals' clothes or immortality recipes, but just [finds it] difficult to give them to man. Since man does not make a great contribution to Heaven and Earth . . . Heaven therefore withholds from man the immortality recipes and immortals' clothes, which are to be reserved for people of extraordinary merit. . . . For comparison's sake, we may take the example of the grain of the imperial granaries and government cloth. There are numerous *hu* and *dou* of grain in the imperial granaries, but people possessing neither merit nor virtue cannot expect to receive even a *sheng* of them. . . . Now man is so wicked that [his conduct] is not in accord with the will of Heaven; therefore, Heaven no longer produces good drugs and recipes. . . . So from ancient times through the middle ages [down to the present day], the true *Dao* has been declining day after day, and authentic immortality recipes have thus become inaccessible.[133]

One can easily discern in this passage an apologetic tone. For centuries, people had been seeking immortality drugs and recipes to no avail. Not only were such rationalistic thinkers as Wang Chong skeptical about their existence, but the illiterate masses must also have been keenly disappointed. With the help of the theory of retribution, the belief in immortality was capable of a better theoretical defense against the intellectual attacks of the literati and was reinvigorated as one of the primary tenets of religious Daoism, which was thus enabled to attract more followers.

Another statement in the *Scripture of Great Peace* suggests that the Daoist immortals were in the early *fangshi* tradition, that is, seekers of immortality drugs and recipes for the sovereign. There it is argued that those who know only how to serve the sovereign loyally and obediently in a passive fashion are people of medium goodness. People of extreme goodness are those who make all possible effort to acquire strange recipes and immortality drugs for their sovereign so that his life may be infinitely prolonged.[134]

At this juncture, it may be relevant to take a look at the relations between the cult of immortality and the Han emperors after Han Wudi. Generally speaking, immortality seems never to have ceased to appeal to the sovereigns throughout the two Han dynasties. A few instances will suffice as illustrations. During the reign of Emperor Xuandi (73–49 B.C.E.), the cult of immortality was revived and some recipes for immortality and alchemical formulas,[135] which had formerly been in the possession of the Prince of Huainan, were rediscovered. Thereupon, the emperor chose a famous scholar, Liu Xiang 劉向, to take charge of the experiments made with them.[136] Wang Mang, the reformer and usurper, is reported to have believed in some kind of immortality grain;[137] moreover, he was associated with a *fangshi* named Zhao Jun 昭君.[138] In the Later Han Period, Emperor Huandi (C.E. 147–167) is particularly well known for the enthusiasm with which he paid homage indiscriminately to both Daoism and Buddhism.[139] It is interesting to note that the emperor was interested in Daoism primarily, if not solely, because he wanted to achieve physical immortality. We are told that he occupied himself with matters concerning physical immortality and, on this account, not only sent envoys to perform sacrifices to Laozi at Huxian 苦縣 (Henan), the reputed birthplace of the sage, but also personally performed sacrifices to Laozi in the palace.[140] Other evidence tends to show that toward the end of the Later Han, the cult of Laozi was already fused with that of immortality.[141] From these facts, it seems clear that Daoism succeeded in establishing itself at the Han court through the medium of the immortality cult. It may be further conjectured that in the Later Han, many *fangshi* and *daoshi* (Daoist priests) carried on the practice of their predecessors by winning the trust and favor of sovereigns with extravagant promises of immortality.

This historical background provides us, I believe, with an important clue to understanding what the *Scripture of Great Peace* says about seeking immortality drugs and recipes for the sovereign.[142] Unfortunately, unlike the *Records of the Grand Historian* and the *History of the Former Han Dynasty*, the *History of the Later Han Dynasty* tells us almost nothing about the activities of *daoshi* and *fangshi* at the imperial court.[143] However, the following case is indicative of the close association of the Daoists with some of the Later Han emperors. "The Empress He (wife of Emperor Ling, 168–188 B.C.E.) . . . gave birth to a prince [named] Bian [who was] brought up in the family of a Daoist by the surname of Shi 史, [and the child was thus] known as Shi Hou (Marquis Shi)." The commentary quotes a passage from the *Xiandi chunqiu* 獻帝春秋 (Spring and Autumn of Xiandi), which explains the event thus: "Emperor Ling had several times lost his sons. Therefore, he dared not give a formal name [to the child and] had him brought up in the family of Daoist name Shi Zimiao 史子眇 and called him Shi Hou."[144] The importance of this story, simple as it is, can hardly be overstressed, because it throws much light on Daoist influence in the imperial court of Later Han times. At least two tentative conclusions can be drawn from it. First, the fact that a prince could be entrusted to the care of a Daoist family shows the extent to which the Daoists had won the general confidence of the court. Second, the practice of having a child brought up in a Daoist family for the sake of safety, which became rather common in the period that immediately followed, must be somewhat related to the popular belief in Daoist immortality and longevity. A parallel case may be drawn from the period of the Six Dynasties (222–589). The famous poet, Xie Lingyun 謝靈運 (385–433), was sent right after his birth to a Daoist family named Du 杜 for fosterage, because the Xie family had not been prolific in offspring. He did not return to his own family until he was fifteen.[145]

Lastly, let us examine the worldly transformation of *xian* in light of the *Scripture of Great Peace*. The traditional, seclusive type of *xian* as typified by Wang Ziqiao or Chi Songzi had no connection with the human world. In the *Scripture of Great Peace*, however, a *xian* could serve as a minister in case the True Man becomes the supreme ruler.[146] Moreover, in earlier literature, all *xian*, whether they were Divine Men (shenren 神人), True Men, or others, were taken as equals. They were not graded into higher or lower classes. Yet strangely enough, in the *Scripture of Great Peace*, the Heavenly world and the human world are hierarchically linked as follows: Divine Man, True Man, *xian*, Man of the Way, sages, Worthy Man, common people, and slaves.[147] In this way, the Heavenly and human worlds are actually connected and made into one. In later times, as we have noted, a sort of earthly *xian* was to be created (see note 111). But in the *Scripture of Great Peace*, we already encounter such worldly immortals in their primordial form. For instance, the work actually mentions famous mountains and great rivers as places to accommodate those *xian* immortals who are not yet able to ascend to Heaven.[148]

The last point that has an important bearing on the worldly character of *xian* may be seen in the emphasis on the family tie. According to the *Scripture of Great Peace*, he who learns the *Dao* merely for personal salvation is a man of the lower grade, but a man who studies the *Dao* to transcend this world with his family is of the middle grade.[149] This is obviously a strong rejection of the traditional, seclusive, and individualistic idea of immortality. Elsewhere in the work, leaving behind one's parents, wife, and children to go in search of the *Dao* is ferociously attacked as the very opposite of the true *Dao*.[150]

SUMMARY

The whole development of immortality both as an idea and as a cult from its beginning in the late Warring States Period down through Han times may be best characterized by one word: worldliness. This worldly spirit, as has been observed, not only has its historical origin in the universal desire for longevity traceable to ancient China; ideologically, it is also entrenched in the general humanistic emphasis on life characteristic of Chinese thought.

The process of the worldly transformation of immortality is particularly well illustrated by the changing views on the life of *xian* immortals. In pre-Qin literature, the *xian* is portrayed only as a secluded individual wandering in the sky, in no way related to the human world. In Han literature, however, we begin to find that the *xian* may sometimes also enjoy a settled life by bringing with him to paradise not only his family but also all chattels of his human life. This change, it seems to me, should not be isolated from the development of Han society, in which the individual's family ties were increasingly emphasized. Without such a readjustment to the new environment, it is not likely that the idea of *xian* could have survived the rapid and extensive social changes that sharply separated the Qin and Han Period from earlier times.

Another important aspect of the worldly spirit of the immortality cult lay in its political entanglements. It is a commonplace in Chinese history that the Daoist religion exerted no small influence of one sort or another on political developments through its close association with the imperial court.[151] In light of what has been said above, we can be certain that the tradition of such an association was first established by the *fangshi* of the late Warring States Period and then greatly strengthened by those of Qin and Han times, always with the quest for immortality as a medium. This point is amply evidenced by the intensity with which the *Scripture of Great Peace* urges people to seek immortality drugs or recipes for their sovereign. And the keen political interest of the *fangshi* or Daoist immortals also makes it more likely that they were in some way related to the so-called Huang-Lao Daoism of the early Former Han Period.

APPENDIX: HAN USE OF LONGEVITY TERMS IN PROPER NAMES

In Han times, the idea of longevity was expressed by various terms. In addition to *yishou* and *yanshou*,[152] other names reflecting the imperial quest for immortality were in use, such as *yannian* 延年 (prolongation of life), *yingnian* 迎年 (praying for long life), and, according to Yan Shigu's commentary, *mingnian* 明年, which Yan takes to mean "showing that prolongation of life may be obtained."[153] Such names were not an imperial monopoly, but were widely used in Han China for places and persons. Whether imperial use helped to popularize them or whether their popularity prompted the court to adopt them, we have no way of knowing, although the former seems more likely. In either case, they indicate the worldly transformation and popularization of the cult of immortality, as borne out by the place and personal names in the Han documents on wooden slips discovered at Edsin Gol, which cover roughly the period from 102 B.C. to 31 C.E.

		Hanjian			Jiabian	
	Number of mentions	Page	Number of mentions	Page	Number of mentions	Page
Shou 壽	109	3	5,737	120	1,403	59
	532	12	5,860	123	1,489	62
	601	13	6,579	136	2,103	87
	4,500	92	6,833		141	(Appendix)
	4,520	93	7,394	152	6	106
	4,667	96	9,048	183		
Yanshou 延壽	150	4[1]	6,175	129	33	3
	857	18	7,215	148	941	40
	1,091	22	7,303	150		
	3,566	71	7,670	159		
	3,749	75	7,677	159		
	4,543	93	8,013	165		
	4,690	97	9,438	190		
	5,329	110	9,941	199		
Changshou 長壽	1,230	25	4,093	83		
	4,061	82				
Yishou 益壽	1,954	40				
Shangshou 上壽	7,216	148				
Yannian 延年	221	5	1,005	21	636	28
	715	15	3,114	62	1,500	62
	768	16	3,603	72	2,554A	104
	885	18	7,439	153		
Changsheng 長生	1,627	33				

[1] Yishou 益壽: According to *Jiabian*, no. 538, 24. The original character is not clear in the plate.

In the case of place names, we find three Shouli 壽里,[154] one Changshouli 長壽里,[155] and two Yanshouli 延壽里.[156] There is even one watchtower bearing the name Yanshou.[157]

As for personal names, examples are much more numerous. Besides such famous names as Li Yannian 李延年, Yan 嚴 Yannian, and Han Yanshou 韓延壽, which are given biographical entries or are repeatedly mentioned in the *Records of the Grand Historian* and *History of the Former Han Dynasty*, the following personal names appear most frequently in Han wooden documents:

The above list makes no claim to completeness. Names of those who are known or suspected to be of a later period have not been included (e.g., see *Hanjian*, no. 223, 5, and no. 669, 14). Repetitions have also been avoided as far as determinable (e.g., *Hanjian*, no. 6234, 130; no. 7176, 147; no. 7676, 159). On the other hand, omissions due to carelessness are inevitable; therefore, this list is at best a good sample. Whatever its shortcomings, it reveals two important facts about the worldly transformation and popularization of the immortality cult in Han China. First, the fact that men bearing such names were mostly officers and soldiers in frontier watchtowers shows that the common

people shared with emperors the desire for longevity or immortality, an indication of the permeation of the idea of *xian* immortality in society. Second, the
fact that the people so named came from various provinces of the empire further indicates that the concept had spread rather quickly as well as widely.
Among the localities represented by these persons are Hanzhong 漢中 (*Hanjian*,
no. 150), Nanyang 南陽 (ibid., no. 5737), Dongjun 東郡 (ibid., no. 6579), Juyan
居延 (ibid., no. 7216), Chang-an, the capital (*Jiabian*, no. 1500), and Changyi 昌
邑 in Shanyang 山陽 (ibid., no. 2130). This distribution gives some notion of the
popularity of the immortality cult in geographical terms.

NOTES

1. James Legge, trans., *The Chinese Classics*, vol. 1, *Confucian Analects* (Hong Kong: HKU
   Press, 1960), 241. This chapter in the present volume is a slightly revised and expanded
   version of chapter 1 of my doctoral dissertation written in 1961 at Harvard University. I
   wish to take this opportunity to express my gratitude to Professor Lien-sheng Yang,
   under whose guidance its first draft was completed. Grateful acknowledgment also
   goes to Professor Benjamin I. Schwartz, who read the manuscript and made valuable
   suggestions as well as criticisms. Neither of them, of course, is responsible for any
   errors or faults that may remain.

2. S. Kierkegaard, *The Sickness Unto Death*, trans. Walter Lowrie (New York: Anchor
   Books, 1954), 144.

3. See Fu Sinian 傅斯年, "Xingming guxun bianzheng" 性命古訓辨證, in *Fu Mengzhen
   xiansheng ji* 傅孟真先生集 (Taipei: Taiwan daxue, 1952), 1–201.

4. For a general study of views of life and death in early Confucian thought, see Shizukui-
   shi Kōkichi 靜石鑛吉, "Jukyō no shiseikan to tōitsu no ichishiki" 儒教の死生觀と統一の
   意識, *Tokyo Shina gakuhō* 東京支那學報 7 (June 1961): 69–79.

5. *Laozi*, SBBY, 51.9b–10a; J. J. L. Duyvendak, *Tao Te Ching* (London: John Murray, 1954),
   113.

6. James Legge, trans., *The Yi King*, SBE, 16.381. For modern discussions on the date of the
   "Great Appendix" to the *Yijing*, see Gu Jiegang 顧頡剛, in *Gushi bian* 古史辨, 7 vols., 1926–
   1941 (Shanghai: Guji 1982 [reprint]), 3:37–70; Li Jingchi 李鏡池, in *Gushi bian*, 3:95–132;
   and Guo Moruo, "Zhouyi zhi zhizuo shidai" 周易之制作時代, reprinted in *Qingtong shidai*
   青銅時代 (Beijing: Kexue, 1954), 66–94.

7. Legge, *Yi King*, 356.

8. For these two lines of development of early Daoist views, see Tsuda Sōkichi 津田左右吉,
   Dōka no shisō to sono tenkai 道家の思想と其の展開 (Tokyo: Iwanami Shoten, 1939),
   313–332; Xu Dishan 許地山, *Daojiao shi* 道教史 (Shanghai: Shangwu, 1934), 114–119; Arthur Waley, *The Way and Its Power* (New York: Grove Evergreen, 1958), 39–50.

9. Wang Xianqian 王先謙, *Xunzi jijie* 荀子集解, WYWK, 2.13; Fung Yu-lan, *A History of Chinese Philosophy*, trans. Derk Bodde (Princeton: Princeton University Press, 1952), 1:140.
   Yang Zhu 楊朱 has been known as the arch-hedonist Chinese history, but considering

that the hedonistic theory attributed to him is found mainly in the "Yang Zhu" chapter of the *Liezi*, which has been proved by modern scholars to be a forgery of the Wei (220–264 C.E.) or Jin (265–420 C.E.) period, I have avoided mentioning him among the ancient hedonists. As Fung Yu-lan has successfully shown, the theory of hedonism in this chapter of *Liezi* differs considerably from Yang Zhu's own doctrine, which still can be seen, though in a fragmentary manner, in various pre-Qin philosophical works (Fung, *History*, 1:133–143). For the controversy surrounding *Liezi*, see Zhang Xincheng 張心澂, *Weishu tongkao* 偽書 通考, 2 vols. (Shanghai: Shangwu, 1939, 2:699–712, and Shanghai: Shangwu, 1954). More recently, almost all important arguments concerning the forgery of *Liezi* have been collected by Yang Bojun 楊伯峻, in part or in entirely, in Appendix 3 to his *Liezi jishi* 列子集 釋 (Shanghai: Longmen, 1958), 185–245. For a full recent study, see A. C. Graham, "The Date and Composition of *Liehtzyy*," *AM* 8, no. 2 (1961): 139–198.

10. For discussion of the term *quansheng*, see Fung Yu-lan, *History*, 1:139–140; Waley, *Way and Power*, 42–43; Joseph Needham, *Science and Civilisation in China* (Cambridge: Cambridge University Press, 1956), 2:67.

11. *Guanzi* 管子, "Lizheng" 立政, *GXJB* (Shanghai: Shangwu, 1936), 1:15.

12. See Xu Weiyu 許維遹, *LSCQJS* (Beijing: Zhongguo shudian, [1955] 1985), 2.7a–8a; for English translation, see Fung Yu-lan, *History*, 1:139. Cf. also *Liezi jishi*, 7.145–146.

13. *LSCQJS*, 1.11a; Fung, *History*, 1:137; *Huainanzi* (Hangzhou: Zhejiang shuju, 1879), 7.13b.

14. *LSCQJS*, 2.10a.

15. Ibid., 1.7a. According to Fu Sinian, the so-called nature (*xing* 性) of man should be interpreted throughout this passage as "life" (*sheng* 生). Fu Sinian, "Xingming guxun bianzheng," 67.

16. Tsuda, *Dōka no shisō*, 319; Waley, *Way and Power*, 44.

17. With probably the sole exception of Fukui Kōjun 福井康順, *Dōkyō no kisoteki kenkyū* 道 教の基礎の研究 (Tokyo: Shoseki Bunbutsu Ryûtsûkai, 1952 [1958]), 214–255, it seems that scholars now agree that most of the *Taipingjing* was composed during the Later Han Period or, more precisely, during the middle of the second century C.E. See, e.g., Tang Yongtong 湯用彤, "Du Taipingjing shu suojian" 讀太平經書所見, *GXCK* 1 (1935): 1–32; Yang Kuan 楊寬, "Lun Taipingjing" 論太平經, *Xueshu yuekan* 學術月刊 (September 1959): 26–34; Ōfuchi Ninji 大淵忍爾, "What Is Told in *Taipingjing*, a Daoist Canon" 太平經の思 想について [in Japanese], *Tōyō Gakuhō* 東洋學報 28 (1941): 619–642; Oyanagi Shigeta 小 柳司氣太, *Tōyō shisō no kenkyū* 東洋思想の研究 (Tokyo: Seki shoin, 1934), 440–551; and a recent comprehensive reexamination of the problem by Xiong Deji 熊德基, "The Authorship and Doctrines of the *Taipingjing*, and Its Alleged Relationship with the Huang Jin and Tianshi Dao" [in Chinese], 太平經的作者和思想及其與黃巾和天師道的關係, *LSYJ* 4 (1962): 8–25.

Still, such a book as the *Taipingjing* must have been continuously subject to later additions and interpolations. For instance, the first part (甲部) of the *Taipingjing chao* 鈔, generally believed to be a résumé of the original work, has long been suspected by scholars of Daoism (see Ōfuchi Ninji, "History of the Transmission of the Daoist Canon *Taipingjing* and Its Textual Relation to the *Taipingjing lingshu*" 太平經の來歷について [in Japanese], *Tōyō Gakuhō* 27 [1940]: 272; cf. also Fukui Kōjun, *Dōkyō no kisoteki kenkyū* 217n1). It has now definitely been proved to be a much later interpolation than Later Han (see Wang Ming 王明, "Problems on the Authenticity of the Part 'Jia pian' of *Taipingjing*" 論太平經鈔 甲部 [sic 篇] 之偽 [in Chinese], *ZYYY* 18 [1948]: 375–384, and the same author's foreword in *TPJHJ* [Beijing: Zhonghua, 1960], 11–15). It may also be noted that the Dunhuang hand-written fragments of the *Taipingjing* (Stein no. 4226) seem to suggest both that the extant version is of a very early origin and that it contains interpolations at least as early as pre-Tang (see Xiong Deji, "Authorship and Doctrines of the *Taipingjing*," 8n2, and Yoshioka Yoshitoyo 吉岡義豐, "On the Dunhuang Copy of *Taipingjing*" 敦煌本太平經について [in Japanese], *Tōyō bunka kenkyūjo kiyō* 東洋文化研究所紀要 22 [1961]: 1–103).

18. See, e.g., *TPJHJ*, 113–220; 207–208; 392. The Confucian scholar Dong Zhongshu 董仲舒 and his followers must have popularized this idea widely during the Han Period. In one place, the *Chunqiu fanlu* 春秋繁露 (Luxuriant Dew of the Spring and Autumn Annals) states: "It is Heaven that produces (life), Earth that nourishes, and man that accomplishes" (天生之，地養之，人成之), WYWK, 6.93. Cf. also the translation in William Theodore de Bary, Wing-tsit Chan, and Burton Watson, *Sources of Chinese Tradition* (New York: Columbia University Press, 1960), 178. For Dong Zhongshu's development of Han Confucianism, see Yang Xianggui 楊向奎, *Xi-Han jingxue yu zhengzhi* 西漢經學 與政治 (Chongqing: Duli chubanshe, 1945), esp. pp. 64–78; Zhou Fucheng 周輔成, *Lun Dong Zhongshu sixiang* 論董仲舒思想 (Shanghai: Shanghai renmin, 1961). Here the addition of man to form a trinity with Heaven and Earth is particularly characteristic of Han Confucianism. Cf. de Bary, Chan, and Watson, *Sources*, 222–223. It is against this teleological theory of life that Wang Chong launched his attack in *Lunheng*. See especially Liu Pansui 劉盼遂, *LHJJ* (Beijing: Guji, 1957), 365–371; English translation by Alfred Forke, *Lun Heng* (Leipzig: Harrassowitz, 1907), 1:92–102.

19. *TPJHJ*, 218–219.

20. The two important studies on this work are Rao Zongyi 饒宗頤, *Laozi Xiang-er zhu jiao-jian* 老子想爾注校箋 (hereafter *Xiang-er Commentary*) (Hong Kong: Dongnan shuju, 1956; Shanghai: Shanghai guji, 1991), in which the whole text of the manuscript is collated and punctuated, and 陳世驤, "On the Historical and Religious Significance of the Tun-huang Manuscript of *Laozi*, book 1, with Commentaries by 'Xiang-er'" 想爾老子道經敦煌殘卷 論證 [in Chinese], *Guoxue xuebao* 國學學報, n.s., 1, no. 2 (April 1957): 41–62.

21. *Xiang-er Commentary*, 35. For a discussion of the importance of the idea of life in this work, see Rao's note on p. 68.

22. Ibid., 22, 35. Cf. the original text in *Laozi*, 16.9a, 25.14ab; Duyvendak, *Tao Te Ching*, 49–50, where *wang* is rendered "great," and p. 65.

23. *TPJHJ*, 658.

24. *TPJHJ*, 701. Wang Ming punctuates this passage wrongly as 道乃主生，道絕萬物，不生萬物，不生則無世類，無可相傳，萬物不相生相傳則敗矣, which is obviously self-contradictory as far as the nature and function of 道 is concerned. The correct reading is 道乃主生；道絕，萬物不生；萬物不生，則無世類.

25. *Xiang-er commentary*, 10.

26. *TPJHJ*, 36.

27. *TPJHJ*, 37; cf. also 221.

28. See Xu Zhongshu 徐中舒, "Jinwen guci shili" 金文嘏辭釋例, *ZYYY* 4 (1936), esp. pp. 15–18. Cf. also H. G. Creel, *The Birth of China* (New York: F. Ungar, 1937), 333; Hiraoka Teikichi 平岡禎吉, "On the Making of the Idea of Qi" 氣の思想成立について [in Japanese], *Shinagaku kenkyû* 支那學研究 13 (September 1955): 34–35.

29. Guo Moruo, "*Zhouyi* zhong zhi chuantong sixiang kao" 周彝中之傳統思想考, in *Jinwen congkao* 金文叢考, rev. ed. (Beijing: Renmin, 1954), 8a.

30. See, e.g., H. G. Creel, "What Is Taoism?," *JAOS* 76 (1956): 147.

31. Xu Zhongshu, "Terms and Forms of the Prayers," 25.

32. For the term 保身, see ibid., 26.

33. For the term 登遐 or 登霞, see Sun Yirang 孫詒讓, *Mozi jiangu* 墨子間詁, WYWK, 113, and Sun's commentary.

34. For the term "unit-ideas," see Arthur O. Lovejoy, *The Great Chain of Being* (Cambridge, Mass.: Harvard University Press, 1936), 3–6; cf. also his *Essays in the History of Ideas* (New York: George Braziller, [1948] 1955), 8–10. A criticism of Lovejoy's "unit-ideas" approach may be found in René Wellek and Austin Warren, *Theory of Literature* (New York: Harcourt, Brace, 1956), esp. pp. 99–101.

35. Xu Zhongshu, "Terms and Forms of the Prayers," 24–25.

36. For instance, Xu Zhongshu insists that the idea of physical immortality was brought into China by the northern Di 狄 people at the beginning of the Eastern Zhou Period (771–256 B.C.E.). Ibid., 43. Wen Yiduo 聞一多 is of the opinion that immortality in the sense of "no death" was imported to China by the Qiang 羌 people from the west. See his "Shenxian kao" (A Study on Immortals) 神仙考, in *Shenhua yu shi* 神話與詩 (Beijing: Guji, 1956), esp. pp. 154–157. However, both authors fail to produce evidence strong enough to substantiate their theories. I rather agree with Tsuda Sōkichi, who says that the transition from the idea of longevity to that of immortality in the sense of "no death" is a natural one. See his "Shinsen shisō ni kansuru ni-san no kosatsu" 神僊思想に關する二三の考察 (hereafter "Shinsen shisō"), in *Man-Sen chiri rekishi kenkyū hōkoku* 滿鮮地理歷史研究報告 10 (1924): 235, an article that is still the most comprehensive study on the Chinese idea of immortality.

37. E.g., Tsuda Sōkichi interprets the development of the immortality cult mainly in terms of the traditional desire for longevity and "no death" (see "Shinsen shisō," esp. pp. 235–237). This view is shared by Xu Dishan, *Daojiao shi*, 139–140. Takeuchi Yoshio 武內義雄, following a suggestion made by Gu Yanwu 顧炎武 in his *Tianxia qunguo libing shu* 天下群國利病書, SBCK, 18:36ab, advanced the theory that the cult originated in the imagination of the coastal people of Qi and Yan (Shantung and Hebei) stimulated by views of mirages. See his *Shinsen setsu* 神僊說 (Tokyo: Iwanami Shoten, 1935), 5–8. The theory was accepted by Uchida Tomō 內田智雄, "Dōkyō shi" 道教史, in *Shina shukyō shi* 支那宗教史, *Shina chiri rekishi taikei* 支那地理歷史大系, vol. 11 (Tokyo: Hakuyôsha, 1942), esp. pp. 237–238, and further elaborated by Ōfuchi Ninji in "Shoki no sen-setsu ni tsuite" 初期の僊說について, *Tōhō shūkyō* 東方宗教 1, no. 2 (September 1952), esp. p. 25. Among the many Chinese historians who favor this theory, see, e.g., Lü Simian 呂思勉, *Xian Qin shi* 先秦史 (Shanghai: Shanghai guji, 1941), 463–464, and Qian Mu 錢穆, *Guoshi dagang* 國史大綱 (Shanghai: Guoli bianyiguan and Shangwu, 1947), 1:254.

38. Chen Yinke doubts importation by the sea route (see his "Tianshidao yu binhai diyu zhi guanxi" 天師道與濱海地域之關係), *ZYYY* 3, no. 4 (1934): 439–440. For a recent criticism of Chen's theory, see Yang Xiangkui, *Zhongguo gudai shehui yu gudai sixiang yanjiu* 中國古代社會與古代思想研究 (Shanghai: Shanghai guji, 1962), 1:477–478. Wen Yiduo, while admitting that the cult of immortality was related both to the earlier idea of "no death" and to the geography of the coastal state of Qi, advances a theory that the concept of *xian* derived from the practice of cremation by the Qiang people of the west, who migrated to Qi. See his "A Study on Immortals," 153–180.

39. Gu Yanwu is probably the earliest scholar to point out that the idea of the *xian* does not antedate the late Zhou (i.e., Warring States, 481–221 B.C.E.) Period (see his *Rizhi lu* 日知錄 [1869 edition], 30:28a). Since most scholars agree on this point, it requires no further discussion.

40. *ZZ*, Duke Chao, 20; Legge, *The Chinese Classics*, 5:684.

41. Wang Xianshen 王先慎, *Hanfeizi jijie*, "Shuo-lin," *shang*, WYWK, 2.48. Cf. also *Zhanguoce*, Chu 4, WYWK, 2.38. For complete translation of the *Zhanguoce*, see J. I. Crump, trans., *Intrigues: Studies of the Chan-kuo ts'e* (Ann Arbor: University of Michigan Press, 1964).

42. *Hanfeizi jijie*, "Waichu," 3.22.

43. For dates of these kings, I have followed the chronological tables in Qian Mu, *Xian Qin zhuzi xinian* 先秦諸子繫年, rev. ed. (Hong Kong: HKU Press, 1956), 2:548–566.

44. *SJ*, Zhonghua, 28.6a; Burton Watson, *Records of the Grand Historian of China* (New York: Columbia University Press, 1961), 2:26.

45. *Shanhaijing*, SBCK, 2:37b; *Huainanzi*, 4.111b.

46. *Shanhaijing*, SBCK, 2:69a. There are also other terms such as 不死鄉; see "Yuanyou" 遠遊 in Dai Zhen 戴震, *Qu Yuan fu zhu* 屈原賦注 (Shanghai: GXJBCS, [1933] 1968), 52, and *LSCQJS*, 22.13a, and 不死之野 in *Huainanzi*, 5.23a.

47. *Shanhaijing*, 2:84b.

48. Ibid., 2:54a. According to *Huainanzi*, 4.7b, there was also a "no-death grass."

49. *Huainanzi*, 4.3b.

50. See, e.g., Xu Dishan, *Daojiao shi*, 140; Holmes Welch, *The Parting of the Way: Lao Tzu and the Taoist Movement* (Boston: Beacon Press, 1957), 89. Creel's "What Is Taoism?" (145) dates the rise of what he calls the "cult of immortality" to around 300 B.C.E.

51. *Chuang-tzu*, trans. Feng Youlan (Beijing: Foreign Languages Press, 1989), 36–37. Citation refers to the 1933 edition. Cf. Legge, *The Texts of Taoism*, SBE, 39:170–171, and the discussion of this passage in Tsuda Sōkichi, "Shinsen shisō," 248–250.

52. For the text, see *Qu Yuan fu zhu*, 5:40–54. For a discussion of the "Yuanyou" as a poem of early Han times, see James R. Hightower, "Ch'ü Yüan Studies," *Silver Jubilee Volume of the Zinbun-Kagaku-Kenkyusyo* (Kyoto: Kyoto University, 1954), 196–200; David Hawkes, *Ch'u Tz'u: The Songs of the South* (Oxford: Clarendon Press, 1959), 81. Cf. also Tsuda, "Shinsen shisō," 220–222.

53. Wen Yiduo, "A Study on Immortals," 161.

54. Cf. Hightower, "Ch'ü Yüan Studies," 199; Hawkes, *Ch'u Tzu*, 81; Wen Yiduo, "A Study on Immortals," 161–162.

55. *Zhanguoce*, Qin, 3, 1.48.

56. *SJ*, 55.6b.

57. *Huainanzi*, 20.9a.

58. *Quan Han wen* 全漢文, in *Quan Shanggu Sandai Qin Han Sanguo Liuchao wen* 全上古三代秦漢三國六朝文, ed. Yan Kejun 嚴可均 (Beijing: Zhonghua, 1958 [reprint]), 42.10b.

59. Lu Jia 陸賈, *Xinyu* 新語, *SBBY*, 2.11a. This work has not received the detailed study of other Han writings; for a general discussion, see Hu Shi, 述陸賈的思想 in *Zhang Jusheng xiansheng qishi shengri jinian lunwenji* 張菊生先生七十生日紀念論文集 (Shanghai: Shangwu, 1937), 83–94.

60. *SJ*, 6.9ab.

61. Ibid., 28.6a; Watson, *Grand Historian*, 2:25–26.

62. *Yan tie lun*, *GXJB*, 59. This passage is not translated in Esson M. Gale's *Discourses on Salt and Iron* (Leiden: E. J. Brill, 1931).

63. *SJ*, 6.12b.

64. Ibid., 6.15a.

65. Ibid., 6.12b–13a.

66. Ibid., 28.13b; Watson, *Grand Historian*, 2:47–48. Cf. also *SJ*, 12.5b, 9a.

67. For more details concerning *fangshi*, see *SJ*, 28; Watson, *Grand Historian*, 2:13–69.

68. *HS* (Shanghai: Shangwu, 1927), 25B.7a; *Quan Han wen*, 46.7ab.

69. *HS*, 25B.6a. According to Qian Mu, during the time of Qin Shi Huang and Han Wudi, the most convenient and important method of achieving immortality was sacrificial offerings to gods or *xian* rather than consumption of drugs or other devices. See his "Zhouguan zhuzuo shidai kao" 周官著作時代考, in *Liang Han jingxue jin gu wen pingyi* 兩漢經學今古文平議 (Hong Kong: Xinya yanjiusuo, 1958), 433. This theory has been accepted by Tang Yongtong 湯用彤 in his *Han Wei Liang-Jin Nanbeichao Fojiao shi* 漢魏兩晉南北朝佛教史 (Beijing: Zhonghua, 1955 [reprint]), 1:52–53.

70. On the Western Queen Mother and Mount Kunlun, see Kume Kunitake 久米邦武, "Konron Seiôbo kô" 崑崙西王母考, *Shigaku zasshi* 史學雜誌 4 (1893): 197–214, 288–302; Nomura Gakuyô 野村岳陽, "Bunken jô yori mitaru Konron shisô no hattatsu" 文獻上より見たる崑崙思想の發達, *Shigaku zasshi* 29 (1918): 458–494, 583–601; Nakayama Heijirô 中山平次郎, "Shina ko shômei no Seiôbo ni tsuite" 支那古鐘銘の西王母に就て, *Kōkogaku zasshi* 考古學雜誌 11 (1921): 324–332. Recently, Du Erwei 杜而未, in a suggestive but rather one-sided study, *Kunlun wenhua yu busi guannian* 崑崙文化與不死觀念 (Taipei: Xuesheng, 1962), tries to relate the *xian* immortality of Mount Kunlun to the moon myth by drawing parallels from other primitive cultures. Another new interpretation, advanced by Su Xuelin 蘇雪林 in *Kunlun zhi mi* 崑崙之謎 (Taipei: Zhongyang wenwu gongyinshe, 1956), apparently derives the name of the mountain, as a residence for immortals, from Khursag Kurkura, the mythical mountain in ancient Babylonian tradition. Since I have not been able to consult this work, I have had to depend on the paraphrase given by Du Erwei (50).

71. Shiratori Kurakichi 白鳥庫吉, *Saiiki-shi kenkyū* 西域史研究 (Tokyo: Iwanami, 1944), 2:328–331.

72. *HS*, 22.10b; cf. also Zhang Weihua 張維華, 漢武帝伐大宛與方士思想 "The Influence of the Thought of the Magicians Upon the Conquest of Dawan During the Reign of Han

Wudi" [in Chinese], *Zhongguo wenhua yanjiu huikan* 中國文化研究彙刊 3 (1943), esp. pp. 6–7.

73. See Lü Simian, *Qin Han shi* 秦漢史 (Shanghai: Shanghai guji, 1947), 1:120; Qian Mu, *Qin Han shi* (Hong Kong: Xinhua, 1957), 133; Ise Sentaro 伊瀬仙太郎, *Saiiki keiei-shi no kenkyū* 西域經營史の研究 (Tokyo: Nihon Gakujutsu Shinkôkai, 1955), 81; Hatani Ryōtai 羽溪了諦, *Xiyu zhi Fojiao* 西域之佛教, Chinese translation by He Changqun 賀昌羣 (Shanghai: Shangwu, 1956), 33.

74. Ise Sentaro, *Saiiki keiei-shi no kenkyū*, 82; Shiratori Kurakichi, *Saiiki-shi kenkyū*, 2:330.

75. See Zhang Weihua, "The Influence of the Thought of the Magicians," 1–12. A similar view is found in Arthur Waley, "The Heavenly Horses of Ferghana: A New View," *History Today* 5, no. 2 (February 1955): 95–103. See also the defense of the traditional interpretation by Yu Jiaxi in *Yu Jiaxi lunxue zazhu* 余嘉錫論學雜著 (Beijing: Zhonghua, [1963] 1977), 1:175–180.

76. *SJ*, 28.11a; Watson, *Grand Historian*, 2:39; *HS*, 25A.8b–9a.

77. *SJ*, 28.17b; Watson, *Grand Historian*, 2:63. Watson reads 故衰耗 as "the power of Yüeh had declined," but I believe "the population became weakened and exhausted" suits the context better; *HS*, 25B.1a.

78. The problem of the Longevity Hall needs some elucidation. According to *SJ*, 28.17b, only one hall, named Yiyanshou guan 益延壽觀, was built at Ganquan. *HS*, 25B.1a, gives the name Yishou Yiyanshou guan 益壽延壽館, which the Tang commentator Yan Shigu 顏師古 interprets as two names for two separate halls. Yan's interpretation has been generally accepted (see Burton Watson on "Long Life and Increased Life Towers," *Records of the Grand Historian*, 2:63), but it was challenged as early as Song times by Huang Buosi 黃伯思, who convincingly argued on the basis of Han tiles bearing the name Yiyan shou, which had been unearthed in the locality of the hall, that Yan was wrong in taking it as two buildings and that the name given in *SJ* was correct. (See *Dongguan yulun* 東觀餘論, Shaowu xushi congshu edition 邵武徐氏叢書, 2:43b–44a.) In recent times, more such Han tiles, and even large Han bricks bearing the name Yiyanshou presumably used in building the hall, have come to light. See Chen Zhi 陳直, *Hanshu xinzheng* 漢書新證 (Tianjin: Tianjin renmin chubanshe, 1959, 119). Archaeological evidence, therefore, tends to support Huang's theory rather than Yan's. It may not be out of place to add here that the construction of the Longevity Hall by Han Wudi had considerable influence in shaping the pattern of imperial court life in later periods. For instance, during the Tang, the well-known Changsheng dian 長生殿, or Changsheng yuan 院, which may also be rendered as "Longevity Hall," was built in various palaces both at Chang-an and Loyang. I agree with Zhou Yi-liang, "Tantrism in China," *HJAS* 8 (1945): 310–311, and Chen Yinke, *Yuan-Bo shi jianzheng gao* 元白詩箋證稿 (Beijing: Wenxue guji kanxing she, 1955), 37–40, that halls bearing this name during Tang times were used primarily for religious purposes rather than as living quarters. Evidence tends to show that in most cases, Tang emperors (including the Empress Wu) stayed in the Longevity Hall only to offer sacrifices to Daoist gods, and the hall is often described by Tang writers as a place where deities (or rather, *xian* immortals) would descend (Zhou, "Tantrism in China," 311). It seems to follow, then, that the Longevity

Hall in Tang times must have been associated with the imperial quest for immortality or longevity, modeled closely on that of the Han dynasty. Both Zhou and Chen, however, fail to invoke this obvious historical precedent to strengthen their arguments.

79. For a general and comprehensive study of the *feng* and *shan* sacrifices, see Fukunaga Mitsuji 福永光司, "On the Evolution of Fengshan Theory" 封禪說の形成, *Tōhō shūkyō* 1, no. 6 (November 1954): 28–57, and 1, no. 7 (February 1955): 45–63.

80. For this Confucian political interpretation, see Chen Li 陳立, *Bohu tong shuzheng* 白虎通疏證 (Huainan: Huainan shuju, 1875), 6.16a–19a; T'an Tjoe Som, trans., *Po Hu T'ung: The Comprehensive Discussions in the White Tiger Hall* (Leiden: Brill, 1949–1952), 1:239–241.

81. *SJ*, 28.11a, 16a; Watson, *Grand Historian*, 2:56.

82. *SJ*, 28.5a; Watson, *Grand Historian*, 2:23–24.

83. *SJ*, 87.5b.

84. Cf. Kurihara Tomonobu 粟原朋信, *Shin Kan shi no kenkyū* 秦漢史の研究 (Tokyo: Yoshikawa Kôbunkan, 1961), 35–37.

85. *SJ*, 28.16a; Watson, *Grand Historian*, 2:57.

86. Cf. Fukunaga Mitsuchi, "Evolution of Fengshan Theory," esp. pp. 38–39.

87. Kurihara, *Shin Kan shi no kenkyû* (29–37), discusses the difference between the two *fengshan* performances.

88. *SJ*, 28.15a; Watson, *Grand Historian*, 2:52.

89. *SJ*, 117.18a.

90. See Xu Zhongshu, "On the Four Bronze Vessels of the Dian Family of Qi" 陳侯四器考釋 [in Chinese], *ZYYY* 3, no. 4 (1934), esp. pp. 499–502; Ding Shan 丁山, "A Glimpse Into the Tradition of the 'Five Emperors' with the Help of the Inscriptions on a Vessel of Dian" 由陳侯因資錞銘論五帝, *ZYYY* 3, no. 4 (1934): 517–535. As Ding Shan demonstrates, the so-called Chen Hou Yinzi is the name of King Wei of Qi (517). Guo Moruo's identification with King Xuan of Qi is probably in error; see *Shi pipan shu* 十批判書, rev. ed. (Shanghai: Qunyi chubanshe, 1950), 158.

91. *SJ*, 1.16a.

92. See Xu Zhongshu, "On the Four Bronze Vessels," 502; Gu Jiegang, *Qin Han di fangshi yu* 秦漢的方士與儒生 (Shanghai: Shanghai renmin, [1955] 1962), 32.

93. Xu Zhongshu, "On the Four Bronze Vessels," 502; Guo Moruo, *Shi pipan shu*, 158.

94. Wen Yiduo, "A Study on Immortals," 154.

95. *SJ*, 74.2b; cf. Guo Moruo, *Shi pipan shu*, 160.

96. Qian Mu, *Xian Qin zhuzi xinian*, 224–226.

97. Ibid., 376.

98. During the former Han, so-called Huang-Lao Daoism referred primarily to the Daoist political philosophy of "nonaction." Only during the Later Han did Huang-Lao Daoism gradually acquire religious elements, in particular an interest in *xian* immortality. On Huang-Lao during the Han, see Akitsuki Kanei 秋月觀瑛, "Genealogy of the Huang-Lao Concept" 黃老觀念の系譜 [in Japanese], *Tōhōgaku* 東方學 10 (April 1955): 69–81.

99. Creel, "What Is Taoism?," 145.

100. *SJ*, 80.4b (the Grand Historian's comment).

101. *SJ*, 28.11b. For Anqi Sheng, see also Qian Mu, *Xian Qin zhuzi xinian*, 1:224–226.

102. Wen Yiduo, "A Study on Immortals," 170–172n12; Chen Pan 陳槃, "Some Remarks on Fangshi (Alchemists) of the Period from Seven Princedoms to the Han Dynasty" 戰國 秦漢間方士考論, *ZYYY* 17 (1948): 26–27.

103. Laozi's elevation to a *xian* by the *fangshi* followed long after the Yellow Emperor's, probably early during the Later Han (cf. Akitsuki, "Genealogy," 71–73). In the "Treatise on Literature" in *HS*, of the ten works classified under the School of *Xian* Immortals 神仙 家, four bear the name of the Yellow Emperor, but none is associated with Laozi (*HS*, 30.29a; cf. also Akitsuki, "Genealogy," 73). The name of the Yellow Emperor is also associated with all the schools or arts in which the *fangshi* were involved, such as the Daoist School, the Ying-Yang School, the School of the Five Elements 五行, the art of astrology, the art of divination, the art of medicine, and the art of sexual techniques (the last four fall under the categories of *shushu* 術數 and *fangji* 方技). On the other hand, the name of Laozi is found only in connection with the Daoist School (*HS*, 30.2a). This fact shows that during the Former Han Period, Laozi was still considered a Daoist philosopher, while the Yellow Emperor had already become the common ancestor of all kinds of *fangshi*. The distinction between the Yellow Emperor and Laozi in Han times made by the Qing scholar Fang Dongshu 方東樹 (1772–1851) is a useful one. According to him, although the two were often mentioned together in Han times, the name of Laozi was used by those who talked of the Way and its Virtue, whereas that of the Yellow Emperor was used by those who talked about supernatural and extraordinary things. See *Hanxue shangdui* 漢學商兌, Huailu congshu 槐廬叢書, 1:4a.

 The term *fangshi* was used loosely during Han times to mean those who practiced any, more often several, of the arts mentioned above. In this broad sense, the term was interchangeable with such terms as *shushi* 術士, *fangshushi* 方術士, *daoshi* 道士, and *daoren* 道人. See Chen Pan, "Some Remarks on Fangshi," 7–33; cf. also Tsuda, "Shinsen shisō," 263–265. On the terms *fangshi* and *daoshu*, see Sakai Tadao 酒井忠夫, "*Fangshu* and *daoshu*, Religious and Political Art in Daoism" 方術と道術 [in Japanese], *Tōyō shigaku ronshū* 東洋史學論集 1 (1953): 49–59. Therefore, as a general term, *fangshi* may be translated as "religious Daoists" or "popular Daoists," since all such arts were later incorporated in the Daoist religion. Only in specific cases depending on context should the term be translated as "magicians," "alchemists," or "immortals."

104. *SJ*, 12.2a, 28.11a; *HS*, 25A.9a.

105. *SJ*, 12.7a, 28.14b–15a; Édouard Chavannes, *Les Mémoires historiques de Se-ma Ts'ien*, 5 vols. (Paris: E. Leroux, 1895–1905), 3:488; *HS*, 25A.12b. Modern scholars agree that the legend of the Yellow Emperor's ascension to Heaven originated during the time of Han Wudi, not earlier (see, e.g., Ōfuchi, "Shōki no sen-setsu ni tsuite," 33–36). One passage in the inner chapters of the *Zhuangzi* mentions that the Yellow Emperor attained the *Dao* and by it ascended to Heaven (see Fung Youlan, *Zhuangzi*, 118; Legge, *The Texts of Taoism*, *SBE*, 39:244), but this dubious passage is probably a later interpolation. See Qian Mu, *Zhuangzi zuanjian* 莊子纂箋, 3rd ed. (Hong Kong: Dong nan yin wu, [1955] 1957), 52. Citation refers to the 1957 edition.

106. Thus considered, one is justified in saying that the Daoist idea of a Heavenly world where *xian* immortals live is the result of worldly desires pushed to the extreme and is hence a prolongation of the human world. See Wen Yiduo, "A Study on Immortals," 162–163; Murakami Yoshimi 村上嘉實, *Chūgoku no sennin* 中國の仙人 (Kyoto: Heirakuji Shoten, 1956), 76.

107. See biography in *SJ*, 118.3b–9a.

108. For a more detailed account, see *LHJJ*, 147; Forke, *Lun Heng*, 1:335; Ying Shao 應劭, *Fengsu tongyi* 風俗通義, SBCK, 2.15–16a.

109. See Ying Shao, *Fengsu tongyi*, 2.16a.

110. Yan Kejun, *QHHW*, 106.1b–2a.

111. *HS*, 30.29a. Later in the third and fourth centuries C.E., *xian* acquired a still more worldly character with the advent of a new type, the "earthly immortal" 地仙 (see *BPZ*, *neipian*, 2.27). Sometimes the earthly immortal refused to ascend to Heaven because of a reluctance to give up worldly pleasures, as in the case of a Mr. Puoshi 白石先生 (see Ge Hong 葛洪, *Shenxian zhuan* 神仙傳, 3–4b). Cf. also Murakami Yoshimi, *Chūgoku no sennin*, 76–84, and Tu Erwei, *Kunlun wenhua yu busi guannian*, 117–122.

112. For instance, the Han etymologist Xu Shen defines 僊 as "to live long and leave this world as *xian*" 長生僊去 (*Shuowen jiezi*, 8A). Another Han etymologist, Liu Xi, in his *Shiming* (cf. N. C. Bodman, *A Linguistic Study of the Shih Ming* [Cambridge, Mass.: Harvard University Press, 1954], 110, no. 1025) defines 仙 as, "to live on to old age and not die," 老而不死, SBCK, 21a.

113. For instance, in the *Lunheng* and the *Taipingjing*, 度世 and 不死 are freely interchangeable.

114. *Fayan* 法言, SBCK, 12.3b–4b; see Fung Yu-lan, *History*, 1:149; E. von Zach, "Fa Yan," *Sinologische Beitrage* (Batavia) 4, no. 1 (1939): 67–68.

115. See *QHHW*, 15.7a; cf. also *Huanzi xinlun* 桓子新論, *SBBY*, 17b. Elsewhere, Huan emphatically stated that there was no such thing as "the Way of cultivating *xian* immortality," which was but a fabrication of those who were curious about strange things (無仙道, 好奇者為之, *QHHW*, 15.5b). According to Zhang Hua 張華 (*Buowuzhi* 博物志, Shili ju congshu 士禮居叢書, 4.1a), Huan shared this view with Yang Xiong. Huan's position on the matter has been the subject of much controversy, but we need to point out here only that some fragmentary statements attributed to him appear to mean just the contrary. E.g.: "Why should the (ancient) sages have died instead of learning to achieve *xian* immortality? (The answer is that the sages had become immortals by releasing [themselves] from their corpses.) That they are said to have died is just to show the people that there is an end for them" (*QHHW*, 15.5b). Huan also wrote a "Xian fu" in praise of Wang Qiao and Chi Songzi, in which he says something to the effect that cultivation of physical immortality as described by the *fang shih* is possible (*QHHW*, 12.7b; cf. also *Huanzi xinlun*, 15b). He seems, therefore, to have held two conflicting views, and if we take him to represent one, we must explain away the other.

The *Xinlun* now exists only in collected fragments, which even if actually by Huan, may not accurately represent his views. It was his practice to quote first the statements of others or popular views of his time and then follow these with his own opinions. Those few statements that seem to represent him as a Daoist immortal may, therefore, be such quotations and not Huan's opinions. Moreover, the "Xian fu" was composed in his youth, when as a courtier under the Emperor Chengdi, he composed the *fu* on the occasion of the emperor's visit to the Jiling Palace 集靈宮, built by Han Wudi at the foot of Mount Hua in honor of Wang Qiao and Chi Songzi. A literary piece composed under such circumstances is probably too conventional to be considered a true expression of the author's views. Even if we take the "Xian fu" at its face value, however, it is a youthful work, whereas the *Xinlun* was written during the early years of the Later Han (*HHS* [Shanghai: Shangwu, 1927], 58A.3a) when Huan was about seventy and can therefore be taken to represent his mature opinion on the subject. For Huan Tan, see a series of important studies by T. Pokora, especially "The Life of Huan T'an," *Ada Orientalia* 31 (1963): 1–79, 521–576. He has discussed and translated the "Xian fu" in *Archiv orientální* 28 (1960): 353–367.

116. *LHJJ*, 145–157; Forke, *Lun Heng*, 1:332–350.

117. Ying Shao, *Fengsu tongyi*, 2.I7a.

118. *LHJJ*, 150; Forke, *Lun Heng*, 1:339.

119. *LHJJ*, 155; Forke, *Lun Heng*, 1:346.

120. *LHJJ*, 156; Forke, *Lun Heng*, 1:347.

121. *LHJJ*, 157; Forke, *Lun Heng*, 1:348.

122. *LHJJ*, 29–33, 147; Forke, *Lun Heng*, 1:325–331, 336. As Forke rightly points out, metamorphosis is of a much earlier origin, and he cites (336) the transformation of sparrows into clams after they dive into the water, an idea mentioned in ancient Chinese works. The *Guoyu* (Discourses of the States) records that Zhao Jianzi 趙簡子 envied the metamorphoses of lower animals and deplored the fact that man could not achieve bodily transformation ("Jinyu," WYWK, 178). This reference would seem to indicate that the idea of human metamorphosis had not come into being during the Spring and Autumn Period (771–481 B.C.E.); however, the idea of "man with plumage" (*yumin* 羽民, *yuren* 羽人) can be found in later works such as the *Shanhaijing* (Classic of Mountains and Seas; presumably of the Warring States Period), *Lüshi chunqiu*, and *Huainanzi* (see Tsuda Sōkichi, "Shinsen shisō," 242–246). It is probably safe to conclude that the idea of human metamorphosis grew contemporaneously with the general notion of physical immortality, for the concept was so fully developed by the Han Period that feathered immortals were represented in both poetry and painting. See Liu Pansui's commentary in *LHJJ*, 32–33. For such Han depictions, see M. I. Rostovtzev, *Inlaid Bronzes of the Han Dynasty in the Collection of C. T. Loo* (Paris and Brussels: G. Vanoest, 1927), plate 12, and Mizuno Seiichi 水野清一, "Supernatural Motif in the Design of the Han Dynasty in China" 漢代の仙界意匠について [in Japanese], *Kōkogaku zasshi* 考古學雜誌 27 (1937–1938): 501–507.

123. See especially the "Daoxu" and "Wuxing" chapters and Forke, *Lun Heng*, vol. 1, chaps. 27 and 28.

124. E.g., Wang Chong quotes from a work no longer extant that "the fluid-eaters live long without dying" (*LHJJ*, 156; Forke, *Lun Heng*, 1:348).

125. *LHJJ*, 153; Forke, *Lun Heng*, 1:343.

126. *TPJHJ*, 222–223.

127. *TPJHJ*, 596. *Tian*, or Heaven, is used in this paragraph as well as throughout the *Taipingjing* in two senses: one referring to the place of ultimate happiness where immortals take permanent residence (i.e., paradise), the other a personified Heaven or divinity that governs the entire universe. This confusion of usage represents a popular version of Professor Y. L. Jin's distinction: "If we mean by *Tian* both nature and divinity which presides over nature, with emphasis sometimes on the one and sometimes on the other, we have something approaching the Chinese term." Quoted in Fung Yu-lan, *A Short History of Chinese Philosophy* (New York: Macmillan, 1948), 192. To show the distinction, I have capitalized "Heaven" to denote the second meaning of the term.

128. For a study of the Chinese theory of retribution, see Lien-sheng Yang, "The Concept of Pao as a Basis for Social Relations in China," in *Chinese Thought and Institutions*, ed. John K. Fairbank (Chicago: University of Chicago Press, 1957), 291–309.

129. On the theory of retribution during the Han, see Uchiyama Toshihiko 内山俊彦 漢代の應報思想, "Retribution in Han Thought" 漢代の應報思想 [in Japanese], *Tokyo Shinagakuhō* 6 (June 1960): 17–32.

130. For biographies, see *HHS*, 92.

131. *HHS*, 112B.8a. According to the *Taipingjing*, the date of ascension is set in advance and a sort of amulet (符) must be placed on the breast before ascension, presumably for identification (*TPJHJ*, 608–609; cf. also 532–533 and 710).

132. *BPZ*, neipian, 5.999. The story is also found in Zhang Hua, *Buowuzhi*, 7.3a.

133. *TPJHJ*, 138–139.

134. Ibid., 131–133; cf. also 230.

135. During the Han Period, the cult of immortality involved alchemy. See Henri Maspero, *Le taoïsme* (Paris: Gallimard, 1950 [1971], 89–90). Citation refers to the 1950 edition. According to Huan Tan, immortality drugs could be made from transmuted gold (see *QHHW*, 15.6b).

136. *HS*, 36.3b.

137. *HS*, 25B.10a. Wang Mang is also said to have believed in other ways of achieving immortality, such as selecting virtuous girls for his harem as well as using a particular kind of carriage (華蓋) in which the Yellow Emperor was believed to have ascended to Heaven (*HS*, 99B.7a).

138. *HS*, 99B.10b.

139. *HHS*, 7.8a and 60B.10b. Cf. also Tang Yongtong, *Fojiao shi*, 55–57.

140. *HHS*, 18.4b. In the year 165–166 c.e., the emperor actually sent envoys to Huxian three times. Only the first and last missions are recorded in *HHS*, 7; the second was added by the Qing scholar, Hui Dong 惠棟, in his *HHSbuzhu* 補注, *CSJC*, 1.100.

141. There is considerable evidence for Laozi as one of the central figures of the immortality cult in the latter part of the second century c.e. According to the "Inscription on Laozi" by Bian Shao 邊韶 (on this authorship, see Erik Zürcher, *The Buddhist Conquest of China* [Leiden: Brill, 1959], 2:429–430n31), Daoists of the time distorted the idea of immortality in Laozi and deified its author. See Bian Shao, "Laozi ming," in *QHHW*, 62.3a–4a; cf. also Kusuyama Haruki 楠山春樹, "*Laozi Ming* According to Bian Shao"

邊韶の老子銘について [in Japanese], *Tōhō shûkyō* 11 (October 1956): 49–54. Another
more controversial example is the worship of Huang-Lao Jun 黃老君 for prolongation of
life (*HHS*, 80.1b). One commentator, Liu Bin 劉邠, takes the term as a corruption of
"Huangdi Laojun," 黃帝老君 an interpretation that has been challenged by Wu Renjie
吳仁傑, who does not believe that Huangdi and Laozi were "Heavenly gods" 天神 and
points out that there was a Huang-Lao Jun in the Daoist pantheon according to Daoist
literature of the Six Dynasties Period (*Liang Han kanwu buyi* 兩漢刊誤補遺, Zhipuzu
zhai 知不足齋 edition, 10.3b–4a). Hui Dong suggests that Huang-Lao Jun was one of the
five "Heavenly emperors" 天帝, who might also be known as "Heavenly gods" (*HHSbuzhu*, 5.317). None of the three scholars offers evidence in support of these guesses, and
in Han literature, the term appears only in *HHS*, 80. Probably misled by Wu and Hui,
Maspero advances a theory that this particular cult was established early during the
Former Han and that the Yellow Turbans regarded Huang-Lao Jun as the Supreme Deity. In other words, he does not consider the term related to Huangdi and Laozi, but derived from *huang* (yellow), the color of the center, and *lao* (old) (see Maspero, *Le taoïsme*,
219–222). More recently, Akitsuki Kanei has advanced another theory according to
which the name represents the deification of both the Yellow Emperor and Laozi into a
single god, as well as the incarnation of the *Dao*, and worship of Huang-Lao Jun was
thought to bring about immortality or longevity (Akitsuki, "Genealogy," 77). Since, as
we have seen above, Emperor Huan's worship of Laozi was motivated by his craving for
immortality, Huang-Lao Jun must have been related to Huangdi and Laozi. See also
Tsuda, *Dôha no shisô*, 346–347; Creel, "What Is Taoism?," 149n97; and Holmes H. Welch,
"Syncretism in the Early Daoist Movement," Papers on China (Cambridge, Mass.: East
Asian Research Center, Harvard University, 1956), 13–14. It should be noted that even as
late as the early fourth century C.E., the term Huang-Lao was still used to indicate the
Yellow Emperor and Laozi rather than a single deity (*BPZ*, *neipian*, 10.178). For our pur-
poses, however, the origin of the name of the cult is of less importance than the fact that
it was primarily a cult of immortality.

142. Yu Xun 余遜, "Political Thoughts of Early Daoists" 早期道教之政治信念 [in Chinese],
Furen xuezhi 輔仁學誌 11 (1942): 101.

143. Examination of the relations of some Later Han princes with *daoshi* or *fangshi* show
similarities to those of the Prince of Huai-nan. In 70 C.E., Prince Ying 英 of Chu was
also accused of dealing with such *fangshi* as Wang Ping 王平 and Yan Zhong 顏忠, and
of making preparations for rebellion. He too committed suicide (*HHS*, 72.2b–3b).
According to the *Lunheng*, a *daoshi* 道士 named Liu Chun 劉春 induced the same prince
to eat filth (*LHJJ*, 139; Forke, *Lun Heng*, 1:290). These incidents show how active *fangshi*
or *daoshi* were in the court of one prince. And Tang Yongtong has pointed out that almost all the brothers of the Prince of Chu were involved in witchcraft and shared the
prince's religious beliefs (*Fojiao shi*, 1.51–52). Yan Zhong also turns up at the court of
Prince Kang of Jinan 濟南王康, where he instigated him to commit sedition (*HHS*,
72.3b–4a). Liu Chun, Hui Tong suggests, is to be identified with Liu Zichan 劉子產,
who was also at the court of Prince Kang (*HHSbuzhu*, 5.447). In 147 C.E., Prince Suan of
Qinghe 清河王蒜 won the support of a "Wizard rebel" (妖賊) named Liu Yu 劉鮪 in his

bid for the empire. The term in *HHS* refers in most cases to a Daoist (cf. He Changchun 賀昌羣, "Popular Slogans During the Uprising of the Yellow Turbans in the Han Dynasty" 論黃巾農民起義的口號 [in Chinese], *LSYJ*, 6 [1959]: 34). As a final example, in 173 C.E., Prince Chong of Chen 陳王寵 was accused of sacrificing to the Heavenly God with his chancellor Wei Yin 魏愔, with seditious intent. This "Heavenly God" was later discovered to be none other than Huang-Lao Jun (*HHS*, 80.1b).

144. *HHS*, 10.6a.

145. Zhong Rong 鍾嶸, *Shipin* 詩品, WYWK, 1.6.

146. Ibid., 25.

147. Ibid., 221.

148. Ibid., 698. This passage may be read in conjunction with *BPZ*, *neipian*, 2.27.

149. *TPJHJ*, 724.

150. Ibid., 676. Cf. also Tang Yongtong, "Du Taipingjing shu suojian," 26, and *Fojiao shi*, 104–105.

151. Cf. Chen Yinke in *ZYYY* 3, no. 4 (1934): 439–466; Yu Xun, "Early Daoists," 92–102.

152. According to Chen Zhi (*Hanshu xinzheng*, 120), there was actually another palace, the Yanshou Guan, in Lantian 藍田, also in modern Shaanxi.

153. *HS*, 25B.2b.

154. Lao Gan 勞榦, *Juyan Hanjian* 居延漢簡 (hereafter *Hanjian*) (Taipei: Zhongyang yanjiuyuan lishi yuyan yanjiu suo, 1960), Shiwen 釋文, no. 2038, 42; no. 2145, 44; no. 4092, 83.

155. *Hanjian*, no. 509, 11.

156. Ibid., no. 3999, 81; *Juyan Hanjian Jiabian* 甲編 (Beijing: Kexue chubanshe, 1959), no. 1192, 50.

157. *Hanjian*, no. 1274, 26.

3. "O Soul, Come Back!"

A Study in the Changing Conceptions of the Soul and Afterlife in Pre-Buddhist China

In this study, I propose to investigate indigenous Chinese conceptions of the afterlife in the period before the arrival of Buddhism in China. I shall take the ritual of *fu* 復, "Summons" or "Recall," as the point of departure, for in my judgment, this ritual embodied the crystallization of a variety of ideas about human survival after death that had developed in China since high antiquity. After a reconstruction of the ritual of *fu*, I shall proceed to inquire into the origin and development of the notions of *hun* 魂 and *po* 魄, two pivotal concepts that have been, and remain today, the key to understanding Chinese views of the human soul and the afterlife. Finally, I shall examine the changing conceptions of the two afterworlds before Buddhism transformed them into "Heaven" and "Hell."

A study of this kind must be based on every type of evidence now available—historical as well as archaeological, written as well as pictorial. My central purpose is to identify a common core of beliefs in Han China that were shared by the elite and popular cultures. In this particular area of Han thought, the boundaries between Confucian ideology and popular Daoist religion, which was a syncretism of all the indigenous religious beliefs and practices at the popular level, are blurred and often impossible to distinguish. For example, views about the *hun*-soul and *po*-soul found in the Han Confucian *Liji* 禮記 (Classic of Rites) bear a strong resemblance to those found in the *Laozi heshang zhu* 老子河上注 (Heshang Commentary on the Laozi), a popular Daoist text of

Han origin.[1] Such blurring also occurs in the *Taipingjing* 太平經 (Scripture of Great Peace) popular beliefs concerning the afterlife at the end of the Han Period. Portions of this text are clearly traceable to the Han times and can throw important new light on our subject, especially when they are used with caution and in combination with other newly discovered documents proven to be from the Han Period.[2]

Finally, a word about the problem of cultural unity or diversity is also in order. The general picture presented below reflects what all our evidence tells us, but no claim is made that the beliefs described constitute in any strict sense a unified belief system, much less the only one, embraced by all the Chinese of the Han Empire throughout the four centuries of its existence. Some of the beliefs and practices discussed in this study may well have been of only local subcultural importance. On the other hand, however, it would not be worthwhile to attempt to identify every belief or practice with the regional culture from which it originally arose. For example, the idea of *hun*, though possibly of a southern origin, had already become universally accepted by the Chinese by the third century B.C.E. at the latest, and the Taishan cult had also assumed a nationwide religious significance by the second century C.E., if not earlier. Throughout this study, I shall identify, whenever possible, the date and local origin of each piece of supporting evidence. Nevertheless, given our present stage of knowledge, it is not always clear what sorts of conclusions can be drawn from such identifications.

THE *FU* 復 RITUAL

In Han China there was an important death ritual called *fu*, "the Summons of the Soul." It was the first of a series of rituals to be performed for the newly dead. Although this *fu* ritual, as variously reported in the *Zhouli* 周禮 (Rites of Zhou), the *Yili* 儀禮 (Book of Etiquette and Ceremonial), and the *Classic of Rites* is a highly complex one, it may nevertheless be briefly described. As soon as a person dies, a "summoner" (*fuzhe* 復者), normally a member of the family, climbs from the east eaves to the top of the roof with a set of clothes belonging to the deceased. The summoner faces the north, waves the clothes of the deceased, and calls him by name aloud: "O! Thou so-and-so, come back!" After the call has been repeated three times, the summoner throws down the clothes, which are received by another person on the ground. The receiver then spreads the clothes over the body of the dead. Afterward, the summoner descends from the west eaves. Thus, the ritual of *fu* is completed.

According to the Han commentator Zheng Xuan 鄭玄 (127–200), the purpose of the *fu* ritual is "to summon the *hun*-soul of the dead back to reunite with its *po*-soul" (*zhaohun fupo* 招魂復魄). In fact, the ritual is predicated on the belief that when the *hun* separates from the *po* and leaves the human body, life comes to an end. At the moment when death first occurs, however, the living cannot bear to believe that their beloved one has really left them for good. The living must first assume that the departure of the *hun*-soul is only temporary. It is possible, then, that if the departed soul can be summoned back, the dead may be brought back to life. A person can be pronounced dead only when the *fu* ritual has failed to achieve its purpose, after which the body of the dead will be placed on the bed in his or her own chamber and covered with a burial shroud called *hu* or *fu* 幠.[3]

Remarkably, this Han ritual practice has been confirmed by recent archaeological discoveries. From 1972 to 1974, three Han tombs were excavated at Mawangdui, in Changsha, Hunan. At the time of its excavation, Tomb No. 1 aroused worldwide attention primarily because of the well-preserved body of its occupant, the wife of Licang 利蒼, the Marquis of Dai 軑, who probably died sometime after 175 B.C.E. (hereafter "Countess of Dai"). In Tomb No. 3, dated 168 B.C.E. and belonging to Licang's son, a large quantity of silk manuscripts of lost ancient writings were found. Since their discovery, the scholarly literature on these two tombs and their unusually rich contents has been enormous and is still growing. My discussion below will be confined to the light that this spectacular discovery sheds on the *fu* ritual. For this purpose, I will focus on the two T-shaped polychrome paintings on silk from Tombs No. 1 and No. 3, respectively. In addition to these two, similar paintings have also been found in other Han tombs. A Chinese archaeologist has summarized the contents of the Han paintings as follows:

> They are all of silk and are painted with fine colored pictures. The picture is divided into three sections, depicting, from top to bottom, Heaven, man's world, and the underworld. Both Heaven and the underworld are represented by mythological images; the Heaven picture has sun, moon, and sometimes stars, and the sun has a golden crow and the moon has a toad and a white rabbit, and sometimes a picture of Chang-e, the Goddess of the moon. The underworld picture shows various aquatic animals, representing an aquatic palace at the bottom of the sea. As for man's world, the picture depicts scenes from daily life and also a portrait of the master of the tomb.[4]

This characterization is on the whole accurate, taking as it obviously does the painting from Tomb No. 1 at Mawangdui as typical of its kind. Scholars are generally agreed that the central theme of the painting is the "Summons of the Soul." According to Yu Weichao 俞偉超, the two male figures above the aged woman, who can be clearly identified as the Countess of Dai, are most likely the "summoners." Judging by the position they occupy and the robes and hats they wear, these two men are represented as calling the departed soul back from a rooftop.[5] While other identifications have also been suggested, Yu's seems to fit with the main theme of the painting best, especially, as we shall see momentarily, when the function of the painting is clarified.[6] Moreover, the lady below the moon, instead of being the goddess of the moon (Chang-e 嫦娥 or Heng-e 姮娥), may well have been a representation of the departed soul of the Countess of Dai herself. A comparison with the T-shaped silk painting from Tomb No. 3 shows that the most noticeable difference between the two heavenly scenes lies in the absence of the so-called Chang-e in the latter.[7] Michael Loewe has also made an interesting suggestion that the beautiful woman's figure ending in a serpentine tail at the central apex of the painting may not be intended to represent any of the mythological figures that scholars have put forth. Instead, it may have been the artist's intention to represent the final stage of the countess's journey to Heaven when she has reached her destination.[8] In other words, one of the two figures must be a representation of the countess's *hun*-soul. It is important to note that in the round central space of the second painting, the female figure is replaced by a male figure. This difference of gender makes better sense when we take into consideration the gender of its occupant. It is quite reasonable to assume that the male figure in this case is also a representation of the soul of the countess's son in Heaven.[9]

The establishment of the central theme of the T-shaped paintings as the summons of the soul also helps to identify the function of the silk painting. While the suggestion that the painting was a banner used in funeral processions cannot be completely ruled out, it is more likely that it was the burial shroud, *hu*, frequently referred to in Han texts in connection with the *fu* ritual. In the Han inventories of funeral furnishings found in both tombs, there is an item listed as "*feiyi*, twelve feet long," which has been identified with the T-shaped silk painting.[10] The identification seems firmly grounded. *Feiyi* 非衣 means "mantle," "shroud," or "cover." Moreover, in ancient ritual texts, *fei* and *hu* are interchangeable in meaning. According to Han commentators, a *hu* was a cloth painted red and used to cover the corpse of the newly dead and, later, the coffin.[11] This description agrees perfectly with the silk painting. The current view that it was a *mingjing* 銘旌, or "funerary banner," is therefore questionable, to say the least; literally, *mingjing* means "inscribed funerary banner." The basic purpose of a *mingjing* was "to identify the departed *hun*-soul" by means of a name inscribed on a banner. The use of the *mingjing*, widespread at the time of Xunzi (third century B.C.E.), continued throughout the Han Period.[12] In fact, none of the *mingjing* excavated from Han tombs in recent decades lacks such an inscription.[13] Since the names of neither the mother nor her son are inscribed on the T-shaped paintings, they must not be *mingjing*.

To conclude this section, it seems reasonable to assert that the T-shaped paintings not only take the ritual of *fu* as their main theme, but their function is also closely related to that same ritual. We may say that these paintings provide archaeological confirmation of the ritual of *fu* as recorded in the various Han writings on ritual.

THE *HUN* AND *PO* SOULS

The ritual of *fu*, as pointed out earlier, is based on the belief in *zhaohun fupo*, to summon the *hun*-soul to reunite with the *po*-soul. To grasp the full meaning of this ritual practice, we must proceed to trace the evolution of the Chinese concept of soul from antiquity to the Han times.

Before the dualistic conception of *hun* and *po* began to gain currency in the middle of the sixth century B.C.E., *po* alone seems to have been used to denote the human soul. The character *po* 魄 (or its variant *ba* 霸) means "white," "bright," or "bright light," deriving originally from the growing light of the new moon. The earliest form of the character has recently been found on a Zhou oracle bone inscription datable to the eleventh century B.C.E. It is used in the term *jipo* 既魄, which, according to Wang Guowei, stood for the period from the eighth or ninth to the fourteenth or fifteenth of the lunar month. The term *jisipo* 既死魄 may also be found or another piece of oracle bone indicating the period from the twenty-third or twenty-fourth to the end of the month.[14] These two terms were later used repeatedly in early Zhou historical documents as well as bronze inscriptions in the standard forms of *jisheng ba* 既生霸 and *jisi ba* 既死霸, which may be translated, respectively, as "after the birth of the crescent" and "after the death of the crescent."[15]

Since the ancient Chinese took the changing phases of the moon as periodic birth and death of its *po*—its "white light" or soul—by analogy, they eventually came to associate, by the early sixth century B.C.E. if not earlier, the life or death of a man with the presence or absence of his *po*.[16] Two examples from the *Zuozhuan* 左傳 (Zuo Commentary to the Spring and Autumn Annals), the chronicle of the state of Lu compiled probably in the fourth century B.C.E., will serve to illustrate our point. In 593 B.C.E., a man named Zhao Tong 趙同 behaved erratically at the court of Zhou. One official made the following prediction: "In less than ten years Zhao Tong will be sure to meet with great calamity. Heaven has taken his *po* from him."[17] Fifty years later, in 543 B.C.E., a nobleman named Boyou 伯有 in the state of Zheng (in central Henan) had shown a marked decline in reasoning power and judgment, which also led a contemporary to remark: "Heaven is destroying Boyou and has taken away his *po*."[18] In both cases, the *po* is identified as the soul of the man, something that when taken away, by Heaven, causes the man to lose his intelligence. Clearly, the *po* must have been conceived as a separate entity that joins the body from outside.

Toward the end of the sixth century B.C.E., however, the concept of *hun* as a soul had also become widespread. In 516 B.C.E., Yue Qi 樂祁, an official at the court of the state of Song (in eastern Henan), had the following to say about the Duke of Song and a guest named Shusun 叔孫 from Lu because both had wept during a supposedly joyful gathering: "This year both our lord and Shusun are likely to die. I have heard that joy in the midst of grief and grief in the midst of joy are signs of a loss of mind (or heart, *xin* 心). The essential vigor and brightness of the mind is what we call the *hun* and the *po*. When these leave it, how can the man continue long?"[19] Here, both the *hun* and the *po* are regarded as the very essence of the mind, the source of knowledge and intelligence. Death is thought to follow inevitably when the *hun* and *po* leave the body. We have reason to believe that around this time, the idea of *hun* was still relatively new. To the mind of an ordinary Chinese, it was probably not very clear in precisely what way the *hun* and *po* were related to each other. In 534 B.C.E., the state of Zheng was deeply disturbed by a series of events resulting, reportedly, from a nobleman's ghost having returned to take revenge on his murderers. This nobleman was the above-mentioned Boyou, who had been not only expelled from Zheng but also assassinated by his political enemies. As a result of the loss of his hereditary office, his spirit was also deprived of sacrifices. The disturbances supposedly caused by this avenging ghost terrified the entire state. The wise statesman and philosopher, Zichan 子產, therefore reinstated Boyou's son in his former office. Finally, as our story goes, the ghost was satisfied and disappeared. Afterward, a friend asked Zichan whether there was any explanation for this strange phenomenon: What does a ghost consist of? How is it possible for a ghost to disturb the human world? The following answer given by Zichan is of central importance to our study because it is the locus classicus on the subject of the human soul in the Chinese tradition:

> When man is born, that which is first created, is called the *po* and, when the *po* has been formed, its positive part (*yang* 陽) becomes *hun* or conscious spirit.
>
> In case a man is materially well and abundantly supported, then his *hun* and *po* grow very strong, and therefore produce spirituality and intelligence. Even the *hun* and *po* of an ordinary man or woman, having encountered violent death, can attach themselves to other people to cause extraordinary troubles. . . . The stuff Boyou was made of was copious and rich, and his family great and powerful. Is it not natural that, having met with a violent death, he should be able to become a ghost?[20]

To begin with, it is important to point out that the very fact that Zichan found it necessary to offer such a detailed explanation of the relationship between the *po* and the *hun* indicates that the *hun* as a concept of soul was not yet familiar to the Chinese mind. This point can be further seen from the fact that he took the *po* to be fundamental and the *hun*, derivative. In his emphasis on physical nourishment as the foundation of the soul, Zichan's analysis strongly suggests a materialistic point of view. On the whole, I believe, this interpretation is best understood as reflecting Zichan's personal view of the subject rather than being a common conception in sixth-century B.C.E. China. It is true that Zichan's statement, as quoted above, later became the orthodox doctrine of *hun* and *po* in the Confucian (including neo-Confucian) philosophical tradition.[21] As we shall see later, however, it was not the view to be accepted by the common man in China in subsequent, especially Han, times.

We know relatively little about the origin of *hun* as a concept of soul. It is quite possible that the concept was more fully developed in the south and then spread to the north sometime during the sixth century B.C.E.[22] This possibility finds some support in the textual evidence at our disposal.

According to the "Tangong" 檀弓 chapter of the *Classic of Rites*, generally believed to be a pre-Han text, Prince Jizha 季札 of the southern state of Wu (in Jiangsu) lost his son while traveling in the north in 515 B.C.E. At the burial ceremony, he is reported to have expressed the following view about the dead: "Destined it is that his bones and flesh should return to the earth. As for his soul-breath (*hunqi* 魂氣), it goes everywhere, everywhere."[23] It is important to note that in this passage, the idea of *po* is conspicuously missing, which seems to indicate that it was not as widespread a concept as in the north, for the "bones and flesh" refers to the corpse, not the *po*-soul. At any rate, there can be little doubt that in the southern tradition, the *hun* was regarded as a more active and vital soul than the *po*. This is clearly shown in the ancient *Chuci* 楚辭 (Elegies of Chu). Two of the songs, datable to the early third century B.C.E., describe the shamanistic ritual of "soul summons." The following lines appear repeatedly in these two songs: "O soul, come back! In the east you can not abide. O soul, come back! In the south you cannot stay. O soul, go not to the west! O soul, go not to the north! O soul, come back! Climb not to Heaven above. O soul, come back! Go not down to the Land of Darkness."[24] The "soul" in each and every case refers invariably to the *hun* and therefore confirms completely the belief of the southern prince Jizha that the *hun*-soul indeed goes everywhere.

Probably as a result of the fusion of cultures, by the second century B.C.E. at the latest, the Chinese dualistic conception of soul had reached its definitive formulation. A most succinct statement of this dualistic idea may be found in the "Border Sacrifices" (Jiao te sheng 郊特牲) chapter of the *Classic of Rites*: "The breath-soul (*hunqi* 魂氣) returns to Heaven; the bodily soul (*xingpo* 形魄) returns to earth. Therefore, in sacrificial offerings, one should seek the meaning in the *Yin* and *Yang* 陰陽 principle."[25] It may be noted that several dualities are involved in this formulation. In addition to the basic duality of *hun* and *po*, we also see the dualities of *qi* and *xing*, Heaven and Earth, and *Yin* and *Yang*. We shall explain the ideas of *qi* and *xing* at a later juncture. Briefly, the dualism may be understood in the following way. Ancient Chinese generally believed that the individual human life consists of a bodily part as well as a spiritual part. The physical body relies for its existence on food and drink produced by the earth. The spirit depends for its existence on the invisible life force called *qi*, which comes into the body from Heaven. In other words, breathing and eating are the two basic activities by which a human being continually maintains life.

But the body and the spirit are each governed by a soul, namely, the *po* and the *hun*. It is for this reason that they are referred to in the passage just quoted above as the bodily soul (*xingpo*) and the breath-soul (*hunqi*), respectively.

The identification of the *hun-po* duality with the *Yin* and *Yang* principles was a later development, evidently resulting from the rise and popularity of the *yin-yang* cosmology in the late fourth and early third centuries B.C.E. Although in the above-quoted statement by Zichan the *hun* is defined as the *yang* or positive part of the *po*, the *po* itself, or the remainder of it, is not described as *yin*. The equation of the paired concept of *hun-po* with that of *yin-yang* had yet to be developed. Now, according to the *yin-yang* cosmology, there are two basic opposite but complementary forces at work in the cosmos. *Yin* is the supreme feminine force, while *yang* is its masculine counterpart. As two basic principles, the *yin* is characterized, among other things, by passivity and negativity, and the *yang* by activity and positivity. But life, whether cosmic or individual, comes into being only when the two forces begin to interact with each other. Heaven and Earth, for instance, being the highest embodiment of *yang* and *yin*, operate in response to each other to form cosmic life. It was, therefore, quite natural for ancient Chinese to fit the *hun-po* duality into this *yin-yang* framework. By Han times at the latest, as the above-quoted passage from the *Classic of Rites* shows, it already became a generally accepted idea that the *hun* belongs to the *yang* category and is hence an active and heavenly substance, whereas the *po* belongs to the *yin* category and is hence a passive and earthly substance.

This identification led to a new conception of the relationship between the *hun* and the *po*. During the Han dynasty, there was a widely shared belief in both elite and popular culture that in life, the *hun* and *po* form a harmonious union within the human body, and at death, the two souls separate and leave the body. This belief may have originated during a much earlier period because we already find a clear expression of the idea of "the separation of the *hun* from the *po*" in the *Elegies of Chu* of the early third century B.C.E.[26]

When the *hun* and *po* separate, however, they also go their separate, or more precisely, opposite, ways. The *hun*-soul, being a breathlike light substance (*hunqi*), has a much greater freedom of movement. By contrast, the *po*-soul, being associated with the physical body, is conceived as a heavier substance with only restricted mobility. Therefore, at death, the *hun*-soul goes swiftly upward to Heaven, whereas the *po*-soul moves downward to earth at a much slower pace. This explains why, in the ritual of *fu*, it is the *hun*, but not the *po*, that has to be recalled from the rooftop. For the same reason, the *Elegies of Chu* speak of "summoning the *hun*-soul" but never "summoning the *po*-soul."[27]

To clarify the term *hunqi*, a word may be said about the complex and difficult concept of *qi* as the "source of life." The concept has a broad as well as a narrow meaning. In its broad sense, *qi* is a primal and undifferentiated life force that permeates the entire cosmos. However, when the *qi* becomes differentiated and individuated to form all the things in the universe, it then varies in purity.

Thus, as succinctly summed up by D. C. Lau: "the grosser *qi*, being heavy, settled to become the earth, while the refined *qi*, being light, rose to become the sky. Man, being halfway between the two, is a harmonious mixture of the two kinds of *qi*."[28] It is in this broad sense that a Daoist philosophical treatise of the second century B.C.E. says that the *hun* is made up of the refined, heavenly *qi* and the *po* the grosser, earthly *qi*.[29] But in its narrow sense, the *qi* refers specifically to the heavenly *qi*. It is in this narrow sense that the *hunqi*, or the breath-soul, is distinguished from the *xingpo*, or bodily soul.

We have seen that it was a general belief in Han China that the *hun* owes its existence to the refined *qi* from Heaven, whereas the *po*, always being associated with the body, is composed of the coarse *qi* from Earth. But how are the two souls, *hun* and *po*, distinguished from each other in terms of specific functions? According to Zheng Xuan (127–200), *qi* or *hun*-soul forms the basis of a man's spirit and intelligence, whereas the function of the *po*-soul is specifically defined as "hearing distinctly and seeing clearly."[30] In other words, the *hun* governs man's spirit (*shen* 神, including *xin*, mind or heart) and the *po* governs his body (including the senses). It is interesting to point out that a similar distinction between the *hun* and the *po* can also be found in Han Daoist literature. According to the *Heshang Commentary on the Laozi*, Heaven feeds man with five kinds of *qi*, which enter his body from the nostrils and are stored in his heart (or mind). The five kinds of *qi* are pure and subtle, and therefore go to form man's spirit, senses, voice, etc. Thus, a man has a soul called *hun*. The *hun* is masculine; it goes out and comes in through the nostrils and communicates with Heaven. Earth feeds man with five tastes, which enter his body from the mouth and are stored in the stomach. The five tastes are impure and therefore go to form a man's body, bones and flesh, blood and veins, as well as six emotions. Thus, a man has a soul called *po*. The *po* is feminine; it goes out and comes in through the mouth and communicates with Earth.[31] Although there are differences between the Confucian and Daoist versions with regard to the respective functions of the *hun* and *po*, the basic structural similarity is nevertheless unmistakable. This similarity testifies fully to the universality of the distinction between the *hun* and *po* in Han China, the former being a "spiritual" soul and the latter a "bodily" soul.

BELIEF IN AFTERLIFE

The above discussion of the changing Chinese conception of soul from antiquity to the Han Period naturally leads to the problem of afterlife. Does the departed soul continue to possess knowledge and feelings? Can the soul exist as an independent entity forever? Where does the soul go after its separation from the body? Admittedly, these are not easy questions to answer owing to the paucity of the sources on the subject. Thanks to recent archaeological discoveries, however, it is now possible to attempt a reconstruction of a general picture.

Long before the rise of the dualistic conception of the soul, there had already been a common Chinese belief in an afterlife. The notion that the departed soul is as conscious as the living is already implied in Shang-Zhou sacrifices. Shang people generally took sacrifice to be an actual feeding of the dead.[32] According to a Zhou bronze inscription, the kinds of animals offered sacrificially to ancestral spirits were identical with those presented to the reigning king as food.[33] As far as daily needs were concerned, no sharp distinction was drawn between the departed soul and the living. In fact, ancient Chinese were extremely concerned about what they believed to be their ancestors' hunger in the afterworld. In 604 B.C.E., a nobleman from the house of Ruo-ao 若敖, apprehending the forthcoming disaster of extermination of his whole clan, wept and said: "The spirits of the dead are also in need of food. But I am afraid those of our Ruo-ao clan will be sure to suffer starvation."[34] What he meant is that when the entire clan is wiped out, there will be no one left to offer regular sacrifices to the ancestral spirits. His concern lies at the very cornerstone of Chinese ancestor worship, for the Chinese have believed until recent decades—indeed some may still continue to believe today—that a spirit cannot, as a rule, enjoy the sacrifices offered by someone other than his own flesh and blood, namely, his male descendant, owing to the incommunicability between different kinds of the individuated qi. Apparently, it was believed that without sacrificial food, the hungry ancestral spirits would disintegrate more quickly. The original Chinese term for "the spirits of the dead" in the above passage is gui. As clearly shown in oracle inscriptions, the character gui 鬼 had already acquired the meaning of "the soul of the dead" as early as the Shang Period.[35] The po or the hun, on the other hand, were distinguished from gui by being names for "the soul of the living."

The belief that the departed soul actually enjoys the sacrificial food offered by the living was widely held in the popular culture of Han China. As vividly described by the critical philosopher Wang Chong 王充 (27–100? C.E.) from Guiji (in Zhejiang), "People never desist from urging the necessity of making offerings, maintaining that the departed are conscious, and that ghosts and spirits eat and drink like so many guests invited to dinner."[36] This description has been archaeologically confirmed by the large quantities of food and food vessels found in Han tombs excavated over the past four decades.[37]

On the other hand, the idea that the individual soul can survive death indefinitely seems to have been alien to the Chinese mind. In this regard, once more, we may take the Zhou sacrificial system as an illustration. Perhaps partly as a result of the shift from the predominantly lateral succession of the Shang Period to the lineal succession, the Zhou system set a limit to the number of generations in ancestor worship according to social status. The royal house, for example, would offer sacrifices to no more than seven generations of ancestors, while the common people did so for only two generations, that is, their dead parents and grandparents. Therefore, every new generation would have to suspend sacrifices to the uppermost generation previously sacrificed to. An exception was made for the founding ancestor, who had to remain as a symbol of the collective identity of the lineage. The system was apparently predicated on the assumption that after a certain period of time, the spirits of the dead gradually dissolve into the primal *qi* and lose their individual identities. As for the differences in number of generations for different social groups, the justification was probably based on a materialistic interpretation of the relationship between the body and the soul. As Zichan's remark, quoted earlier, makes abundantly clear, the soul of a nobleman is stronger than that of an ordinary man or woman because, being from a great and powerful family, his physical body is much better nourished than a common person's. As a result, his departed soul disintegrates more slowly.

The idea that the departed soul gradually shrinks with the passing of time is well attested to by the ancient saying "the spirit of a newly dead is large and that of an old one is small" (*xingui da, gugui xiao* 新鬼大, 故鬼小).[38] The same idea was later expressed in a slightly different way. In a literary work of the early fourth century C.E., the soul of a newly dead is described as much heavier than that of an old one.[39] Thus, both the elite culture and the popular thought in ancient China shared the belief that the departed soul can survive, in the words of Hu Shih, "only for a time varying apparently in length according to its own strength, but [it] gradually fades out and ultimately disintegrates entirely."[40] This materialistic conception of the soul explains the great importance that ancient Chinese had attached to the body of the dead. As archaeological discovery has shown, people in the Han Period often went to great lengths to preserve the body of the dead. Evidently, ancient Chinese, just like ancient Egyptians, believed that the soul could not survive much longer unless the body itself were preserved.[41]

THE AFTERWORLD: SEPARATE ABODES
FOR THE *HUN* AND THE *PO*

Finally, to answer the question of where the soul goes after its separation from the body, we must take a closer look at the conception of the afterworld. Before we proceed, however, we must correct a deep-rooted misconception about the origin of the Chinese belief in an afterworld. Early in the seventeenth century, Gu Yanwu 顧炎武, based on a preliminary historical investigation, came to the conclusion that the Chinese did not have a clear notion of an afterworld until the end of the Han dynasty when Buddhism arrived on the scene.[42] In modern times, this thesis has received further support from Hu Shih's study of the history of Chinese Buddhism. He emphatically maintained that it was Buddhism that gave the Chinese the idea of tens of heavens and many hells.[43] More recently, Joseph Needham, taking issue with the distinction between "this-worldly" and "otherworldly" xian 仙 immortality I proposed two decades ago, has said: "If one bears in mind the conceptions of different peoples (Indo-Iranian, Christian, Islamic, etc.) there was no such thing as an 'other world' in ancient Chinese thought at all—no Heaven or hell, no creator God, and no expected end of the universe once it had emerged from primeval chaos. All was natural and within Nature. Of course, after the permeation of Buddhism, 'the case was altered.' "[44] Indeed, it is true that in ancient Chinese thought, the contrast between "this world" and the "other world" was not as sharp as in other cultures. One may also legitimately argue that, put in a comparative perspective, the early Chinese idea of an "other world" appears to be "refreshing" because it is rather differently conceived. But to say that there was no such thing as an "other world" and no Heaven or hell at all is obviously an exaggeration and a position that is contradicted by known historical and archaeological facts.

We have noted that as early as the Shang Period, there had already arisen the idea of a "heavenly court," which, however, may have been reserved only for the long-lasting, if not immortal, souls of the kings and lords as a depository of social authority.[45] From about the eighth century B.C.E. on, the term Yellow Springs (huangquan 黄泉) began to be used in historical and literary writings to denote the home of the dead. The Yellow Springs was imagined to be located beneath the earth, a place conceived of as dark and miserable. On the whole, the idea is a vague one, however, and very little detail about it exists in the written record.[46] As we have seen, in the "Summons of the Soul," one of the *Elegies of Chu*, the soul is advised "not to climb Heaven above" or "go not down to the Land of Darkness" (youdu 幽都). Thus, for the first time, we encounter both "Heaven" and "hell" in the same poem. However, Chinese imagination of the afterlife did not become fully developed until the Han Period. Tremendous progress in Han archaeology has allowed us to reconstruct in its general form the early Chinese conception of afterlife, including the related beliefs of Heaven and hell.

As noted earlier, the two T-shaped silk paintings from Mawangdui clearly reveal the belief that at death the *hun*-souls immediately "return to Heaven," just as the above-quoted *Classic of Rites* passage says. Although we are in no position, given our present state of knowledge, to identify each and every one of the mythological elements in these paintings, the two paintings do provide us with concrete evidence that by the second century B.C.E., the Chinese already had a vivid conception of a heavenly world above and an underworld below.

The notion of a government in Heaven overseeing human activities was developed later in Han popular culture. In the earliest Daoist canon *Scripture of Great Peace*, datable to the second century C.E., that is, before appreciable Buddhist influence on Chinese life and thought, we find at least four *cao* 曹 or "departments" in the celestial government. They are the *mingcao* 命曹 ("Department of Fate"), *shoucao* 壽曹 ("Department of Longevity"), *shan-cao* 善曹 ("Department of Good Deeds"), and *e-cao* 惡曹 ("Department of Evil Deeds").[47] The term *cao*, it may be noted, is a direct borrowing from the Han governmental organization. There were, for instance, four *cao* in the office of the *shangshu* 尚書 ("Masters of Documents"), which, since the time of Emperor Wu, had become "the key organ of the state."[48] This also explains why in the *Laozi Xiang-er zhu* 老子想爾注 (Xiang-er Commentary on the Laozi), the celestial government is also referred to as the *Tiancao* 天曹 ("Heavenly Departments"), an idea that has been perpetuated in Chinese popular culture ever since.[49] The *Scripture of Great Peace* also reveals something about how the various departments conduct their business. Each department keeps detailed personal dossiers on all living persons. When a person has accumulated enough merits, for instance, his dossier, after evaluation, may be transferred to the Department of Longevity.[50] On the other hand, there is also the possibility that a person formerly of good conduct may eventually end up in the Department of Evil Deeds, if he is later found to have committed many sins. Thus, not only are the personal records of all living beings updated on a daily basis, these records are also constantly subject to transfer from one department to another. Indeed, activities of this kind constitute a major function of the celestial bureaucracy.[51]

Now, let us turn to the idea of "underworld" in Han times. On this subject, fortunately, very interesting evidence has also been found in the Mawangdui Tomb No. 3. A wooden document from this tomb reads as follows: "On the twenty-fourth day, second month, the twelfth year [of Emperor Wen's reign, 168 B.C.E.], Household Assistant Fen to the *langzhong* 郎中 in charge of the dead: 'A list of mortuary objects is herewith forwarded to you. Upon receiving this document, please memorialize without delay to the Lord of the Grave (Zhuzang Jun 主藏君).'"[52]

This document reveals two interesting points about Han beliefs about an underworld. First, since the silk painting from the same tomb shows that the *hun*-soul of the dead goes to Heaven, the present document makes sense only if understood as dealing with the journey of his *po*-soul to the underworld. Second, the bureaucratic structure of the underworld is, like that of the heavenly world, modeled on that of the human world. It is interesting to note that before 104 B.C.E., there was an office of *langzhongling* 郎中令 ("Supervisor of Attendants") whose function it was to render personal services to the emperor.[53] Thus, the analogy between the status of Household Assistant Fen in the marquisate of Dai and the *langzhong* in the underworld is unmistakable. In other words, Family Assistant Fen was notifying his counterpart in the court of the Underworld Lord of the arrival of the newly dead, in this case, the son of the Marquis of Dai. This practice is also confirmed by two similar wooden documents found in the Han tombs at Fenghuang Shan 鳳凰山 (in Jiangling 江陵, Hubei) in 1975. The first one, from Tomb No. 168, dated 167 B.C.E., was issued in the name of the Assistant Magistrate of Jiangling and sent to the Underworld Assistant Magistrate. The former informed the latter of the immigration of a newly dead under his jurisdiction to the underworld and requested the case be reported to the Underworld Lord.[54] The second one, dated 153 B.C.E., is found in Tomb No. 10. In this case, the document was submitted to the Underworld Lord (Dixia Zhu 地下主) directly in the name of the dead, Zhang Yan 張偃 himself. Unlike the Mawangdui case, the two occupants of the Feng-huang Shan tombs were neither noblemen nor officials, but common people of some means, a fact that testifies fully to the universality of this belief.[55]

Since the po-soul is closely associated with the body, therefore, at death it returns to earth when the body is buried. However, it seems to have been a widespread idea during Han times that the life of the po-soul in the underworld depends very much on the condition of the body. If the body was well preserved and properly buried, then the po-soul would not only rest in peace and remain close to the body but probably also last longer. Lavish interment and body preservation are thus quite characteristic of Han tombs belonging to families of some means. Needless to say, not every family could afford the Mawangdui type of burial. The simplest way to preserve the body was, according to Han death ritual, to put a piece of jade into the mouth of the dead.[56] This ritual practice has been amply confirmed by archaeological discovery.[57] It was generally believed in ancient China that jade can prevent the body from decay. The world-renowned "jade shrouds," discovered in the tomb of an early Han prince at Mancheng, Hebei, in 1968, were obviously intended to have this effect.[58]

To sum up, the combination of textual and archaeological evidence suggests that pre-Buddhist Chinese beliefs about a heavenly world above and an underworld below were closely related to the dualistic conception of soul, the hun and the po. At death, the hun and po were thought to go separate ways, with the former returning to Heaven and the latter to earth. The idea of Heaven and hell as opposing sites as reward and punishment in the afterlife was not fully developed in Chinese thought until the coming of Buddhism.

THE RISE OF *XIAN* IMMORTALITY AND THE RESTRUCTURING OF THE AFTERWORLD

A historical account of the Chinese conception of afterlife would remain incomplete without a brief discussion of the fundamental transformation it underwent during the reign of Emperor Wu of Han (140–87 B.C.E.). The transformation in question pertains to the development of the cult of *xian* 仙 immortality.[59]

Xian was a unique idea in ancient Chinese thought and probably began as a romantic conception of total spiritual freedom. A prototype of a *xian* immortal may be found in the beginning chapter of the *Zhuangzi* 莊子, where a Divine Man is described as follows: "There is a Divine Man living on faraway Kuyeh [Guye] Mountain, with skin like ice or snow . . . [who is] gentle and shy like a young girl. He doesn't eat the five grains, but sucks the wind and drinks the dew, climbs up on clouds and mists, rides a flying dragon, and wanders beyond the four seas."[60] The important thing to note here is that the Divine Man does not eat anything earthly such as the five grains but only "sucks the wind and drinks the dew," phenomena that come from Heaven. Elsewhere the *Zhuangzi* also mentions the method of regulating or manipulating the *qi* or breath (*dao-yin* 導引) as a way of cultivating long life.[61] It seems then that the idea of the *xian* was originally conceived in terms of the *hun*-soul, which, being made up entirely of the Heavenly *qi*, is able to ascend to Heaven.

The only difference between the *hun* and the *xian* is that while the former leaves the body at death, the latter obtains its total freedom by transforming the body into something purely ethereal, that is, the Heavenly *qi* 氣. Thus, regulation of *qi* or breath and "abstention from grains" were widely believed to be the two most important means of achieving *xian* immortality.[62] The "Yuanyou" 遠遊 (Far-Off Journey) in the *Elegies of Chu* describes a scene of some ancient *xian* immortals' ascension to Heaven in the following lines: "With the ether's (i.e., *qi*'s) transformations they rose upwards, with godlike swiftness miraculously moving. Leaving the dust behind, shedding their impurities—never to return again to their old homes."[63] In view of the fact that both the *Zhuangzi* and the *Elegies of Chu* are products of the Chu culture in the south, the family resemblance between the idea of *xian* and *hun* can hardly be a matter of historical coincidence.

As we have seen, in early philosophical and literary imagination, a *xian* immortal is someone who rejects this human world. He must "leave the dust behind" and "never return home again." However, as soon as the idea of *xian* immortality attracted the attention of the worldly rulers, such as princes of the Warring States Period and emperors of the Qin and Han dynasties, it began to develop into a cult of a this-worldly character. Princes and emperors were not interested in transforming themselves into *xian* immortals because they had suddenly developed a renunciatory attitude toward the honors and pleasures they enjoyed in this world. On the contrary, they were motivated by a strong desire to prolong their worldly pleasures forever.

This worldly cult of *xian* immortality had already gained considerable popularity among the princes of various states before the unification of China in 221 B.C.E., but it reached its zenith during the time of Emperor Wu of Han. Emperor Wu was led to believe, by a number of professional "necromancers," that a meeting could be arranged between him and some *xian* immortals on the top of Mount Tai 泰山, the sacred mountain in ancient China, as a preparation for his final ascension to Heaven. At this time, a story had been fabricated that the legendary Yellow Emperor did not really die but flew to Heaven on a dragon's back together with his court assistants and palace ladies after having performed imperial sacrifices to Heaven and Earth at the central peak of Mount Tai. Taken in by this story, Emperor Wu made his imperial pilgrimage to Mount Tai in 110 B.C.E. and carried out all the religious rituals supposedly in the tradition of the Yellow Emperor. He returned to the capital assured that he would eventually join the Yellow Emperor in Heaven as a *xian* immortal. By the turn of the first century C.E., at the latest, the cult of *xian* immortality had already spread from royal and aristocratic circles to the common people. A Han stone inscription relates that, in 7 C.E., a yamen underling in the local government of Hanzhong 漢中 (in modern Shaanxi) named Tang Gongfang 唐公房 succeeded in his pursuit of *xian* immortality. Consequently, he ascended to Heaven with not only his whole family but also his house and domestic animals.

The great popularity of this cult transformed the Han conception of the afterlife in a fundamental way. According to the *Scripture of Great Peace*, only the *xian* immortals who had embodied the great *Dao* were admitted to Heaven.[64] Since the immortal *xian* and the dissolvable *hun* were conceived as belonging to two completely different categories of beings, they were not supposed to mix in the same Heaven. As a result, a new abode had to be found to accommodate the *hun* souls. Thus, the governmental structure of the underworld was expanded. Based on a variety of historical and archaeological evidence, this new conception of the underworld may be briefly reconstructed as follows. First, from around the end of the first century B.C.E., a belief gradually arose that there was a supreme ruler called Lord of Mount Tai (Taishan Fujun 泰山府君) whose capital was located in a place named Liangfu 梁父, a small hill near Mount Tai.[65] Liangfu, it may be noted, was traditionally the place at which imperial sacrifices had been made to the supreme earthly deity, the Lord of Earth (Dizhu 地主).[66] It was indeed only a small step to transform the Lord of Earth into the Lord of the Underworld (Dixia Zhu 地下主). The title Lord of Mount Tai—Taishan Fujun—also requires a word of explanation. The term *fujun* must not be taken to mean "lord" in a general sense. In fact, it was a popular name referring specifically to provincial governors in Han times. Nor should "Taishan" in this case be understood as the sacred mountain itself. Instead, it was a reference to the province named after the sacred mountain in which Liangfu was also located.[67] In other words, calling the supreme ruler of the underworld Taishan Fujun was to indicate both the location of his residence and the bureaucratic rank of his office. Since he was in charge of the dead, he was therefore assigned an official position lower than the supreme ruler of the human world, the emperor, by one rank. This fits perfectly well with some other popular names by which he was also known. For example, stone inscriptions found in Han tombs often refer to him either as "Lord of Mount Tai" or as "the provincial governor in the underworld."[68] Moreover, a popular Han religious tract says that he is the "grandson of the Heavenly God."[69] The last instance is particularly revealing. Clearly, the idea of "grandson of the Heavenly God" was derived analogously from that of the "Son of Heaven," that is, the emperor.

Second, like the supreme ruler of the human world, it was believed that the Lord of Mount Tai also had a bureaucracy to assist him in governing the dead. Judging by the various official titles found in Han tombs and other texts, the bureaucratic structure of the underworld was closely modeled on the administrative system of the Han Empire. The first thing the newly dead had to do was to go to the capital of the underworld to register. There is further evidence suggesting that the underworld government could send for the souls of those whose allotted span on earth, according to the Register of Death, was up. As time wore on, the idea of postmortem punishment also found its way into the Han belief about the afterlife. The *Scripture of Great Peace* of the second century C.E. has the following vivid description of the administration of justice in the underworld:

> If a man commits evils unceasingly, his name will then be entered into the Register of Death. He will be summoned to the Underworld Government (*tufu* 土府) where his body is to be kept. Alas! When can he ever get out? His soul will be imprisoned and his doings in life will be questioned. If his words are found to be inconsistent, he will be subject to further imprisonment and torture. His soul is surely going to suffer a great deal. But who is to blame?[70]

This new conception of the underworld may well have been a faithful reflection of the cruel realities of interrogation and torture in the imperial and provincial prisons, especially during the second century C.E.[71]

Third, we have reason to believe that as the supreme ruler of the underworld, the authority of the Lord of Mount Tai was originally conceived to be exercised over the *hun*-souls. Several historical and literary sources specifically link the *hun*, but not the *po*, to Mount Tai, which itself calls to mind the underworld in which the Lord of Mount Tai reigns supreme. The *hun*-soul is said to be either "returning" or "belonging" to Mount Tai.[72] It may be recalled that Heaven was now populated by the *xian* immortals; it was no longer a place to which the *hun*-souls could return. For the Han Chinese, therefore, Mount Tai was the highest place imaginable, second only to Heaven. Strictly speaking, however, the *hun*-souls could not even ascend the central peak of that sacred mountain because it had also been transformed into a meeting place between the emperor and the *xian* immortals. The *hun*-souls could only travel to Liangfu, the capital of the underworld in which the Lord of Mount Tai operated his central administration. It may be further noted that in Han popular culture, Mount Tai itself, especially its peak, was a symbol of life and immortality, whereas Liangfu was that of death. However, the simple fact that Liangfu not only was located in the vicinity of Mount Tai but also fell under the jurisdiction of the province bearing the name of the holy mountain gradually gave rise to widespread confusion in Han popular beliefs about the afterlife. With the province bearing the name of Mount Tai inextricably confused with the mountain itself, texts from the second century c.e. on often speak of the departed *hun*-souls as if they were to "return" to the holy mountain. But it is important to point out that in all probability the original conception was that the *hun*-soul of the newly dead would go to the Liangfu hill in Taishan Province, to register its name with the underworld government.

Finally, a word about the *po*-soul is in order. Since the *hun*-soul now went to the underworld instead of Heaven, what happened to the *po*? It is interesting to observe that the *po* was under the care of a separate department of the underworld government. According to Dongfang Shuo (ca. 160 B.C.E.–ca. 93 B.C.E.), the court jester of Emperor Wu's time, the office in charge of the dead was called *bo* 柏. Clearly, *po* and *bo* share the same etymological root; the name *bo* may well have been derived from the belief that it was the abode of *po*-souls. Moreover, the same jester also defined *bo* as "the court of the ghosts" (*guiting* 鬼廷).[73] In Han times, the term *ting* commonly designated the yamen of a county magistrate, just as *fu* was the popular name of the office of a provincial governor.[74] This fits perfectly well with the bureaucratic hierarchy of the Han underworld: the deity in charge of the *po*-souls was lower by one level in rank than the deity in charge of the *hun*-souls, the Lord of Mount Tai. In approximately the middle of the first century B.C.E., the name Gaoli (or Haoli) 蒿里, suddenly gained popularity as an abode for the dead. It is interesting to note that it turns out that Gaoli was another place of deep religious significance at the foot of Mount Tai, where Emperor Wu performed the ritual of sacrifice to the Lord of Earth in 104 B.C.E.[75] Later in Han popular literature, Gaoli also came to be identified as the Lower Village (Xiali 下里) or the Yellow Springs in which the dead take their permanent residence.[76] At first it seems puzzling that there should be two different places in the Han underworld for the departed souls. However, the puzzle disappears as soon as we remember that each person was believed to be in possession of two separate souls, the *hun* and the *po*. There is clear evidence from inscriptions found in Later Han tombs that both the *hun* and the *po* are subject to the call of the underworld government.[77] This suggests the good possibility that the *po*-soul of the newly dead would be required to report to the underworld government in Gaoli in a way similar to the *hun*-soul's journey to Liangfu. As a response to the rise of the popular cult of *xian* immortality, which prevented the *hun*-soul from returning to Heaven, the Chinese underworld seems to have been fundamentally restructured along a dualistic line to accommodate the *hun* and the *po*, respectively.

This dualistic structure of the pre-Buddhist Chinese underworld is clearly reflected in the following four lines from a song about Mount Tai by the famous writer Lu Ji 陸機 (261–303):

On the hill of Liangfu there are hostels (*guan* 舘),

In Gaoli, there are also lodges (*ting* 亭) for the travelers,

Along the dark path stretch ten thousand ghosts (*gui*), one
   following the footsteps of another,

In the spiritual houses (*shenfang* 神房) are gathered hundreds of
   spirits (*ling* 靈).[78]

Here the poet is describing imagined scenes of the trips of both the *hun*-souls and the *po*-souls to their separate destinations—Liangfu and Gaoli. In his imagination, the poet introduces the Han system of travelers' inns (*guan* and *ting*) into the underworld.[79] There can be no question that the term *gui* (ghosts) refers specifically to the *po*-souls and the term *ling* (spirits) to the *hun*-souls. In a Confucian treatise from the Han Period, "Jiyi" 祭義 (The Meaning of Sacrifice), *gui* and *shen* are given as the names of *po* and *hun*, respectively, when the pair separate at death.[80] The identification of *gui* as the name for *po* after death is already confirmed by the saying of Dongfang Shuo, quoted above. The term *ling* in the poem can also be shown to be a variant of *hun* or *shen*. For example, Lu Ji's brother, Lu Yun 陸雲 (262–303), in his "Dengxia song," 登遐頌 uses *ling-po* 靈魄 instead of *hun-po*.[81] It is therefore safe to conclude that even as late as the third century, the Han dualistic conception of afterlife was still very much alive in the Chinese mind, namely, at death when the *hun* and the *po* part company, the former returns to Liangfu and the latter to Gaoli. It is important to note, however, that neither the nature of the two souls nor their relationship underwent any basic change as a result of the restructuring of the underworld. The original idea that the *hun*, being made of the Heavenly *qi* and light, moves upward, while the *po*, being made of the earthly *qi* and heavy, moves downward, was retained without change. Indeed, in this new conception, the destination of the *hun*-soul is located high on the Liangfu hill, whereas that of the *po*-soul is down in Gaoli, identified as the Lower Village (Xiali) in popular culture. This point is also further borne out by another poem of the same writer in which it is explicitly stated that after death, the *hun* "flies" and the *po* "sinks."[82]

In conclusion, it is important to point out that the popular belief in Han China linking the underworld to Mount Tai prepared the ground for the Chinese people to adjust themselves to the much more powerful Buddhist idea of "hells" in the centuries to come. It is interesting to note that in some of the earliest Chinese translations of Buddhist sûtras attributed to the Parthian monk An Shigao 安世高 (?–168) and the Sogdian monk Kang Senghui 康僧會 (?–280), the term *niraya* (hell) is often rendered as "the underworld prison in Mount Tai" (Taishan Diyu 泰山地獄). One translated text even says something to the effect that both the *hun*- and *po*-souls are harshly tortured in the Taishan Diyu.[83] This description agrees remarkably well with the indigenous Chinese idea of postmortem punishment as found in the *Scripture of Great Peace* quoted earlier. Needless to say, as Buddhism gradually gained ground in China, Chinese conceptions of the soul and afterlife were to be totally transformed. As a result, the pre-Buddhist belief in a dualistic underworld was eventually replaced by the Buddhist belief in "Ten Hells" each governed by a "King" (*yamarāja*). Nevertheless, the Han tradition about the Lord of Mount Tai in charge of the dead survived this radical transformation. Instead of being completely forgotten, the Lord of Mount Tai secured a permanent place in the Buddhist underworld as one of the Ten Kings—King of Mount Tai.[84] It is a point worth stressing that popular Chinese beliefs about the afterlife in their post-Han form, which developed under the influence of Buddhism, cannot be fully understood without knowledge of indigenous beliefs in pre-Buddhist China.

NOTES

1. This commentary, usually referred to as *Laozi heshang zhu* 老子河上注, has been traditionally thought to be a post-Han work due to the vulgarity of its language. See Zhang Xincheng 張心澂, *Weishu tongkao* 偽書通考, 2 vols. (Shanghai: Shangwu, 1954), 2: 743–745. However, with the discovery of several Dunhuang manuscripts of earlier commentaries on the *Laozi*, the origin of the Heshang text can now be traced to the second century C.E. or earlier. See Rao Zongyi 饒宗頤, *Laozi Xiang-er zhu jiao-jian* 老子想爾注校箋 (Hong Kong: Printed by the author, 1956), 87–92, and Kobayashi Masayoshi 小林正美, "Kajo shinjin shoku no shisô to seiritsu" 河上真人章句の思想と成立, *Tōhō shūkyō* 東方宗教 65 (May 1985): 20–43.

2. Particularly important are various kinds of inscriptions found in Han tombs. For the dating of the *Taipingjing*, see note 47 below.

3. On the ritual of *fu* 復, see *Liji zhushu* 禮記注疏, in *Shisan jing zhushu* 十三經注疏 (1815 edition), 4.20b, 21.9b–11a, 44.3a–5a; Hu Peihui 胡培翬, *Yili zhengyi* 儀禮正義, *GXJBCS*, 26.2–6; Sun Yirang 孫詒讓, *Zhouli zhengyi* 周禮正義, *GXJBCS*, 5.16.20–22. See also James Legge, trans., *The Texts of Confucianism Part 3; The Li Ki*, 2 vols., *SBE*, 1.368–369; John Steele, trans., *The I-li or Book of Etiquette and Ceremonial* (London: Probsthain, 1917), 1:45.

4. Wang Zhongshu, *Han Civilization* (New Haven: Yale University Press, 1982), 181. [Quoted with minor editorial changes—Eds.]

5. See Yu Weichao's 俞偉超 view in a symposium on the Han Tomb No. 1 at Mawangdui in *WW* 9 (1972): 60–61.

6. *Changsha Mawangdui yihao Hanmu* 長沙馬王堆一號漢墓, 2 vols. (Beijing: Wenwu, 1973), 1:41, identifies the two men as "the guardians of the heavenly gate," and An Zhimin 安志敏 "Changsha xin faxian di Xi-Han buohua shitan" 長沙新發現的西漢帛畫試探, *KG* 1 (1973): 45–46, identifies them as *da siming* and *shao siming*. For a detailed and technical study of this painting in English, see Michael Loewe, *Ways to Paradise: The Chinese Quest for Immortality* (London: Allen and Unwin, 1979), chap. 2.

7. Wang Buomin 王伯敏, "Mawangdui yihao Hanmu buohua bingwu Chang-e benyue" 馬王堆一號漢墓帛畫並無嫦娥奔月, *KG* 24, no. 3 (1979): 274.

8.   Loewe, *Ways to Paradise*, 59.

9.   See Jin Weinuo 金維諾, "Tan Changsha Mawangdui sanhao Hanmu buohua" 談長沙馬
     王堆三號漢墓帛畫, *WW* 11 (1974): 43.

10. For Tomb No. 1, see Shang Zhitan 商志香覃, "Mawangdui yihao Hanmu 'feiyi' shishi"
     馬王堆一號漢墓'非衣'試釋, *WW* 9 (1972): 43–47. For Tomb No. 3, see also *KG* 1 (1975): 57.

11. For *fei* and *hu* as interchangeable words in ancient ritual texts, see the views of Tang Lan
     唐蘭 and Yu Weichao in *WW* 9 (1972): 59–60.

12. Sun Yirang, *Zhouli zhengyi*, 50.35–36.

13. An Zhimin "Changsha xin faxian di Xi-Han buohua shitan," 50–51; Ma Yong 馬雍, "Lun
     Changsha Mawangdui yihao Hanmu chutu buohua di mingcheng he zuoyong" 論長沙
     馬王堆一號漢墓出土帛畫的名稱和作用, *KG* 2 (1973): 119–122; Xu Zhuangshu 許莊叔,
     "Fupo Jingzhao kao" 復魄旌旐考, *Wenshi* 文史 17 (June 1983): 261–263. It is somewhat
     puzzling that in spite of the fact that a *mingjing* is, by definition, "inscribed" and that all
     the *mingjing* excavated from Han tombs so far invariably bear the names of the dead,
     both An and Ma still insist on identifying the two uninscribed T-shaped paintings as
     "inscribed funerary banner."

14. See "Shaanxi Qishan Fengchu cun faxian Zhou chu jiaguwen" 陝西岐山鳳雛村發現周
     初甲骨文, *WW* 10 (1979): 41 and figure 5 on p. 43. See also the original *jisipo* inscription
     reproduced in plate 6, 2 (H11:55). For the identification of *jipo* and *jisipo*, see further discus-
     sions summarized in Wang Yuxin 王宇信, *Xi Zhou jiagu tanlun* 西周甲骨探論 (Beijing:
     Zhonghua, 1984), 82–83. The only Chinese scholar who has expressed some reserva-
     tions is Yan Yiping 嚴一萍. See his "Zhouyuan jiagu" 周原甲骨, *Zhongguo wenzi*, n.s., 1
     (March 1980): 166.

15. See Wang Guowei's 王國維 classic study "Shengba siba kao" 生霸死霸考, in *Guantang
     jilin* 觀堂集林 (Beijing: Zhonghua, 1959), 1:19–26. According to the statistics recently
     worked out by the Institute of Archaeology at CASS (Chinese Academy of Social Sci-
     ences), out of more than 390 Zhou bronze inscriptions, the term *jishengba* appears 59
     times and the term *jisiba* 26 times. See Liu Yu 劉雨, "Jinwen 'chuji' bianxi" 金文初吉辨
     析, *WW* 11 (1982): 77. For further discussions of Chinese ideas of life and death related
     to the changing phases of the moon, see my "New Evidence on the Early Chinese
     Conception of Afterlife," *JAS* 41, no. 1 (November 1981): 81–85.

16. See Hu Shih, "The Concept of Immortality in Chinese Thought," *Harvard Divinity
     School Bulletin* (1945–46): 30. See also Nagasawa Yōji 永澤要二, "Paku kō" 魄考, *Kan-
     gaku kenkyū* 漢學研究, n.s., 2 (March 1964), esp. p. 51.

17. *The Ch'un Ts'ew with the Tso Chuen* (hereafter *Tso Chuen*), in James Legge, trans., *The
     Chinese Classics*, 5 vols. (Hong Kong: HKU Press, 1961), 5:329.

18. *Tso Chuen*, 551.

19. Ibid., 708.

20. Ibid., 618. Here the English translation is adapted from Alfred Forke, trans., *Lun Heng*
     (New York: Paragon, 1962), part 1, pp. 208–209.

21. The orthodox Confucian view is best presented in Qian Mu 錢穆, *Linghun yu xin* 靈魂與
     心 (Taipei: Lianjing, 1976). It is interesting to note that Zichan's view may be compared
     to Aristotle's, as expressed in *De Anima*, 413a/4: "The soul is inseparable from its body,

or at any rate that certain parts of it are (if it has parts)—for the actuality of some of them is nothing but the actualities of their bodily parts. Yet some may be separable because they are not the actualities of any body at all." Richard McKeon, ed., *The Basic Works of Aristotle* (New York: Random House, 1941), 556.

22. Hu Shih, "Concept of Immortality," 31–32.

23. *Liji zhushu*, 10.19b.

24. These lines can be found in David Hawkes, *Ch'u Tz'u: The Songs of the South* (Boston: Beacon Press, 1962), 104–105, 110.

25. *Liji zhushu*, 26.21b. For a comprehensive discussion of the relationship between the *hun* and the *po* on the one hand, and the idea of *qi* as a cosmic life force on the other, see Kurita Naomi 粟田直躬, *Chûgoku jôdai shisô no kenkyû* 中國上代思想の研究 (Tokyo: Iwanami shoten, 1949), 75–146.

26. The original expression is *hun-po li san* 魂魄離散, but in Hawkes's translation (103), it is rendered simply as "His soul has left him."

27. See Wen Yiduo 聞一多, *Wen Yiduo quanji* 聞一多全集, 4 vols. (Shanghai: Kaiming, 1948), 2:458.

28. D. C. Lau, introduction to *Mencius* (Harmondsworth: Penguin Books, 1970), 24, with change in romanization of *qi*.

29. Liu Wendian 劉文典, *Huainan honglie jijie* 淮南鴻烈集解, *GXJBCS*, 9.2a.

30. *Liji zhushu*, 47.14a–15a. In this connection, I wish to call the reader's attention to Mencius's famous distinction between the *dati* 大體 and *xiaoti* 小體 ("The parts of greater importance and the parts of smaller importance of the person of a man"). According to him (*Mencius*, 6A.14 [D. C. Lau's translation]), the *xiaoti* consists of "the organs of hearing and sight," which "are unable to think and can be misled by external things," whereas the *dati* is identified as "the organ of the mind or heart" whose function it is "to think." Mencius specifically singles out this thinking organ of the mind or heart as the gift that man alone receives from Heaven. Therefore, he defines "a great man" as one who is guided by the interests of his *dati* (i.e., the thinking mind) and "a small man" as one who is guided by the interests of his *xiaoti* (i.e., the organs of hearing and sight). Moreover, Mencius further holds that there is a "floodlike *qi*" (*haoran zhi qi* 浩然之氣) in the cosmos that is, in the highest degree, vast and unyielding. It is this *qi* that provides the mind or heart with the very source of moral power (*Mencius*, 2A.2). Clearly, then, Mencius must have shared the cosmological view current in the fourth century B.C.E. that man's body consists of the grosser, earthly *qi*, while his mind or heart is the seat of the refined, Heavenly *qi* (see D. C. Lau's introduction in *Mencius*, 24). Although Mencius did not mention the ideas of *hun* and *po* in his philosophical discussions, it is nevertheless unmistakable that his distinction between the *dati* and the *xiaoti* bears a resemblance to the distinction between the *hun* and *po* as defined by Zheng Xuan, not only structurally but also functionally. In view of the gradual fusion of the ideas of *hun* and *po* since the sixth century B.C.E., I find it difficult to resist the temptation to link this Mencian formulation to a contemporary dualistic conception of the soul as a possible model. If so, then Zheng Xuan's interpretation of the different functions of the *hun* and the *po* may well have been of a much earlier (i.e., pre-Han) origin. Traditionally, it has

been contended, especially by the Qing philologists, that the commentaries written by Han Confucian exegetes may, by and large, be viewed as depositories of ideas of classical antiquity transmitted orally from generation to generation down to Han times. It seems likely that Zheng Xuan's ideas about *hun* and *po* have precisely such ancient origins.

31. *Laozi Daodejing* 老子道德經, SBCK, A.3b. Here the *hunqi* is clearly described as a breathlike life force. In this respect, the Chinese idea of *hun* is certainly comparable to its counterparts in other ancient cultures. The Greek *psyche* and *thymos*, the Roman *animus* and *anima*, and the Jewish *nephesh*, for instance, were all associated with breath. See Richard Broxton Onians, *The Origins of European Thought About the Body, the Mind, the Soul, the World, Time, and Fate* (Cambridge: Cambridge University Press, 1954), esp. chap. 4, pp. 16 and 66–69 (for *thymos*); 93–95 (for *psyche*); 168–173 (for *anima* and *animus*); 481–482 (for *nephesh thymos*). Onians is basically right in pointing out the similarity between the Chinese idea of *hunqi* and the Greek and Roman ideas of soul, although his discussions of the "Chinese conception of the soul" (520–530) are full of factual errors and anachronisms. For *psyche* as something airy and breathlike, see the classic study by Erwin Rohde, *Psyche*, trans. W. B. Hillis (New York: Harper & Row, 1925 [1966]), 4–5; citations refer to the 1925 edition. See also Emily Vermeule, *Aspects of Death in Early Greek Art and Poetry* (Berkeley: University of California Press, 1979), 212–213 (chap. 1, n11), and, for a discussion of *psyche* and *thymos*, Bruno Snell, *The Discovery of the Mind: The Greek Origins of European Thought*, trans. T. G. Rosenmeyer (Cambridge, Mass.: Harvard University Press, 1953), 8–12.

32. H. G. Creel, *The Birth of China* (New York: Reynal and Hitchcock, 1937), 198–199.

33. Guo Moruo 郭沫若, *Jinwen congkao* 金文叢考, rev. ed. (Beijing: Renmin, 1954), 8b–9a.

34. *Tso Chuen*, 297.

35. It may be noted that in oracle bone inscriptions, *gui* and *wei* 畏 (fear) are sometimes interchangeable. See the various interpretations of the two characters in Li Xiaoding 李孝定, ed., *Jiagu wenzi jishi* 甲骨文字集釋 (Taipei: Academia Sinica, 1965), 9:2903–2904 (*gui*) and 2909–2912 (*wei*). For a more recent discussion, see Ikeda Suetoshi 池田末利, *Chûgoku kodai shūkyōshi kenkyū* 中國古代宗教史研究 (Tokyo: Tōkai daigaku-shuppankai, 1981), 155–198.

36. A. Forke, *Lun Heng*, part 1, 509.

37. See Wang Zhongshu, *Han Civilization*, 206–207. See also Ying-shih Yü, "Han," in *Food in Chinese Culture: Anthropological and Historical Perspectives*, ed. K. C. Chang (New Haven: Yale University Press, 1977), 53–84.

38. *Tso Chuen*, 234.

39. Gan Bao 干寶, *Soushen ji* 搜神記, GXJBCS, 28.

40. Hu Shih, "Concept of Immortality," 33.

41. See Loraine Boettner, *Immortality* (Grand Rapids, Mich.: Wm. B. Eerdmans, 1956), 61–62.

42. Gu Yanwu 顧炎武, *Rizhi lu* 日知錄, WYWK (Taipei: Taiwan Shangwu, 1965), 10:28–29.

43. Hu Shih, "The Indianization of China: A Case Study in Cultural Borrowing," in *Independence, Convergence and Borrowing in Institutions, Thought, and Art* (Cambridge, Mass.: Harvard University Press, 1937), 224–225. However, it must be mentioned that in his

later years, Hu Shih apparently modified this extreme view considerably and came to realize that there was also an indigenous Chinese origin of the idea of hell. See *Hu Shi shougao* 胡適手稿, eighth collection, vol. 1 (Taipei: Hu Shi jinian guan, 1970), where a vast amount of early materials relating to the idea of the underworld in ancient China may conveniently be found.

44. Joseph Needham, *Science and Civilization in China*, vol. 5, book 2 (Cambridge: Cambridge University Press, 1974), 98 (note c).

45. Jacques Choron, *Death and Western Thought* (New York: Collier Books, 1963), 24.

46. Needham, *Science and Civilization*, 84–85.

47. Wang Ming 王明, ed., *TPJHJ* (Beijing: Zhonghua, 1960), 526, 546, 551, 552. The dating of the *TPJHJ* has been highly controversial. See B. J. Mansvelt Beck, "The Date of the *Taipingjing*," *TP* 66, nos. 4–5 (1980): 149–182. However, modern scholars generally agree that although it contains many later interpolations, parts of the work can be dated to the second century. See Ying-shih Yü, "Life and Immortality in the Mind of Han China," *HJAS* 25 (1964–65): 84n17, and Max Kaltenmark, "The Ideology of the *T'ai-p'ing ching*," in *Facets of Taoism*, ed. Holmes Welch and Anna Seidel (New Haven: Yale University Press, 1979), 19–45. More recently, further efforts have been made by two Chinese scholars to establish the Han origin of the text. See Wang Ming 王明, "Lun *Taipingjing* di chengshu shidai he zuozhe" 論太平經的成書時代和作者, *Shijie zongjiao yanjiu* 世界宗教研究 1 (1982): 17–26, and Tang Yijie 湯一介, "Guanyu *Taipingjing* chengshu wenti" 關於太平經成書問題, *Zhongguo wenhua yanjiu jikan* 中國文化研究集刊 1 (March 1984): 168–186.

48. Wang Yü-ch'üan, "An Outline of the Central Government of the Former Han Dynasty," in *Studies of Governmental Institutions in Chinese History*, ed. John L. Bishop (Cambridge, Mass.: Harvard-Yenching Institute, 1968), 38.

49. Rao Zongyi, *Xiang-er zhu*, 33, 77.

50. *TPJHJ*, 602, 625.

51. Ibid., 552.

52. "Changsha Mawangdui ersanhao mu fajue jianbao" 長沙馬王堆二三號墓發掘簡報, *WW* 7 (1974): 43 and plate 12, no. 11.

53. Wang Yü-ch'üan, "Central Government," 52n52 and 20–21.

54. See "Hubei Jiangling Fenghuang Shan yiliuba hao Hanmu fajue baogao" 湖北江陵鳳凰山168號漢墓發掘報告, *WW* 9 (1975): 4 and plate 3, no. 1. See also the remarks by Yu Weichao in a symposium published in the same issue, pp. 12–14, where other similar documents are compared. For further discussions of the document, see Chen Zhi 陳直, "Guanyu Jiangling Chengao 'Dixia Cheng'" 關於江陵丞告'地下丞', *WW* 12 (1977): 76, and Huang Shengzhang 黃盛璋, *Lishi dili yu kaogu luncong* 歷史地理與考古論叢 (Jinan: Qilu shushe, 1982), 201–206, where the social status of the occupant of Tomb No. 168 is discussed in considerable detail.

55. Quoted in Yu Weichao's remarks in *WW* 9 (1975): 13.

56. Yang Shuda 楊樹達, *Handai hun sang lisu kao* 漢代婚喪禮俗考 (Shanghai: Kaiming, 1933), 73–74.

57. For examples, see *WW* 12 (1972): 12, and *WW* 9 (1975): 7.

58. See *Man cheng Hanmu* 滿城漢墓 (Beijing: Wenwu, 1978), 25–26. See also Shi Wei 史為, "Guanyu 'jinlou yuyi' ziliao jianjie" 關於金縷玉衣資料簡介, *KG* 2 (1972): 48–50.

59. For a more comprehensive study of the Han cult of *xian* immortality, see my "Life and Immortality in the Mind of Han China."

60. Burton Watson, trans., *The Complete Works of Chuang Tzu* (New York: Columbia University Press, 1968), 33.

61. Ibid., 168n.

62. *SJ* (Beijing: Zhonghua, 1959), 55.2048. Both practices have now been confirmed by the discovery of a pre-Qin text at Mawangdui. See *WW* 6 (1975): 1, 6–13, 14–15.

63. Hawkes, *Ch'u Tz'u*, 82.

64. *TPJHJ*, 138.

65. For the development of the cult of Mount Tai as a place for the dead, see also Zhao Yi 趙翼, *Gaiyu congkao* 陔餘叢考 (Shanghai: Shangwu, 1957), 35.751–752; Édouard Chavannes, *Le T'ai Ch'an* (Paris: Leroux, 1910), chap. 6; Sakai Tadao 酒井忠夫, "Taizan shinko no kenkyû" 泰山信仰の研究, *Shichō* 史潮 7, no. 2 (June 1937).

66. Due to space limitations, the following discussion is highly condensed. For a detailed study, see my Chinese article, "Zhongguo gudai sihou shijie guan di yanbian" 中國古代死後世界觀的演變, in *Yanyuan lunxue ji* 燕園論學集 (Beijing: Beijing daxue, 1984), 177–196. *SJ*, 28.1367; Burton Watson, trans., *Records of the Grand Historian of China*, 2 vols. (New York: Columbia University Press, 1961), 2:24.

67. This is rightly pointed out in Hu Sanxing's 胡三省 commentary on *Zizhi tongjian* 資治通鑑 (Beijing: Zhonghua, 1956), 20.678.

68. Quoted in Fang Shiming 方詩銘, "Zailun dijuan di jianbie" 再論地券的鑑別, *WW* 8 (1979): 84. For more details of the transformation of the Lord of Mount Tai, see Okamoto Saburō 岡本三郎, "Taizan fukun no yurai ni tsuite" 泰山府君の由來について, *Tōyōgaku kenkyū* 東洋學研究 1 (November 1943): 63–98.

69. We owe this information to a fragment of the *Xiaojing yuanshen qi* 孝經援神契, preserved in Zhang Hua's 張華 (232–300 C.E.) *Bowu zhi*; see Fan Ning 范寧, ed., *Bowu zhi jiaozhu* 博物志校注 (Beijing: Zhonghua, 1980), 12. This perhaps also explains why, as recent archaeology amply shows, the Heavenly God was thought to send envoys to warn underworld officials of all levels that they must not harass the souls under their jurisdictions. See Hayashi Minao 林巳奈夫, "Kandai kijin no sekai" 漢代鬼神の世界, *Tohō gakuhō* 東方學報, 46 (March 1974): 227–228 and 297–298n14. Obviously, Han Chinese believed that the souls in the underworld were subject to the taxes and labor services demanded by underworld officials. See the inscription from a Han tomb dated 173 C.E. in Guo Moruo 郭沫若, *Nuli zhi shidai* 奴隸制時代 (Beijing: Renmin, 1972), 94.

70. *TPJHJ*, 615; see also 598–599. In contrast to ancient Greece, the Chinese idea of postmortem punishment is a much later development. See Vermeule, *Aspects of Death*, 8, and E. R. Dodds, *The Greeks and the Irrational* (Berkeley: University of California Press, 1951), 137, 150–151.

71. Lu Simian 呂思勉, *Qin-Han shi* 秦漢史, 2 vols. (Shanghai: Kaiming, 1947), 2:704–709.

72. *HHS* (Beijing: Zhonghua, 1965), 90.2980. It is important to point out that here the fragment of the *Xiaojing yuanshen qi* preserved in the *Bowu zhi* (see note 69 above) is

also quoted by the Tang commentator to support the statement of the *HHS*. The *HHS* text says, "The *hun*-soul (*hunshen* 魂神) of the dead returns to Mount Tai," and the commentary, quoting *Bowu zhi*, says, "Mount Tai, the Grandson of the Heavenly God, is responsible for summoning the human *hun*-souls" (90.2981). The two passages agree with each other exactly.

73. *HS* (Beijing: Zhonghua, 1962), 33.2845.

74. For *fu* 府 and *ting* 廷 as popular names of the governor's and the magistrate's offices, respectively, see vol. 1 of Yan Gengwang 嚴耕望, *Zhongguo difang xingzheng zhidu shi* 中國地方行政制度史, part 1 (Taipei: Zhongyang yanjiuyuan lishi yuyan yanjiusuo, 1961), 216.

75. *HS*, 38.1991.

76. For the term "Gaoli" meaning underworld, see *HS*, 63.2761, and Yan Shigu's commentary on p. 2762. For Gaoli and Xiali in Han popular literature, especially in inscriptions, on tombstones, see Wu Rongzeng 吳榮曾, "Zhenmuwen zhong suo jiandao di tong Han Dao wu guanxi" 鎮墓文中所見到的東漢道巫關係, *WW* 3 (1981): 59. In his *Taoism and Chinese Religion*, trans. Frank A. Kierman Jr. (Amherst: University of Massachusetts Press, 1981), Henri Maspero gives a brief account of the Taishan Fuzhun in later Daoist tradition in which the underworld is localized in "the hillock Haoli" (102–104). Here "Haoli" is a variant reading of Gaoli. Though much distorted, this later tradition nevertheless shows unmistakable traces of its Han origin.

77. See some examples given in Wu Rongzeng, "Zhenmuwen," 60–61. It has often been pointed out that Han beliefs in the afterlife as revealed in the vast amount of literary and archaeological sources are full of contradictions and inconsistencies. I would argue that on the whole, the various ideas about death rituals, Heaven, and Hell discussed above make good sense if we keep in mind that in Han times people generally believed not only in the separation of the *hun* and the *po* at death, but also in the possibility of achieving *xian* immortality and ascension to Heaven. While contradictions and inconsistencies are certainly there, they do not invalidate or render meaningless the cluster of Han beliefs we have been examining. On the contrary, there is every reason to think that these beliefs occupied a central place in the daily life of Han Chinese irrespective of their social status. Moreover, as recent religious studies in the West have shown, beliefs in Heaven and the afterlife do not depend on logical consistency for their validity. On this point, see Robert N. Bellah, "Christianity and Symbolic Realism," *Journal for the Scientific Study of Religion* 9 (Summer 1970): 89–96, and Bradley R. Hertel, "Inconsistency of Beliefs in the Existence of Heaven and Afterlife," *Review of Religious Research* 21, no. 2 (Spring 1980): 171–183.

78. See *Lu Shiheng wenji* 陸士衡文集, SBCK, 7.28.

79. See Ying-shih Yü, *Trade and Expansion in Han China* (Berkeley: University of California Press, 1967), 32–34.

80. See *Liji zhushu*, 47.14a–b, and Kong Yingda's 孔穎達 *Zhengyi* 正義, in *Zuozhuan zhushu*, *Shisan jing zhushu* (1815 edition), 44.13a–14a: 改生之魂曰神, 改生之魄曰鬼. [After death] the name of *hun* in life is changed to *shen* and that of *po* to *gui*.

81. *Lu Shilong wenji* 陸士龍文集, SBCK, 6.33. It may be pointed out that the *HHS* (90.2980) also uses *hun-shen* 魂神 and *shen-ling* 神靈 interchangeably to refer to the *hun*-soul.

82. See the poem "Zeng congxiong Cheqi" 贈從兄車騎, in *Lu Shiheng wenji*, 5.18: 營魄懷茲土, 精爽若飛沉. Here *ying* 營 is a variant of *hun*. See *Laozi*, chap. 10.

83. *Hu Shi shougao*, eighth collection, 1:83–107.

84. Ibid., 1:13–42. For the popular version of the "Ten Kings of the Underworld," see Anthony C. Yu, trans., *The Journey to the West*, 4 vols. (Chicago: University of Chicago Press, 1977), 1:110.

4. New Evidence on the Early Chinese Conception of Afterlife

The spectacular discovery of the three Han tombs at Mawangdui in Chang-sha, Hunan, in 1972–1974 was indeed an event of singular importance in the history of Han studies. Of the three tombs, 1 and 3 in particular aroused worldwide attention. Tomb 3 is known for its preservation of a large quantity of silk manuscripts, some of which were long assumed lost. Tomb 1 made headline news at the time of its excavation, primarily for the well-preserved body of its occupant, the wife of the Marquis of Dai 軑, who probably died around 168 B.C.E. When the full report was published in 1973, it turned out that the tomb was also unusually rich with furnishings of all sorts, including textiles, lacquerware, musical instruments, pottery, inscribed bamboo slips, and food remains. However, the single most significant discovery from this tomb was that of a polychrome painting on a silk banner that was presumably used in the funerary processions of the dead. Since the painting reveals a great deal about early Chinese mythology, art, religion, and ritualism, it has been extensively studied by specialists of several disciplines in China and Japan, as well as in the West. It is also this painting that forms the core of Michael Loewe's *Ways to Paradise: The Chinese Quest for Immortality* (London: George Allen & Unwin, 1979).

In *Ways to Paradise*, Loewe examines three related subjects: the conception of paradise as shown in the silk painting from Mawangdui; the Han views of the cosmos as revealed in the so-called TLV mirrors, which were particularly in fashion between about 50 B.C.E. and 100 or 150 C.E.; and the rise of the cult of the Queen Mother of the West since the later part of the Former Han dynasty. There is nevertheless a common thread that runs through all three separate subjects of this study, namely, "the underlying beliefs of the Han Chinese regarding death and the hereafter" (vii). It is also this unifying theme that makes the reading of *Ways to Paradise* an extremely thought-provoking experience.

As is customary with all his scholarly writings, Dr. Loewe's treatment of each of the three topics in the book is careful, thorough, detailed, and technical. He uses every bit of literary and historical evidence at his disposal to make the otherwise silent archaeological data talk, often sensibly. It is also commendable that the author occasionally brings a comparative perspective into this study. In chapter 5, for instance, the symbols of the bird and the hare in other mythologies are compared as well as contrasted with the Chinese case. The result is both fruitful and illuminating.

In my opinion, the discovery of the silk painting and other related funerary objects in the Mawangdui tombs is of revolutionary importance to the study of religious thought in ancient China. For the first time, we have unmistakable and direct evidence that testifies fully as well as vividly to the indigenous Chinese imagination of death and afterlife in pre-Buddhist antiquity. The dominant modern theory that there was no "other world" in Chinese thought until the advent of Buddhism is thus proved to be untenable. For example, the late Dr. Hu Shih held Buddhism responsible for giving Chinese the idea of tens of heavens and many hells.[1] Recently, Dr. Joseph Needham also expressed a similar view.[2] According to him, there was no heaven or hell in ancient Chinese thought; this was altered only after the permeation of Buddhism. It is one thing to say that the indigenous Chinese conception of heaven or hell is different from its Buddhist counterpart, but it is quite another matter to suggest that the idea of heaven or hell was totally alien to the Chinese mind. Now, thanks to the Mawangdui discovery, this problem has been fundamentally solved.

Loewe agrees with most scholars that the silk painting is a description of the pilgrimage of the soul of Lady Dai to Heaven. In light of a similar painting found in Mawangdui Tomb 3, this identification may be considered as firmly established. Interestingly enough, Tomb 3 also provides us with an important piece of evidence concerning the Han Chinese belief in the underworld. There is a document on wood written in the name of a "Family Assistant" (*jiacheng* 家丞) of the Marquis of Dai and addressed to an official in charge of the dead (*zhuzang langzhong* 主臧 [藏] 郎中) in the underworld. It may be translated as follows: "On *wuchen* [twenty-fourth] day, second month, the twelfth year [of Emperor Wen's reign, 168 B.C.E.], Household Assistant Fen 奮 to the *langzhong* in charge of the dead: 'A list of mortuary objects is herewith forwarded to you. Upon receiving this document, please memorialize without delay to the Lord of the Grave (Zhuzang Jun 主臧 [藏] 君).'"[3] Clearly, here Household Assistant Fen is notifying his counterpart in the underworld bureaucracy of the arrival of the newly deceased. Recent archaeology has shown that the belief in an underworld bureaucracy taking care of the departed souls was already widespread in China by the second century B.C.E. In 1975, two similar pieces of evidence were found in Han Tombs 10 and 168, respectively, at Fenghuang Shan, Jiangling, Hubei. The document from Tomb 168, dated the thirteenth of the fifth month, 167 B.C.E., was issued in the name of the Assistant Magistrate of Jiangling (Jiangling Cheng 江陵丞) and sent to the Underworld Assistant (Dixia Cheng 地下丞). As in the Mawangdui case, this Han local official of Jiangling was also notifying his counterpart of the immigration of the occupant of the tomb, a man under his jurisdiction, to the underworld and requesting that the case be reported in due course to the Lord (Zhu 主). The document from Tomb 10, dated 153 B.C.E., is of a slightly different form. It was a memorial presented directly to the underworld Lord (Dixia Zhu 地下主) by the deceased named Zhang Yan 張偃.[4] There can be little doubt that this underworld Lord (Dixia Zhu), or Lord of the Dead (Zhuzang Jun), was the predecessor of the famous Lord of Mount T'ai (Taishan Fujun 泰山府君) of the later Han Period, who was to be, eventually, transformed into one of the ten kings or judges of Buddhist hells.

At this point, however, an interesting question arises: Why was it that, as shown especially in the case of the Mawangdui Tomb No. 3, the ancient Chinese made arrangements for the departed soul to go to heaven and the underworld at the same time? The answer may best be sought from the dualistic Chinese view of the soul. As Loewe rightly points out, the Chinese of the Han Period distinguished two souls in every individual human being, the *hun* 魂 and the *po* 魄. The *hun* was characterized as *yang* 陽—male and active—and the *po* as *yin* 陰—female and receptive. Moreover, it was also believed that at death, the *hun* and the *po* separated, with the result that the former went to paradise and the latter to the underworld (see 9–10). This idea, it may be pointed out, is most clearly formulated in a passage in the *Liji* (Classic of Rites): "the soul-breath (*hunqi* 魂氣) returns to Heaven; the bodily substance (*xingpo* 形魄) returns to earth. Therefore, in sacrifice-offering, one should seek the meaning in the principles of *yin* and *yang*" ("Jiao te sheng 郊特牲"). Although this particular formulation is of Han date, the idea itself can be traced back to a statement of Prince Jizha 季札 of Wu 吳 made in 515 B.C.E.[5]

The evolution of the *hun* and *po* in the mind of pre-Han China is a long and complicated story, which cannot be fully told here. Suffice it to say that, originally, the term *po* alone had been used by the primitive Chinese to denote the "soul." Etymologically, *po* means white, whiteness, or bright light and probably derives from the growing light of the new moon. In the *Shujing* or *Shangshu* (Book of History) as well as in many Zhou bronze inscriptions, we often encounter the expressions *jishengba* 既生霸 (*ba* being a variant of *po*), meaning "after the birth of the crescent," and *jisiba* 既死霸, meaning "after the death of the crescent." As Hu Shih rightly observed, "the primitive Chinese seem to have regarded the changing phases of the moon as periodic birth and death of its *po*, its 'white light' or soul."[6] On the other hand, textual evidence seems to suggest that it was from the middle of the sixth century B.C.E. onward that the idea of *hun* began to gain currency and eventually replaced *po* as the more important and active part of the soul.

This primitive association of the soul with the growing light of the new moon is of tremendous importance to our understanding of certain myths related to the seventh day of the months discussed in the *Ways to Paradise*. As a matter of fact, it is a key to both the story of the Weaving Maid and the Oxherd and that of the Queen Mother of the West. As the two Han stories go, the annual meeting of Emperor Wu of Han with the Queen Mother of the West took place on the seventh day of the first month and that between the Weaving Maid and the Oxherd on the seventh day of the seventh month. Loewe is certainly correct in seeing the two stories as part of a much larger myth—one that "saw the continuity of the universe as depending on two annual meetings that took place in summer and winter" (119). On the authority of Kominami Ichirō, he further calls our attention to the interesting fact that in light of early Japanese folklore, "the importance of the seventh day of the month lay partly in its function as marking the phases of the moon" (120). This is indeed an insightful observation.

However, it seems somewhat odd, to say the least, that the meaning of the myth has to be grasped by way of folklore of a much later date. In fact, the classical Chinese expression *jishengba* ("after the birth of the crescent") has already provided us with the most important key to understanding the myth. According to Wang Guowei's four-quarter theory of the lunar month,[7] in early Zhou times, *jishengba* probably stood for the second quarter from the eighth or ninth to the fourteenth or fifteenth. Wang's theory ties in extremely well with the fact that the two annual meetings actually took place at midnight of the seventh day.[8] There can be little doubt that in the minds of the ancient Chinese, midnight of the seventh day marked the beginning of the *jishengba* quarter of the month. It is also significant that in referring to the birth of the *po*-soul in man, the passage in the *Zuozhuan* (Zuo Commentary to the Spring and Autumn Annals), dated 534 B.C.E., actually uses the expression *jishengpo* 既生魄.[9] This proves conclusively that the primitive Chinese conception of the soul was derived analogously from the birth of the crescent.

In conclusion, it may be noted that the recent anthropological analyses of death rituals also bear importantly on our understanding of the subjects with which the *Ways to Paradise* is centrally concerned, for death as transition concerns not only the dead but the living as well. "During the burial ritual itself," as Richard Huntington and Peter Metcalf point out, "the deceased, the living, and even the cosmos go through a period of transition."[10] As a result, the themes of rebirth and sexuality often dominate the symbolism of funerals. Only by bearing this in mind can we then grasp more fully the symbolic meanings of the silk painting from Mawangdui, the designs of TLV mirrors, and the myth of the Queen Mother of the West, as these are all burial-related objects found in Han tombs.

With regard to the woman's figure with a serpentine tail in the upper part of the silk painting, Loewe has made the interesting suggestion that it may have been the artist's intention to represent the final stage of Lady Dai's journey to Heaven when she has reached her destination sloughing off her mortal coil (59). This interpretation particularly makes sense when death is viewed as "the transition of the deceased from the world of the living to the realm of the dead." It seems permissible to take the final scene of the painting as a symbolization of the fact that the difficult and risky process of transition is at last completed.[11] The cosmic significance of the TLV mirrors is also worth noticing, because they were intended, as Loewe says, "to set a man permanently in his correct relation with the cosmos and to escort him to a life in the hereafter" (83). I am inclined to think that one of the symbolic meanings of the mirrors may have been to assure the restoration of a cosmic order that has been upset by death.

Finally, in the myth of the Queen Mother many layers of symbolic meaning can be readily discerned. To begin with, the Queen Mother was conceived as possessing the power to renew the cosmic cycle as well as life. In the second place, the pairing of the Queen Mother of the West with the King Father of the East, which often appears in stone reliefs and bronze mirrors found in Han tombs, clearly symbolizes sexuality and rebirth. The same may also be said of the symbolic representation of Fu Xi 伏羲 and Nü Gua 女媧 with interlaced tails, which has an equally wide archaeological distribution in Han tombs.[12] Last, but not least, the story of the meeting of Emperor Wu of Han and the Queen Mother of the West also suggests something more than meets the eye. On the basis of archaeological evidence, Kominami has offered the interesting interpretation that in the original myth, the Queen Mother may have been an androgynous figure representing primordial cosmic unity and order.[13] I am not quite convinced of the Queen Mother's hermaphroditism. There is reason to believe, however, that the myth of the Queen Mother may indeed have had something to do with unity and order. In view of the Han frame of mind, which stressed the harmony between the two cosmic forces of yin and yang and the intimate relationship between Heaven and Man, the meeting of Emperor Wu of Han with the Queen Mother seems to suggest the symbolic balancing of yin with yang, Heaven with Man, and life with order. According to the Han Wu gushi 漢武故事 (Stories of Emperor Han Wudi), in their meeting, the Queen Mother only discussed matters pertaining to the human world with Emperor Wu of Han and refused to talk about affairs concerning the supernatural world (see 117–118). This may well be taken as evidence that the emperor stands for the human order.

On the other hand, the symbolic representation of the Queen Mother in this story is unmistakably that of life and immortality. In this connection, the pairing of Fu Xi with Nü Gua also helps us to grasp the meaning of this symbolic meeting. In Han popular culture, Nü Gua was conceived as a female creator of man and therefore symbolized life, whereas Fu Xi was described as possessing the power to maintain cosmic unity and order.[14] It is clear that in both cases, a fundamental balance between life and order is maintained. Thus, the various death-related myths of pre-Buddhist origins not only reveal early Chinese beliefs about the hereafter but also express basic Chinese values regarding the nature and meaning of life, as does the symbolism of funeral rituals in practically all cultures.

NOTES

1. Hu Shih, "The Indianization of China: A Case Study in Cultural Borrowing," in *Independence, Convergence and Borrowing in Institutions, Thought, and Art* (Cambridge, Mass.: Harvard University Press, 1937), 224–225.

2. Joseph Needham, *Science and Civilisation in China* (Cambridge: Cambridge University, 1974), 2:98.

3. The Hunan Provincial Museum and IAAS, No. 7, "Excavation of Han Tombs Nos. 2 and 3 at Ma-wang-tui, Changsha" [in Chinese], *WW* 7 (1974): 43.

4. Archeological Team of Han Tomb 168, No. 9, "Excavation of Han Tomb No. 168 at Fenghuangshan in Jiangling County, Hubei Province" [in Chinese], *WW* 9 (1975): 4; "Guanyu Fenghuangshan yiliubahao Hanmu zuotan jiyao," *WW* 9 (1975); and The Hunan Provincial Museum and IAAS, "Excavation of Han Tombs Nos. 2 and 3 at Mawangdui, Changsha" [in Chinese], *WW* 7 (1974): 39–48, 63, 95–111.

5. *Liji zhushu*, in *Shisan jing zhushu* (Nanchang edition, 1815), chap. 10, 19b.

6. Hu Shih, "The Concept of Immortality in Chinese Thought," *Harvard Divinity School Bulletin*, no. 122 (1945–1946): 30.

7. Wang Guowei, "Shengba siba kao," in *Guantang jilin* (Beijing: Zhonghua, 1959), 1: 19–26.

8. See the various versions of the myth quoted in Kominami Ichirō, "Seiōbo to shichi seki densho," *Tōhō gakuhō* 46 (March 1974): 36–40.

9. See the Chinese text in James Legge, *The Ch'un Ts'ew with the Tso Chuen* (Hong Kong: HKU Press, 1960), 613.

10. Richard Huntington and Peter Metcalf, *Celebrations of Death: The Anthropology of Mortuary Ritual* (Cambridge: Cambridge University Press, 1979), 117.

11. Ibid., 116.

12. See Wen Yiduo, "Fu Xi kao," in *Wen Yiduo quanji* (Shanghai: Kaiming, 1948), 1:3–68; Zhong Jingwen, "Mawangdui Hanmu bohua di shenhua shi yiyi," *Zhonghua wenshi luncong* 2 (1979): 78–80.

13. Kominami Ichirō, "Seiōbo to shichi seki densho," 62–74.

14. See Zhong Jingwen, "Mawangdui Hanmu bohua di shenhua shi yiyi," 30, quoting a fragment of a lost Han work, *Yi qiankun cuodu*.

5. Food in Chinese Culture

The Han Period (206 B.C.E.–220 C.E.)

In 558 B.C.E., a nobleman of the Rong people told a Chinese statesman, "Our drink, our food, and our clothes are all different from those of the Chinese states" (*Zuozhuan* [Zuo Commentary to the Spring and Autumn Annals], fourteenth year of Duke Xiang). Thus, in one simple sentence, this Rong nobleman of the Spring and Autumn Period (771–481 B.C.E.) aptly distinguished the Chinese from the non-Chinese. Culture may sometimes be defined as a way of life. If so, can we think of anything more fundamental to a culture than eating and drinking? It is on this assumption that I shall attempt, in what follows, to understand Han culture through a study of food and eating in Han China.[1]

Recently, some very distinguished anthropologists have embarked on the ambitious undertaking of finding universal food meanings common to all humankind. Being a historian by training, I am far from qualified to play this new anthropologist's game. The central task I set for myself in this study is therefore confined primarily to finding out what sorts of food and drink were available to the Han Chinese and how they ate and drank them. Fortunately, in the last three or four years, Chinese archaeology has shed tremendous light on Han culinary history. Important and interesting as they are, however, archaeological finds are not easy to use fruitfully. For one thing, they are extremely scattered. For another, they require a historical context to make them meaningful to us, for we are some twenty centuries too late to eat and drink together with the Han Chinese. I shall not consider it a complete failure if my efforts in the pages that follow can provide no more than the beginnings of such a historical context. I reserve the intriguing and fascinating question of why the Han Chinese ate and drank in the way they did for those who are wiser and more learned.

FOOD AND FOODSTUFFS FOUND IN HAN TOMB NO. 1 AT MAWANGDUI

In 1972, China made a spectacular archaeological discovery on the eastern outskirts of Changsha, Hunan, uncovering what is now known as "Han Tomb No. 1 at Mawangdui." The worldwide renown of this discovery was earned initially on the basis of the owner of the tomb, whose body had been so remarkably preserved that her skin, muscles, and internal organs still retained a certain elasticity when the coffin was opened. Originally, this tomb was dated from between 175 and 145 B.C.E. Thanks to the excavation of Tombs No. 2 and No. 3 in 1973, however, the identity of the woman in this tomb can be more positively determined. She was most likely the wife of Licang, the first Marquis of Dai 軑 (reigned 193–186 B.C.E.), and died a few years after 168 B.C.E. at about the age of fifty.[2] It has been rightly claimed that the preservation of the corpse in such an excellent condition over the long span of some twenty-one centuries must be regarded as a miracle in medical history, but what particularly interests us here is the extreme importance of the entire discovery for our knowledge of food and eating in Han China.

In the woman's esophagus, stomach, and intestines 138 1/2 yellowish-brown musk melon seeds were found, clearly indicating that she had eaten musk melons not too long before she joined her husband, who was buried in Tomb No. 2, which borders hers on the west side. Musk melon turned out to be only one of the many foodstuffs that she had enjoyed in life. Among the rich burial remains unearthed from Tomb No. 1 are forty-eight bamboo cases and fifty-one pottery vessels of various types. Most of them contained foodstuffs. In addition, several hemp bags of agricultural products were also uncovered from the side compartments of the tomb chamber. All of these food remains have been identified and the whole list is as follows:[3]

Grains:
rice (Oryza sativa L.)
wheat (Triticum turgidum L.)
barley (Hordeum vulgare L.)
glutinous millet (Panicum miliaceum Linn.)
millet (Setaria italica [L.] Beauv.)
soybean (Glycine max [L.] Men.)
red lentil (Phaseolus angularis Wight)

Seeds:

hemp (Cannabis sativa L.)

malva (Malva verticillata L.)

mustard (Brassica cernua Hemsl.)

Fruits:

pear (Pyrus pyrifolia Nakai)

jujube (Zizyphus jujuba Mill. var. inermis [Bunge] Rehd.)

plum (Prunus mume [Sieb.] Sieb. et Zucc.)

strawberry (Myrica rubra Sieb. et Zucc.)

Roots:

ginger (Zingiber officinale Roscoe)

lotus root

Animal Meats:

sheep (Ovis aries Linn.)[4]

Bird Meats:

wild goose (Anser sp.)

mandarin duck (Aix galericulata L.)

duck (Anatidae)

bamboo chicken (Bambusicola thoracica Temminck)

chicken (Gallus gallus domesticus Brisson)

pheasant (Phasianus colchicus L.)

crane (Grus sp.)

pigeon (Streptopelia sp.)

turtledove (Oenopopelia tranquebarica Temminck)

owl (Strigidae)

magpie (Pica pica L.)

sparrow (Passer montanus L.)

Fish:

carp (Cyprinus carpio L.)

crucian carp (Carassius auratus L.)

bream (Acanthobrama simoni Bleeker)

two other kinds of carp (Xenocypris argeuteus Gunther and Elopichthys
    bamausa Richardson)

perch (Spiniperca sp.)

Spices:

cinnamon bark (Cinnamomum chekiangense Nakai)

huajiao ["fagara"] (Zanthoxylum armatum D.C. and Z. planispinum Sieb.
    et Zucc.)

xingyi (buds of the Magnolia denudata Desr.), galangal (Alpinia officinal-
    rum Hance)

Apart from food remains, there are also 312 inscribed bamboo slips that give additional information not only on food but on cooking as well. The slips itemize a number of foodstuffs that are not found among the remains, such as melon, bamboo shoots, taro, wild ginger, and goosefoot in the vegetable category, together with quail, wild duck, and eggs within the bird group. Altogether, these make a good supplementary list. More important, the slips tell us a lot about seasonings and methods used in Han-period cooking. The seasonings included salt, sugar, honey, soy sauce (*jiangyou* 醬油), *shi* 豉 (salted darkened beans), and leaven (*qu* 麴). Cooking and preserving methods consisted of roasting, scalding, shallow frying, steaming, deep frying, stewing, salting, sun drying, and pickling.

A variety of dishes mentioned in these bamboo slips also merit attention. The first kind of dish to be noted is *geng* 羹 (stew), a thick liquid dish with chunks of meat or vegetables or both. The list of dishes begins with nine *ding* 鼎 (tripod cauldrons) of "Grand [meat] Stew" (*Yugeng* or *Dageng*).[5] *Geng*, it may be pointed out, was the most common kind of Chinese main dish from antiquity through the Han Period. As will be shown below, while *geng* was characteristically made of mixed ingredients, the *Dageng*, or Grand Stew, alone was not. Han Confucianists, like the author of *Liji* (Classic of Rites) and Zheng Zhong (first century C.E.), were all in agreement that the *Dageng*, whether as a sacrificial offering or as a dish for guests, should always be unseasoned to honor its simplicity.[6] Wang Chong (27–100? C.E.) also said, "The Grand Stew must of necessity be flavorless."[7] The nine *Dageng* listed on the bamboo slips are respectively made of ox, sheep, deer, pig, suckling pig, dog, wild duck, pheasant, and chicken.

The mixed *geng* was normally a seasoned combination of meat with grain or vegetables. Bamboo slip number 11 names *niubaigeng* 牛白羹, which has been correctly identified as "beef-rice stew."[8] It is important to note that meat-grain stew was a very common type of *geng* in Han times. Other *geng* mixtures recorded on the bamboo slips include the following: deer meat–salted fish–bamboo shoots, deer meat–taro, deer meat–small beans, chicken–gourd, crucian carp–rice, fresh sturgeon–salted fish–lotus root, dog meat–celery, crucian carp–lotus root, beef–turnip, lamb–turnip, pork–turnip, beef–sonchus (a wild grass), and dog meat–sonchus.

The bamboo slips also reveal how discriminating Chinese taste had become in terms of the use of the various parts of different animals by the Han Chinese. The slips mentioned, among other things, deer flank, beef flank, dog flank, lamb flank, beef chuck, deer chuck, pork shoulder, beef stomach, lamb stomach, beef lips, beef tongue, beef lungs, and dog liver. Slip number 98 lists a pottery vessel of horse meat sauce. No remains of horse have been found, however,[9] although it is well known from literary sources that horse meat was a favorite dish in Han China. The only part of the horse that was inedible in Han times was the liver. Emperor Jing (reigned 156–141 B.C.E.), a contemporary of the owner of Han Tomb No. 1 at Mawangdui, once said, "No one accuses a man of lacking good taste in food because he eats other meats but refrains from eat-ing horse liver."[10] Emperor Wu (reigned 140–87 B.C.E.) also told the court necro-mancer Luan Da that Shaoweng, Luan's predecessor, had died, not because he was executed on an imperial order, but because "he happened to eat some horse liver" (*Shiji* [Records of the Grand Historian], 1.1390; hereafter *SJ*, with refer-ence given in parentheses in text).[11] True or false, in Han times, it was generally believed that horse liver was deadly poisonous. The absence of horse liver in the extensive food lists from the tombs helps confirm that this was a popular belief.

According to a preliminary report on the two other Han tombs at Mawang-dui, similar food remains and food lists have also been found in Tomb No. 3. Grains and meats are essentially the same as those of Tomb No. 1. However, some additional fruits have been identified, such as orange, persimmon, and water caltrops.[12] It must be emphasized that to date, the excavation of these Han tombs at Mawangdui is the single most important archaeological contribution to the study of food and eating in Han China.

What makes the Mawangdui discovery doubly interesting is the amazing degree to which the food list from Tomb No. 1 agrees with the list given in the "Neize" 內則 (Internal [Family] Regulations) chapter of the *Classic of Rites*. Vir-tually all the foodstuffs and prepared dishes listed above can be found in that chapter.[13] For well over twenty centuries, however, the food list in the "Internal [Family] Regulations" chapter had remained a regulation on paper, which, like a drawing of a cake, as the Chinese proverb goes, can hardly satisfy our hunger. It was the archaeological finds at Mawangdui that finally transformed the regu-lation into a reality.

Recent archaeology adds still another important dimension to the study of food and eating in Han China. By this I refer particularly to the discovery of many kitchen and feast scenes in mural paintings and stone reliefs in Han tombs. Han literature, especially poetry and *fu* 賦 (prose-poetry) often contains descriptions of kitchen and feast scenes, but none of them can compare in viv-idness and vitality with the scenes shown in the murals and reliefs. In this sec-tion and the next, I shall discuss such scenes in paintings and stone reliefs from several Han tombs, while, at the same time, introducing additional ar-chaeological and literary evidence to supplement my discussion.

A very elaborate kitchen scene has been found among the mural stone re-liefs of a Han tomb at Dahu Ting in Mi *xian* 縣 (county), Henan, excavated from 1960–1961.[14] The scene shows ten people working in the kitchen. In the upper middle of the picture, one man is stirring meat that is cooking in a huge *ding* 鼎 (cauldron). On the other side of the *ding*, a man is carrying firewood toward the stove in the upper right-hand corner. Another man to the side of the stove seems to be cooking something over the stove. Left of the center of the picture, two people appear to be walking out of the kitchen, the one in front hold-ing a dish of fish, the other carrying a round tray with drinking cups and other food-serving vessels on it. In the lower left-hand corner stands a large-sized *fu* 釜

(pot) in which it looks as if *geng* is being made since the man to the side of the *fu* is using a long-handled ladle, possibly to spoon the *geng* out of the *fu*. Facing him, toward the lower center of the picture, is another man in a squatting position washing or mixing something in a basin with his left hand while he gestures with his right hand. It looks as if the squatting man is showing the man with the ladle where to put the *geng*. Behind the squatting man and to the right, a man is working with both hands in a big container. Finally, to the lower right, there is a well with a wooden frame over it, from which a well bucket suspends. Between the well and a large jar to the right stands a man who is drawing water from the well, and on the other side of the jar, a man holding a basin is coming to fill it with water.

In addition to the activities described above, this lively tableau also reveals other things about a Han kitchen. For instance, it gives us a picture of the various types of Han food vessels and utensils, which are scattered throughout the picture, and their uses. What is even more interesting are the two meat racks, from which different kinds of meat are hanging, in the upper left corner. Although the meats are not readily identifiable, they definitely range from birds to animals. Right beneath the two racks, however, we can clearly see an ox head and an ox leg lying on the ground.

Another important kitchen scene comes from a mural-painted tomb of late Later Han date, situated in Bangtaizi in the northwestern suburbs of the city of Liaoyang (in southern Manchuria). This tomb was first discovered by villagers in the autumn of 1944, but no detailed account of it was given until 1955.[15] In the summer of 1945, the tomb and its mural paintings became known to a group of Japanese who were skilled copiers in Liaoyang but nevertheless named it the Dongwayaozi tomb. The Japanese group had made copies of the paintings, but unfortunately, they were not able to make the fruits of their long months of labor known to the scholarly world as they left Manchuria empty-handed after the end of World War II.[16] Thus far, no copy of the kitchen scene from the Bangtaizi tomb has been produced. The following discussion is based entirely on Li Wenxin's report and line drawings.

The cooking operation in this kitchen scene is on a scale that is even larger than that of the Dahu Ting tomb described just above. Altogether, twenty-two people are shown working in the kitchen. Unlike the scene from the Dahu Ting tomb in which the cooks and helpers are all men, the present scene includes at least four women. The women's jobs look less strenuous, however, compared with the activities of the eighteen men in the kitchen. For instance, one woman is about to take a vessel from the stove while another takes one from a cabinet. The other two are sitting on the ground apparently doing some kind of light work. By contrast, the men's jobs, such as meat roasting, food mixing, or pounding some sort of food into pulp, require either skill or greater physical strength. The range of different tasks here is also much wider than in the scene from

Dahu Ting. The chores vary from butchering an ox or a pig to removing duck's feathers.

Like the Dahu Ting scene, meats are also shown hanging from a wooden rack in the kitchen. In this case, however, the various meats are so well painted that most of them are recognizable. According to Li Wenxin, they are, from left to right, turtle, animal head, goose, pheasants, birds (of unknown kind), monkey, animal heart and lungs, suckling pig, dried fish, and fresh fish. Each is hung on an iron hook that seems firmly nailed to the rack. This kind of meat rack, it may be noted, must have been very common in Han kitchens since at least five iron meat hooks have recently been found in a Han tomb in Henan.[17]

There is another kind of meat holder in this kitchen scene from the Bangtaizi tomb that has not yet been found in other Han mural paintings. It is a high pole with two horizontal rods near the top. On these rods are hung meat strips, intestines (possibly sausages), stomachs, and so on. The rods are up so high that a man is shown using a long-handled hook to reach the food. Meats were placed this high, understandably, to prevent land creatures, such as dogs, from getting them. To illustrate this point, right below the pole we find a dog, undoubtedly with watering mouth, depicted gazing up at the meats on the rods.

Similar kitchen scenes have been discovered in other mural-painted Han tombs, especially in Liaoyang, such as Sandaohao clay pits No. 2 and No. 4, and Sandaohao Tomb No. 1.[18] In the famous Han stone reliefs of Wu Liang Ci and the Yinan tomb (both in Shandong), kitchen scenes are also present.[19] Particularly worth mentioning are two such scenes found in Inner Mongolia. In May 1956, a Han tomb rich with mural paintings was excavated in Duoketuo *xian*, Inner Mongolia, the first of its kind ever found in that region. A kitchen scene is painted on the rear, left, and front walls of the left chamber. Illustrated in the scene are containers, a stove, a black pig, a yellow dog, two chickens, and a meat rack, on which are hung a pair of pheasants, a piece of meat, a pair of fish, a pair of chickens, and a piece of beef.[20] Recently, in 1972, another important mural-painted Han tomb was found in Helin-ge-er (Suiyuan). The kitchen scene there shows people cooking and drawing water, as well as a meat rack on which hang such foodstuffs as an animal head, intestines, fish, meat, pheasant, and hare.[21] The two scenes described here are almost identical with those found in Liaoyang, Henan, and Shandong. One is very tempted to say that in Han China, the upper-class kitchen setup was more or less standardized, whether in inland China, such as Henan and Shandong, or in the frontier region, such as Manchuria and Inner Mongolia.

Hanging meats on a wooden rack or beam, for instance, was a universal practice in Han times. A painted brick from Sichuan and a newly discovered mural painting from Jiayu Guan, Gansu, both show cooking scenes in which a meat rack is in a dominant position.[22] It was the sight of meats hanging from a rack that gave rise to the descriptive term "meat forest" (*roulin* 肉林, *Hanshu*

[History of the Former Han Dynasty], 61.76; hereafter *HS*, with reference given in parentheses in text). This practice apparently had a pre-Han origin, however, for Sima Qian already spoke of Zhou, the last king of Shang, as having "hung meats to make a forest" (*xuanrou wei lin* 懸肉為林; *SJ*, 2, 3.11a). On the whole, from Han mural paintings discovered in various places, one can hardly detect any regional differences in terms of foodstuffs and cooking utensils. It is particularly interesting to note that animal meats of the three major categories (land, air, and water) that are shown hung on the racks basically tally with the list of meats found in Mawangdui Tomb No. 1.

There is, however, one interesting feature of the Han kitchen that has not yet been found in kitchen scenes in mural paintings, namely, an ice chamber, which had been in use since antiquity.[23] According to Wang Chong, Han Chinese broke ice in winter to make an "ice chamber" (*bingshi* 冰室) for food storage. How to keep food, especially meat, cold so that it would not spoil must have been a problem that bothered Han Chinese constantly. Wang Chong further reports that some imaginative scholars even dreamed up a kind of "meat fan" in the kitchen, which would automatically make wind to keep food cool.[24]

HAN FEASTS IN PAINTING AND IN REALITY

Feast scenes are even more numerous in Han mural paintings than kitchen scenes. For convenience, we again begin our discussion with a scene from the Dahu Ting tomb and then will bring in other archaeological and historical evidence to amplify it.

The scene unfolds from the middle with a man sitting on a very low, rectangular, presumably wooden couch (*ta* 榻), which has screens both to the back and to the sitter's right.[25] In all likelihood, the man on the couch is the host. To his right, we see a seated guest looking in the direction of the host; on the host's left-hand side, two guests sit together and are apparently engaged in polite conversation. The guests are sitting on mats instead of couches. At the right end of the scene behind the host, a servant is ushering in two more guests. In addition, four manservants are represented serving drinks and food.

In front of the host's couch, there is a low, rectangular serving table, known as *an* in Han times. On the table are placed wine cups and dishes. This kind of long table seems to have been specially made to match the size of the wooden couch. Two identical screened couches with tables of matching size can be found in mural paintings from Sandaohao Tomb No. 4. It is very interesting to note that a writing brush is clearly shown to be sticking into one of the Sandaohao tables.[26] It seems safe to conclude that a table matching a screened couch was not made exclusively for serving food and drink. It was also used as a sort of writing desk. Ordinary food-serving tables are much smaller in size, such as the ones placed before the guests in this feast scene. This explains why the virtuous Lady Meng Guang was able "to raise the table as high as her eyebrows" each time she served a meal to her husband, Liang Hong (*Hou Hanshu* [History of the Later Han Dynasty], 83.14a; hereafter *HHS*, with reference given in parentheses in text). Generally speaking, Han food-serving tables are of two shapes: round and rectangular (sometimes square). When not being used, they are piled up in the kitchen, as shown in the kitchen scene from Bangtaizi and by earthenware tables found stacked in this manner at Shaogou, Luoyang.[27] If the table was round, it was called a *qiong*.[28]

We do not know what the occasion was for this feast in the Dahu Ting scene. The owner of the tomb has been tentatively identified as Zhang Boya, governor of Hongnong in Henan during the Later Han dynasty. Possibly the scene shows one of the feasts he gave to his subordinates in the governor's mansion. At any rate, the host in this scene occupies a central position, perhaps the seat of honor. Such a seating arrangement was quite logical for a governor and his subordinates in Han China. A similar seating arrangement is also discernible in feast scenes in stone reliefs from the famous Han shrine at Xiaotang Shan, Shandong.[29]

The Dahu Ting scene shows only the beginning of a feast. Thus, in the painting, only drinks are being served and no food is visible. We must therefore turn to some of the recorded historical feasts for more concrete knowledge as to what constituted a "feast" in Han times. The best-known feast during this period is "The Banquet at Hong Men," which took place in 206 B.C.E. Before coming to that great historical event, however, let us first introduce a Han mural painting that has been identified by Guo Moruo as the artistic representation of the Banquet at Hong Men. The painting, which is done in vermilion, green, blue, yellow, and brown, comes from an Earlier Han tomb excavated at Luoyang in 1957. The tomb has been dated from between 48 and 7 B.C.E. Since all the mural-painted Han tombs we know are of Later Han date, this one can surely claim to be the oldest tomb with mural paintings ever found in China.[30]

A synopsis of Guo Moruo's explanation of the painting is as follows: The back wall of the chamber is decorated with scenes depicting the story of the Banquet at Hong Men. On the right side of the design, a man is shown broiling a joint of beef over a stove, while another man with a staff stands by watching. The wall behind the people is hung with joints of beef and an ox head. To the left of the stove, two men are shown seated on the floor, drinking. The one holding a drinking horn probably represents Xiang Yu, while the other, who is more elegant in appearance, represents Liu Bang. The man standing by the side of Liu Bang represents Xiang Bo. A huge seated tiger to the left of Liu Bang is actually a design painted on a door. Two men standing with folded hands to the left of the tiger design represent Zhang Liang and Fan Zeng. A fierce-looking man with a sword in his hand who is about to stab Liu Bang represents Xiang Zhuang.[31]

There can be no doubt that the scene depicts a feast held in a military camp. It is debatable, however, whether it is a description of the Banquet at Hong

Men. A full and lively account of the banquet is given by the Grand Historian in *Records of the Grand Historian*, as follows:

> Xiang Yu invited Liu Bang to stay for a banquet. He and Xiang Bo sat facing east, the patriarch Fan Zeng faced south, Liu Bang faced north, and Zhang Liang, who was in attendance upon him, faced west. Several times Fan Zeng shot Xiang Yu meaningful glances and three times, as a hint, raised his jade *que*. But Xiang Yu did not respond. Finally Fan Zeng rose and went out. Summoning Xiang Zhuang, he said:
>
> "Our lord is too kindhearted. Go in, drink a toast, and offer to perform a sword dance. Then strike the Lord of Bei [Liu Bang] down where he sits. If you don't do this, we will all end up his captives."
>
> Xiang Zhuang went in to offer a toast, after which he said, "Our prince is drinking with the Lord of Bei, but we have no entertainers in the army. May I perform a sword dance?"
>
> "Very well," said Xiang Yu.
>
> Xiang Zhuang drew his sword and began the dance, and Xiang Bo followed suit, shielding Liu Bang with his body so that Xiang Zhuang could not strike him.
>
> Zhang Liang went out to the gate of the camp to see Fan Kuai, who asked, "How are things in there?"
>
> "Touch and go," replied Zhang Liang. "Xiang Zhuang has drawn his sword to dance. He means to kill the Lord of Bei."
>
> "This is serious!" said Fan Kuai. "Let me go in and have it out with him."
>
> Sword and shield in hand he entered the gate. Guards with crossed halberds tried to bar the way, but he charged and knocked them down with his tilted shield. Bursting into the tent, he lifted the curtain and stood facing west, glaring at Xiang Yu. His hair bristled; his eyes nearly started from his head. Xiang Yu raised himself on one knee and reached for his sword.
>
> "Who is this stranger?" he asked.
>
> "This is the lord of Bei's bodyguard, Fan Kuai," answered Zhang Liang. "Stout fellow!" said Xiang Yu. "Give him a stoup of wine."
>
> Wine was poured and presented to Fan Kuai, who bowed his thanks and straightened up to drink it standing.
>
> "Give him a leg of pork," directed Xiang Yu.
>
> A raw leg of pork was given to Fan Kuai, who set his shield upside down on the ground, placed the pork on it, carved it with his sword, and began to eat.
>
> "Stout fellow!" cried Xiang Yu. "Can you drink any more?"
>
> "I am not afraid of death; why should I refuse a drink?" retorted Fan Kuai. . . . Xiang Yu could not answer.

"Sit down," he said.

Fan Kuai took a seat next to Zhang Liang. Presently Liu Bang got up and went out to the privy, beckoning Fan Kuai to go with him.[32]

Checking this account against the mural painting, we immediately find that there are more discrepancies than correspondences between the two pieces. The seating arrangement and the absence of Fan Kuai in the painting are very difficult to explain if the story is about the Banquet at Hong Men. The fierce man at the left end whom Guo takes to be Xiang Zhuang looks more like Fan Kuai in the Grand Historian's description. But then, Xiang Zhuang would be missing from the scene. Moreover, both Xiang Zhuang and Xiang Bo are supposed to be performing a sword dance together in the banquet.

Identification of the feast scene in the Luoyang mural painting is not our main concern here, however. What particularly interests us is the light the Banquet at Hong Men throws on our understanding of a Han feast. The first thing to be noted is the seating arrangement of the banquet, which is recorded in *Records of the Grand Historian* but not in the *History of the Former Han Dynasty*. As we have seen above, in this banquet, Xiang Yu and his uncle, Xiang Bo, sat facing east. Xiang Yu thus shared the seat of honor with his uncle. Evidence reveals beyond a doubt that the seat facing east was the place of honor at a Han feast. Take the following case of Tian Fen, prime minister under Emperor Wu's reign, as an example: One day, Tian Fen invited guests to a drinking party and made his elder brother, the marquis of Kai, sit facing south while he took the place of honor facing east. He explained that family etiquette must not be allowed to detract from the prime minister's dignity.[33] Moreover, in 32 B.C.E., Prime Minister Kuang Heng was also accused of having violated the rules of propriety by assigning the east-facing seat of honor to one of his subordinates during an official banquet (*HS*, 76.25a). It must be pointed out that this particular rule was not a Han invention but traceable to at least the late Zhou Period.[34] The seating arrangement at the Banquet at Hong Men was therefore definitely a meaningful one. It conveys the important message that Liu Bang had actually accepted Xiang Yu as his superior. This perhaps explains why Xiang Yu no longer had the heart to do away with Liu Bang after everyone had taken his seat at the banquet. Indeed, the way of eating could also become a subtle political art.

Another observation I wish to make about this historical banquet concerns the cooking of meat. The feast scene from the Luoyang mural-painted tomb shows a man broiling (or roasting) a joint of beef on a stove. The rectangular-shaped four-legged stove was possibly painted after the model of an iron one as was found in the immediately neighboring Han cemetery at Shaogou.[35] Interestingly enough, the whole operation in the painting strikes the modern eye very much as a scene of an outdoor open-fire barbecue. But perhaps it would not be too farfetched if we take this portion of the mural painting to be suggestive of the way meat was cooked for the Banquet at Hong Men. It may be recalled that Fan Kuai had been given a raw, uncut leg of pork to eat. It is not inconceivable that the "raw" pork leg was but a halfway, or even less than halfway, broiled piece of meat not ready for serving. Xiang Yu's order was given so suddenly that the cook simply had no time to finish the broiling. A careful reader of the textual account would agree that the chain of events, from Xiang Yu's giving the order to Fan Kuai's eating the leg of pork, makes much better sense if the food was prepared right in the feasting place, as shown in the aforementioned painting. After all, we must remember, the banquet took place in a wartime military camp. Furthermore, broiled or roasted meat was a prized dish for the Han Chinese. Jia Yi (d. 169 B.C.E.), for instance, included it in his proposed menu for Han restaurants on the border to attract the Xiongnu to China's side. In his optimistic estimation, "When the Xiongnu have developed a craving for our cooked rice, *geng* stew, roasted meats, and wine, this will have become their fatal weakness."[36] Roasted or broiled meat also has been found in a mural-painted tomb of late Later Han date at Jiayu Guan, Gansu. In this case, however, the meat is cut into small pieces skewered on a three-pronged fork, ready for serving.[37]

Finally, in the Banquet of Hong Men, Xiang Zhuang made the excuse to perform a sword dance by saying, "We have no entertainment in the army." Thus, he introduces us to another component of a Han feast: entertainment. A formal Han feast was often, though not always, accompanied by amusements of various kinds, including music, dance, and acrobatics. As a matter of fact, in many of the Han mural paintings and stone reliefs, the feast scene includes diversions of some sort as an integral part. Archaeologically, this point can be vividly illustrated by the recent discovery of a whole set of figurines in an earlier Han tomb at Wuying Shan, Jinan. The figurines may be conveniently divided into four different groups: two girls dancing face to face, four men performing acrobatics, two girls and five men playing music, and three gentlemen drinking together while enjoying the show.[38] Ordinarily, however, it was music and dance that went together with a feast in Han times. In literature, both Fu Yi's and Zhang Heng's *fu* entitled "Dance" clearly indicate that a formal banquet is usually accompanied by music and dance.[39] Zhang Heng (78–139 C.E.) provides us with even more specific information about the order of such performances in a feast. According to him, when music begins, wine will be served, and when the drinkers become intoxicated, beautiful girls will then rise to perform dances. Even at an informal dinner party, musical entertainment was sometimes present. Zhang Yu (d. 5 B.C.E.) often brought his favorite student, Dai Chong, to the inner hall for drink and food in the company of a band (*HS*, 81.14a).

Feast scenes in Han mural paintings can only provide us with a skeleton of a Han feast in real life. Historical records are also, as a rule, silent about the sorts of food and drink that were offered and how. Therefore, for the flesh and blood, so to speak, of a Han feast, we must turn to the descriptive literary pieces. Here we run into difficulties of another nature, however: many of the foods mentioned in such literary pieces are only names to us today. This is the case with names from about a dozen or so *fu* by Han writers from Mei Cheng (second century B.C.E.) to Xu Gan (early third century C.E.).

I have found that, among the recognizable items, the following are often mentioned as foodstuffs or prepared dishes in a Han feast:

MEATS: beef flank, fatted dog, bear's paw, panther's breast, suckling pig, deer meat, lamb shoulder.

BIRDS: baked owl, wild duck stew, sparrow broth, roasted wild goose, chicken, snow goose, crane.

FISH: finely minced fresh carp, perch (from Lake Dongting), turtle stew, boiled turtle.

VEGETABLES: bamboo shoots, edible rush shoots, leeks, turnips.

SPICES: ginger, cinnamon, fagara.

FRUITS: lychee, pear, hazelnuts, melon, orange, apricot.

SEASONINGS: peony sauce, salt, plum sauce, meat sauce, sugar, honey, vinegar.[40]

Needless to say, the above list is by no means an exhaustive one, but it does give us some idea of the sorts of foods the Han Chinese usually enjoyed at a feast.

A few supplementary remarks are necessary to make the list more meaningful, however. First, cooking methods mentioned include stewing, boiling, frying, roasting, baking, steaming, and pickling. The mixture of the "five flavors" (bitter, sour, hot, salty, sweet) to achieve "harmony" was also considered to be fundamental to the art of cooking. In this respect, cooking in Han China was more traditional than innovative. However, the art of cutting seems to have been stressed more emphatically than in previous periods. Several Later Han writers speak of mincing and slicing fish and meat to the thinnest degree as a built-in feature of fine food. In fact, as we shall see later, there were also significant new developments in the history of food and cooking during the Han Period. It would be wrong to assume that Han Chinese simply followed the eating tradition of classical antiquity.

Second, as always, grain food is ever present in the Han literary descriptions of a feast. Rice (both ordinary and glutinous) and millet (especially *liang* 粱, *Setaria italica* Beauv. var. *maxima*) are particularly praised as being delicious. We can therefore assume that they were preferred to other kinds of grains available.

Third, wine was by definition an indispensable part of the feast. A second century B.C.E. writer, Zou Yang, in his *fu* on wine distinguishes between the two alcoholic beverages *li* 醴 and *jiu* 酒 and, further, says that wines are manufactured from rice and wheat.[41] The *li* and *jiu* contrast is also found in Zhang Heng's "Qi bian," where we are told that *jiu* is dark in color whereas *li* is white.[42] In the early Earlier Han dynasty, a Confucian scholar named Mu, at the court of

Prince Yuan of Chu, did not like *jiu*, so the prince always prepared *li* for him at a feast. According to the Tang commentator Yan Shigu, *li* tastes sweet. It is manufactured with less "starter" (*qu* 麴) and more rice than are required for the preparation of *jiu* (*HS*, 36.26). Since antiquity, both *li* and *jiu* were put in two separate *zun* beakers during a feast (*Yili* [Book of Etiquette and Ceremonial], "Xiangyin jiu li" [Rites of the District Symposium]). This practice was still followed during the Han Period. As a Later Han song says, "[For] entertaining guests in the north hall . . . there are two *zun* 尊 containers, one for clear (*jiu*), and the other for white (*li*)."[43] On the other hand, *jiu* (or *qingjiu* 清酒, "clear wine") seems to have been a more popular beverage. Conceivably, *jiu* is much stronger than *li*. The Later Han dictionary *Shiming* 釋名 (Explaining Words) tells us that *li* could be made overnight,[44] whereas according to Jia Sixie of the sixth century, the fermentation of clear wine is a very complicated process and therefore takes a much longer time.[45]

In the two Mancheng tombs (in Hebei) of Earlier Han date, altogether thirty-three pottery wine jars were found in 1968. Several of the jars bear inscriptions describing such wines as "*Shu* 黍 [glutinous panicled millet] wine," "Sweet *lao* 醪," "Rice wine," and "*Shu* wine of *shangzun* 上尊 quality."[46] *Li* wine made from wheat is also mentioned in Cai Yong's letter to Yuan Shao in the early third century C.E.[47] Thus, we know that wines in Han times were made from virtually all kinds of grain, including rice, millet, and wheat.[48]

The term *shangzun* needs a word of explanation. According to a Han law quoted by Rushun, wine made from rice is classified as *shangzun* (upper grade), wine made from *ji* 稷 (*Setaria italica* Beauv. var. *maxima*) is *zhongzun* 中尊 (middle grade), and wine made from *su* 粟 (*P. miliaceum*) is *xiazun* 下尊 (lower grade). However, Yan Shigu believes that the grade of wine had nothing to do with the kind of cereal from which it was made. Rather, the grade of wine in Han times was determined by the degree of its thickness: the thicker the wine, the better its quality (*HS*, 71.12b). Now, with the discovery of the inscription "*Shu* wine of *shangzun* quality" from tombs of none other than Prince [Liu] Sheng of Zhongshan and his wife, it seems that Yan Shigu's theory is correct after all.

We have found out, above, what sorts of food and drink were commonly available at a Han feast. It is now time that we try to reconstruct the relative order in which food and drink were served to the guests. First, wine would be offered to the guests. This is shown not only in the above-quoted song of the Later Han Period but also in the Banquet at Hong Men. It may be recalled that Fan Kuai was first given a cup of wine and then a leg of pork. After this initial wine serving, *geng* (stew) would be the opening dish of the feast. The *Book of Etiquette and Ceremonial* says, "When *geng* is ready, then the host asks the guests to take their seats."[49] Ying Shao of the second century C.E. also reports that in his day, *shu*-meat stew was always the first dish presented to the guests at a feast.[50] After *geng*, other dishes, if any, would follow. We are reasonably sure that grain food was the last to be served. The Later Han song quoted above further reveals that toward the end of the feast, the host would hurry the kitchen to prepare grain food (lit. "rice") so that guests might not be detained too long.[51] Han Chinese, like their descendants today, considered a meal incomplete if grain food of some kind were not offered. Thus, Ge Gong of the early second century C.E. found it necessary to write apologetically to a friend about the fact that when the latter visited him some evening before he had only shrimp to offer and no grain food.[52]

Finally, at the end of the meal, fruit would be presented to the guests, perhaps not as a part of the meal, but in the sense of the Western dessert. Wang Chong, for instance, considers it the correct order of eating when he comments on the story that Confucius had eaten millet first and peach later.[53] Fu Yi (early second century C.E.) also makes this very clear in his "Qi Ji" when he describes pears from Yongzhou being offered after the meal.[54] Evidently, the end of a feast was not necessarily the end of eating and drinking, however. According to Ying Shao, sometimes it happened that when the feast was finished, the host still wanted to continue drinking with his guests. In such cases, it was already too late for the kitchen to prepare any fresh food, so dried meat and fish seasoned with fagara, ginger, salt, and *shi* (salted darkened beans) were served instead.[55] This story seems to indicate that as early as the Later Han Period, Chinese had already developed the habit of always having some kind of food when drinking wine.

To conclude our discussion of the Han feast, let us quote a passage from the famous "Tongyue" 僮約(Contract for a Slave) by Wang Bao of the first century B.C.E. The "Contract," dated 59 B.C.E., is a semihumorous account of Wang Bao's purchase of a bearded slave named Bianliao at Chengdu, Sichuan. Among the numerous household tasks Wang Bao assigned to the slave was to prepare feasts for guests. The "Contract" says: "When there are guests in the house he [the slave] shall carry a kettle and go after wine; draw water and prepare the evening meal; wash bowls and arrange food trays; pluck garlic from the garden; chop vegetables and mince meat; pound meat and make stew of tubers; slice fish and roast turtle; boil tea and fill the utensils."[56] The passage speaks for itself. The only point to be briefly noted is whether or not tea was already in use in China this early.[57] However, based on various pieces of literary evidence, including the "Contract," Gu Yanwu came to the conclusion that tea drinking had begun in the Sichuan region even before the Han dynasty.[58] The spread of tea drinking as a habit in the rest of China, especially in the north, probably came much later.[59]

FOOD AND EATING IN EVERYDAY LIFE

Because of the nature of the evidence at my disposal, I have thus far confined my discussion of food and eating in Han China to the upper classes. Food remains and food lists from Mawangdui, kitchen and feast scenes from various mural-painted tombs, the historic Banquet at Hong Men, the numerous delicacies described in a mouth-watering fashion by men of letters—all these belonged exclusively to the rich and powerful who constituted but a small fraction of the sixty million Han Chinese. Now I must try to find out what sorts of foods were generally available to the great majority of people in their everyday life during the Han Period. This is easier said than done, for historical records and archaeological finds normally reflect the life of people of at least some means. Moreover, it is also desirable at times to bring the well-to-do into the discussion that follows both for contrast and comparison.

Grain was the main food for the Han Chinese, as it still is for Chinese today. What, then, were the major categories of grain that were cultivated in Han China? The Han Chinese, following the ancients, often talked about "five grains," "six grains," "eight grains," or "nine grains," but scholars from Han times down to the present have never come to a complete agreement as to the identification of these grains.[60] Thanks to recent archaeological discoveries, however, we are now on a much more solid ground to determine the staple grains on which the Han Chinese lived, philological confusion notwithstanding.

As listed at the beginning of this study, the following grain remains were uncovered in Han Tomb No. 1 at Mawangdui: rice, wheat, barley, two kinds of millet, soybean, and red lentil. With the exception of red lentil, all have long been included, one way or another, in the identification lists of traditional exegetes and philologists. Grain remains have also been found elsewhere. At Shaogou (northwestern outskirts of Luoyang) in 1953, a total of 983 earthenware grain containers were unearthed from 145 tombs datable from middle Earlier Han to late Later Han. Grain remains of the following were found in many of the containers: millets of various kinds (P. *miliaceun* Linn., *Setaria italica* Beauv. var. *maxima*, spiked millet, etc.), hemp, soybean, rice, and Job's tears (*Coix lacryma-jobi*). Moreover, most of the containers bear inscribed labels indicating the food content of each. In addition to the grains just given above, we also find the following names: wheat, barley, bean, lesser bean, hulled white rice, and others.[61] The rice remains from Shaogou, it is interesting to note, were analyzed by a Japanese expert and turned out to be closer to the Indian rice, *Oryza saliva* var. *indica*.[62] In 1957, more such inscribed grain containers with remains were discovered at another Luoyang site, at Jin-guyuan village.[63] Based on these archaeological finds, we can now say with confidence that the major categories of grain generally accessible to the Chinese in Han times included millets of various kinds, rice, wheat, barley, soybeans, lesser beans, and hemp. It is particularly noteworthy that this archaeological list matches very closely the "nine grains" recorded in the agriculturist book by Fan Shengzhi of the first century B.C.E.[64] Unlike Han exegetes such as Zheng Xing and Zheng Xuan, whose knowledge of agriculture was mainly bookish, Fan was a professional agriculturist and had actually taught people in the vicinity of Chang-an the art of farming.[65]

It is almost superfluous to say that not all these grain foods were equally available in all parts of Han China. Since antiquity, various kinds of millet had been the grain staple in north China, whereas rice had been the main starch food for southern Chinese. This situation seems to have continued well into the Han Period. Moreover, we have reasons to believe that on the whole, Han China produced much more millet than rice.[66] According to the *Huainanzi*, only water from the Yangzi River was suitable for rice cultivation.[67] Ban Gu (32–92), in the geographical section of his *Hanshu*, also singles out Sichuan and the Chu region (mainly Hunan and Hubei) as the two major rice-producing areas (*HS*, 28b.20a, 33b–34a). This point has been born out recently in archaeological excavations. In 1973, a group of nine tombs of early Western Han date was excavated at Feng-huang Shan, in Jiangling, Hubei. From Tombs 8, 9, and 10, food remains of various kinds and over four hundred inscribed bamboo slips were found. The remains include rice, melon seeds, kernels of fruit, eggs, millet, chestnuts and vegetable seeds. Many of the bamboo slips also yield information on grain.[68] The slips record rice, glutinous rice, millet, wheat, beans, and hemp. Judging by the number of slips and quantity of the remains, it seems safe to conclude that rice and millet, but especially the former, were the grain staples of this area during the Han.[69] By contrast, it is interesting to note that millet of various kinds comes in much greater quantities than rice from the Shaogou in Luoy-ang.[70] Allowing for this geographical difference between the north and the south, it still may not be too far-fetched to say that millet by and large was more common than rice as the main grain food in Han China. In antiquity, rice had been regarded as an expensive and delicious grain food even by nobility. There is no evidence to suggest that the situation had undergone a drastic change during the Han dynasty.

Next to rice and millet in popularity were wheat, barley, soybeans, and hemp. A word about hemp first. It is common knowledge that hemp fiber provided the basic material for manufacturing cloth in traditional China, but hemp seed proved to be edible also, and for that reason, it was often classified by the an-cients as a "grain." The *Yantielun* (Discourses on Salt and Iron) reports that the early Han Confucian scholar Baoqiu Zi had hemp seed for his grain food.[71] However, hemp seed as food did not appear to assume an importance compa-rable to that of other grains.

For the existence of the very poor, soybeans and wheat could be even more vital than millet. Although Han China undoubtedly produced more millet (of various kinds) than other grains, the consumption of millet was probably even greater. There was therefore always a pressing demand for soybeans and wheat as substitutes. Indeed, Ban Gu points out that the poor only had soybeans to chew and water to drink (*HS*, 91.3a).[72] The *Discourses on Salt and Iron* also men-tions "bean stew" as the simplest kind of meal.[73] Fan Shengzhi has given us a good explanation as to why this was the case. He says: "From soybeans a good crop can be easily secured even in adverse years, therefore it is quite natural for the ancient people to grow soy as a provision against famine. Calculate the acre-age to be covered by soybeans for members of the whole family according to the rate of 5 mou *per capita*. This should be looked at as 'the basic' for farming."[74] Wheat was regarded as a coarse grain food together with beans. There is a fa-mous story about bean conjee (gruel) and wheat food being prepared as a hur-ried meal by Feng Yi for Emperor Guangwu and his soldiers during a period of military campaigns. Many years later, the emperor wrote to Feng Yi apologiz-ing that he had not yet returned the latter's favor of bean conjee and wheat food (*HHS*, 17.3a and 12a). Wang Chong also says, "although bean and wheat are coarse, they can nevertheless satisfy our hunger."[75] In 194 C.E., when there was a great famine in the vicinity of the capital, prices for grains went sky-high: 500,000 coins for only one *hu* 斛 of unhusked grain (millet) and 200,000 coins for one *hu* of beans or wheat (*HHS*, 9.8a).[76] This shows conclusively that beans and wheat were considered much inferior to millet as grain food. An official would be highly praised for having led a simple life if after his death it was found out that he had left behind only a few bushels (*hu*) of wheat or barley (*HHS*, 31.22b, 77.4b).

But even the same grain varied considerably from fineness to coarseness. In Han times, one *hu* of unhusked grain (*gu* 穀 or *su* 粟) would normally yield six parts to every ten of the same grain husked (*mi* 米).[77] The husked grain was considered coarse (*li* 糲) if its ratio to the unhusked grain was seven to ten.[78] Sometimes grain food for the poor was even coarser. *Zao* 糟 (distilled grain) and *kang* 糠 (husks) are also mentioned as grain food (*HHS*, 41.18b–19a). The "Suoyin" in *Records of the Grand Historian* even defines *zaokang* as food for the poor (*SJ*, 1, 61.8b), but this could be just a literary exaggeration. According to Meng Kang (ca. 180–260 C.E.), the so-called *kang* was merely leftover unhusked wheat (*HS*, 40.11b). In any case, *zaokang* was an expression for grain food of the coarsest kind.

What sorts of dishes, if any, went along with grain food for the Han Chinese in their everyday life? *Geng* is the usual answer. The *Classic of Rites* says, "*Geng* was eaten by all, from the princes down to the common people, irrespective of status." Zheng Xuan comments that *geng* was the main food in a meal.[79] Here the Han commentator was obviously speaking from his own daily experience. *Geng* could be cooked with or without meat. The following is the only clear description known to me of meat *geng* in reality under the Han. During Emperor Ming's reign (58–75 C.E.), Lu Xu of Kuaiji (in modern Zhejiang) was imprisoned in the capital, Luoyang. One day when he was given a bowl of meat *geng* to eat, he im-mediately knew that his mother had come to Luoyang to see him. He told the people around that the kind of *geng* he had just received could have been cooked by none other than his mother. As he described it, "When my mother cuts the meat, the chunks always come in perfect squares, and when she chops the scal-lions, the pieces always come in sections exactly one inch long" (*HHS*, 81.21a–b). From this story we know that meat stewed with scallions was a common type of *geng.* But meat *geng* was more a luxury than a daily necessity in Han China. During Wang Mang's reign (9–23 C.E.), a eunuch bought fine millet food and meat *geng* from the marketplace to deceive Wang Mang about what the residents in Chang-an ordinarily had for meals (*HS*, 9c.21b–22a). This act of deception on the part of the eunuch proves that meat *geng* was beyond the reach of people of ordinary means. A first-century scholar, Min Zhongshu of Taiyuan (in Shanxi), being impoverished, of ill health, and advanced in age, could not afford meat, which he badly needed. Instead, he daily bought a piece of pork liver from the meat shop, without perhaps knowing that it was rich in vitamins (*HHS*, 53.2a). In Min's case, the meat he wished to have was probably pork, although beef and mutton seem to have been more in demand in the Han market.[80] Beef was especially prized because the ox was such a useful animal that the government occasionally prohibited its slaughter (*HHS*, 41.3a–b).[81] In theory, meat was exclusively reserved for the aged and nobility.[82] In an imperial decree of 179 B.C.E., Emperor Wen ordered the government to provide the aged (those age eighty or older) in the empire with monthly provisions of grain food, meat, and wine (*HS*, 4.6b–7a). Throughout the Han dynasty, similar decrees had been issued from time to time. Evidence shows, however, that officials in charge rarely took such orders seriously.

Of all animal meats, chicken was probably more within the reach of the common people than other kinds. Local officials also made special efforts to encourage people to raise pigs and chickens as a supplementary household occupation (*HS*, 89.5a–b, 13a). Pottery chickens, pigs, and pig houses have been found in many Han tombs, especially those of Later Han date.[83] This may well be taken as a faithful reflection of an ordinary Han household. Pig butchering was, however, a rather large operation for an individual family. According to Cui Shi, it took place only once a year in the family a few days before the New Year—a practice that had generally been followed by the rural Chinese until the present century.[84] When one or two guests came for dinner, therefore, the Han Chinese, like their ancestors in the time of Confucius, usually had only chicken to offer. In fact, chicken paired with glutinous millet (*shu*) was regarded as a very presentable food for guests both in pre-Han and in Han times.[85] Even the pleasure of chicken meat was denied to the very poor, however. Mao Rong of the second century C.E. had only one chicken for his aged mother and none for his honorable guest Guo Linzong (*HHS*, 68.4b). Also under the Later Han, it is said that an old lady had to steal her neighbor's chicken, which she cooked for herself and her daughter-in-law (*HHS*, 84.14a–b).

We have shown that both meat and poultry were not as readily available to the common people as they were to the rich and the powerful. The only other category of dishes that occupied an important place in everyday meals of the great majority of Han China was, therefore, vegetable dishes of various kinds. As mentioned above, *geng* was by no means necessarily associated with meat, though the list of *geng* from Mawangdui does seem to create such an impression. In fact, it was perfectly legitimate to speak of vegetable *geng* in Han as well as pre-Han times. Han Fei, for example, already mentioned *lihuo zhi geng* 藜藿之羹 with coarse grain food.[86] *Huo* was bean leaves, which, according to Fan Shengzhi, "can be sold as greens."[87] We are not sure what *li* was, but it has been described as a scallionlike plant.[88] The *lihuo* expression later became so stereotyped that it came to mean collectively any kind of coarse vegetable eaten by the poor.

In history we find only a few dietary details concerning the poor. The afore-mentioned Min Zhongshu was, on another occasion, given some garlic by a friend, to go with beans and water (*HHS*, 53.1b). Also, in the first century C.E., Jing Dan was once offered wheat grain and scallions for a meal that he neverthe-less refused to eat (*HHS*, 83.10b–11a). Thus, we know that garlic and scallions were most likely to be on the food list of the impoverished. I must hasten to add, however, that scallions could sometimes be very expensive during the Han Period depending on who ate them. In 33 B.C.E., Shao Xinchen obtained the approval of Emperor Yuan to close down an imperial "greenhouse" for the cul-tivation of out-of-season vegetables, among which were scallions and leeks. As a result, the court saved several tens of millions (of coins) a year (*HS*, 89.15a).[89] Nevertheless, generally speaking, scallions, garlic, and leeks appeared to be quite common in Han times. Their cultivation has been reported in various sources (*HS*, 89.13a; *HHS*, 51.b).[90]

Another kind of vegetable easily within the means of the common people was taro or yam. Under the reign of Emperor Cheng (32 to 7 B.C.E.), the prime minister Zhai Fangjin (whose courtesy name was Ziwei) had caused the break-down of a major irrigation dam in Runan commandery (in Henan). Agriculture in the whole region was therefore seriously affected. To register their complaint against Zhai, the people of Runan created a song that reads:

> It was Zhai Ziwei who destroyed our dam,
> Now all we have for food is soybeans and yam.

As the commentary by Yan Shigu makes clear, the second line means that the people cooked soybeans as grain food (*fan* 飯) and yam as *geng* (*HS*, 84.22a). That yam or taro was a staple vegetable in Han China is fully testified to by Fan Shengzhi's agriculturist book in which detailed instructions on planting and cultivating it are given.[91]

In the everyday life of the Han Chinese there is yet another category of food to mention, namely, dried grain food known as *bei* 糒, *hou* 餱, or *qiu* 糗. It is difficult to distinguish clearly the three kinds of dried provisions from one an-other except that both *bei* and *hou* are said to be dried boiled grain (*ganfan* 乾飯), whereas *qiu* is sometimes described as being made from pulverized grain. Moreover, *qiu* is also believed to be dried by fire such as by baking or roasting. Rice, wheat, barley, millet, and beans could all be transformed into dried grain food.[92] Dried grain food had probably already been extensively used by soldiers and travelers as early as the Zhou Period.[93] However, it was under the Han that this kind of food came to play a role of vital importance in the daily lives of millions of Chinese.

First, it was the main food for all Han travelers irrespective of status. Wang Mang, for example, ordered his imperial attendant to prepare dried grain food and dried meat for his tour of inspection in c.e. 14 (*HS*, 99B.26b). Empress Deng, wife of Emperor He (89–105 c.e.), also had large quantities of dried grain food stored in her royal residence (*HHS*, 10A.28b). In fact, there was an official in the court whose duty was to select grain for making dried provisions for imperial use (*HHS*, "Zhi" section, 26.2b). Second, repeated large-scale military campaigns against the Xiongnu in the north caused Han warriors to rely entirely on dried grain food for survival. According to Yan You (first century c.e.), the Chinese soldiers, once sent to fight the Xiongnu in the desert, lived on dried provisions and water in all seasons. In Yan's estimation, for an expedition of three hundred days, each soldier would need eighteen *hu* of *bei*. This put a man's consumption of *bei* at exactly 0.6 *sheng* 升 per day (*HS*, 94B.24a, 25a). In 99 B.C.E., when Li Ling's army was surrounded by the Xiongnu in the neighborhood of Dunhuang, he gave each of his fighting men two *sheng* of *bei* and a piece of ice to get out of the encircled area one by one and later reassemble in a Han fort (*HS*, 54.12b). Obviously, the fort must have been within a three-day journey from the battlefield. Third, the Han government always kept large quantities of dried grain food in store for uses besides military ones. Thus, in 51 B.C.E., some thirty-four thousand *hu* of *bei* were sent to the Xiongnu by the Han court as a reward for their recent submission: this was the largest single amount of dried provisions ever recorded in Han history (*HS*, 94.4b). Last, but not least, dried grain food was also consumed by men working in the field. As Ying Shao pointed out, both warriors and farmers carried *hou* with them.[94] Cui Shi's *Simin Yueling* 四民月令 (Monthly Ordinances for the Four Classes [Scholars, Farmers, Artisans, and Merchants]) advises that people make as much *bei* as possible out of the newly harvested wheat.[95] Indeed, we can surely say that in Han China, hardly a day passed without some people eating dried grain food.

Before I bring this section to a close, I wish to say a word about food vessels in Han China. The subject of food vessels is so important and complicated that an extensive treatment would definitely involve at least another chapter. In the following I will therefore merely point out a few salient features of Han food vessels, with special reference to the distinction between vessels shown in kitchen scenes in mural paintings and those actually used by the common people in their everyday lives.

One safe generalization scholars have been making from time to time is that in Han times, the upper classes used mainly lacquerware while the common people relied entirely on earthenware for cooking, eating, and drinking.[96] Previously, in speaking of Han lacquerware, people always turned to the two important archaeological discoveries in Luolang and Noin-Ula for illustration.[97]

Now Luolang and Noin-Ula have both been dwarfed in this respect by Mawang-dui Tombs No. 1 and No. 3.[98] It is certainly no exaggeration to say that the Mawangdui finds "represent the largest and best preserved group of Western [Earlier] Han lacquer ware, as well as the most diversified in vessel types, ever unearthed in China."[99] Lacquerware found in Mawangdui Tombs No. 1 and No. 3 consists mostly of food and drink vessels.

In ancient China, there had been a fundamental contrast between eating and drinking.[100] That the same contrast persisted during the Han Period is fully attested to by many of the examples given above. Lacquerware from the two Mawangdui tombs reveals that the contrast is also reflected in the vessels. It is very interesting to note that food vessels and drink vessels are clearly distinguished from each other by the two contrasting inscriptions *Jun jin shi* 君進食 ("Please eat food, sir") and *Jun jin jiu* 君進酒 ("Please drink wine, sir"). Another interesting point to observe is that vessels for food and those for drink seem to have come in separate sets.

On the basis of the two contrasting inscriptions, then, we can easily distinguish the set of drink vessels from that of food vessels. The former includes *fang* vases, *Zhong* 鍾 vases, *yi* 匜 pitchers, *zhi* 觶 cups, *shao* 勺 and 杓 ladles, and winged wine cups; the latter includes *ding* tripods, cake boxes, *lian* 奩 food boxes, plates, and winged food cups. Some of the food and drink vessels still contained remains at the time of their excavation, and their actual functions were therefore unmistakably indicated. Moreover, cups and plates came in different sizes. For instance, wine cups have a capacity of 4 *sheng*, 2 *sheng*, 1.5 *sheng*, or 1 *sheng*.[101] Scholars who actually examined the finds already have indicated that some of the vessels can be better understood if taken in sets rather than in individual pieces.[102] It may be additionally noted that among the lacquerware pieces, the *zhi* cups, winged cups, and *yi* pitchers were the most common types of vessels for drink used by the Han Chinese, and the food cup *bei* was a vessel for *geng*. None of them was the monopoly of the upper classes.[103] Needless to say, although the common people used the same types of vessels, the materials from which theirs were made—earth or wood—were much inferior in quality. Archaeological finds show, however, that pottery vessels in Han China sometimes were also made in sets, perhaps in imitation of lacquerware.[104] As we know, the price of lacquerware in Han times was much higher than not only earthenware or woodenware but bronze as well. Lao Gan is certainly right in saying that, under the Han, lacquer food vessels basically replaced ancient bronze ones.[105]

The Han Chinese were status conscious as far as the material of their vessels for food and drink was concerned. Toward the end of the Earlier Han dynasty, a ranking official, Tang Zun, was accused of hypocrisy because he used earthenware vessels (*HS*, 72.30a). Under Emperor Guangwu's reign, Huan Tan, in a memorial essay for the monarch, attacked some of the hypocritical court officials in ministerial positions who sought to achieve reputations for frugality by using plain wooden cups for eating and drinking.[106] It is interesting to note that Liu Xiang (77–6 B.C.E.) also has a disciple of Confucius making comments that clearly imply that earthen food vessels and boiled food (zhushi 煮食) befit only the poor.[107] Boiled food was considered inferior, presumably because the poor always cooked their wheat, beans, and bean leaves by boiling.

Finally, what were the most essential cooking utensils for the Han Chinese? The answer can be given without the slightest hesitation: fu and zeng. These two utensils were basic to every Han Chinese kitchen, rich and poor alike. The fu 釜 (cauldron) was used mainly for cooking geng and the zeng 甑 (steamer) primarily for steaming or boiling grain food. In actual cooking, the zeng was always placed on top of the fu. Archaeologically, therefore, the two are always found together as if they were an inseparable pair. Most of the fu and zeng were made of clay, such as those found at Mawangdui, Youceng in Shandong, Canton, and Shaogou.[108] Metal fu were also made, however. An iron fu was found at Shaogou, and seven bronze ones with a lot of fish bones in them were discovered in tombs in Canton.[109] From Han tombs at Lizhu, Shaoxing (in Zhejiang) a number of fu of all three materials—pottery, bronze, and iron—were unearthed in 1955, but the number of iron fu was greater than the other two kinds.[110] In historical writings, we also often find mention of the fu accompanied by the zeng (SJ, 2, 7.10a; HS, 31.14a; HHS, 81.28b). It is probably safe to conclude that since geng (stew) and fan (grain food) were the two most basic kinds of food for the Han Chinese, the pairing of fu with zeng simply reflects this fundamental dietary reality in Han China.

TOWARD A CULINARY REVOLUTION

Thus far in this study, no special reference has been made regarding what was significantly new in Han culinary history. Now, by way of conclusion, I wish to point out emphatically that Han Chinese were as innovative as they were traditional in matters pertaining to food and eating. In the following, I shall first list a few important exotic edibles that were brought to China for the first time, and then proceed to discuss two major Han contributions to the art of cooking that, in my biased view, produced far-reaching revolutionary consequences in Chinese culinary history.

The Han dynasty is marked, among other things, by expansion, and expansion inevitably opened China to things non-Chinese, including foods. Post-Han literary works credit Zhang Qian, the greatest traveler of early Han times, with the introduction of almost all the exotic edibles from the western regions. The list includes, for instance, grape, alfalfa, pomegranate, walnut, sesame, onion, caraway seeds, peas, coriander from Bactria, and cucumber. In fact, however, as Kuwabara Jitsuzo has convincingly shown, none of these plants was introduced to China by Zhang Qian himself.[111] Nevertheless, there can be little doubt that some of the foreign foods listed above were brought to the Han soon after Zhang Qian. Grape and alfalfa seeds were brought back to China by Han envoys from Ferghana around 100 B.C.E. (*SJ*, 2.280). Grape is further mentioned in a Later Han literary piece.[112] Grape wine imported from the western regions was greatly prized as late as the end of the second century C.E.[113] Kong Rong wrote a thank-you note to a friend for a gift of walnuts.[114] In *Monthly Ordinances for the Four Classes*, we find alfalfa, sesame, peas, and onion.[115] Sesame seems to have been particularly important, for it alone appears three times in the text. The kind of "barbarian grain food" (*hufan* 胡飯) enjoyed by Emperor Ling (168–188 C.E.) was, in all likelihood, grain food cooked with the flavorful sesame (*HHS*, "Zhi" section, 13.8b).

Mention may also be made of the renowned *longyan* 龍眼 and *lizhi* 荔枝 (lychee, *Litchi chinensis*), which, though coming from the tropical southern border of the Han, were still considered more or less new and exotic throughout this period. Both fruits were sent to the court by special fast horses from Guangdong (*HHS*, 4.25a–b). During Emperor Shun's reign (126–144 C.E.), Wang Yi, in his *fu* on the lychee (*lizhi*), praised it as the leading tributary fruit.[116] At the end of the Han, Zhongchang Tong still criticized his contemporaries for having overindulged in the taste of lychee.[117]

Earlier we have seen that both soybeans and wheat were primarily foods for the common people. It was due to soybeans and wheat, however, that a quiet culinary revolution began in Han China. By this I refer particularly to the manufacturing of *shi* (salted, darkened beans) and the making of wheat flour. As Shi Shenghan pointed out:

> *Shi* is very popular in a vast area of China, especially among the rustic population leading a very simple life. . . . It was almost the only relish they could afford to enjoy. The date of *shi* is not yet well traced, but Sima Qian mentioned it in the *Records of the Grand Historian* as one of the products in cities, so it must already have been produced in large quantities in his time. The *Qimin Yaoshu* (Important Arts of the People) gives the first known instructions for its preparation.[118]

In the learned opinions of Kong Yingda of the Tang and Zhou Mi of the Song, however, *shi* was invented sometime around 200 B.C.E.[119] It had already become a basic condiment in the early Han, and it was on a very short list of food supplies that Prince Liu Chang received from the government after his revolutionary plot had been discovered (*SJ*, 1, 2.364). The name *shi* even found its way into an elementary Han textbook, the *Jijiu pian* (Handy Primer or Dictionary for Quick Use)—a clear indication of its great popularity.[120] Now, with the excavation of Mawangdui Tomb No. 1, *shi* remains have become a concrete archaeological fact for the first time.[121] The earliest bean curd is also reported to have been made during the Han Period, but the textual evidence is too weak to support such a claim.[122]

However, what we today call *mian* 麵 (noodles) was clearly a unique contribution by the Han to Chinese culinary art. In Han times, "noodle food," in a broad sense, was known as *bing* 餅 (cakes), while the character for *mian* was defined as wheat flour in the standard dictionary *Shuowen jiezi* 說文解字 (Explaining Wen and Analyzing Zi).[123] That noodle foods came into existence during the Han Period but not earlier may be explained by the simple fact that the techniques required for large-scale flour grinding were not available to the Chinese until the Han. Such techniques were probably introduced to China from the West in the latter part of the Earlier Han dynasty as a result of the Han expansion.[124] For instance, the flour mill is suspected to have been adopted from another culture rather than an indigenous Chinese invention.[125] Three stone mills have been found in Shaogou tombs datable to the end of the Earlier Han and beginning of the Later Han.[126] We can therefore assume that the Han Chinese made wheat flour around the second half of the first century B.C.E. at the latest. The word *cuo* 䃺 was specifically coined for wheat grinding.[127]

Under the Later Han, a great variety of noodle foods were cooked, including boiled noodles, steamed buns (modern *mantou* 饅頭), and baked cakes with sesame seeds.[128] According to *Explaining Words*, noodle food was called *bing* 餅, because the word indicates the idea of blending (*bing* 并) flour with water.[129] In connection with this, a flour-kneading scene has been found in Han and Wei-Jin tombs such as Yinan and Jiayu Guan.[130] Boiled noodles and swung noodles are also mentioned in *Monthly Ordinances for the Four Classes*.[131] Boiled noodles were so popular in the second century C.E. that even the emperor ate them (*HHS*, 63.14b–15a). It was probably no accident that from Wang Mang's time on, selling noodle food became a notable business (*HS*, 99B.18b; *HHS*, 64.23b, 82B.12a.[132]

The Western Jin writer Shu Xi (late third and early fourth centuries) composed a *fu* on noodle food ("Bing *fu* 餅賦"). According to him, people in Zhou times were acquainted with wheat grain food but not noodles, which had developed only in the very recent past. He made a special reference to the art of flour kneading by describing vividly how the cook's skillful hands and fingers moved in molding the flour dough into a variety of shapes. He also mentioned how noodle food could be delicately cooked with meats (especially mutton and pork) and seasonings (including ginger, scallions, fagara, and above all, *shi*). From a historical point of view, however, the following observation that he made on the origins of noodle food interests us even more: "The various kinds of noodles and cakes were mainly the invention of the common people, while some of the cooking methods came from foreign lands."[133] In other words, it was the ingenuity of the Han Chinese in experimenting with the most common of eating materials, coupled with a willingness to learn from other cultures, that eventually led to the opening of an entirely new chapter in Chinese culinary history.

NOTES

1. As I was finishing this chapter, Hayashi Minao's 林巳奈夫 detailed study of food and drink in Han times (in Japanese) came to my attention. Like my work, Hayashi's is also based on both archaeological and textual evidence, although our approaches are different. The reader is therefore referred to Hayashi's valuable work for additional information on the subject. See Hayashi, "Kandai no inshoku" 漢代の飲食, *Tōhō gakuhō* 東方學報 48 (1975): 1–98.

I wish to take this opportunity to thank the Institute of Chinese Studies, Chinese University of Hong Kong, for providing me with research assistance in the fall term, 1974–1975, which facilitated the original preparation of this chapter. I am indebted to Susan Converse for her research and editorial help.

2. Hunan sheng 湖南省, "Changsha Mawangdui er sanhao Hanmu fajue jianbao" (hereafter "Fajue jianbao") 長沙馬王堆二三號漢墓發掘簡報, *WW* 7 (1974): 46–48.

3. Hunan sheng bowuguan 湖南省博物館, *Changsha Mawangdui yihao Hanmu* (hereafter *Mawangdui yihao Hanmu*) 長沙馬王堆一號號漢墓 (Beijing: Wenwu Press, 1973), 1:35–36.

4. See also Gao Yaoting 高耀亭, "Mawangdui yihao Hanmu suizang pin zhong gong shi yong di shoulei" 馬王堆一號漢墓隨葬品中供食用的獸類, *WW* 9 (1973): 76–78.

5. However, in light of bamboo slips found in Han Tomb No. 3 at Mawangdui, the identification of *Yugeng* with *Dageng* may still be an open question. See Zhongguo kexue yuan kaogu yanjiusuo 中國科學院考古研究所, and Hunan sheng bowuguan, *WW* 1 (1975): 55.

6. *Liji*, 8.8a; cf. James Legge, *Li Chi: Book of Rites* (New York: University Books, 1967), 1:35. *Zhouli zheng zhu*, *SBBY* (Shanghai: Zhonghua, 1936), 4.35.

7. *Lunheng* 論衡 (Shanghai: Renmin, 1974 edition), 452.

8. Hunan sheng bowuguan, *Mawangdui yihao Hanmu* (1973), 131–132.

9. Gao Yaoting, "Mawangdui yihao Hanmu suizang pin," 78.

10. Sima Qian 司馬遷, *Shiji* 史記 (Beijing: Zhonghua, 1959), 1:3123.

11. Burton Watson, *Records of the Grand Historian* (New York: Columbia University Press, 1961), 2:46.

12. Hunan sheng, "Fajue jianbao," 45.

13. *Liji*, 8.19a–21b; Legge, *Li Chi*, 1, 459–463.

14. An Jinhuai 安金槐 and Wang Yugang 王與剛, "Mixian Dahu Ting Handai huaxiang shimu he bihua mu" 密縣打虎亭漢代畫像石墓和壁畫墓, *WW* 10 (1972): 61.

15. Li Wenxin 李文信, "Liaoyang faxian di sanzuo bihua gumu" 遼陽發現的三座壁畫古墓, *WWCKZL* 5 (1955): 15–42.

16. Wilma Fairbank, *Adventures in Retrieval* (Cambridge, Mass.: Harvard University Press, 1972), 146–147, 174–178.

17. Henan sheng bowuguan 河南省博物館, "Jiyuan Sijian Hanmu di fajue" 濟源泗澗漢墓的發掘, *WW* 2 (1973): 47–48.

18. Li Wenxin, "Liaoyang faxian"; Dongbei bowuguan 東北博物館, "Liaoyang Sandaohao Liangzuo bihuamu di qingli jianbao" 遼陽三道壕兩座壁畫墓的清理簡報, *WWCKZL* 12 (1955): 52–54.

19. Ôsamu Shinoda 篠田統, *Chûgoku Tabemono shi* 中国食べ物史 (Tokyo: Shibata shoten, 1974), 49; Huadong wenwu gongzuodui Shandong zu 華東文物工作隊山東組, "Shandong Yinan Han huaxiang shimu" 山東沂南畫像石墓, *WWCKZL* 8 (1954): 41; Zeng Zhaoyu曾昭燏, Jiang Baogeng 蔣寶庚, and Li Zhongyi黎忠義, *Yinan gu huaxiang shimu fajue baogao* 沂南古畫像石墓發掘報告 (hereafter *Fajue baogao*) (Beijing: Wenhuabu wenwu guanliju, 1956), 20–21, pl. 48.

20. Luo Fuyi 羅福頤, "Nei Menggu zizhiqu Tuoketuo xian xin faxian di Hanmu bihua" 內蒙古自治區托克托縣新發現的漢墓壁畫, *WWCKZL* 9 (1956): 43.

21. Nei Menggu wenwu gongzuodui 內蒙古文物工作隊, "Helinge-er faxian yizou zhongyao di Dong Han bihuamu" 和林格爾發現一座重要的東漢壁畫墓, *WW* 1 (1974): 11; Museum of Fine Arts, North Kyûshû, "Zhonghua Renmin Gonghe Guo Han-Tang bihuazhan" 中華人民共和國漢唐壁畫展 (Tokyo: Kitakyûshû Shiritsu Bijutsukan, 1974), pl. 19; Anonymous, *Han Tang bihua* 漢唐壁畫 (Beijing: Foreign Language Press, 1974), pl. 26.

22. He Haotian 何浩天, *Hanhua yu Handai shehui shenghuo* 漢畫與漢代社會生活 (Taipei: Zhonghua, 1958), 96. Jiayu Guan Shi wenwu qingli xiaozu 嘉峪關市文物清理小組, "Jiayu Guan Han huaxiang zhuan mu" 嘉峪關漢畫像磚墓, *WW* 12 (1972): 40, fig. 34.

23. Lin Naishen 林乃燊, "Zhongguo gudai di pengtiao yu yinshi" 中國古代的烹調與飲食, *Beijing daxue xuebao* 北京大學學報 2 (1957): 136–137.

24. *Lunheng*, 268.

25. We know that this kind of couch was not uncommon in the Han Period because we find it not only in the Bangtaizi mural painting (Li Wenxin, "Liaoyang faxian," 17–18) but also in a painted brick from Sichuan, though in the latter case the couch has no screens on the sides. See Chongqing Shi bowuguan, *Sichuan Hanmu huaxiang zhuan xuanji* (Beijing: Wenwu Press, 1957), 20. Moreover, the *Gaoshi zhuan* 高士傳 also reports that Guan Ning 管寧 of the third century often sat on a wooden couch (quoted in *Sanguo zhi* 三國志, "Wei zhi" 魏志, 11.27b).

26. Li Wenxin, "Liaoyang faxian," 30, figs. 18–20.

27. Ibid., 27, fig. 14; Luoyang qu kaogu fajuedui 洛陽區考古發掘隊, *Luoyang Shaogou Hanmu* 洛陽燒溝漢墓 (Beijing: Kexue, 1959), 137–319, fig. 64, pl. 35.

28. Xu Shen 許慎, *Shuowen jiezi* 說文解字 (Hong Kong: Taipei, 1969 edition), 122; Qu Xuanying 瞿宣穎, *Zhongguo shehui shiliao congchao* 中國社會史料叢鈔 (Shanghai: Shangwu, 1937), 131.

29. Lao Gan 勞榦, "Lun Luxi huaxiang sanshi" 論魯西畫像三石, *Bulletin of the Institute of History and Philology, Academia Sinica* 8 (1939): 100.

30. Henan sheng 河南省, "Jiyuan Sijian Hanmu di fajue," 107–125, pl. 2; Anonymous, *Han Tang bihua*, pls. 2, 3.

31. Guo Moruo 郭沫若, "Luoyang Hanmu bihua shitan" 洛陽漢墓壁畫試探, *KG* 2 (1964): 6.

32. *SJ*, Yang Xianyi and Gladys Yang, trans., *Records of the Historian* (Hong Kong: Commercial Press, 1974), 218–219.

33. Ibid., 361. According to *HS*, 52.4b, however, the marquis of Gai faced north.

34. Shang Binghe 尚秉和, *Lidai shehui fengsu shiwu kao* 歷代社會風俗事物考 (hereafter *Shiwu kao*) (Shanghai: Shangwu, 1938), 283–284.

35. Luoyang qu, *Luoyang Shaogou Hanmu*, pl. 58, figs. 3, 4.

36. Jia Yi 賈誼, *Xinshu* 新書 (Shanghai: Shangwu, 1937 edition), 4, 41.

37. Jiayu Guan Shi, "Jiayu Guan . . . zhuan mu," 25, pl. 7, fig. 1, and fig. 34 on p. 40.

38. Jinan shi bowuguan 濟南市博物館, "Shitan Jinan Wuying Shan chutu di Xi Han yuewu zaji yanyin taoyong" 試探濟南無影山出土的西漢雜技陶俑, *WW* 5 (1972): 19–24.

39. Yan Kejun 嚴可均, *QSW* (Beijing: Zhonghua, 1958), 705–706, 769.

40. These are based on many literary pieces collected in *QSW*, 238, 403, 623, 624, 644, 706, 713, 714, 768, 775, 827, 963, 975, 976.

41. Ge Hong 葛洪, *Xi jing zaji* 西京雜記, *Han Wei congshu* 漢魏叢書 (1937 edition), 4, 4a–5b.

42. *QSW*, 775.

43. Guo Maoqian 郭茂倩, ed., *Yuefu shiji* 樂府詩集, vol. 2 (Beijing: Wenxue guji, 1955 edition), *juan* 37: 2.

44. Liu Xi 劉熙, *Shiming* 釋名 (Shanghai: Shangwu, 1939), 66.

45. Shi Shenghan 石聲漢, *Qimin Yaoshu jinshi* 齊民要術今釋 (Beijing: Kexue, 1958), 460–462.

46. Zhongguo kaogu yanjiusuo 中國考古研究所, "Mancheng Hanmu fajue jiyao" 滿城漢墓發掘紀要, *KG* 1 (1972): 14.

47. *QSW*, 872.

48. See also Shi Shenghan, *Qimin Yaoshu gailun* 齊民要術概論 (Beijing: Kexue, 1962), 81.

49. *Yili*, WYWK (Shanghai: Shangwu, 1933), 89.

50. *QSW*, 680.

51. Guo Maoqian, *Yuefu shiji*, *juan* 37: 1b.

52. *QSW*, 780.

53. *Lunheng*, 451.

54. *QSW*, 706.

55. Ibid., 676.

56. Translated by C. Martin Wilbur in *Slavery in China During the Former Han Dynasty, 206 B.C. to A.D. 25* (New York: Russell and Russell, 1943), 385, with minor alterations.

57. Wilbur, *Slavery in China*, 391n19.

58. Gu Yanwu 顧炎武, *Rizhi lu* 日知錄, WYWK (Shanghai: Shangwu, 1929), 3, 55–57.

59. Lü Simian 呂思勉, *Liang Jin Nanbeichao shi* 兩晉南北朝史 (Shanghai: Shangwu, 1948), 2:1136–1137.

60. See, e.g., Qi Sihe 齊思和, "*Mao Shi* gu ming kao" 毛詩穀名考, *Yenching Journal of Chinese Studies* 36 (1949): 266–269.

61. Luoyang qu, *Luoyang Shaogou Hanmu*, 112–113, table 26.

62. Nakao Sasuke 中尾佐助, "Henan sheng Luoyang Hanmu chutu di daomi" 河南省洛陽漢墓出土的稻米, *KG* 4 (1957): 79–82.

63. Huang Shibin 黃士斌, "Luoyang Jin-guyuan cun Hanmu zhong chutu you wenzi di taoqi" 洛陽金谷園村漢墓中出土有文字的陶器, *Kaogu tongxun* 考古通訊 1 (1958): 36–41.

64. Shi Shenghan 石聲漢, *On "Fan Sheng-chih Shu* 氾勝之書*": An Agriculturalist's Book of China Written by Fan Sheng-chih in the First Century B.C.* (Beijing: Science Press, 1959), 8–11.

65. Ibid., 42–44.

66. Qi Sihe, "*Mao Shi* gu ming kao," 304–305.

67. Liu Wendian 劉文典, annotator, *Huainan Honglie jijie* 淮南鴻烈集解 (Taipei: Shangwu, 1974), 4, 10a.

68. Changjiang . . . xunlian ban 長江 . . . 訓練班, "Hubei Jiangling Fenghuang Shan Xi-Han-mu fajue jianbao" 湖北江陵鳳凰山西漢墓發掘簡報, *WW* 6 (1974): 41–54.

69. Huang Shengzhang 黃盛璋, "Jiangling Fenghuang Shan Hanmu jiantu yu qi zai lishi dili yanjiu shang di jiazhi" 江陵鳳凰山西漢墓簡牘與其在歷史地理研究上的價值, *WW* 6 (1974): 76–77.

70. Luoyang qu, *Luoyang Shaogou Hanmu*, 112–113.

71. Huan Kuan 桓寬, *Yantielun* 鹽鐵論 (Shanghai: Renmin, 1974), 41; for Baoqiu Zi, see Wang Peizheng 王佩諍, *Yantielun zhaji* 鹽鐵論札記 (Beijing: Shangwu, 1958), 65.

72. Nancy Swann, trans., *Food and Money in Ancient China: The Earliest Economic History of China to A.D. 25* (Princeton: Princeton University Press, 1950), 419.

73. Huan Kuan, *Yantielun*, 41.

74. Shi Shenghan, *On "Fan Sheng-chih Shu,"* 19–21.

75. *Lunheng*, 131.

76. Normally the price of one *hu* of unhusked grain was around one hundred coins only. See Lao Gan 勞榦, *Juyan Hanjian kaoshi* 居延漢簡考釋 (Taipei: Institute of History and Philology, Academia Sinica, 1960), 58–59.

77. Lien-sheng Yang, *Studies in Chinese Institutional History* (Cambridge, Mass.: Harvard University Press, 1961), 154.

78. See Zhang Yan's 張晏 commentary to the *Shiji*, 1:130, 5a.

79. *Liji*, 8.22a.

80. *Lunheng*, 221.

81. Ying Shao 應劭, *Fengsu tongyi* 風俗通義, *Han Wei congshu* (Shanghai: Shangwu, 1937 edition), 9:5a–6a; *QSW*, 543–544.

82. Lü Simian, *Qin Han shi* 秦漢史 (Shanghai: Shangwu, 1947), 571–572.

83. Luoyang qu, *Luoyang Shaogou Hanmu*, 140–142; Guangzhou shi wenwu guanli weiyuanhui 廣州市文物管理委員會, "Guangzhou shi wenguanhui 1955 nian qingli gumu zang gongzuo jianbao" 廣州市文管會 1955 年清理古墓葬工作簡報, *WWCKZL* 1 (1957): 74; Guizhou sheng bowuguan 貴州省博物館, "Guizhou Qianxi xian Hanmu fajue jianbao" 貴州黔西縣漢墓發掘簡報, *WW* 11 (1972): 44.

84. Cui Shi 崔實, *Simin yueling* 四民月令 (Beijing: Zhonghua, 1965), 74–76.

85. Shang Binghe, *Shiwu kao*, 105.

86. Chen Qiyou 陳奇猷, *Hanfeizi jishi* 韓非子集釋 (Hong Kong: Zhonghua, 1974), 2:1041.

87. Shi Shenghan, *On "Fan Sheng-chih Shu,"* 38–39.

88. Yan Shigu's 顏師古 commentary in *HS*, 62, 4a; Wang Niansun 王念孫, *Guangya shuzheng* 廣雅疏證, *CSJC* (Shanghai: Shangwu, 1939), 7:1170.

89. On this greenhouse, see Jiang Mingchuan 蔣名川, *Zhongguo di jiu cai* 中國的韭菜 (Beijing: Caizheng jingji, 1956), 14.

90. Cui Shi, *Simin yueling*, 13–15.

91. Shi Shenghan, *On "Fan Sheng-chih Shu,"* 24–27, 40–41.

92. Wang Niansun, *Guangya shuzheng*, 6:935–936.

93. Qi Sihe, "*Mao Shi* gu ming kao," 293.

94. Ying Shao 應劭, "Han Guanyi" 漢官儀, in *Han Guan Qizhong* 漢官七種, compiled by Sun Xingyan 孫星衍 (Taipei: Zhonghua, 1962), 1:35b.

95. Cui Shi, *Simin yueling*, 43.

96. Zhongguo kaogu yanjiusuo, *Kaoguxue jizhu* 考古學集注 (Beijing: Kexue, 1958), 133; C. S. Wang Zhongshu 王仲殊, "Handai wuzhi wenhua lüeshuo" 漢代物質文化略說, *Kaogu tongxun* 1 (1956): 71.

97. Ying-shih Yü, *Trade and Expansion in Han China* (Berkeley: University of California Press, 1967), 24.

98. *KG* (1972), 41.

99. Hunan sheng bowuguan, *Mawangdui yihao Hanmu* (1973), English abstract, 5.

100. Chang Kwang-chih, "Food and Food Vessels in Ancient China," *Transactions of the New York Academy of Sciences* 35 (1973):509–510.

101. Hunan sheng bowuguan, *Mawangdui yihao Hanmu* (1973), 76–96; ibid. (1974), 44–45.

102. *WW* 5 (1972): 67.

103. Wang Zhenduo 王振鐸, "Zai lun Handai jiuzun" 再論漢代酒樽 *WW* 11 (1963): 1–12.

104. Ibid., 13–15; Luoyang qu, *Luoyang Shaogou Hanmu*, 149.

105. Lao Gan, "Lun Luxi huaxiang sanshi," 99.

106. *QSW*, 536.

107. Liu Xiang 劉向, *Shuo Yuan* 說苑, *Han Wei congshu* (Taipei: Yiwen yinshu guan, 1967 edition), *juan* 20: 13a.

108. Hunan sheng bowuguan, *Mawangdui yihao Hanmu* (1973), 124–125; Shandong sheng wenwu guanli weiyuanhui, *WWCKZL* no. 6 (1955), 86; Mai Yinghao, "Guangzhou huaqiao xincun Xi Han mu," *KG* 2 (1958): 64; Luoyang qu, *Luoyang Shaogou Hanmu*, 135.

109. Luoyang qu, *Luoyang Shaogou Hanmu*, 196; Mai Yinghao, "Guangzhou huaqiao xincun Xi Han mu," 68.

110. Zhejiang sheng wenwu guanli weiyuanhui 浙江省文物管理委員會, "Shaoxing Lizhu di Hanmu" 紹興漓渚的漢墓, *KG* 1 (1957): 137.

111. Kuwabara Jitsuzô 桑原騭藏, *Zhang Qian xizheng kao* 張騫西征考, 2nd ed., trans. Yang Lian 楊鍊 (Shanghai: Shangwu, 1935), 47–52, 117–127.

112. *QSW*, 784.

113. Ying-shih Yü, *Trade and Expansion in Han China*, 196.

114. *QSW*, 922

115. Cui Shi, *Simin yueling*, 13, 20, 26, 41, 46, 56.

116. *QSW*, 784.

117. Ibid., 956.

118. Shi Shenghan, *Qimin Yaoshu gailun*, 86.

119. ZZ, Zhao gong ershinian 昭公二十年, online text: *Shisan jing zhushu* edition of *Chunqiu Zuozhuan Zhengyi*, 十三经注疏-春秋左传正义.txt, p. 1047; Zhou Mi 周密, *Qidong yeyu* 齊東野語, *CSJC* (Shanghai: Shangwu, 1959 edition), 2, 115.

120. Wang Guowei 王國維, commentator, *Jiao Songjiang ben Jijiu pian* 校宋江本急救篇, in *Wang Zhongque Gong yishu* 王忠愨公遺書 (1929 edition), 10b; Shen Yuan 沈元, "*Jijiu pian* yanjiu" 急救篇研究, *LSYJ* 3 (1962): 66.

121. Hunan sheng bowuguan, *Mawangdui yihao Hanmu* (1973), 127, 138.

122. Li Qiaoping 李喬平, *Zhongguo huaxue shi* 中國化學史, 2nd ed. (Taipei: Shangwu, 1955), 200.

123. Duan Yucai 段玉裁, commentator, *Shuowen jiezi zhu* 說文解字注 (Taipei: Yiwen yinshu guan, 1955), 234.

124. Ôsamu Shinoda, *Chûgoku Tabemono shi*, 54.

125. Berthold Laufer, *Chinese Pottery of the Han Dynasty* (Leiden: Brill, 1909), 15–35.

126. Luoyang qu, *Luoyang Shaogou Hanmu*, 206, pl. 62.

127. Duan Yucai, *Shuowen jiezi zhu*, 234.

128. Qi Sihe, "*Mao Shi* gu ming kao," 294–295.

129. Liu Xi, *Shiming* (Shanghai: Shangwu, 1939), 62.

130. Zeng Zhaoyu 曾昭燏, Jiang Baogeng 蔣寶庚, and Li Zhongyi 黎忠義, *Fajue baogao*; Jiayu Guan shi, "Jiayu Guan . . . zhuan mu," 40, fig. 31.

131. Cui Shi, *Simin yueling*, 44–45.

132. Shang Binghe, *Shiwu kao*, 105.

133. *QSW*, 1962–1963.

6. The Seating Order at the Hong Men Banquet

In "Xiang Yu benji" (The Basic Annals of Xiang Yu) in the *Shiji* (Records of the Grand Historian), Sima Qian writes:

> Xiang Yu on the same day asked the Lord of Pei [Liu Bang] to stay and join in feasting. Xiang Yu and Xiang Bo sat facing east. Uncle sat facing south. Uncle was Fan Zeng, whom Xiang Yu treated as if he were a younger brother of his father. The Lord of Pei sat facing north, with Zhang Liang in attendance facing west. Fan Zeng several times eyed Xiang Yu, and thrice lifted the jade girdle that he wore as a signal. But Xiang Yu remained silent and did not respond.

This is the Grand Historian's description of a most exciting and important scene during the Hong Men Banquet (Hong Men Yan 鴻門宴). The "Chen Sheng Xiang Ji zhuan" ("Biography of Xiang Yu"") in the *Hanshu* (History of the Former Han Dynasty) contains nothing about this incident, however, and the "Gao Di benji" ("Basic Annals of Gao Di [Liu Bang]") in recording the Hong Men Banquet, makes no mention of its seating arrangements. As a matter of fact, the Grand Historian's detailed account of the seating order was certainly not a casual one. Concealed between the lines is a message of grave consequences. Scholars before us, in their reading of *Records of the Grand Historian*, have paid attention to some extent to the question of seating. The *Shiki kaichū kôshô* 史記會注考證 of Kametaro Takigawa 瀧川龜太郎 may be cited as a basis for discussion. Under the entry "Fan Zeng as *Ya Fu*" (Xiang Yu's Veritable Paternal Uncle), Takigawa has the following commentary:

Huang Chunyao 黃淳耀 says:

"The ancients esteemed the right side. So ritual regulations regarding the direction of the ancestral temple all provided that it faced south, whereas the occupant of the temple faced east. The etiquette concerning the seating of the host and guests was governed by the same principle."

The "Xiang yinjiu" (Rites of the District Symposium) 鄉飲酒 section in the *Yili* 儀禮 (Book of Etiquette and Ceremonial) states: "When the guests resume their places, they should be in the local school's western apartments facing east."

In the "Huaiyinhou liezhuan" ("Biography of Han Xin"), in the *Records of the Grand Historian* it is stated that the Lord of Guangwu sat on the east side and that Han Xin faced him from the west and treated him like a tutor.

Upon capturing Wang Ling's mother, Xiang Yu incarcerated her in an armed camp. When Wang Ling's emissary arrived, Xiang Yu placed her in a seat facing east in an attempt to beckon Wang Ling to surrender.

Zhou Bo disliked literature. Each time he summoned disputatious scholars to his Grand Marshal's office for mediation, he sat facing east to upbraid them.

The above all indicates that east was the honorable side.

By this token, the order of seating at the Hong Men Banquet was as follows: "First Xiang Yu and Xiang Po, next Fan Zeng, then the Lord of Pei."

Sekitoku Nakai 中井積德 says: "At a court of office where upper seat and lower seat faced each other, the direction facing south was deemed honorable. Otherwise, the direction facing east was deemed honorable; no longer was the south side esteemed."

Although the explanations of Huang and Nakai differ, they both agree that eastward is the esteemed direction. And Mr. Huang's discussion of the order of precedence especially tallies with the actual conditions then existing. From antiquity to the Han dynasty, the sitting mats facing east were deemed honorable. In his essay entitled "Sit Facing East" in *juan* 28 in the *Rizhi lu* 日知錄 (Record of Daily Knowledge), Gu Yanwu 顧炎武 quoted profusely from the classics and histories, and reached a most closely reasoned conclusion. Unfortunately, this essay has not been incorporated into the *Shiki kaichû kôshô*. Two recent scholars, Yang Shuda 楊樹達[1] and Shang Binghe 尚秉和,[2] have also come to the same conclusion. This, then, is a nearly settled question.

However, the "Quli" 曲禮 (Summary of the Rules of Propriety) chapter in the *Liji* (Classic of Rites) asks, and answers: "In giving a feast, how should the guests be seated? . . . When the mats face north and south, the west is the superior side. When the mats face east and west, the south is the superior side." According to this passage, then, there are two different kinds of seating arrangements. It comes closer to Nakai's description, and yet there is a variance.

What deserves attention is that there is a distinction between *fang* 方 (side) and *xiang* 向 (direction). If we say, "when the mats face north and south, the west is the superior side," then that which faces east should be the most honored. But in saying "when the mats face east and west, the south is the superior side," are we to understand that facing north is the most honored? It seems that there is a considerable problem there. So as far as this point is concerned, we must leave the question open. From here on, we had better confine ourselves to discussing the significance of the seating order at the Hong Men Banquet on the basis of historical examples.

In reporting the polite declination of the imperial throne by Emperor (Xiao) Wen (then Prince of Dai), the "Basic Annals of Emperor Xiao Wen" in *Records of the Grand Historian* states, "The Prince of Dai faced west and declined thrice; then (he) faced south and declined twice" (same in the *HS*). Pei Yin's 裴駰 *Jijie* 集解 (Collected Interpretations) on the *Records of the Grand Historian* quotes Ruchun 如淳 as saying:

> [Emperor Wen was] declining the courtiers' urging. Some say: the seats of the guest and the host faced east and west, respectively; the seats of the sovereign and ministers faced south and north, respectively. So the Prince of Dai sat facing west thrice, declining the offer of the throne. However, when all the ministers present still insisted that he was the appropriate choice, then the Prince of Dai shifted his seat to face south, indicating his change of mind and a gradual readiness to ascend the throne.

This is to say that at the very beginning, when receiving the courtiers, Emperor Wen (as Prince of Dai) insisted on the prescribed rite of a host facing west. Later, he changed direction and faced south. Orally, he was still politely declining, but by facing south, he had already hinted at his readiness to accept the offer of the throne. From this example we can best see the ritual occasions that gave the places of honor to the sides that faced east and south. However, Hu Sanxing 胡三省 disagreed with Ruchun's explanation. Under the entry of the eighth year of Empress Gao, in *juan* 13 of the *Zizhi tongjian* 資治通鑑 (Comprehensive Mirror for Aid in Government), Hu's commentary says:

> In my opinion, Ruchun's theory that the Prince of Dai's sitting southward was a sign of his gradual readiness to ascend the throne may not have caught the thought behind his repeated declination. Since the courtiers had arrived soon after the Prince of Dai entered his official residence, he received them as their host. Therefore, he faced west. When the courtiers

urged him to accept the throne, he thrice declined. The courtiers then steered the Prince to a seat directly facing south. Again he thrice declined. And so it was not of his own accord that the Prince faced south; rather, it was the courtiers who steered him in that direction. How impermissible it is to say that the Prince had suddenly shifted his seat to face south!

Hu Sanxing's commentary that the Prince of Dai's southward-facing position was caused by the steering of the courtiers has no clear proof in history, but it is an excellent example of a commentary that is rich in historical imagination. With such an explanation, we can see the scene as if it were before our eyes. Compared with Ruchun's assumption that the Prince of Dai had himself moved to face south and again declined the throne offer, this explanation is much more reasonable. Ruchun may have correctly stated what was on the mind of the Prince of Dai, but Hu Sanxing has accurately portrayed the actions of the sovereign and ministers of the Han Court at the time.

The statement "the seats of the guest and the host face east and west, respectively; the seats of the sovereign and ministers face south and north, respectively," as cited in Ruchun's annotation, can very well be used to explain the order of seating at the Hong Men Banquet. Based on the principle that "the seats of the guest and the host face east and west, respectively," why was it, then, that Xiang Yu contrarily took a seat facing east, since at the Hong Men feast, Liu Bang was the guest and Xiang Yu the host? This was because at that time (206 B.C.E.), the struggle for the mastery of the empire was still undecided and neither Liu Bang nor Xiang Yu had yet proclaimed themselves sovereigns. The meeting at Hong Men was convoked precisely for the purpose of determining to whom the leadership should belong. Unavoidably, Liu Bang risked exceptional hazards to attend the meeting to show his willingness to accept Xiang Yu's leadership and to indicate that he harbored no ulterior motive. On Xiang Yu's part, he had wanted to avail himself of the opportunity to win Liu Bang's fealty. Political considerations with regard to the relative status of the two men made the Hong Men Banquet something more than an ordinary social occasion. In the "Biographies of the Marquis of Wu-an and the Marquis of Weiqi" in *juan* 107 of *Records of the Grand Historian*, there is the following description of how Tian Fen, the Marquis of Wu-an, entertained his guests: "He frequently summoned guests to drink with him. He placed his elder brother, the Prince of Gai, in a seat facing south, and he himself sat facing east. He considered that his dignity as a prime minister of the Han dynasty should not be undermined by personal consideration and by surrendering the seat of honor to his elder brother." Takigawa's *Shiki kaichû kôshô* says: "According to the *History of the Former Han Dynasty*, facing 'south' is recorded as facing 'north.' This is incorrect. The ancients, in seating, considered facing east as the honored direction. So in sacrifices at the ancestral temple, the tablet of the grand ancestor faced east. Even by the etiquette of social intercourse, the guests also faced east, while the host faced west." This concrete example enables us to know for sure that on a feasting occasion, the seat facing in the eastern direction was considered higher than that facing in the southern direction. According to the "Biography of Prince Daohui of Qi" in *juan* 38 of the *History of the Former Han Dynasty*, it is stated: "When Prince Daohui presented himself at Court in the second year of Emperor Hui Di's reign (193 B.C.E.), the sovereign and the Prince of Qi imbibed in the presence of the Empress Dowager. Emperor Hui Di placed his elder brother, the Prince of Qi, in the seat of honor, observing family rules of etiquette." A commentary of Yan Shigu 顏師古 notes: "Brothers rank in their order of seniority. They do not follow the rites governing the sovereign and his ministers. This is why the text refers to it as family [rules of etiquette]." The Prince of Qi was older than Emperor Hui Di,[3] so the latter bade the former to take the seat of honor, which is understood to be the one facing east. Even as emperor, Hui Di observed the order of fraternal seniority, and yet Tian Fen actually dared to pull his ministerial rank and cast aside the family etiquette governing high and low. It can thus be seen that this seating arrangement is given special attention in *Records of the Grand Historian* to underscore the overbearing nature of the Marquis of Wu-an. In recording in detail the seating order at the Hong Men Banquet, Sima Qian had a similar purpose in mind. By occupying the seat of honor facing east without declining, Xiang Yu had behaved exactly like the Marquis of Wu-an. Both employed their higher political stations as the criterion, but Xiang Yu was even more strongly motivated by his desire to excel.

During the Han dynasty when superiors entertained their subordinates, they themselves frequently occupied the seats of honor and did not follow the customary etiquette governing hosts and guests. This point is most clearly manifested on stone carvings. In discussing the murals of feasting at Wu Liang's Shrine and Xiaotang Shan in Western Shandong Province, Lao Gan touches on the question of seating. He says:

> As to the seat of the host, whether it was on the left or right, the direction does not seem to have been fixed. Since the position of the murals at the Wu (Liang) Shrine can no longer be ascertained, there is no way to tell whether it was related in meaning to the dictum that in an east-west direction the west [i.e., facing east] was the superior and that in a north-south direction the south was the superior. What can still be discerned is that at the Wu (Liang) Shrine, the host's seat, generally speaking, was on the left. As to Xiaotang Shan, the host's seat, on the whole, was on the right. Could it be that the murals of Wu (Liang) Shrine show scenes of entertaining friends and thus the host took the lowest seat, whereas those of the Xiaotang Shan are of a different kind?

Since in the Han dynasty there was a distinction between a prefect and his subordinates as that between a prince and his ministers, the prefect's office, in like manner, could be styled a court. . . . Now as the three Wus served, respectively, only as Assistant to the Zhijinwu ("Superintendent of the Capital"), Chief Officer of The Western Regions (Xiyu zhangshi), and a Circuit Secretary (Zhou congshi), they were actually subordinates of others and could not have treated others as their subjects. So there ought not to be any doubt that at the banquet (at the shrine) they should have occupied the hosts' seats. As for Xiaotang Shan, it decidedly was not the site of Guo Zhu's Shrine. According to *Lixu*, it was probably the site of Zhu Fou's Shrine, or perhaps the Zhong family's. If it was Zhu Fou's Shrine, then the description would fit, for Zhu Fou had been a prefect for a long time. If it was the Zhong family's shrine, then although we do not know now the particulars of that family's official career, we may assume that the Zhongs must have been prefects, for only in a prefectural post could the Zhongs assume the honored seat and receive many guests who came to pay tribute.[4]

In 1959, two Han tombs rich with murals were discovered at Dahu Ting, Whipping Tiger Pavilion, in Mi xian, Henan Province. In Tomb No. 1, there was a side room with a mural depicting a banqueting scene on the west wall. It was 1.53 meters long and 1.14 meters high. The host in this mural (who was also the tomb's occupant) also had his seat on the right side, like that found at Xiaotang Shan. Three guests had already been seated on mats. They were seated on both sides of the host (one at a superior position and two in inferior positions). Two other guests were just arriving. In the mural, there are altogether four servants, each attending to his own business. One is pictured greeting guests. Moreover, he is shown indicating to the guests with his hand as to where they should sit. Of course, their seating directions cannot be found, but it can be seen at a glance that the host had placed himself in an honored seat. According to research, the tomb's occupant appears to be Zhang De (styled Boya), the Prefect of Hongnong, mentioned in a note on the Wei Shui (a small river in Henan) in *Shuijing zhu* 水經注 (Commentaries on the Water Classic). Zhang De's precise dates remain to be verified, but, on the basis of the tomb's construction and the subject matter and content of the murals, archeologists have determined that its construction belongs to the late Eastern Han dynasty. Since Zhang De was Prefect, the guests must have been his subordinates.[5] Thus, in the painting, he is pictured occupying the honored seat. This painting, then, adds yet another new and effective piece of evidence for Lao Gan's theory.

The literary and archaeological data cited above are enough to explain that Xiang Yu's eastward-facing seating at the Hong Men Banquet was a conscious act of political significance. He did not treat Liu Bang as a guest of equal stature;

rather, he regarded Liu Bang as his subordinate. There was a basis for Xiang Yu acting in this way. When Liu Bang first joined the uprising, he once came under the banner of Xiang Yu's uncle, Xiang Liang. After Xiang Liang died in action, Xiang Yu naturally inherited his uncle's power of leadership, and furthermore, at the time of the Hong Men Banquet, Xiang Yu had earned the perfectly justifiable title of "The Supreme General to Whom All Feudal Lords Belong."

In the seating arrangements at the Hong Men Banquet, however, the placement of the Lord of Pei in a "seat facing north" deserves further attention. If, according to Ruchun's theory, "the seats of the sovereign and ministers face south and north," then Liu Bang obviously was formally signifying his intention to become subject to Xiang Yu. In the chapter on "The Way of Sovereigns" in *juan* 1 of his *Shuoyuan* 說苑 (Garden of Stories), Liu Xiang records Guo Wei as having told Prince Zhao of Yan:

> "Now if Your Majesty sits facing east and seeks the services of statesmen by giving orders in a haughty manner through expressions of the eyes and countenance and not in words, then what will arrive are men with the aptitude of menials. But if you seek the services of statesmen by holding court when facing south and not neglecting due propriety, then men of the caliber of ordinary ministers will arrive. If Your Majesty faces west and treats others as equals, and greets them mildly and pleasantly, not taking advantage of your authority to seek the services of statesmen, then men of the caliber of friends will arrive. If Your Majesty faces north and seeks the services of statesmen in a respectful and humble manner, then men of the caliber of teachers and advisers will arrive. . . ." Thereupon, the Prince of Yan invited Guo Wei to take a seat of honor facing south for three years.

Although the story itself may not be believable, what it tells about the order of precedence of seating must have been the customary practice during the days of the Warring States and the Qin and Han dynasties (481 B.C.E.–220 C.E.)—of that there can be no question. From this passage, we know for certain that Ruchun's theory that "the seats of the guest and the host face east and west and the seats of the sovereign and ministers face south and north" was a general rule at that time. The reason Liu Bang occupied a north-facing seat and not a west-facing seat was because the north-facing seat was the lowest for a subject, whereas west-facing seats were for friends who treated each other as equals. Although Zhang Liang occupied a west-facing seat, *Records of the Grand Historian* plainly states that he was "in attendance." Thus, Sima Qian's account of the rank, sequence, and precedence of seating is in strict order. Is this why the brush of the Grand Historian has remained unexcelled thus far?

Records of the Grand Historian narrates yet another incident that is similar to the Hong Men Banquet. It is recorded in the "Account of Southern Yue," and the story provides us with a basis for comparison. During the reign of Emperor Wu Di (140–87 B.C.E.) in the Former or Western Han dynasty (202 B.C.E.–8 C.E.), the King of Southern Yue was a minor and the Empress Dowager ruled. Southern Yue's Prime Minister, Lü Jia, was an elder statesman and a popular figure. Wishing to take advantage of the presence and prestige of the Han envoys, the Empress Dowager plotted to murder Lü Jia at a diplomatic banquet. *Records of the Grand Historian* states: "The Han 'envoys all sat facing east, the Empress Dowager sat facing south, the King sat facing north, Lü Jia, the Prime Minister, and other ministers all faced west, attended, and then sat (on mats) drinking.'" (*Note:* HS merely says: "The envoys and ministers were all attended upon and were seated drinking.") The seating arrangements this time also contained a delicate political meaning. Moreover, they fitted in with the nature of the entire banquet. The Empress Dowager strongly favored the pledging of Southern Yue's allegiance to the Han Court. For this reason, she invited the Han envoys (there were more than one) to take the honored seats facing east. She herself was Southern Yue's supreme ruler, so she occupied the next highest seat facing south. The King of Southern Yue sat facing north so as to signify his submission to Han. This also happened to be the way Liu Bang was seated at the Hong Men Banquet. Prime Minister Lü Jia and other ministers then "faced west, attended, [and then] sat drinking." They were in a situation completely identical to that which faced Zhang Liang. *Records of the Grand Historian* continues: "After the wine cups were passed around, the Empress Dowager said to Lü Jia: 'It is to Southern Yue's advantage to submit to Han. But you as Prime Minister have found this painfully inconvenient. Why?' She said this to provoke the Han envoys." It can be seen, therefore, that this banquet was single-handedly arranged by the Empress Dowager. Her idea, then, was to put on an appearance of submission to the Han Court. Hence, as soon as the passing around of wine cups commenced, she readily and directly raised with Lü Jia the question of "internal submission" that was most distressful to him, because Lü Jia was the leader of the group who most resolutely opposed the policy of Southern Yue becoming a vassal state of the Han. Quite obviously, at this banqueting scene where "internal submission" was the main theme and where a blood-thirsty spirit lurked, the order of seating had the effect of deciding the basic atmosphere of the entire occasion.

By comparison with this Southern Yue court banquet, we have further reason to believe that the seating at the Hong Men Banquet was specially arranged to meet the political requirements at that time. In that case, who arranged the seating? Since *Records of the Grand Historian* is silent on this point, we cannot but readily emulate Hu Sanxing and apply a bit of historical imagination. Among the five people seated at the Hong Men Banquet, Liu Bang and Zhang

Liang were guests. As such, they could not have taken the initiative to arrange their own seating. Fan Zeng was invited to keep the visitors company; moreover, he was the one who most vigorously advocated the slaying of the Lord of Pei. So it was also not possible for him to arrange a seat that proved to be so advantageous to Liu Bang. There remained only Xiang Yu and Hsiang Bo. According to reason, Xiang Yu in his capacity as host was the most likely determinant of the order of seating. A previous writer had suspected this point. In his punctuated commentary on the "Biography of Xiang Yu," Wu Jiansi 吳見思 of the early Qing dynasty said the following regarding the passage "Xiang Yu, Hsiang Bo sat facing east": "At the time, the seat facing east was the most honored. This reflected Xiang Yu's arrogance."[6] This places the responsibility for arranging the seating on Xiang Yu himself. Although Xiang Yu was a rough and ready blusterer, after all, he did begin life as a member of the aristocratic class. His style could not have been like that of Liu Bang, who was haughty and impolite. Han Xin had once analyzed Xiang Yu's personality. In the "Biography of the Marquis of Huaiyin" in *juan 92* of *Records of the Grand Historian*, Han Xin said to Liu Bang:

> When meeting people, Xiang Yu was polite and kind. His words were cordial and consoling. When others had serious ailments, he wept silently and shared (with them) his food and drink. When people had performed meritorious services and deserved to be raised to the nobility, he toyed with the seal of investiture with his hands until its corners were rounded off. So his benevolence may be compared to that of a woman.

It is evident, then, that Xiang Yu's greatest fault was that, politically, he was too narrow-minded, but decidedly he was not conceited to the degree of disregarding etiquette. Deducing from Han Xin's observation that "when meeting people, Xiang Yu was polite and kind," there was certainly no reason he should himself have occupied the most honored seat facing east and, simultaneously, placed Liu Bang in the lowest seat facing north. Therefore, viewing the background and the entire course of developments at the Hong Men Banquet, we must recognize that much of the credit for the final seating arrangements should go to Xiang Bo for his intercession and mediation beforehand. And behind Xiang Yu's back, Liu Bang's cunning patience and Zhang Liang's clever strategy probably also produced an important effect. Even if we go so far as to say that Xiang Bo, Liu Bang, and Zhang Liang had had a tacit understanding beforehand about the seating arrangements, such a possibility is within reason. In light of Xiang Yu's straightforward and self-conceited nature, this was an ingenious chess move to dispel his doubt and appease his anger. In the end, Xiang Yu agreed that he himself should "sit facing east" and that Liu Bang should "sit facing north." This showed that Xiang Yu had considered Liu

Bang as his subordinate and had formally accepted Liu Bang's expression of submission. Therefore, when the host and guests were seated, Xiang Yu no longer cherished the idea of killing Liu Bang.

In recounting the seating order at the Hong Men Banquet, *Records of the Grand Historian* follows closely with this passage: "Fan Zeng several times eyed Xiang Yu. He thrice lifted the jade girdle that he wore as a signal. But Xiang Yu remained silent and did not respond." The foregoing discussion of the seating arrangements provides the most plausible explanation of the action described here. Needless to say, Fan Zeng's private signal had been arranged with Xiang Yu beforehand. However, Fan Zeng could not for the life of him have guessed that his murder plot was already foiled so unobtrusively by the other side.

The Hong Men Banquet was one of the most important and, at the same time, most dramatic incidents in Chinese history.[7] Since Liu Bang managed to escape this confrontation unharmed, from then on, he was, so to speak, like a dragon returning to the high seas. Xiang Yu would never again have an opportunity to exterminate him. After a short period of four years (202 B.C.E.), Liu Bang finally gained Xiang Yu's empire. In looking back, we may say that the success and failure of Liu Bang and Xiang Yu was not decided on the battlefield but at the time of the seating at the Hong Men Banquet, where the outcome was determined. Liu Bang said to Xiang Yu, "I would rather engage in a battle of wits; I cannot engage in a test of strength." And Xiang Yu, when he was about to die, declared, "It is Heaven that destroys me; it is not the fault of combat." In so saying, each in his own way had supplied the key to the rise and fall of Han and Chu. However, there was this difference: Liu Bang was smiling when he made his remark, and when he did so, the seating scene at the Hong Men Banquet probably floated through his mind. As for Xiang Yu, his mind remained muddled up to his death. Consequently, he could only lay the blame on Heaven. If not for Sima Qian's absolutely admirable historiographical brush, we ourselves today at the most could only see the "woman's benevolence" that was revealed by Xiang Yu at the Hong Men Banquet; we would have no way of knowing how Liu Bang and Zhang Liang ingeniously capitalized on the limitations of Xiang Yu's aristocratic outlook in politics and actually dealt Xiang Yu a fatal blow even as they were exchanging toasts at the Hong Men Banquet. (Translated by T. C. Tang)

NOTES

1. Yang Shuda, "Qin-Han zuoci zunbei kao" 秦漢座次尊卑考, in *Jiwei ju xiaoxue shulin* 積微居小學述林 (Beijing: Kexue, 1954), 247–249.

2. Shang Binghe, *Lidai shehui fengsu shiwu kao* 歷代社會風俗事務考, 2nd ed. (Taipei: Shangwu, 1967), 283–284.

3. *SJ*, 8, "The Basic Annals of Gaozu," states: "Emperor Gao Di (Gaozu) had eight sons: The eldest, born of a concubine, was Liu Fei, Prince Daohui of Qi. The second was Xiao Hui, who became Emperor Hui Di)."

4. Lao Gan 勞榦, "Lun Luxi huaxiang sanshi—Zhu Wei shishi, Xiaotang Shan, Wushi ci" 論魯西畫像三石—朱鮪石室, 孝堂山, 武氏祠, *Bulletin of the Institute of History and Philology, Academia Sinica* 8, no. 1 (October 1939): 100. Professor Lao is in error quoting this dictum; he obviously did so from memory without checking the original text. See above for the correct wording of the passage from "Quli" 曲禮 in the *Liji*.

5. An Jinhuai 安金槐 and Wang Yugang 王與剛, "Mixian Dahu Ting Handai huaxiang shimu he bihua mu" 密縣打虎亭漢代畫像石墓和壁畫墓, *WW* 10 (1972): 49–62.

6. Wu Jiansi's punctuated and annotated *Shiji lunwen* 史記論文, (Taiwan: Zhonghua, 1967 photo-offset edition), 1:58b. His punctuated annotation on the same page also states:

    Then Hsiang Yu occupied the place of honor, the Lord of Pei as guest was seated to his right, Fan Zeng as an associate guest was seated to his left. At that time, the right side was esteemed. Zhang Liang as attendant faced the superior side. As Liu Bang's attendant, he was also seated. This can be seen by the fact that Fan Kuai, Liu Bang's carriage attendant, was seated next to Zhang Liang. The description of their seating on four sides was as clear and distinct as a picture.

    However, it looks as if Wu Jiansi was not informed on a point of contemporary ritual. He was obviously wrong when he thought that the Lord of Pei, placed to the right, was seated above Fan Zeng. All that is needed to establish this point is to compare it with the description in the "Account of Southern Yue" about "the Empress Dowager facing south and the King facing north." Wu Jiansi's comment about Zhang Liang, "as attendant, he was also seated," and his subsequent reference to Fan Kuai sitting next to Zhang Liang as proof, may also not be entirely correct. Judging from the statement in the "Account of Southern Yue" that "Prime Minister Lü Jia and other ministers all faced west, attended, then sat drinking" as an example, it was possible that they had first stood in attendance and then sat down to drink. Although it is actually not easy to differentiate between "sitting" and "attending," at least there should be a difference in posture. True, "attending" does not necessarily mean "standing." In the section on "The Ritual Governing the Meeting of *Shi*" in the *Yili*, there is an essay on "The Attending and Seating of Gentlemen." The same section further states, "When sitting, (*zuo*) the eyes are trained on the knees." If so, then *zuo* 坐 and *gui* 跪 (kneel) are close to each other and yet slightly different. Could it be that the "attending" 侍 (*shi*) twice referred to in the *Shiji* was quite close to "kneeling" (*gui*)? This awaits further investigation. Regarding the difference between *zuo* and *gui*, see in detail the essay "On *Gui* (Kneeling), *Zuo* (Sitting), and *Bai* (Saluting)," in Zhu Xi 朱熹, *Zhu Wengong wenji* 朱文公文集, *juan* 68.

7. In 1957, a batch of Western Han murals was discovered at Luoyang (Henan Province). Guo Moruo decided that one of them depicted the Hung Men Banquet. See Guo Moruo, "Luoyang Hanmu bihua shitan" 洛陽漢墓壁畫試探, *KG* 2 (1964). For an illustration, see "A Report on the Excavation of the Murals in Western Han Tombs at Luoyang" in

the same issue, 107–125, and plate 2 in the section on illustrations. In my judgment, although the mural resembles a banquet in a military camp, many difficulties will be encountered if one is to point directly at it and assert that it is a representation of the Hong Men Banquet. I have briefly touched on this in my chapter on "Han China" in *Food in Chinese Culture*, so I shall not repeat that information here. See K. C. Chang, ed., *Food in Chinese Culture: Anthropological and Historical Perspectives* (New Haven: Yale University Press, 1977), chap. 2, "Han China."

7. Individualism and the Neo-Daoist Movement in Wei-Jin China

Both "individualism" and "holism" are Western concepts whose introduction into Chinese intellectual discourse is a matter of only recent historical development.[1] This does not mean, however, that as categories of analysis these two concepts are totally inapplicable to the study of early Chinese thought. As a matter of fact, we find in the long history of Chinese political and social thought a wide range of views that can be legitimately characterized as either holistic or individualistic. In this study, the Neo-Daoist movement since the end of the Han dynasty will be explored as an example of one type of Chinese individualism.

CRISIS IN SOCIAL RELATIONSHIPS AT THE END OF THE HAN

Throughout the Han Period (202 B.C.E.–8 C.E. and 25–220 C.E.), the central issue in Chinese political and social thinking was the problem of collective life at various levels. The problem of the individual, which had figured prominently in classical thought in pre-Qin times, ceased to be a matter of major concern to the Han-dynasty Chinese theorists. As a result, the best-known Chinese theory of social relationships—the so-called three bonds and six rules (*sangang liuji* 三綱六紀)—reached its definitive formulation during this period. The "three bonds" refers to the relationships between ruler and subject, father and son, and husband and wife, whereas the "six rules" pertain to those between paternal uncles, elder and younger brothers, other relatives of the same surname, maternal uncles, teachers, and friends. What is meant by these "bonds" and "rules"? The *Bohu tongde lun* 白虎通德論 (White Tiger Hall Discussions) provides the following answer: "A bond gives orderliness; a rule regulates. What is greater is the bond; what is smaller is the rule. They serve to order and regulate (the relations between) superiors and inferiors, and to arrange and adjust the way of mankind."[2] As the quotation makes apparent, the theory is exclusively concerned with the establishment of order in all social groups, from family to state. Though unmistakably Legalist in origin, the idea of the "three bonds" was nevertheless fully incorporated into Han Confucian ideology.[3] Under Legalist influence, Han Confucianism also systematically developed the *li* 禮 (rites; rituals) in a way similar to the development of the Legalist *fa* 法 (laws). Whatever the differences may have been between the *li* and the law, there can be little doubt that during the Han Period they both functioned, each in its own way, as external constraints on the individual. *Li* and law later became so closely associated that by 94 C.E., the Han Commandant of Justice could even characterize the two as "the outside and the inside of the same thing."[4]

If we take the Han Period to be essentially an age of collectivism, then the end of the Han dynasty witnessed the rise of individualism. As a matter of fact, the period from the end of the second century to the early decades of the fourth century was the only epoch in Chinese history in which individualism flourished, not only in the realm of thought but also in the world of action. To understand this important historical development, we must begin our account with the profound social and intellectual crisis that began at the end of the Han dynasty.

The crisis took place primarily in the realm of social relationships in some radical circles of the elite class and may best be described as dissolution of the "three bonds." Let us first examine the ruler–subject relationship. By the second half of the second century C.E., there were indications that the idea of universal kingship was under fire. In 164 when Emperor Huan 桓帝 of Han made an imperial visit to Yunmeng (in modern Hubei), he attracted a large crowd from the neighborhood. There was, however, one old man from Hanyin who continued to work in the field as if nothing was happening. Surprised, a member of the imperial entourage asked the old man why he alone showed no interest in looking at the emperor. The old man said:

> May I ask: What is our purpose in establishing the Son of Heaven? To bring order to the world? Or to bring chaos to it? Do we establish the Son of Heaven with the hope that he would treat us with paternal love? Or must we enslave the whole world in order to provide the needs of the Son of Heaven? Formerly, the sage-kings, in governing the world, had only thatched huts for shelter. Nevertheless, the people lived in peace. Now,

look at your ruler. He forces the people to work hard so that he can live in self-indulgence and enjoy leisurely trips without limit. I am ashamed for you. Yet you have the nerve to ask me to look up to him with reverence.[5]

This passage immediately raises the question of the legitimacy of universal kingship. Here the authority to rule is based not on the idea of the "Mandate of Heaven," but on the Daoist theory of the state of nature. Thus, when a ruler fails to fulfill the obligations of his part, he has violated the contract and disqualified himself from the throne. The view of the old man from Hanyin, therefore, not only alludes to the disintegration of political order but also anticipates the type of anarchism that was to dominate Chinese political thinking in the next two centuries, as exemplified particularly by the ideas of Ruan Ji 阮籍 (210–263) and Bao Jingyan 鮑敬言 (fourth century C.E.).

In his famous "Daren xiansheng sheng zhuan" (Biography of the great man), Ruan Ji says:

> For there were no rulers and everything was in order; there were no officials and every matter went well. . . . Once rulers were instituted, oppressions arose; once officials were appointed, robbery began. Detached and apart, they instituted the rites and the laws by which to impose the bonds on the common people. . . . The utmost of Heaven, Earth, and the myriad things are exhausted in order to supply their insatiable sensual desires.[6]

There can be little doubt that this anarchist declaration was a culmination of the line of thinking implicit in the words of the old man from Hanyin.[7] Later, Bao Jingyan further developed the anarchist theme by undermining the traditional theoretical foundations of political order. He was the first thinker to openly challenge the myth of the Mandate of Heaven. Political order was not imposed on man by Heaven. Rather, it arose from the simple fact that "the strong suppressed the weak until the weak submitted to them; the clever outsmarted the stupid until the stupid served them." Following the ideas of early Daoists, especially Zhuangzi 莊子, he described the joys of the state of nature as follows: "In remote antiquity, rulers and subjects did not exist. Wells were dug for drinking, and fields tilled for food. At sunrise, the people went out to work; at sunset, they came home to rest. Movement was free and without restriction, and desires did not go unfulfilled. Competition and planning were unknown, as were honor and disgrace."[8] Here Bao Jingyan clearly placed freedom of the individual above social order.

From the second century to the fourth, it may be noted, this type of anarchistic thought gained currency in China. In the *Liezi*, there is a Utopian country called "Utmost North," where "old and young live as equals and no one is ruler or subject."[9] The most celebrated Utopia in Chinese literature, Tao Qian's 陶潛 (372–427) Peach-Blossom Spring, is also a community characterized by the absence of the ruler–subject relationship, as was rightly observed by Wang Anshi 王安石 (1021–1086) long ago.[10] It was on account of this authority crisis that conservatives such as Guo Xiang 郭象 (d. 312 C.E.), Ge Hong 葛洪 (253?–333?), and Yuan Hong 袁宏 (328–376) found it necessary to come to the defense of political order. In their view, a community without a ruler would inevitably end in either chaos or disintegration.[11] The fact of the defense itself testifies to the great popularity, and hence the great danger, of anarchist ideas during this period.[12]

On the other hand, universal kingship was experiencing a crisis not only as an idea but also as an institution. The reference to the Han emperor as "your ruler" by the old man from Hanyin suggests that in his view, no ruler–subject relationship ever existed between the emperor and himself. That such a view gained considerable currency in China at the end of the Han should occasion no surprise, for by the second century C.E., the ruler–subject bond had acquired, in actual practice, a particularized, personal character. To illustrate this point, let me proffer one interesting example. In 199 C.E., Liu Biao 劉表, the overlord of Jingzhou, decided to send a local assistant named Han Song 韓嵩 to the imperial court as his personal envoy, but Han said to Liu:

> When one commits oneself to a ruler–subject relationship, one is bound by it till death. Since I have pledged my allegiance to you, I place myself completely in your service even at the risk of my life. . . . Now Your Excellency sends me to the capital. Should it so happen that the Emperor offers me a position which I cannot decline, then I would become His Majesty's subject and Your Excellency's former subordinate. As a man owes his primary loyalty to the ruler he is currently serving, I am afraid that my duty would then require me to obey His Majesty's orders. Therefore, I would no longer be able to devote my life to Your Excellency.[13]

Han Song's words show clearly that by the end of the Han, a man did not take the emperor as his ruler until he actually accepted the latter's official appointment. Thus, the ruler–subject relationship in second-century China, like the feudal lord–serf bond in medieval Germanic culture, became essentially personal in nature.[14] At any given time, a man had only one particular ruler to serve, and it made no difference whether the ruler was an emperor or a local lord. This new development is further illustrated by the following, widely circulated saying of the time: "When a family has served a lord for two generations, they regard him as their master (*zhu* 主), and for three generations, they regard him as their ruler (*jun* 君)."[15] All of these examples point to the conclusion that the emperor had ceased to be perceived as a universal king.

An equally profound crisis was also taking place in familial relationships. First of all, the idea of *xiao* 孝, or filial piety, being interpreted in purely biological terms was seriously questioned by late Han scholars. Taking up an argument first formulated by the critical thinker Wang Chong 王充 (27–ca. 100 C.E.), Kong Rong 孔融 (153–208 C.E.), a descendant of Confucius, reportedly made the following startling remarks about the parent–child relationship: "Why should there exist a special kind of affinity between father and son? Originally, the father merely intended to satisfy his desire. What exactly is the relationship between mother and son? A son in his mother's womb is no different from a thing in a bottle. Once the thing comes out of the bottle, the two become separate and are no longer related."[16] Later, when Ruan Ji was told that a man had murdered his mother, he immediately remarked, "It is conceivable that someone would kill his father, but this man has indeed gone too far by killing his mother!"[17] Such radical ideas may well have reflected, to a considerable extent, a real crisis in the father–son relationship. At any rate, it had become proverbial by the end of the Han that "those who have been recommended to office on the merit of filial piety often turn out to live separately from their fathers."[18]

There were signs that the husband–wife relationship was also undergoing a fundamental change during the Wei-Jin Period. To begin with, it is important to point out that like the idea of filial piety, the traditional view that *de* 德, or virtue, was the most essential quality in women also became subject to dispute. Xun Can 荀粲, who lived in the first quarter of the third century, startled his contemporaries with the unorthodox view that "a woman's virtue is not worth praising; her beauty should be considered the most important thing."[19] As a matter of fact, elite women during this period generally disregarded the Confucian rules of propriety. Instead of devoting themselves exclusively to household work, they now became actively involved in society. For instance, in about 194, when Xiahou Dun 夏侯惇, governor of Chenliu, gave an official banquet in honor of his newly appointed subordinate, Wei Zhen 衛臻, the invitation also included Wei's wife. Wei, however, being a conservative, criticized the practice as "the custom of an age of decadence that does not agree with the established ritual (*li* 禮)."[20] This "custom" persisted and spread over the next two centuries, however. Writing in the early years of the fourth century, Ge Hong complained that women of his day no longer attended to their household duties. Instead, they were busy taking part in all kinds of social gatherings, especially informal, mixed parties at which they enjoyed conversation, drinking, and music in the company of men. Moreover, it even became fashionable among friends to greet the host's wife in the inner chamber (*ru shi shi qi* 入室視妻).[21] The new lifestyle of elite women of the period is best described in the official history of the Jin dynasty:

> With their makeup and hair-dress and fine clothing, they depend entirely on maids and servants to do for them; they know nothing of women's work in the tasks of silk and linen making, nor of the household work of preparing foods and wines. They marry prematurely; they act just as they

feel. Consequently, they admit no shame for licentious transgressions, and have no compunctions about displaying the fault of jealousy. Their fathers and older brothers do not reproach them, nor does the world condemn them.[22]

THE DISCOVERY OF THE INDIVIDUAL

The foregoing discussion of the political and social crisis provides us with the historical background against which the rise of individualism during the Wei-Jin Period may be evaluated. In his well-known study of the development of the individual in Renaissance Italy, Jacob Burckhardt points out that in the Middle Ages, "man was conscious of himself only as a member of race, people, party, family, or corporation—only through some general category." It was in Renaissance Italy that man first "became a spiritual *individual*, and recognized himself as such."[23] Almost the same can be said of the spiritual transition from Han collectivism to Wei-Jin individualism, for the breakdown of Confucian ritualism at the end of the Han was also closely linked to the self-discovery of the individual.

In the first place, it is significant to note that the classical Daoist idea about the importance of individual life was rediscovered in the second century. The great Confucian scholar Ma Rong 馬融 (79–166), in a critical and decisive moment of his life, said to a friend with a sigh: "The individual life of man is indeed more cherishable than the entire world. It is not in accord with the teaching of Laozi 老子 and Zhuangzi to risk my priceless life on account of a negligible moral point."[24] It was no accident that he became one of the earliest commentators of the *Laozi* and the *Huainanzi*, thus anticipating Wang Bi 王弼 (226–249) by a century.

The search for the authentic self gradually led to the emergence of a type of personality that, to borrow Burckhardt's phrase, neither knew "of false modesty or of hypocrisy," nor was afraid of singularity, of being unlike others. For instance, Dai Liang 戴良 (late second century) was once asked by a friend: "Who in the contemporary world, in your own view, would be your peer?" Dai replied: "I compare myself to Confucius from Eastern Lu and the Great Yu from Western Qiang. I stand alone in the world, and none is qualified to be my peer."[25] Mi Heng 禰衡 praised Kong Rong as "Confucius not dead" and Kong Rong returned the compliment by calling Mi Heng "Yan Hui 顏回 back to life." Neither felt the need to feign modesty.[26] By the end of the Han dynasty, singularity (*yi* 異) had become a positive value. A personality would be favorably judged precisely because it was singular, different, extraordinary.[27] On the other hand, the idea of identity, or sameness (*tong* 同), was held in contempt in a famous essay titled "Bian he tong lun" 辯和同論 (Harmony and Identity). Liu Liang 劉梁 (d. ca. 180) even formulated a radical thesis saying, "all faults arise from identity."[28]

During this period, the development of the art of characterology also attests to the growth of individualism. "Characterology" refers to the technique of analyzing, evaluating, and judging the character and ability of an individual—a practice that had originated in the Han local recommendation system. The judgment thus passed on a person by his own community served as a basis for deciding whether he would qualify for recommendation to office. One basic assumption of this type of characterology was that personal character and ability differ from individual to individual. By the late second century, the art of characterology had acquired, so to speak, a separate life of its own, though it continued to serve the purpose of the recommendation system during the Wei-Jin Period. At the end of the Han, there appeared a number of characterologists whose profound insight and sound judgment made them legends in their own time. Among them were Guo Tai 郭泰 (better known as Lingzong 林宗, 128–169) and Xu Shao 許劭 (ca. 153–198), who distinguished themselves by characterizations that were always terse and to the point. It is particularly important to point out that while making characterizations, their approach was not only physiognomical but psychological as well, with the purpose of capturing the spirit (shen 神) of the individual.

This point is fully borne out in Liu Shao's 劉劭 (early third century) Renwu zhi 人物志 (Treatise on Personalities), the only characterological work that has survived from this period. Liu's treatise begins with an analysis of man's feelings (qing 情) and his nature (xing 性), which are, in his view, the basis of personality. With regard to physiognomical observations, the emphasis is placed on going beyond the physical appearance of a person to reach his spirit. To do this, the entire observational process must end in the study of the eyes, which alone convey the spirit of a person. In Liu Shao's own words: "Every person has a body; every body possesses a spirit. Our study of a person will be exhaustive only when we are able to understand his spirit."[29] Needless to say, characterology must have contributed immensely to the growth of self-awareness of the individual during and after the last decades of Han China.

Closely related to the art of characterology was the development of portraiture, another unmistakable sign of the rise of individualism. The discovery of the individual in the West since the later Middle Ages is evidenced by the emergence of a new type of portraiture that depicted "a concrete image and a human personality in all its individuality."[30] A similar change also took place in Wei-Jin China. Figure painting, to be sure, was no invention of this period; it existed long before the Han dynasty. However, judging from the Han products brought to light by modern archaeology, these are, by and large, portraits of worthies that were intended to be morally inspiring. As the poet Cao Zhi 曹植 (192–232) put it: "When one sees pictures of the Three Kings and Five Emperors, one cannot help assuming an attitude of respect and veneration. . . . By this we realize that painting serves as a moral guide."[31] This didactic tradition in portraiture, it must be emphasized, did not totally disappear with the end of the Han. Nevertheless, a new, individualistic type of figure painting clearly made its debut during the Wei-Jin transition. Under the influence of characterology, the artist set out to capture the spiritual individuality of the human person. How to "convey the spirit" (chuanshen 傳神) became the central problem of portraiture, and the artistic representation of the eyes was once again at the heart of this endeavor. The famous story about Gu Kaizhi 顧愷之, the great fourth-century master of portraiture, will serve to illustrate this point: "Gu Kaizhi would paint a portrait and sometimes not dot the pupils of the eyes for several years. When someone asked his reason, Gu replied: 'The beauty or ugliness of the four limbs basically bears no relation to the most subtle part of a painting. What conveys the spirit and portrays the likeness lies precisely in these dots.' "[32] Thus, in representing a human personality in all its individuality, the Wei-Jin artist chose to focus on the spiritual uniqueness rather than on the physical likeness of his subject.[33] In the West, individual self-discovery was often accompanied by a proliferation of personal verse, especially lyric poetry, through which the emotions of the individual sought expression. Historical examples of this correlation may be found in early Greece and the later Middle Ages, as well as in Renaissance Italy.[34] Interestingly enough, the time of the Han-Wei transition also witnessed the emergence of poetic individuality in China. This was the age in which Chinese poets were mainly concerned with expressing their personal feelings in the face of life's joys and sorrows. For example, the "Gushi shijiu shou" 古詩十九首 (Nineteen Old Poems), generally considered products of the Latter Han Period, show in a highly personal way their authors' inner experiences with the fleetingness of life, the sadness of parting, the emptiness of fame, etc.[35] Starting in the jian-an period (196–219) with the appearance of Cao Cao 曹操 and his two sons Cao Pi 曹丕 and Cao Zhi on the historical scene, a new chapter in Chinese literature was clearly inaugurated. Han rhyme-prose (fu 賦), which was predominantly political in character, lost much of its original vitality and importance. Pentameter verse of a personal and lyrical variety, in the tradition of the "Nineteen Old Poems," now became the main vehicle of literary art,[36] owing to a large extent to the influence of the new poetry of the three Caos. Even Cao Cao in his poetic moments was not totally free from a smack of pessimism and individualism.[37] However, perhaps it is in Ruan Ji's eighty-two "Yonghuai shi" 詠懷詩 (Poems of My Heart) that we meet Chinese lyric in its full maturity. Striving to express thoughts and sentiments from the innermost reaches of his heart, he was not only personal but also, at times, autobiographical.[38] This was also true of many other poets of his time. Xi Kang's 嵇康 "Youfen" 幽憤(Dark Indignations) and "Shuzhi" 述志 (Stating My Aspirations), as well as several of his poems to friends, are all classic examples. Both self-discovery and self-revelation figured centrally in Wei-Jin individualism.

Before moving on to the realm of philosophical thought, I wish to examine briefly some of the new expressions in interpersonal relations. A digression in this direction is valuable because, as modern studies have amply shown, the Wei-Jin Period is characterized in particular by the interesting fact that ideas and social realities were closely interlocked.[39]

Side by side with the breakdown of the Confucian social order during the last years of the Han, a new type of personal relationship began to take shape. According to Ge Hong's observation, personal relationships toward the end of the Han were characterized by "closeness" (qinmi 親密) or "intimacy" (qinzhi 親至). In a gathering of friends, Ge Hong tells us: "People no longer bother to exchange greetings when they see each other. A guest may come to the house and hail the servants; a host may look at the guest while calling the dog. If someone does not act in the same way, he would be considered as having failed to establish intimacy with others. As a result, he would be rejected by his own circle."[40] Close personal relationships also developed in literary circles. Warm feelings among friends were generally expressed through two vehicles: the verse and the letter. The letter as a means of sharing one's innermost thoughts and emotions was practically unknown in ancient times. As far as can evidentially be determined, the purely personal type of letter first appeared in the *jian-an* period. Particularly representative, according to Professor Qian Mu 錢穆 (1895– 1990), are some of the letters of Cao Pi and Cao Zhi.[41] Since the letter provided the individual with an important emotional outlet, both receiving a letter from and writing one to a personal friend were a major source of joy. Thus, in his "Da Fan Qin shu" 答繁欽書 (Letter in Reply to Fan Qin), Cao Pi says, "it gives me so much delight and laughter reading your letter that I can hardly control myself."[42] Cao Zhi's letter to his best friend, Ding Yi 丁廙 (whose courtesy name is Jingli 敬禮), articulates a similar sentiment: "As I am writing this letter to you in a great mood, I hold my brush with delight. Expressing words from my heart amidst laughter is indeed the extreme of joy."[43]

Personal correspondence brought two friends close by making them completely open with each other. It contrasts sharply with the type of correspondence we find in the earlier periods, which is almost invariably formal, impersonal, and business oriented. Exactly the same thing can be said of the exchange of poems between friends. Moreover, it is significant to note that according to the *Wenxuan* 文選 (Anthology of Literature; *juan* 24–26), poetic exchange (*zengda* 贈答) was a completely new device in Chinese culture, first introduced in the *jian-an* era. It was therefore another form in which individual self-awareness manifested itself.

The same sort of intimacy also characterized familial relationships. The following story from the *Shishuo xinyu* 世說新語 (New Account of Tales of the World) is a vivid expression of the emergence of a new type of husband–wife relationship:

Wang Rong's 王戎 (234–305) wife always addressed Rong with the familiar pronoun "you" (*qing* 卿). Rong said to her, "For a wife to address her husband as 'you' is disrespectful according to the rules of etiquette. Hereafter don't call me that again." His wife replied: "But I'm intimate with you and I love you, so I address you as 'you.' If I didn't address you as 'you,' who else would address you as 'you'?" After that he always tolerated it.[44]

For the English reader, it is perhaps necessary to point out that every "you" in this translated passage is *qing* 卿 in the original Chinese text. It may further be noted that usage of the word *qing* as an intimate pronoun was common only during the Wei-Jin Period of Chinese history.[45]

Another family bond, the father–son relationship, also took a decidedly new turn at this time. Humu Fuzhi 胡母輔之 (ca. 264–ca. 312), a second-generation leader of Neo-Daoist conversationalists, was particularly noted for his excessive love of "freedom" (*da* 達). In this respect, however, he was surpassed by his son, Qianzhi 謙之, who even went so far as to call him by his first name. While this practice shocked many contemporaries, the father himself took the matter in stride.[46]

The two examples cited above must not be taken as isolated and exceptional cases. On the contrary, they clearly indicate that a profound change in interpersonal relations had taken place in some quarters of elite society during this period. Toward the end of the third century, Shu Xi 束皙, in a remarkable piece of literary imagination, revealed vividly his unique vision of paradise on Earth. It is surprising to note that he described his Utopia as a place where "all the wives address their husbands as 'you' (*qing* 卿); all the sons call their fathers by first names."[47] This is proof that intimacy as a guiding principle in family life was becoming widespread. Although intimacy may not have been a condition of the development of individualism in the West, in the case of Wei-Jin China, it clearly helped to set the individual free from the various collectivist bonds that had evolved through the centuries of the Han dynasty.

THE TRANSITION FROM CONFUCIANISM TO NEO-DAOISM

Having traced the emergence of individualistic expression in interpersonal relations of the period, we must now proceed to examine the problem of individualism in the realm of thought. In this section, I shall aim to show that apart from the generally accepted political interpretation, the transition from Confucianism to Neo-Daoism in the Wei-Jin Period may be more sensibly viewed as an outgrowth of the discovery of the individual. Moreover, the evidence indicates that the type of philosophic discourse that was to dominate the Neo-Daoist movement from the middle of the third century on had already begun well before the end of the Han.

As is generally acknowledged, Chinese philosophical thought in the third century underwent a radical transformation. Traditionally, this transformation has been characterized as a transition from Confucian classical scholarship (*jingxue* 經學) to Neo-Daoist metaphysics (*xuanxue* 玄學). This is undoubtedly an accurate description. The question we must ask, however, is whether this philosophical shift was linked to the rise of individualism and, if so, in what sense and to what extent? The commonly accepted view with regard to the transition has focused predominantly on political events. According to this view, repeated persecutions of critical and dissident intellectuals by the eunuchs of the imperial court following the two great *danggu* 黨錮 purges, in 166 and 169 gradually transformed the former from political activists to intellectual escapists. After the end of the Han, such persecution intensified under the repressive Legalist politics of the (Cao) Wei 曹魏 dynasty. For many members of the elite, survival demanded a turn away from their Confucian commitments to social and political order; refuge was found in the metaphysical speculation of Laozi and Zhuangzi, which had no immediate bearing on the worldly affairs of their time. As a result, the political discourse of "Pure Criticism" (*qingyi* 清議) in the second century gave way to the philosophical discourse of "Pure Conversation" (*qingtan* 清談) in the third. The intellectual transition from Confucian classical scholarship to Neo-Daoist metaphysics was thereby realized.[48]

While much of this well-established view is indeed accurate, it nevertheless fails to take sufficient account of the positive contributions of the Han-Wei intellectuals to the rise and growth of the movement. It is not entirely true that the intellectuals of the period were coerced into Neo-Daoism by political circumstances; many actually chose to develop this new mode of discourse as a natural outgrowth of their recent self-discovery as individuals. This contention is supported not only by the fact that "conversation" evolved as a way of life for the Han-Wei intellectuals but also by the central philosophic issues that were to be crystallized later in Neo-Daoism (see below).

To begin with, it may be pointed out that the historical relationship between Pure Criticism and Pure Conversation in the traditional view appears to have been somewhat misrepresented. Like the verse and the letter, conversation acquired new importance in the middle of the second century as a medium through which ideas were exchanged between intellectuals. It was not the case, as has often been assumed, that conversation at this time focused only on political and characterological criticisms and then, as a result of the persecution of its practitioners, shifted to philosophical discussion in the third century. On the contrary, the evidence clearly indicates that both elements were already present in late Han conversations. As Wang Fu 王符 (90?–165?) complained, "Scholars nowadays like to talk about matters concerning vacuity and nonbeing (*xuwu* 虛無)."[49] Hence, by the middle of the second century at the latest, it had already become an established practice for intellectuals to discuss Daoist philosophical topics in their daily conversations. In 159 C.E., Zhou Xie 周勰, who had from youth admired Laozi's teachings of "mystery and vacuity" (*xuanxu* 玄虛), earned a great reputation for his generous hospitality. He always invited friends to his home and enjoyed conversations and other entertainments with them.[50] This early case clearly shows how reorientation in thought (i.e., the shift from Confucian learning to Daoist philosophy) and conversation as an art had combined to form an important part of the elite's new lifestyle.

The phenomenal growth of the student body in the Imperial Academy (Taixue 太學) in the middle of the second century also contributed to the rise of this new mode of intellectual discourse. After 146 C.E., as the *Hou Hanshu* (History of the Later Han Dynasty) succinctly summarizes it: "Students in the Academy steadily increased to over thirty thousand. However, they gradually turned away from textual analysis (*zhangju* 章句, lit., 'sentences') of the Classics and came to venerate what was frivolous and ornate (*fouhua* 浮華); the Confucian mode of learning was thus on the wane."[51] It is probably inappropriate to identify the "frivolous and ornate" type of intellectual pursuit with "pure conversation," which was to be referred to pejoratively as "frivolous and vacuous" (*fouxu* 浮虛) in the third century. Nevertheless, there are sure indications that it may well have been a prototype of the latter. For instance, when Fu Rong 符融 came to study at the Imperial Academy in 168, his intellectual brilliance immediately drew the attention of Li Ying 李膺, a leader among the officials. Each time Fu Rong came to call, Li Ying listened to his talk with such intense interest that he sent other guests away in order to avoid distractions. The conversation between Li and Fu always ended with the former holding the latter's hands and sighing with admiration. It is particularly significant that Fu Rong's style of conversation is vividly depicted as follows: "Wearing a kerchief and swinging his sleeves, his words gushed forth like clouds."[52] As is immediately apparent, this is a typical description of Pure Conversation as we encounter it in later literature, except that from the late third century on, the "fly whisk" or "sambar-tail chowry" (*zhuwei* 麈尾) was to replace the "sleeves" as an inseparable accoutrement of the conversationalist.[53] Fu Rong's conversation was extremely influential in the Imperial Academy. His dormitory room was always swarming with visitors. Very much annoyed, a neighbor once chided him thus: "Is it the intention of the Son of Heaven to found this Imperial Academy just for people to engage in conversations?"[54] It is difficult to imagine that all these spirited conversations were devoted exclusively to discussions on politics and personalities (*qingyi* 清議) and had nothing to do with the fermentation of new thought (*qingtan* 清談) that was under way at the time.

In fact, philosophic reasoning was part and parcel of late Han conversation. The case of a young poet named Li Yan 酈炎 (150–177) may be taken as an illustration. He is described as a person who was, among other things, sharp in language and skilled in enunciating principles (*li* 理).[55] Here the association of speech with enunciation of principles is particularly noteworthy. As far as we know, this small but solid piece of evidence provides the earliest historical link between the art of conversation and the emergence of a new mode of thinking in late Han times. It antedates by a century the kind of analysis of "names and principles" (*mingli* 名理) that was central to the Wei-Jin pure conversation.[56]

Historically, the relationship between the art of speech and philosophic reasoning was a symbiotic one; both owed their development to the practice of late Han characterology. According to Liu Shao, two important ways of evaluating the native intelligence of an individual are to "observe his speech" and "examine his argument." "Speech" reveals the quality of a man's training in language and "argument" that of his reasoning power.[57] Moreover, Liu Shao also relates both speech and reasoning to analysis of "principles" (*li*). He distinguishes four categories of "principles": cosmological principles (*daoli* 道理), principles of social institutions (*shili* 事理), moral principles (*yili* 義理), and principles of human feelings (*qingli* 情理). In his view, the main obstacle to a reasonable settlement in intellectual discussions often arises from the confusion of categories of principles on the part of the discussants. Once this obstacle is removed, however, it is possible to determine which side is truly convincing on the linguistic level (*cisheng* 辭勝) as well as on the philosophical level (*lisheng* 理勝).[58]

Since Liu Shao's work is generally thought of as a synthesis of the characterological principles that evolved from the middle of the second century, the influence of Liu's discussions in the *Treatise on Personalities* on the origins of the Pure Conversation movement must be taken seriously. They show clearly how late Han conversation had in practice been pushed, step by step, into the realm of thought by its own inner logic. It is important to point out that Wei-Jin Pure Conversationalists basically discussed philosophical topics in terms of Liu Shao's categories of "principles." Moreover, the two terms *cisheng* (lit., "superior in linguistic skill") and *lisheng* (lit., "superior in philosophical reasoning") are also highly illuminating. They indicate unmistakably that a major technical feature of later Pure Conversation had already been developed in late Han intellectual discussions, namely, a "reasonable settlement" had to be reached in a conversation so as to decide which of the participants was "superior" in language and reasoning. Actually, from the fourth century on, Pure Conversation became a standard intellectual game (like *weiqi* 圍棋, Chinese chess) played by two or more participants. More often than not, someone would in the end emerge triumphant—either linguistically or logically or both. The transition from Confucian classical learning to Daoist metaphysics may well have been precipitated by political events, but a purely political interpretation of an intellectual movement of this magnitude can hardly stand up to close scrutiny.

By the last two decades of the second century, it was becoming quite clear that Han conversationalists were already intensely absorbed in philosophical discussions. The sudden surge of interest in Wang Chong's *Lunheng* 論衡 (Balanced Inquiries) attests to this profound change of intellectual atmosphere.

Balanced Inquiries owed its great popularity during this period primarily to the efforts of two leading scholars. The first one is Cai Yong 蔡邕 (132–192), who discovered the work sometime between 179 and 189 while residing in Guiji (in modern Zhejiang), the hometown of Wang Chong. Cai so cherished the work that he always kept it to himself as an "aid to conversation" (*tanzhu* 談助). The second one is Wang Lang 王朗 (d. 228), who obtained a copy of *Balanced Inquiries* when he was serving as prefect of Guiji from 193 to 196. After his return to the north, as the story goes, his marked improvement in intellectual powers took all his old friends by surprise. When they pressed him for an explanation, he confessed that he had been greatly benefited by *Balanced Inquiries.*[59]

The accuracy of these perhaps somewhat dramatized accounts is corroborated by other evidence. Earlier in this study, we quoted a startling statement by Kong Rong questioning the Confucian idea of filial piety—a statement based entirely on Wang Chong's argument. In view of the intimate friendship between Kong Rong and Cai Yong, it is almost certain that the former must have owed his discovery of *Balanced Inquiries* to the latter.[60] Wang Lang's discovery of the same work also contributed indirectly to the rise of Pure Conversation of Wang Bi and He Yan 何晏. Wang Lang's son Wang Su 王肅 (d. 256), a leading classical scholar of the period, played a crucial role in turning the study of the *Yijing* 易經 (Classic of Changes) in a new direction. He brought a newly developed cosmological framework to bear on the interpretation of that unique Confucian classic (which was destined to form, along with the *Laozi* and the *Zhuangzi*, the "three metaphysical works" [*sanxuan* 三玄] of the Wei-Jin era). Wang Su's interpretation was largely followed by Wang Bi in the latter's commentary to the *Classic of Changes.*[61] Thus, it is clear that Wang Chong's merciless dissection of Confucian values, his pointed rejection of the teleological view of the cosmos, and above all, his emphasis on the Daoist idea of "naturalness" (*ziran* 自然) were already dominant themes of late Han intellectual discourse. Through conversationalists such as Cai Yong, Kong Rong, and Wang Lang, *Balanced Inquiries* exerted a shaping influence on the philosophical development of Pure Conversation. The simple fact that Cai Yong used *Balanced Inquiries* as an "aid to conversation" proves that conversations among intellectuals had assumed a philosophic tone even before the end of the second century.[62]

This active and enduring interest in the exploration of the world of ideas suggests that there was indeed something profound in the consciousness of the conversationalists that sustained it. From the point of view of this study, I am inclined to think that this striking historical phenomenon can be most sensibly explained in terms of the rising individualism of the period. Through the process of self-discovery, the spiritually liberated individual embarked on a search for a new world order in which he might feel completely at home. As clearly shown in Liu Shao's four categories of "principles" listed above, the individual was seeking to redefine the relationship of the ego to the cosmos, to the state, to the moral order, and to other individuals. Enunciation of the "principles" (*li*) of these categories, as we shall see, figured centrally in the philosophic discourse throughout the period. This was the case because the liberated individual refused to settle for anything less than a total understanding of these relationships. Obviously, such principles could nowhere be found in Confucian classical scholarship as it was received in the second and third centuries; it had by then degenerated into meaningless fragments of textual analysis. On the other hand, Daoism, with its ontological concept of "nonbeing" (*wu* 無), its cosmological views of "nonaction" (*wuwei* 無為) and "naturalness" (or "spontaneity," *ziran* 自然), its political and social ideal of "nongoverning" (*wuzhi* 無治), and, most important, its general emphasis on the freedom of the individual, provided the Wei-Jin individualist with precisely the right kind of spiritual resources. This point will become clear as we identify the central issues in neo-Daoist philosophy.

INDIVIDUALISM IN PURE CONVERSATION

Needless to say, this is not the place to discuss Neo-Daoism in all its diversity and complexity. What follows will simply try to show, through a brief analysis of three pairs of key concepts in Pure Conversation, that there was a close connection between the discovery of the individual on the one hand and the Neo-Daoist mode of thinking on the other. These three pairs are, respectively, "nonbeing" (*wu*) and "being" (*you* 有), "naturalness" or "spontaneity" (*ziran*) and the "teaching of names" (*mingjiao* 名教), and "feelings" (*qing*) and "rituals" (*li*). I understand all three pairs as having primarily to do with the problem of the individual vis-à-vis order, but at different levels. Structurally, all three pairs share a similar internal relationship. Just as the origin of being is based on nonbeing, that of the "teaching of names" is based on "naturalness" and that of "rituals" on "feelings." In other words, in the Neo-Daoist view, nonbeing, naturalness, and feelings are taken to be ultimate and primary, whereas being, the "teaching of names," and rituals are derivative and secondary. In terms of schools of thought, the first triad has traditionally been identified with Neo-Daoism and the second with Confucianism. In the present context, however, it may be more fruitful to associate nonbeing, naturalness, and feelings with the problem of the individual, and being, the "teaching names," and rituals with that of order. I am fully aware that in historical inquiry such neat dichotomies can be made only at the risk of oversimplification. Nevertheless, in this case, the risk is a calculated one.

Let us first look at the Neo-Daoist cosmology. According to the *Jinshu* (History of the Jin Dynasty):

During the *zhengshi* reign (240–248) of the Wei dynasty, He Yan, Wang Bi, and others followed the teachings of Laozi and Zhuangzi. They established the theory that Heaven, Earth, and all the myriad things have the basis of their existence in nonbeing. That which is called nonbeing is the beginning of things and the completion of affairs: it exists everywhere. It is by virtue of nonbeing that the *yin* and the *yang* transform into life, all the myriad things take their forms, the worthy establishes his moral worth, and the unworthy (i.e., the common man) keeps his person from being injured.[63]

This central thesis is well explained as follows by Kung-chuan Hsiao:

He Yan's statement, "Heaven, Earth, and all the myriad things have the basis of their existence in nonbeing," is adequate to sum up the cosmology of the Wei-Jin Daoist school. That is, *wu*, or "nonbeing," is the ontological reality of the cosmos. In the "beginning of things and the completion of affairs," it is *you* or "being" that is produced by it. Nonbeing produces (generates), and is being; that concept is not necessarily in conflict with that of *Dao* (道). . . . Xiahou Xuan 夏侯玄 (209–245) said: "Heaven and Earth spontaneously move in their cycles; the Sage spontaneously functions. By spontaneity is meant the *Dao*." To speak in terms of the spontaneous cycles of movement and production of Heaven and Earth and the myriad things, Heaven and Earth do not purposely produce the myriad things, nor do the myriad things know for what they are produced. Heaven and Earth (according to Wang Bi), "take no purposive action with respect to the myriad things, and each of the myriad things adapts to its own functioning."[64]

We can easily see from the views of He Yan, Wang Bi, and Xiahou Xuan quoted above that the Wei-Jin Daoists defined the relationship of the individual to the cosmic order in a totally new way. As we know, cosmology during the Han Period had been both teleologically and hierarchically oriented. Under the Han cosmological system, Heaven not only produces all things, including man, with predetermined purposes, but also imposes a hierarchical order on them. Thus, on the one hand, Dong Zhongshu 董仲舒 states, "Heaven and Earth produce the myriad things for the purpose of nourishing man."[65] On the other hand, he says that Heaven is the "great-grandfather" of the common man—that the common man has access to Heaven, only through the intermediary of the emperor, that is, the Son of Heaven.[66] Now, in Neo-Daoist cosmology, teleology is wholly rejected owing, at least partly, to the influence of Wang Chong.[67] Heaven and Earth no longer produce things. On the contrary, like all the myriad things, they are also produced by nonbeing, the ontological reality of the cosmos. Consequently, the concept of *Dao* also underwent a fundamental change. It was identified, not with what Dong Zhongshu called "the Way of Heaven," but with the ontological creativity of nonbeing, which functions spontaneously. In other words, *wu*, *ziran*, and *Dao* all became synonymous. From the point of view of the individual, this new conception of the cosmos assures the ego of its inner freedom, for in the realm of being, every individual thing comes into being by itself, moves in its natural course, and "adapts to its own functioning." Things are not produced by a higher creator with a predetermined purpose. As Guo Xiang says: "Throughout the realm of things, there *is* nothing . . . which is not 'self-transformed.' Hence the creating of things has no Lord; everything produces itself and does not depend on anything else. This is the normal way of the universe."[68] Indeed, this is a remarkable statement concerning the self-development and self-sufficiency of the individual made on a cosmic scale.

Neo-Daoist cosmology also throws light on the problem of order. The hierarchical conception of *Dao* in the Han Period was considerably modified. Since, as we have seen, *Dao* is redefined as nonbeing and spontaneity in Neo-Daoist thought, neither the Son of Heaven nor the sage is in a position to claim a monopoly on it. Every individual thing in the world, high or low, great or small, worthy or unworthy, is immediate to *Dao* because nonbeing is the basis of existence for all things. This does not mean, however, that Neo-Daoists completely did away with the idea of order in their cosmos. Order does exist, but it exists only in the realm of being and is therefore secondary. Moreover, it is present in a way that fully accords with the principle of naturalness. On this point, again, Guo Xiang is our reliable guide: "For the one whom the age takes to be worthy becomes the ruler, while those whose talents do not correspond to the demands of the age become servitors. It is analogous to the heavens' being naturally high and earth naturally low, the head being naturally on top and the feet occupying naturally the inferior position."[69] It must be noted that Guo Xiang's emphasis here is placed unequivocally on the naturalness of order. As a Neo-Daoist thinker, however, his ultimate concern was not with order but with the individual. Thus, in the very beginning of his commentary to the *Zhuangzi*, he writes: "Although the great is different from the small . . . if they all indulge themselves in the realm of self-fulfillment, then all things are following their own nature and doing according to their own capacity; all are what they ought to be and equally happy. There is no room for the distinction . . . [between] superior and inferior."[70] Clearly, it was this Neo-Daoist vision of the freedom of the individual that necessitated the emergence of a new cosmological system in which all beings must be self-determining as well as self-fulfilling.

Of the three paired concepts of opposites, *ziran* (naturalness) and *mingjiao* (the teaching of names) have been the most extensively discussed in modern historical scholarship. There is therefore no need to go into all the ramifications of this pair in the present essay. This pair shall be examined only insofar as it sheds light on the problem of the individual vis-à-vis order. In a broad sense, the scope of this pair overlaps with that of nonbeing and being on the one hand and that of feelings and ritual on the other. In a narrower sense, however, it deals primarily with the relationship of the individual to political order, i.e., the state. By and large, modern historians have tended to emphasize the political implications of the controversy over naturalness and the teaching of names. For the sake of clarity, I shall use this paired concept in its narrow sense.

In his commentary on the sentence "When there first were institutions and regulations, there were names," Wang Bi says: "When the uncarved block was dispersed . . . there were officials and rulers. When institutions and regulations, officials and rulers, are initiated, it is impossible not to establish names and statutes by which to determine superior and inferior; therefore when first there are institutions and regulations, there will be names."[71] This is Wang Bi's understanding of the origins of political order. Here, the "uncarved block" (*pu* 樸), a term used in the *Laozi*, is a symbol of the primordial naturalness. Like nonbeing, from which being arises, naturalness provides political order with its existential basis. As Chen Yinke rightly points out, the term "names" in this passage is identifiable with that in the teaching of names.[72] If the teaching of names, i.e., political order, originates in naturalness, it then follows that, ideally, it must model itself on the way naturalness operates, which is through "nonaction" (*wuwei*). Nonaction, however, does not imply a total absence of political order.[73] As a matter of fact, the notion of the necessity of political order was, on the whole, not seriously disputed by leading Neo-Daoist thinkers of the period, with the possible exception of Ruan Ji. Even the radical Xi Kang had a very clear idea of what an ideal political order should be. As he described it:

> The Sage comes as though inevitably to rule over the empire without intending to do so, [and] hence takes the (mind of) all the myriad things as his own mind. He leaves all the forms of life to themselves, and guides his own person by means of the Dao, being therein the same as all the world in gaining his own fulfillment. Effortlessly, he takes the absence of involvement in his work; calmly, he looks upon the empire as a commonality.[74]

Thus, the political order that grows out of primordial naturalness and works through nonaction is a minimal order. In terms of general features, if not of concrete conditions, it is quite reminiscent of the minimal state arising from the state of nature in the Lockean tradition. Xi Kang's view may be fruitfully compared to Guo Xiang's formulation of the same thesis:

> If the realm were to lack an enlightened ruler, then nothing would be able to reach its fulfillment. Such fulfillment as there now is must be accounted the achievement of enlightened rulers. Yet that achievement lies in his nonaction and in turning responsibility back to the world. All the (constituent parts) of the world having obtained autonomy, the consequence is

that their (individual fulfillment) does not appear to be the achievement of the enlightened ruler.[75]

Both Xi Kang and Guo Xiang are talking about the minimal political order of nonaction. Yet there appears to be a subtle difference: the former, apparently more concerned with the self-fulfillment of the individual, sees an invisible hand in the order of nonaction; the latter, emphasizing the function of the "enlightened ruler," attributes the order to the work of a hidden hand.[76] Whether by an invisible hand or a hidden hand, however, maintaining order is hardly ever the central issue in the Neo-Daoist political philosophy. For Neo-Daoists such as Wang Bi, He Yan, Xi Kang, and Guo Xiang, political order was at best a "necessary evil."[77] There can be no doubt that as far as the problem of the individual vis-à-vis order was concerned, their emphasis was always on the former, not the latter. As Guo Xiang remarked: "The value of a sage-king does not lie in his ability to govern. It lies in the fact that through nonaction, he allows each individual thing to undertake its own action."[78]

According to this view, then, political order can be justified on the sole ground that it makes possible self-fulfillment for each and every individual. In other words, the state exists for the sake of the individual, but not vice versa. The language of Neo-Daoist philosophy also attests overwhelmingly to its individualistic mode of thinking. Terms such as self-fulfillment (*zide* 自得), self-containment (*zizu* 自足), self-transformation (*zihua* 自化), self-control (*zizhi* 自制), self-action (*ziwei* 自為), self-completion (*zicheng* 自成), self-adjustment (*zishi* 自適), self-complacency (*zizai* 自在), etc., abound in Neo-Daoist texts. If language is a reliable index to thought, then the emergence of these new linguistic expressions clearly indicates the direction in which Chinese intellectual history was moving after the end of the second century.

Finally, we come to the last pair of our concepts of opposites, feelings versus rituals. The bearing of this pair on the problem of the individual vis-à-vis order is self-evident, and requires no elaboration. The controversy over feelings and rituals was most immediately relevant to the social reality of the time. As our earlier discussion of the changing interpersonal relationships clearly shows, the free and spontaneous flow of personal feelings between husband and wife or father and son inevitably led to transgressions of the "rules of etiquette" (*li* 禮). This was the most protracted of all controversies during this period; it began in the second century and continued well into the fourth. As a matter of fact, the controversy was even more intense in the fourth century than in the third. Debates about mourning rites, for instance, dominated the intellectual discourse of the Eastern Jin Period (317–420).[79] The truth is that while the problem of freedom of the individual versus order had been basically resolved in the political domain with the founding of the Western Jin (265–316) dynasty, a regime of "nonaction" very much catered to the interests of the elite. No modus vivendi, however, was worked out in the social sphere until more than a century later.

Chen Yinke's famous thesis that by the early fourth century Pure Conversation had evolved into an intellectual game played by the elite with no reference to actualities of life is valid only on the political level.[80] On the social level, especially in family and clan relationships, the problem of feelings versus rituals was still very real.

The relationship of "feelings" and "rituals" was probably first called into question in the late second century in connection with Dai Liang's mourning for his mother. Like Ruan Ji a century later, Dai Liang, while observing the mourning period, helped himself to meat and wine and wept only when truly overcome by grief. Someone asked him whether he was performing the right kind of rites, to which he replied: "Yes. Rites are to keep feelings from going to excess. If feelings are not excessive, what is the need to talk about rites?"[81] As this case clearly shows, in the initial stages of the controversy, a high tension between "feelings" and "rituals" already existed. The two were not yet, however, diametrically opposed to each other. Unlike Ruan Ji's radical antiritualism, Dai Liang's rejection of *li* was only partial and conditional.

We have reason to believe that, psychologically, the tension between human emotions and ritual originated in the sudden release of personal feelings or emotions that accompanied the self-discovery of the individual after the late second century. The traditional ritual system apparently lacked sufficient flexibility to respond to the deluge of new feelings being allowed expression.

In the realm of ideas, this tension manifested itself essentially in two ways: a fresh interest in the function of feelings in man and a new emphasis on the importance of the spirit, as opposed to the letter, of rituals. As we know, with regard to the idea of "feelings" in Han thought, Dong Zhongshu's view that human nature is good but human feelings are bad had been accepted as more or less orthodox.[82] It is therefore highly significant that at the end of the Han, Xun Yue 荀悅 (148–209) quoted with emphatic approval in his *Shenjian* 申鑒 (Extended Reflections) the heterodox view of Liu Xiang 劉向 (77–76 B.C.E.) that "since human nature corresponds to human emotions, the one cannot be all good and the other all bad." As he further remarked, if one asserted that human feelings are all bad, then he would have to say that sages like Yao 堯 and Shun 舜 had no feelings.[83]

This leads us directly to Wang Bi's influential theory concerning the emotions of the sage:

> He maintained that where the sage is vitally superior to other men is in his spirit-like intelligence, but where he is like other men is in having the five emotions. Being superior in his spirit-like intelligence, he is able to identify himself with the harmonious whole, so that he is imbued with nonbeing; but being like others in his five emotions, he cannot but react to things with emotion. The emotions of the sage are such that though he reacts to things, he is not ensnared by them. It is a great error, consequently,

to say that because he is not ensnared by things, he therefore has no (emotional) reactions to them.[84]

Two observations may be made about Wang Bi's theory. First, it clearly indicates, in conjunction with Xun Yue's view, that during the first half of the third century, new philosophical attention was being paid to the problem of "feelings," though we do not know for sure that Wang Bi had access to Xun Yue's work. Second, the theory admirably serves as a justification of the ever-growing importance of personal feelings in the social life of the day. Evidence shows that by the middle of the fourth century it became one of the most central philosophical topics in Pure Conversation, a testimony to its great popularity.[85]

On the other hand, "rituals" as an idea also received critical reexamination in the hands of philosophers. In his commentary on the phrase "the meaning of rites (li)" in the Zhuangzi, for example, Guo Xiang had this to say:

> For the person who knows the meaning of the rites must roam beyond the realm so as to keep order in the mundane sphere, must cling to the mother in order to preserve the son, must acknowledge his feelings and straightaway act accordingly. Should he display anxiety about his reputation or be restricted by the formalities, then his filial piety will not be sincere and his compassion will not be genuine. Father and son, elder brother and younger (as formalized relationships, make one) hold feelings that lead to mutual deceptions. How can that be the larger meaning of the rites?[86]

Here Guo Xiang charged that the Confucian ritual system of his time was devoid of meaning because it could no longer freely express the true feelings of man. Quite to the contrary, it had been formalized to the point of sheer artificiality.[87] Guo Xiang's interpretation of "rituals" and "feelings" as antithetical to each other proves beyond dispute that in the early fourth century, the Neo-Daoists were still grappling with the problem of freedom of the individual in the face of a strong and deep-rooted Confucian ritual order.

The Neo-Daoist revolt against the ritual order was more radical, widespread, and profound than its attack on the political order. The reason for this is not difficult to see. The conflict between feelings and rituals arose, after all, from the everyday experiences of the spiritually liberated individual who was caught between the growing need to express freely and openly his personal feelings on the one hand and the inadequacy of the existing ritualistic forms on the other. Naturally, the Neo-Daoist individualist would not hesitate to do away with "rituals" whenever and wherever they proved to be in the way of free emotional expression. Thus, when someone chided Ruan Ji for having violated rituals by saying good-bye to his sister-in-law, he replied: "Were the rites established for people like me?"[88] In response to a criticism of his excessive grief over the loss of a son, Wang Rong said: "a sage forgets his feelings; the lowest beings aren't even capable of having feelings. But the place where feelings are most concentrated is precisely among people like ourselves."[89] Needless to say, for individualists like Ruan Ji and Wang Rong, it was far more meaningful to be true to one's authentic self than to conform to a stereotyped social norm. It was precisely this search for inner authenticity that turned individualists of the period away from Confucian ritualism.

An inside view that links the rise of Neo-Daoism to the self-discovery and self-awareness of the individual has been provided by Xi Kang. In a debate on the nature of Confucian learning, he explained why the Six Classics were unacceptable to him:

> The emphasis of the Six Classics is placed mainly on repression whereas human nature experiences joy in the following of desires. Repression goes against a man's inclinations; he attains to naturalness by following his desires. Therefore it follows that attainment of naturalness does not come from the repressive Six Classics, and preservation of man's nature does not need a base in rituals and laws which run counter to feelings.[90]

Thus, in the final analysis, it was Xi Kang's profound resentment of ritualistic repression that led him to reject Confucianism. In a letter to a friend, he further explained how he was drawn to the Daoist view:

> Further, I was long left to my own devices, and my disposition became arrogant and careless, my bluntness diametrically opposed to etiquette; laziness and rudeness reinforcing each other. . . . Besides, my taste for independence was aggravated by my reading of Zhuangzi and Laozi; as a result, my desire for fame and success grew daily weaker, and my commitment to freedom increasingly firmer.[91]

Here, we are told, it was love of independence and freedom that pushed him to Daoism. These two self-revelatory accounts are complementary, and together they reveal most vividly the inner dimensions of the rise of the Neo-Daoist movement.

In view of the evidence we have examined thus far, the transition from Confucian classical scholarship to Neo-Daoist metaphysics may be more intelligently interpreted as what Michel Foucault calls a "rupture" in Chinese consciousness. It was clearly the case that neo-Daoist metaphysics was not established in the places formerly occupied by Confucian classical scholarship, but in an area where the latter simply did not exist.[92] Han Confucianism was ultimately concerned with the collective life in an imperial order, and Wei-Jin Neo-Daoism with the problem of freedom of the individual. The transition from one to the other was by no means a smooth one. Viewed from this perspective, it may justifiably be contended that the central historical significance of the development of Pure Conversation lies in the emergence of a totally new mode of discourse—an individualistic mode of discourse that superseded the old, collectivistic one of the Han Period.

RECONCILIATION BETWEEN DAOIST INDIVIDUALISM AND CONFUCIAN RITUALISM

So as not to overstate the case of Wei-Jin individualism, we must, in concluding, say something about the ritualistic side of the coin. Throughout the period under consideration, Confucian ritualism with its marked emphasis on moral order and conformity never ceased to be a social and intellectual force with vigor and vitality. Side by side with the new individualistic type of familial relationships described above there also existed a sharply contrasting type of family order. The case of He Zeng 何曾 (199–278) may be proffered as an illustrative example. His was probably a family life of the most ritualistic kind. He was not only a well-known filial son of the day but also maintained a highly formalized relationship with his wife throughout his life. In his old age, we are told, he saw his wife only two or three times a year; each time, he was formally dressed and treated her in strict accordance with the Confucian etiquette between host and guest.[93] He was clearly following a ritualistic tradition of the Han Period that managed the private household in the manner of the "government office."[94] Little wonder that he found Ruan Ji's transgression of mourning rites absolutely intolerable and proposed to have him banished "beyond the sea."[95]

It is interesting to note that there are also indications of a struggle between Confucian ritualism and Neo-Daoist naturalism as two competing ways of life. The following story will help to illuminate this contest:

> Wang Rong and He Qiao 和嶠 (d. 292) experienced the loss of a parent at the same time, and both were praised for their filial devotion. Wang, reduced to a skeleton, kept to his bed; while He, wailing and weeping, performed all the rites. Emperor Wu 武帝 (r. 265–290) remarked to Liu Yi 劉毅, "Have you ever observed Wang Rong and He Qiao? I hear that He's grief and suffering go beyond what is required by propriety, and it makes me worry about him."
>
> Liu Yi replied: "He Qiao, even though performing all the rites, has suffered no loss in his spirit or health. Wang Rong, even though not performing the rites, is nonetheless so emaciated with grief that his bones stand out. Your servant is of the opinion that He Qiao's is the filial devotion of life, while Wang Rong's is the filial devotion of death. Your Majesty should not worry about Qiao, but rather about Rong."[96]

In the final analysis, the struggle is clearly reducible to a contest between "rituals" (*li* 禮) and "feelings" (*qing* 情). The story is unmistakably pro-Daoist in tone, however. The judgment that Wang Rong surpassed He Qiao in filial devotion suggests that Neo-Daoist naturalism could beat Confucian ritualism on the latter's own ground. On the other hand, the story also reveals that at the end of the Western Jin, Confucian ritualism, though crippled by a social and spiritual crisis that had lasted for a century, was still very much alive.

The controversy over "feelings" and "rituals" was carried to the south by Western Jin émigrés during the early decades of the fourth century. It took at least another century to bring the debate to a conclusion. The end of the controversy was not as visible and colorful as the beginning had been, but from the historical point of view, it was as important.

By the middle of the fourth century, Neo-Daoist naturalism and Confucian ritualism began to show signs of reconciliation. We find, for example, that the idea of "rituals" was no longer being treated with contempt and resentment by the elite. On the contrary, they came to the realization that interpersonal feelings cannot be meaningfully and fully expressed without a sensitive ritual system in the first place. Thus, speaking of both the ruler–subject and father–son relationships, Yuan Hong (328–376) could now say that their handling required the presence of both "feelings" and "rituals" at the same time.[97] How is such a drastic change in attitude to be accounted for? To answer this question, attention must be drawn to a quiet but enduring movement in ritual reforms traceable to as early as the middle of the third century. It is particularly significant that the emphasis of the reform movement was focused quite specifically on the mourning rites, the very battleground on which, as we have seen, wars had been fought between Confucian ritualists and Neo-Daoist naturalists. The movement was by no means a Confucian monopoly. As a matter of fact, Neo-Daoist participants were just as active in it. Especially with the founding of the refugee regime in the south, the study of the mourning rites gained an unprecedented popularity. Leading specialists in the field included not only Confucianists and Neo-Daoists but Buddhists as well.

Ritual studies during the period are too complicated to be discussed here. For our purposes, however, it will suffice to note that the spirit of the reform movement consisted in the particularization of the rites with a view to satisfying, as much as possible, the individuated feelings of the members of each mourning community.[98] In this way, the reformists claimed that they had completely renovated the ritual system, thereby making it, once again, an effective vehicle for the free expression of personal feelings. Thus, we see that along with the self-discovery and self-awareness of the individual, there was also a genuine search for ritualization throughout the Wei-Jin Period. Ironically enough, even Pure Conversation, the very symbol of Wei-Jin individualism, became highly ritualized in the course of its development. To qualify as a Pure

Conversationalist, for instance, one had to be trained in the art of speech, including voice and logic,[99] to know how to gesticulate the fly whisk properly,[100] to be well versed in the three metaphysical works (the *Classic of Changes*, the *Laozi*, and the *Zhuangzi*), and, above all, to belong to the elite circle.[101] Wang Sengqian's 王僧虔 (426–485) letter to his son contains the following interesting admonition:

> You have read only about five feet each of the scrolls of the *Laozi* and the *Classic of Changes*. You have neither known what Wang Bi and He Yan had to say, nor the differences between the commentaries of Ma (Rong) and Zheng (Xuan), nor (Wang Bi's *Laozi*) *zhi* (-*lüe*) and (*Zhouyi*) *li* (-*lüe*). And yet you have already picked up the fly whisk and styled yourself a Conversationalist. Nothing is more dangerous than this. Suppose Prefect Yuan (Can, 袁粲 420–477) asks you to talk about the *Classic of Changes*, Palace Secretary Xie (Zhuang, 謝莊 421–466) challenges you to a discussion on the *Zhuangzi*, or Mr. Zhang (Xu, 張緒 433?–490?) questions you about the *Laozi*, can you answer by admitting that you have not read them? Pure Conversation is like the game of archery: the player must always be aware of the marks already hit by others. A player who knows nothing about them simply loses the game.[102]

This is a most vivid account of the basic intellectual qualifications of a Pure Conversationalist. Clearly, by the middle of the fifth century, Pure Conversation had developed a ritual framework of its own. It fits remarkably well with Foucault's description of the societies of discourse "whose function is to preserve discourse by producing it in a restricted group."[103] Thus, with the teaching of names firmly established on the basis of naturalness, and "rituals" on that of "feelings," as it were, a balance between order and individuality was restored at long last.

NOTES

1. See Lu Xun 魯迅, "Wenhua pianzhi lun" 文化偏至論, in *Lu Xun quanji* 魯迅全集, 20 vols. (Beijing: Renmin wenxue, 1973), 1:45–46.
2. *Bohu tongde lun*, SBCK chu, 7.58; Fung Yu-lan, *A History of Chinese Philosophy*, trans. Derk Bodde, 2 vols. (Princeton: Princeton University Press, 1953), 2:44.
3. Yü Ying-shih 余英時, *Lishi yu sixiang* 歷史與思想 (Taipei: Lianjing, 1976), 39–41.
4. *HHS*, 12 vols. (Beijing: Zhonghua, 1959), 5.1554; T'ung-tsu Ch'ü, *Law and Society in Traditional China* (Paris: Mouton, 1961), 279.
5. *HHS*, 10.2775.
6. *Ruan Ji ji* 阮籍集 (Shanghai: Guji, 1978), 66. For English translation, see Kung-chuan Hsiao, *A History of Chinese Political Thought*, trans. Frederick W. Mote, 2 vols. (Princeton:

Princeton University Press, 1979), 1:622–623, and Donald Holzman, *Poetry and Politics: The Life and Works of Juan Chi, A.D. 210–263* (Cambridge: Cambridge University Press, 1976), 195–196.

7. For more details, see Yü Ying-shih, "Mingjiao weiji yu Wei-Jin shifeng di zhuanbian" 名教危機與魏晉士風的轉變, originally published in *Shihuo* 食貨 9, nos. 7–8 (November 1979): 2–4; now collected in *Zhongguo zhishi jieceng shilun* 中國知識階層史論 (Taipei: Lianjing, 1980), 333–337.

8. *BPZ*, 4 vols., WYWK, 4:773–774; English translation in Wolfgang Bauer, *China and the Search for Happiness*, trans. Michael Shaw (New York: Seabury Press, 1976), 138–139.

9. Yang Bojun 楊伯峻, *Liezi jishi* 列子集釋 (Shanghai: Longmen, 1958), 102; A. C. Graham, trans., *The Book of Lieh Tzu* (London: John Murray, 1960), 102. As Graham rightly points out in his introduction, the consensus among scholars in China is that the *Lieh Tzu* is a product of the third century C.E. Most of these scholarly opinions are now conveniently collected in Yang Bojun's *Liezi jishi*, 185–245.

10. *Wang Wengong wenji* 王文公文集, 2 vols. (Shanghai: Renmin, 1974), 2:439. See Chen Yinke 陳寅恪, *Tao Yuanming zhi sixiang yu qingtan zhi guanxi* 陶淵明之思想與清談之關係 (Chengdu: Harvard-Yenching Institute, 1945), 52–53.

11. See passages quoted in Yü Ying-shih, "Mingjiao weiji," 336 and n6.

12. For a general study of Wei-Jin anarchism, see Tan Jiajian 譚家健, "Lüe lun Wei-Jin shiqi di wujunlun sichao" 略論魏晉時期的無君論思潮, *Zhongguo zhexue* 中國哲學 2 (March 1980): 120–136.

13. *Fuzi* 傅子 (Writings of Fu Xuan 傅玄), quoted in *SGZ*, punctuated edition, 5 vols. (Beijing: Zhonghua, 1959), 2:213; *ZZTJ*, 20 vols. (Beijing: Zhonghua, 1956), 5:2018–2019.

14. Colin Morris, *The Discovery of the Individual, 1050–1200* (London: S.P.C.K. [for the Church History Society], 1972), 160.

15. *Weishu* 魏書, quoted in *SGZ*, 1:260.

16. *HHS*, 8.2278.

17. *Jinshu* 晉書, 10 vols. (Beijing: Zhonghua, 1974), 5.1360.

18. *BPZ*, 3:509.

19. Richard B. Mather, trans., *Shih-shuo hsin-yü: A New Account of Tales of the World* (Minneapolis: University of Minnesota Press, 1976), 485.

20. *SGZ*, 3:647. See Mori Mikisaburō 森三樹三郎, "Gi-Shin jidai ni okeru ningen no hakken" 魏晉時代における人間の發展, *Tôyô bunka no mondai* 東洋文化の問題 1 (June 1949): 146–147.

21. *BPZ*, 3:598–603.

22. *Jinshu*, 1.136; English translation in Kung-chuan Hsiao, *Chinese Political Thought*, 635–636, with editorial modifications.

23. Jacob Burckhardt, *The Civilization of the Renaissance in Italy*, trans. S. G. C. Middlemore (London: Phaidon Press, 1951), 81. Although Burckhardt's thesis has been variously modified, his basic view of Renaissance individualism still holds well. See Ernst Cassirer, *The Individual and the Cosmos in Renaissance Philosophy*, trans. Mario Domandi (Philadelphia: University of Pennsylvania Press, 1972), 35–36; Paul Oskar Kristeller, "Changing Views of the Intellectual History of the Renaissance Since Jacob Burchkhardt," in *The*

Renaissance: A Reconsideration of the Theories and Interpretations of the Age, ed. Tinsley Helton (Madison: University of Wisconsin Press, 1961), 30.

24. *HHS*, 7.1953.

25. Ibid., 10.2773.

26. Ibid., 8.2278.

27. See Tang Yongtong 湯用彤, *Wei-Jin xuanxue lungao* 魏晉玄學論稿 (Beijing: Renmin, 1957), 8.

28. *HHS*, 9.2635–2639.

29. Liu Shao, *Renwu zhi*, SBCK chu, *shang*, 4–6. Cf. J. K. Shryock, *The Study of Human Abilities: The Jen Wu Chih of Liu Shao* (New Haven: American Oriental Society, 1937), esp. pp. 99–100.

30. See Walter Ullman, *The Individual and Society in the Middle Ages* (Baltimore: Johns Hopkins University Press, 1966), 105; Morris, *Discovery of the Individual*, 86–95.

31. Quoted in William Willets, *Chinese Art*, 2 vols. (Harmondsworth, UK: Penguin, 1958), 2:582. For Cao Zhi's original text, see Yu Jianhua 俞劍華, ed., *Zhongguo hualun leibian* 中國畫論類編, 2 vols. (Hong Kong: Zhonghua, 1973), 1:12.

32. Mather, *Tales*, 368.

33. See the interesting story about Gu Kaizhi adding three hairs to the cheek of the person in a portrait to catch his "spirit" in Mather, *Tales*, 367.

34. See Bruno Snell, *The Discovery of the Mind: The Greek Origins of European Thought*, trans. T. B. Rosenmeyer (New York: Harper, 1960), chap. 3; Morris, *Discovery of the Individual*, 68–70; Burckhardt, *Civilization of the Renaissance*, esp. pp. 184–188.

35. Sui Senshu 隋森樹, *Gushi shijiu shou jishi* 古詩十九首集釋 (Hong Kong: Zhonghua, 1958).

36. Yu Guanying 余冠英, "Lun *jian-an* Caoshi fuzi di shi" 論建安曹氏父子的詩, in *Wenxue yichan zengkan* 文學遺產增刊 (Beijing: Zuojia, 1955), 1:137–158.

37. Étienne Balazs, *Chinese Civilization and Bureaucracy*, ed. Arthur F. Wright (New Haven: Yale University Press, 1964), 177.

38. According to the classification of Zhang Zhiyue 張志岳, thirteen out of the eighty-two are autobiographical poems. See his "Lüe lun Ruan Ji ji qi *Yonghuai shi*" 略論阮籍及其詠懷詩, in *Wei-Jin Liuchao shi yanjiu lunwen ji* 魏晉六朝詩研究論文集 (Hong Kong: Zhongguo yuwen, 1969), 66.

39. I refer mainly to the works of Chen Yinke, Tang Yongtong, and Tang Changru 唐長孺.

40. *BPZ*, 3:604.

41. Qian Mu, "Du *Wenxuan*" 讀文選, in his *Zhongguo xueshu sixiangshi luncong* 中國學術思想史論叢, 8 vols. (Taipei: Dongda tushu gongsi, 1977), 3:107.

42. Yan Kejun 嚴可均, *QSW*, 5 vols. (Beijing: Zhonghua, 1958), 2:1088.

43. Ibid., 1141.

44. Mather, *Tales*, 488.

45. See Zhang Hao 張昊, *Yungu zaji* 雲谷雜記 (Shanghai: Zhonghua, 1958), 97; Zhou Fagao 周法高, *Zhongguo gudai yufa: chengdai pian* 中國古代語法稱代篇 (Taipei: Academia Sinica, 1959), 83–84. See also Mather, *Tales*, 161, where the intimate "you" is used with a friend.

46. *Jinshu*, 5.1379–1380; Mather, *Tales*, 12.

47. *QSW*, 2:1962.

48. For this standard view, see Chen Yinke, "'Xiaoyao you' Xiang-Guo yi ji Zhidun yi tan-yuan" 逍遙遊向郭義及支遁義探源, *Qinghua xuebao* 清華學報 12, no. 2 (April 1937): 309, and *Tao Yuanming zhi sixiang*, 3; Tang Yongtong, "Du *Renwu zhi*" 讀人物志, in *Wei-Jin xuanxue lungao*, 16; Aoki Masaru 青木正男, "Seidan" 清談, in *Aoki Masaru zenshû* 青木正男全集, 10 vols. (Tokyo: Shunjü Sha, 1969), 1:208–240.

49. Wang Fu, *Qianfu lun* 潛夫論, annotated by Wang Jipei 汪繼培, *GXJBCS*, 11, and Wang Jipei's note.

50. *HHS*, 7.2031.

51. Ibid., 79.2547.

52. Ibid., 78.2232.

53. Mather, *Tales*, 56.

54. *HHS*, 9.2481.

55. Ibid., 79.2647. For more examples of this kind, see the case of Xie Zhen 謝甄 and Bian Rang 邊讓 (ibid., 78.2230) and that of Kong Gongxu 孔公緒 (ibid., 78.2258).

56. Fung Yu-lan, *History*, 2:175–179.

57. Liu Shao, *Renwu zhi, shang*, 22–23.

58. Ibid., *shang*, 11–12.

59. *HHS*, 6.1629.

60. Ibid., 8.2277.

61. For Wang Su's influence on Wang Bi, see Meng Wentong 蒙文通, *Jingxue jueyuan* 經學抉原 (Taipei: Shangwu, 1966 [reprint]), 38. Cai Yong probably contributed more than anyone else to the widespread circulation of Wang Chong's *Lunheng*. For instance, after his death, Cai's entire library was obtained by Wang Ye 王業, Wang Bi's father. It is therefore more than probable that Wang Bi had direct access to Cai's copy of the *Lunheng* (see *Bowu ji* 博物記, quoted in *SGZ*, 3:796). On the other hand, Ruan Yu 阮瑀, Ruan Ji's father, had been a disciple of Cai (*SGZ*, 3:600). This important fact explains why both Ruan Ji and his nephew Ruan Xiu 阮脩 were so familiar with Wang Chong's ideas. For details, see Yü Ying-shih, *Zhongguo zhishi*, 339n7.

62. Miyazaki Ichisada 宮崎市定 thinks that the transition from Pure Criticism took place in the early decades of the third century; see his "Seidan" 清談, *Shirin* 史林 1, no. 31 (January 1946): 5. Shiba Rokurô 斯波六郎 classifies late Han "conversation" in terms of two different types he calls "critical conversation" and "inquisitive conversation." The former focused on personalities, the latter on ideas. He further states that the former flourished during the reigns of Emperors Huan (147–167) and Ling (168–188), and the latter during the reigns of Emperors Lin and Xian (189–220); see his "Kô-Kan makki no danron ni tsuite" 後漢末期の清談について, *Hiroshima daigaku bungakubu kiyô* 廣島大學文學部紀要 8 (October 1955): 213–242. I have examined this question in considerable detail in "Han-Jin zhi ji shi jin xin zijue yu xin sichao" 漢晉之際士之新自覺與新思想, originally published in *Xinya xuebao* 新亞學報 4, no. 1 (August 1959): 50–60, now included in my *Zhongguo zhishi*, 236–249. For a more thorough study, see Okamura Shigeru 岡村繁, "Kô-Kan makki no heiron-teki kifû ni tsuite" 後漢末期の評論的氣風に

ついて, in *Nagoya daigaku bungakubu kenkyû ronshû* 名古屋大學文學部研究論集 (Nagoya: Nagoya University Press, 1960), 67–112.

63. *Jinshu*, 4.1236. For a good general discussion of the idea of nonbeing and its relationship to the self-awareness of the individual during this period, see Matsumoto Gamei 松本雅明, "Gi-Shin ni okeru mu no shiso no seikaku" 魏晉における無の思想の性格, *Shigaku Zasshi* 史學雜誌 51, no. 2 (February 1940): 13–42; 51, no. 3 (March 1940): 74–105; 51, no. 4 (April 1940): 63–90. However, Professor Qian Mu is one of the earliest modern scholars to characterize Wei-Jin Neo-Daoism in terms of the self-awareness of the individual. See *Guoxue gailun* 國學概論, 2 vols. (Shanghai: Shangwu, 1931), 1:150.

64. Kung-chuan Hsiao, *Chinese Political Thought*, 1:610–611. For a general study of the thought of He Yan and Wang Bi, see Itano Chôhachi 板野長八, "Ka An O Hitsu no shisô" 何晏王弼の思想, *Tohō gakuhō* 東方學報 14, no. 1 (March 1943): 43–111.

65. *Chunqiu fanlu* 春秋繁露, WYWK, 2 vols., 1:85. See also *HS*, punctuated edition, 8 vols. (Beijing: Zhonghua, 1962), 6.2516. Dong Zhongshu never explicitly stated for what purpose Heaven finds it necessary to produce man. However, he believed that Heaven endows man with a nature so that he can practice *ren* 仁 (humanity) and *yi* 義 (righteousness) (*Chunqiu fanlu*, 1.28). He further held that "humanity" is the embodiment of Heaven's will and "righteousness" that of Heaven's principle (*Chunqiu fanlu*, 2.175). Therefore, if hard pressed, he probably would say that Heaven creates man for the purpose of bringing itself to moral perfection.

66. *Chunqiu fanlu*, 2.175.

67. See Wang Chong's essay on "Ziran" 自然 in Chan, *SB*, 296–299.

68. Guo Qingfan 郭慶藩, *ZJS*, 4 vols. (Beijing: Zhonghua, 1961), 1:111–112; English translation in Fung Yu-lan, *History*, 2:210.

69. *ZJS*, 1:58; English translation in Kung-chuan Hsiao, *Chinese Political Thought*, 1:612.

70. *ZJS*, 1:1; English translation slightly modified from Fung Yu-lan, *Chuang Tzu: A New Selected Translation with an Exposition of the Philosophy of Kuo Hsiang*, 2nd ed. (New York: Paragon, 1964 [reprint]), 27.

71. Kung-chuan Hsiao, *Chinese Political Thought*, 1:612.

72. Chen Yinke, *Tao Yuanming zhi sixiang*, 5–6.

73. Guo Xiang says: "Nonaction does not mean that (the ruler) just sits there silently with arms folded. Rather he allows each individual thing to undertake its own action so that, ultimately, it may rest in the true form of its nature and life" (*ZJS*, 2:369). For a general study of the thought of Guo Xiang, see Murakami Yoshimi 村上嘉實, "Kaku Chô no shisô ni tsuite" 郭象の思想について, *Tôyôshi kenkyû* 東洋史研究 6, no. 3 (May 1941): 1–28.

74. Dai Mingyang 戴明揚, *Xi Kang ji jiaozhu* 嵇康集校注 (Beijing: Renmin wenxue, 1962), 171; translated in Kung-chuan Hsiao, *Chinese Political Thought*, 1:618.

75. *ZJS*, 1:296; translated in Kung-chuan Hsiao, *Chinese Political Thought*, 1:616–617.

76. For the distinction between "invisible hand" and "hidden hand," I have followed Robert Nozick, *Anarchy State, and Utopia* (New York: Basic Books, 1974), 18–20.

77. *ZJS*, 2:348. Commenting on the statement "the sage brings little benefit to the world, but much harm," Guo Xiang says: "How true is this statement: Although this statement

is true, we nevertheless cannot do without the sage. For before all types of knowledge have disappeared from the world, we still need the Way of the sage to control them. If all other kinds of knowledge are around while the sagely knowledge alone is gone, then the world would suffer more harm than it does because of the sage. It therefore follows that in spite of the fact that the sage brings much harm to the world, it is still far better than a world without the sage in which disorder reigns supreme."

78. *ZJS*, 2:364.

79. See Mou Runsun 牟潤孫, *Lun Wei-Jin yilai zhi chongshang tanbian ji qi yingxiang* 論魏晉以來之崇尚談辯及其影響 (Hong Kong: CUHK Press, 1966).

80. See Chen Yinke, *Tao Yuanming zhi sixiang*, 2; Tang Changru, *Wei-Jin Nanbei chao shi luncong* 魏晉南北朝史論叢 (Beijing: Sanlian, 1955), 336–339. This view is followed by Richard Mather in "The Controversy Over Conformity and Naturalness During the Six Dynasties," *History of Religions* 9, nos. 2–3 (November 1969/February 1970): 161.

81. *HHS*, 10.2773.

82. Fung Yu-lan, *History*, 2:32–33.

83. *Shenjian*, SBCK chu, 5:32–33; translated in Ch'i-yün Ch'en, *Hsün Yüeh and the Mind of Late Han China* (Princeton: Princeton University Press, 1980), 187–188.

84. He Shao's 何劭 biography of Wang Bi, quoted in the commentary of *SGZ*, 3:795; translated in Fung Yu-lan, *History*, 2:188. For an excellent discussion of the philosophical significance of this thesis, see Tang Yongtong, *Wei-Jin xuanxue lungao*, 72–83.

85. For example, see Mather, *Tales*, 122.

86. *ZJS*, 2:260; English translation slightly modified from Kung-chuan Hsiao, *Chinese Political Thought*, 1:636–637. It is significant to point out that in his commentary to the Confucian *Lunyu*, Wang Bi also stressed the importance of the "meaning" as opposed to the mere forms of the "rites." He specifically remarked, "all the five grades of mourning rites must each fit the feelings of the individual mourner." Quoted in Huang Kan 皇侃, *Lunyu jijie yishu* 論語集解義疏 (Taipei: Guangwen, 1968 [reprint]), 2.4a–b. This point, as will become clear below, bears importantly on the reform movement in mourning rites of the period.

87. See Graham, *Lieh-tzu*, 145.

88. Mather, *Tales*, 374.

89. Ibid., 324.

90. Dai Mingyang, *Xi Kang ji jiaozhu*, 261.

91. Ibid., 117–118; English translation by J. R. Hightower in *Anthology of Chinese Literature from Early Times to the Fourteenth Century*, ed. Cyril Birch (New York: Grove Press, 1965), 163.

92. Michel Foucault, *The Order of Things: An Archaeology of the Human Sciences* (New York: Vintage, 1973), 207. See also Hayden V. White, "Foucault Decoded: Notes from Underground," *History and Theory* 12, no. 1 (1973): 23–54.

93. *Jinshu*, 4.997.

94. *HHS*, 3.573, 4.1119. See also the illuminating discussion by Gu Yanwu 顧炎武 in his *Rizhilu* 日知録, WYWK, 12 vols., 5:40.

95. Mather, *Tales*, 372.

96. Ibid., 10–11.

97. *Jinshu*, 8.2396. See also Tang Changru, "Wei-Jin xuanxue zhi xingcheng ji qi fazhan" 魏晉玄學之形成及其發展, in *Wei-Jin Nanbei chao*, esp. pp. 336–337.

98. A comprehensive study of mourning rites in this period is provided by Fukikawa Masakazu 藤川正數 in *Gi-Shin jidai ni okeru sôfukurei no kenkyû* 魏晉時代における喪服禮の研究 (Tokyo: Keibun Sha, 1960). For more details about this movement in ritual reform, see Yü Ying-shih, *Zhongguo zhishi*, 358–372.

99. For speech and voice, see examples listed and discussed in Yü Ying-shih, *Zhongguo zhishi*, 243–249. For the importance of logic in conversation, see He Changqun 賀昌羣, *Wei-Jin qingtan sixiang chulun* 魏晉清談思想初論 (Shanghai: Shangwu, 1947), 7–8.

100. See Zhao Yi 趙翼, "Qingtan yong zhuwei" 清談用麈尾, in *Nian ershi zhaji* 廿二史劄記 (Taipei: Huashi, 1977), 167–168.

101. For example, Chen Xianda 陳顯達, a military man of humble social origin, told his son: "The fly whisk is something belonging exclusively to such distinguished families as the Wangs and the Xies. It is not the sort of thing that you should carry around." See *Nan Qi shu* 南齊書, punctuated edition, 3 vols. (Beijing: Zhonghua, 1992), 2:490.

102. Ibid., 2:598. The text does not give personal names for these conversationalists. The identifications of Yuan Can, Xie Zhuang, and Zhang Xu have been established as a result of an extensive search in various biographies of the dynastic histories. My reasons for these identifications may be briefly stated as follows:

   In Wang Sengqian's biography, Yuan Shu 袁淑 (408–453) and Xie Zhuang are mentioned as Wang's intimate friends (2:591). However, Yuan Shu died too early to fit into the picture. On the other hand, the identification of Xie Zhuang is unmistakable because he is referred to in the letter by his official title *zhongshu ling* 中書令 (Prefect of the Palace Secretariat), a position he did, in fact, hold (*Songshu* 宋書, punctuated edition [Beijing: Zhonghua, 1974], 8, 2167–2177). Therefore, the letter must have been written sometime before Xie's death in 466 when Wang was about forty, an age old enough to have a son in his late teens or early twenties. Yuan Can was Yuan Shu's nephew. He changed his personal name to Can after the famous Pure Conversationalist Xun Can 荀粲 of the third century. Moreover, he served as prefect of various provinces and was well known for his study of the *Yijing* (*Songshu*, 8, 2229–2234). This fits perfectly well with the reference in the letter. As for Zhang Xu, he was a man of Wuxing with a great reputation as a Pure Conversationalist. Although he was particularly known for his knowledge of the *Yijing*, there can be little doubt that he must also have been versed in the *Laozi* (*Nan Qi shu*, 2:600–602). His first cousin, Zhang Rong 張融 (444–497), for instance, was a famous Neo-Daoist conversationalist with a special interest in the *Laozi* (*Nan Qi shu*, 3:721–730). The simple fact that both Wang Sengqian's and Zhang Xu's biographies are included in the same chapter also indicates a close relationship between the two men.

   Without giving his reasons, however, Professor Qian Mu has identified the three conversationalists as Yuan Can, Xie Fei, and Zhang Xu (*Guoxue gailun*, 1:163). The first and third identifications agree with my findings. However, his identification of Xie *zhongshu* as Xie Fei 謝朏 (441–506), son of Xie Zhuang 謝莊, may be in error. To raise an obvious objection, Xie Fei started his bureaucratic career in 483 and was appointed to the position of *zhongshu ling* as late as 489 or 490, by which time Wang Sengqian had already been dead for four or five years. Wang could not have possibly referred to Xie Fei by his official title. See *Liangshu*, 8 vols., punctuated edition (Beijing: Zhonghua, 1974), 1:261–264.

103. Alan Sheridan, *Michel Foucault: The Will to Truth* (London: Tavistock, 1980), 127.

8. Intellectual Breakthroughs in the Tang-Song Transition

Viewed from inside and understood in its own terms, the long intellectual tradition of China can be discerned to have three major breakthroughs. The earliest breakthrough took place in classical antiquity around the time of Confucius (551–479 B.C.E.), when various philosophical visions such as the Confucian, the Mohist, and the Daoist began to emerge out of the primeval cultural tradition that the author of the last chapter of the *Zhuangzi* identifies as "the original unity of Heaven and Earth" or, simply, the original *Dao* 道. The same author is also the first historian of Chinese thought to introduce the idea of "intellectual breakthrough." With the emergence of the various philosophical schools, he says, "The system of the *Dao* was being broken into fragments and scattered throughout the world."[1]

The second major breakthrough occurred during the Wei-Jin Period, in the third and fourth centuries (220–316 C.E.), when Confucianism as the dominant intellectual mode throughout the Han dynasty (202 B.C.E.–220 C.E.) gave way to the Neo-Daoist discourse, which was soon to converge with Buddhism to form the main flow of thought in China for many centuries to come. The transition from Confucianism to Neo-Daoism and Buddhism is a most severe rupture in Chinese intellectual history because the ontological mode of thinking of the former and the radical otherworldliness of the latter were established, not in the places previously occupied by the classical exegesis and cosmology of Han Confucianism, but in an area where such ways of looking at the world did not exist. As a result, the Han Confucian tradition was not only revised but transcended, and a new tradition began to take shape.

The third and last major intellectual breakthrough in traditional China is, by general consent, the rise and development of Neo-Confucianism. The present chapter addresses some of the central issues involved in this last breakthrough.

Before my discussion begins, I wish to make clear that the emphasis in this study will be more on the interplay of intellectual breakthrough with sociocultural change than on the inner logic of the breakthrough itself. It is not my intention to present a synoptic view of Neo-Confucianism as a finished product of the breakthrough. From the point of view of a historian, it is rather the historical process leading to the Neo-Confucian breakthrough that particularly deserves examination.

It is common knowledge that the rise of Neo-Confucianism was involved with Buddhism in a dialectical, twofold relationship. On the one hand, it was a total root-and-branch rejection of the radical otherworldliness of Buddhism together with its antisocial values. On the other hand, in its philosophical reformulation, Neo-Confucianism borrowed conceptual categories from Buddhism. This common-knowledge view is correct in its general outline, and there is indeed much evidence to support it. Nevertheless, it seems to be a result of a narrow historical perspective. To see the rise of Neo-Confucianism in this way, it seems to me, one must assume that Buddhism had retained its original otherworldly character without change through the centuries since it first arrived in China. This is clearly contrary to all the known historical facts, however. Another underlying assumption is that the revival of Confucianism during the late Tang and early Song as a conscious response to social changes was self-generated. Considering, however, that during this period it was Buddhism and, to a lesser extent, Daoism that captured the Chinese mind and soul, one cannot help asking: Given the stereotyped and lifeless state of Confucian classical scholarship in the time of Han Yu 韓愈 (768–824) and Li Ao 李翱 (772–841), what source of inspiration could these two men have possibly drawn from the Confucian tradition to initiate an intellectual breakthrough of this magnitude?

The truth of the matter is that if we broaden our perspective and try to discern the general trends in the development of Chinese spirituality from the late Tang to the early Song, we would find that this last major breakthrough far transcended the boundaries of the intellectual movement generally identified as the rise of Neo-Confucianism, even though the latter's central importance from the eleventh century on is beyond dispute. Viewed as a whole, the breakthrough may be broadly defined as a spiritual movement taking a decidedly "this-worldly turn" (*rushi zhuanxiang* 入世轉向). The "prime mover" of the breakthrough, so to speak, was not Confucianism but the new Chan Buddhist School founded by Huineng 惠 (or 慧) 能 (638–713). It was this new Chan sect that started the whole process of the "this-worldly turn," which then set first Confucianism and later religious Daoism in motion.

The social origin of the new Chan School is beyond the scope of the present inquiry. Suffice it to say that the new Chan differed from the traditional one in that while the latter, as represented by Shenxiu 神秀 (600–706), enjoyed the patronage of the aristocracy, the former generally appealed more to people of the lower social strata. According to tradition, Huineng, the founder, was at best semiliterate. Moreover, after he had supposedly received the patriarchal robe from the Fifth Patriarch, he spent no less than sixteen years among the common people, including peasants and merchants. As is well known, his teaching consists primarily of a theory about complete and sudden enlightenment, which can be attained by directly pointing to one's original mind and seeing one's true nature without the use of written texts. It also shows a strong iconoclastic tendency with regard to such matters as Buddhas, bodhisattvas, and rituals. Needless to say, this kind of "simple and easy" teaching was better suited to the spiritual needs of the masses than the elite of the time. The famous writer Liang Su 梁蕭 (753–793) once remarked about the teaching of the new Chan in the following words: "When they preach these doctrines to the average man, or men below the average, they are believed by all those who live their lives of worldly desires."[2] Little wonder that it was the new Chan that had developed out of "the lives of worldly desires" of the ordinary people that took the first step in the "this-worldly turn."

The "this-worldly turn" of the new Chan School is nowhere more clearly revealed than in *Liuzu tanjing* 六祖壇經 (The Platform Sutra of the Sixth Patriarch). Section 36 of the Dunhuang text reads, in part, as follows: "The Master said: 'Good friends, if you wish to practice, it is all right to do so as laymen; you don't have to be in a temple. If you are in a temple but do not practice, you are like the evil-minded people of the West. If you are a layman but do practice, you are practicing the good of the people of the East. Only I beg of you, practice purity yourselves; this then is the Western Land.' "[3] The long verse in the same section also has the following lines:

> From the outset the Dharma has been in the world;
> Being in the world, it transcends the world.
> Hence do not seek the transcendental world outside,
> By discarding the present world itself.[4]

To us today these words are commonplace, but to the ears of Huineng's audience, they must have sounded like a "lion's roar" or a "tidal wave." Huineng's message is quite clear: lay believers need not abandon this world and seek salvation in the temples, for the Dharma has always been in this world. On the contrary, only after one has practiced one's faith in the daily life of the world can this world be transcended. As the common Chan saying expresses it so well, "in carrying water and chopping firewood: therein lies the wondrous *Dao*."[5]

After the An Lu-shan Rebellion, imperial and aristocratic patronage of Buddhism declined markedly. Economically, the Buddhist monks in the monasteries had to rely more and more on their own hard work for support. As a result, a new worldly work ethic began to emerge in the Buddhist communities. Again it was the new Chan School that took the lead in this further development of the "this-worldly turn." As we know, according to original Buddhist texts of discipline (*vinaya*), the clergy were not allowed to engage in agricultural work for fear of killing living beings (e.g., insects, plants, and trees). Begging and collecting donations were the normal way of their economic life. However, in the late eighth or early ninth century, the Chan Master Baizhang Huaihai 百丈懷海 (720–814) of the Baizhang Mountains in modern Jiangxi introduced a new principle in his revised text of monastic rules known as the *Baizhang qinggui* 百丈清規 (Pure Rules of Baizhang), which required all the monks in the monastery, irrespective of age and rank, to work equally to earn their own living. He also invented the famous motto, "a day without work, a day without meals,"[6] which not only was generally followed by Buddhist monks but even became proverbial in the lay society. This motto certainly reminds us of the saying of St. Paul, "If a man will not work, neither shall he eat," as emphatically quoted with approval by John Calvin.

It is important to note the psychological tension created by this new monastic rule. One of Huaihai's disciples asked him: "Is it sinful to cut grasses, chop trees, dig the field, and turn over the soil?" The Master answered: "I cannot say that it is definitely sinful. Whether it is sinful or not depends on how the person does it. If he does it with a worldly sense of gain and loss, then surely he has committed a sin. However, if he does it with a transcendent state of mind, then he has committed no sin at all."[7] The tension shown in the above dialogue is sufficient proof that the new rule laid down by Huaihai was a sharp break with tradition, and thus a "breakthrough," for the process of breakthrough must of necessity be pregnant with tension until the breaking point is reached. To illustrate the pre-breakthrough Buddhist practice in this area, allow me to cite the following example: A monk in Shansi named Sengxi 僧襲 (578–641) was in charge of the rice cultivation as a "superintendent" of his monastery. However, when he saw that numerous insects in the field were killed in the process of work, he found the cruelty too much to bear. As a result, he gave up his "superintendent" post.[8] This example gives us a clear notion of the seriousness with which the Buddhists viewed the sin of killing of lives in agricultural work.

Even though Sengxi was not personally engaged in the work, mere supervision already created more guilty feelings than his conscience could possibly take. The profound meaning of the above-quoted conversation between Huaihai and his disciple must be grasped in light of this long-established practice in Buddhism.

After the breakthrough, however, the case was altered. Everyday worldly activities such as agriculture were no longer viewed in a negative way. On the contrary, they were given a religious significance. Consider the following conversation between Lingyou of the Wei Mountains 溈山靈祐 (771–853) and his disciple Huiji of the Yang Mountains 仰山慧寂 (807–883) when the latter came to pay tribute at the end of a summer: "Lingyou said to Huiji: 'I have not seen you here for a whole summer. What sort of things have you been doing down there?' Huiji replied: 'I ploughed a piece of land and sowed a basketful of seeds.' Lingyou remarked: 'In that case, your summertime has not been wasted.'"[9] Since Lingyou was Huaihai's disciple, we can assume that he not only accepted the latter's new teaching but also passed it on to the next generation. In this conversation, which took place only a few decades later than Huaihai's discussion quoted above, the idea that killing living beings in agricultural work is a sin is totally absent. Instead we find that productive labor is praised as a virtue and that wasting time in the sense of failing to do one's share of everyday activities is among the worst of sins. Max Weber obviously overstates his case when he says: "Labour is an approved ascetic technique, as it always has been in the Western Church, in sharp contrast not only to the Orient but to almost all monastic rules the world over."[10] As a matter of fact, in its emphasis on the Dharma always being in this world, on every individual being's immediate access to transcendent reality (without the intermediaries of either the Buddhist sangha or even the sûtras), and above all, on combining productive activity in this world with an otherworldly aim, the new Chan School is definable in every sense in terms of "inner-worldly asceticism" in the Weberian typology of religion. Thus, its emergence clearly marks the end of otherworldly asceticism and the beginning of the "this-worldly turn" at the same time.

From the ninth century on, Chan masters always stressed the point that the Way or Truth is nowhere to be found apart from the ordinary daily life. When a newcomer went to seek instruction from Master Congshen of Zhaozhou 趙州從諗 (778–897), the Master asked him, "Did you have your pottage for breakfast?" "Yes, I did," he answered. "Then go clean your pot," said the Master.[11] Master Yixuan of Linji 臨濟義玄 (d. 867) said it all when he lectured to his audience with the following words: "My fellow monks, the Buddhist Dharma is not something that you can find a specific way to search for. It consists of nothing but the ordinary life: To move the bowels and pass water, to put on clothes and eat, and when you are tired, to go take a rest. Stupid people would surely laugh at me, but the wise would understand what I mean."[12] What Yixuan is really saying is that the monastic life should not be different from the lay life. Someone asked Master Wenyan of Yunmen 雲門文偃 (864–949) what a Buddhist monk ought to do when he behaves like an ordinary human being. The Master said: "In the morning, he brings the plough to the field and in the evening he pulls it back."[13] Here we see how the new Chan School gradually transformed otherworldly asceticism into inner-worldly asceticism. Sebastian Franck once said, "You think you have escaped from the monastery, but everyone must now be a monk throughout his life." According to Weber, this statement sums up "the spirit of the Reformation."[14] In the Chinese case, I imagine, a Chan Master probably would say to the monks: "You think you have escaped from the world, but every monk in the monastery must now be a man of the world throughout his life." The emphasis may be different, but the result is similar. Unlike the ascetic dogmas of Protestantism, however, Chan Buddhism did not create an adequate ethics for the full development of Chinese inner-worldly asceticism. It was in the Neo-Confucian breakthrough that such an ethical foundation was eventually established.

Han Yu has long been held as the first precursor of Neo-Confucianism. This historical view is established on so solid a foundation that to defend its validity is superfluous and to question it is unwise. We must, however, ask some new questions about this well-established view. Why was it Han Yu rather than somebody else who started the Neo-Confucian breakthrough? Why did Han Yu find it necessary to revive the Confucian tradition by way of the *Mencius* and the *Daxue* 大學 (Great Learning), both texts, but particularly the latter, being relatively obscure in the Tang Period? Why were the Confucian *Dao* and its transmission conceived by Han Yu in such a peculiar way? Needless to say, to answer these questions fully requires more space than allowed here. What can be attempted below will be no more than an overview.

There are two inseparable and interrelated aspects to Han Yu's breakthrough, namely, criticism of Buddhism (and Daoism) on the negative side and revival of the Confucian *Dao* on the positive side. In his own day, he was primarily known for the negative side, especially his anti-Buddhist memorial of 819. Since the Song dynasty on, however, he has been more appreciated for the positive side, especially his famous essay on the *Dao*, written sometime before 805. But paradoxically, it is generally agreed among scholars today that his criticism of Buddhism is singularly lacking in originality, as all of his arguments can be found in anti-Buddhist writings of earlier critics, beginning with Fu Yi's 傳奕 memorial of 621. On the other hand, it has also been often pointed out that from a strictly philosophical point of view, Han Yu's exposition of the Confucian *Dao* is unsophisticated and uninteresting. Such being the case, how are we to justify his historical role as the first precursor in the Neo-Confucian breakthrough?

I would suggest that Han Yu's importance lies neither in critical originality nor philosophical profundity, but in his creative synthesis of both the negative and the positive aspects that laid the ground for Confucianism to carry the "this-worldly turn" to a new historical stage. Unlike the anti-Buddhist critics before him who had nothing positive to offer, Han Yu clearly showed a way to return to this world without abandoning the other world, which all along had been the main attraction of Buddhism to the Chinese. Citing Confucian texts, particularly the *Great Learning* and the *Mencius*, as his authority, he tried to show, in his "Yuandao" 原道 (Essentials of the Moral Way) and other essays, that political and social order in this world is ultimately grounded in a transcendent reality known as the Heavenly Law (or Heavenly Constancy; *Tianchang* 天常).

The ancient sages had discovered this great truth long ago and called it the *Dao*. This true Confucian *Dao*, he emphatically pointed out, is to be distinguished from the Buddhist *Dao*, known as nirvana, which is the cessation of all existence.

In "Essentials of the Moral Way," Han Yu says:

> Now what is this *Dao*? I reply that what I call the *Dao* is not what has hitherto been so called by the Daoists and Buddhists. Yao transmitted it to Shun; Shun transmitted it to Yu; Yu transmitted it to (King) Wen and (King) Wu, and the Duke of Zhou; Wen and Wu and the Duke of Zhou transmitted it to Confucius; Confucius transmitted it to Mencius. After Mencius died, it was no longer transmitted.[15]

This is his most famous theory of the transmission of the *Dao* (*daotong* 道統). But where did he get such an idea? Is it really the case, as has been generally assumed, that his inspiration came from a reading of the last section in the *Mencius*? If we believe with Hans-Georg Gadamer that understanding is always "the fusion of horizons" of the past and the present, and that "every encounter with tradition that takes place within historical consciousness involves the experience of the tension between the text and the present," then we must also take into account the horizon Han Yu acquired in his own present time.[16] Noticing that Han Yu had spent two or three years in his early life (from 777 on) in Shaozhou, the birthplace of the new Chan School, and moreover that it also happened to be the time when the new Chan movement was at its height, Chen Yinke suggested that Han Yu's theory of the transmission of the *Dao* was actually modeled on the Chan legend about the transmission of the Dharma, which had been very much in vogue since the time of Huineng, the Sixth Patriarch.[17]

There is indeed much in Han Yu's writings that would lend support to Chen Yinke's thesis. In the essay "Essentials of the Moral Way," he criticized the Buddhist idea of "governing the mind" (*zhixin* 治心) to "escape from the world," and countered it with the Confucian theory of "rectifying the mind" (*zhengxin* 正心) as the spiritual basis for eventually "bringing order to the world." On the surface, it would seem that he was proposing something diametrically opposite to the new Chan School in which the exclusive concern was the cultivation of the mind. In reality, however, it was no more than an imitation in disguise, for to do exactly the opposite is also a mode of imitation.

In Han Yu's essay "Shi shuo" 師說 (On Teachers), traces of the Chan influence are no less obvious.[18] In his day, the ordinary Confucian teacher was generally held in contempt, a fact to which the writings of Liu Zongyuan 柳宗元 (773–819) and Lü Wen 呂溫 (771–781) fully testify. Han Yu, therefore, knew very well that unless the dignity of the Confucian teacher were reestablished, efforts to revive Confucianism would be doomed. By contrast, the Chan master as teacher commanded tremendous respect in late Tang society. It is quite clear that Han Yu's definition of an ideal Confucian teacher in terms of "transmission of the *Dao*" (*chuan Dao* 傳道) and "removal of delusion" (*jiehuo* 解惑) was modeled on the Chan master. The term *huo* (delusion) may even be identified as Chan language. As a common Chan saying of the time goes, "Bodhidharma came to the East with only one purpose in mind: To find someone who was free from delusions." Two further points in "On Teachers" also deserve comment. First, the essay stresses the point that "whoever is in possession of the *Dao* is a teacher, irrespective of his social status and age."[19] This is particularly characteristic of a Chan master such as Huineng, who was not only of humble social background but also had disciples older than he in age. Second, the essay concludes with the notion that a disciple may not necessarily be inferior to his teacher in wisdom. This idea also smacks of the Chan conception of the teacher–disciple relationship. As another of Master Lingyou's mottos goes, "A disciple worthy of teaching is one who surpasses his teacher in wisdom."[20]

Hitherto, the genesis of Han Yu's thought has been examined mainly in the Confucian context; its relation to Buddhism is noted only in a general and imprecise way. Once it is shown that his reformulation of the Confucian *Dao* was specifically linked to the prevailing mode of thinking of the new Chan School, many puzzles about it disappear. Given Han Yu's sensitive mind, it would indeed be incomprehensible that he could have remained totally oblivious to the most powerful religious movement of the time. As a matter of fact, his poetic and epistolary pieces show that throughout his life he had extensive contact with Chan monks. He often expressed admiration for their spiritual praxis but had no sympathy for their renunciation of this world. At any rate, the evidence clearly suggests that Han Yu was sufficiently familiar with the new Chan School to be able to appropriate its teaching for his own Confucian use. What he appropriated from Chan Buddhism, however, was not individual ideas or concepts but the total paradigm evolved in the process of the Chan breakthrough. To the extent that Han Yu proposed to rebuild Confucian society, he was pushing to its logical end the "this-worldly turn" initiated by the Chan movement. To the extent that he reformulated the Confucian *Dao* after the model of the new Chan School, he was seeking to ground this world in a transcendent reality radically different from its Buddhist counterpart. It is true that his actual accomplishments in both areas are very limited, but as far as the Neo-Confucian breakthrough was concerned, it was he who set the direction as well as the basic guidelines for its development in the Song Period.

As we all know, the Chinese term for "Neo-Confucianism" is *Lixue* 理學, derived from the central concept of *li* (principle) or, better, *Tianli* 天理 (Heavenly Principle). Hence, the emergence of the idea of Heavenly Principle may be taken as the most characteristic feature of Neo-Confucianism that distinguishes it from its classical past. *Ren* 仁 (humanity), the key concept in the *Lunyu* (Analects), for example, has to be redefined in Zhu Xi's 朱熹 (1130–1200) commentary as "the principle of love." The Heavenly Principle is a fundamental and absolute concept of Neo-Confucianism, central not only to the Cheng-Zhu School but to the Lu-Wang School as well. Wang Yangming 王陽明 (1472–1529), therefore, unequivocally identifies his *liangzhi* 良知 as the Heavenly Principle.

Leaving aside the subtle differences with regard to its interpretation, we must ask why the idea of Heavenly Principle was central to the Neo-Confucian breakthrough. Before we can answer this question, it is necessary to say a word about the Buddhist response to Han Yu's initial breakthrough prior to Cheng Hao 程顥 (1032–1085) and Cheng Yi 程頤 (1033–1107). In this connection, two Buddhists thoroughly familiar with Han Yu's work may be mentioned together. The first is Monk Zhiyuan 智圓 (976–1022) of the Tiantai School, a great admirer of Han Yu. Under the latter's influence, he turned to the study of the Confucian classics, especially the *Mencius* and "Zhongyong" 中庸 (Doctrine of the Mean) late in his life. Unlike other Buddhists in late Tang and early Song who found the "Doctrine of the Mean" close to the Buddhist teachings in a general way, he specifically compared it to the Doctrine of the Middle Path (*Mâdhyamika*) of Nâgârjuna. His love of this Confucian text was so profound that he styled himself "Master of the Zhongyong." It is very significant that he not only accepted Han Yu's line of orthodox transmission of the Confucian *Dao* as historical fact but was also totally convinced by the latter's argument concerning the necessity of political and social order in this world. Confucianism and Buddhism, he believed, must complement each other. He has the following to say about the function of the two teachings:

> Confucianism is the teaching about governing the body, hence its name "The External Law," whereas Buddhism is the teaching about cultivating the mind, hence its name "The Internal Law." Alas! Confucianism and Buddhism—aren't they the outside and the inside of the same thing? People whose vision is confined only to this world often distort our teaching seriously and say that it ought to be discarded. But on the other hand, people who are restricted to Buddhism often take Confucianism as no more than a game. Do they realize that without the teachings of Confucius, neither can the state be governed, nor the family stabilized, nor the body settled? Then where is the Buddhist way to be practiced?[21]

The case of Zhiyuan shows clearly that by early Song times, the "this-worldly turn" had already spread from the Chan to other Buddhist schools. It is also important to note that before Han Yu's breakthrough was rediscovered by later Neo-Confucians, it had deeply touched the sensitive nerves of some Buddhists.

Our second case is Master Qisong 契嵩 (1007–1072) of the Yunmen sect, which dominated Chan Buddhism throughout the Song Period. He was a leading Buddhist prose writer after the style of Han Yu and a close friend of Ouyang Xiu 歐陽修 (1007–1072). Like Zhiyuan, he also studied Confucian classics ex tensively and held a very positive view about the basic Confucian social values, especially filial piety. Unlike Zhiyuan, however, he was best known for his powerful countercriticism of Han Yu's criticism of Buddhism. He said: "Alas! Master Han was nearsightedly concerned with human affairs and failed to see the far-reaching principles of life. Wasn't this perhaps a result of the fact that he only followed the outside but was oblivious to the inside?"[22] He also distinguished Buddhist teaching from Confucianism in the following way: "Mind is the basis of the Sage's (i.e., Buddha's) Way and its meaning. The worldly way depends on the Buddhist way for its root."[23] It may be readily observed that although Qisong's emphasis is somewhat different from Zhiyuan's, both of them nevertheless shared the view that Buddhism and Confucianism must cooperate with each other by each taking care of its own world. From the Buddhist point of view, however, the Confucian world is only an illusion created by the mind. It therefore follows that the real, transcendent world of mind is the exclusive concern of Buddhism. Obviously, they were only willing to yield to Han Yu's argument about the importance of this world, but remained totally unconvinced with regard to the transcendent nature of the Confucian *Dao*, a point that Han Yu merely assumed but did not argue for. It is against the background of this Buddhist response to Han Yu's breakthrough that the Neo-Confucian idea of Heavenly Principle must be understood.

Even as late as the eleventh century, the Chinese intellectual world was still very much under the spell of Chan Buddhism. True, since the beginning of the Song dynasty, Confucianism had been gradually but steadily gaining ground with renewed vigor and vitality. Generally speaking, however, it was viewed by Buddhists and non-Buddhists alike as a worldly teaching concerned entirely with political and social order without the support of any transcendent, metaphysical principles. The following conversation of Cheng Hao (or perhaps Cheng Yi) may be taken as evidence attesting to the great popularity of Chan Buddhism at that time:

> Yesterday in a gathering, everyone present was talking enthusiastically about Chan Buddhism. But I could not bring myself to do it. Alas! Since the trend has long been formed, what can we do to rectify it? In earlier times when Buddhism was at its height, its teaching consisted mainly of worshipping the Buddha's image. It was therefore less injurious to society. But today when people speak of Buddhism, they all insist that when it comes to topics such as "human nature," "Heavenly decree," "the Way," and "virtue," we must turn to the study of Buddhism. So it is the intelligent people who are the first to be misguided.[24]

It is quite clear, then, that the Neo-Confucian breakthrough would not be complete unless and until Neo-Confucians could succeed in developing a metaphysical vision of the transcendent reality of their own that took the place of

Chan Buddhism. In other words, the vital area in which Neo-Confucianism must compete with Chan Buddhism was not this world but the other world. As we have seen above, the followers of Chan had been willing all along to cede this world to the Confucians. It was for this reason, I believe, that the Song Neo-Confucians, from Zhou Dunyi 周敦頤 (1017–1073) onward, set as their central task the metaphysical construction of the Confucian other world, culminating in the idea of Heavenly Principle.

There is no need to elaborate on the idea of *Tianli* and all its ramifications here. Two observations, however, may be made on the nature of the Neo-Confucian other world in contrast to its Buddhist counterpart. In the first place, unlike the Buddhist "mind," which is defined in terms of void, annihilation, or nonbeing, the Neo-Confucian Heavenly Principle is real. As Cheng Yi explains: "Heaven is in possession of this Principle, which has been followed and practiced by the sages. This is the so-called Way (*Dao*). Our sages take Heaven as their base, whereas the Buddhists take the mind as their base."[25] The Heavenly Principle must be both transcendent and real at the same time to provide the existence of this world with a permanent basis. The Buddhists, by contrast, believe that the phenomenal world has no permanent existence, being a "net of delusion" arising out of "ignorance" (*wuming* 無明 or *avidyā*). In the second place, in Buddhism, the Chan School included, this world and the other world may well be envisioned as running in opposite directions. Even after taking a "this-worldly turn," a Chan Buddhist would ultimately still have to abandon "this shore" in order to be able to land in the "other shore." This is the tenet that Buddhists of all persuasions must keep. Thus, in contrast to the Buddhist other world that, so to speak, turns its back against this world, the Neo-Confucian other world turns its face toward this world. Instead of abandoning this world, the Neo-Confucians seek to improve this world on the model of the other world. This is possible because the Confucian other world is conceived as a source of power with which this world can be transformed through the agency of man.

In the foregoing I have suggested that the Neo-Confucian other world of Heavenly Principle was developed as a direct response to the Buddhist claim of the day that the function of Confucian teaching is strictly confined to this world while Buddhism assumes full responsibility for the other world. This is tantamount to saying that Buddhism is the *ti* 體 (substance) and Confucianism is the *yong* 用 (function). In Western terminology, it comes close to a division between the world of value and the world of fact. Needless to say, such a formulation was totally unacceptable to the Neo-Confucians.

Earlier in this paper, I also proposed to view the whole development from the new Chan School to Neo-Confucianism as a spiritual movement taking a "this-worldly turn." Seen in this way, the construction of the Neo-Confucian other world of Heavenly Principle must be recognized as an event of singular importance in the whole movement. Within the Confucian tradition, we may even say that it constitutes the very essence of the Neo-Confucian breakthrough. This is the case because the Neo-Confucian other world, with its emphasis on life and creativity, provided the this-worldly movement during the Tang-Song transition with the support of an Archimedean point it very much needed. By contrast, the Buddhist other world of nirvana was too negative to serve this purpose. It is true that the Chan School did bring the other world much closer to this world by identifying nirvana with the original substance of the Buddha-mind present in all men. Since nothing, however, is ultimately gained in the attainment of Buddhahood through enlightenment, the Chan other world still falls short in providing this world with a transcendent power necessary for its transformation.

On the surface, the emergence of the Confucian other world marks a sharp break with Buddhism in Chinese intellectual history. There can also be no doubt that at the explicit level of consciousness, the Neo-Confucians were making every effort to distinguish themselves from the Buddhists. In a deeper sense, however, the Neo-Confucian breakthrough may be better understood as continuous with the this-worldly turn initially taken by the new Chan School in the eighth century. In fact, during much of the Song Period, the paradigm of the Chan breakthrough continued to inspire the Neo-Confucians in many aspects. A few examples may be proffered to illustrate this point. Cheng Hao once said that the Chan Buddhists talk only of "knowing one's mind and seeing one's nature" but have nothing comparable to what the Confucians call "preserving one's mind and nourishing one's nature," a reference to the Confucian type of moral cultivation.[26] But Xie Liangzuo 謝良佐 (1050–1103), a leading disciple of the two Chengs, is reported to have told the story that Cheng Yi had at one time studied spiritual exercises with a Chan monk and learned all of his methods. He then "stole" these methods from the monk and appropriated them for his own use. Commenting on this story, Zhu Xi remarked:

> In the beginning, all Buddhism could offer were words; spiritual practice of "preserving and nourishing" was lacking. It was the Sixth Patriarch of the Tang dynasty who began to teach the method of "preserving and nourishing." His followers, however, only talked about it but did not actually apply it to themselves. It was Yichuan (Cheng Yi) who began to teach people how to apply it to themselves. This is perhaps why it is said that Yichuan had stolen it from Buddhism for his own use.[27]

It is truly amazing that Xie Liangzuo could have openly accused his teacher of "stealing" the method of cultivation from a Chan monk. As we can see, Xie's report is directly contradictory to Cheng Hao's statement. It is even more amazing, however, that Zhu Xi could have been so honest as to admit without the slightest hesitation that the method of "preserving and nourishing" was indeed first developed by Huineng. The only part of Zhu Xi's conversation that is untrue is probably the suggestion that Huineng's "followers only talked about it but did not actually apply it to themselves." Moral cultivation, as we all know, is at the very center of the Neo-Confucian project, and yet, by their own admission, it was an adaptation from the Chan paradigm.

Our second example concerns the regulations of the Neo-Confucian school for children. Lu Jiuling 陸九齡 (Lu Xiangshan's brother) once discussed ways of establishing such regulations with Zhu Xi. The latter replied: "It would be better if we could just follow the example of the *Chan Yuan qinggui* 禪苑清規 (Pure Rules of Chan Yuan)."[28] The *Pure Rules of Chan Yuan*, it may be noted, is a revised text of the famous *Pure Rules of Baizhang*, compiled by Zongze in 1103. It is revealing that Zhu Xi should consider the monastic regulations and rules of Chan Buddhism worth following as a model for Neo-Confucian elementary education. This story also shows how closely the Neo-Confucians in Song times had followed the development of the Chan School.

Our last example is about the spiritual rather than the technical influence of Chan Buddhism on the Neo-Confucian breakthrough. One of the most obvious social consequences of the breakthrough was the emergence, among the *shi* 士 (scholar) class, of a high sense of mission and responsibility toward this world. This new self-consciousness of the *shi* class, of course, had much to do with the social changes during the Tang-Song transition. The total disappearance of a hereditary aristocracy in Song China promoted the *shi* class to the leading position in society. As a result, there appeared on the scene a number of Neo-Confucian reformers who, though of obscure origin, took it as their responsibility to rebuild society. Among them, Fan Zhongyan 范仲淹 (989–1052) and Wang Anshi 王安石 (1021–1086) are two outstanding examples. Even before he had passed the civil examinations, Fan Zhongyan already expressed the view that a Confucian scholar is one who must take the whole world as his personal responsibility. Later he introduced the new ideal of the Confucian scholar as "one who is first in worrying about the world's troubles and last in enjoying its pleasures." There can be little doubt that Neo-Confucians such as Fan and Wang must have been more or less inspired by the earlier exemplary personalities in the Confucian tradition, particularly Mencius. Fan's maxim, for instance, can be shown to be an adaptation from a sentence in the *Mencius*, and Wang also, in a poem, openly expressed his great admiration for the moral idealism of Mencius. It is also reasonable, however, to assume that Neo-Confucian idealists such as Fan and Wang may have also been, to varying degrees, influenced by the new spirit of Chan Buddhism resulting from a this-worldly reorientation. The late Arthur F. Wright made an interesting observation that Fan's maxim was probably the bodhisattva ideal cast in secular Chinese terms.[29] I would like to suggest that if Fan's maxim should indeed prove to be partly of Buddhist origin, it may not have been the bodhisattva ideal in general but rather the Yunmen branch of the Chan School in particular. The Yunmen sect not only occupied a central and dominant place in Song Buddhism but was particularly noted for its "love of mankind" (*ai zhongsheng* 愛眾生) and "inner worldly asceticism" (*rushi kuxing* 入世苦行). The case of Wang Anshi can lend support to my contention. According to the famous Chan monk-poet Huihong 惠洪 (1071–1128), when he lived a quiet, retired life in Jinling (Nanjing) in his later years, Wang Anshi once reminisced with a friend about his political career. He said, "You know, I accepted the appointment of the prime ministership only because I had been moved by a saying of the Chan master Xuefeng 雪峰 (822–908)." The friend then asked him what that saying was. He quoted from memory the following sentence: "You old fellow, what have you ever done for mankind?"[30]

Master Xuefeng (Yicun 義存), it must be noted, was none other than the teacher of Master Wenyan (864–949), the founder of the Yunmen sect. This anecdote is by no means unreliable hearsay. On the contrary, its historical authenticity can be fully established on the basis of Wang Anshi's poems in which his compassion to save humankind in the Buddhist sense finds deeply touching expressions.

In concluding, I must make it clear that I am not repeating the outworn traditional charge against Neo-Confucianism by suggesting that it is no more than Chan Buddhism in disguise. There is not the slightest doubt in my mind that Neo-Confucianism is a renewal of the Confucian tradition in its main outlines. All I am saying is that the Neo-Confucian breakthrough as a historical phenomenon cannot be fully understood without also taking the Chan breakthrough into account. As a matter of fact, the rise of Neo-Confucianism makes better sense if viewed in a broader historical perspective as the culmination of the long-lasting spiritual movement initially activated by the new Chan School in the eighth century.

NOTES

1. Burton Watson, *The Complete Works of Chuang Tzu* (New York: Columbia University Press, 1968), 364, renders this passage from *Zhuangzi jishi*, 10B.1069 as follows: "and 'the art of the Way' in time comes to be rent and torn apart by the world (*daoshu jiang wei tianxia lie*)."

2. Liang Su, "Tiantai famen yi" 天台法門議, *QTW, juan* 517, *ce* 22 (Taipei: Huiwen, 1961 [reprint]).

3. Philip B. Yampolsky, *The Platform Sutra of the Sixth Patriarch* (The Text of the Tun-Huang Manuscript with Translation, Introduction, and Notes) (New York: Columbia University Press, 1967), 159.

4. Ibid., 161.

5. *Chuandeng lu* 傳燈録, *juan* 8: 263, CBETA, vol. 51, no. 2076; cited with a somewhat different translation in Fung Yu-lan, *A History of Chinese Philosophy*, trans. Derk Bodde (Princeton: Princeton University Press, 1953), 2:403.

6. Pu Ji 普濟, *Wudeng huiyuan* 五燈會元, *juan* 3 (Beijing: Zhonghua, 1984).

7. Zecangzhu 賾藏主, ed., *Guzun suyu lu* 古尊宿語録, *juan* 1 (Beijing: Zhonghua, 1994).

8. Daoxuan 道宣, *Xu gaosengzhuan* 續高僧傳, in *Gaosengzhuan* 高僧傳, *ji* 2, *juan* 21, "Seng Shan zhuan fu Seng Xi zhuan" 僧善傳附僧襲傳, *ce* 3 (Taipei: Yinjingchu 印經處, 1961).

9. *Wudeng huiyuan, juan* 9.

10. Max Weber, *The Protestant Ethic and the Spirit of Capitalism*, trans. Talcott Parsons (New York: Charles Scribner's Sons, 1958), 158.

11. Zecangzhu, *Guzun suyu lu, juan* 16.

12. Ibid., *juan* 4. See also Chan, *SB*, 446.

13. *Wudeng huiyuan, juan* 15.

14. See Max Weber, *Essays in Economic Sociology* (Princeton: Princeton University Press, 1999), 165, and his *General Economic History*, trans. Frank H. Knight (Glencoe, Ill.: Free Press, 1927).

15. *Changli xiansheng ji* 昌黎先生集, SBCK, *juan* 11. See also Wm. Theodore de Bary and Irene Bloom, eds., *Sources of the Chinese Tradition from Earliest Times to 1600*, 2nd ed. (New York: Columbia University Press, 1999), 1:569–573; this passage is on p. 573.

16. Hans-Georg Gadamer, *Truth and Method*, 2nd rev. ed. (New York: Crossroad, 1989, 317, or New York: Continuum Books, 1997, 306).

17. Chen Yinke 陳寅恪, "Lun Han Yu" 論韓愈, in *Jinmingguan conggao chubian* 金明館叢稿初編 (Shanghai: Guji, 1980), 286.

18. *Changli xiansheng ji*, SBCK, *juan* 12.

19. Ibid.

20. Zecangzhu, *Guzun suyu lu, juan* 5, "Linji chanshi yulu zhiyu" 臨濟禪師語録之餘; the phrase "zhihui guoshi" 智慧過師 is also in *Jingde chuandeng lu* 景德傳燈録, *juan* 16, "Quanhuo zhuan" 全豁傳, SBCK.

21. "Zhongyongzi zhuan" 中庸子傳, in *Xianju bian* 閑居編, *juan* 19, *Xuzangjing* 續藏經本.

22. "Fei Han shang diyi" 非韓上第一, *Tanjin wenji* 鐔津文集, *juan* 14, SBCK.

23. "Quanxue diyi" 勸學第一, ibid., *juan* 1; "Wanyan shu shang Renzong huangdi" 萬言書上仁宗皇帝, ibid., *juan* 9.

24. "Lunxue pian" 論學篇, *Er Cheng ji* 二程集, *Chengshi cuiyan* 程氏粹言, *juan* 1 (Beijing: Zhonghua, 1981).

25. *Er Cheng ji* 二程集, *Chengshi yishu* 程氏遺書, *juan* 21B.

26. See *Mencius*, 7A.1, translated in De Bary and Bloom, *Sources of Chinese Tradition*, 1:155.

27. ZYL (Beijing: Zhonghua, 1986), *juan* 126.

28. Ibid., *juan* 7.

29. Arthur F. Wright, *Buddhism in Chinese History* (Stanford, Calif.: Stanford University Press, 1959), p. 93.

30. Hui Hong 惠洪, "Shengren duo sheng Ru Fo zhong" 聖人多生儒佛中, *Lengzhai yehua* 冷齋夜話, *juan* 10, SKQS edition.

9. Morality and Knowledge in Zhu Xi's Philosophical System

MORAL NATURE VERSUS INQUIRY AND STUDY

In a letter to Xiang Anshi 項安世 (Xiang Pingfu 項平父, 1153–1208), Zhu Xi (1130–1200) wrote:

> Generally speaking, since the time of Zisi 子思 "honoring the moral nature" (*zun dexing* 尊德性) and "following the path of inquiry and study" (*dao wenxue* 道問學) have been the two basic methods of instruction according to which people are taught to exert themselves.[1] Now, what Zijing 子靜 [Lu Xiangshan 陸象山, 1139–1193] talks about are matters pertaining exclusively to "honoring the moral nature," whereas in my daily discussions I have placed a greater emphasis on "inquiry and study." . . . From now on, I ought to turn my attention inwardly to self-cultivation. Thus, by removing weakness on the one hand and gathering strength on the other, I probably would be able to prevent myself from falling into one-sidedness.[2]

This letter was written in 1183 in response to a criticism made by Lu Xiangshan. However, when Lu later learned about the letter, he remarked pointedly, saying: "Zhu Yuanhui 朱元晦 [Zhu Xi] wanted to get rid of the defects and combine the merits of both sides. But I do not think this is possible. If one does not know anything about honoring the moral nature, how can there be inquiry and study in the first place?"[3] These exchanges have led later scholars to believe that the basic difference between Zhu and Lu lies in the fact that the former stressed the importance of "inquiry and study" (*dao wenxue*), whereas the latter stressed that of "moral nature" (*zun dexing*). Wu Cheng 吳澄 (1249–1333) was probably more responsible than anybody else for the initial dissemination of this view.[4] By the time of the Ming dynasty (1368–1644), this view had become so firmly established that even Wang Yangming 王陽明 (1472–1529) found it difficult to alter.[5] Although Wang Yangming's powerful refutation was generally accepted by his followers without question,[6] it nevertheless failed to eradicate completely this popular view. Thus, we find the very same distinction perpetuated in the *Song-Yuan xue-an* 宋元學案 (Scholarly Cases of Song and Yuan Classical Scholars), where Huang Zongxi 黃宗羲 (1610–1695) explicitly remarks that Lu Xiangshan's teaching was focused on *zun dexing* and Zhu Xi's was on *dao wenxue*. While neither side completely ignored the emphasis of the other, the difference between the two in terms of priority was nevertheless a real one.[7]

However, my purpose here is not to discuss the philosophical differences between Zhu and Lu. Instead, I set as my central task in this study to examine the relationship between morality and knowledge in Zhu Xi's philosophical system. Like *li* 理 (principle) and *qi* 氣 (material force), *Tianli* 天理 (Heavenly Principle) and *renyu* 人欲 (human desire), or *yin* and *yang* 陰陽 (passive and active cosmic forces), morality and knowledge form a polarity in Zhu Xi's thought.[8] Because of its central position in his system, Zhu Xi used many different paired concepts in the Confucian tradition to express this polarity. Apart from *zun dexing* and *dao wenxue*, which are clearly an overarching pair in this category, there are also other polarized pairs such as "seriousness" (*jing* 敬) and "learning" (*xue* 學), "self-cultivation" (*hanyang* 涵養) and "extension of knowledge" (*zhizhi* 致知), "exercise of seriousness" (*jujing* 居敬) and "exhaustive investigation of principle" (*qiongli* 窮理), "essentialism" (*yue* 約) and "erudition" (*bo* 博), and "a single thread" (*yiguan* 一貫) and "extensive knowledge" (*duoshi* 多識). Each and every one of these pairs of polarized concepts describes in its own way the relationship between morality and knowledge. It is therefore necessary to treat them below as "unit-ideas," borrowing the terminology of Arthur O. Lovejoy.[9]

To begin with, we must try to understand Zhu Xi's statement, quoted above, about his emphasis on "inquiry and study." Does this mean that he assigned a greater importance to knowledge than to morality? Needless to say, this could not possibly have been the case. "Honoring the moral nature" was a central and fundamental assumption in Neo-Confucianism shared by all individual thinkers irrespective of their different views on other matters. Zhu Xi was certainly no exception. Like Lu Xiangshan, he also took "honoring the moral nature" to be the primary and ultimate goal toward which all "inquiry and study" must be directed. Morality not only takes precedence over, but also gives meaning to knowledge.[10]

The question then inevitably arises: If this is the case, why did Zhu Xi, by his own admission, place a greater emphasis on "inquiry and study"? First of all, it is important to point out that in the letter to Xiang Anshi quoted above, Zhu Xi is not talking about the relative importance of knowledge vis-à-vis morality in Confucian learning as a whole. There, it may be recalled, he is merely referring to "honoring the moral nature" and "following the paths of inquiry and study" as two "methods of instruction." In other words, his emphasis on "inquiry and study" was made, not on the general theoretical level, but on the practical, pedagogic level.[11] I am not suggesting, however, that their overall differences are reducible to a pedagogic one. As we shall see below, Zhu Xi's emphasis on "inquiry and study" is very much a reflection of his philosophical views on such key concepts as "principle" (*li*) and "mind" (*xin* 心). All I am saying is that the traditional distinction between Zhu and Lu in terms of *zun dexing* versus *dao wenxue* is more apparent than real; its validity is rather limited in scope.

Having clarified this point, the above question must be modified as follows: Why was it necessary for Zhu Xi to say a great deal about "inquiry and study" but relatively less about "honoring the moral nature" in his instructions? The answer is provided by Zhu Xi himself. He says:

> The actual work in the realm of inquiry and study involves many items, but that in the realm of "honoring the moral nature" is rather simple. For instance, Yichuan 伊川 [Cheng Yi 程頤, 1033–1107] only said: "To be serious is to concentrate on one" and "to concentrate on one means not to go away from it." That is all ["honoring the moral nature"] is about and there is nothing else. However, in the past my discussions on the side of "honoring the moral nature" have been rather light. Now I feel this to be a mistake. The first part of the phrase ["honoring the moral nature"] provides a general framework so that the work of "inquiry and study" can be carried out meaningfully.[12]

Hence, according to Zhu, while "honoring the moral nature" is a matter of the first order, there is nevertheless very little that can be directly said about the former. In his view, the so-called honoring the moral nature involves mainly establishing as well as maintaining a moral state of mind, which is identifiable with Cheng Yi's "seriousness" or "reverence" (*jing*). This brings us naturally to Cheng Yi's best-known formula, "Self-cultivation requires seriousness; the pursuit of learning depends on the extension of knowledge."[13]

SELF-CULTIVATION VERSUS EXTENSION OF KNOWLEDGE: STRUGGLE WITH CHENG YI'S FORMULA

As we know, throughout his long intellectual life, Zhu Xi placed this formula at the very center of his teaching. As a matter of fact, he regarded this formula as a most satisfactory reformulation of the polarity of *zun dexing* and *dao wenxue*.[14] Although he discussed a great deal more about "seriousness" or "reverence" than about "honoring the moral nature," his conception of the relationship between "seriousness" and "extension of knowledge" bears a remarkable resemblance to that between *zun dexing* and *dao wenxue*. "Seriousness" is not a separate task to be accomplished before everything else can be carried out. Rather, it is a state of mind or mental attitude under which knowledge can be effectively extended.[15] In other words, "exercise of seriousness" and "extension of knowledge" must begin simultaneously.[16] It is in this reformulation that his views of the relationship between morality and knowledge are most fully revealed.

There can be no doubt that the first part of Cheng Yi's formula, "self-cultivation requires seriousness," falls exclusively into the category of morality and therefore constitutes the key to Confucian learning.[17] However, the second part, "the pursuit of learning depends on the extension of knowledge," requires a word of explanation. Zhu Xi says: " 'The investigation of things' simply means that in regard to a thing that comes to our attention we make an exhaustive study of all its principles. 'The extension of knowledge,' on the other hand, means that after we have studied exhaustively the principles of a thing, our knowledge of it becomes complete. We obtain this knowledge as if we have extended it [from our minds]."[18] "The investigation of things" (*gewu* 格物) and "the extension of knowledge" (*zhizhi* 致知) are, in this case, taken as two different descriptions of the same operation seeking to discover the "principles" of things. We use the term *gewu* when we speak of this operation from the point of view of the object of investigation and the term *zhizhi* when we speak of it from the point of view of the knowing subject. In light of the above discussion, Cheng Yi's formula as understood and interpreted by Zhu Xi may be seen as involving altogether three aspects. First, a moral attitude of "seriousness" or "reverence" must be established and maintained at all times; second, an intellectual activity of *gewu* or *zhizhi* must be pursued in a spiritual state of "seriousness" or "reverence"; third, as a result, "principles" (*li*) of things become known. In Zhu Xi's view, this operation is an endless, ongoing process in the life of every truly confirmed Confucian. It is through this spiritual journey that a Confucian seeks to bring his moral nature to perfection. Thus, taken as a whole, these three aspects constitute a total system of moral practice. Yet even in such a system of primarily moral character, we find that the role assigned to knowledge by Zhu Xi is essential even though it is, paradoxically, also secondary at the same time.

On the surface, it is true that "seriousness" and "reverence" are moral language and that "principles" are also primarily principles of the moral kind. A closer examination shows, however, that "investigation of things" or "extension of knowledge"—the central and operative part of the entire system—is clearly a reference to an intellectual process by which knowledge is gained about "principles of things." That this process is necessarily intellectual can be explained by the fact that in Zhu Xi's conception, the mind (xin) is identified with material force (qi), the most intelligent and sensitive of all the material forces.[19] In investigating things, internal or external, the mind only seeks to know their constitutive principles in an objective way; it does not engage in moral activities of any kind on this level. Even though the initial decision to investigate a thing is a moral one and the knowledge thus gained is only to serve moral ends, there is nevertheless no indication that in Zhu Xi's system morality is ever allowed to interfere directly with the intellectual operation of gewu or zhizhi. Moral considerations always take place on a different (from the Neo-Confucian point of view, however, higher) level.

Throughout his life, Zhu Xi never swerved from the view that knowledge must precede practice or action (xing 行). While this cannot be taken to mean that he valued knowledge above everything else in life, it does reveal nonetheless his central concern with the intellectual foundation of morality. He said: "Knowledge and practice always require each other like the eyes and legs of a man. Without legs, a man cannot walk although he has eyes, but without eyes, he cannot see although he has legs. With respect to order, knowledge comes first; with respect to importance, however, a greater weight must be attached to practice."[20] Here Zhu Xi is clearly talking about the relationship between knowledge and morality. By "knowledge" he is referring to "extension of knowledge," which, as explained above, is basically an intellectual operation; by "practice" or "action" he is referring to moral practice—practice based on the "principles" obtained from the "extension of knowledge." Since, according to him, the pursuit of knowledge can be justified not on its own ground but only on the ground of its relevance to moral life, it is therefore natural that between knowledge and morality, his emphasis lay ultimately on the latter. However, his insistence that "knowledge must precede practice" reveals unmistakably the crucial role that knowledge plays in his total system.

In response to a questioner, Zhu Xi said:

With regard to the question you raised yesterday about the order of self-cultivation, extension of knowledge and practice, I think self-cultivation should come first, extension of knowledge next, and practice still next. Without self-cultivation, you cannot become your own master.... Having cultivated yourself, you must extend your knowledge, and having extended your knowledge, you must put it into practice. Knowledge without practice is no different from having no knowledge, but all the three things must be done simultaneously. The order should not be taken to mean that you cultivate yourself today, extend your knowledge tomorrow and then practice it day after tomorrow.[21]

We can sense that he was at pains trying to establish the order of this triad. Clearly, the order here is conceived more as a logical one than a temporal one. In the actual temporal order, he always took the "extension of knowledge" to be the starting point of Confucian learning. Thus, when really hard pressed, he would not even hesitate to reverse the original order in Cheng Yi's formula by placing the "extension of knowledge" before "self-cultivation."[22] From his point of view, this is necessary because self-cultivation, like practice, must also be predicated on principles of the right kind. Without a correct knowledge of the principles involved, cultivation or practice would be blind.[23]

THE ROLE OF BOOK LEARNING

The above analysis shows that although Zhu Xi used Cheng Yi's formula as a heuristic principle throughout his long teaching career and always spoke of it with worshipful reverence, in practice he reinterpreted it in such a way that the role played by knowledge was clearly more active and central than in the original formulation. To clarify Zhu Xi's conception of knowledge, it is desirable that we now turn to his views on book learning and its relation to morality. Of all the Song dynasty (960–1279) Neo-Confucian philosophers, Zhu Xi alone emphasized the importance of book learning to the attainment of the Way and, moreover, developed a systematic methodology about it. It was this aspect of his thought that led to the criticism of a seventeenth-century thinker that "Master Zhu's learning consists wholly of book learning and nothing else."[24] While this is undoubtedly an overstatement, it nevertheless serves well as an illustration of the influence that his emphasis on book learning exerted on the subsequent development of Neo-Confucianism. Even his admirers characterized a central part of his teaching as "Study the principles thoroughly through book learning so that one's knowledge may be extended."[25]

To be fair to Zhu Xi, we must begin by pointing out that he never advocated the primacy of scholarship in Confucian learning. On the contrary, he made it very clear in his instructions that "Book learning is only a matter of the second order."[26] It is nevertheless true that on the whole, he was convinced that to be a good Confucian does commit one to a basic understanding of the original Confucian teaching and its tradition. In a memorial presented to the throne in 1194, he said:

> With regard to the way of learning, nothing is more urgent than a thorough study of principles; and a thorough study of principles must of

necessity consist in book learning.... All principles in the world are wondrous and subtle, each perfect in its own way, and eternally valid. However, only the ancient sages had been able to grasp them in their entirety. As a result, the words and the deeds [of the ancient sages] have all become permanent and fundamental exemplars for the later generations to emulate. Those who followed them were gentlemen and blessed; those who contradicted them were small men and accursed. The most blessed can preserve the empire and therefore serve as a positive example; the most accursed cannot even preserve his own person and would therefore serve as a negative example. These visible traces and necessary results are all contained in the classics and histories. A person who wishes to have a thorough knowledge of the principles in the world without first seeking them [in the classics and histories] is one who wishes to go forward but ends up standing right in front of a wall. This is why we say, "a thorough study of principles must of necessity consist in book learning."[27]

In this connection, two related observations may be made about Zhu Xi's theory of book learning. First, it appears that he honestly believed that the ancient sages had not only discovered most, if not all, of the principles but also embodied them in what they said and what they did. Because the words and the deeds of the sages are preserved in books, book learning naturally provides "the study of principles" with a most logical starting point. Little wonder that he identified book learning as a matter of "investigation of things."[28] In fact, it forms the most substantial part of his teaching of "investigation of things." In his famous "emendation" to the text of the *Daxue* 大學 (Great Learning), he says, "the first step in the education of the adult is to instruct the learner, in regard to all things in the world, to proceed from what knowledge he has of their principles, and investigate further until he reaches the limit."[29] There can be little doubt here he is primarily talking about knowledge derived initially from book learning as a basis for further study.

Second, book learning in his system is always morality oriented. He never advocated book learning for its own sake and without a moral focus. He specifically singled out, in the above memorial, classics and histories as the two kinds of books for study. This is because he believed that moral principles discovered by the sages are clearly recorded in the Confucian classics and their actualization in the past is amply illustrated in historical works. According to his disciple Yang Ji 楊楫, Zhu Xi's general educational program runs in the following order: The Four Books, the Six Classics, and histories. As for the literary art of the post-Qin and Han Period (221 B.C.E.–220 C.E.), he discussed it with students only in his spare time.[30] This testimony concerning the order of book learning not only agrees with the above memorial but is also corroborated by Zhu Xi's conversations. For instance, he once gave the following instruction to a student: "You should first read *Lunyu* [Analects], *Mencius*, and the 'Zhongyong' 中庸

[Doctrine of the Mean]. Then you turn to study one of the Confucian Classics. Finally, you should read histories. You will find [this order of book learning] easy to follow."[31] The criterion according to which Zhu Xi established his order of priority in book learning was knowledge of moral principles. Study of the *Analects* and *Mencius* should precede that of the Six Classics because, in his view, the former takes less time but yields more results while in the case of the latter, the contrary is true.[32] Historical works, on the other hand, report moral principles in actual operation.[33] However, history can only reveal the changes of the past and the present, and teach moral and practical lessons. It is quite irrelevant as far as moral cultivation of the self is concerned.[34] Hence, while Zhu Xi fully recognized the importance of history as a subject of study in Confucian learning, he nevertheless assigned it a low priority.

In a letter to his friend Lü Zuqian 呂祖謙 (1137–1181), Zhu Xi attributed the establishment of this order of study—the Four Books, Classics, histories—to Cheng Yi.[35] This may well have been the case. However, a close look at the recorded sayings of the two Cheng brothers does not exactly bear out Zhu Xi's statement.[36] It was in the hands of Zhu Xi that the scope of book learning was greatly enlarged. Moreover, as we shall see, he also developed a comprehensive methodology to cope with the problem of how to understand the meaning of a Confucian text on all levels. The intellectual foundation of morality thus became firmly established in the Neo-Confucian tradition.

Zhu Xi further justified book learning on the ground that the moral mind is constantly in need of the support of knowledge obtained from the study of Confucian texts. In this respect, he actually followed a line of thinking first developed by Zhang Zai 張載 (1020–1077). Zhang says: "If one does not read enough, one will not be able to investigate and examine moral principles to the minutest details. Book learning can always give support to one's mind. The moment one stops reading is the moment one's moral nature lapses into laxity. As one reads, one's mind is always on the alert. But one is surely not to see any moral principles without engaging in book learning."[37] Zhu Xi often quoted this passage with approval in preaching his gospel of book learning. On one occasion, he offered the following remark: "The expression 'to give support to' is extremely well said. As is usually the case, when the mind is not occupied with book learning, it has no place to apply itself. Nowadays, there are people who are unwilling to pursue principles of things with thoroughness once they have caught a glimpse [of the Way]. As a result, they indulge their minds in empty speculation."[38] But what exactly did he mean when he praised Zhang Zai's expression "book learning gives support to the mind?" The answer may be found in the following statement: "In learning, one cannot afford not to learn from books. As for the method of book learning, it ought to include intimate familiarity with, deep reflection on, and total immersion in [the text]. As [knowledge] accumulates inch by inch, the effort will eventually come to fruition. In the end,

not only do the principles become clear but the mind also naturally gets settled."[39] Clearly, in his view, a profound intellectual understanding of principles
can keep the mind in a moral state, thereby preventing it from being disturbed
by selfish desires. On this problem, however, Zhu Xi must not be regarded as a
slavish follower of Zhang Zai. As a matter of fact, he took a further step by giving
knowledge a more positive role to play in the cultivation of moral nature. Zhang
Zai's view in terms of "support" implies that the function of knowledge is passive; it only "supports" moral nature from collapse but does not add anything to
it. Zhu Xi, on the other hand, relates knowledge to morality in terms of growth.
In one place, he speaks of book learning as being capable of cultivating the root
of moral nature.[40] In another context, he is even more explicit, saying, "A thorough study of the principles enunciated by the sages and the worthies can
nourish the root so that the branches and the leaves may grow luxuriantly by
themselves."[41] Here his organismic language contrasts vividly with Zhang Zai's
mechanistic language. In Zhu Xi's deep consciousness, knowledge does more
than just "give support to" morality; it provides morality with nourishment for
its continuous growth.[42]

   In his discussion of the polarity of "erudition" (*bo*) and "essentialism" (*yue*),
Zhu says:

> In learning, we must first establish a base. Its beginning is rather simple,
> starting with what is essential [to moral practice]. The middle part is very
> broad. In the end, however, it returns to what is essential. Scholars nowa-
> days are fond of the essentialist approach and do not pursue broad knowl-
> edge. The problem is: without extensive knowledge, how can we test [the
> authenticity or falsity] of what we hold to be essential? . . . There are other
> scholars who are only after erudition but never return to what is essential.
> They study one institution today and another institution tomorrow, exert-
> ing themselves only in the investigation of the functional aspects [of the
> Way]. They are even worse than the essentialists.[43]

Obviously, Zhu Xi was fighting on two different fronts at the same time. Moral
essentialism without intellectual base and erudition without moral focus were
both detestable to him. His own position may be described as a centrist one,
always seeking to combine "essentialism" and "erudition" in a most creative
way. In the realm of knowledge, as he once remarked, "essentials come entirely
from erudition."[44] This conception of the relationship between *bo* and *yue*, it
must be emphatically pointed out, presupposes the autonomy of book learning.

   In the above-quoted passage, Zhu Xi spoke of a moral beginning as well as a
moral end in learning, but his emphasis was clearly placed on the broad "middle
part," which is an autonomous intellectual realm. It is very revealing that with
all his admiration for Cheng Yi, he was nevertheless profoundly dissatisfied

with the latter's *Chengshi Yizhuan* 程氏易傳 or *Yichuan Yizhuan* 伊川易傳 (Commentary on the Classic of Changes) precisely for its disregard for the autonomy of the original text. He sharply criticized this work as follows: "Yichuan intended to give moral instructions [in the *Commentary*]. But he should have provided them elsewhere, not in connection with the *Classic of Changes*."[45] This is clear evidence that he was very much conscious of the autonomy of the world of knowledge with which morality must not be allowed to interfere directly.

Zhu Xi also extended his respect for autonomy to the world of arts. The *Analects* contains the following statement by Confucius (551–479 B.C.E.): "I set my heart on the Way, base myself on virtue, lean upon benevolence for support and take my recreation in the arts."[46] Zhang Shi 張栻 (1133–1180) explained the meaning of the last phrase, "take my recreation in the arts," as follows: "The arts are only to nourish our moral nature." Zhu Xi raised a strong objection to this explanation, pointing out:

> This statement is especially fallacious. Although the arts occupy the lowest place [in the Confucian scheme of things], they nevertheless have a raison d'être all their own and each follows its own natural pattern. The expression "take recreation in the arts" shows that [Confucius] only intended, in each and every case, to respond to things without going contrary to their principles. By not going contrary to principles, our moral nature is naturally nourished. But we do not, in the beginning, count on the arts for the cultivation of our moral nature. Your explanation also has its origin in a contemptuous attitude toward the arts because of their low place. It is probably because you regard it as shameful to "take recreation in the arts" that you offer this interpretation to justify your point of view. . . . But the arts are entitled to their own right of existence. We take recreation in them not necessarily because they can nourish our moral nature.[47]

The importance of this passage can hardly be overstated. Here Zhu Xi comes very close to the view of "art for art's sake." Each of the Six Arts (ceremonies, music, archery, carriage-driving, writing, and mathematics), in this view, follows its own "natural pattern" or "principle" and each is to be played according to its own rules. All together they constitute an autonomous realm that tolerates no external interference, not even moral interference. They may very well produce moral effects and serve moral ends, but their existence needs no moral justification. Clearly, Zhu Xi's conception of human culture is pluralistic and hierarchical at the same time. It is pluralistic because morality, knowledge, and arts all have their separate realms; it is hierarchical because the Way 道 (*Dao*) holds all these realms together with the highest one reserved for morality.

INTERPRETATION AND OBJECTIVITY:
ZHU XI'S NEO-CONFUCIAN HERMENEUTICS

In Zhu Xi's cultural order, knowledge is next only to morality. Since, as we have seen above, knowledge for him is primarily knowledge gained through book learning, especially the Confucian classics, it requires a comprehensive and systematic methodology for the interpretation and understanding of texts. This is precisely the area wherein lies one of his monumental contributions to Neo-Confucian learning. The autonomy of knowledge, in his case, depends almost entirely on his methodology of book learning; this methodology led to a full-blown development of what may be called Neo-Confucian hermeneutics.

Zhu Xi's hermeneutics covers practically all levels of interpretation ranging from the philological, the historical, the literal, the reconstructive, to the existential. To interpret a classical text, according to him, it is necessary to begin with the philological and historical explications of early exegetes. In addition to the text, he says, a student must also be able to familiarize himself with the commentaries to such an extent that he can grasp all the details in the commentaries that bear directly on the meaning of the text.[48] What is even more important on this level is to compare closely all the different interpretations of a text offered by various exegetes through the ages. Truth will emerge only through cross-examination and comparison of all these differences.[49] Philological interpretation in his hermeneutical system is only the first step, however. Although it cannot be bypassed, it must be transcended. At the end of this stage, one sees no commentaries at all, only the text.[50]

According to Zhu Xi, reading a text usually requires a person to undergo three stages. In the beginning, he learns how to set his mind attentively on the text. In the second stage, he penetrates into the text by following correct rules of textual analysis. Being bound by these rules, he can describe the text in its general outlines, but the description is lifeless. Only when he reaches the final stage can he bring the text to life.[51] We can ignore the beginning stage and proceed directly to say a word about the second and final stages.

The second stage involves at least two levels of understanding, namely, the literal significance of the text and the original intention of the author. The literal level of understanding is relatively simple; it consists mainly of a grasp of the language of the text.[52] However, the line between the literal and the intentional levels of understanding is by no means clear-cut. As is often the case, our determination of the literal significance of a text very much depends on our understanding of the intentional meaning of its author and vice versa. Throughout his numerous discussions on the problem of textual interpretation, Zhu Xi's central concern is always with how to understand the "original intention" (*benyi* 本意) of the author of a classical text, in his case, the author being either a sage or a worthy. In a letter to a friend, he says: "To study a text requires the interpreter to be open-minded and cool-headed. His understanding follows closely the literal meaning of the text. He must not come to the text with his preconceived ideas . . . which prevent him from seeing the original intentions of the sages and the worthies."[53] Here what he is actually saying is that the reader cannot reach the intentional level without first going through the literal level. On the other hand, he was also quite aware that the latter is no absolute guarantee of the former. Otherwise, he would not have criticized his disciples for engaging only in literal interpretation but neglecting the intention of the sages.[54]

Special attention must be paid to both his plea for "open-mindedness" and his warning against "preconceived ideas" in the understanding of a classical text. A basic principle in his theory of interpretation is formulated as follows: "To read a text, one must not forcibly impose one's own view on it. Instead, one must remove one's ideas and find out the meaning in it exactly as the ancients intended."[55] In this regard, Zhu Xi is indeed very close to some of the modern theorists of interpretation, especially Emilio Betti, for Zhu Xi, like Betti, was also centrally concerned with the autonomy of the object of interpretation (text) as well as the possibility of objective knowledge derived from textual interpretation.[56] Because of the unique nature of his object of interpretation—the Confucian text—Zhu Xi always took the problem of the author's original intention very seriously. This does not mean, however, that he was totally unaware of what Paul Ricouer calls the problem of "distanciation." On the contrary, his great emphasis on the necessity to compare and contrast all the different interpretations of a classical text and, indeed, his lifetime work in the realm of exegesis fully testify to the fact that he had all along been grappling with the difficulties arising from the distance between the autonomy of the text and the original intention of the author.[57]

Zhu Xi's concern with the objectivity of textual interpretation also led him to stress the importance of doubt in book learning. This is equivalent to what Betti calls the "critical moment" within the process of interpretation—a moment that "is called upon in cases requiring a questioning attitude, such as the emergence of incongruences, illogical statements or gaps in a line of argument."[58] Zhu Xi said:

I used to tell friends that in book learning, one ought to think and seek points of doubt. However, I have now come to realize that it is better to study with an open mind. After working closely at a text for a long time, you will naturally benefit by it, but at the same time, you will also encounter points where doubt naturally arises. For a close reading will inevitably lead to places that block your path and cause you perplexity. Thus, doubts will come to your consciousness and require you to compare, to weigh, to ponder over. It is not fruitful to start out with the intention of finding things to doubt. . . . When I studied the *Analects* in my early years, my doubts were immediately raised. The simple fact that the same passage had been given widely different explanations by various commentators led me to doubt.[59]

Dr. Hu Shih 胡適 (1891–1962) may have somewhat exaggerated his case when he said that Zhu Xi's "doubt with an open mind" has led to the growth of a "scientific tradition" in China.[60] It may not be too far-fetched, however, to suggest that Zhu Xi's emphasis on the importance of open-mindedness, removal of "preconceived ideas," and, above all, the critical spirit of doubt in textual interpretation did lead him to establish a methodology of Chinese *Geisteswissenschaften* with which objective knowledge of the Confucian message may be fruitfully pursued.

Now let us turn to Zhu Xi's final stage of interpretation in which the text comes to life. "Once we obtain principles," he says, "we also have no need of the classics."[61] This clearly means that the classical text itself is also eventually to be transcended. It is at this point that the text comes to life in the sense that what is interpreted is transformed into an organic part, so to speak, of the interpreter's spiritual life. He pointed out: "The reason that we have to learn from books is to discover moral principles. However, once we have understood these principles, we will find that they are originally inherent in our own nature, not imposed on us from the outside."[62] He further clarified the meaning of this statement as follows: "In book learning, we must not only seek moral principles from the text. Instead we must also reverse the process by seeking them in ourselves. There are [principles] that had already been clearly stated by the sages but of which we are still ignorant. In light of the words of the sages, we will be able to acquire them by examining ourselves."[63] What he is saying here is that not only do we interpret the classics but, more important, the classics interpret us. In this regard, he is no different from his philosophical opponent Lu Xiangshan, who has been particularly known for the statement "All the Six Classics are my footnotes."[64] Thus, Zhu Xi reaches the level of existential interpretation, which presupposes some kind of preunderstanding. In his terminology, it is an "inner experience relevant to the self" (*qieji tiyan* 切己體驗). Ultimately, as he repeatedly stressed, all the classical texts must be understood beyond literalism and as an inner experience relevant to the interpreter's self.[65] He testified that this was exactly how he had studied the Confucian texts all along.[66] What is actually involved here is, to borrow Bultmann, "a preceding living relationship to the subject matter which finds expression in a text either directly or indirectly." It is a kind of inquiry that "is always guided by a pre-existing and preliminary understanding of human existence, i.e., a definite existential understanding."[67]

I must hasten to add, however, that in the case of Zhu Xi, "human existence" can only be understood in a moral sense of the Confucian type. For him, what is "relevant to the self" is always morally relevant. Although his "inner experience relevant to the self" involves preunderstanding of a moral kind, there is no reason to believe that this moral element interferes directly with the objective interpretation of a text. What it actually affects is rather the decision to select and order texts for interpretation. His order of book learning—the Four Books, the Five Classics, and histories, for example—was established precisely on the basis of "moral relevance to the self." But once the interpreter sets out to work on his text, he must follow strictly the methodological rules of textual interpretation and relegate all moral considerations to the background. It is only at the very end of the investigations of a text that moral relevance to the self of the interpreter comes into full play. He must then be able to rise above the text to seek existential understanding, which alone can give meaning to his moral existence. It is precisely at this point that *dao wenxue* returns to *zun dexing*, *bo* to *yue*, and *zhizhi* to *jing*. In a word, knowledge is transformed into moral practice. The transformation undoubtedly involves a "leap" in understanding—a "leap" from the intellectual level to the moral level. Such a "leap" is possible only if the desire to understand arises from the actual moral needs of the interpreter. Thus, Zhu Xi's view of the role of knowledge in life may be seen as necessarily presupposing spiritual cultivation at the same time. Without self-cultivation, how can one possibly distinguish authentic moral needs from disguised selfish desires? Intellectual progress and spiritual progress must go side by side to reach the meeting ground on which the "leap" finally takes place. Here, I believe, lies the central significance of Zhu Xi's lifetime efforts to reinterpret Cheng Yi's formula, "self-cultivation requires seriousness; the pursuit of learning depends on the extension of knowledge."

KNOWLEDGE AS THE FOUNDATION OF MORALITY: A PHILOSOPHICAL OVERVIEW

As indicated earlier, Zhu Xi's emphasis on "inquiry and study" in his debate with Lu Xiangshan is deeply rooted in his philosophical system. In this concluding section I propose to discuss, briefly, a few of his philosophical ideas directly related to the central thesis of this study.

The logical place to begin is Zhu Xi's view of the function of "intelligence" (or "wisdom" *zhi* 智) in human nature. Of the four cardinal virtues inborn in man according to Mencius (372–289 B.C.E.)—humanity (*ren* 仁), righteousness (*yi* 義), propriety (*li* 禮), and intelligence (*zhi*)—it is noteworthy that Zhu Xi considered "humanity" and "intelligence" to be the more active pair. While "humanity" is undoubtedly an all-embracing virtue, "intelligence," by virtue of its power to "accomplish things from beginning to end," is no less important.[68] When a student asked him why Mencius placed "intelligence" at the end of the list, he answered thus: "Mencius was actually talking about a circle. In fact, humanity, righteousness, and propriety are all stored in intelligence. You can act in a certain way only when you know it."[69] Elsewhere he further pointed out, "[Like humanity] intelligence also includes all [the four virtues] because knowledge comes first"[70] and "Humanity and intelligence are inclusive while righteousness and propriety are not."[71] To say that Mencius's list is actually a "circle" is to refute in a subtle way the traditional interpretation that "intelligence" is the last of the four cardinal virtues. His description of "intelligence" in terms of its "power to accomplish things" and "inclusiveness" refers primarily to its active and dynamic character, which alone can set the other three virtues in motion. For example, he explicitly stated: "Consciousness is clearly something arising from intelligence. . . . The reason that intelligence is close to humanity is that it is the point at which the circle of the 'Four Beginnings' starts to move. Without intelligence, humanity cannot be set in motion."[72] This also explains why he defined, elsewhere, "intelligence" as the "masculine way" (*qiandao* 乾道), that is, possessing active, vigorous, aggressive, productive qualities.[73] For this reason, he held the view that sagehood (*sheng* 聖) must also require "intelligence" for completion.[74] "Without intelligence, sagehood gets nowhere."[75]

With his emphasis on the importance of "intelligence" (better, in his case, "intellect"), it is only natural that his philosophical system admits of no such distinction as moral knowledge (*dexing zhi zhi* 德性之知) versus sense knowledge (*wenjian zhi zhi* 聞見之知). In the history of Neo-Confucianism, this distinction was first proposed by Zhang Zai;[76] it received the following reformulation in the hands of Cheng Yi: "The knowledge obtained through hearing and seeing is not the knowledge through moral nature. When a thing (the body) comes into contact with things, the knowledge so obtained is not from within. This is what is meant by extensive learning and much ability today. The knowledge obtained from moral nature does not depend on seeing and hearing."[77] The language suggests Mencius's distinction between the function of the senses and that of the mind.[78] Mencius did not distinguish two types of knowledge, however. In a different place, Zhang Zai speaks of the two types of knowledge in a slightly different way: "Knowledge gained through enlightenment that is the result of sincerity is the innate knowledge of one's natural character. It is not the small knowledge of what is heard or what is seen."[79] The term "small knowledge" is obviously a borrowing from Zhuangzi 莊子 (369?–286? B.C.E.). Although Zhuangzi contrasts "small knowledge" with "great knowledge," the difference between the two is most likely one of degree rather than kind.[80] Clearly, the distinction must be credited to Zhang Zai and Cheng Yi.

According to this distinction, then, moral knowledge lies in a higher realm, to which human intellect has no access. This is even more so with Cheng Yi than with Zhang Zai, for while the latter only said that moral knowledge does not originate from senses, the former held that moral knowledge does not depend on the senses. If this is the case, then all Zhu Xi's talk about "investigation of things," "extension of knowledge," and book learning would be pure nonsense. Therefore, from Zhu Xi's philosophical point of view, this distinction is false and must be rejected. When a student asked him whether there is something called sense knowledge, he replied with a contemptuous tone:

"There is only one kind of knowledge! What is at issue is whether our knowledge is true or not true. Why should we argue on such a matter? It is definitely not the case that [after we have acquired sense knowledge], we later obtain another kind of knowledge."[81] Discussing Zhang Zai's conception of sense knowledge, he further remarked:

> In order to be able to learn, we must possess senses of seeing and hearing (*jianwen* 見聞). How can we possibly do without them? We work hard with our senses until we achieve a wide and far-reaching penetration. Ordinarily, when we study something by relying on senses, the knowledge obtained is only limited to a single principle. However, when we reach the stage of a general penetration, all the principles become one.[82]

In his view, even if we call knowledge arrived at in the final stage "moral knowledge," it differs from sense knowledge only in degree. In his terminology, it is rather a difference between shallowness and depth as well as between coarseness and refinement.[83] Moreover, moral knowledge, a term he never really adopted, can only be developed out of sense knowledge. What is even more revealing is his sharp criticism of Zhang Zai with respect to this distinction:

> QUESTION: What about Hengqu's 橫渠 [Zhang Zai] distinction between sense knowledge and moral knowledge?
> ANSWER: It is fallacious. Sense knowledge also follows the same principle. I do not understand, given such an extraordinary intelligence as his, how he could possibly make so glaring a mistake.[84]

He knew very well that Cheng Yi not only had subscribed to the same view but even developed it to a more rigid form. So his criticism of Zhang Zai was equally applicable to Cheng Yi. Because of his great respect for the latter, however, he purposely omitted the latter's name in his discussions. This is clear evidence that although he basically followed Cheng Yi's teaching, he nevertheless consciously went beyond him in the intellectualization of the Confucian way.[85] It was largely because of his great influence that the distinction between moral knowledge and sense knowledge had fallen into almost complete oblivion until Wang Yangming arrived on the scene.

Zhu Xi's emphasis on knowledge as a foundation of morality must also be understood in light of his views of *li* (principle) and mind. To begin with, it is necessary to clarify a common misunderstanding concerning one aspect of the relationship between principle and mind in his system. Zhu Xi often makes such statements as "the mind possesses a multitude of principles and responds to the myriad affairs," "the mind embraces all the principles," "the myriad principles are completely embodied in a mind," and "all the principles are originally within the mind, not obtained from the outside."[86] These statements have given rise to the interpretation that he was not really interested in objective knowledge of the external world. His "investigation of things," according to this interpretation, is therefore nothing but seeking confirmation of the knowledge of "principles" already contained in one's own mind. Dai Zhen's 戴震 (1724–1777) sharp criticism of his view that "principle is received from Heaven and completely embodied in the mind,"[87] for example, is based on such an interpretation. This is not the place to go into details concerning this important matter. I merely wish to point out that despite his sometimes loose and therefore misleading language, Zhu Xi did not hold that the mind possesses knowledge of principles before the "investigation of things." As he makes clear in his famous "emendation" to the *Great Learning*, the mind is only "formed to know." He also states unequivocally, "Although the myriad principles are embodied in our minds, the mind must still be made to know them."[88] I believe it would make much better sense if we took his "principles embodied in the mind" as a priori forms of understanding—something akin to, though not the same as, "categories" in the Kantian spirit. He seems to think that for each and every "principle" of a thing or event, there is a corresponding a priori form in the mind. Apparently, he also believes that eventually all the principles can be shown to be differentiations from a single unitary principle. This is clearly expressed in the celebrated dictum he inherited from Cheng Yi, "The principle is one, but its manifestations are many" (*liyi fenshu* 理一分殊).[89] However, these a priori forms in the mind are empirically empty. The postulation of a priori forms corresponding to principles of things and events in the external world is necessary because from his point of view, it alone can explain how our minds are "formed to know" the latter. Yet on the other hand, as amply shown in his conversations as well as writings, no positive knowledge of principles is possible without the "investigation of things." Seen in this way, not only was he genuinely interested in objective knowledge of the external world but his whole philosophical system also required it. It is true, as we have already noted, that he was much more concerned with knowledge of the human world than that of the natural world. Nevertheless, his objective curiosity about and keen observation of natural phenomena were clearly without match among the Neo-Confucians.[90] This sustained interest in the natural world came partly from his intellectual temper; his earliest wonder, which occurred at the age of five or six (Chinese counting), was about heavenly bodies.[91] But it was undoubtedly also closely related to his firm belief that principles are inherent in things in the external world, including "a blade of grass or a tree." He once told his students: "Principles are universally inherent in all things in the world. But it is the mind that takes charge of them. Being in charge, the mind therefore makes use of them. It may be said that the substance of principles is in things themselves while their functions depend on the mind." Yet the next morning he added the following: "I stated the case in this way because I was taking myself as the [knowing] subject and things as objects [of knowledge]. However, the important truth is that there is really no difference between saying that principles exist in things and that they exist in us [i.e., the mind]."[92] Both the original statement and the afterthought are highly illuminating. The original statement shows that he fully recognized the objectivity of principles. In terms of substance, they exist in things and are independent of the mind. By saying that "the mind takes charge of principles," he obviously refers to the fact that the mind can discover, order, and apply them. The afterthought shows, on the other hand, that he became aware of the possibility that the original statement might mislead his students to question the validity of his postulation about a priori forms in the mind that correspond to principles inherent in things of the external world. To say "there is really no difference between saying that principles exist in things and that they exist in us" is to stress the point that in the actual practice of "investigation of things" and "extension of knowledge," the subjectivity of a priori forms and the objectivity of principles are ultimately to become unified.[93]

In a letter to Zhang Shi, Zhu Xi wrote:

> Confucian learning on the whole begins with a thorough study of principles. Each individual thing has its own principle. Only when a person has a clear knowledge of principles can he get hold of an exact standard (*zhunze* 準則), as of weight and measurement, for his mind to follow in its functioning. If he does not extend his knowledge in this [realm of principles] thereby being left, generally, without an exact standard, and is rather content with the sole claim that he has obtained such and such a knowledge and understanding of the mind, then how would it be possible for what is preserved in and issued from his mind to conform unerringly to principles?[94]

Nowhere is the necessity of "the investigation of things" and "the extension of knowledge" in Zhu Xi's philosophical system more clearly explained than this letter. Because his trust of the material and fallible human mind was always less than total, he therefore wanted to find an objective standard for the mind to follow so that it may not mistake selfish desires for moral principles. This exact standard, in his view, can only be established on the basis of a thorough knowledge of principles that exist objectively in things and events in the external world. Thus, we see that at least in theory, knowledge of the natural world and knowledge of the human world are equally important as far as the objectivity of principles is concerned. As he emphatically pointed out, "principles of things are identical with moral principles. The world does not possess two kinds of principles."[95] This is a logical conclusion easily derivable from his fundamental presupposition that all the individual principles in the world are but differentiations from a single unitary one that is none other than what he calls the Great Ultimate (*Taiji* 太極). Hence, in the final analysis, the cosmic order and the moral order follow the same pattern; law for things and moral law are of the same kind.[96] Through "inquiry and study," an objective standard can be discovered in either world, which, from his point of view, would guarantee the objectivity as well as the stability of moral truth.

It was also his distrust of the ordinary human mind and his search for an exact standard that led him to see the necessity of book learning. He said:

> As I see it, the reason that we have to study is because our minds are not yet as [purified as] the sages' minds. Since our minds are not yet as purified, we therefore cannot see principles clearly and do not have an exact standard to conform to. As a result, we often follow our personal inclinations, which generally fail to meet the standard by either going beyond or falling below it. But we are usually unaware of our excesses or deficiencies. If our minds are from the very beginning not at all different from the sages' minds or the cosmic mind, then what do we need study for? For this reason, it is necessary that we as learners first seek to understand the ideas or intentions of the sages through early commentaries and then search for universal principles in the light of the ideas or intentions of the sages. Our search proceeds from the superficial to the profound as well as from what is at hand to what is far-reaching. We do this by following a step-by-step order, not by jumping to the conclusion with burning impatience. Once we have reached the ultimate limit, our minds will become naturally rectified. By then, even the sages' minds or the cosmic mind cannot be very different from ours. But I do not mean to suggest that we be satisfied with what is superficial and at hand [book learning] and forget about what is profound and far-reaching [moral principles]. Nor do I mean that we simply go after the minds of the sages at the expense of our own minds and follow uncritically the interpretations of early commentators at the expense of our own interpretations.[97]

This letter speaks remarkably well for itself. I only want to call attention to a few important points. First, the "exact standard" he was seeking to establish is ultimately to be found in the objectivity of principles of things and events of the external world, not in the subjectivity of the sages' minds, for the search must eventually go beyond "the ideas or intentions of the sages." This is entirely consistent with his hermeneutical principle that in the end our understanding must be able to transcend the classical text. Second, it was never his idea that we must follow the sages blindly. As a matter of fact, his critical spirit of "doubt" led him to the contrary. As he explicitly stated elsewhere: "We should always read a text with open mind and fair spirit in order to scrutinize the principles enunciated in it. If there is a valid point, we do not cast it aside simply because it is made by a common man. On the other hand, if there is a doubtful point, we must examine it carefully even though it is attributed to a sage or worthy."[98] Third, it is true that book learning is central to his teaching at the methodological level.

However, his insistence on learning from the sages and the worthies of the past can by no means be construed as arising out of an uncritical and idolatrous attitude on his part. Nor is it a result of sheer antiquarianism. It is rather based on his belief that the past sages had bequeathed to us numerous objective principles that they had discovered through "investigation of things." They can serve as our models because their minds had been extremely well cultivated (or purified) through "inquiry and study." As learners, we must also cultivate our minds in the same way. We do this not only by following their examples but, more important, by also standing on their shoulders. This is precisely why he says in his "emendation" to the *Great Learning* that the learner, in regard to all things in the world, must "proceed from what knowledge he has of their principles, and investigate further until he reaches the limit." The knowledge of principles of things and events now at our disposal is the richest and the most valuable legacy we have inherited from the past sages and worthies. It must of necessity serve as the starting point of our new investigations. He said:

> It is of course true that in high antiquity, before the writing system had been invented, the learners had no books to read. Moreover, it is also true that people with above-average intelligence sometimes can attain the Way through self-realization and without book learning. However, ever since the sages and worthies began their creative work, a good deal of the Way has been preserved in the classics. Therefore, even a sage like Confucius could not have possibly pursued learning apart from them.[99]

There cannot be the slightest doubt, as Professor Qian Mu 錢穆 points out, that he must have written this passage with the question posed by Lu Xiangshan during their Goose Lake Temple meeting in mind: "Before the time of Yao 堯 and Shun 舜, what books were there for people to read?"[100] From his point of view, this is asking the wrong question, one that borders on sophistry. The historical situation between now and "the time before Yao and Shun" has been fundamentally changed. The simple truth is that we now do have the Confucian classics, which define the Way in its main outlines as well as in its minute details. If we are in quest of the very same Way, as Lu Xiangshan apparently was, then what possible justification do we have for our refusal to start the search with the classics? Zhu Xi's keen historical consciousness naturally led him to emphasize the importance of the tradition of Confucian scholarship. For him, knowledge of principles of things and events is always an accumulative enterprise.

Lastly, Zhu Xi's statement in the above passage, "Nor do I mean that we simply go after the minds of the sages at the expense of our own minds," is an outright rejection of the idea of "transmission of mind," then in wide currency.

In his view, what can be transmitted is not the mind but the Way, which consists of the principles objectively discovered by the sages' minds in things and events.[101] Since the mind is essentially a knowing mind, the best a person can hope to accomplish is to raise his mind to the level of purification as high as the sages' minds. There is no way he can take the sage's mind as his own, however. He is convinced that only the sage's words exhibit the sage's mind, which is nothing but the embodiment of the principles in the world. Only by studying carefully and step by step the sage's words can one expect to grasp these principles. But Lu Xiangshan believes, according to Zhu Xi, that a person can obtain the principles by relying only on his own mind without the help of the sages' words. It is indeed excellent, says Zhu Xi, if a person is able to obtain, all by himself, the right kind of principles. But what if the principles he gets turn out to be of the wrong kind?[102] Here again Zhu Xi displays his deep distrust of the subjectivity of mind on the one hand and his basic concern with the objective validity of moral principles on the other. Seen in this light, the roots of his differences with Lu Xiangshan on the pedagogic level indeed strike deep in their different conceptions of such key Neo-Confucian ideas as "principle" (*li*) and "mind" (*xin*).

Unlike Zhu Xi, Lu Xiangshan's concern is not with the objectivity of principles but rather with the subjectivity of mind. Needless to say, I cannot deal with his theory of mind here.[103] All I need to say is that his trust of the subjectivity of mind is unlimited.[104] His well-known proposition, "Mind is Principle," his identification of the mind with the (spatio-temporal) cosmos, his emphasis on the "recovery of the original mind," and many other similar formulations all point in the same direction. "Mind" conceived in this way cannot possibly be identified with that as understood by Zhu Xi, which, as we have seen, is essentially "formed to know." It makes sense only if interpreted as the absolute moral mind.[105] With regard to this mind, there cannot be principles external to it; all objectivity is absorbed into subjectivity. Zhu Xi's question of an "objective standard," therefore, will never arise in the context of Lu Xiangshan's philosophy. Moreover, according to Lu Xiangshan, this absolute moral mind that is shared by everyone does not change with time. History, therefore, makes little difference, and tradition is of no fundamental importance. The "recovery of the original mind" depends entirely on everyone's own effort; it cannot count on the words or minds of the sages and the worthies for help in an essential way. Lu once reminisced that his understanding of Confucian learning was self-attained on the occasion of reading the *Mencius*.[106] Obviously, he here placed the emphasis more on self-attainment than on the book, which only provided the occasion for his enlightenment. It is also very interesting to note that he reached the same conclusion as Zhu Xi did with regard to the problem of "transmission of mind," but for completely different reasons. In the Goose Lake Temple meeting, he was dissatisfied with the second line of his brother Jiuling's 九齡 poem composed specifically for the occasion. It reads: "Ancient sages pass on this mind." In response, the same line of his own poem says: "'Tis man's indestructible mind through all ages."[107] Clearly, in his view, recovery of the original mind depends primarily on everyone's "self-attainment," whereas "transmission of mind" implies a dependence on the minds, and consequently, also the words, of the sages.[108] It was in this way that Lu Xiangshan's view of mind led, by its inner logic, to an attitude toward book learning diametrically opposed to Zhu Xi's.

NOTES

1. This is a reference to the "Zhongyong" 中庸, which provides the locus classicus of *zun dexing* and *dao wenxue*. The "Zhongyong" has been traditionally ascribed to Zisi (483–402 B.C.E.?), Confucius's grandson.

2. *Zhu Wengong wenji* 朱文公文集 (hereafter *Wenji*), SBCK, chap. 54, 962, "Reply to Xiang Pingfu."

3. See Lu Xiangshan's "nianpu" 年譜 in the *Xiangshan xiansheng quanji* 象山先生全集, SBCK, chap. 36, 321, and *Yulu* 語錄 in SBCK, chap. 34, 261. I have followed Lu's *nianpu* in dating Zhu's letter to Xiang Anshi. Wang Maohong 王懋竑 (1668–1741) is clearly wrong in assigning this letter to 1181, for this was the year that Xiang Anshi first came to know Lu Xiangshan. See Wang Maohong, *Zhuzi nianpu* 朱子年譜, GXJBCS, 100.

4. See Yu Ji's 虞集 (1272–1348) "Xingzhuang" 行狀 of Wu Cheng in *Daoyuan xuegu lu* 道園學古錄, SBCK, chap. 44, 386–387.

5. See Wang Yangming's two letters to Xu Chengzhi 徐成之, written in 1522, in the *Yangming quanshu* 陽明全書, SBBY, 21:5a–8b.

6. For example, see Xu Jie's 徐階 (1503–1583) "Xueze bian" 學則辨, in *Xiangshan xiansheng quanji*, "Fulu" 附錄, 14–15.

7. See SYXA, WYWK, chap. 58, 6–8. Huang Zongxi's view was also followed by his son Bojia 黃百家 (ibid., 8) and Quan Zuwang 全祖望 (1705–1755) in *Jieqi ting ji, waipian* 鮚埼亭集, 外篇, SBCK, chap. 44, 656–657.

8. For the term "polarity," see B. I. Schwartz, "Some Polarities in Confucian Thought," in *Confucianism in Action*, ed. David S. Nivison and Arthur F. Wright (Stanford, Calif.: Stanford University Press, 1959), 51–52.

9. For "unit-ideas," see Arthur O. Lovejoy, *The Great Chain of Being* (Cambridge, Mass.: Harvard University Press, 1936), 3–6.

10. ZYL (Taipei: Zhengzhong, 1973), chap. 64, 2524.

11. See Zhu Hengdao's 朱亨道 letter quoted in *Xiangshan xiansheng quanji*, chap. 36, 319.

12. ZYL, chap. 64, 2521–2522. Similar discussions on the relationship between *zun dexing* and *dao wenxue* may also be found in chap. 117, 4504–4505, and chap. 118, 4568–4569. For the quoted saying of Cheng Yi, see *Yishu* 遺書 in the *Er-Cheng quanshu* 二程全書, SBBY, 15, 20a.

13. See *Yishu*, 18:5b; English translation in Chan, *SB*, 562.

14. For instance, see ZYL, chap. 64, 2522–2523.

15. Ibid., chap. 115, 4425.

16. Ibid., chap. 115, 4415.

17. For instance, he says: "The concept 'seriousness' truly constitutes the key link (*gangling* 綱領) in the teachings of the sages. It is also the chief method for moral cultivation." Ibid., chap. 12, 335.

18. *Wenji*, chap. 51, 897, "Reply to Huang Zigeng 黃子耕."

19. For instance, Zhu Xi says: "The mind is the refined essence of material force," *ZYL*, chap. 5, 138.

20. Ibid., chap. 9, 235. Similar views may also be found in his writings. See *Wenji*, chap. 50, 875, "Reply to Cheng Zhengsi 程正思," and chap. 54, 972, "Reply to Guo Xilü 郭希呂."

21. Ibid., chap. 115, 4425.

22. Ibid., chap. 9, 241.

23. Ibid., chap. 9, 241–242.

24. Yan Yuan 顏元 (1635–1704), *Sicun bian* 四存編 (Shanghai: Guji, 1957), 104.

25. Chen Jian 陳建, *Xuebu tongbian* 學蔀通辨, *CSJC*, "Tigang" 提綱, 102; Chen's view is quoted with approval in Gu Yanwu 顧炎武, *Rizhi lu* 日知錄, *WYWK*, chap. 18, 118.

26. *ZYL*, chap. 10, 255.

27. *Wenji*, chap. 14, 204. For the dating of this memorial, see Wang Maohong, *Zhuzi nianpu*, chap. 2, 197–200.

28. *ZYL*, chap. 10, 264.

29. Chan, *SB*, 89.

30. Wang Maohong, *Zhuzi nianpu*, chap. 4, 340–341. The Four Books are *Daxue* (Great Learning), "Zhongyong" (Doctrine of the Mean), the *Lunyu* 論語 (Analects), and the *Mencius* (Mengzi 孟子). The Six Classics are the *Shijing* (Classic of Poetry), 詩經 the *Shujing* or *Shangshu* 書經, 尚書 (Classic or Book of History), the *Yijing* 易經 (Classic of Changes), the *Liji* 禮記 (Classic of Rites), the *Chunqiu* 春秋 (Spring and Autumn Annals), and the *Yuejing* 樂經 (Classic of Music). Since the *Classic of Music* has long been lost, however, the Six Classics are also referred to as the Five Classics.

31. *ZYL*, chap. 11, 309. See also 298, 200–201.

32. Ibid., chap. 19, 689. His discussions throughout this chapter make it clear that his emphasis in classical studies is placed on knowledge of moral principles.

33. Ibid., chap. 11, 301.

34. *Wenji*, chap. 46, 800, "Reply to Pan Shuchang 潘叔昌."

35. Ibid., chap. 35, 558, "Reply to Lü Bogong 呂伯恭."

36. For Cheng Hao's 程顥 (1032–1085) rather negative attitude toward book learning, see *Yishu*, 3:1b and 2a; Xie Liangzuo 謝良佐, *Shangcai yulu* 上蔡語錄, *Zhengyi Tang quanshu* 正誼堂全書, 2:11b. For Cheng Yi's limited approval of study of the Classics, see *Yishu*, 15:12a; 16a; "Cuiyan" 粹言, in the *Er-Cheng quanshu*, 1:25a. On this problem, see Ichikawa Yasuji 市川安司, *Tei I-sen no tetsugaku no kenkyû* 程伊川哲學の研究 (Tokyo: Tokyo University Press, 1964), 137–140. Professor Qian Mu is right in saying that it was Zhu Xi who introduced history into the Cheng-Zhu curriculum of Neo-Confucian learning. See his *Zhuzi xin xue-an* 朱子新學案 (Taipei: Sanmin, 1971), book 5, 113.

37. *Zhangzi quanshu* 張子全書, *GXJBCS*, chap. 6, 108.

38. *ZYL*, chap. 119, 4584. See also chap. 114, 4399–4400, where he says: "Only by a constant engagement in book learning can the functioning of one's mind be prevented from being interrupted."

39. *Wenji*, chap. 64, 1188, "Reply to Jiang Duanbo 江端伯."

40. Ibid., chap. 44, 764, "Reply to Jiang Degong 江德功."

41. Ibid., chap. 49, 855, "Reply to Chen Fuzhong 陳膚仲."

42. This idea comes from a passage in the *Yijing* 易經; see James Legge, trans., *Yi King*, *SBE*, 300. Zhu Xi actually quoted it in another conversation. See *ZYL*, chap. 120, 4639.

43. *ZYL*, chap. 11, 298–299. Here he referred, respectively, to the essentialists of the Lu Xiangshan School and the many-angled scholars of the Lü Zuqian School. See Qian Mu, *Zhuzi xin xue-an*, book 1, 676.

44. *ZYL*, chap. 33, 1336.

45. Ibid., chap. 69, 2767.

46. *The Analects of Confucius*, trans. D. C. Lau (劉殿爵) (New York: Penguin, 1979), 86.

47. *Wenji*, chap. 31, 494, "Comments on Zhang Shi's 'Interpretations of the *Analects* of 1173.'"

48. *ZYL*, chap. 11, 304. However, he also points out that if the names of things and institutions in a text are not central to our understanding of its meaning, we may be satisfied with a general knowledge of them. See ibid., 301.

49. Ibid., 305.

50. Ibid.

51. Ibid., 282.

52. Ibid., 292, 306.

53. *Wenji*; chap. 53, 943, "Reply to Liu Jizhang 劉季章."

54. *ZYL*, chap. 36, 1581.

55. Ibid., 293. This compares well with the following maxim in contemporary Western hermeneutics: "Meaning has to be derived from the text and not imputed to it." See Josef Bleicher, *Contemporary Hermeneutics* (London: Routledge and Kegan Paul; Boston: Henley, 1980), 36.

56. See Emilio Betti's discussion of the need of an "intellectual open-mindedness" for interpretations in his "Hermeneutics as the General Methodology of the *Geistewissenschaften*," translated by Bleicher in *Contemporary Hermeneutics*, 85.

57. Paul Ricoeur, "The Hermeneutical Function of Distanciation," in his *Hermeneutics and the Human Sciences*, ed. and trans. John B. Thompson (Cambridge: Cambridge University Press, 1981), 131–144.

58. Bleicher, *Contemporary Hermeneutics*, 40.

59. *ZYL*, chap. 11, 295.

60. Hu Shih, "The Scientific Spirit and Method in Chinese Philosophy," in *The Chinese Mind*, ed. Charles A. Moore (Honolulu: East West Center Press, 1967), 104–131.

61. *ZYL*, chap. 11, 305.

62. Ibid., chap. 10, 255.

63. Ibid., 287.

64. *Xiangshan xiansheng quanji*, chap. 34, 256–261.

65. *ZYL*, chap. 11, 286–288.

66. Ibid., chap. 30, 1235–1236.

67. Quoted in Bleicher, *Contemporary Hermeneutics*, 105–106.

68. *ZYL*, chap. 6, 175. The locus classicus of these four virtues is the *Mencius*, 6A.6 and 7A.21.

69. Ibid., chap. 53, 2048.

70. Ibid., chap. 20, 766.

71. Ibid., chap. 6, 172.

72. Ibid., chap. 20, 771. As taught in the *Mencius*, 2A.6, the Four Beginnings are: the sense of compassion is the beginning of humanity, the sense of shame and dislike is the beginning of righteousness, the sense of deference is the beginning of propriety, and the sense of right and wrong is the beginning of intelligence.

73. Ibid., chap. 42, 1719; chap. 104, 4162.

74. Ibid., chap. 58, 2173.

75. *Wenji*, chap. 58, 1062, "Reply to Zhang Jingfu 張敬夫."

76. *Zhangzi quanshu*, chap. 2, 45. English translation in Chan, *SB*, 515.

77. *Yishu*, 25:2a; English translation by Chan, *SB*, 570. On the connection between Zhang Zai and Cheng Yi, see A. C. Graham, *Two Chinese Philosophers, Ch'eng Ming-tao and Ch'eng I-ch'uan* 程明道 / 程伊川 (London: Lund Humphries, 1958), 176–178.

78. *Mencius*, 6A.15.

79. *Zhangzi quanshu*, chap. 2, 40; Chan, *SB*, 507.

80. Guo Qingfan 郭慶藩 (1844–1897), *Zhuangzi jishi* 莊子集釋 (Beijing: Zhonghua, 1961), chap. 1, 11 and 51.

81. *ZYL*, chap. 34, 1440.

82. Ibid., chap. 98, 4002.

83. On this point, see also Qian Mu, *Zhuzi xin xue-an*, book 2, 388–389, and Zhang Liwen 張立文, *Zhu Xi sixiang yanjiu* 朱熹思想研究 (Beijing: CASS Press, 1981), 411–416.

84. *ZYL*, chap. 99, 4031.

85. Zhu Xi's intellectualism also led him to distinguish two types of approach to the Confucian Way. He said that among Confucius's leading disciples, Zigong 子貢 took the "intellectual approach" (*zhishi* 知識), whereas Zeng Can 曾參 took the "practical approach" (*jianlü* 踐履). By the former he meant inquiry and study, and by the latter, he meant practicing filial devotion and other moral virtues in daily life (*ZYL*, chap. 27, 1088–1089). This distinction is interesting in two ways: On the one hand, the very idea that there is an "intellectual approach" to the Way reveals his emphasis on the role of knowledge in Confucian teaching as a whole. On the other hand, the idea of a "practical approach" to the Way suggests that he was very much conscious of the problem of how to relate Confucianism to the life of the common (and in most cases also unlettered) man. This is an important subject needing further investigation. His view contrasts sharply with that held by both Lu Xiangshan and Wang Yangming. Both philosophers spoke highly of Zeng Can and slighted Zigong precisely because of the latter's "intelligence" and pursuit of many-sided "knowledge." See *Xiangshan xiansheng quanji*, chap. 1, 20, "Letter to Hu Jisui 胡季隨"; *Yangming quanshu*, 1: 24b; and Wang Yangming, *In-*

structions for Practical Living and Other Neo-Confucian Writings, trans. Wing-tsit Chan (New York: Columbia University Press, 1963), 71–72. It may be further noted that Zhu Xi's distinction continued to provoke strong reactions among scholars as late as the Qing Period (1644–1912). For example, Cheng Tingzuo 程廷祚 (1691–1767), a great admirer of Yan Yuan, understandably rejected the distinction of two types as nonsense. See Dai Wang 戴望 (1837–1873), Yanshi xueji 顏氏學記, WYWK, chap. 9, 115. But Quan Zuwang, in his Jingshi wenda 經史問答, chap. 6, Jieqi ting ji, 451, and Dai Zhen, in Mengzi ziyi shuzheng 孟子字義疏證 (Beijing: Zhonghua, 1961), 56, accepted it as valid.

86. See the examples conveniently collected together in Qian Mu, Zhuzi xin xue-an, book 2, 1–24.

87. See Dai Zhen's criticism translated in Chan, SB, 715–717. For further analysis, see Ying-shih Yü, "Dai Zhen and the Zhu Xi Tradition," in Essays in Commemoration of the Golden Jubilee of the Fung Ping Shan Library, ed. Chan Ping-leung, Lai Shu-tim, Yeung Kwok-hung, Wong Tak-wai, Lee Ngok, Chiu Ling-yeung (Hong Kong: Fung Ping Shan 馮平山 Library, HKU, 1982), 390–391.

88. ZYL, chap. 60, 2263.

89. Ibid., chap. 1, 2; cf. Chan, SB, 639.

90. This area of Zhu Xi's thought has been extensively explored in a monographic study by Yamada Keiji 山田慶兒; see his Shushi no shizenkaku 朱子の自然學 (Tokyo: Iwanami, 1978).

91. Wang Maohong, Zhuzi nianpu, chap. 1, 1–2.

92. ZYL, chap. 18, 669.

93. On this point, a roughly similar interpretation may also be found in Takahashi Susumu 高橋進, Shu Ki to o Yōmei 朱熹と王陽明 (Tokyo: Kakusho kankokai, 1977), 108–117 and 225–236.

94. Wenji, chap. 30, 473, "Reply to Zhang Jingfu."

95. ZYL, chap. 15, 471.

96. On this problem, see also the analysis by Tomoeda Ryûtarô 友枝龍太郎, in his Shushi no shisô keisei 朱子の思想形成 (Tokyo: Shun-ju-sha, 1969), esp. pp. 354–366.

97. Wenji, chap. 42, 712–713, "Reply to Shi Zizhong 石子重."

98. Ibid., chap. 31, 484, "Reply to Zhang Jingfu."

99. Ibid., chap. 43, 724, "Reply to Chen Mingzhong 陳明仲."

100. Qian Mu, Zhuzi xin xue-an, book 3, 616. Yao and Shun were legendary sage-emperors.

101. Wenji, chap. 70, 1291, "Notes on Some Doubtful Points."

102. ZYL, chap. 120, 4657.

103. For general discussions of Lu Xiangshan's theory of mind, the reader is referred to Tang Junyi 唐君毅, Zhongguo zhexue yuanlun, yuanxing pian 中國哲學原論原性篇 (Hong Kong: New Asia Institute, 1968), esp. pp. 538–552, and Kusumoto Masatsugu 楠本正繼, So-Min jidai jugaku shisô no kenkyû 宋明時代儒學思想の研究 (Tokyo: Hiroike Gakuen Press, 1972), 341–367.

104. See a saying of Lu Xiangshan's ("I only trust this mind of mine") preserved in SYXA, chap. 77, 27.

105. Professor Fung Yu-lan [Feng Youlan] 馮友蘭 holds that both Zhu Xi and Lu Xiangshan shared the same view of "mind"; *History of Chinese Philosophy*, trans. Derk Bodde (Princeton: Princeton University Press, 1953), 2:587–588. Recent studies, however, suggest that the contrary is true. See Mou Zongsan 牟宗三, *Cong Lu Xiangshan dao Liu Jishan* 從陸象山到劉蕺山 (Taipei: Xuesheng, 1979), chap. 2, and Lao Siguang 勞思光, *Zhongguo zhexue shi* 中國哲學史 (Taipei: Sanmin, 1980), book 3, part 1, 409–414.

106. *Xiangshan xiansheng quanji*, chap. 35, 307.

107. Ibid., chap. 34, 279. For a complete English translation of the two poems, see Julia Ching 秦家懿, "The Goose Lake Monastery Debate (1175)," *Journal of Chinese Philosophy* 1 (1974): 165.

108. Qian Mu, *Zhuzi xin xue-an*, book 3, 299–301.

10. Confucian Ethics and Capitalism

Since the publication of *The Protestant Ethic and the Spirit of Capitalism* in 1905 and later in an expanded form in 1920, studies of Max Weber's thesis have grown into a heavy industry.[1] The main controversy, of course, centers around the "link" between a "Protestant ethic" and the "spirit of capitalism." By linking the two together, does Weber mean to say there is a definite causal relationship between them? If so, in what sense? Does it mean that Weber is so extreme in his idealistic interpretation of history that he believes "Protestant ethic" to be the necessary and sufficient cause for the rise of "capitalism"? Needless to say, this is far from Weber's view. A general consensus has now been reached that Weber's is causal pluralism, which admits of both ideals and material factors as agents of social change. However, he did seem to insist that relevant material preconditions alone are not sufficient to explain the development of modern capitalism unless combined with the Protestant ethic and vice versa.

By "Protestant ethic," as we all know, Weber meant, specifically, Calvinism (and its English version, Puritanism). He took a few Calvinist ideas such as "calling" and "predestination" to be the theological foundation of a work ethic uniquely suited to the development of modern capitalism. In his view, Calvinism is unique in the West because it alone unintentionally provides a psychological sanction for profit making and thereby gives the search for salvation a this-worldly direction. By contrast, the Lutheran conception of the "calling," according to him, remained traditionalistic, and Luther viewed the pursuit of material gain beyond personal needs as "a symptom of lack of grace." Salvation in Lutheranism, in other words, must be pursued in the otherworldly direction. In this comparative perspective, Weber saw the Puritan work ethic as one factor, among others, responsible for capitalism to have been developed first in England.

Finally, Weber's comparative historical sociology led him to a comprehensive study of what he called the "economic ethics of world religions" encompassing Confucianism, Hinduism, and Buddhism, Judaism, Islam, and Christianity. He did this with the explicit purpose of establishing his Protestant ethic thesis on firmer empirical grounds. He thus came to the conclusion that only ascetic Protestantism completely eliminated magic and the supernatural quest for salvation and created the religious motivations for seeking salvation primarily through immersion in one's worldly vocation. In contrast to it, none of the major religions such as Confucianism, Buddhism, Islam, and Judaism provided any path to "a rational, methodical control of life."[2]

In this connection, a brief mention of Weber's view of Confucianism is in order. Toward the end of *The Religion of China*, Weber offers a comparison between Confucianism and Puritanism that contains numerous fascinating insights of a great mind. In essence, his fundamental position in accounting for the absence of capitalistic development in China seems to be the following: Confucianism was only interested in affairs of this world. Moreover, "the Confucian wished neither for salvation from life which was affirmed, nor salvation from the social world, which was accepted as given."[3] In other words, Confucianism was an exclusively this-worldly teaching and had little or no serious concern for the world beyond either in the religious or metaphysical sense. Thus, its rationalism meant only rational adjustment to the world, as contrasted to Puritan rationalism, which meant rational mastery of the world on God's command.

Having thus reviewed Weber's famous thesis and his negative view of the Confucian ethic with regard to the "capitalist spirit," how are we going to relate Confucian ethics and capitalism in a meaningful new way today when we are on the very threshold of the twenty-first century? First of all, I wish to emphasize that even if Weber's thesis is valid and his characterization of Confucianism is tenable, the thesis itself is largely of historical significance and no longer directly relevant to the question of religious belief versus economic development in the contemporary world. Whatever its historical explanation may be, the fact has been established beyond dispute that modern capitalism was a unique creation of Western civilization and as a system of economic production and organization, it has spread to every corner of the world since the nineteenth century. We need not be concerned any more with its historical origins.

Weber's thesis as a historical explanation of the genesis of capitalism in the West has been vigorously as well as rigorously reexamined by historians and sociologists in recent decades, especially since the 1980s. As a result, important modifications of the original thesis have been made. Weber's critics now seriously question his interpretation of certain key theological ideas in Puritanism, such as "calling" and "predestination." According to them (such as Malcolm H. MacKinnon), Puritanism did not give religious sanction to secular callings because by "works," Puritan pastors still meant otherworldly labor such as "meditation" or "introspection." Richard Baxter, whom Weber quoted so much in *The Protestant Ethic* to support his thesis, for example, never urged the pursuit of private profit as a way of earning favor from God. The emphasis of the Puritan doctrine of the "calling" was also placed squarely on the "spiritual" side, not earthly or temporal obligations, which are at best indifferent to salvation and at worst sinful. The immersion of self in earthly success is viewed as sinning against God because it inevitably leads to exclusion of dedicated worship. Even defenders of the Weber thesis (such as Gordon Marshall) also concede that the line between the Reformation and pre-Reformation with regard to the real beginning of economic rationality, the very quintessence of "the spirit of capitalism," may have been overdrawn. The activities of the medieval businessmen, judged by standards of their own times, are just as rational as those of the ascetic Protestant of the Reformation era.[4]

Needless to say, Weber's understanding of Confucianism was severely limited by the level of European sinology of his own day, which made no distinction between classical Confucianism and Neo-Confucianism in late imperial China. His characterization of Confucianism in terms of world accommodation may find empirical support in behavior patterns of many practically oriented Chinese, but as a theoretical interpretation, it is clearly wide of the mark. As the sociologist C. K. Yang pointed out in 1963, in classical Confucianism the transcendental world was often disguised under the name of the *Dao*, or the "golden past." The Confucian scholar as the guardian of *Dao* never accepted this world "as given." On the contrary, more often than not, he found the sociopolitical order in this world at ethical variance with the ideal world of *Dao* and, moreover, it was his sacred duty to transform the given world in conformity to the *Dao*. This is essentially a sum-up of the views developed by Confucians themselves over the centuries. If we accept this interpretation, then Weber's statements such as Confucianism "was (in intent) a rational ethic which reduced tension with the world to an absolute minimum" or "completely absent was any tension between ethical demand and human shortcoming, religious duty and sociopolitical reality"[5] would require radical revision, to say the least. I think C. K. Yang is on a much firmer ground when he said, "Confucian rationalism and asceticism stemmed from this tension between the *Dao* and worldly realities, especially during historical crisis when mass suffering reigned."[6]

This tension was greatly heightened in Neo-Confucianism of the Song and Ming periods when, again, contrary to Weber's assertion, a metaphysical dimension was fully developed in response to the Buddhist domination of the Chinese spiritual world. In this regard, I agree completely with Thomas A. Metzger's observation that the Neo-Confucian idea of "heavenly principle" and its elusiveness expresses some of the very "tension" Weber was looking for.[7]

In view of the above criticisms of Weber's famous thesis and his treatment of the Confucian ethic in comparative perspective, I cannot help feeling that we have reached a dead end in seeking a definite answer to the question why China did not develop capitalism. Further speculation is not likely to produce results proportionate to the effort. Instead, I propose to ask a different question, namely, why have Chinese businessmen (and businesswomen) in Taiwan, Hong Kong, and the Chinese mainland been so successful in embracing and developing Western capitalism in recent decades? It is in connection with this new question that I shall discuss the possibility of Confucianism as a contributory factor. In a sense, this question has already been anticipated by Weber himself. Toward the end of *The Religion of China*, Weber said:

> The Chinese in all probability would be quite capable, probably more capable than the Japanese, of assimilating capitalism which has technically and economically been fully developed in the modern culture area. It is obviously not a question of deeming the Chinese "naturally ungifted" for the demands of capitalism. But compared to the Occident, the varied conditions which externally favored the origin of capitalism in China did not suffice to create it.[8]

Now, as I shall stay away from the question of "origin," I would choose to focus on the question of why the Chinese are capable of assimilating capitalism. As a matter of fact, this is precisely why the Weber thesis has attracted so much scholarly attention in the first place. "Sociologists of religion," as Hartmut Lehman observes in his preface to *Weber's Protestant Ethic*, "used Weber's thesis on the relationship of ascetic Protestantism and the spirit of capitalism in order to gain arguments for constructing universally applicable laws of development that, in turn, could be used to strengthen the work ethic, and thus capitalism, in developing countries."[9] However, as a historian of early China, it is not my business to construct any "laws." In what follows, I shall outline the evolutions of business culture and its relation to Confucian ethics in Chinese history in the hope that it may shed some light on the contemporary development of capitalism in East Asian societies as a whole.

Fernand Braudel insisted that capitalism must be separated from market economy and therefore rejected what he called the a priori argument—"no capitalism, no market economy."[10] With the two thus separated, he then went on to suggest that nondevelopment of capitalism in no way prevented China from having had "a solidly established market economy" in the Ming-Qing times.

Now, following Braudel's useful distinction, I would relate Confucian ethics, not to capitalism, which I take to be a unique creation of the West, but to market economy, which seems common to all societies.

To begin with, it may be noted that the so-called Confucian ethics, which has gradually evolved in China since the eleventh century, cannot be considered as purely "Confucian" because of the active interactions between Confucianism on the one hand and Buddhism and Daoism on the other. Talk of *Sanjiao heyi* 三教合一 (Three Teachings in One) was increasingly common from the twelfth century to Wang Yangming 王陽明 (1472–1529). Historically, it was Chan (Zen) Buddhism that initiated what Weber called "this-worldly asceticism" in the Chinese spiritual world. According to original Buddhist texts of discipline (*vinaya*), the clergy were not allowed to engage in agricultural work for fear of killing living beings (e.g., insects, plants, and trees). In the late eighth or early ninth century, however, the Chan Master Baizhang Huaihai 百丈懷海 (720–814) introduced a new principle in his revised text of monastic rules that required all of the monks to work equally in order to earn their own living. One disciple asked the Master: "Is it sinful to cut grasses, chop trees, dig the field, and turn over the soil?" The Master answered: "It depends on how the person does it. If he does it with a worldly sense of gain and loss, then surely he has committed a sin. However, if he does it with a transcendent state of mind, then he has committed no sin at all."[11]

This answer immediately reminds us of the Calvinist attitude of combining practical sense and cool utilitarianism with an otherworldly aim. It was also this same Chan Master who has been credited with the invention of the famous motto, "A day without work, a day without meals," which not only was followed by Buddhist monks but also became proverbial in the lay society.[12] Again, we cannot help think of the saying of St. Paul, "If a man will not work, neither shall he eat," as emphatically quoted with approval by Calvin.

Chan Buddhist asceticism may have been originally of an otherworldly nature, but it soon took a this-worldly turn and thereby converged with as well as strengthened Confucian asceticism. Industry, frugality, cherishing time—these are all virtues promoted by Confucian sages since classical antiquity. Nevertheless, they received new emphasis in Neo-Confucianism due largely to the example of Chan Buddhist asceticism. Both Zhang Zai 張載 (1020–1077) and Zhu Xi 朱熹 (1130–1200) not only urged their students to be industrious in learning but also advised them to divide the day into three sections for "accumulation of effort," clearly following the example of the Chan practice of "thrice-daily sûtra-reading." Zhu Xi even explicitly quoted a Buddhist saying, "Apart from dressing and eating, do not get your mind involved with other things during the entire day."[13] Another Confucian (Su Song 蘇頌, 1020–1102) exhorted people of all occupations, not just scholars, to practice this virtue: "Life lies in being industrious: with industry, one will lack nothing."[14] And with "industry" came the consciousness of cherishable time. One poet wrote:

> Daylight is like a galloping steed.
> Youth is not staying forever. . . .
> If you truly think of this,
> Then what leisure is there for meals during the day,
> What leisure for sleep during the night?[15]

The Chan Buddhist motto "a day without work, a day without meals" also found its sympathetic echoes in the Neo-Confucian's mind. Fan Zhongyan 范仲淹 (989–1052) once remarked: "When I lie down at night, I reckon the cost of my consumption for the day, as well as the work I have done. If my expenditure and work stand in balance, I can fall into sound sleep; if not, then all through the night I cannot rest in peace, determined to make good the balance the next day."[16] Zhu Xi even considered it a violation of the Heavenly Principle for anyone living in this world not to do any useful work after taking his meals. The work ethic thus developed in the Confucian elite was also accepted by other social classes, including the merchants. A late Qing *Manual for Apprentices in Trade* begins with the sentence: "Whoever leaves his home to learn a trade, no matter what role he plays, should always be diligent and careful." The rest is a detailed description of the work schedule for the apprentice, including getting up on time and using leisure time for moral and intellectual improvement. Thus, he is advised to "set up his mind upright, and not be selfish or greedy," or "practice the abacus and calligraphy."[17]

There is ample evidence that Confucian ethics spread from the educated elite to the merchant class between 1600 and 1800 when the market economy was growing quickly in many parts of China. Beginning with the sixteenth century, a quiet but active social movement known as "abandoning Confucian studies for commercial pursuits" swept China. Because of the ever-increasing competitiveness of the examination system on the one hand and the prosperity of the market economy on the other, numerous Confucian scholars gave up their hopes on bureaucratic careers and turned to become merchants. There was a widely current belief at the time that "while one out of ten scholars will attain success in examinations, nine out of ten will in business." This is not unlike the "commercial wave" in today's China, which has thrown numerous "intellectuals" into the "ocean of business."

In his introduction to a series of studies under the general title "The Economic Ethic of the World Religions," Weber said: "Confucianism was the status ethic of prebendaries, of men with literary educations who were characterized by a secular rationalism. If one did not belong to this *cultured* stratum, he did not count. The religious (or if one wishes, irreligious) status ethic of this stratum has determined the Chinese way of life far beyond the stratum itself."[18] Obviously, here he identified Confucianism as the exclusive ethic of what we call scholar-officials even though he was very much aware of the profound and pervasive influence of Confucianism in Chinese society. It is also misleading to characterize Confucianism as "secular" or "irreligious." In any case, the Western category of "religious versus secular" does not readily apply to Confucianism.

What Weber was unaware of at the time of writing this paragraph is that from the sixteenth century on, large numbers of educated Chinese, well trained in Confucian learning including classics and histories, turned away from the bureaucratic toward the business world. As a result, Confucianism was no longer the monopoly of the literati; the merchants now felt that they were entitled to an equal share of the Confucian *Dao*. In 1523, Li Mengyang 李夢陽 (1473–1529), a leading Confucian writer, composed an epitaph for a Shanxi merchant named Wang Xian 王現 (1469–1523) in which the merchant is quoted as having made the following statement: "Merchants and scholars pursue different occupations but share the same mind."[19] I consider this statement extremely significant because never before had the Chinese merchant been so assertive as to suggest that he was a social equal of the scholar.

As we all know, according to the traditional conception of social hierarchy, the merchant was the last of the four major categories of occupations, the other three being, in descending order, the scholar, the farmer, and the artisan. From the sixteenth century on, however, we often find the merchant asking this question: "Why must a merchant always be placed below the scholar?" Even the scholars also openly expressed their sympathy for the merchants. Wang Daokun 汪道昆 (1524–1593), for example, not only questioned the long-established state policy of "light taxes on the farmer and heavy taxes on the merchants," but also went so far as to say, "Is a fine merchant necessarily inferior to a great scholar?"[20] What is even more amazing is the following statement made by Wang Yangming, arguably the greatest Neo-Confucian philosopher of the Ming Period. In a tomb inscription for a scholar-turned-merchant named Fang Lin 方麟, written in 1525, he said:

> In olden times, the four categories of people were engaged in different occupations but followed the same *Dao*; they were at one in giving full realization to their minds. Scholars maintained government services, farmers provided for subsistence needs, artisans prepared tools and implements, and merchants facilitated commodity flow. Each person chose his vocation according to the inclination of his talent and the level of his capacity, seeking to give full realization to his mind.[21]

For the first time in the history of Confucianism, a philosopher of Wang Yangming's eminence openly recognized the right of the merchants to their share of *Dao*. Elsewhere he also said, "Engagement in trade all day long will not stand in one's way of becoming a sage or worthy,"[22] which further confirms that Wang Yangming's conception of the Confucian *Dao* had indeed been recognized to accommodate the new social reality centering around a massive scholar-turned-merchant movement.

It is highly significant to note that from the sixteenth century on, Chinese merchants began to take an active interest in Neo-Confucian philosophy. The ethical and ritual teachings of Zhu Xi were generally promoted in the communities of Xin-an merchants in big cities all over China because Xin-an (in modern Anhui Province) happened to be this great Neo-Confucian master's birthplace. Zhan Ruoshui 湛若水 (1446–1560), whose philosophical message consisted in "experiencing and realizing Heavenly Principles anywhere in this world," attracted many rich salt merchants of Yangzhou of his day.[23] They not only sought his enlightenment on the Neo-Confucian Way (*Dao*) but also made generous contributions to the founding of his Ganquan Academy in Yangzhou. One widow of a wealthy merchant in Nanjing, for example, sent one of her sons to study Neo-Confucianism with Zhan Ruoshui and donated several hundred silver *taels* to Zhan's private academy.[24] In the early years of the seventeenth century, a Zhejiang merchant by the name of Zhuo You was a true believer in Wang Yangming's theory of "the unity of knowledge and action." His biographer even suggested that his great success in business owed very much to his Confucian education: cardinal Confucian virtues such as wisdom (*zhi* 智), humanity (*ren* 仁), courage (*yong* 勇), and strength (*qiang* 強) were also essential to the establishment, management, and expansion of large-scale commercial enterprises.

Limited by time here, let me briefly discuss two aspects of the complicated relationships between Confucian ethics and Ming-Qing market economy: the work ethic in the Chinese market and what Weber referred to as "Confucian rationalism." It is hoped that this discussion may shed some light on the possibility of continuing relevance of Confucian ethics to the development of modern capitalism.

As mentioned earlier, central to Confucian asceticism are such precepts as industry, frugality, and preciousness of time, which, it is interesting to note, also happen to be among the core virtues of the Protestant ethic. Using Benjamin Franklin to illustrate his case, Weber said: "Now, all Franklin's moral attitudes are colored with utilitarianism. Honesty is useful, because it assures credit; so are punctility, industry and frugality, and that is the reason they are virtues."[25] According to Weber, however, while Protestant utilitarianism was to serve a higher otherworldly purpose, the Confucian sense of economic utility was utterly this-worldly without a corresponding dimension of transcendence. Again, I believe, Weber's distinction between Confucian asceticism and Protestant asceticism is overdrawn. Weber defined the Protestant ethic in terms of a commitment to proving one's moral worth in and through the practice of one's worldly calling, which, in turn, arose from one's salvation anxiety induced by the dogma of predestination. It was this particular version of worldly asceticism that turned, under certain circumstances, into "the spirit of capitalism."[26] Let us leave aside the difficulties involved in this complicated causal chain (as analyzed by Gianfranco Poggi)[27] and assume that Weber's inference is valid. Then there can be no question that this peculiar sort of "salvation anxiety" was indeed absent from Confucianism. But it is obviously untrue to say that Confucian ethics completely lacks an otherworldly dimension. Let me illustrate my point by giving some concrete examples. In sixteenth-century biographical literature, ethical concepts such as "sincerity" (*cheng* 誠), "trustworthiness" (*xin* 信), and "nondeception" (*buqi* 不欺) are always emphasized as the quintessential qualities of the merchant. These qualities may well be regarded as the Chinese counterpart of the Western notion of "honesty." Like "honesty," "sincerity," "trustworthiness," and "nondeception" are also useful because they can guarantee the reputation of credibility of a merchant's enterprise. Both the Xin-an merchants and Shanxi merchants—the two most famous merchant groups in Ming-Qing China—have been particularly known in history for their practice of these ethical qualities. Yet when the merchants spoke of such virtues, they never regarded them as purely human. Instead, they always associated them with the "Way of Heaven" or "Heavenly Principles." For example, a Xin-an merchant named Huang Jifang (1499–1559) practiced "sincerity" in business transactions throughout his entire life. He was first attracted to this idea through reading a story about Sima Guang in a Neo-Confucian text entitled *Xiaoxue* 小學 (Primer of Confucian Learning) edited by Zhu Xi and his disciples. The story runs as follows: A junior scholar who had worked with Sima Guang for five years later confided in his friends that he only learned the single word "sincerity" from this famous statesman-historian. Sima Guang explained to him, "Sincerity is the Way of Heaven, while aspiring to embody sincerity is the way of man." One also earnestly exhorted his descendants saying, "All my life, I have only held to Heavenly Principles; the constant way of human relations and the boundless good are all derived from them."[28] Thus, we see that Confucian ethics does have its religious or metaphysical foundation.

Now I wish to further suggest that although the Calvinist "salvation anxiety" was wholly alien to the Confucian tradition, we can nevertheless find a functional equivalent to it underlying the work ethic of Chinese merchants from the sixteenth century on. For reasons to be explained later, I shall call it "immortality anxiety." By the sixteenth century, the merchants had grown fully confident of the social worth of their calling and they often compared their big business enterprises to the establishment of dynastic empires. Biographers often described the business activities of successful merchants in a language heretofore reserved exclusively for dynastic founders. "Imperial power base" or "imperial capital" was frequently used to refer to the headquarters of business operations of a merchant. In a more extreme case, even the expression "starting an imperial enterprise and leaving a dynastic tradition to be carried on" (*chuangye chuitong* 創業垂統) was usurped to praise the founder of a "business empire."[29] One Xin-an merchant named Xu Zhi 許秩 (1494–1554) spoke of his own social ambition in these words: "Although I am but a merchant, do I not cherish the aspirations of Duanmu, who wherever he went, stood up to the prince as an equal?"[30] Duanmu Ci (Zigong 子貢), it may be noted, was a leading disciple of

Confucius who was famous for being at the same time a wise scholar and a wealthy merchant. When he visited the royal court of a state, he was always honored by the prince as his equal.

This "immortality anxiety" was also shown in the merchants' great enthusiasm for their biographies being written by famous scholars and writers. The above-quoted biography of a merchant named Fang Lin by Wang Yangming was one among thousands of cases in Ming-Qing China. Merchants in the late imperial age were generally very anxious to have their lifetime accomplishments recorded to be passed on to posterity. This anxiety was by no means confined to the rich and powerful merchants, however. It was equally shared by the commonest of the market people. Writing in 1550, the famous scholar Tang Shunzhi 唐順之 (1506–1560) said:

> During my leisure, I often reflect on one or two things in our world to which we have long been accustomed but which are nonetheless absolutely ridiculous. One is that a man of lowly social standing such as a butcher or restaurateur, as long as he is able to earn a living, would be sure to have an epitaph in his honor after death. . . . This is something that was unheard of not only in high antiquity but even before Han or Tang.[31]

Yet it is a great irony that Tang himself also did the very thing he ridiculed by composing several biographies for merchants.

Zhang Han 張瀚 (1511–1593), a scholar-official with firsthand familiarity with the merchant network in sixteenth-century China, also complained about too many "epitaphs" being produced in his own day. "In ancient times," he said, "only those who had great accomplishments in moral virtue and deeds deserved such epitaphs."[32] Zhang's statement is a clear reference to the Confucian idea of immortality, which calls for a word of explanation.

In 548 B.C.E., when Confucius was only a child of three, a wise man of the state of Lu made the remarkable statement that there are three kinds of immortality. The best course is to establish virtue or character, the next best is to establish achievement, and still the next best is to establish words. When these do not perish with the passing of time, it may be called immortality. This Chinese belief in immortality has satisfied many educated Chinese over the last twenty-five centuries. As Hu Shih (1891–1962) rightly pointed out: "It has taken the place of human survival after death. It has given the Chinese gentleman a sense of assurance that although death doth end his toil, the effect of his individual worth, his work, and his thoughts and words will long remain after he is gone."[33] This Confucian notion of immortality was always the source of anxiety for the Chinese political and intellectual elite, but in the sixteenth century, many a Chinese merchant also began to succumb to its pressure. As a result, the merchants not only had their share of Confucian *Dao* but also their share of the "immortality anxiety," which was part and parcel of the *Dao*.

Finally, I shall conclude by briefly commenting on the question of Confucian rationalism. Weber insisted that Confucianism developed the most rational form of adjustment, but this rationalism was not linked to a "transcendental goal." However, I believe that the above discussion of the "immortality anxiety" raises a serious question about this view. Particularly problematic is the following statement in *The Religion of China*:

> A well-adjusted man, rationalizing his conduct only to the degree requisite for adjustment, does not constitute a systematic unity but rather a complex of useful and particular traits. Such a way of life could not allow man an inward aspiration toward a "unified personality," a striving which we associate with the idea of personality. Life remained a series of occurrences. It did not become a whole placed methodically under a transcendental goal.[34]

This is tantamount to saying that the Chinese are not "capable of a complete and inwardly motivated personal devotion to a cause that transcends individuality."[35] I don't think any serious scholar today can take such an extreme position.

Closely related to rationalism is the problem of rationalization. In the *Protestant Ethic*, Weber used two examples to illustrate what he called "the process of rationalization" in the West. The first was "the principle of low prices and large turnover" and the second "rational bookkeeping."[36] It is interesting to note that it happened that both features were also present in the Chinese market economy between 1500 and 1800. The famous writer Kang Hai 康海 (1475–1541) recorded the following criticism his merchant-uncle once made of another merchant who waited for prices to go up before selling his commodities: "This merchant does not understand the way of business. To wait for a fixed price before selling is the way of the mediocre trader who seeks to avoid loss, but who can pass a whole year without making a single transaction. Those who do as I do can effect more than ten transactions a year, and so can make more than ten times the profit the mediocre merchant can manage."[37] There cannot be a slightest doubt that the way of business enunciated here is exactly "the principle of low prices and large turnover." He Xinyin 何心隱 (1517–1579), a radical philosopher of the Wang Yangming school, is also reported to have given wise counsel to a young merchant in two different formulas: "buy a bit: sell a bit" and "buy wholesale: sell retail."[38] As a result, the latter made a fast fortune in the market. Again both formulas, but especially the first one, are identical with Weber's principle. In the eighteenth century, a book dealer in Beijing once revealed the secret of his success to a friend as follows: "Since I like profit, I shall also let the purchasers of my books get their share of profit. After all, who does not desire profit as much as I do? If I try to monopolize the profit so that the goods remain stagnant rather than circulating, this means losing the profit altogether."[39]

Thus, we see that from the sixteenth century to the eighteenth, the same principle was consistently followed in the Chinese market.

The application of arithmetic to commerce also began in the sixteenth century at the latest. As the famous spokesman for the merchants, Wang Daokun, pointed out, in the Huizhou region, the hometown of Xin-an merchants, arithmetic was studied with a much greater enthusiasm than Confucian classics. In fact, commercial arithmetic was so popular in this region that housewives often learned it to help with their husbands' business bookkeeping. Recent studies indicate that as early as the Ming Period, the Chinese already developed "The Three-Legged Account Book," which is a single-entry system with some features of double-entry. This was then followed by an improved system known as the "Four-Legged Account Book" in the Qing Period, which a recent writer calls "an indigenous Chinese double-entry methodology, without the influence from Western double-entry bookkeeping techniques." Even if we grant that Western double-entry did influence Chinese bookkeeping, the Chinese case of rationalization probably would not be weakened to any significant degree. As well argued by Jack Goody, "When the Chinese adopted 'rational' or 'scientific' bookkeeping, they surely must have already had the 'rationality' or 'science' to do so." At any rate, Wang Daokun once described a typically "fine merchant" as someone whose calculations were so precise that he neither made a slightest error nor missed a single business opportunity.[40] This is indeed market rationality idealized to its highest possible degree.

Taking the above two central features together, it may not be too far-fetched to suggest that the Chinese market did undergo a "process of rationalization" between 1500 and 1800 even though it did not lead to the rise of capitalism.

NOTES

1. The material in this chapter arose from a 1998 Symposium on "Confucian Ethics and Capitalism." Max Weber, *The Protestant Ethic and the Spirit of Capitalism* (London: Unwin Paperbacks, 1985; also George Allen & Unwin Paperback, 1976, from Charles Scribners's Sons, 1958). Page numbers are from this edition. For works discussing Weber's thesis, one can see Kurt Samuelsson's negative and Gordon Marshall's supportive views. Marshall's book also provides a reflective discussion on various other works on the Weberian thesis. See Kurt Samuelsson, *Religion and Economic Action: A Critique of Max Weber* (New York: Harper Torchbooks, 1964 [1957 in Sweden]). A 1993 University of Toronto Press edition is further subtitled *The Protestant Ethic: The Rise of Capitalism and the Abuses of Scholarship.* Gordon Marshall, *In Search of the Spirit of Capitalism: An Essay on Max Weber's Protestant Ethic Thesis* (New York: Columbia University Press, 1982), 82–96.

2. Max Weber, *Economy and Society: An Outline of Interpretive Sociology*, ed. Guenther Roth and Claus Wittich, trans. Ephraim Fischoff et al. (Berkeley: University of California Press, 1978), 630.

3. Max Weber, *The Religion of China: Confucianism and Taoism* (New York: Free Press, 1951), 156.

4. See Marshall, *In Search of the Spirit of Capitalism*; Malcolm H. MacKinnon, "Part I: Calvinism and the Infallible Assurance of Grace: The Weber Thesis Reconsidered," *British Journal of Sociology* 39, no. 2 (June 1988): 143–177, and "Part II: Weber's Exploration of Calvinism: The Undiscovered Provenance of Capitalism," *British Journal of Sociology* 39, no. 2 (June 1988): 178–210.

5. Weber, *The Religion of China*, 227, 235

6. Quoted in Kai-wing Chow, On-cho Ng, and John B. Henderson, eds., *Imagining Boundaries: Changing Confucian Doctrines, Texts, and Hermeneutics* (Albany, N.Y.: SUNY Press, 1999), 231.

7. Thomas A. Metzger, *Escape from Predicament: Neo-Confucianism and China's Evolving Political Culture* (New York: Columbia University Press, 1977).

8. Weber, *The Religion of China*, 248.

9. Hartmut Lehmann and G. Roth, eds., *Weber's Protestant Ethic: Origins, Evidence, Contexts* (Cambridge: Cambridge University Press, 1993), viii.

10. Fernand Braudel, *Civilization and Capitalism, 15th–18th Century: The Wheels of Commerce* (Berkeley: University of California Press, 1982), 588.

11. See "Dajian xia sanshi—Huaihai" 大鑑下三世—懷海, in Zecangzhu 賾藏主, ed., *Guzun suyu lu* 古尊宿語録 (Beijing: Zhonghua, 1994), *juan* 1. See also Michael John Walsh, *Sacred Economies: Buddhist Monasticism and Territoriality in Medieval China* (New York: Columbia University Press, 2010), 56. Further references to Huaihai in notes on pages 169 and 170.

12. For the origin of this saying, see Yü Ying-shih, *Zhongguo jinshi zongjiao lunli yu shangren jingshen* (hereafter *Shangren jingshen*) 中國近世倫理與商人精神 (Taipei: Lianjing, 1987), 23n26.

13. Li Jingde 黎靖德, ed., *ZYL* 朱子語類 (Beijing: Zhonghua, 1986 edition), *juan* 121: 2935.

14. See Su Song, "Tan Xun" 談訓, cited in the appendix to "Su xiansheng Song 蘇先生頌," in *Song Yuan xue-an buyi* 宋元學案補遺, ed. Wang Zicai 王梓材 and Feng Yunhao 馮雲濠 (Taipei: Shijie, 1980), *juan* 2.

15. This poem is by Shi Jie 石介, see the appendix to "Culai meiren" 徂徠門人, in *Song Yuan xue-an buyi, juan* 2.

16. For Fan Zhongyan's words, see Shao Bo 邵博, *Shaoshi wenjian houlu* 邵氏聞見後録 (Beijing: Zhonghua, 1983), *juan* 22.

17. On such manuals for apprentices, see James Hayes, "Specialists and Written Material in the Village World," in *Popular Culture in Late Imperial China*, ed. David Johnson, Andrew J. Nathan, and Evelyn S. Rawski (Berkeley: University of California Press, 1985), 83, as noted in Richard John Lufrano, *Honorable Merchants: Commerce and Self-Cultivation in Late Imperial China* (Honolulu: University of Hawaii Press, 1997), 19n50.

18. Max Weber, introduction to "Die Wirtschaftsethik der Weltreligionen" (The Economic Ethic of the World Religions [1913, 1915]), in *Gesammelte Aufsaetze zur Religionssoziolgie* (Tubingen: Mohr, 1922–1923), 1:237–268. Translation in H. H. Gerth and C. Wright Mills, eds., *From Max Weber: Essays in Sociology* (New York: Oxford University Press, 1946), 267–301; this passage is on page 268.

19. Li Mengyang, *Kongtong ji* 空同集, SKQS, *juan* 44: 420. For details, see Yü Ying-shih, *Shangren jingshen*, 108.

20. See Wang Daokun, "Yubu Chen Shijun quezheng bei" 虞部陳使君榷政碑, cited in Yü Ying-shih, *Shangren jingshen*, 150.

21. *Wang Yangming quanji* (Shanghai: Guji, 1992), vol. 1, *juan* 25: 940–941. For details, see Yü Ying-shih, *Shangren jingshen*, 104.

22. *Wang Yangming quanji*, vol. 2, *juan* 32: 1171.

23. See He Liangjun 何良俊, *Siyouzhai congshuo* 四友齋叢說 (Beijing: Zhonghua, 1983), *juan* 4: 32. See also Yü Ying-shih's discussion in his *Shangren jingshen*, 125–126.

24. Tang Shunzhi 唐順之, *Jingchuan xiansheng wenji* 荊川先生文集, SBCK, *juan* 16: 337.

25. Weber, *The Protestant Ethic*, 52.

26. Ibid., esp. chaps. 4 and 5.

27. Gianfranco Poggi, *Calvinism and the Capitalist Spirit: Max Weber's Protestant Ethic* (London: Macmillan Press, 1983).

28. *Shaoshi wenjian houlu*, *juan* 20, as discussed in Yü Ying-shih, *Shangren jingshen*, 141.

29. *Ming-Qing Huishang ziliao xuanbian* 明清徽商資料選編 (hereafter MQHS), compiled by Zhang Haipeng 張海鵬, Wang Tingyuan 王廷元, and Tang Lixing 唐力行 (Hefei: Huangshan, 1985), 234. It is extremely revealing that in a late Ming popular handbook for merchants, the successful businessman is also described as "in possession of extraordinary qualities endowed by Heaven" as the dynastic founder and the top successful candidate in metropolitan examinations. See Li Jinde, *Keshang yilan xingmi* (Taiyuan: Shanxi renmin, 1992), 312. See also Yü Ying-shih, *Shangren jingshen*, 148.

30. MQHS, 216.

31. *Jingchuan xiansheng wenji*, *juan* 6: 119.

32. Zhang Han, *Songchuang mengyu* 松窗夢語 (Beijing: Zhonghua, 1985), *juan* 7: 141.

33. Hu Shih, "The Concept of Immortality in Chinese Thought," *Harvard Divinity School Bulletin* 122 (1945/1946): 23–46; reprinted in Chou Chih-p'ing, ed., *English Writings of Hu Shih*, vol. 2, *Chinese Philosophy and Intellectual History* (Berlin: Springer, 2013), 193–207, this quote is on p. 207.

34. Weber, *The Religion of China*, 235.

35. Wilhelm Hennis, "Personality and Life Orders: Max Weber's Theme," in *Max Weber, Rationality and Modernity*, ed. Scott Lash and Sam Whimster (London: Allen & Unwin, 1987), 52–74.

36. Max Weber, *The Protestant Ethic and the Spirit of Capitalism*, 24–25, 68.

37. See Yü Ying-shih, *Shangren jingshen*, 1987, 158; also quoted in Terada Takanobu 寺田隆信, *Sansei shonin no kenkyū* 山西商人の研究 (Kyoto: Toyoshi kenkyukai, 1972), 296.

38. Gu Xiancheng 顧憲成, *Xiaoxinzhai zhaji* 小心齋劄記 (Taipei: Guangwen, [1877] 1975), *juan* 14: 344–345.

39. Sun Xingyan 孫星衍, "Wusong yuan wengao" 五松園文稿, in *Sun Yuanru shiwen ji* 孫淵如詩文集, SBCK, 112.

40. Jack Goody, *The East in the West* (Cambridge: Cambridge University Press, 1996), 78–81; the Four-Legged Account Book is also discussed here.

11. Business Culture and Chinese Traditions

Toward a Study of the Evolution of Merchant Culture in Chinese History

As indicated by the title, this chapter will relate "business culture" to "Chinese traditions." To begin with, let me explain briefly what sort of things will be discussed. In the first place, business culture must be distinguished from business itself. The former may be understood as a way of life grown out of the ever-evolving business world that involves ideas, beliefs, values, ethical code, behavior patterns, etc. It is mainly to these cultural aspects, not the business world itself, that I shall address myself. In the second place, from the very beginning, business culture has been an integral part of Chinese culture as a whole and it must not be misconceived as an isolated phenomenon confined only to the business world. As a matter of fact, in the everyday world, business culture constantly interacts as well as intermingles with cultures arising from different realms of life. Special attention, therefore, will be called to the mutual influences between business culture on the one hand and Chinese political, intellectual, and religious traditions on the other. In the third place, I shall also give a brief account of the changing position of the merchant class, particularly vis-à-vis the intellectual elite over the centuries. Business culture is, after all, largely the creation of the merchant community. The relative importance (or unimportance) of business culture in any given period of Chinese history can be more precisely measured by the place of the merchant in the social scale.

What follows is essentially a historical overview divided into three sections. The first section covers the ancient period to the unification in 221 B.C.E., a period that witnessed the origins and development of the market as well as the first remarkable effervescence of Chinese business culture. The second section deals with the long imperial age down to the sixteenth century. It has been generally believed that during this long period, Chinese society was guided by the principle known as "emphasizing the importance of agriculture at the expense of commerce" (*zhongnong qingshang* 重農輕商), with the result that merchants were held in extremely low esteem—at the bottom of the social ladder, at least in theory. Finally, in the third section, I shall outline the sustained growth of business culture with ramifications in different directions from the sixteenth century on, which may well have reached the limits of the Chinese tradition with its often strong antimerchant bias.

In his last book, *The Fatal Conceit: The Errors of Socialism*, F. A. Hayek argues forcefully that our civilization owes its origin and preservation to what he calls "the extended order of human cooperation," which, in the final analysis, may be shown to have been an outgrowth of the evolution of the market. He further speculates, on the basis of Old World archaeology and European history, that not only the market is much older than the state, but the role of the state in the history of civilization has also been greatly exaggerated.[1] One may or may not agree with Hayek's central thesis. It is undeniable, however, that the problem of the market vis-à-vis the state is one of fundamental importance common to all societies, ancient or modern. Let us now begin with the idea of the market in ancient China.

ANCIENT TIMES TO THE 221 B.C.E. UNIFICATION

According to tradition, the Chinese state recognized the importance of the market at a very early date. An often-quoted passage from the *Yijing* 易經 (Classic of Changes) attributes the institutionalization of the market to the legendary emperor Shennong or Divine Farmer. It says: "He had markets to be held at midday, thus bringing together all the people, and assembling in one place all their wares. They made their exchanges, and retired, everyone having got what he wanted.[2] The text in question is generally considered to be of a much later date, probably of the third century B.C.E., and the quoted passage cannot be accepted as a historical account of the origin of the market in China. Nevertheless, it clearly shows that in the ancient Chinese mind, the state and the market were inseparable from the very beginning. This point is also amply borne out by many other preunification sources including the *Zhouli* 周禮 (Rites of Zhou) and the chapter on King's Regulations ("Wangzhi" 王制) in the *Liji* 禮記 (Classic of Rites). The *Rites of Zhou*, in particular, describes a very complex official market system. Under the General Directorship of the Market (*sishi* 司市), we find specialized departments in charge, respectively, of price fixing, security, sales certificates, weights and measures, etc. There can be no question that the system presented in *Rites of Zhou* is an idealized picture. From Sun Hang's detailed annotations, however, it is now clear that the idealization is not wholly devoid of historical basis. In all likelihood, it can be taken as an indication of the intentions and efforts on the part of the state to bring under control the ever-growing market forces from the sixth century B.C.E. onward, if not earlier.[3]

For illustration, let me give the following interesting example. In 525 B.C.E., an envoy from the powerful state of Jin visited the state of Zheng, then under the administration of the wise statesman Zichan. This envoy wanted Zichan to use his authority as Chief Minister to force a merchant to sell him a jade ring. Much as he wished to maintain a good relationship with the state of Jin, Zichan nevertheless resolutely rejected the envoy's request. According to Zichan, there had been in existence for generations a "covenant" between the government and the merchants of Zheng, which runs as follows:

> If you do not revolt from me, I will not violently interfere with your traffic. I will not beg or take anything from you, and you may have your profitable markets, precious things, and substance, without my taking any knowledge of them.
>
> Zichan therefore said to the envoy:
>
> "Now your Excellency having come to us on a friendly mission, and asking our State to take away [the ring] from the merchant by force, this was to request us to violate that covenant."
>
> Thereupon the envoy withdrew his request.[4]

A few observations may be made about this extraordinary story. First, the "covenant" between the state of Zheng and the merchant community was, to the best of my knowledge, an exception rather than the rule of the time. The historical background of the covenant suggests that when the state of Zheng was founded two centuries earlier by Duke Huan, who moved eastward with the royal house of Zhou as a result of barbarian invasions, he was joined and helped by a group of merchants of Zhou. This perhaps accounts for the privileged position of the merchants in this state. It was by no means accidental that during the Spring and Autumn Period, the merchants of Zheng were much more politically active than their counterparts in other states. For instance, in 626 B.C.E., the famous merchant Xiang-ao, upon learning about an imminent surprise attack of the Qin army against his state on his business trip, disguised himself as an official representative of Zheng and thereby succeeded in persuading the Qin commander to turn back.[5] Again in 587 B.C.E., a merchant of Zheng formed a secret plan to rescue a statesman of Qin imprisoned in the state of Chu.[6] Merchants of other states, so far as I know, were not so politically involved. Thus, the mutual trust between the government and the merchants must be understood as unique in the state of Zheng.

Second, by contrast, there is no evidence that merchants in other states were so respected and well treated by the ruling nobility. The envoy from Jin, for instance, simply took it for granted that the chief minister of Zheng could take the jade ring from a merchant by force. This may well have been the way he dealt with merchants in his own state.

Third, even in the state of Zheng where the merchant community was allowed greater freedom and autonomy, the state still maintained some kind of control over the marketplace. According to his biography in the *Shiji* 史記 (Records of the Grand Historian), two years after Zichan had been appointed as chief minister, "no one overcharged in the markets."[7] This would seem to suggest the existence of an official market system in charge of price regulations as mentioned in *Rites of Zhou*. Moreover, around 600 B.C.E., when Sun Shu-ao was prime minister of Chu, he was reported to have helped the "Master of the Marketplace" (*shiling* 市令) to restore the order of the market when it ran into confusion due to an erroneous monetary policy whimsically adopted by the king. The title of *shiling* further lends support to the historicity of *sishi* in the *Rites of Zhou*. Since concrete descriptions of the relationship between the state and the market in ancient China are extremely rare, I believe it justifiable to quote the story in its entirety:

> One time King Zhuang, deciding that the coins then in use were too light, had them replaced by larger ones, but the people found the new currency inconvenient and all of them abandoned their occupations. The master of the marketplace came to Sun Shu-ao and said, "The market is in complete confusion! The people are milling around restlessly and no one knows where to set up shop."
>
> "How long has it been this way?" asked Sun Shu-ao.
>
> "For the past three months," replied the Master of the Market.
>
> "You may go now," said Sun Shu-ao. "I will see that things are put back the way they were." Five days later Sun Shu-ao appeared at court before the king and said, "Some time ago the currency was changed because it was thought that the old coins were too light, but now the master of the marketplace comes and tells me that the market is in complete confusion and that the people are milling around restlessly and cannot decide where to set up their shops. I beg that things be put back the way they were before."
>
> The king gave his consent, and three days after the order was issued the market had returned to normal.[8]

I must hasten to add that there is no guarantee that the event actually happened in the sixth century B.C.E., or even in the state of Chu, for that matter. However, we may assume that it can be taken as a representation of the state of affairs perhaps in the late fourth or early third century when urbanization and commercialism reached their peak. The story reveals both sides of the relationship between the state and the market. While the state always interfered with the operation of the market, the market, by the early third century B.C.E. at the latest, had already generated its own forces vast enough to resist the arbitrary intervention of state power.

It is truly remarkable that as the market was growing in an ever-increasing pace from the sixth century to the third, Chinese statesmen, thinkers, and merchants also gradually discovered that certain market laws must have been at work. Let me give one or two examples. I am quite sure that they grasped the notion of "supply and demand" in its rudimentary essentials. In 538 B.C.E., the Duke Jing of Qi asked Yan Ying, a famous statesman, whether he knew anything about prices in the market since his residence was close to a marketplace. It happened that the Duke had recently punished numerous people by cutting off their toes. In a remonstrative mood, Yan Ying replied: "Shoes for people whose toes have been cut off are dear, and other shoes are cheap."[9] This reminds us immediately of what Adam Smith says when he discusses the variations in the market price of commodities: "A public mourning raises the price of black cloth. But as the demand for most sorts of plain linen and woolen cloth is pretty uniform, so is likewise the price."[10] Here, of course, Smith is enunciating the principle of supply and demand. Needless to say, I am not in the least suggesting that Yan Ying could compare with Smith in his understanding of this principle. It is nevertheless unmistakable that he was linking market price to the law of supply and demand in an elementary way. As time went by, their understanding of market laws also deepened. In the early fifth century, a man named Ji Ran in the southern state of Yue elaborated the art of manipulating the market for profit as follows:

> The fundamental principle of accommodations and storage is to make sure that articles are paid for in full, in order that money will not cease [to circulate] for profit. Let articles be exchanged the one for the other; no merchandise for consumption that is perishable should be retained [for long in storage], and one should not risk storing it for high prices [to come]. By taking into consideration over-supply and under-supply [of merchandise], then one will know whether [merchandise will be] cheap or dear.
>
> When high prices have risen to the apex, then comes the turn downward to low [prices]; when low prices have fallen to the antipode, then comes the turn upward to high prices. When [merchandise] is dear, one should get rid of it as if it were [as worthless as] dung or dirt, but when it is cheap, one should gather it as if it were [as valuable as] pearls or jade. It is desirable that media of exchange [including money], should be circulated as flows water.[11]

Then, about a century later, came Bai Gui, a native of Zhou, who was universally acknowledged as the foremost leading expert on economic affairs. Not unlike John Maynard Keynes, Bai Gui was not only a theorist but also made a fortune in the market. His neat formulation, "What others throw away, I take; what others take, I give away," which may be inserted into the text of the *Laozi* 老子 without ever being detected, has become one of the most often quoted of ancient sayings up to this day. What he originally intended to say is probably the idea "buy cheap and sell dear." A saying so generally formulated obviously has much wider philosophical applications, however. He is said to have been very watchful of the opportunities presented by the changes of the times in the market. When he wanted to increase his money supply, he bought cheap grain, and when he wanted to increase stock, he bought up high-grade grain. He said that he would invest his money in grain when the harvest year was good and sell silk and lacquer, but he would reverse the course when the harvest year was bad.[12] The following statement based on his personal experience in the market particularly deserves our close attention:

> I manage my business affairs in the same way that the statesmen Yi Yin and Lu Shang planned their policies, the military experts Sunzi and Wuzi deployed their troops, and the Legalist philosopher Shang Yang carried out his laws. Therefore, if a man does not have wisdom enough to change with the times, courage enough to make decisions, benevolence enough to know how to give and take, and strength enough to stand his ground, though he may wish to learn my methods, I will never teach them to him.[13]

Here, he is not speaking as a moral philosopher explaining to us the meanings of Confucian ideas such as "wisdom," "courage," "benevolence," and "strength." Instead, he is talking in the capacity of a "worldly philosopher" in the sense as Robert L. Heilbroner has used it.[14] In this remarkable statement, we find a calculating mind who is actually trying to enlighten us about how to ride with the tides in the vast ocean of the market by relying purely on cold reason. Drawing on the analogies of political action, military deployment, and legal enforcement, he is unmistakably promoting what in substance is referred to as "instrumental rationality" by Max Weber without that term.

Now, I wish to relate the market to the larger world. Due to space, I can only briefly indicate, first, the general impact of the market on human relations in the political domain, and second, the way of life arising from the market as reflected in the philosophical thinking of ancient China. Both may be considered as important aspects of what we call business culture, but as far as I know, have not been adequately dealt with in modern historical scholarship.

Max Weber made an interesting observation on the impersonality of the market as follows:

> The market community as such is the most impersonal relation of practical life into which humans can enter with one another. . . . The reason for the impersonality of the market is its matter-of-factness, its orientation to the commodity and only to that. Where the market is allowed to follow its own autonomous tendencies, its participants do not look toward the persons of each other but only toward the commodity; there are no obligations of brotherliness or reverence, and more of those spontaneous human relations that are sustained by personal unions. They all would just obstruct the free development of the bare market relationship, and its specific interests serve, in their turn, to weaken the sentiments on which these obstructions rest. Market behavior is influenced by rational, purposeful pursuit of interests.[15]

As usual, Weber is speaking of an ideal type pushed to its logical extreme; it is nowhere to be found in any real market community. Moreover, he has in mind, specifically, the Western market in its fully developed modern stage, which does not readily apply to ancient China. However, his notion of impersonality is relevant to our discussion here, for we do find in the market relationship in the late Warring States Period (481–221 B.C.E.) a touch of impersonality.

Around the middle of the third century B.C.E., a new concept called "market way" (shidao 市道) suddenly emerged. The well-known general Lian Po of Zhao was rehabilitated as field commander after having been dismissed for over a decade. All of his former followers ("guests" or "retainers") abandoned him upon learning of his dismissal. Now, with his reinstatement, they returned to him to offer their services. Not yet recovered from his deeply hurt feelings, he ordered them to leave, but one of them said to him: "How come your lordship discovers things so late? In this world of ours, people build their relations with each other according to the market way (shidao). When your lordship is in power, we follow you, and out of power, we leave you. This is a generally acknowledged principle. Why have a grudge against us?[16] A few decades earlier, a similar case also happened to Lord Mengchang of Qi, best known for his generosity in keeping thousands of "guests" under his patronage. When he was reappointed prime minister of Qi in the early years of the third century, his "guests" all requested to see him for employment. He then privately told the only protégé he trusted that he would humiliate them when they arrived. The protégé gave him the following counsel:

> The wealthy and powerful attract many followers, while the poor and lowly have few friends. This is how things naturally are. Don't you ever see those who go to the market? At dawn, they turn sideways to get into the gate, and at dusk, they don't even care to give it a glance as they pass by. It is not that they like the market at dawn and resent it at dusk. It is because the profitable goods they look for are no longer there after dusk.

Now it is only natural that all the guests left you when you lost your position. It is therefore not worthy of you now to hold grudge against them, thereby cutting yourself off completely from all those who want to be your guests.[17]

Lord Mengchang is said to have found this argument utterly convincing.

The above two stories in the *Records of the Grand Historian* may well have been exaggerated or even fictionalized, but there can be no doubt that they represent the Chinese perception of a new social reality closely associated with the ever-growing importance of the market from the sixth century to the third.

Two core elements emerge clearly from the above account. First, the relationship between a feudal lord and his followers seems to have undergone a change from personal to impersonal. It was the impersonal forces of wealth and power, not personal ethics of trust and loyalty, that ultimately determined their mutual relations. Second, the paradigm of this impersonality was believed to be provided by the market relationship—hence, the new term market way (*shidao*). On the one hand, the so-called "guests" thought of their services in terms of a commodity and offered them to a feudal lord as such. On the other hand, a feudal lord who kept "guests" under his patronage was also not really different from a customer who made business transactions in the market.

It is extremely revealing that the Legalist philosopher Han Fei (280–233 B.C.E.) even defined government offices in market terms. He quoted a father's instructions to a son in the following words: "A prince sells his government offices and rank just as a minister sells his intelligence and work. So you depend on yourself, not others." A Japanese commentator explains this passage thus: "A person obtains office and rank through his intelligence and work as if it were a business exchange in the market."[18] Han Fei further elaborated this idea elsewhere. He said: "A minister makes a market deal (*shi* 市) with a prince by working to the utmost of his ability for him and a prince makes a market deal (*shi*) with a minister by bestowing on him rank and emolument. The relationship between prince and minister is not a natural one as between father and son. It is based on mutual calculations." According to a commentary, the last sentence means: "The prince calculates the service rendered by the minister while the minister calculates the emolument received from the prince."[19] Thus, we see that office, rank, intelligence, and work were all transformed into goods for exchange in the political market.

But most astonishing of all, by the third century, even the throne was conceived as a commodity. This is vividly shown in the rise of Lü Buwei 呂不韋 (290–235 B.C.E.) from wealthy merchant to prime minister of Qin. Lü had been engaged in long-distance interstate trade between Qin and Zhao with considerable success until he met a hostage prince from Qin in the capital of Zhao. His sharp business sense immediately told him that this prince was "an extraordinary commodity worth hoarding" (*qihuo kezhu* 奇貨可居). He then went home to seek advice from his father. The following is said to be the resulting conversation:

> LÜ: How many times of profit can be gained in agriculture?
> FATHER: Ten times.
> LÜ: How many times in the trade of pearls and jade?
> FATHER: A hundred times.
> LÜ: Then how many times in putting a king on the throne?
> FATHER: Numerous.

Thereupon Lü made the most critical and decisive move in his life from the economic market to the political market.[20]

Again, the details of Lü Buwei's phenomenal rise to political prominence have long been questioned.[21] However, the basic fact about his merchant background remains undeniable. The conversation between father and son may have been a fiction and the remark about the prince as an "extraordinary commodity" may also have been put into his mouth. Nevertheless, for social history of ideas in general, the evidential value of such stories can hardly be exaggerated. There can be no doubt about these ideas being dated to the late third century prior to the unification. Moreover, it was rather common among scholars at that time to think of power and honor in market terms as amply shown in the writings of Han Fei, quoted above.

The reason is not far to seek. With the unprecedented prosperity of the market in the third century, the merchant class also became interested, more than ever, in investing their money in power and honor. Here again, Han Fei is our best guide. He said:

> Nowadays, however, if a man can enlist the private pleading of someone at court, he can buy offices and titles. When offices and titles can be bought, you may be sure that merchants and artisans will not remain despised for long; and when wealth and money, no matter how dishonestly gotten, can buy what is in the market, you may be sure that the number of merchants will not remain small for long.[22]

It is an unexpected good fortune for us that the above observations about the market are further confirmed by newly discovered texts from the famous Mawangdui silk manuscripts. In a collection of third-century texts belonging to the School of *zongheng* 縱橫 Strategists, "market" is mentioned in two of them. No. 21 refers to the "marketplace" meeting at dawn as going very fast, which agrees exactly with the account given in the case of Lord Mengchang of Qi, discussed above.[23] No. 26 speaks of the state of Wei in the late third century as being in possession of "seventeen large-sized *xian* 縣 (counties) and more than thirty small-sized *xian* with marketplaces."[24] It is very significant that the author of this text should find it necessary to mention, specifically, "market-places" in connection with small-sized *xian*. It seems to imply that the political and economic importance of a *xian* was to be judged by whether it included marketplaces or not. We can also assume the mention of "marketplace" to-gether with the administrative unit of *xian* is an indication that an official mar-ket system more or less along the lines described in the *Rites of Zhou* must have been in existence in most, if not all, of the states prior to unification.

To bring our discussions of the ancient period to a close, let me now turn to the intellectual tradition. It is my assumption that the mere use of things re-lated to the market for analogical, illustrative or some other purposes on the part of thinkers and scholars during the period from the sixth to the third century attests to the importance of the market in their everyday lives. It is be-side the point whether their views with regard to commercial pursuits were sympathetic or antagonistic.

Zigong 子貢 (Duanmu Ci 端木賜) is the only disciple of Confucius who has an entry in "Huozhi liezhuan" (The Biographies of the Money Makers) in the *Records of the Grand Historian*. According to the Grand Historian, in his capac-ity as a wealthy merchant he was always treated by the feudal lords as an equal when he visited them. It was also due to his efforts that Confucius's fame was spread all over China.[25] The authenticity of this account is fully corroborated by Confucius's *Lunyu* (Analects). Confucius once made a contrast between the poverty-stricken Yan Hui 顏回 and the wealthy Zigong in these words: "Hui is perhaps difficult to improve upon; he allows himself constantly to be in dire poverty. Ci (Zigong) refuses to accept his lot and indulges in money making, and is frequently right in his conjectures."[26] This is one of the very controversial passages in the *Analects*. Deeply biased against the merchant class, many tra-ditional commentators tend to read it as a criticism of Zigong.[27] We need not be concerned about the controversy itself, however. The important point here is rather that Confucius probably owed his knowledge of the market to his student-turned-merchant.

Two conversations between Confucius and Zigong in the *Analects* may be cited in support of this point. On one occasion, Zigong asked his teacher: "Poor without being obsequious, wealthy without being arrogant. What do you think of this saying?" Confucius said, "That will do, but better still poor yet delight-ing in the way, wealthy yet observant of the rites" (1.5). I strongly suspect that when Zigong was asking this question, he must have been either already rich or on his way to becoming rich. Moreover, he may well have had in mind, spe-cifically, the contrast between Yan Hui and himself, which also seems implied in Confucius's answer. This interpretation is definitely not far-fetched in view of the controversial passage (11.19) quoted above. The second conversation is even more interesting. It runs as follows: "Zigong said, 'If you had a piece of beautiful jade here, would you put it away safely in a box or would you try to sell it for a good price?' The Master said, 'Of course I would sell it. Of course I would sell it. All I am waiting for is the right offer' " (9.13). Here, Zigong's question is about the scholar's acceptance of a government appointment but veiled behind the language of the market. It is not entirely clear, however, whether the question is formulated generally as a matter of principle or raised specifically with respect to Confucius or himself. Commentators are agreed that in this case, Zigong was urging his teacher to take office because Confucius's answer clearly referred to himself. However, there is another possibility, namely, Confucius showed his good sense of humor by imitating the typical expression of a jade merchant—hence, the repetition of "sell" as well as the last sentence. Whatever the case may have been, it is nevertheless unmistakable that both teacher and disciple were speaking the merchant's language. I would also like to point out that it was a general practice in the market of the day that valuables such as jade and pearls were put in a "box." One ritual text mentions: "the merchant opens the box to take out the jade."[28] In the *Hanfeizi* 韓非子, there is also a famous story about a merchant of Zheng who bought a pearl with a beautifully decorated box from a merchant of Chu. More fascinated with the box than its contents, the former ended up by buying the box without the pearl.[29] Jade and pearls were probably the most profit-making businesses in ancient China, as shown in Lü Buwei's conversation with his father, quoted earlier. Was Zigong a trader in jade and pearls? One wonders.

Most fascinating of all, however, is to listen to Confucius talk about the marketplace. He once said: "If wealth were a permissible pursuit, I would be willing even to act as a guard holding a whip outside the marketplace. If it is not, I shall follow my own preferences" (*Analects*, 7.12). The "guard holding a whip outside the marketplace" is known as *xu* 胥 in the *Rites of Zhou*, the lowest-ranked of all personnel in a marketplace. Each *xu* was in charge of two shops and as security guard, it was his duty to watch the gate as well as maintain order.[30] Needless to say, Confucius never really wanted to abandon his own preferences. However, his familiarity with the marketplace is truly amazing, perhaps again thanks to Zigong.

Living in the fourth century, Mencius was not only more aware of the pervading presence of the market but also made certain evaluative statements about it. To begin with, he held a peculiar theory about the origins of taxation in the market:

> In antiquity, the market was for the exchange of what one had for what one lacked. The authorities merely supervised it. There was, however, a despicable fellow who always looked for vantage point and, going up on it, gazed into the distance to the left and to the right in order to secure for himself all the profit there was in the market. The people all thought him despicable, and, as a result, they taxed him. The taxing of merchants began with this despicable fellow.[31]

As a historical account, it probably cannot be taken seriously. However, two observations may be made here. First, it suggests the recency of taxing the merchants. This is further supported by his talk of the absence of levy at border stations and marketplaces during the time of King Wen of Zhou (1B.5) and his proposal to do away with "custom and market duties" altogether (3B.8). Second, his imagination about "a despicable fellow" is actually a reference to the competitiveness of the market in his own day.

His long debate with a follower of Xu Xing of the Agriculturalist School reveals not only his own attitude toward the market but also how other schools responded to it. Xu Xing wanted to turn the clock backward to the time before social division of labor had taken place. In such a wholly undifferentiated primitive society, neither the state nor the market can really be said to have been in existence. The follower of Xu Xing was convinced that once we succeeded in reversing the process of social evolution: "There will be only one price in the market and dishonesty will disappear from the capital. For equal lengths of cloth or silk, for equal weights of hemp, flax, or raw silk, and for equal measures of five grains, the price will be the same; for shoes of the same size, the price will also be the same." It seems clear that the Agriculturalist School was particularly disgusted with the pervading dishonesty with respect to price in the marketplace. For his part, however, Mencius took social division of labor for granted. For him, therefore, the market was here to stay and it was unrealistic to speak of "one price in the market." In refuting Xu Xing's theory, Mencius argued: "That things are unequal is part of their nature. Some are worth twice or five times, ten or a hundred times, even a thousand and ten thousand times, more than others. If you reduce them to the same level, it will only bring confusion to the Empire. If a roughly finished shoe sells at the same price as a finely finished one, who would make the latter?" (3A.4). What particularly deserves our attention is his theory of price. As his example about two kinds of shoe indicates, he links the price of a commodity to its intrinsic value. Following Ricardo, Marx holds that "the value of a commodity is the amount of labor it has within itself. If it takes twice as much labor to make hats as shoes, then hats will sell for twice as much the price of shoes."[32] Mencius seems to have a vague sense of this problem. Thus, it may be justifiable to say that on the problem of price, Mencius was different, at least in emphasis, from many thinkers of the period who tended to see price being determined more by "supply and demand" than anything else.

In this connection, I wish to introduce the Mohist view on price. In the Mohist *Canons* and *Explanations*, we find two logical formulations that display an amazingly profound grasp of the inner workings of price mechanism. To avoid being technical, let me quote A. C. Graham's summary, which, by virtue of being terse and to the point at the same time, serves our purpose remarkably well:

The two *Canons* on economics show that for him there really is a right price, the one fixed by supply and demand. The first *Canon* approaches it from the buyer's point of view, the latter from the seller's. A price cannot be too high if the buyer will pay it or too low if the trader cannot sell for more. The proof that the price is right is that you make the deal, which requires that both parties want to make it: "whether it is right or not decides whether people want to or not."[33]

These sections show the proper capitalist spirit both in the ruthlessness of the illustration (for example, people in a defeated state selling their houses and marrying off their daughters) and in the plausibility of the moral justification. Money and grain are each the price of the other, money is constant in quantity but grain variable, so that their relative values fluctuate inversely with the harvest; in time of scarcity you pay more, but in money which will buy less.

The Mohist *Canons* (*jing* 經) are of a late date, some even as late as the end of the third century. Now I wish to turn to an early Mohist text for an example to make my point. In the "Gongmeng" 公孟 chapter, Mozi is reported to have said something to the effect that one cannot count the "indentations" on other people's tallies as if they were one's own wealth.[34] The original sentence is too brief to be comprehensible. As a late Qing commentator rightly pointed out, its full meaning can be grasped only in light of the following story in the *Liezi* 列子: "There was a man of Song who was strolling in the street and picked up a half tally someone had lost. He took it home and stored it away, and secretly counted the indentations of the broken edge. He told a neighbor: 'I shall be rich any day now.'"[35] The "tally" (*qi* 契) was a most commonly used document in business transactions in the ancient period. It was a sort of "contract" or "agreement" divided into two halves held by buyer and seller, respectively. Money or goods can be collected only when the "indentations" on the two half tallies fitted each other perfectly. The very fact that Mozi used this analogy so readily in a debate with his Confucian rival Gongmeng attests to his familiarity with the market language. It is relevant to note that the same "tally" also appears in the text of *Laozi*: "The sage, holding the left-hand tally, performs his part of the covenant."[36] In the *Zhuangzi* 莊子, however, "left-hand and right-hand tally" is replaced by "inner part and outer part of a *juan*" 券 which, according to commentators, performs the same function as the tally (*qi*). Hence, the text says, "one [who holds the outer part *juan*] with his mind wholly set on the hoarding of goods is a mere merchant."[37] Without getting too technical about it, I need only to point out that *qi* or *juan* "tally" as a legal document was a component part of the official market system in ancient times. According to the *Rites of Zhou*, the market system included a special office in charge of these legal documents for prevention of litigation related to business transactions.[38]

It is interesting to note that if we take the story in the *Liezi* as a text of possible pre-Qin origin, as I now do, then the Daoists were equally knowledgeable about the market in spite of their otherworldliness in philosophical orientation relative to other schools. To illustrate my point a little further, I would like to remark briefly on the text of *Laozi*. We are still not sure about its date. To the best of my knowledge and judgment, the text may have gradually evolved from the fourth to the third century. What strikes me as particularly noteworthy is the fact that in this 5,000-word text, *huo* ("goods" or "hard-to-get goods") appears no less than five times, *qi* (tally) once, and *shi* (market) once. The sentence involving "market" (chapter 62) says, "Fine words will find their market" (or rather, "Fine words may lubricate business"). In this case, the *Heshanggong Commentary* is very illuminating. It says, "Fine words alone are adequate to the marketplace . . . Because the buyer is anxious to get the commodity while the seller is anxious to sell it."[39] If this interpretation is correct, the author of the *Laozi* text must indeed be recognized as an unusually keen observer of business culture of his day. As a matter of fact, there is good reason to believe that Heshanggong is probably right. In his biography in the *Records of the Grand Historian*, Laozi is credited with the following quote: "A good merchant is deep in concealment that gives the appearance of emptiness," which has become proverbial to this day.[40] This is a worldly wisdom whose discovery requires a spirit as otherworldly as the author of the *Laozi* to discover.

The three intervening centuries between Confucius and Han Fei witnessed the expansion of the market, the growth of the merchant class, and the emergence and evolution of business culture in China. As shown above, practically all philosophical schools responded to changes resulting from these new developments to varying degrees, and each in its own way. None of these schools may be characterized as wholly positive about these new developments, but the differences among them seem very vast. To conclude, let me single out the question of state-versus-market for a brief comment. Contrary to the conventional view that Confucianism has been mainly responsible for the traditional attitude known as "emphasizing the importance of agriculture at the expense of commerce," during this early period, Confucians actually recognized the importance of the market more than any other school. Of course they also considered agriculture to be a more fundamental occupation, but definitely not at the expense of commerce and trade. Mencius's wholehearted acceptance of the principle of social division of labor committed him to a favorable view of trade. Thus, he said: "If people cannot trade the surplus of the fruits of their labors to satisfy one another's needs, then the farmer will be left with surplus grain and the women with surplus cloth. If things are exchanged, you can feed the carpenter and the carriage-maker" (3B.4). As we have seen earlier, he was strongly against "custom and market duties." Taking these two points together, we may justifiably say that it was his basic view that the interference in the market by the state ought to be kept to a minimum. It is interesting to note that on these two points, Xunzi's views are essentially identical with those of Mencius.[41]

By contrast, it was the Legalists who viewed both the market and the merchant class with extreme hostility. The Legalist statesman Shang Yang 商鞅 (Lord Shang, ca. 390–338 B.C.E.), not only proposed heavy taxation on the market but also advocated a policy by which, he hoped, the growth of the merchant class could be effectively checked.[42] Han Fei's hostility toward the merchants was even more pronounced: he took them to be one of the five groups who constituted what he called "the vermin of the state."[43] It was also he who for the first time proposed to call agriculture "the fundamental occupation" (benwu 本務) while at the same time reducing commerce and trade to a place called "nonessential work" (mozuo 末作), thereby giving rise to the idea of "emphasizing the importance of agriculture at the expense of commerce."[44] In short, the Legalist advocacy of state control over the market was complete.

In the second century B.C.E., Daoist-oriented scholars such as the Grand Historian developed a very favorable view of the business world that may have been rooted in the Daoist notions of "nonaction" (wuwei 無為) and "spontaneity" (ziran 自然). However, in preunification times, Daoists, as represented by authors of the Laozi and Zhuangzi, were equally negative about both state and market. Suffice it to say that under the Former Han dynasty, Daoists became Confucians' natural ally in their common opposition to the Legalist policy of government monopoly of salt and iron, which marked the beginning of a full-scale state intervention of the market in Chinese history.

221 B.C.E. TO THE SIXTEENTH CENTURY

If we follow the wise counsel of Fernand Braudel to separate, conceptually, market economy and capitalism, then we can say that with ups and downs, market economy was ever-present throughout the imperial age.[45] From the late eighth century on, it was clearly on its way to steady growth and expansion. In what follows, however, I shall discuss, not market economy itself, but business culture, which arose from its base in the market. To begin with, a word of clarification seems in order with regard to the relationship between the market and the state after the unification in 221 B.C.E.

In this regard, two broad generalizations have been generally accepted almost as self-evident truths. First, the all-powerful state was the main obstacle to the free development of the market. Second, the merchant, being placed at the bottom of the social order, was always held in contempt by the ruling class, including, of course, the educated elite. The first generalization may be considered valid but requires all sorts of modification. As for the second one, the situation was even more complicated. It not only varied from period to period but also often vacillated between idealized fiction and social reality. To be sure, social biases against the merchant in the entire imperial age were both deep-seated and widespread. But the Chinese merchant was not necessarily held in lower esteem than his counterpart in medieval Europe, say, up to the twelfth century. In the European feudal system, merchants also occupied an inferior place. Moreover, the Canon Law was even more severe in its condemnation of commercial gain than Confucian ideology. The Church viewed it, honest or otherwise, as sinful.[46]

In imperial China, the primary source of anticommercialism was the state, not religion. Han Fei said it all when he proposed, "An enlightened ruler will administer his state in such a way as to decrease the number of merchants, artisans, and other men who make their living by wandering from place to place, and will see to it that such men are looked down upon."[47] As we know, the central purpose of Legalist philosophy was to make the state stable and all-powerful. According to this philosophy, wealth as a source of power must also remain in the state treasury, not fall into the hands of private individuals. When the founding emperor of the Han dynasty unified China, one of the first things he did was to transform Han Fei's proposal into law even though he may not have heard the name of the philosopher. Thus, he prohibited the merchants from wearing garments of silk and riding in carts on the one hand and increased their taxes on the other with the explicit purpose of "hampering and humiliating them."[48] It is very significant that as late as 1381, the same attitude was still shared by the founding emperor of the Ming dynasty. To turn people away from commercial pursuits to the "fundamental occupation" of agriculture, he made it a law that the use of silk would be allowed to the farmer's family but denied to the merchant's. The law was so strict that even if only one member of a farmer's family should become a merchant, the whole family would be deprived of the right to silk.[49]

However, law is one thing and its enforcement quite another. Evidence is overwhelming that throughout the imperial age, merchants could always use their wealth to get whatever they most wanted. The Han founding emperor's law was no sooner promulgated than ignored. In 178 B.C.E., a high-ranking court official already bitterly complained that rich merchants daily wandered about in large cities and market towns. They wore "embroidered" clothes and ate "fine" food. In his own words, "At the present time the laws and regulations disesteem the merchant, but the merchant is already rich and honored."[50] This description can actually apply to all the later dynasties.

It was not true to say that the ruling elite from the emperor to the scholar generally held the merchant and the market in contempt. Numerous examples show that envy was also a feeling characteristic of many among them, especially in an age when commercialism reigned supreme. Let me cite two extraordinary cases to illustrate my point. At the end of Han Period, Emperor Ling (r. 168–188) was fond of playing the merchant game with his court ladies in the inner palace. He would have the ladies playing the role of "hostess" of private inns while he himself impersonated a traveling merchant checking into each and every inn to enjoy the entertainment of the "hostess." It was one of his most favorable games, which he is reported to have played repeatedly.[51] Thirteen centuries later, another emperor, in this case, the Zhengde Emperor of the Ming dynasty (r. 1506–1521), again played the same game, perhaps without knowledge of his Han predecessor. He transformed the storage houses in the palace into six different "shops" and he pretended to be a merchant doing business with them one by one. Wherever he went, he made a great deal of noise haggling with "shopkeepers" over prices.[52] Both emperors played the game for more than mere fun; they were really envious of the merchant's lifestyle and of their wealth as well. The former was known for selling top government posts at fixed prices as well as for appointing a large number of traders in marketplaces to the secretariat of the Heir-Apparent.[53] The latter turned himself into an enterprising businessman by sending, in 1513, his trusted eunuchs to open up and manage "imperial business establishments" of various kinds in the capital and other big cities. Backed by the state, needless to say, he pushed many a private merchant out of business.[54] It was by no means accidental that Emperor Ling of Han and the Zhengde Emperor of Ming behaved in the same way, for both happened to live in the centuries in which commerce and trade were highly flourishing. But how doubly ironical it was that none other than both emperors' founding ancestors specifically laid down the law to "humiliate and hamper" the merchants. Forces generated by the market could prove to be, at times, irresistible indeed.

Among high-ranking officials and high-minded scholars, we also find interesting cases of the influence of commercialism. Wang Rong 王戎 (234–305), one of the "Seven Worthies of the Bamboo Grove," possessed all the worst features of the vulgar market man. He was fond of making money and accumulated enormous wealth. His bonds of indebtedness were so numerous that every night he and his wife spent hours calculating the sums. The plums in his garden were of the best kind, which he frequently sold, but fearing that other people might get possession of the pits, he always bored holes through their kernels. Once his daughter who had borrowed money from him came home for a visit without immediately paying the debt; he showed a long face until the money was repaid.[55] Even if these "tales" may not be wholly reliable, there must have been some individuals among the intellectual elite who more or less behaved this way.

However, there is another case whose historical authenticity is definitely beyond doubt. In a letter of instruction to his son, Xu Mian 徐勉 (466–535) said:

> I have been politically prominent for almost thirty years. My former disciples and friends made all kinds of suggestions to me as to what I ought to do. Some proposed acquisition of estates, some urged establishment of warehouses and wholesale stores, again others advised obtaining boats for water transportation, and still others said I should engage in trade and moneylending. I refused to take up any of these engagements.[56]

Xu was a leading scholar of Confucian rites and rose to the position of prime minister (*zhongshu ling* 中書令) in the southern court of Liang (502–557). Clearly, it must have been a common practice among high court officials of the time to engage in commercial pursuits. From this letter, we also know precisely what sorts of business possibilities were open to men wielding great power in the government.

The cases of Wang Rong and Xu Mian thus provide us with a historical context to appreciate the famous piece of social satire entitled "Qianshen lun" 錢神論 (On the Divine Power of Money) by a certain Lu Bao at the end of the third century. What it says, in essence, may be summed up in one simple sentence, "with money, one can do anything." The writer made an emphatic point of telling us that men of power and honor in the capital (Luoyang) all loved that little bronze thing with a "square hole" in it called "money" (i.e., the standard coin).[57] Thus, money was a medium of exchange not only in the business world but also between the business world and the rest of the world, including, especially, the political.

Down to the Tang-Song Period, business culture grew considerably in depth and scope as commerce and, especially, foreign trade expanded to a new height.[58] In a seminal study on the Tang market system, Denis Twitchett describes its breakdown in the late eighth and ninth centuries as follows:

> The abandonment by the government of their attempts to preserve a rigid and direct control over prices and markets coincides with the relaxation, in the late eighth and ninth centuries, of the extreme physiocratic theories which had led all administrations to adopt a generally repressive and hostile attitude toward trade and industry. During the late Tang and early Song periods, for instance, many of the laws and policies designed to underline the inferior status of the merchant in society—the strict sumptuary laws regarding dress, ceremonial, houses, carriages, the sorts of animals upon which the merchant might ride, the denial of participation in official examinations for sons of merchants—were gradually relaxed and abandoned.

Moreover, a similar change of attitude toward commerce also took place in the field of taxation: "Where before commerce had been considered something fundamentally undesirable which, since it was, after all, a necessary evil, had to be strictly controlled and kept within limits, it was now accepted that since trade could neither be suppressed nor adequately controlled, the best solution was to exploit it as a source of revenue."[59] These observations based on solid historical scholarship are extremely important for our discussion here. In the first place, they provide us with an excellent historical background of changes in Tang-Song business culture. In the second place and more important, they serve to caution against any simplistic overgeneralizations regarding the relationship between the state and the market in imperial China. Contrary to the popular view that the state control of the market was at all times nearly total,[60] we now see that long-term growth of market forces could also force the state to make compromises at both policy and institutional levels.

Although we cannot be certain about the power of the merchants under the Tang dynasty due to insufficiency of evidence, I am nevertheless inclined to believe that they were politically more influential than under any of the preceding dynasties. It is truly astonishing that in the beginning of the eighth century, several merchants from Shu (modern Sichuan) got themselves invited to a formal banquet in the inner palace hosted personally by Empress Wu Zetian. Among the guests were Prime Minister Wei Anshi and other high-ranking officials. The prime minister strongly protested, saying, "Merchants belong to a mean class, and should not be seated here." Our source is not clear, however, as to whether the empress actually expelled them from the banquet.[61] Thus, while traditional prejudice persisted, it did not appear to be always effective against the aggressiveness of the merchant class.

Central Asian merchants (shanghu 商胡; literally, "barbarian merchants"), especially of Sogdian origin, were particularly active in Tang China not only in trade but in politics as well.[62] One Sogdian merchant named Kang Qian rose to the position of Protector of Annan and, later, was even promoted to chief minister in charge of the reception of foreign envoys on account of his large contributions to state finance after the outbreak of the An Lushan Rebellion.[63] As the great medievalist Chen Yinke has conclusively shown, the Central Asian and other non-Han ethnic composition of the population in northern and northeastern China in the Tang Period was the power base of this rebellion. He specifically called our attention to two important facts. First, prior to the rebellion of 755, there had existed settlements of large numbers of Central Asian merchants (shanghu) in the city of Yingzhou, the birthplace of An Lushan (in modern Rehe). Second, both rebel leaders, An Lushan and Shi Siming, were of mixed central Asian (Sogdian) and Turkish origins, and spoke many languages, a fact that explains why both men had been appointed "brokers in border markets" in their early careers.[64] The following sentence cited by Chen Yinke in support of his thesis strikes me as particularly noteworthy: "[Prior to the rebellion, An Lushan] secretly sent barbarian merchants to various regions [to engage in trade] and contributed millions of cash and goods each year."[65] A check of the original text has led me to realize that the "merchants" part is as significant as, if not more than, the "barbarian" part. The narrative immediately following this sentence says:

> During a mass meeting, Lushan was seated on a raised chair, with incense burning, rare valuables displayed, and hundreds of barbarians attending to the left and right. Merchants were ushered in to have audience with him while he was deifying himself by having sacrificial offerings

placed before him and shamanic priestesses drum and dance in front of him. He then secretly asked the merchants to buy embroidered silk clothes in red and purple, several tens of thousands in number, in preparation for [the forthcoming] rebellion.[66]

The above description strongly suggests that the meeting was designed as a fund-raising campaign with Central Asian merchants as the primary target. The religious atmosphere probably helped to strengthen their faith in An Lushan's success as an empire bidder. From this whole account, we know that Central Asian (especially Sogdian) merchants had for many years contributed huge amounts of money and goods to finance An Lushan's secret planning for rebellion. There can be little doubt that the active participation of the Central Asian merchants in the rebellion must have been motivated by the prospect of establishing their dominant trading position in China under An Lushan's dynasty. This observation seems further confirmed by the revolt of Central Asian merchants in Wuwei (modern Gansu) in 757, slightly over a year after the break-out of the rebellion. In this case, the merchant leader's name was An Menwu, showing unmistakably that his ethnic identity was the same as An Lushan's. This merchant group must have been powerful and of a considerable size, for they were able to take five of the seven cities in Wuwei and hold them for seventeen days.[67]

On the other side, it is equally significant to note that the Tang court also relied on "forced loans" from rich merchants of the Yangzi valley and of Sichuan to finance its war against the rebels.[68] Furthermore, I must mention that the Uighurs' (Huihu) decision to side with China against An Lushan was not only prompted by the promise of Emperor Suzong to allow them to plunder the wealth of the two capitals after their recapture from the rebels but, more important, by the prospect of a long-term exchange trade between Uighurs' horses and Tang's silk.[69] The Uighurs and Central Asian merchants were rivals in the Chinese market. It was only after the rebellion that the latter became dependent on the privileged position of the former to do business in China, but the tension between the two groups never really eased. Thus, around 780, the Uighurs massacred thousands of Central Asians in their state while Central Asian merchants in Chang-an, in retaliation, also seized an opportunity to urge a Tang general to execute the Uighur envoy and merchants, more than nine hundred in number.[70] Naturally, the Uighurs viewed An Lushan's rebellion with deep hostility from its very beginning.

If my interpretation is not too far-fetched, then I must say that barbarian merchants played no small role in the entire historical process of the An Lushan Rebellion, which has been generally recognized as one of the most important turning points in Chinese history. There is also evidence that even Chinese merchants showed some interest in bearing arms. For example, when the rebellion broke out in 755, the imperial guards proved to be incapable of defending the capital because all of them came from marketplaces, originally either trades-men or peddlers.[71] Another interesting example is provided by a case dated 844 in Xingzhou (in modern Hebei). There the regional commander Pei Wen's army consisted largely of "sons and younger brothers of wealthy merchants."[72] The second case is especially puzzling. Why should young men from such rich families choose to serve as ordinary soldiers? In both cases, apparently, these people of merchant background joined the military forces of their own accord. This phenomenon seems to reveal something new about Tang merchants, but exactly what still needs further exploration.

One important way to measure the political and social status of merchants in imperial China is to examine their relationship with the examination sys-tem. As we have learned from Han Fei, it was already a common practice in the Warring States Period for wealthy merchants to purchase offices and titles. After the unification, this practice was by and large continued throughout the imperial age. Since it was an irregular channel, however, offices and titles ob-tained through it carried less power than "business connections" in high places. But it was a wholly different matter with the examination system, which was traditionally held as the "right path" (zhengtu 正途) to officialdom. The "exami-nation system" has a broad definition as well as a narrow one. Broadly defined, it may be traced back to 124 B.C.E. when the Imperial Academy (Taixue 太學) was founded. Narrowly defined, it began only in the early years of the seventh century during the reign of Emperor Yang of Sui (604–616), with the presti-gious jinshi 進士 degree as its central feature. In this chapter, I use the term in the latter sense, which is generally known as keju 科舉. During the Sui-Tang Period, the system was legally closed to the merchants and their sons, and in practice, we have yet to find evidence to the contrary.

It was under the Song dynasty that the ban imposed on the merchant class was relaxed. The late Professor Lien-sheng Yang (Yang Liansheng) discovered a regulation, dated 1044, in the Song huiyao jigao 宋會要輯稿 (Collected Impor-tant Documents of the Song), which throws new light on this problem. The regulation only required that "the candidate himself (shen 身) was not a mer-chant or artisan and had not formerly been (cengwei 曾為) a Buddhist monk or Daoist priest." According to Professor Yang's interpretation, "The use of the words 'himself' and 'formerly' seems to indicate that family members of mer-chants, or even ex-merchants themselves, would be allowed to take the exami-nations." I believe this interpretation is very reasonable. I also agree with his overall judgment, based not only on the regulation itself but also on other per-tinent facts, that "[For] the last several hundred years, the merchants had re-ceived a kind of political emancipation."[73]

Let me illustrate this point by selecting two or three examples from the huge collection of anecdotes and stories, Yijian zhi 夷堅志 (Stories of Yijian, Records of the Listener), by Hong Mai 洪邁 (1123–1202). During the zhenghe reign of

Emperor Huizong (1111–1125), an old man named Wu of the city of Rao (modern Jiangxi) was locally known for his hat-making business. His constant contact with those customers who were candidates for prefectural examinations made him envious of their social status. He was therefore determined to send his bright son to school with the hope of making him one of them someday. Finally, the son succeeded in the examinations and rose to the position of prefectural supervisor of ever-normal granaries.[74] Another story of a similar nature happened to a poor merchant named Pan of Jinyun (modern Zhejiang). A pouring rain came while he was trading in the city. He went to a nearby house for shelter, unaware of its being a brothel. He stayed in the corridor overnight. One of the girls in her dream saw a black dragon in the corridor and discovered him the next morning. Greatly impressed, she offered help by entrusting all her savings for his management. Eventually, he became enormously wealthy and married her. They had a son who passed the *jinshi* examination and had a successful career leading to prefectural governorship.[75] In both cases, Hong Mai as a twelfth-century story narrator simply took it for granted that sons of merchants were completely free to take the examinations. Our second story is doubly interesting. The "black dragon" symbolized a person of great importance in the popular culture of the time. In the story that immediately precedes this one, which supposedly also took place in the city of Jinyun, the same symbolism is applied to a future "prime minister."[76] It seems to suggest that a rich merchant was considered comparable to a top-ranking official in social importance, at least in popular thought.

Still another anecdote indicates that it was indeed possible for an "ex-merchant" to become an examination candidate, as the regulation of 1044 says. A scholar of Panyang (in modern Jiangxi) named Huang Andao failed several times in examinations. He almost made up his mind to pursue a business career and even had considerable beginner's luck in his inter-regional trade between the capital, Luoyang, and Chang-an. At the insistence of his friends, however, he gave the other alternative a last try only a few days before his scheduled departure on a business trip from the capital to the west. This time, he passed the metropolitan examination.[77] In this case, our hero actually vacillated between his two career choices, showing the blurring of the line between scholar and merchant. With the breakdown of the official market system, it was probably difficult to determine who was a merchant. The credibility of this story is amply confirmed by numerous examples of the Northern Song Period (960–1127) showing that it was a common practice for provincial candidates to bring local commodities to the market in the capital (Kaifeng) when they came to take metropolitan examinations. As the early eleventh-century state councilor Song Xiang remarked, "Of all the provincial candidates coming for metropolitan examinations, can we find a single person who has taken the trip without bringing some goods to sell?"[78] As a matter of fact, examination candidates were by no means the only group turning into part-time merchants. As a detailed study by Quan Hansheng shows, government officials' private business activities under the Song reached monstrous proportions.[79]

It may be questioned that the *Stories of Yijian, Records of the Listener*, in addition to being a work of fiction, is also somewhat late as evidence for the regulation of 1044 regarding the qualified acceptance of the merchants to the examination system. To remove this doubt, let me give two eleventh-century examples whose historical authenticity is beyond dispute. In a memorial to the throne, dated 1067, Su Che proposed to enhance the intellectual quality of the *jinshi* degree by raising the candidate's age and cutting down the total number. One reason he gave was that the current system was so loose that "families of farmers, artisans and merchants have all abandoned their old occupations to pursue scholarly careers."[80] Obviously, this could have happened only if the regulation of 1044 had been enforced. Wang Pizhi 王闢之 (b. 1031 and *jinshi* 1067), a scholar-official from Shandong, told a story about a merchant family in Caozhou (also in Shandong). A certain market man named Yu Lingyi 于令儀 was known for his kindness and generosity. He became very rich in his old age and established a private school for the children of his clan. As a result, one of his sons and two nephews all succeeded in *jinshi* examinations years later.[81] This case proves conclusively that sons of merchants were free to take regular examinations by the second half of the eleventh century, if not earlier.

On the whole, the social place of the merchant in the Song Period undoubtedly improved. We must not overstate our case, however. In the eyes of a brothel girl, a rich merchant may have been just as important as a prime minister, but the intellectual elite still refused to take someone with a merchant background as a social equal. Thus, in the twelfth century when Meng Sikong 孟思恭 was appointed the envoy to the Jurchens, his colleagues at the court derided him by imitating a line of Su Shi's 蘇軾 famous poem to his brother on a similar occasion, saying: "Tell them, you are the son of a salt merchant."[82] This story reminds us of a parallel development in contemporary Europe. The hereditary warriors in the twelfth century were also much disturbed by those rich merchants who aspired to knighthood for themselves or their sons. The German barons also spoke of the nouveau riche contemptuously as "men in trades and crafts."[83] It is indeed an interesting coincidence that in exactly the same century, the ruling elite in both China and Europe equally felt the powerful presence of the emerging merchant class.

Before leaving the Tang-Song Period, I wish to briefly mention contributions of the expanding market to Chinese elite culture of the period. In his long letter to Yuan Zhen 元稹 written probably in 816, the most widely read poet, Bo Juyi 白居易, told his friend the following story. A sing-song girl in the capital told her potential employer that since she was able to sing the "Changhen ge" 長恨歌 (Song of Everlasting Sorrow) of Bo Juyi, she ought not be treated as any ordinary girl. As a result, the employer agreed to pay her a much higher price. Bo also mentioned to his friend that just the day before, he was invited to a drinking and singing party and all the sing-song girls immediately recognized him as the writer of the "Song of Everlasting Sorrow."[84] Poetry was the crowning achievement of Tang culture, but it obviously owed much to the thriving entertainment business for its wide dissemination. The Tang entertainment world also included wine shops with beautiful Central Asian dancers and singers located in the Western market of Chang-an. These wine shops were established primarily for the convenience of foreign visitors, especially Central Asian, Persian, and Uighur merchants. However, they also turned out to be the favorite places of Chinese poets, including the great Li Bo 李白. Many of them described these exotic beauties and their performing arts in vivid verses.[85] This tradition continued well into Song times and beyond. The nationwide popularity enjoyed by *ci* 詞 poetry in Song society such as those of Liu Yong 柳永 and Su Shi was inconceivable without the improvisation of the numerous sing-song girls, both official and private.[86]

The emerging book market was another central feature of the Tang-Song business world. In his preface to Bo Juyi's collected works dated 824, Yuan Zhen said that for the past two decades many of Bo's poems as well as his own had been, without authorization on their part, either hand-copied or printed from woodblocks and then sold in the market. He specifically pointed out that copies of their miscellaneous poems were largely produced by people in Yang and Yue (modern Jiangsu and Zhejiang), and circulated in bookstores in the cities.[87] There has been some dispute with regard to the term "printing" (*mole*) among specialists, but it does not concern us here. Suffice it to know that the book market already played an important role in the wide circulation of poetry in Tang China by the beginning of the ninth century.

By the eleventh century, the printing business in China was in full swing. However, I shall leave aside government printing offices either in the capital or in the prefectures, whose primary purpose was not for profit making. For our purpose here, only a simple observation on the private book market is needed. As early as 1044, a court official was demoted because, among other offenses, he privately printed books and forced local governments to buy them for huge personal profit.[88] As a matter of fact, the book trade was a favorite commercial pursuit for Song officials at the court as well as in the prefectures. As a general practice, it continued throughout the Song Period, as shown particularly in the much discussed case of Tang Zhongyou 唐仲友 at the end of the twelfth century.[89] More noteworthy, however, was the private printing business.[90] Writing in 1128 or later, Ye Mengde 葉夢得 (1077–1148) mentioned four printing centers of his time: Hangzhou, Sichuan, Fujian, and the capital (recently lost to Jurchens). Of the first three, he considered books printed in Hangzhou to be of the highest quality, those of Sichuan next, and the worst came from Fujian. But he concluded, "Now books from Fujian have practically dominated the market throughout China precisely because they are easiest to produce."[91] Books printed in Fujian are generally known as Masha editions in the history of Chinese printing, notorious for carelessness in proofreading.[92] This was obviously due to the fact that the publishers were private merchants with every intention to compete for quick profit in the book market. As a result, book prices began to decline significantly from the second half of the eleventh century and the same trend continued into the next two centuries.[93] Therefore, from the point of view of cultural history, the book market in Song China deserves the credit for having made large numbers of texts, in all varieties, accessible to the reading public. Moreover, as Susan Cherniack says: "The commercialization of printing, which transformed books into commodities, gave new ideas tangible worth. It encourages their production."[94] It may be suggested that the revival of learning and the dissemination of Neo-Confucian ideas in the Song Period were both the unintended consequences of the growth of the book market, to a greater or lesser degree.

GROWTH OF BUSINESS CULTURE FROM THE SIXTEENTH CENTURY TO 1800

A new wave of business culture swept China in the late imperial age beginning with the sixteenth century, if not earlier. It deserves our special attention on account of its long-lasting and pervasive influences on various aspects of the Chinese tradition unmatched in the preceding dynasties, including Tang and Song. Let me begin by quoting an overview offered by the nineteenth-century historian Shen Yao 沈垚 (1798–1840) as a basis for discussion:

> Emperor Taizu of the Song (r. 960–976) took back the entitlements [of officials] to [fringe] benefits (i.e., extra incomes from government-owned lands such as zhifentian 職分田 or "lands pertaining to office" and gongxietian 公廨田 "lands of the public administration" under the Tang dynasty) and placed all [of the revenues] in the state treasury. In consequence of this, scholar-officials began to find it necessary to engage also in agricultural pursuits in order to support their families; everything had changed from the past. Since officials thus vied with the common people for profit, and scholars who had not entered government service had to depend on agricultural pursuits for self-sustenance before they could afford to concentrate on their studies, management of family finance became ever more pressing, and the tendency towards trade and commerce grew stronger. Indeed, without fathers and elder brothers managing some business in the first place, sons and younger brothers would have no means to engage in studies through which they might enter officialdom. Thus, while in the olden days, the four categories of people (i.e., scholar, farmer, artisan, and merchant) were differentiated from one another, in later times,

they were not differentiated. While in olden days, sons of scholars forever remained as scholars, in later times, only sons of merchants could become scholars. This is the general picture of the change since the Song, Yuan, and Ming dynasties.

Meanwhile, with most of the scholars coming from merchant families, a spirit of parsimony and stinginess steadily intensified. Yet while it is often difficult these days to witness an amiable and philanthropic spirit in the scholar-officials, one sees it instead in the merchants. Why is this so? Because the empire's center of gravity has tilted toward commerce, and consequently, heroes and men of intelligence mostly belong to the merchant class; by profession, they are merchants, in character, they are heroes. And being the heroes they are, they understand perfectly the affairs of the world; and so they can manage what others cannot, but cannot bear to see what others are indifferent to. Thus, the situation comes to pass that the scholars turn ever more stingy, while the merchants come more and more to cherish the morals of the past. This is again the general picture of the ways and mores of the world.[95]

Despite his intended exaggerations and occasional overstatements, the two "general pictures" Shen Yao has drawn above are marvelously close to what we call sociologically oriented generalizations in history. The first one is a summing up of the changes in social structure resulting from the rise of the merchant class and the second one describes the emergence of a new culture ultimately rooted in the changing social structure. In a nutshell, Shen Yao's view is that the scholar and the merchant had changed places in society and, consequently, the social role of leadership that traditionally had been the monopoly of the former was now largely assumed by the latter. On the basis of my own research, I can say without hesitation that both pictures are by and large truthful representations of the social reality in China from the sixteenth century on. It is also astonishing that Shen Yao praised the merchants in such laudatory terms. In contrast to the past as sketched in the previous two sections, the language seems wholly new. As I shall try to show below, however, it was actually continuous from the sixteenth century, if not earlier.

To begin with, let me point out that by the sixteenth century, big business networks on a nationwide scale had already come into existence. Rich merchants from Huizhou (in Anhui)—known in history as "Xin-an merchants"—were particularly famous for building such networks. One example will serve well as a concrete illustration. According to the biography of a man named Ruan Bi 阮弼 (1504–1586?) by Wang Daokun 汪道昆 (1525–1593), Ruan was a successful merchant from She, a county in Xin-an, and established his business headquarters in the entrepôt of Wuhu (also in Anhui). He engaged in paper manufacturing and selling. At the height of his success, he had branch offices in the big cities of many provinces including Jiangsu, Zhejiang, Hubei, Henan, Hebei, and Shandong. He hired many talented assistants to take charge of various provincial offices while he himself was giving instructions from the headquarters. He is said to have had such an extremely good business sense that he knew exactly when and how to expand his enterprise. He was also widely respected for the absolute trustworthiness of his promise. Once given, with or without a written agreement, he never violated it.[96] But Ruan Bi was only one among many such newly emerging entrepreneurs of his time.[97] In the seventeenth century, a merchant from Dongting (in Jiangsu) named Xi Benzhen 席本禎 (1601–1653) also developed a similar business network with many warehouses in large cities all over China. He never visited his branch offices and simply directed his business by sending written instructions to them, some of which were even one to two thousand (Chinese) miles away. His instructions were always carried out faithfully by his managerial staff in the various branches.[98]

Such networks seem equally qualified to be nicknamed "business empires" as those in the modern West. It is therefore all the more interesting to see that sixteenth-century Chinese merchants indeed began to speak of them in exactly such terms. In the case of the above-mentioned Ruan Bi, for example, Wang Daokun said that he took his native county of She as a place for "retirement," but considered Wuhu to be his "Fengpei" 豐沛, the geographical base from which the founding emperor of Han started his "empire-building" career.[99] If this was only an isolated description, then we could perhaps dismiss it as an abuse of analogy on the part of a writer imprisoned in the house of the classical language. An analogy of this sort occurred frequently in the sixteenth century, however. Take another Xian-an merchant named Li Dahong, for example. His biography in the clan genealogy says that he ran pawnshops in the city of Gushu (Dangtu in southern Anhui), which became his "Guanzhong" 關中, a reference to Chang-an, "within the passes."[100] In other words, Gushu was the capital of his "business empire." An even more startling case is provided by Cheng Zhou, a merchant who had many business establishments in Jiangxi ranging from pawnshops to salt trading. His biography in the *Xin-an mingzu zhi* 新安名族志 (dated 1551) (Records of Famous Clans in Xin-an) describes him as a person "starting an enterprise and leaving a tradition to be carried on." The original Chinese expression is *chuangye chuitong* 創業垂統, which, though originally used in a general sense by Mencius (*Mencius*, 1B.14), had been exclusively reserved for a dynastic founder after the unification of 211 B.C.E.[101] In the latter two cases, the biographers were family members, and therefore both can be taken as reflecting the merchants' self-image.

From the sixteenth century on, the merchant class grew increasingly self-confident and, indeed, even self-conceited. Biographies of successful merchants often characterize them as men of "great aspirations or visions" early in life, a characterization previously applied only to political and intellectual leaders.[102] In the words of a Xian-an merchant named Xu Zhi 許秩 (1494–1554): "Although

I am but a merchant, do I not cherish the aspirations of Duanmu (i.e., Zigong) who wherever he went, stood up to the king as an equal?"[103] It was also around this time that the merchants became more assertive than ever of their own social worth. For the first time, they raised the question "Why must the merchant always be placed below the scholar?"[104] For their part, the scholars also began to recognize the legitimacy of their claim. Thus, Wang Daokun jumped onto their bandwagon and asked: "Is a fine merchant necessarily inferior to a great scholar?"[105] He openly questioned not only the time-honored tradition of *chong-ben yimo* 崇本抑末, meaning "upholding essentials (agriculture) and eliminating nonessentials (commerce and industry)," but also the established financial policy of "light taxes on the farmer and heavy levies on the merchant." In his view, the two occupations ought to be given equal treatment. "Why is the merchant necessarily inferior to the farmer?" he again asked. On this matter, his view was widely shared by his contemporaries, including Zhang Juzheng 張居正 (1525–1582) and Zhang Han 張瀚 (1511–1593).[106]

Thus, we see that by the sixteenth century, merchants no longer passively accepted the low status assigned to them by tradition. On the contrary, they made every effort to prove that they were the social equals of scholars as well as farmers. A comparison with an early case will fully reveal the revolutionary implications of the rise of this new merchant ideology. A rich man of the eleventh-century from Hunan named Li Qianzhi 李遷之 once related to Ouyang Xiu 歐陽修 (1007–1072) what he thought about his social role as a merchant vis-à-vis people of other occupational categories. He said:

> The common people exert their labor for a livelihood. Those who toil hard will receive a large return, while those who work leisurely will receive a meager return. The size of their return is always dependent on and proportionate to the amount of labor they put in. And then each lives on his labor without shame. Scholars are beyond the match of my type. . . . I consider myself equal to the artisans and farmers . . . but what [the farmers and artisans] receive does not exceed the value of their labor. Now for me it is different . . . I expend labor in a most leisurely and easy manner, and yet what I receive in return far exceeds my labor. I feel ashamed before them.[107]

Here we encounter a merchant who embraced without a demur the traditional four-tiered social hierarchy in the descending order of scholars, farmers, artisans, and merchants. There cannot be the slightest doubt that between the eleventh and the sixteenth centuries, Chinese business culture must have undergone changes of a fundamental nature.

At this juncture, let me turn to the realm of social thought, where a new theory about the social division of labor was being developed in response, essentially, to the growing importance of the merchant class in Chinese society.

In this regard, the most significant documentary evidence is provided, quite unexpectedly, by the leading Neo-Confucian philosopher Wang Yangming 王陽明. In a tomb inscription for a merchant called Fang Lin 方麟, written in 1525, the philosopher offered the following view:

There was a gentleman from the Kunshan County of Suzhou Prefecture called Fang Lin, whose courtesy name was Jie-an. He started off as a scholar, studying for the civil service examinations. But he left off after a short while and went to live with his wife's family, the Zhus, who had been merchants for a long time. One of Fang's friends said to him: "So now you have left the world of scholarship for commerce?" Fang smiled and replied: "How do you know that a scholar does not engage in commerce, and that a merchant cannot be a scholar?"

The Hanlin scholar Gu Jiuhe said to me: "I once read Fang's letter to his two sons. His words of advice were all earnest exhortations to loyalty, filial piety, integrity, and righteousness; they were above popular vulgar talk and rather like those of a man of ancient times who knew the Way (*Dao*)."

I replied: "In olden times, the four categories of people were engaged in different occupations but followed the same Way; they were at one in giving full realization to their minds. Scholars maintained government services, farmers provided for subsistence needs, artisans prepared tools and implements, and merchants facilitated the flow of commodities. Each person chose his vocation according to the inclination of his talent and the level of his capacity, seeking to give full realization to his mind.

"Hence, in terms of the final objective of advancing the way of human life, their vocations were the same. . . . But with the Kingly Way extinguished and learning gone astray, people lost their [original] minds and craved for gains, vying to surpass one another. It was then that people began to think highly of scholars, look down on farmers, to honor officialdom and despise being artisans and merchants. If one investigates the facts objectively, however, one will realize that the scholars were even more opportunistic and blinded by considerations of profit, only under a different name. . . . Looking into Mr. Fang's statement on the occupations of the scholar and the merchant, I see it as reminiscent of the truth pertaining to the ancient four categories of people; it was as if he were aroused in some way to say what he did. Alas, it is a long time since such truth was lost; did Mr. Fang perhaps hear about it somewhere? Or is it that the superiority of his innate qualities enabled him to assimilate it silently within his heart? Thus, I came to ponder deeply on the subject."[108]

I quote this inscription at some length because it reveals changes in sixteenth-century Chinese society in several important ways. Moreover, it may also be regarded as an epoch-making document in the history of Neo-Confucian social thinking to which, unfortunately, due attention has not been given thus far. In what immediately follows, I shall try to bring out some of its most important implications by way of a running commentary.

First, Fang Lin's was an early case typical of numerous scholars-turned-merchants in Ming (1368–1644) and Qing (1644–1911) times. In the sixteenth and seventeenth centuries, a quiet but active social movement known as "abandoning Confucian studies for commercial pursuits" (*qiru jiugu* 棄儒就賈) swept China. The basic pattern may be simply characterized. Having repeatedly failed in provincial examinations (*juren* 舉人), a scholar in his twenties would give up his studies and choose to pursue the career of a merchant. Of course individual cases of this type occurred much earlier. We have already seen a Northern Song case in the story of Huang Andao mentioned above. During the Ming Period, it became noticeable as early as the fifteenth century.

Judging by the date of Wang Yangming's tomb inscription (1525), Fang Lin's shift of career must have happened in the second half of the previous century. According to Sang Yue 桑悅 (1447–1530), his father, Sang Lin 桑琳 (1423–1497), also married into a merchant family and then abandoned his studies for the *juren* examinations to take charge of a large shop, exactly as Fang Lin did.[109] The same trend also continued well into later centuries. For example, in the single county of Wuyuan (in Xin-an) no less than fifty such cases can be found in the local gazetteer for the Qing Period alone,[110] but the largest concentration of scholar-turned-merchant cases, as far as can be confirmed by the sources, was between 1500 and 1700. This phenomenon requires an explanation.

Tentatively, I would like to suggest that the ever-increasing competitiveness of the examination system on the one hand and the prosperity of the market economy on the other seemed equally responsible for it. A rough estimate indicates that China's population probably rose from some 65 million in the late fourteenth century to the neighborhood of 150 million by 1600.[111] But the quotas of the *jinshi* and *juren* degrees remained basically stationary throughout the Ming-Qing Period. As Wen Zhengming 文徵明 (1470–1559) pointed out in 1515, in the eight counties of Suzhou Prefecture, there were altogether no less than fifteen hundred *shengyuan* 生員 in the local schools. Out of this large number, however, only twenty *gongsheng* 貢生 and thirty *juren* were produced in every three-year period, so he proposed a liberal increase of the *gongsheng* quotas as a solution.[112] At about the same time, Han Bangqi 韓邦奇 (1479–1556) also remarked that both the *jinshi juren* quotas ought to be greatly expanded to cope with the situation that the *gongsheng* generally had little opportunities for official appointment.[113] By contrast, the chances of success in the sixteenth-century business world were extremely good. It was believed that "while one out of ten scholars will attain success in examinations, nine out of ten merchants will in business."[114] A man named Huang Chongde 黃崇德 (1469–1537) was persuaded by his father to give up his preparations for examinations and went to coastal

Shandong for the salt trade. A year's work brought him a 10 percent profit, which soon rose to doubling his capital.[115] Thus, we see that the "push" of the examination system and "pull" of the market jointly created the first and long-lasting "commercial wave," which threw numerous "intellectuals" into the "ocean of business," to borrow the language now very much in vogue in China.[116]

Second, when Wang Yangming, endorsing and elaborating Fang Lin's view, said that scholars of his day were more profit-minded than merchants, while among merchants there were individuals who lived up to the ideals of the Sagely Way of antiquity, he was making essentially the same criticism of the same social reality that Shen Yao did three centuries later. The main difference was a linguistic one. Wang spoke a language of philosophical idealism, whereas Shen spoke that of historical realism. Many writers between them also made similar observations but expressed in different ways. The most common of them were "a scholar in occupation but a merchant in conduct" and "a merchant in occupation but a scholar in conduct," or, in a morally neutral sense, "the scholar-merchant" or "the merchant-scholar," which are too numerous to require documentation. What really happened, however, was that by the sixteenth century, it was hardly possible to draw a clear social line between the scholar and the merchant; more often than not, both lived under the same roof. Shen Yao's point about "the four categories of people being undifferentiated in later times" had already been common knowledge in Wang Yangming's time. Gui Youguang 歸有光 (1507–1571) also said that nowadays "scholar," "farmer," and "merchant" were often "mixed" in the same person,[117] and this observation of his was only to be reconfirmed by his great-grandson, Gui Zhuang 歸莊 (1613–1673), a century later.[118] This new development is indeed noteworthy but should occasion no surprise given our knowledge of the earlier interpenetration between elite culture and business culture in Song times. Nor is it unique to Chinese history. In fifteenth-century England, there was also a movement toward a "fusion" between merchants and gentry to the extent that "the gentleman merchant" even emerged as a legal term that is certainly comparable to "the scholar-merchant" (*shi er shang* 士而商), a social term in the Chinese case. According to Sylvia Thrupp, in medieval England, "The movement from the merchant class into the landed gentry exceeded the reverse movement."[119] In Ming-Qing China, however, I suspect it was probably the other way around.

Last but not least, our greatest attention must be drawn to Wang Yangming's statement that "the four categories of people were engaged in different occupations but followed the same Way (*simin yi ye er tong Dao* 四民異業而同道)." For the first time in the history of Confucian thought, a philosopher of Wang Yangming's eminence openly acknowledged that the merchants are equally entitled to their share of the sacred Way. That Wang Yangming really meant what he said can be corroborated by a remark he made in a wholly different context that "Engagement in trade all day long will not stand in one's way of becoming a sage or worthy."[120] From the sociohistorical point of view, a distinction must be made between the general proposition that "everyone can become a sage" and the specific one saying that "a merchant can become a sage or worthy," even though logically, the latter is implied in the former, for the general proposition, long worn out with the passing of time, could sometimes become a cliché devoid of existential meaning. It was rather unlikely that a member of the Confucian elite would spontaneously associate this general idea with a merchant, or even with a farmer or artisan for that matter. Here, I believe, lies the central significance of Wang Yangming's redefinition of the four categories of people in terms of *Dao*.

I must hasten to add, however, that it may not be completely fair to credit the originality of this idea to Wang Yangming. Two years before Wang wrote the tomb inscription for Fang Lin, his literary friend Li Mengyang 李夢陽 (1473–1529) had composed an epitaph for a Shanxi merchant named Wang Xian 王現 (1469–1523) in which the merchant is quoted as having said to his sons that "scholars and merchants pursue different occupations but share the same mind."[121] Wang Yangming could have had access to this widely circulated epitaph of Li's and for him, "mind" and *Dao* were interchangeable in meaning. If Wang Xian's remark had inspired the philosopher in some way, then it was the merchant who first made his claim to an equal share of the sacred Way. As a matter of fact, merchants from the sixteenth century on appeared to take an active interest in Neo-Confucian philosophy and Zhu Xi 朱熹, Lu Xianshan 陸象山, Zhan Ruoshui 湛若水 (1466–1560), and Wang Yangming all had their admirers among them. It goes without saying that Xian-an merchants generally worshipped Zhu Xi as a great moral teacher from their own locality.[122] An early seventeenth-century merchant from Zhejiang named Zhuo Yu 卓禺 was also a true believer in Wang Yangming's theory of "the unity of knowledge and action."[123] The case of Zhan Ruoshui is even more interesting. In the 1530s when he was appointed minister of rites in Nanjing, many salt merchants of Yangzhou came to him for philosophical instructions.[124] Also around this time, the widow of a rich merchant sent one of her sons to study with Zhan Ruoshui to learn how to "embody the Heavenly Principle." When Zhan Ruoshui was short of funds for building his Ganquan Academy in Yangzhou, she made a contribution of several hundred silver taels.[125] Huang Chongde, mentioned earlier, turned from scholar to merchant because he was convinced by his father's argument that "the learning of Lu Xiangshan takes the securing of a livelihood as its first priority."[126] Confronted with evidence like this, the conclusion seems inevitable that merchants not only actively sought to take part in the *Dao* but also reinterpreted it in their own way. In this light, Wang Yangming's new formulation may well be taken more as a response to a changing social reality than as an original idea created purely from the mind of a philosophical genius, which he undoubtedly was.

Wang Yangming was one of the earlier writers who honored merchants with biographical accounts. From this time on, we can hardly go through the collected

work of a Ming-Qing author of note without encountering some positive statements about the social functions of merchants, which usually took the forms of
epitaph, biography, and birthday essay. This is definitely a new development in
Ming-Qing business culture, for we have yet to discover even a single merchant
biography in the works of pre-Ming writers. In the sixteenth century, some
writers may be justifiably called spokesmen for the merchant class, notably
Wang Daokun and Li Weizhen 李維楨 (1546–1626). Wang not only came from
a merchant family but also married the daughter of a rich merchant.[127] It must
be emphatically pointed out that intermarriage between scholar families and
merchant families was extremely common during the Ming-Qing Period,
which also accounted for the rich biographical information about the merchants
in the literary productions. For example, Qian Daxin 錢大昕 (1728–1804), a most
respected scholar of the Qianlong era, wrote an epitaph for a wealthy merchant
named Qu Lianbi 瞿連璧 (1716–1786) because his daughter was married to the
latter's grandson.[128] Li Weizhen was especially famous for his service to rich
merchants in this regard, for which he was paid handsomely.[129] In both Wang
Daokun's and Li Weizhen's collected writings alone, hundreds of merchant biographies can be found. This new trend was by no means confined only to the
circles of rich and powerful merchants, however. By the sixteenth century, even
the commonest of the market people were equally determined to honor their
fathers and grandfathers in this way. In his letter to a friend, dated 1550, Tang
Shunzhi 唐順之 (1506–1560) wrote:

> During my leisure, I often reflect on one or two things in our world to
> which we have long been accustomed but which are nonetheless abso-
> lutely ridiculous. One is that a man of lowly social standing such as a
> butcher or restaurateur, as long as he is able to earn a living, would be sure
> to have an epitaph in his honor after death. . . . This is something that was
> unheard of not only in high antiquity but even before Han or Tang.[130]

This is a piece of evidence of vital importance for our understanding of the
merchant mentality in Ming China. It is further corroborated by a writer fifty
years later who commented that what Tang said was indeed "a true fact."[131]
Moreover, Zhang Han must also have had the merchants in mind when he
complained about too many "epitaphs" being produced in his own day. In ancient times, he said, "only those who had great accomplishments in moral virtue
and deeds deserved such epitaphs."[132]

How are we going to interpret this new social phenomenon in the sixteenth
century? Traditionally, it has been generally assumed that the merchants, being
envious of the intellectual elite, made every effort to imitate the lifestyle of the
scholar-official. The standard expression is *fuyong fengya* 附庸風雅, lit. "para-
sitic on [the scholar's] cultural elegance." Even modern historians rarely question this interpretation, which undeniably, does contain a grain of truth. It is

also obvious, however, that the very assumption itself was part and parcel of the millennia-long and deep-seated prejudice against the merchant class. From the merchant's point of view, however, it seems more sensible to say that their newly gained self-confidence led them to think that they were equally entitled to the recognition and honor that had long been the monopoly of the scholars. This is simply Wang Yangming's "different occupations but the same Way" interpreted in its most worldly sense.

There is considerable evidence showing that not all merchants aspired to become scholar-officials. According to a late Ming short story, the social custom in Huizhou took commerce and trade as the occupation of primary importance and considered success in examinations to be secondary.[133] Wang Daokun also told us that people in this region "prefer merchant to scholar and substitute the *Nine Chapters [of Arithmetic]* for the Six Classics."[134] Still another testimony is provided by the great ancient-style prose master Wang Shizhen 王世貞 (1526–1590), who said, "The custom of Huizhou has been such that the social worth of a man is often measured by his wealth."[135]

Taking all three general characterizations together, it seems safe to assume that among Huizhou merchants of the Ming Period, there must have been many who were wholeheartedly devoted to business as their calling. Space here does not allow me to substantiate this conclusion with individual cases, but I shall touch on this point again later.[136] It is interesting to see that this custom of Huizhou was paralleled by that of Shanxi, another province famous for providing China with countless enterprising merchants since the Ming dynasty. In 1724, the provincial governor memorialized to the throne, pointing out that it was the established custom in Shanxi that "the majority of the talented and outstanding young men join the trading profession. . . . Only those whose talents are below average are made to study for the examinations." In response, the Yongzheng Emperor said that he had long been aware of this "extremely ridiculous custom."[137] Moreover, even if a merchant sent a son to government service or the Imperial Academy as a "graduate student" (*jiansheng* 監生), his motivation could be other than "envy" or power for its own sake. A sixteenth-century rich merchant of Hebei, for instance, was greatly relieved when his son was transferred from the Censorate to the Board of Revenue, for the former was too close to the center of power. He was absolutely delighted when his son was finally made an official in charge of customs duties in the Suzhou area. As the father saw it, his son was now in a position to keep the merchants from being harshly treated by the customs office.[138] In the case of the *jiansheng*, it was a status that would give its holder direct access to scholar-officials in general and government authorities in particular.[139] It is not difficult to see that "envy" or "imitation" is too simple to be adequate to the task of historical explanation.

By the sixteenth century, merchants were often honored by the government for their generous monetary contributions to emergency needs or philanthropic deeds. For example, in the late sixteenth century, a shrine was built, with the emperor's blessing, in memory of a public-spirited merchant named Huang Zongzhou in Jiangyin on account of the enormous funds he had provided in the 1550s for the defense of the city against the *wokou* pirates, as well as for the relief of the poor.[140] A Huizhou merchant Jiang Keshu 蔣克恕 (1520–1581) was honored by the local government with a stone stele because he had single-handedly taken care of the vast expenses for the construction, near his hometown, of a huge stone bridge and a long road dotted with pavilions for travelers' rest. Greatly excited by the grandeur and glory this gigantic project had brought to their town, local residents remarked: "It is quite enough to be a merchant. Why should anyone care to be a scholar?" From a different perspective, his son-in-law, a scholar himself, also commented, "A well-groomed scholar can indeed discourse a great deal on abstract principles, but he could do little to help other people. My father-in-law has done enormously for others. What's the point for him to become a scholar?"[141] As these two cases clearly show, what Shen Yao called "the philanthropic spirit of the merchants" had, over time, brought them broader and more lasting recognition from both state and society. From this time on, the entire social atmosphere seemed to be changing slowly but steadily in the merchants' favor. It was by no means unrealistic to say that a late Ming merchant could feel that a life wholly devoted to business was a life worth living. With merchants and scholars being increasingly undifferentiated, they not only came to share more of the old values but also developed new values together. As I have shown elsewhere, interpenetration between business culture and elite culture was not a one-way traffic with the merchant always imitating the scholar. It worked in reverse as well.[142]

Before closing, I wish to take a quick look at the business culture of the Ming-Qing Period and its relations to Chinese traditions. Due to space limitations, I can do no more than make a few brief comments.

First, the new business culture. A term that we often encounter in the biographical literature on merchants of this period is *gudao* 賈道 ("merchant way" or "way of business"). Its meaning seems to vary from one context to another. However, in one particular sense, it is clearly a reference to certain market laws that one must follow to make his business a success. I shall discuss the term only in this technical sense. Kang Hai 康海 (1475–1541), a famous writer from Shaanxi, reported a criticism his deceased uncle made of a merchant who waited for prices to go up before selling his commodities. It runs as follows: "He does not understand the way of business (*gudao*). To wait for a fixed price before selling is the way of the mediocre trader who seeks to avoid loss, but who can pass a whole year without making a single transaction. Those who do as I do can effect more than ten transactions a year, and so can make more than ten times the profit the mediocre merchant can manage."[143] What is particularly interesting in this passage is that the critic seems to have rediscovered the principle first enunciated by Jiran in the fifth century B.C.E. that "one should not risk a merchandise for high prices to come," as quoted earlier. Throughout the sixteenth and seventeenth centuries, scholars' writings on the merchants are pervasively infiltrated with the language of Sima Qian's 司馬遷 chapter on "Money-Makers." This was obviously the inevitable result of the literary fashion of the day, which looked up to the Grand Historian of Han as the model prose writer. So what I just referred to as "rediscovery" of the pre-unification ideas about the market may well have been a linguistic illusion. There is another possibility, however: it was the extralinguistic reality that invited the use of the specific language in question. What the merchants of the day did and said probably reminded these writers of the pre-unification "money-makers." Whatever the case may be, it is important to point out that Ming-Qing merchants developed market rationality to a much higher level than their pre-Qin predecessors.

I shall mention only two features in the Ming-Qing "way of business," namely, the application of arithmetic to commerce and the emergence of "the principle of low prices and large turnover." Both features happen to be taken by Max Weber as illustrative examples of "the process of rationalization" in the rise of Western capitalism.[144] I am not suggesting that Ming-Qing China developed anything even remotely resembling "capitalism," however. I agree with Weber that capitalism is a peculiar Western system. All I am saying is simply that these two features, central to the Chinese "way of business" in the Ming-Qing Period, fit in well with Weber's definition of rationality. There is no reason to assume that rationality, even market rationality, must of necessity lead to capitalism of the Western type.

We have already quoted Wang Daokun that Huizhou people were more interested in arithmetic than the Confucian classics. This general statement can be amply substantiated. Cheng Dawei's 程大位 (1533–1606) *Suanfa tongzong* 算法統宗 (General Compilation of Arithmetic), completed in 1593, was a famous textbook on arithmetic designed specifically to give solutions to problems by means of the abacus. It was clearly intended to apply to business calculations due to the author's early background as a merchant.[145] Another example from Huizhou was Wang Tingbang 汪廷榜 (1729–1803), who also turned from a merchant to mathematician.[146] Commercial arithmetic was so popular in Huizhou that even a housewife learned it in order to help her husband's business bookkeeping.[147] But enthusiasm for commercial arithmetic was a nationwide phenomenon, not confined to Huizhou. Some late Ming commercial handbooks also devoted sections to it for the convenience of traveling merchants.[148] While there was admittedly no double-entry bookkeeping in China, the commercial arithmetic of the sixteenth century was nevertheless sophisticated enough to be comparable to its contemporary counterpart in Europe.[149] In this connection, I may also mention that in merchant biographies of this period, the term "mental calculation" (*xinji* 心計) is often emphasized as a desirable quality. A typically "fine merchant" is described as someone whose calculations are so precise that he will neither make the slightest error nor miss a single opportunity.[150] This is instrumental rationality idealized to its highest possible degree without that term.

The principle of low prices and large turnover was also universally accepted and widely practiced in the Ming-Qing market. As a matter of fact, it is already implied in the above quoted remark of Kang Hai's uncle about the "way of business." The following anecdote is more revealing, however. According to Gu Xiancheng 顧憲成 (1550–1612), the radical thinker He Xinyin 何心隱 (1517–1579) was once asked for advice by a young man on his way to becoming a merchant. He Xinyan gave him two formulas. The first one was in six words: "buy one bit; sell one bit." The second one was in four words: "buy wholesale; sell retail." Following He's advice, the young merchant made a fast fortune in the market.[151] The story cannot be verified, but whoever said them had a profound understanding of the market economy, indeed. In effect, what the first formula meant is to sell quickly what one has bought, which is almost identical with Weber's principle. Now let me cite two examples to show that the principle was continually practiced by merchants with good business sense through the Ming-Qing Period. Jin Runai 金汝鼐 (1596–1645), a merchant from the Suzhou region, is described as follows: "While other merchants preferred to detain market commodities and wait for prices to soar before releasing them, Jin always sold them at a lower price, passing on what he had bought in and discharging what he had stored up, his objective being that his commodities should not be left unsold."[152] The other example was Tao Zhengxiang 陶正祥 (1732–1797), a book dealer of Suzhou. According to Sun Xingyan 孫星衍 (1753–1818), Mr. Tao once told a friend about his way of doing business thus: "Since I like profit, I shall also let the purchasers of my books get their share of profit. After all, who does not desire profit as much as I do? If I try to monopolize the profit so that the goods remain stagnant rather than circulating, this means losing the profit altogether." But Mr. Tao was not the only one who had a firm grasp of this principle. Sun Xingyan also knew two other merchants in the capital, art dealer Wang and antique dealer Gu, who held exactly the same view as Tao's. All three flourished at the time.[153]

Taking these two central features together, I think it is reasonable to suggest that the Chinese business world also underwent a "process of rationalization" between 1500 and 1800. In the Chinese case, however, this process was linked, not to capitalism, but to a more advanced market economy, to follow the distinction made by Braudel.

Second, the "way of business," discussed above, may be regarded as the nucleus of Ming-Qing business culture. The concept of business culture is extremely broad, however. If understood as a way of life associated with the business world, then we must say that business culture in the Ming-Qing times was practically coextensive with Chinese culture itself, for it touched every part of the Chinese tradition. A simple and easy way to explain this situation is to use a commercial handbook as an illustration, for such works were all compiled by merchants. Take the *Shishang leiyao* 士商類要 (Classified Essentials for Scholars and Merchants), dated 1626, as an example. It consists of four chapters (*juan* 卷). Chapter 1 is a travel guide including commercial routes. Chapter 2 is really the core, for it tells the merchant everything he needs to know about the business world. More interesting to note is that it contains popularized versions of general principles about the "way of business," such as a rhymed prose on "trade" and an essay on "business management." In the last two chapters, however, we find "essentials" of every important aspect of the Chinese world, past and present. The topics range from history, cosmology, ethics, and religion to social relations, medicine, and political institutions. As its title clearly indicates, the handbook was designed to meet the needs of both traveling merchants and examination candidates in their everyday life. This is a concrete example showing how the social intermingling of merchants with scholars inevitably led to the interpenetration of culture between them.

In this connection, let me also give a most amusing example to show that when our merchant-author laid his hand on something in the elite culture, he sometimes also changed it by way of reinterpretation. In a section on "Basic Guidelines for the Traveling Merchant," the author discussed price mechanism in the market and quoted the *Daodejing* to support it. The quoted sentence says: "One who desires dear [goods] must have cheap [goods] as his root; one who desires high [prices] must take the opportunity when [prices] are low."[154] In the original text of the *Laozi*, however, it reads, "the humble is the stem upon which the mighty grows; the low is the foundation upon which the high is laid" (chap. 39). Whatever it means, it speaks to "princes" and "barons" about their power base, having nothing to do with the market. Here our merchant-author not only quoted it completely out of context but also distorted its meaning through whimsical emendations, such as adding "one who desires" and changing "foundation" (*ji* 基) to "opportunity," which happens to be a homophone (*ji* 機). This concrete case serves well as an illustration of the fact that by actively participating in the culture of the scholar, the merchant also transformed it.

The imprint of business culture on the Chinese tradition was not spread evenly everywhere, however. It was more deeply felt in some areas than others. As we all know, its influences on the developments of popular religion and popular literature in the late Ming were enormous. Merchants of this period were generally very religious, and one of them, Cheng Yunzhang 程雲章 (1602–1651), even became the founder of a popular sect on the model of the Three-Teachings-in-One of Lin Zhao-en 林兆恩 (1517–1598).[155] There is also evidence that the so-called morality books (*shanshu* 善書), a type of semireligious tract that gained widespread popularity in the sixteenth and seventeenth centuries, made special efforts to encourage merchants to be generous with their money for charities and public works.[156] On the other hand, fiction, drama, and oral literature not only created tremendous profit for merchants in the book market[157] but also provided other merchants with their most favorite reading materials. As an early nineteenth-century Huizhou merchant remarked, "Merchants invariably turn to romances and novels as their pastimes,"[158] but this reading habit had already begun as early as the fifteenth century.[159] For the sixteenth century, I can cite the remarkable example of Gu Xue 顧學, the merchant-father of Gu Xiancheng. In his early years, he was an avid reader of novels, especially the *Shuihu zhuan* 水滸傳 (Water Margin), and late in life, he became an enthusiastic follower of Lin Zhao-en's Three-Teachings-in-One sect.[160] This example is remarkable because it kills two birds with one stone, showing beyond dispute the pivotal role of the merchant class in the promotion of popular literature and popular religion in Ming-Qing China.

Finally, allow me to conclude by making an observation on the reorientation of the Confucian tradition in the Ming-Qing Period. Generally speaking, it seemed to exhibit a tendency toward relaxation of moral absolutism. Polarities such as "principle versus desire," "common good versus self-interest," "righteousness versus profitableness," "frugality versus luxury," etc., had long been understood as opposites with the first part ("principle," "common good," "righteousness," and "frugality") identified as positive values and the second part ("desire," "self-interest," "profitableness," and "luxury") as negative ones. From the sixteenth century on, however, many Confucian scholars and thinkers tended to reinterpret them as mutually complementary rather than mutually exclusive. What is more important is that "desire," "self-interest," "profitableness," and "luxury" were all given a positive revaluation to a greater or lesser extent. It is impossible to trace the evolutionary processes of these ideas here. Based on my previous research, I shall summarize my findings on three of them whose relationship to business culture can be established on clear evidence.

Self-interest. In the postclassical Confucian tradition, it was a generally accepted principle that self-interest (*si* 私) must at all times be subordinate to common good (*gong* 公), which was predicated on the more fundamental principle of the priority of community to individual. Now suddenly, during the Ming-Qing transition, this received view was being seriously questioned. Each in his own way, Li Zhi 李贄 (1527–1602), Chen Que 陳確 (1604–1677), Huang Zongxi 黃宗義 (1610–1695), Gu Yanwu 顧炎武 (1613–1682) and, later, Dai Zhen 戴震 (1724–1777) and Gong Zizhen 龔自珍 (1792–1841) all proposed revisions as regards the relationship between *gong* and *si*. In the interest of simplicity, allow me to take Gu Yanwu's neat formulation as representative of this new line of thinking. It runs as follows:

> It is natural and normal for everyone in the world to be concerned about his own family and cherish his own children. The Son of Heaven may care for his subjects, but he cannot possibly do better than they can for themselves. This has been the case even before the Three Dynasties. What the [ancient] sage [kings] did was to transform self-interest of every individual person into a common good for all, with his own person serv-

ing as the key link. In this way, a universal order is established. . . . Therefore, what is self-interest to every individual person in the world is common good to the Son of Heaven.[161]

What he is really saying is, in a nutshell, that "self-interest" and "common good" are not opposed to each other and the only function the government [symbolized by the "Son of Heaven"] is to perform in the name of the "common good" is to see to it that the "self-interests" of all the people in the world are to be fulfilled each in his individual way. This point was further sharpened when he remarked elsewhere, "with all the self-interests in the world combined, the common good is thus formed."[162] Clearly, in this new formulation, common good is conceived as but the sum total of all the individual self-interests and therefore depends entirely on the latter for its very existence. Now, the point I wish to emphasize is that this new idea already had its beginning in the first half of the sixteenth century and the person who expressed it earlier than all the great names listed above happened to be a scholar-turned-merchant. Yu Xie 喻燮 (1496–1583) of Jiangxi once said to his nephew in no uncertain terms: "Common good can be established only if self-interest is realized in the first place."[163] I take this to be the quintessence of the new conception of self-interest vis-à-vis common good to be fully developed a century later. By citing this early example, however, I am not suggesting that the new conception began as a merchant ideology and Confucian scholars who developed it all served the specific interests of the merchant class. All I am saying is that between elite culture and business culture, there was an overlapping consensus in which each endorsed this new conception from its own point of view.

Profitableness. The polarity of "righteousness versus profitableness" underwent a similar change. The early sixteenth-century merchant Wang Xian, whose remark about "scholar and merchant pursuing different occupations but sharing the same mind" already noted above, also offered his view about this polarity as follows:

> A truly good merchant can cultivate lofty conduct while amidst the arena of money and trade, and consequently remain undefiled in spite of any profit they may make. On the other hand, a truly good scholar is guided by the classics of former sages to keep away from the path of money and profit, and consequently is bound to gain [deserved] fame and make accomplishments. And so profit is regulated by righteousness while fame is cultivated by purity of mind, as each abides by his chosen vocation.[164]

Here Wang Xian is making two important points. First, the Confucian moral principle of "righteousness versus profitableness" should not be regarded as something exclusively worthy of the scholars; it is equally applicable to the merchants. Second, one must not assume that the merchant has no moral concern about what is right and what is wrong simply because he happens to be in a profit-making occupation. On the contrary, his profit-making activity is also subject to the regulation of the very same moral principle that governs the behavior of the scholar. This is another piece of evidence vividly illustrative of the merchants' self-awareness of their growing importance in society.

On the scholars' part, this view was also sympathetically received. A few decades later, Han Bangqi wrote much in the same vein in an epitaph for his merchant-student. He said of the merchants, "Amidst the hubbub of business transactions, righteousness is to be found." On the other hand, he also pointed out that a scholar may be profit-minded all the way through his Confucian schooling if it is understood in terms of investment and emolument. The latter point, of course, was not new, but it gained new significance when the criticism was made of the scholar vis-à-vis the praise of the merchant.[165] Gu Xiancheng gave this problem a neat philosophical formulation. In an epitaph he wrote for a merchant who died in 1604, he constructed two opposing views. One was that righteousness and profitableness are completely separated and always at war with each other. The other was that the two are united and mutually complementary. In the later case, "righteousness regulates profitableness while profitableness assists righteousness." He dismissed the first view as erroneous and praised the deceased merchant for his success in practicing the second one during his lifetime.[166] With his strong merchant background, it was only natural that he should make such a liberal interpretation of this principle when applied specifically to a merchant. By contrast, however, he would not give even an inch when the same principle was applied to scholar-officials who, as trusted public custodians of the common good, were no longer entitled to "self-interest" or "profit."[167] Therefore, he cannot be accused of applying a double standard. In later centuries, it was the view of mutual complementarity that dominated the business culture. In 1715, even an imperial censor in the capital did not hesitate to endorse it publicly when he was requested to contribute an essay to a stone monument in commemoration of the founding of a merchant association.[168]

Luxury. In 1957, two leading economic historians, one in China and one in America and independently of each other, called our attention to a sixteenth-century essay in favor of spending by Lu Ji 陸楫 (1515–1552). Fu Yiling in China compared it to Bernard de Mandeville's *The Fable of the Bees or Private Vices, Public Benefits* (1727), while Lien-sheng Yang of Harvard University considered it the closest thing to an economic analysis of "spending for prosperity."[169] The central thesis of the essay is that luxury, while a private vice, turns out to be a public virtue, and frugality, while a private virtue, turns out to be a public vice. In support of this thesis, he cited many examples to show that "in general, if a place is accustomed to extravagance, then the people there will find it easy to make a living, and if a place is accustomed to frugality, then the people there will find it difficult to make a living." He further explained what he called the principle of "one person's loss, another person's gain" in this way: "But what is generally referred to as extravagance is merely the fact that rich merchants and powerful families spend much for their own houses, carts, horses, food, drink and clothing. When they are extravagant in meat and rice, farmers and cooks will share the profit; when they are extravagant in silk textiles, weavers and dealers will share the profit." Here, both in language and in reasoning, the resemblance between Lu Ji and Mandeville is truly amazing. The latter also argued, "it is the activities of the 'sensual Courtier,' the 'fickle Strumpet,' the 'profuse Rake' and the 'haughty Courtesan'—in short, all those who live a life of 'Pride and Luxury'—which sets the Poor to Work, adds Spur to Industry and encourages the skilful Artificer to search after further improvements."[170] Needless to say, we must not push historical parallelism beyond its limit. The differences between sixteenth-century China and eighteenth-century England were too vast to be ignored. Nevertheless, the emergence of a positive view of luxury vis-à-vis frugality in late Ming China was no less historically significant than releasing luxury from moral strictures in seventeenth-century England.

I shall make three analytical observations on Lu Ji's essay in favor of spending. In the first place, it was not an isolated idea suddenly coming into existence from nowhere. On the contrary, it was part and parcel of a much larger new trend in the history of social and economic thought dating from the sixteenth century and involving many other ideas in the Confucian tradition, such as the two polarities analyzed above. It is extremely important to note that the subtle change in the structure of this polarity was exactly the same as the other ones. Frugality and luxury also turned from mutually exclusive opposites to mutually complementary elements of an inseparable unit. In the second place, an investigation of the family background of our essayist throws considerable light on the relationship between this new idea and business culture. Lu Ji was the son of Lu Shen 陸深 (1477–1544), a famous scholar and writer who at one time held the prestigious position of Director of National University. However, for a succession of four generations from his great grandfather to his elder brother, Lu Shen's had been very much a merchant family.[171] From more than one hundred letters he wrote to his son over the years, we know that Lu Ji never served in the government due to both his poor health and his repeated failures in metropolitan examinations. Though a scholar in his own right, Lu Ji, as the only son, was nevertheless entrusted with the management of family business.[172] Thus, we see that his advocacy of luxury as a way to provide employment for the general population grew directly out of his personal experiences in the business world.

In the third place, unlike a comet that disappears quickly without a trace, Lu Ji's idea was not only transmitted to later centuries but also translated into local policies in the commercially prosperous cities in the south, notably Yangzhou and Suzhou. At the end of the sixteenth century, Li Yuheng 李豫亨 gave a summary of Lu's essay in his *Tuipeng wuyu*, which was, in turn, quoted by Fa-shi-shan 法式善 (1753–1813), a scholar of Mongolian ancestry, in his *Taolu zalu* (1799) without Lu's name.[173] It is interesting that by the eighteenth century, the idea of luxury as a way to provide employment gained great popularity in the Lower Yangtze region with its authorial origin completely forgotten. Gu Gongxie 顧公燮, an eighteenth-century Suzhou scholar, also spoke of the local custom of extravagance with approval from a communitarian point of view. It was unmistakably a derivation from Lu Ji's essay, though he probably got it second- or thirdhand, but he must be given the credit for giving the idea a new formulation when he made this statement: "Extravagance of thousands of people in one group provides the job opportunities for thousands of people in another. If you try to change the habit of extravagance of the former and force them to return to simplicity, then you will inevitably run the risk of eliminating the job opportunities of the latter."[174] This explains why he was adamantly opposed to prohibition of luxury as a policy.[175] Most significant of all, even the emperor also came to recognize the social importance of luxury in this specific sense. During his imperial tour to Yangzhou in 1765, the Qianlong Emperor remarked in a note to his poem: "It is a great benefit [to society] that rich merchants spend their money in this way with the result that people trained in various skills and crafts are all able to make their livings. It is indeed easy to impose prohibitions on their lavish style of life involving all those singing and dancing entertainments. However, since the wealthy are generally parsimonious, what else can we do to make them help the poor?"[176] What a sharp contrast to tradition when we recall the Ming founding emperor's law of 1381 denying the use of silk to the merchant! We cannot but be aware that between the fourteenth century and the eighteenth, a sea change had occurred. Here and there, even the state had to give ground to the impersonal forces of the ever-expanding market.

Now we have come to the end of our story about the evolution of business culture in China up to 1800. It is neither necessary nor possible to draw specific conclusions from the above account, which is self-explanatory most of the time. To bring this chapter to a close, however, I wish to make the following three brief points.

First, the importance of business culture and its influences in Chinese history have been heretofore much underrecognized due to no small extent to the deep-seated traditional bias on the part of the Chinese ruling elite. With the notable exceptions of the beginning and the end, during much of the long middle period, roughly from the end of the Former Han to early Ming, the social existence of merchants was so blatantly ignored by the intellectual elite that they were accorded no biographical status. I hope I have somewhat succeeded in redressing this gross injustice in this chapter. Business culture has always been an integral part of Chinese culture and it has, to a greater or lesser degree, helped to shape many a Chinese tradition while at the same time also being conditioned by the larger culture as a whole.

Second, in this chapter, I have tried to give an account of business culture in traditional China from the vantage point of the inner world of the merchants so long as it is possible for a historian on the threshold of the twenty-first century, but I am fully aware that the picture that emerges from the vast amount of sources I have selectively canvassed can only be a partial one. It is also in the very nature of historical analysis that the subject matter under investigation be isolated from its total context. The many new and subtle changes I have shown in the last section did take place during the Ming-Qing Period. However, I must also point out that they took place in a traditional world in which resistance was very strong and at times even fierce. People were indeed not lacking who refused to underwrite the social value of the merchant and who continued to stubbornly hold to the tradition of moral absolutism.

Third, to the best of my judgment, social and intellectual changes in late imperial China had created a frame of mind that made it possible for some Confucian scholars to be receptive to certain types of Western values and ideas at the end of the nineteenth century.[177] As we have shown above, this new frame of mind was inseparable from the new business culture that had gradually evolved since the sixteenth century. Viewed in this light, the role of business culture in China's transition from tradition to modernity certainly deserves our most serious attention. In any case, it seems that the modern transformation of the Chinese business world followed, relatively, a course of gradual and quiet growth in sharp contrast to the violence and disruptiveness of political and intellectual revolutions. Given the present state of our historical knowledge, we are not yet in a position to offer responsible answers to many of the fascinating questions related specifically to the modernization of Chinese business culture. It is therefore hopeful that the above picture, painted in broad brushes, may serve to stimulate fellow scholars to make more penetrating inquiries.

NOTES

1.   F. A. Hayek, *The Fatal Conceit: The Errors of Socialism*, ed. W. W. Bartley III, vol. 1 of *The Collected Works of F. A. Hayek* (Chicago: University of Chicago Press, 1989), esp. pp. 29–45. For a general comparison with the West, the reader is referred to Thomas L. Hasken and Richard F. Teichgraeber III, eds., *The Culture of the Market: Historical Essays* (Cambridge: Cambridge University Press, 1996).

2.   *Zhouyi* 周易, SBCK chubian suoben 初編縮本, *juan* 8: 48; James Legge, *Texts of Confucianism* (Oxford: Oxford University Press, 1982), part 2, 383.

3.   Sun Yirang 孫詒讓, *Zhouli zhengyi* 周禮正義 (Taipei: Shangwu, 1967), *juan* 27: 7.77–98; *juan* 28: 8.1–5.

4.   James Legge, *The Chinese Classics*, vol. 5, *The Ch' un Ts' ew with the Tso Chuen* (Hong Kong: HKU Press, 1960), 664.

5.   Ibid., 224.

6.   Ibid., 353. On the unique relationship between merchants and the court in the state of Zheng, see Takezoe Koko 竹添光鴻, *Saden kaisen* 左傳會箋 (Taipei: Fenghuang, 1974 [reprint]), chap. 7, p. 59.

7. *SJ* (Beijing: Zhonghua, 1972), 10.3101. All dynastic histories used in this study are from this punctuated edition. Burton Watson, trans., *Records of the Grand Historian of China* (New York: Columbia University Press, 1961), 2:415.

8. *SJ*, 10.3100; Watson, *Records*, 2:414.

9. Legge, *Tso Chuen*, 589.

10. Adam Smith, *An Inquiry Into the Nature and Causes of the Wealth of Nations*, ed. Edwin Cannan (Chicago: University of Chicago Press, 1976), 1:129.

11. *SJ*, 10.3256; Nancy Lee Swann, trans., *Food and Money in Ancient China* (Princeton: Princeton University Press, 1950), 426–427.

12. *SJ*, 10.3258–3259; Swann, *Food and Money*, 428–429.

13. *SJ*, 10.3259; Watson, *Records*, 11:483.

14. Robert L. Heilbroner, *The Worldly Philosophers*, 6th ed. (New York: Touchstone Books, 1992).

15. Max Weber, *Economy and Society*, ed. Guenther Roth and Claus Wittich (Berkeley: University of California Press, 1978), 1:636.

16. *SJ*, 8.2448.

17. *SJ*, 7.2362. See also *Zhanguoce* 戰國策, *WYWK*, *juan* 11: 1.93–94.

18. Chen Qiyou 陳奇猷, *Hanfeizi jishi* 韓非子集釋 (Shanghai: Renmin, 1974), 2:772–773.

19. Ibid., 2.800. See the old commentary cited on p. 803.

20. *SJ*, 8.2505–2509; *Zhanguoce*, *juan* 7: 1.61–63.

21. See Qian Mu 錢穆, *XianQin zhuzi xinian* 先秦諸子繫年, 2nd ed. (Hong Kong: HKU Press, 1956), 2:485–489; 491–493.

22. *Hanfeizi jishi*, 2.1075–1076; English translation by Burton Watson, *Han Fei Tzu, Basic Writings* (New York: Columbia University Press, 1964), 116.

23. Mawangdui Hanmu boshu zhengli xiaozu 馬王堆漢墓帛書整理小組, *Zhanguo congheng jia shu* 戰國縱橫家書 (Beijing: Wenwu, 1976), 91. See also note 11 on p. 93.

24. Ibid., 115.

25. *SJ*, 10.3258.

26. D. C. Lau, *Confucius: The Analects* (Harmondsworth: Penguin, 1979), 11.19.

27. See Liu Baonan 劉寶楠, *Analects zhengyi*, 論語正義, *WYWK*, 3.37–38.

28. *Yili* 儀禮, *juan* 19: 7a, *Shisan jing zhushu* 十三經注疏 edition (Nanchang, 1815). See the annotation by Hu Peihui 胡培翬 in *Yili zhengyi* 儀禮正義, *WYWK*, 7.40–41.

29. *Hanfeizi jishi*, 2.623.

30. *Zhouli zhengyi*, *juan* 8: 8.4.

31. *Mencius*, trans. D. C. Lau (New York: Penguin, 1970), 2B.10.

32. Heilbroner, *Worldly Philosophers*, 156.

33. A. C. Graham, *Later Mohist Logic, Ethics and Science* (Hong Kong: CUHK Press, 1978), 397. For further discussion, see Hu Jichuang 胡寄窗, *Zhongguo jingji sixiangshi* 中國經濟思想史 (Shanghai: Renmin, 1962), 1:129–134, and Liu Cunren 柳存仁, "Mojing jianyi" 墨經箋疑, in his *Hefeng Tang wenji* 和風堂文集 (Shanghai: Guji, 1991), 1:118–120.

34. Sun Yirang, *Mozi jiangu* 墨子閒詁, *WYWK*, 3:31.

35. *The Book of Lieh-tzu: A Classic of the Tao*, trans. A. C. Graham (New York: Columbia University Press, 1990), 179.

36. Lao Tzu, *Dao Teh Ching*, trans. John C. H. Wu (Boston: Shambhala, 1989), chap. 79, p. 161.

37. Wang Xianqian 王先謙, *Zhuangzi jijie* 莊子集解 (Beijing: Zhonghua, 1954), 11.37–38; Burton Watson, trans., *The Complete Works of Chuang Tzu* (New York: Columbia University Press, 1968), 255.

38. For details, see *Zhouli zhengyi*, juan 27: 7.92–94.

39. *Laozi Daodejing*, SBCK, *hsia*: 12a.

40. *SJ*, 7.2140.

41. John Knoblock, *Xunzi: A Translation and Study of the Complete Works* (Stanford, Calif.: Stanford University Press, 1990), 2:102.

42. Zhu Shiche 朱師轍, *Shangjun shu jiegu dingben* 商君書解詁定本 (Hong Kong: Zhonghua, 1974), 82–83.

43. *Hanfeizi jishi*, 11.1078; Watson, *Han Fei Tzu*, 17.

44. Luo Genze 羅根澤, "Gudai jingjixue zhong zhi bennong moshang xueshuo" 古代經濟學中之本農末商學說, in *Guanzi tanyuan* 管子探源 (Shanghai: Zhonghua, 1931), 234–238.

45. Fernand Braudel, *Civilization and Capitalism, 15th–18th Century*, vol. 2, *The Wheels of Commerce*, trans. Sian Renolds (Berkeley: University of California Press, 1992), 588–589.

46. M. M. Postan, E. E. Rich, and Edward Miller, eds., *Cambridge Economic History of Europe* (Cambridge: Cambridge University Press, 1963), 3:46–47.

47. *Hanfeizi jishi*, 11.1075; Watson, *Han Fei Tzu*, 116.

48. Swann, *Food and Money*, 231.

49. Xu Guangqi 徐光啓, *Nongzheng quanshu* 農政全書 (Shanghai: Guji, 1979), 1:65.

50. Swann, *Food and Money*, 164–166.

51. Ying-shih Yü, *Trade and Expansion in Han China: A Study in the Structure of Sino-Barbarian Economic Relations* (Berkeley: University of California Press, 1967), 218.

52. Mao Qiling 毛奇齡, *Xihe wenji* 西河文集, WYWK, 14:2204; Chen Hongmo 陳洪謨, *Jishi jiwen* 繼世紀聞 (Beijing: Zhonghua, 1985), 69. Chen Hongmo (1474–1555) was a contemporary of the Zhengde Emperor.

53. *HHS*, 2:339 and 342.

54. See Zheng Kecheng 鄭克晟, *Mingdai zhengzheng tanyuan* 明代政爭探源 (Tianjin: Guji, 1988), 274–283.

55. Richard B. Mather, trans., *Shih-shuo hsin-yü: A New Account of Tales of the World* (Minneapolis: University of Minnesota Press, 1976), 455–456. See also *Jinshu*, 4:1234.

56. *Liangshu*, 梁書, 2:384.

57. *Jinshu* 晉書, 8:2437–2438.

58. Studies of Tang-Song commerce and foreign trade are legion. However, works by Quan Hansheng 全漢昇, Kato Shigeshi 加藤繁, and Shiba Yoshinobu 斯波義信 are indispensable.

59. Denis Twitchett, "The T'ang Market System," *AM*, n.s. 12, no. 2 (1966): 205–206.

60. For example, see Braudel, *Civilization and Capitalism*, 586–589.

61. *JTS*, 9:2956. According to Sima Guang 司馬光, *ZZTJ* (Beijing: Zhonghua, 1956), this event occurred in 700. See vol. 14, p. 6553.

62. E. G. Pulleyblank, *The Background of the Rebellion of An Lushan* (London: Oxford University Press, 1955), p. 41 and chap. 4, 134n7.

63. *XTS*, 20:6425, where it is also stated that Kang Qian's son-in-law was a follower of An Lushan.

64. *Chen Yinke xiansheng lunji* 陳寅恪先生論集 (Taipei: Academia Sinica, 1971), 126–138.

65. Ibid., 129 citing the biography of An Lushan in *XTS*, 20:6414.

66. *XTS*, 20:6414; *ZZTJ*, 15:6905.

67. *ZZTJ*, 15:7015.

68. Tao Xisheng 陶希聖 and Ju Qingyuan 鞠清遠, *Tangdai caizheng shi* 唐代財政史 (Changsha: Shangwu, 1940), 99; Denis Twitchett, *Financial Administration Under the Tang Dynasty* (Cambridge: Cambridge University Press, 1963), 35 and 247n109.

69. Chen Yinke, *Yuan Bai shi jianzheng gao* 元白詩箋證稿 (Beijing: Wenxue guji, 1955), 240–246.

70. *ZZTJ*, 16:7287–7288; *XTS*, 19:6121–6122.

71. *JTS*, 16:5370.

72. *ZZTJ*, 17:8005.

73. Lien-sheng Yang, "Government Control of Urban Merchants in Traditional China," in his *Sinological Studies and Reviews* (Taipei: Shihuo, 1982), 30–31.

74. Hong Mai 洪邁, *Yijian zhi* 夷堅志 (Beijing: Zhonghua, 1981), 4:1562–1563.

75. Ibid., 1:98.

76. Ibid., 1:97–98.

77. Ibid., 2:670.

78. Quoted in Quan Hansheng, "Bei Song Bianliang de shuchuru maoyi" 北宋汴梁的輸出入貿易, in his *Zhongguo jingji shi luncong* 中國經濟史論叢 (Hong Kong: New Asia Institute, 1972), 1:120.

79. Quan Hansheng, "Songdai guanli de siying shangye" 宋代官吏的私營商業, in his *Zhongguo jingji shi yanjiu* 中國經濟史研究 (Hong Kong: New Asia Institute, 1976), 2:1–74.

80. Su Che 蘇轍, *Luancheng ji* 欒城集, SBCK, *juan* 21: 228.

81. Wang Pizhi 王闢之, *Shengshui yantan lu* 澠水燕談錄 (Beijing: Zhonghua, 1981), 30.

82. *Yijian zhi*, 2, 840.

83. See Marc Bloch, *Feudal Society*, trans. L. A. Manyon (Chicago: University of Chicago Press, 1961), 322.

84. *Boshi Changqing ji* 白氏長慶集, SBCK, *juan* 28: 143.

85. Xiang Da 向達, *Tangdai Chang-an yu Xiyu wenming* 唐代長安與西域文明 (Beijing: Sanlian, 1957), 34–40.

86. See the various anecdotes collected in Ding Chuanjing 丁傳靖, *Songren yishi huibian* 宋人軼事彙編 (Beijing: Zhonghua, 1981), 2, 465–466; 596; 612–613; 621–622.

87. *Yuanshi Changqing ji* 元氏長慶集, SBCK, *juan* 51: 161.

88. See an edict dated 1044 cited in Quan Hansheng, *Zhongguo jingji shi yanjiu*, 2, 62.

89. See Lien-sheng Yang, "The Form of the Paper Note *Hui-tzu* of the Southern Sung," in his *Studies in Chinese Institutional History* (Cambridge, Mass.: Harvard University Press, 1961), 216–223.

90. See, for examples, Zhang Xiumin 張秀民, *Zhang Xiumin yinshua shi lunwen ji* 印刷史論文集 (Beijing: Yinshua gongye, 1988), 84–95; 96–117; Zhang Xiumin, *Zhongguo yinshua shi* 中國印刷史 (Shanghai: Renmin, 1989), 70–74; 78–79; 88–92.

91. Ye Mengde, *Shilin yan yu* 石林燕語 (Beijing: Zhonghua, 1984), 116.

92. Ibid., 115.

93. Ming-sun Poon, "Books and Printing in Song China, 960–1279," Ph.D. diss., University of Chicago, 1979, 95 and 180, cited and further discussed in Susan Cherniack, "Book Culture and Textual Transmission in Song China," *HJAS* 34, no. 1 (June 1994), 43–45.

94. Cherniack, "Book Culture and Textual Transmission," 79–80.

95. Shen Yao, *Luofanlou wenji* 落帆樓文集, *juan* 24: 11b–12b, Wuxing congshu 吳興叢書 edition (Beijing: Wenwu, 1987 [reprint]). I am grateful to Professor Charles Y. T. Kwong for a draft translation of this passage.

96. Wang Daokun, *Taihan ji* 太函集 (hereafter *THJ*) (Nanjing, 1591), *juan* 35: 11b–16a.

97. For more examples of such networks of Huizhou merchants, see Fujii Hiroshi 藤井宏, "Shinan shōnin no kenkyū" 新安商人の研究, *Tōyō gakuhō* 東洋學報 36, no. 3 (December 1953): 85–87.

98. Wu Weiye 吳偉業, *Meicun jiacang gao* 梅村家藏稿, SBCK, *juan* 47: 207.

99. *THJ*, 35:14a–b.

100. *Ming-Qing Huishang ziliao xuanbian* 明清徽商資料選編 (hereafter *MCHS*), compiled by Zhang Haipeng 張海鵬 and Wang Tingyuan 王廷元 (Hefei: Huangshan, 1985), 296–297.

101. *MCHS*, 234. It is extremely revealing that in a late Ming popular handbook for merchants, the successful businessman is also described as "in possession of extraordinary qualities endowed by Heaven" as the dynastic founder and the top successful candidate in metropolitan examinations. See Li Jinde 李晉德, *Keshang yilan xingmi* 客商一覽醒迷 (Taiyuan: Shanxi renmin, 1992), 312.

102. *MCHS*, 87. For more examples, see pp. 223 and 259.

103. *MCHS*, 216.

104. Ibid., 439.

105. *THJ*, 55:1a. The same point is also repeated in 29:20b.

106. See Yü Ying-shih 余英時, *Zhongguo jinshi zongjiao lunli yu shangren jingshen* 中國近世宗教倫理與商人精神 (Taipei: Lianjing, 1987), 150.

107. *Ouyang Wenzhong Gong wenji* 歐陽文忠公文集, SBCK, *juan* 63: 477–478.

108. *Wang Yangming quanji* 王陽明全集 (Shanghai: Guji, 1992), vol. 1, *juan* 25: 940–941. I am grateful to Professor Charles Y. T. Kwong for a draft translation of this passage.

109. Sang Yue, *Sixuan ji* 思玄集, *juan* 7: 1a–b, Ming edition in the Gest Oriental Library of Princeton University.

110. See Shigeta Atsushi 重田德, *Shindai shakai keizaishi kenkyū* 清代社會經濟史研究 (Tokyo: Iwanami shoten, 1975), 294–349.

111. Ping-ti Ho, *Studies on the Population of China, 1368–1953* (Cambridge, Mass.: Harvard University Press, 1959), 264.

112. Wen Zhengming 文徵明, *Futian ji* 莆田集, SKQS (Taipei: Shangwu, 1984 [reprint]), *juan* 25: 415.

113. Han Bangqi 韓邦奇, *Yuanluo ji* 苑洛集, SKQS, *juan* 19: 4–5.

114. *MCHS*, 251.

115. *MCHS*, 74–75.

116. For a general description of the prosperity of the market economy in sixteenth-century China, see Zhang Han 張瀚 (1511–1593), *Songchuang mengyu* 松窗夢語 (Beijing: Zhonghua, 1985), 80–87; Timothy Brook, "The Merchant Network in 16th Century China: A Discussion and Translation of Zhang Han on Merchants," *Journal of Economic and Social History of the Orient* 24, no. 2 (1981): 165–214. For a survey of the ten great geographically based merchant groups in Ming-Qing China, see Tang Lixing 唐力行, *Shangren yu Zhongguo jinshi shehui* 商人與中國近世社會 (Hangzhou: Zhejiang renmin, 1993), 43–71.

117. Gui Youguang, *Zhenchuan xiansheng ji* 震川先生集, SBCK, *juan* 13: 188.

118. *Gui Zhuang ji* 歸莊集 (Shanghai: Guji, 1984), vol. 2, *juan* 6: 359–360.

119. Sylvia Thrupp, *The Merchant Class of Medieval London* (Chicago: University of Chicago Press, 1948), chap. 6, "Trade and Gentility." The quotes are on p. 269 and pp. 286–287, respectively.

120. *Wang Yangming quanji*, vol. 2, *juan* 32: 1171.

121. Li Mengyang, *Kongtong ji* 空同集, SKQS, *juan* 46: 420. For a detailed study of Wang Xian and the genealogy of the Wang family, see Ono Kazuko 小野和子, *Minki tōsha ko* 明季黨社考 (Kyoto: Dohosha, 1996), 79–82.

122. See Tang Lixing, *Shangren yu Zhongguo jinshi shehui*, 93; 200–201.

123. *Meicun jiacang gao, juan* 50: 222.

124. He Liangjun 何良俊, *Siyouzhai congshuo* 四友齋叢說 (Beijing: Zhonghua, 1983), 32.

125. Tang Shunzhi 唐順之, *Jingchuan xiansheng wenji* 荊川先生文集, SBCK, *juan* 16: 337.

126. *MCHS*, 74.

127. *THJ*, 13:6b–8b; 19:18b–20b.

128. Qian Daxin 錢大昕, *Qianyantang wenji* 潛研堂文集, SBCK, *juan* 28: 461–462.

129. *Mingshi* 明史, 24:7386.

130. *Jingchuan xiansheng wenji, juan* 6: 119.

131. Li Le 李樂, *Jianwen zaji* 見聞雜記, preface dated 1601 (Shanghai: Guji, 1986), 1:285.

132. *Songchuang mengyu, juan* 7: 141.

133. Ling Mengchu 凌濛初, *Erke pai-an jingqi* 二刻拍案驚奇 (first printed in 1632, *juan* 37), quoted in *MCHS*, 46.

134. *THJ*, 77:8b.

135. Wang Shizhen, *Yanzhou sibu gao* 弇州四部稿, SKQS, vol. 4, *juan* 95: 539.

136. See, nevertheless, the case of Zhang Yuanhuan of the early sixteenth century in *MCHS*, 93.

137. Quoted and discussed in Terada Takanobu 寺田隆信, *Sansei shonin no kenkyū* 山西商人の研究 (Kyoto: Tōyōshi kenkyū kai, 1972), 285–288.

138. Li Weizhen 李維楨, *Taibi shanfang ji* 太泌山房集 (Wanli, 1573–1615 edition), *juan* 70: 17b.

139. Ibid., 106:24a; 114:17a–b.

140. *Yanzhou sibu gao*, vol. 3, *juan* 76: 281–283.

141. Wang Shizhen, *Yanzhou xugao* 弇州續稿, SKQS, vol. 3, *juan* 93: 344.

142. See my "Shi-shang hudong yu Ruxue zhuanxiang—Ming Qing shehuishi yu sixiang-shi zhi yi mianxiang" 士商互動與儒學轉向——明清社會史與思想史之一面相, in *Zhong-guo jinshi zhi chuantong yu tuibian: Liu Kwang-ching yuanshi qishiwu sui zhushou lunwen ji* 中國近世之傳統與蛻變: 劉廣京院士七十五歲祝壽論文集, ed. Hao Yanping 郝延平 and Wei Xiumei 魏秀梅 (Taipei: Zhongyang yanjiuyuan jindaishi yanjiusuo, 1998), 3–52.

143. Quoted in Terada Takanobu, *Sansei shonin no kenkyū*, 296.

144. See Max Weber, *The Protestant Ethic and the Spirit of Capitalism* (London and Sydney: Unwin Paperbacks, 1985), 24–25; 68.

145. Tang Lixing, *Shangren yu Zhongguo jinshi shehui*, 220–221.

146. *MCHS*, 461–462.

147. *THJ*, 52:12a.

148. Terada Takanobu, *Sansei shonin no kenkyū*, 321–324. See the case of the sixteenth-century merchant from Shanxi named Zhang Sijiao 張四教 quoted and discussed in Ono Kazuko, *Minki tōsha ko*, 84–85.

149. Takeda Kusuo 武田楠雄, "Tōzai jūroku sekai shōsan no taiketsu" 東西十六世紀商算の對決, *Kagakushi kenkyū* 科學史研究 36 (October–December 1955): 17–22; 38 (April–June 1956): 10–16; 39 (July–September 1956): 7–14. For a recent discussion on this point, see Jack Goody, *The East in the West* (Cambridge: Cambridge University Press, 1996), 78–81.

150. *THJ*, 54:20a. The term *xinsuan* was first applied by Sima Qian to the famous merchant-turned-official Sang Hongyang 桑弘羊 of the Han dynasty. See *SJ*, vol. 4, *juan* 30: 1428.

151. Gu Xiancheng 顧憲成, *Xiaoxinzhai zhaji* 小心齋劄記 (Taipei: Guangwen, [1877] 1975), *juan* 14: 344–345.

152. Wang Wan 汪琬, *Yaofeng wenchao* 堯峰文鈔, SBCK, *juan* 16: 175.

153. Sun Xingyan 孫星衍, "Wusong yuan wengao" 五松園文稿, in his *Sun Yuanru shiwen ji* 孫淵如詩文集, SBCK, 112.

154. Cheng Chunyu 程春宇, *Shishang leiyao* 士商類要 (Nanjing: Wenlin ke, 1626), *juan* 2: 44b.

155. See Sakai Tadao 酒井忠夫, *Chūgoku no zensho no kenkyū* 中國の善書研究 (Tokyo: Kōbundō, 1960), 282.

156. See Cynthia J. Brokaw, *The Ledgers of Merit and Demerit, Social Change and Moral Order in Late Imperial China* (Princeton: Princeton University Press, 1991), 212–215.

157. Zhang Xiumin, *Zhongguo yinshua shi*, 466–470; 605–608.

158. *MCHS*, 216.

159. Ye Sheng 葉盛, *Shuidong riji* 水東日記 (Beijing: Zhonghua, 1980), 213–214.

160. Gu Xiancheng, *Jinggao canggao* 涇臯藏稿, SKQS, *juan* 21: 117.

161. Gu Yanwu 顧炎武, *Gu Tinglin shiwen ji* 顧亭林詩文集 (Beijing: Zhonghua, 1959), 15.

162. Gu Yanwu, *Yuan chaoben Rizhi lu* 原抄本日知錄, punctuated by Xu Wenshan 徐文珊 (Taipei: Minglun, 1970), 68.

163. Li Weizhen, *Taibi shanfang ji*, 105:28a. At the end of the epitaph, Li Weizhen describes Yu Xian as a *sufeng* 素封, or "untitled nobility," a term Sima Qian coined specifically for rich merchants. See *SJ*, vol. 10, *juan* 129: 3272.

164. *Kongtong ji, juan* 46: 420. Zhang Siwei 張四維 (1526–1585), a Shanxi scholar-official from a salt merchant family, expressed a view almost identical to that of Wang Xian. See Ono Kazuko, *Minki tōsha ko,* 77–78.

165. *Yuanluo ji, juan* 7: 447.

166. *Jinggao canggao, juan* 17: 196.

167. *Xiaoxinzhai zhaji, juan* 2: 44.

168. Li Hua 李華, comp., *Ming-Qing yilai Beijing gongshang hui beike* 明清以來北京工商會碑刻 (Beijing: Wenwu, 1980), 16.

169. Fu Yiling 傅衣凌, *Mingdai Jiangnan shimin jingji shitan* 明代江南市民經濟試探 (Shanghai: Renmin, 1957), 107–108; Lien-sheng Yang, "Economic Justification for Spending: An Uncommon Idea in Traditional China," in his *Studies in Chinese Institutional History,* 58–74. An English translation of Lu Ji's essay may be found on 72–74. This article was originally published in *HJAS,* vol. 20, 1957.

170. Christopher J. Berry, *The Idea of Luxury: A Conceptual and Historical Investigation* (Cambridge: Cambridge University Press, 1994), 130–131.

171. See Lu Shen, *Yanshan ji* 儼山集, SKQS, vol. 2, *juan* 81: 516–517; 520–521, *juan* 82: 523–527.

172. For examples, see ibid., 97, 631; *juan* 99: 640; 642.

173. See Fashihshan, *Taolu zalu* 陶盧雜錄 (Beijing: Zhonghua, 1959), 161. I have not been able to locate Li Yuheng's *Tuipeng wuyu* 推篷寤語. For Li Yuheng, see SKQS *zongmu tiyao* 四庫全書總目提要, WYWK, vol. 24, p. 58, where *Tuipeng wuyu* is mentioned.

174. Gu Gongxie, *Xiaoxia xianji zhaichao* 消夏閑記摘抄, Hanfenlou miji 涵芬樓秘笈, 2nd ser., *juan shang,* 27.

175. Ibid., 44.

176. *Chongxiu Yangzhou fu zhi* 重修揚州府志 (Yangzhou, 1810), *juan* 3: 2b. See also Wang Zhenzhong 王振忠, *Ming-Qing Huishang yu Huaiyang shehui bianqian* 明清徽商與淮陽社會變遷 (Beijing: Sanlian, 1996), 137.

177. For a discussion of this problem, see Yü Ying-shih, *Xiandai Ruxue lun* 現代儒學論 (River Edge, N.J.: Global Publishing, 1996), 1–59.

12. Reorientation of Confucian Social Thought in the Age of Wang Yangming

W ang Yangming (1472–1529) was the center of attention in the Chinese intellectual world from the sixteenth century to the early decades of the eighteenth before the rise of Qing philology. During this long period of two and a half centuries, Confucian scholars either argued against him or with him, but rarely without him. I therefore propose to call this period the age of Wang Yangming.

My topic today, however, does not deal primarily with Wang Yangming and his philosophical views, which have been amply and thoroughly examined by other scholars. The task that I set for myself is of a different kind. In recent years, I have been engaging in a more comprehensive study of Ming-Qing social and intellectual history, with particular emphasis on the interplay between social changes on the one hand and the emergence of new ideas on the other. As a result, I am more certain than before that in the realm of social and political thought, Confucianism took a decidedly new turn in the sixteenth century, and this new trend continued well into the eighteenth century.[1]

To begin with, I wish to point out that there was a subtle shift of interest and attention from the imperial state to society among the creative minority of the Confucian elite. They seem to have come to the realization that the traditional Confucian project known as "bringing *Dao* to the world with the support of the throne" (*dejun xingdao* 得君行道) was but an illusion.[2] As Confucians, however, they did not retract their fundamental commitment to the ideal of "the amelioration of human affairs"—to borrow the apt phrase of J. S. Mill. Thus, they had no sooner turned their eyes away from the imperial court than they began to explore the new possibilities of opening up and expanding social and cultural spaces. Some founded private academies, some tried to convey their messages directly to the masses through public preaching or even quasi-religious activities, others devoted their lives to the rebuilding of local communities (including the well-known *xiangyue* 鄉約, or "community compact"), and still others threw themselves into the business world. In short, they steered Confucianism into a new course, which led to what I interpret as a profound reorientation of Chinese social thinking.

To obtain a holistic understanding of the cultural and intellectual changes in the age of Wang Yangming, I propose to examine the new turn of Confucian thinking in its historical context. In what follows I shall therefore deal with four distinct but closely interrelated aspects of the whole process of transformation, namely, Ming despotism, Wang Yangming's revision of the Confucian project, the rise of merchants, and reorientation of Confucian social thought.

THE *SHI* VIS-À-VIS MING DESPOTISM IN CONTRAST TO SONG POLITICAL CULTURE

The Ming imperial system has often been described as "autocratic" or "despotic" in the sense that the emperor exercised his ultimate and absolute power in a cruel and repressive way, about which a great deal has been written.[3] In the present context, however, I shall examine Ming despotism with special reference to how it stood in relation to the educated elite—*shi* 士 (scholar)—of the Ming times as a whole. More specifically, I wish to gauge the plight of *shi* in the political world vis-à-vis the absolute authority of the throne.[4]

The best way to begin such a discussion is to contrast the political culture of the Ming dynasty (1368–1644) to that of the Song dynasty (960–1279) under which the *shi* as the cultural elite was able, to the best of my knowledge, to form a nearly equal partnership with the emperor in governing the empire for, arguably, the first and only time. This partnership is nowhere more clearly shown than in the relationship between Emperor Shenzong (r. 1067–1085) and Prime Minister Wang Anshi 王安石 (1021–1086) during the reform period when both men were making joint efforts to carry out the New Policies (*xinfa* 新法).

As generally known, it was Wang Anshi who took the initiative to propose and formulate the bold reform program, whereas Emperor Shenzong, having enthusiastically embraced it, not only put his full authority into its implementation but often yielded to his prime minister whenever serious differences of opinion occurred between them. The respect so generously shown by Emperor Shenzong to Wang Anshi was not purely personal as traditionally held. As a matter of fact, the Song imperial respect for the *shi* as the cultural elite was symbolically expressed in the person of Wang Anshi. There can be no question that during the early stage of the reform movement, Wang was generally acknowledged as the leader of *shi*. Even prominent conservative scholars who later turned against him, such as Cheng Hao 程顥 (1032–1085), Su Che 蘇轍 (1039–1112), and Liu Yi 劉彝 (1017–1086) all participated in the work of the Finance Commission (Sansi Tiaoli Si 三司條例司), the headquarters of the reform movement, in 1069.

It is by no means an exaggeration to say that by the middle of the eleventh century, there was a general consensus among Confucian scholars that the time for a thoroughgoing political reform had arrived. Shenzong as a sensitive young emperor responded to the needs of the time more positively than his predecessors. It was under such circumstances that he readily accepted the reform proposals from Wang Anshi. With Shenzong and Wang being thus allied to the idea of reform, a new form of political partnership between the *shi* and the throne emerged that was identified by Cheng Hao and Cheng Yi 程頤 (1033–1107) as the classical example of what Mencius once called "bringing *Dao* to the world with the support of the throne" (*dejun xingdao*).

At this juncture, a word about the nature of the Song dynasty is necessary. This sustained belief in *dejun xingdao* as a real possibility among Song Confucians grew and developed in the course of the steady civilianization of imperial governance that began with the founding of the dynasty. In the late Tang and during the Five Dynasties (907–960), the empire in the north as a whole was under the domination of the military, which extended from the imperial court to local governments of all levels. Ironically, even the administration of the civil service examinations had been shifted from the Board of Rites to the Board of War. As a result, the legitimacy as well as the authority of the central court throughout the entire period depended mainly on the allegiance and support of the military, especially the regional commanders.

The founding emperor, Zhao Kuangyin (r. 960–976), who had also been placed on the throne by the armed forces under his command, was nevertheless determined to get rid of the military threat hanging over his new dynasty once and for all. Thus, he made it a cornerstone of the Song Empire to entrust, almost exclusively, its administration to the *shi* scholars chosen through civil examinations.

By the early decades of the eleventh century, there was a general awakening on the part of *shi* that it was they who must assume the responsibilities of putting the empire in good order, as explicitly expressed by Fan Zhongyan 范仲淹 (989–1052). It is particularly worth noting that out of this new awareness, the very idea of partnership between the emperor on the one hand and the *shi* on the other was crystallized later during the reform period. Two examples will suffice to illustrate our point.

First, trying to persuade the conservative Sima Guang (1019–1086) to agree to his reform program, Emperor Shenzong appealed to the ancient concept of *guoshi* (國是 literally, "What is right for the state"). He pointed out that the reform as *guoshi*, a policy decision of the highest order as well as a matter of the utmost importance to the destiny of the empire, was not unilaterally imposed by him in his capacity as emperor. On the contrary, it was a joint decision made through deliberations between him and ranking *shi*-officials in the imperial court. Clearly, this reference to *guoshi* as a joint decision implies partnership.

Second, toward the end of a heated argument in 1071, Wen Yanbo (1006–1097), another conservative leader, emphatically stressed the following point to Emperor Shenzong: "Giving the world a good order is the shared responsibility between Your Majesty and the *shi*-officials!" The emperor acquiesced to this sharp remark. Here we see the same idea of partnership expressed in a different way.

Finally, a classical formulation of the idea by Cheng Yi is worth quoting: "The way to be an emperor is basically to select and appoint the worthy and the talented to the government. Once they are found, he must then share with them the responsibilities of bringing order to the world." This formulation sums up all the basic Song Confucian views with regard to the relationship between the emperor and the *shi* to which practically all scholars of different philosophical persuasions subscribed. It was this political culture that provided the fertile soil in which the *dejun xingdao* project could grow and flourish.[5]

By contrast, the Ming political culture is of an entirely different nature. Ming Taizu (r. 1368–1398), the founding emperor, came from a peasant family with little or no education during childhood. He rose to power from the rank and file of a millenarian rebel group known as Mingjiao 明教 (Teachings of Light), a popular religious sect consisting of mixed beliefs taken from Buddhism and Manichaeism, whose followers were recruited mainly from among the uneducated masses.[6] In short, he did not have much contact with the *shi* circles until a few years before the founding of his dynasty in 1368. Guided by a keen political sense, however, he did indeed make serious efforts to cultivate the friendship of leading scholars in the south. Some of them, notably, Liu Ji 劉基 (1311–1375) and Song Lian 宋濂 (1310–1381), served as his senior advisers. For he was fully aware that, unlike a conquest dynasty based mainly on military power, an indigenous dynasty must of necessity seek and obtain the cooperation of Chinese *shi* for effective imperial rule.

Nevertheless, the peasant-turned-emperor's alliance with *shi* proved to be an extremely uneasy one from the beginning. Generally speaking, he was highly suspicious of *shi* and found remonstrative Confucians in the imperial court particularly intolerable. His suspicion of *shi*-officials in the central government as potential or actual usurpers of his imperial power grew with time and culminated in the bloody purges of 1380 in which the prime minister Hu Weiyong 胡惟庸 (?–1380) and thousands of his alleged followers were executed in the name of "treason."[7] As a consequence, the emperor finally decided to do away with the traditional office of prime minister (*zaixiang* 宰相), an institution that had begun with the unification of the Qin in 221 B.C.E., if not earlier.

Under the Song dynasty, Confucians such as Cheng Yi viewed *zaixiang* as the institutionalized leader of officialdom who, therefore, ought to be responsible for keeping the empire in good order. Ming Taizu, however, rejected this Confucian notion outright, and moreover, from his Legalist point of view, the institution was a great mistake from the very beginning because it had ever since seriously trespassed the absolute power of the throne. That he was a wholehearted advocate for Legalism is now a well-established historical fact. As clearly shown in many of his writings, especially the "Dagao" 大誥 (Great Announcements), he not only held true to the Legalist principle of "the superiority of the sovereign vis-à-vis the servility of the officialdom" but also believed, with Han Fei, the third-century B.C.E. Legalist thinker, that "reward" and "punishment" are the two best methods for a ruler to exercise effective control over those who serve under him.[8] It was precisely for this reason that he found many passages in the *Mencius* so objectionable that in 1394 he ordered all of them excised from the original text.[9]

Given this basic Legalistic orientation in the background, it is obvious that Ming Taizu's espousal of the Cheng-Zhu Confucian orthodoxy was more apparent than real. He needed Confucianism for the legitimization of his newly founded dynasty, but rejected each and every one of its critical functions as an infringement on his absolute imperial authority. Similarly, his emphasis on the importance of *shi* was also squarely placed on their instrumental value. He needed *shi* to run the empire for him at all levels, but only as he willed it. On the other hand, however, he differed decidedly from his counterpart under the Song dynasty in making policy criticism in the imperial court a decidedly life-risking exercise. Allow me to give the following "kill two birds with one stone" example to support my observations. When Li Shilu 李仕魯 (?–1383), a leading Zhu Xi scholar, was recommended to the court, Emperor Taizu appeared to be extremely pleased, and said to him: "I have been looking for you for a long time. I only regret that we haven't met sooner." However, a few years later, true to his Cheng-Zhu tradition, Li repeatedly memorialized the throne against the excessive imperial patronage of Buddhism. Needless to say, his words fell on deaf ears. Frustrated and angry, he abruptly submitted his resignation in an audience with the emperor in protest. In a great rage, the emperor immediately ordered the guards to have him beaten to death on the steps of the palace hall. In the case of Li Shilu, I believe, Ming Taizu's attitudes toward both the Cheng-Zhu orthodoxy and the *shi* are fully revealed.[10]

How did the *shi* respond to this harsh political reality in which they found themselves? A memorial presented to Taizu in 1376 by Ye Boju 葉伯巨, a prefectural school instructor, gives us a firsthand account. The following is a passage relevant to our discussion here:

In ancient times the *shi* considered government service an honor and dismissal from office a humiliation. But today they take complete obscurity

as a blessing and failure to be recruited on account of questionable reputation as good luck. For once in government service they can surely count
on hard labor as inevitable punishment and flogging and beating as all-
too-common humiliation. In the beginning the imperial court tried very
hard to bring all the *shi* in the empire into government service with not
even a single one being left out. However, by the time they were to be
rushed to take the journey to the capital they were treated by the authorities in charge of the operations as if they were the most-wanted criminals
being arrested. When they arrived in the capital they were more often
than not appointed to offices according to their physical appearances with
the result that their expertise and assigned work did not exactly match.
Finally, during their tenure of office a slight mistake on their part would
lead to, if not execution, then surely the punishment of hard labor.[11]

The truthfulness of this general picture is beyond reasonable doubt, for many
of its factual details such as "executions," "flogging and beating," "hard labor,"
etc., can be easily confirmed in the historical record. The memorial infuriated
Emperor Taizu so much that he had Ye thrown into the imperial prison, where
he later died, presumably from torture. The very fact that our memorialist paid
his life for telling the truth further enhances the truth-value of his statements.
He was not exaggerating at all when he said that during the early years of the
Ming, the *shi* in general chose to remain obscure or unpopular to avoid being
called to government service.

With executions, torture, and humiliations as the common lot of *shi*-turned-
officials, some individual *shi* even took very extreme measures to prevent themselves from being recruited by the imperial court. For example, a Confucian
scholar named Xia Boqi 夏伯啟 from Guixi 貴溪 (in Jiangxi) and his nephew
both cut off their fingers, thereby declining the call to serve on grounds of
physical disability. There were also other *shi* such as Yao Run 姚潤 and Wang
Mo 王謨 of Suzhou (in Jiangsu) who bluntly turned down the founding
emperor's summons to the court without even caring to give any reason.

Such noncooperation or defiance on the part of the *shi*, however, was not to
be tolerated by Ming Taizu. As a countermeasure, he created a completely new
category of "crimes" in the penal code known as "the refusal of *shi* to serve the
emperor," a "crime" punishable by death and enslavement of the whole family.
It was in the name of this new "crime" that Yao Run, Wang Mo, Xia Boqi, and
his nephew were all executed.[12] Finally, I must add that this unique "law" did
not end with the reign of Taizu; it remained, as far as our evidence indicates,
very much in effect as late as 1509.[13]

The political atmosphere after Taizu as a whole also remained unchanged. It
turned out that just as both Li Shilu and Ye Boju had rightly predicted, every
word said, and every action taken by the founding emperor were destined to
become exemplary for his successors.[14] As a matter of fact, only four years after

his death in 1402, his fourth son, Zhu Di (1360–1424), took the throne by force from the young emperor Jianwen, Taizu's eldest grandson and legitimate successor, and proclaimed himself Emperor Yongle. To consolidate his imperial power, the usurper killed hundreds of officials loyal to Emperor Jianwen together with members of their families closely following the example of his father's great purges of 1380. In the infamous case of the leading Confucian scholar Fang Xiaoru 方孝孺 (1357–1402), who openly denounced Zhu Di's usurpation, all his kin, all his associates, all his students, all his friends, and even many of his neighbors were executed, totaling almost 1,000 lives.[15]

The continuation and, indeed, intensification of despotism during the reign of Yongle (r. 1402–1424) had a further adverse effect on the relationships between the throne on the one hand and the *shi* on the other. True, the Yongle emperor did try very hard to create more loyal officials from among the *shi* through civil examinations. At the same time, he also made serious efforts to establish the Cheng-Zhu orthodoxy in the examination system as a means of legitimizing his rule. Like his father, however, he had no intention to take *shi* as political partners on a more or less equal footing as in the Song times, nor did his promotion of the Cheng-Zhu orthodoxy as state ideology win the support of true intellectual heirs to the Cheng-Zhu tradition of his day.

According to Huang Zongxi's 黃宗羲 (1610–1695) account in *Mingru xue-an* 明儒學案 (Scholarly Cases of Ming Classical Scholars), Wu Yubi 吳與弼 (1391–1469) was the most influential Cheng-Zhu philosopher of the early Ming Period. As early as 1410, he had already made the most important decision in his life not to serve the imperial court by abandoning examination studies altogether. Later he turned down every request of the provincial or prefectural authorities to recommend his name to the court for appointment. Even when he was finally forced to report to the court in 1457 following an imperial summons, he still managed to return home a free man. He gave a simple and straightforward but very revealing answer to the question as to why he had been so resistant to government service all along: "I want to preserve my own life." Growing up during the Yongle Period, the large-scale executions of officials in connection with Zhu Di's usurpation, especially the most tragic fate of Fang Xiaoru, must have produced an enduring negative effect on his youthful political orientation.[16] Under his influence, his leading disciples such as Chen Xianzhang 陳獻章 (1428–1500), Hu Juren 胡居仁 (1434–1484), and Xie Fu 謝復 (1441–1505) all stopped taking examinations and none showed enthusiasm in pursuing a political career.[17]

The alienation of leading Confucian scholars of the early Ming from the despotic imperial system developed by Taizu and Yongle is also clearly reflected in the realm of thought. It has been observed that the Cheng-Zhu school of the early Ming placed its emphasis almost exclusively on moral cultivation of the individual self.[18] While this observation is undoubtedly true, there is nevertheless more to it than meets the eye. Unlike Song Confucians in general and the two Cheng brothers and Zhu Xi in particular (who were firmly committed to the project of *dejun xingdao*), their early Ming followers, under the severe restraints of despotism, had all but to abandon it altogether. The Song principle of political partnership between the throne on the one hand and the *shi* on the other was no longer valid because "bringing *Dao* to the world" was the responsibility that the emperor now took to be his and his alone. In the eyes of the throne, scholars-turned-officials by way of examinations were not political partners but "instruments" at his personal disposal. Thus, with the road to establishing a public order in accordance with *Dao* closed, it was inevitable that early Ming Cheng-Zhu Confucians carried their quest for *Dao* to the personal domain, with self-edification as the main focus.

Allow me to give a few examples as illustration. As clearly shown in his diaries, Wu Yubi constantly expressed his contentedness with simple and plain living but never touched any political topic. Throughout his life, he was outwardly occupied with virtuous conduct and inwardly sought to achieve serenity of mind.[19] Among his disciples, Chen Xianzhang was famous for his emphasis on the importance of acquiring spiritual enlightenment for oneself (*zide* 自得), whereas Hu Juren took the practice of reverence (*jing* 敬) to one's inner self to be the quintessence of the Confucian way of life.[20] Last but not least, the case of Xue Xuan 薛瑄 (1389–1464), a leading Cheng-Zhu philosopher in the north (from Shanxi) is also revealing. He passed the *jinshi* examinations in 1421 and led a relatively successful career in the court. However, in 1443, he was sentenced to death for having offended the powerful eunuch Wang Zhen 王振 and his life was spared only hours before execution. Finally, he resigned from the high office of Grand Secretary in 1457 when the whimsical and irrational Yingzong emperor retook the throne in a palace coup. Toward the very end of his life, he composed the following two famous lines: "In the seventy-six years of my life, not a thing leaves a single trace. In the end, only the mind of mine senses the oneness with Nature (*xing* 性) and Heaven (*tian* 天)."[21] The first line suggests how disillusioned he must have been that a life devoted to imperial service eventually amounted to nothing. The second line shows that like Wu Yubi who refused in principle to serve the state, he also came to the realization that his quest for *Dao* as a Cheng-Zhu Confucian was strictly confined to the private realm of spiritual enlightenment.

WANG YANGMING'S REVISION OF THE CONFUCIAN PROJECT

Against this early Ming historical background, as adumbrated above, I shall proceed to examine the reorientation of Confucian political and social thinking in the age of Wang Yangming, beginning with the philosopher of genius himself.

Unlike early Ming Confucians, Wang Yangming showed an unusually strong interest in reactivating the Confucian project of "bringing *Dao* to the world with the support of the throne" (*dejun xingdao*) in the early years of his bureaucratic career up to 1506. Immediately after his success in *jinshi* examination in 1499, he presented an eight-point long memorial on frontier defense to Emperor Xiaozong (r. 1487–1505), for which he was much acclaimed.[22] As he recalled it in old age, his memorial carried "too many airs of arrogance and sharpness" to be practicable even though the action itself had grown out of his deep Confucian sense of responsibility toward the public order of the empire.[23] Clearly, he shared the comprehensive conception of *Dao* of Song Confucians, including Zhu Xi, and thereby refused to follow the examples of his early Ming predecessors who deliberately limited their quest for *Dao* to the private realm of self-cultivation. In 1504, he served as the chief provincial examiner of Shandong. One of the examination questions he gave reads: "The so-called great ministers in the imperial court are those who serve their monarch with *Dao*. Otherwise, they ought to stop serving." In a model essay he provided for the candidates, he emphatically stressed the point that the main task of the "great ministers" in the court is to guide the monarch into *Dao* (*yinjun yudao* 引君於道).[24] I take this to be strong evidence for his commitment to the Confucian project of *dejun xingdao* in the early stage of his life.

At this juncture, however, one cannot help but wonder why Wang Yangming thought it possible to resuscitate the Confucian project that had been suspended since the beginning of the Ming dynasty. An important part of the answer lies in the reign of Emperor Xiaozong, for during this period, Wang Yangming grew from a teenager with a highly sensitive and inquisitive mind to a man of full intellectual and political maturity. It happened that Xiaozong had received a very good Confucian education in his early years, and apparently embraced many of the Confucian ethical values. He was also a man of modest nature who seldom showed his temper during court gatherings. Even when offended by an official, he neither humiliated him by "court beating" (*tingzhang* 廷杖) nor subjected him to any inhuman, cruel punishment. As a result, his reign came to be characterized, generally, as harmonious and uneventful.[25] Wang Yangming developed an active interest in the Confucian project of *dejun xingdao* because he was probably under the illusion that the temporary dormancy of the Ming despotic system during Xiaozong's reign would become the normal state of affairs. It was this illusion that brought about the greatest crisis in his life, leading to his most famous "sudden enlightenment" in 1508, which turned out to be the beginning of a major intellectual breakthrough in late imperial China.

In the second month of the beginning year (1506) of the *zhengde* reign (正德, 1505–1521), Wang Yangming presented a memorial to the new emperor, Wuzong 武宗, in support of several censorial officials attacking eunuch power in the court.[26] In this connection, it may be relevant to mention his special reading of the "beginning year" in Confucius's *Chunqiu* 春秋 (Spring and Autumn

Annals). According to him, the "beginning year" marks the beginning of the new king's "rectification of mind," leading, eventually, to the renewal of everything in the human world. Therefore, we can safely assume that he intended to use his memorial to start his project of guiding the new emperor into *Dao*.[27] Unfortunately, the new emperor, unlike his father, was a most irresponsible and capricious ruler who had no sooner been enthroned than he set the despotic machine in motion by allowing a notoriously sycophantic eunuch named Liu Jin 劉瑾 to run the imperial court for him. As a result, in the four years when Liu Jin was in power (1506–1510), he had every court official who had offended him severely punished. Wang Yangming thus fell victim to the very eunuch power he was trying to persuade the new emperor to get rid of. Immediately after the presentation of his memorial, Wang Yangming was thrown into imperial prison and received a humiliating "court beating." Finally, in 1508, he was banished to a mountainous town called Longchang 龍場 in the border province of Guizhou.

The trilogy of imprisonment, "court beating," and banishment jointly produced a traumatic effect on Wang Yangming's life and thought, culminating in his "sudden enlightenment" during a sleepless night at Longchang. As an important event in his life history, this "enlightenment" has been repeatedly examined by scholars, past and present, but mainly in terms of its philosophical or religious implications, which lie outside the scope of this chapter. In my recent study of Ming Confucianism and political culture, however, I have come to a different understanding of the "enlightenment." Due to space, my detailed arguments are too complicated even to be sketched here. In what follows, I can only give a brief report of my findings about his "enlightenment" as specifically related to Ming despotism.

For a whole decade (1499–1508) in government service, Wang Yangming, as shown above, had been working hard toward resuscitating the Confucian project of *dejun xingdao*. Now, banished to Longchang, his faith in the project was totally shattered. With an irresponsible despot like Wuzong on the throne, he finally realized that "the support of the emperor" (*dejun*) as the precondition of "bringing *Dao* to the world" (*xingdao*) was a mere illusion. Thus, in an essay written after the "enlightenment," he questioned whether as a genuine Confucian, he should continue to remain in government service since he was no longer able to bring *Dao* to the world.[28] According to his biographers, the "enlightenment" suddenly took place just as he was pondering the following question: "What would a sage do in my situation?"[29] Putting the two questions together, we are fully justified to believe that Wang Yangming must have found the way out of his deep crisis in the "enlightenment," which showed him exactly "what a sage would do" in his situation. The greatest breakthrough in the "enlightenment" was his fundamental revision of the Confucian project, which consisted of a negative as well as a positive aspect.

On the negative side, he completely abandoned the traditional view assigning to the throne the pivotal role in making *Dao* fully actualized in the world. More important, keenly aware of the destructive power of the despotic system, he decided to avoid direct confrontation with it. Immediately after the "enlightenment," he showed every intention to retire from public service. However, circumstances did not permit him to do so without further adversely affecting his father, who had already been, on his account, dismissed from the office of vice-minister of rites and transferred to Nanjing.[30] From this time on, as we shall see later, there was a marked change in his attitude toward the throne and the imperial court.

On the positive side, he discovered that there was another way of "bringing *Dao* to the world," namely, by awakening the innate moral sense of every individual member of society. For many years he had been struggling with Zhu Xi's theory of *gewu zhizhi* (格物致知, "the investigation of things and extension of knowledge"), which, according to his understanding, assumes that "principles" (*li* 理) are in "things" and therefore external to the "mind/heart" (*xin* 心). He was always uncomfortable with this theory and somehow felt that "principles" and "mind/heart" must be one and the same. In his Longchang "enlightenment," it was suddenly revealed to him that indeed he had been right all along. The truth is, as he stated it, that "the way to sagehood lies within one's own nature."

It is not difficult to see how admirably well this new theory fits in with his revised Confucian project. When "moral principles" (*li*) are identified with the "mind/heart" (*xin*) or "the way to sagehood lies within one's nature," then *Dao* must of necessity be accessible to every individual person, including the illiterate. By contrast, Zhu Xi's emphasis on "the investigation of things and the extension of knowledge" as the prerequisite for the quest of "moral principles" does place the well-educated elite, from *shi* scholars up to the emperor, in a specially privileged position as far as access to *Dao* is concerned. This perhaps explains to a large extent why the Cheng-Zhu Confucianism readily lends support to the project of *dejun xingdao*, whose successful implementation requires the collaboration between *shi* on the one hand and the emperor on the other. Now, Wang Yangming believed that every human being is capable of seeing the light of *Dao* by relying solely on the guidance of one's innate moral sense (which he later identified with the Mencian term *liangzhi* 良知, or "innate knowledge"). Armed with this new faith, he decided to turn to people of all walks of life for support in his endeavor to establish a public order according to *Dao*. Thus, he revised the traditional Confucian project in a fundamental way and thereby ushered in a new era of social and political thinking in the history of Confucianism.

So much for the Longchang "enlightenment." Let us now pursue a little further Wang Yangming's post-"enlightenment" political actions and ideas in relation to Ming despotism.

When Wang Yangming was called back to government service, his mentality was radically different from the pre-"enlightenment" period. Though still a conscientious and dutiful official just as before, he now deliberately avoided criticizing the throne or the imperial court at the policy level. Allow me to illustrate my point by citing a few interesting examples.

In 1515, Emperor Wuzong decided to sponsor an extravagant Tibetan-style Buddhist festival in the capital. Many ranking officials in the court memorialized against it to no avail. To show solidarity and support, Wang Yangming also drafted a long memorial stating in no uncertain terms his opposition to the scheduled event on Confucian grounds. What is particularly significant about this memorial, however, is that he finally decided not to submit it to the throne.[31]

How are we to understand this inconsistency on his part? I think it makes sense only if we take into account his Longchang "enlightenment." What really happened was probably something as follows: When he first drafted the memorial, he was merely following the established practice of many Confucian officials in the court who felt duty-bound to protest against an irrational action taken by the emperor, such as the promotion of a costly Buddhist festival. After he had finished writing it, however, he must have come to the realization that it was contrary to his decision during the Longchang "enlightenment" never again to get entangled with the despotic system. Hence, his last-minute change of mind.

The above case alone, however, is insufficient to establish my point. Now I would like to bring your attention to my next and more interesting evidence. In 1520, Wang Gen 王艮 (1483–1541) met Wang Yangming for the first time, but their conversation is more fully recorded in the chronological biography of the former than in that of the latter. According to the fuller version, Wang Gen turned the conversation into "an unrestrained discussion on current affairs of the world" meaning, of course, political criticisms. Wang Yangming immediately stopped him by quoting a saying in the *Yijing* 易經 (Classic of Changes; in the section of hexagram 52, *Gen* 艮): "The superior man does not permit his thoughts to go beyond his assigned place." But Wang Gen continued to argue that even though he was a mere "common fellow" (*pifu* 匹夫), never for a single day had his mind strayed from the idea that the emperor ought to govern his people like Yao and Shun. Then Wang Yangming remarked, "Sage Shun preferred to live in a deep mountain intermingling with deer, pigs, trees, and rocks. He was thoroughly contented with his happy life and forgot about the world completely." Still, Wang Gen refused to give in and retorted, "It was because at that time, Yao happened to be the emperor." It is quite obvious that Wang Gen still pinned his hope for social improvement on the sageliness of the emperor. For his part, however, Wang Yangming was keenly aware not only of the utter futility of this traditional approach but also its disastrous consequences. Based on his own experience, he knew only too well what would happen to a mere "common fellow" should he be so audacious as to beard the lion of despotism exercised through eunuch power.

In light of this conversation, we finally also understand why it was necessary for Wang Yangming to change his new disciple's personal name from Yin (銀 "Silver") to Gen and, in addition, give him the complementary courtesy name Ruzhi 汝止, both taken from the text of the same hexagram in the *Classic of Changes*: it was to serve as a constant reminder that Wang Gen must stop thinking beyond his position. "Ruzhi" simply means "you stop."[32]

To establish my interpretation beyond a reasonable doubt, allow me to submit as evidence his letter of 1525 to another disciple named Tong Kegang 童克剛. Tong, a private scholar, drafted an eight-point memorial advocating basic governmental changes. Twice he showed it to Wang Yangming for critical suggestions, with every intention to present it to the imperial court. Wang Yangming tried to dissuade him from doing it, once without success. The second time, he simply committed the draft memorial to flame without the author's prior consent. In the letter, he again quoted the same saying from the text of hexagram *Gen* warning the author not to allow his thoughts to go beyond his social role. In this case, however, Wang Yangming was quite explicit in expressing his fear that taking such an unwise course of action would inevitably get the author into deep political trouble.[33]

We have no information concerning Tong's response, but Wang Gen did get his teacher's message eventually. Later, after several of his like-minded friends in government service had been either killed because of remonstrations or banished to far-away places on political grounds, he wrote the famous essay "Mingzhe baoshen lun" 明哲保身論 (Clear Wisdom and Self-Preservation), dated 1526.[34] His conception of *shen* 身 (self), as rightly observed by Wm. Theodore de Bary, refers mainly to the "bodily self or person."[35] By then, he must have fully embraced his teacher's "fear" and therefore came to see politics (*zheng* 政) as a "dangerous ground" (*weidi* 危地).[36]

It is now time to turn to Wang Yangming's central teaching, especially the doctrine of innate knowledge (*liangzhi*), to see exactly how it was related to his revision of the Confucian project. As indicated earlier, the doctrine had its beginnings in his "enlightenment" at Longchang in 1508. It is a well-established fact, however, that this doctrine did not reach its final, definitive formulation until as late as 1521. On the other hand, his new ideas about the Confucian project, also traceable in origin to the "enlightenment," became crystallized, too, in the same period, the last stage of his thought. This symbiotic growth clearly suggests that the two aspects of his thinking, *liangzhi* and the Confucian project, are inseparably interrelated and must therefore be appreciated in the spirit of what he calls "the unity of knowing and acting."

To illustrate my point, let me briefly examine his most famous essay "Baben saiyuan" 拔本塞源 (Pulling Up the Root and Stopping Up the Source). Written in 1525, it has since been held as a major breakthrough in Confucian social thought in late imperial China.[37] To the best of my judgment, the essay is a succinct statement of his revised project. It not only describes vividly the ideal

Confucian order of human relations his new project is aiming at, but more important, also proposes a completely different course of action through which the project may be successfully carried out. Due to space limitations, I shall make two observations, as follows.

First, in "Pulling Up the Root and Stopping Up the Source," Wang Yangming did not assign any role to the throne, the imperial court, or the state as a whole in his revised project. Describing his idealized antiquity he, indeed, did pay tribute to the legendary sage-kings such as Yao, Shun, and Yu and their wise ministers for their great contributions to the establishment of a perfectly harmonious public order. Nevertheless, he spoke of all of them only as "teachers" and "transmitters" of *Dao*, not wielders of political power. This contrasts sharply to the original project of *dejun xingdao*, explained above in the first section.

Turning his eyes away from the throne, the imperial court, and the state, Wang Yangming looked to all individual members of society to make the *Dao* prevail in the world. Furthermore, unlike his Song predecessors, including Wang Anshi and Zhu Xi, who appealed exclusively to the educated elite (*shi*) for a joint and concerted effort to carry out the Confucian project, he made an unprecedented bold move to include farmers, artisans, and merchants in his revised project on a par with the educated elite.[38] This move, however, must be understood as logically implied in his revision of the project, which consists primarily in turning a top-to-bottom state-centered reform movement into a bottom-to-top individual-based social movement. To launch a full-scale grassroots movement aiming at the building of a social order based on the Confucian *Dao*, it was absolutely essential that his teaching of *liangzhi* directly reach people of all walks of life. This is precisely why he chose the awakening of every individual's *liangzhi* as the starting point of his project. As he explicitly stated in "Pulling Up the Root and Stopping Up the Source": "The reason why the learning can easily be achieved and the ability easily perfected is because the fundamentals of the doctrine consist only in recovering that which is common to our original minds, and are not concerned with any specific knowledge or skill."[39] Here he is actually talking about his own doctrine of *liangzhi*. Particularly noteworthy is his unwavering faith in the "recovery" of *liangzhi* being achievable by every individual irrespective of social and/or cultural status. No less important is the downgrading of "specific knowledge and skill" in his *liangzhi* system. By "knowledge and skill," he was obviously referring to what the educated elite of his day was all about. Since he was convinced that "knowledge and skill," the distinguishing characteristics of the educated elite are irrelevant to the awakening of *liangzhi*, he therefore accorded the *shi* no greater function than any other social groups in his revised project. Thus, as individual members of society, scholars, farmers, artisans, and merchants would all become, he believed, active agents of the project on equal footing once their "innate knowledge" became sufficiently activated.

In his final formulation of the doctrine of *liangzhi*, there is also a subtle point deserving notice. A disciple once asked him: "Innate knowledge is one . . . why did each [sage] view principle (*li* 理) differently?" In reply he said: "How could these sages be confined to a rigid pattern? So long as they all sincerely proceed from innate knowledge, what harm is there in each one's explaining in his own way? . . . You people should just go ahead and cultivate innate knowledge. If all have the same innate knowledge, there is no harm in their being different here and there."[40] This emphasis on the individual differences of *liangzhi* from person to person is closely related to his revised project, which, as pointed out above, is individual based. In his later years, he made various efforts to put his project in practice by spreading his teaching of *liangzhi* to individuals of diverse backgrounds ranging from the well-educated to the illiterate.

We have reason to believe that the highly diversified responses he obtained during these personal communications must have contributed to his emphasis on the individual differences of *liangzhi*. Here again the interconnectedness between the doctrine of *liangzhi* and his revised Confucian project is clearly revealed.

Second, in a letter to Nie Bao 聶豹 (1487–1563) dated 1526, he said: "Thanks to divine guidance I happen to entertain certain views on innate knowledge, believing that only through it can order be brought to the world (*tianxia zhi* 天下治). Therefore whenever I think of people's degeneration and difficulties I feel pitiful and have a pain in my heart. I overlook the fact that I am unworthy and wish to save them by this doctrine."[41] This is also an extremely important statement about his doctrine of *liangzhi*. Generally speaking, *liangzhi* ("innate knowledge," or its vernacular expression *liangxin* 良心, "conscience") has been understood as something more individual than social. Consequently, traditional metaphysically minded Confucians and modern philosophers alike have tended to emphasize its individual dimension to a degree, as if the doctrine were only concerned with spiritual cultivation of the individual self. Now, the above-quoted letter clearly shows that the social dimension of his teaching is no less, if not more, important. Thus, we see that in his doctrine, *liangzhi* is designed to serve dual purposes: it begins individually as spiritual awakening of each and every person but ends collectively in bringing a desirable order to the world. Read in this light, it dovetails perfectly well with the last paragraph of his essay "Pulling Up the Root and Stopping Up the Source" where he made an impassioned plea to fellow-Confucians to use their "intelligence of innate knowledge" for the realization of his revised project "without further delay."[42]

It was on account of his commitment to the ideal of "bringing order to the world" as powerfully expressed in this essay that he was recognized, posthumously, as a most outstanding "transmitter of *Dao*" in the Confucian tradition. For illustration, allow me to cite two examples. In his memorial to the new emperor, Muzong (r. 1566–1572), Geng Dingxiang 耿定向 (1524–1596) requested

that Wang Yangming be honored to receive sacrificial offerings in the Confucian temple; as grounds for this honor, he specifically cited "Pulling Up the
Root and Stopping Up the Source." The essay, he emphatically pointed out,
"has enlightened us on the human mind in a most articulate and penetrating
way. If generally heeded, it would surely contribute to the establishment of an
order of great peace."[43] The second example is provided by Chen Longzheng
陳龍正 (1585–1645), a scholar associated with the famous Donglin Academy. He
characterized Wang Yangming's teaching as follows: "The doctrine of 'Pulling
Up the Root and Stopping Up the Source' is the place where the Master's ideas
and the Tradition of *Dao* (*Daotong* 道統) meet in unison. . . . He was singled-
minded in securing a peaceful life for all the people as well as establishing an
enduring public order in the world. In this sense, he may be said to have really
felt the pulse of the Learning of *Dao* (*Daoxue*)."[44] It is highly significant that
both Geng and Chen focused on the same essay and took the idea of "bringing
order to the world" to be the quintessence of Wang's teaching. Moreover, both
scholars' views also converged on the recognition of Wang as a true standard-
bearer of the Confucian tradition. To single out the above-discussed essay
("Pulling Up the Root and Stopping Up the Source") of all of Wang's writings
and link it directly to "the Tradition of *Dao*" and "the Learning of *Dao*" was actually to emphasize the continuity between Wang and his pre-Ming predecessors from Confucius, Mencius, and all the way down to Zhu Xi. Clearly, here
both scholars were talking about the continuity of the Confucian tradition, not
in general terms, but with special reference to the ideal of a well-ordered society
in accordance with *Dao*, which for convenience has been referred to in this
chapter as "the Confucian project."

　　To sum up, the doctrine of innate knowledge and the revised Confucian
project constitute the inside and the outside of Wang's teaching as an interrelated and inseparable whole, corresponding closely to the paired ideas of "sageliness within" (*neisheng* 內聖) and "kingliness without" (*waiwang* 外王) in Confucian parlance. On the one hand, to the extent that Wang was ultimately
committed to the project of a public order guided by *Dao*, he remained indeed
very much within the tradition from Confucius to Zhu Xi. On the other hand, to
the extent that his doctrine of innate knowledge was intended to supersede Zhu
Xi's interpretation of "investigation of things and extension of knowledge," his
break with mainstream Confucianism of his day—the Cheng Zhu orthodoxy—
was nearly complete. However, an underlying functional similarity between
the two opposing philosophical systems is unmistakable. Just as *gewu zhizhi*
had been conceived of as the intellectual basis for the top-to-bottom state-based
reformism in Zhu Xi's system, *liangzhi* was also taken by Wang as the prime
mover of his bottom-to-top individual-based project.

　　The Qing scholar Jiao Xun 焦循 (1763–1820) once made the following observation about the difference between Zhu Xi's and Wang Yangming's teachings
from a social point of view: The former was intended to morally enlighten the

learned, whereas the latter was intended to morally enlighten the undereducated or illiterate. The reason, he explained, is not far to seek: While, on the one hand, *gewu zhizhi* requires extensive reading and rigorous thinking on the part of those who wish to pursue it, *liangzhi*, on the other hand, refers to what is popularly known as "conscience" (*liangxin*), which, being inborn in every individual human, can be readily activated without any prior intellectual cultivation.[45]

Jiao Xun was the first scholar to pinpoint the social difference between the two leading Confucian schools of thought, even though he may have somewhat overdrawn the distinction. In the case of Wang Yangming, his intended audience included all the four major categories of people (*simin*), namely, scholars, farmers, artisans, and merchants. However, there are clear indications that he was indeed particularly interested in getting his messages across to the masses. For example, he once reminisced that after his "enlightenment" at Longchang in 1508, he was in the company of exiled criminals, émigrés, and the aboriginals. But much to his surprise and delight, when he explained to them about his newly developed doctrine of "the unity of knowing and acting," an early version of *liangzhi*, they turned out to be his most sympathetic and appreciative audience. Years later, he further related, it was rather in scholars' circles that his new doctrine met with much resistance and skepticism.[46] This early experience must have been very encouraging, thereby making him ever more determined to reach out to the common people. The following instruction to his disciples is highly revealing: "You assumed the bearing of a sage to lecture to people on learning. When they saw a sage coming they were all scared away. How could you succeed in lecturing to them? You must become one of the people of simple intelligence and then you can discuss learning with them."[47] I take this to be yet another piece of evidence that his new teaching was conceived from the beginning as part and parcel of his fundamental revision of the Confucian project. He placed so much emphasis on the importance of "lecturing to the people of simple intelligence" because the very success of his revised project would depend on their active participation. Moreover, when he insisted that one must first become one of "the people" and then "lecture" to them, he was clearly speaking from his personal experience. As noted above, he was rather proud of his success in conveying his ideas to people with little education around him at Longchang. He continued to exercise this art of communication whenever the occasion arose. A vivid example is his "lecture" to a deaf-mute conducted through writing. The text is written entirely in the spoken tongue and contains no technical philosophical terms. The two key words, "Heavenly principle" (*tianli* 天理) and "mind/heart" (*xin*), in the "lecture" happened to be in the vocabulary of everyday conversation of common people at the time.[48] This is exactly what he meant by "becoming one of the people" in order to "lecture" to them. In this way, he personally set the example for his disciples to follow regarding how to bring *Dao* to the world from the grassroots.

Finally, I wish to end this section with a brief clarification of Wang Yang-ming's relationship with the famous Taizhou school 泰州學派. Generally speaking, there were two side-by-side tendencies in Wang Yangming's teaching of *liangzhi*, the theoretical and the practical. The former was continuing the metaphysical debate of Principle (*li*) versus Mind (*xin*) between Zhu Xi and Lu Xiangshan. This line of work was carried on by his most learned disciples of the Zhezhong 浙中 and Jiangyou 江右 branches, notably Wang Ji 王畿 (1498–1583), Qian Dehong 錢德洪 (1496–1574), Ouyang De 歐陽德 (1496–1554), Nie Bao, and Luo Hongxian 羅洪先 (1504–1564). The latter, the practical tendency, was deeply rooted in his commitment to the Confucian project. According to his revised version, as shown above, the social practice of the project required a large-scale participation of people from all walks of life including, especially, farmers, artisans, and merchants. It was the Taizhou school that fulfilled Wang Yangming's cherished hope of awakening the *liangzhi* of a large number of commoners through popular lectures and other social activities. Apart from Wang Gen, other members of the school who made distinctive contributions in this respect also included Yan Jun 顏鈞 (1504–1596) and He Xinyin 何心隱 (1517–1579). Now the question is why did the Taizhou school alone, out of all the different groups of Wang Yangming's disciples, succeed in promoting the practical tendency to such a remarkably high degree?

A comprehensive answer obviously lies beyond the scope of the present inquiry. However, I would like to make two points about Wang Gen, the founder of the school. First, unlike other leading disciples of Wang Yangming, he did not come from a well-educated family. His father was a salt farmer and small businessman. In his early years, he also underwent training as a tradesman, often accompanying his father on business trips. With the founder being one of the common people, it was only natural that the school attracted a large number of commoners as its members, such as a potter, a woodcutter, a yamen clerk, farmers and merchants, etc.[49] Second, he had not only developed a similar teaching independently of Wang Yangming but also had been as enthusiastic in "bringing *Dao* to the world" as the latter before they met in 1520. However, it may be recalled that in their first meeting, Wang Gen, who was then still adhering to the traditional notion of "making *Dao* prevail in the world with the blessing of the throne" (*dejun xingdao*), pushed Wang Yangming very hard for political criticisms. In the end, he was stopped by the latter, who showed him what a perilous path he was treading given the recklessness of Ming despotism. Taking the teacher's warning much to heart, Wang Gen, ever after, kept clear of all political entanglements. As a result, he redefined *Dao* in terms of "the daily activity of the common people" (*baixing riyong* 百姓日用),[50] which fitted in remarkably well with Wang Yangming's conception of the social practice of *Dao* from the grassroots. Thus, it is no exaggeration to say that of all of Wang Yangming's disciples, Wang Gen alone had the firmest grasp of the teacher's intentions with regard to the implementation of the revised Confucian project. Although tension sometimes did exist between the teacher and the disciple, Wang Gen and his Taizhou school were nevertheless mainly responsible for transforming the teaching of *liangzhi* into a powerful popular movement that continued well into the early seventeenth century.

The rise of a sustained popular movement and, indeed, the very emergence of a well-organized sociointellectual group such as the Taizhou school, which opened up a new chapter in the social history of Confucianism, clearly indicate that some profound social changes must have occurred in sixteenth-century China. The next sections will be devoted to a brief discussion of the basic changes in social structure and value orientation in the age of Wang Yangming.

MERCHANTS AND CONFUCIANISM

As already mentioned in the beginning of this chapter, the budding business culture in sixteenth-century China constituted a major historical force, beside despotism, that helped set in motion the reorientation of Confucian social thinking. To begin with, let me give a brief sketch of the origins and development of this culture based on my previous studies.

From about the middle of the fifteenth century on, market economy was fast growing in many parts of the Ming Empire; large business establishments with networks on an empirewide scale ranging from salt, grain, textile, paper, to pawnshop, etc., became a new social reality. As a result, the business world offered, for the first time since the unification of China in 221 B.C.E., far better opportunities to young members of the educated elite than did the bureaucratic world by way of examinations. According to a sixteenth-century estimate, "while one out of ten scholars will attain success in examinations, nine out of them will be in business."[51] Further studies show that this is rather an understatement. By this time, the examination system had already become indeed a very narrow "thorny gate" (*jimen* 棘門) as population increased markedly while the quota of the *jinshi* (進士), *juren* (舉人), and *gongsheng* (貢生) degrees remained stationary. In 1515, for example, Wen Zhengming 文徵明 (1470–1559), a famous scholar, calligrapher, and painter, reported that his native Suzhou Prefecture alone had no less than 1,500 *shengyuan* (生員), out of which only about 20 *gongsheng* and 30 *juren* were produced in every three-year period. The ratio of success was actually 30 to 1. As a possible solution to this urgent problem, Wen therefore proposed that the quota of *gongsheng* be drastically increased.[52] However, the overpopulation of *shengyuan* was not a phenomenon unique to the economically and culturally advanced lower Yangzi region like Suzhou. As a matter of fact, the pressure was empirewide, including even in the northwest, then the economic and cultural backwater of China.[53] For instance, Han Bangqi 韓邦奇 (1479–1556), a prominent scholar and high-ranking official from Shaanxi Province, also took this problem most seriously and suggested a different solution, namely, to expand the quota of *jinshi* in each metropolitan examination to one thousand and that of *juren* in provincial examinations proportionally.[54]

On the other hand, the business world became so increasingly attractive that more and more educated young men turned away from the examination system and pursued careers in the market. As far as we can determine from the sources now at our disposal, this new social trend that had begun sporadically in the fifteenth century grew into a powerful, empirewide movement in the sixteenth century and beyond. In its own time, it was generally labeled as *qiru jiugu* (棄儒就賈), literally, "abandoning Confucian studies for commercial pursuits." The label is somewhat misleading, however, because what was really "abandoned" was not Confucianism itself but "studies of Confucian texts for examinations."

This *qiru jiugu* movement was nowhere more clearly shown than in Huizhou (in Anhui), a region particularly famous for producing numerous enterprising merchants in Ming-Qing China, where, as a late Ming short story says, the social custom was such that people generally took commerce and trade as the occupation of primary importance and considered success in examinations to be secondary.[55] Here the storyteller, Ling Mengchu, 1580–1644, gives us not fiction, but vivid description of social reality, which happens to be corroborated by other serious writings of the period. Wang Daokun 汪道昆 (1525–1593), arguably the best-known biographer of merchants of Huizhou, also offers this observation: "In Xiuning and She (i.e., two counties of Huizhou), people prefer merchants to scholars and thereby substitute the *Nine Chapters [of Arithmetic]* for the Six Classics."[56] This is simply a different expression of the idea of *qiru jiugu*. I may add that a similar social custom also developed in Shanxi, another province famous for having produced large numbers of merchants during the Ming-Qing Period. In a memorial submitted to the throne in 1724, Liu Yuyi, the director of education (*xuezheng* 學政) of Shanxi, reported: "The age-old established custom in Shanxi is that wealth is valued far above fame. Talented young men are mostly encouraged to join the trading profession; the less talented ones would rather choose to serve as yamen clerks (who have better opportunities to earn money by irregular means). Only those with below-average intelligence are made to study for the examinations."[57] Needless to say, this "age-old custom" of Shanxi can be easily traced to Ming times, for, like Huizhou during the same period, a similarly widespread "scholar-turned merchant" movement also took place in Shanxi.

Against this historical background, I shall try to relate Wang Yangming's revised Confucian project and the popular movement led by the Taizhou school to the new wave of business culture. To begin with, allow me to quote, in part, an epitaph Wang Yangming wrote in 1525, in honor of a merchant named Fang Lin 方麟:

There was a gentleman from the Kunshan County of Suzhou Prefecture called Fang Lin . . . who started off as a scholar, studying for the civil service examinations. But he left off after a short while and went to live with his wife's family, the Zhus, who had been merchants for a long time. A friend said to him: "So now you have left the world of scholarship for commerce?" Fang smiled and replied: "How do you know that a scholar dose not engage in commerce, and that a merchant cannot be a scholar?"

The Hanlin scholar Gu Jiuhe (Gu Dingchen 顧鼎臣, 1473–1540) said to me: "I once read Fang's letter to his two sons. His words of advice were all earnest exhortations to loyalty, filial piety, integrity and righteousness; they were above popular vulgar talk rather like those of a man of ancient times who knew the Way (*Dao*)."

I replied: "In olden times, the four categories of people were engaged in different occupations but followed the same Way; they are at one in giving full realization to their minds. Scholars maintained government services, farmers provided for subsistence needs, artisans prepared tools and implements, and merchants facilitated commodity flow. Each person chose his vocation according to the inclination of his talent and the level of his capacity, seeking to give full realization to his mind. . . . But with the Kingly Way extinguished and learning gone astray, people lost their original minds and craved for gains, vying to surpass one another. It was then that people began to think highly of scholars, look down on farmers, to honor officialdom and despise being artisans and merchants. . . . Looking into Mr. Fang's statement on the occupations of scholars and merchants, I am reminded of our classical theory of division of labor among the four categories of people once prevalent in ancient times.[58]

The importance of this epitaph as a historical document reflecting societal change in sixteenth-century China cannot be overestimated. In the first place, never before did a major Confucian philosopher honor a merchant with an epitaph, let alone one of Wang Yangming's stature. In fact, of all the famous Ming writers, Wang Yangming was among the earliest to write epitaphs for merchants. As a result of an intensive and extensive search, I have come to the tentative determination that the extension of such literary genres as "epitaph" and "birthday-celebrating essay" to the merchant class probably began in the second half of the fifteenth century but reached a peak in the sixteenth, with such famous prose writers as Wang Shizhen 王世貞 (1526–1590), Wang Daokun, and Li Weizhen 李維楨 (1547–1626). From then on, we can hardly go through the collected work of a Ming or Qing author of note without encountering some literary pieces paying tribute to the social functions of individual merchants. In the present context, the following testimony by Tang Shunzhi 唐順之 (1507–1560), a philosophical follower of Wang Yangming, is sufficient to bear my point out. In his letter to a friend, dated 1550, he wrote:

During my leisure, I often reflect on one or two things in our world to which we have long been accustomed but which are nonetheless absolutely ridiculous. One is that a man of lowly social standing such as a butcher or restaurateur, as long as he is able to earn a living, would surely have an epitaph in his honor after death. . . . This is something that was unheard of not only in high antiquity but even before Han or Tang. Fortunately, these so-called epitaphs . . . no sooner appear than they perish. Despite however many perished, what has survived is still enough to fill several houses.[59]

I take this to be the best simple piece of evidence showing beyond doubt that the mass production of epitaphs in honor of merchants and the social movement of *qiru jiugu* ran exactly in parallel. With the scholar and the merchant class becoming less and less socially distinguishable, even a Confucian philosopher as eminent as Wang Yangming felt fully justified to openly praise a scholar-turned-merchant such as Fang Lin. Although Tang Shunzhi spoke disapprovingly of the new literary fashion, ironically, he couldn't help but contribute to its continuing growth by composing several biographies for merchants at the request of their families.

In the second place, Fang Lin, the hero of Wang Yangming's epitaph, happens to provide us with one of the earliest examples of the scholars-turned-merchants. Wang's epitaph does not give his dates, but we can safely assume that Fang Lin must have been active during the second half of the fifteenth century. A very similar case may be found in the person of Sang Lin 桑琳 (1423–1497), a native of Changshu (in Jiangsu) and father of the noted writer Sang Yue 桑悦 (1447–1503). At first, Sang Lin studied for provincial examinations. However, poverty compelled him to enter into a matrilocal relationship with a merchant family named Zhou. From then on, he abandoned his studies and took charge of a large shop for the Zhous.[60] This is the earliest case of *qiru jiugu* I have discovered so far in fifteenth-century China, earlier than that of Fang Lin by about two decades or so. It is interesting to note that both also happen to be among the earliest cases of intermarriage between scholar families and merchant families, a social phenomenon quite common from the sixteenth century on.

"Scholar-turned-merchant" was by no means a local phenomenon in the Lower Yangzi region; it occurred elsewhere in the same period as well. The following two examples from Shaanxi Province will suffice for illustration. Kang Luan 康鑾 (1446–1507), the fourth uncle of the prose master Kang Hai 康海 (1475–1540) had for years specialized in the study of the *Liji* (Classic of Rites) with the intention to pass the provincial examinations. However, he later chose business as his occupation and earned a good reputation for his entrepreneurship. Toward the end of his life, he became considerably wealthy and made generous cash contributions to the court for border defense for which he was awarded imperial recognition.⁶¹ The second example is a man named Zhang Tong 張通 (1458–1523) who was a prodigy and at fifteen already understood the general meanings of the *Daxue* (Great Learning) all by himself. Greatly impressed, his father sent him to study in school, but a downturn of family fortune eventually forced him to engage in trade. Within the short span of a few years, he traveled all over the empire and made a great success of his business. He became the role model of businessmen in the entire region.⁶²

With examples like these from the southeast to the northwest, it seems safe to assume that "scholar-turned-merchant" as a social phenomenon had become highly visible by the end of the fifteenth century, to which Wang Yangming's 1525 epitaph for Fang Lin was a sensitive early response. This leads to my final point about the epitaph.

Last but not least, we must take most seriously Wang Yangming's statement that "the four categories of people were engaged in different occupations but followed the same Way (*simin yiye er tongdao* 四民異業而同道); they were at one in giving full realization to their minds." As far as I know, this is the first time in the history of Confucianism that the merchant class as a social group was formally as well as openly recognized as being equally entitled to its share of the sacred *Dao*. Now the question is whether this was a mere rhetorical expression or did he really mean what he said? On the following grounds, I find it difficult to doubt the sincerity and seriousness of Wang Yangming's words. First of all, the statement basically agrees with his views of merchants and commercial activities. In reply to a student's question about whether, when driven by poverty, a scholar ought to engage in commercial pursuit to make a living, he said: "If you can manage to keep the equilibrium of your mind undisturbed, then not even engagement in business transactions all day long will stand in your way of becoming a sage or worthy."⁶³ If a merchant could also become a sage, then what he does must of necessity lie within the realm of *Dao*. Second, this statement is also in full accord with the revised Confucian project developed in his 1525 essay "Pulling Up the Root and Stopping Up the Source." As already shown in the previous section, he was convinced that scholars, farmers, artisans, and merchants could all become active agents of the project on equal footing once their "innate knowledge" was awakened. The phrase "giving full realization to one's mind" (*jinxin* 盡心) in the epitaph is actually a reference to "innate knowledge." As he explicitly stated in another essay written in the very same years, "The learning of mind is nothing but learning to give full realization to one's mind."⁶⁴ Third, two years earlier, in 1523, Li Mengyang 李夢陽 (ca. 1473–ca. 1529), leading prose master of the day and friend of Wang Yangming, composed a well-known epitaph for a scholar-turned-merchant from Shanxi named Wang Xian 王現, courtesy name Wenxian文顯, (1469–1523) in which the merchant is quoted as having given his sons the following instruction: "Merchants and scholars pursue different occupations but share the same mind. Hence, those who are truly good at commerce can cultivate lofty conduct while amidst the arena of money and trade. As a result, they make profit without be-ing corrupted."[65] I suspect that Wang Yangming's statement may well have been influenced by Li Mengyang's epitaph in some way. At any rate, the idea that "merchants and scholars pursue different occupations but share the same mind" (*shang yu shi yishu er tongxin* 商與士異術而同心) not only gained wide currency in the sixteenth century but was also espoused by merchants them-selves. Seen in this light, the idea was not exactly original with Wang Yang-ming. Instead, he apparently took it over from the rising business culture of the time and reformulated it to suit the needs of his revised Confucian project, al-ready explained above. I may also add that decades later, this very idea became so deeply rooted in the Chinese mind that scholars and merchants alike ac-cepted it as self-evidently true. Thus, Zhang Siwei 張四維 (1526–1585), a scholar from a salt merchant family of Shanxi, in a "Farewell" essay for his merchant friend Zhan Yuquan 展玉泉 who was to leave the commercial world and join government service, justified the latter's shift of career on the following grounds:

> To serve in the government does not involve a *Dao* differently from work-ing in the market (*shi gu wu yi Dao* 仕賈無異道). It all depends on how one does one's job. To work in the market is to seek self-interest. However, as long as the seeking of self-interest does not impair one's moral conduct in any way, such as demonstrated by the Zhan family for generations, one would be even more respected by others. On the other hand, to serve in the government is supposedly to advance the interests of people other than one's own. However, should the governmental position a man holds gives rise to profit-mindedness, then already he is not too far away from the way of the market![66]

In language as much as in logic, Zhang's argument reminds us immediately of the two epitaphs by Wang Yangming and Li Mengyang, particularly the latter. Li's epitaph, it may be noted, has proven to be more widely read by later biogra-phers of merchants. In a sixteenth-century genealogical work, for instance, a writer of Xin-an specifically quoted it to praise a local merchant named Wang Hong 汪弘.[67]

It is clear from the various types of evidence presented above that the rise of the merchant class to unprecedented social and cultural prominence was the single most important change in sixteenth-century China without which the emergence of Wang Yangming's revised Confucian project would have been hardly conceivable. To say this, however, is not to suggest that Wang Yangming or his disciples, including especially the Taizhou school, developed Confucian-ism in such a way as to link it specifically to the market and the merchant class, even though the reorientation of Confucian social thought, as will be shown below, did bear the mark of business culture of the time. The point I wish to emphasize here consists of two closely related aspects of societal change. First, the sustained "scholar-turned-merchant" movement of the fifteenth and sixteenth centuries gradually loosened the hold of the hierarchical order known as the Four Categories of People (*simin* 四民) and bridged considerably the social gap between *shi* (scholars) of the first category on the one hand and people of the next three categories on the other. As a result, not only did the everyday interactions between the educated elite (*shi*) and the common people become ever-increasingly closer and deeper, but the common people, especially merchants, also began to develop a public-spiritedness that heretofore could have been expected only from the educated elite. As most succinctly stated by Shen Yao 沈垚 (1798–1840) when he tried in earnest to portray the social and moral character of merchants of the Ming-Qing Period:

> While it is often difficult these days to witness an amicable and philan-thropic spirit in a member of the educated elite (*Shidafu* 士大夫, or "scholar-official"), one sees it instead in merchants. Why is this so? Because the empire's center of gravity has tilted toward commerce, and consequently heroes (*haojie* 豪傑) and men of intelligence come mostly from the mer-chant class; by profession they are merchants, in character they are he-roes. And being the heroes they are, they understand perfectly the affairs and things of the world; and so they can manage to accomplish what others cannot, but cannot bear to see [human sufferings] to which others are indifferent.[68]

I must add that to pay homage to merchants in terms of "heroes" (*haojie*, literally, "an outstanding man of power and generosity") already began in the late Ming: Li Weizhen used exactly the same term to describe a Huizhou merchant.[69]

Second, the other aspect is that commercial wealth created or at least consid-erably expanded the cultural and social space for the educated elite to develop and carry out a variety of projects. Specifically related to Confucius in the age of Wang Yangming, I may mention the founding of academies, the organization of "Lecture" meetings, the printing of books, etc. All of these activities, needless to say, required funding, and in numerous cases, the money can be shown to have come, directly or indirectly, from the market. For instance, patrons of academies are often listed as "scholars" (*shi*), "commoners" (*min*), "local gentry" (*xiangshen* 鄉紳), or "graduate students of the Imperial Academy" (*jiansheng* 監生). We know for certain from the above discussion, however, that people of any of these categories could also have come from families engaged in commer-cial pursuits.[70] Allow me to give just one illustrative example: Ge Jian 葛澗, who was from a rich salt merchant family of Yangzhou, was sent by his widowed mother to study under the famous Zhan Ruoshui 湛若水 (1466–1560). Later, when Zhan had a funding problem with the building of his Ganquan Academy (甘泉書院), Ge Jian turned to his mother for help. Considering it a very worthy cause or, in her own language, "a righteous thing" (*yishi* 義事), she contributed several hundred taels of silver to the project.[71]

I must add that the public-spiritedness of the merchant class as shown in this case was already so widely known by the sixteenth century that it found its way into the popular semireligious tracts called *shanshu* (善書, morality books). Some of the authors made it quite a point to encourage merchants to be generous with their money for charities and public works.[72]

Thus, we see that as a result of the growing prosperity of the market, Ming society became increasingly dynamic. It was this new social dynamism vis-à-vis the stubbornness of the despotic system that pushed Wang Yangming, step by step, to turn away from the state above and toward the society below in his lifetime quest for "bringing *Dao* to the world." Eventually, it led to his fundamental revision of the Confucian project. Toward the end of the last section, I already pointed out that Wang Yangming's revised Confucian project was translated into social practice mainly by Wang Gen and members of his Taizhou school. Now I wish to take a further step by finding out exactly how some of the most influential leaders of the school tried to relate the project to the non-elite masses in general and merchants in particular.

Let me begin with Wang Gen, the founder of the school. His early life as a small trader has already been noted in the second section above. In later years, however, he continued to keep close company with merchants either in his teaching career or in connection with his social activities. According to the eyewitness account of Li Chunfang 李春芳 (1511–1585), who stayed in his home for more than a month, farmers and merchants often came to his residence in groups for moral instruction during evenings.[73] This is a very valuable piece of evidence showing beyond a shadow of doubt that he did indeed make serious efforts to spread his new version of the Confucian teaching to the non-elite. In light of Li Chunfang's testimony, we can now fully understand why his famous disciple Wang Dong 王棟 (ca.1503–ca.1581) claimed that it was actually Wang Gen who rediscovered the true meanings of the sagely learning of Confucius and Mencius and then passed it on to enlighten "the simple man and uncouth fellow as well as the absolute illiterate."[74] On the other hand, out of a deep concern for the impoverished and the unfortunate, Wang Gen often turned to merchants for aid in his philanthropic undertakings. In the summer of 1523, for instance, a great famine occurred around his hometown near Yangzhou. For relief, he managed to get two thousand bushels of rice from a rich merchant named Wang of Zhenzhou (in Jiangsu), who always admired and respected him. Wang Gen did it again in the winter of 1535, this time with the help of local families of wealth, especially a certain Lu Cheng 盧澄, who alone contributed one thousand bushels of soybean and barley. In appreciation, he agreed to the marriage proposal between Lu's son and his granddaughter.[75] Clearly, here Wang Gen was continuing his teacher's project but on a gigantic scale.

In this connection, the case of his disciple Han Zhen 韓貞 (1509–1585) may be briefly examined. Han came from a family engaged in pottery for generations. In 1527, mourning for his parents first led him to Buddhist beliefs, but he was soon attracted through lectures to the Confucian teachings of Zhu Shu 朱恕 (courtesy name Guangxin 光信), a woodcutter by trade who had become an active member of the Taizhou school. Then he started his elementary education under Zhu's guidance in the *Xiaojing* 孝經 (Classic of Filial Piety) as a text. Impressed by his devotion to learning and moral practice, Zhu, in 1533, brought him to meet Wang Gen in the latter's hometown, Anfengchang 安豐場 (in Jiangsu), where he stayed until the spring of 1535. During this period, due to the fact that he was still a beginner in Confucian learning, Wang Gen made his young son Wang Bi 王襞 (1511–1587) do the actual instruction but always kept a watchful eye on his spiritual development. At one point, Wang Gen is reported to have made this remark to his son: "This young fellow Han seems to be the only person capable of carrying on our *Dao*!" At any rate, after returning home, Han Zhen did take it to be his calling to teach the ignorant, with a view to transforming society for the better.[76] His work thereafter has been described by his biographers roughly as follows: "Whenever an occasion allowed him, he would seize upon it to enlighten people. Thousands of them, including artisans, merchants, farmhands, and even bond servants, followed him. In the autumn, when farmers were at leisure, he would gather disciples for lectures, going from one village to another, as he sang and others responded, so that the voice of songs filled the countryside."[77] The above two cases, Wang Gen and Han Zhen, together give us a vivid picture as to how Wang Yangming's bottom-to-top project eventually evolved into a powerful popular movement in sixteenth-century China.

Next, He Xinyin (1517–1579), a highly influential leader of the Taizhou school, provides us with a wholly different but no less illuminating case. He does not seem to have had any merchant background, nor is there any evidence that he had direct dealings with merchants. Nevertheless, he alone among his contemporaries showed a firm grasp of the significance of the profound social change arising from the "scholar-turned-merchant" movement as well as the mechanism of the new market. In an essay on "Self-Mastery" (*zuozhu* 作主), he said: "Merchants are greater than farmers and artisans; scholars are greater than merchants." To elaborate this point, he further wrote: "Farmers and artisans would like to be their own masters, yet they cannot but let themselves be directed by merchants. Merchants would like to be their own masters, yet they cannot but let themselves be directed by scholars. In any case, the greatness of merchants and scholars are visible to everyone."[78] I consider the above quotation a remarkable piece of evidence regarding the elevated social status of the late Ming merchant. A closer analysis clearly shows that the traditional conception of the so-called Four Categories of People (*simin*), namely, scholar, farmer, artisan, and merchant, was no longer valid. Instead, they had to be realistically rearranged in the descending order of scholar, merchant, farmer, and artisan. It is also significant that the four categories were further subsumed under two broad divisions, with "scholar" and "merchant" characterized as "great" (*da* 大) on the top, and "farmer" and "artisan" placed together at the bottom. Though perhaps wholly unintended on the part of its author, this little piece of writing can nevertheless be read as a candid reflection of the changing social reality of its time.[79]

He Xinyin's deep knowledge of the market is fully revealed in the following anecdote told by Gu Xiancheng 顧憲成 (1550–1612) the leader of the famous Donglin 東林 school:

> It is because of their total immersion in greed and covetousness, He Xinyin and his kind can manage to incite people. Nevertheless, he does have one kind of intelligence that is beyond the reach of others. Minister of Revenue Geng [Dingxiang] once picked up four of his servants and gave each two hundred taels of silver, asking them to engage in commercial pursuits. One of them sought advice from Xinyin, who taught him the tricks of the trade in six words, "one bit bought, one bit sold," and another formula in four words, "buy wholesale, sell retail." The servant followed his instructions and eventually made a fortune amounting to tens of thousands.[80]

The two formulas taken together fit in perfectly well with what Max Weber calls "the principle of low prices and large turnover";[81] as the embodiment of market rationality, this was widely practiced in Ming-Qing China. This anecdote also betrays Geng Dingxiang's involvement with the business world despite his being a high-ranking official. I may further point out, family background may well have made Gu Xiancheng so readily appreciative of He's two formulas because his father and two elder brothers were all successful businessmen. Being a younger contemporary as well as a very serious author, Gu's story seems trustworthy, at least in its general outlines.[82]

Lastly, let me end with a brief note on Li Zhi 李贄 (1527–1602). In a letter to Jiao Hong 焦竑 (1540–1620), after having sharply criticized Confucian hypocrites of his day as "outwardly sages but inwardly merchants," he had the following to say about merchants:

> On what possible ground are we justified to hold merchants in contempt? As a rule, carrying several tens of thousands worth of silver taels, they travel through perilous roads and stormy waters, endure many humiliations from tax collectors and swallow insults in the market place. They work extremely hard with a huge investment but only a small gain. And yet they would not be able to make profit and avoid harm unless they had succeeded in entering into collusion with powerful officials.[83]

This compassionate expression of sympathy for merchants on Li Zhi's part ought to be understood in the context of the gradual stretching of despotism's long arm to the market during the late sixteenth century. Earlier in the *longqing* period (1567–1572), traveling merchants had already been heavily taxed along the roads and rivers by local officials without the authorization of the Ministry of Revenue. Emperor Shenzong (r. 1572–1620) was enthroned before turning ten and when he came fully of age a decade or so later, he became particularly known for "avariciousness" (*shili* 嗜利). This is because he personally appointed his trusted eunuchs as commissioners in charge of collection of commercial taxes from merchants on the road as well as in market places, a practice that eventually evolved into an empirewide system in 1598.[84] As vividly described by a memorialist in 1615, "over-twenty years, resident merchants have been distressed in market places while traveling ones worried about their trips."[85] This may well have been what are referred to as "humiliations" and "insults" in the above-quoted letter. Moreover, Li Zhi's remark about the relationship between merchants and officials is also fully borne out by late Ming handbooks written primarily for merchants. For instance, almost all of them contain a warning called "Be Respectful to All Officials," which reads, in part, as follows: "Whether high-ranking or low, an official is an appointed representative of the imperial court, and his power is sufficient to harass people. We cannot be disrespectful and imprudent simply because his rank is low, for while he may not be able to bring us honor, it is within his capacity to humiliate us if we provoke him to anger."[86] Like He Xinyin whom he very much admired, Li Zhi kept a constant and close watch over activities in the growing market of his day. Obviously, in their lifetime efforts to put the *Dao* into social practice, both men were following Wang Gen's new teaching that "*Dao* consists in the daily activity of the common people."

Because of the nature of our sources, we know a great deal more about how Wang Yangming, Wang Gen, and their disciples tried in various ways to involve the non-elite, especially merchants, in implementing their new Confucian project. However, this tendency in the written record must not be taken to mean that the common people were all passively led by the educated elite as far as the quest for *Dao* was concerned. Earlier, we have already quoted the statement of Wang Xian, a Shanxi merchant, that "merchants and scholars pursue different occupations but share the same mind." Just a moment ago, we have again seen that farmers as well as merchants came to Wang Gen "in groups" seeking his instructions. There seems little doubt that individuals from among the non-elite also actively participated in the project each in his own way. To further illustrate my point, I would like to give as evidence a few examples showing merchants' enthusiasm for the Confucian philosophical ideas current in the age of Wang Yangming.

Allow me to begin with a newly discovered case. *Xin-an mingzu zhi* 新安名族志 (Records of Famous Clans in Xin-an; 1551) contains the following entry: "Huang

Shou 黃綬 from Tandu 譚渡, village of She 歙 County, also named Shuangquan 雙全, abandoned his commercial pursuits and devoted himself wholeheartedly to the Learning of Mind (*xinxue* 心學). He went to study under Master Wang Yangming and Master Zou Shouyi 鄒守益 (1491–1562). He styled himself Weizhai (畏齋, "Studio of Fearfulness") and wrote a work entitled 'Weizhai yulu' 畏齋語錄 (Recorded Sayings of Weizhai)."[87] Brief and simple as it is, the importance of this biographical account of Huang Shou cannot be exaggerated. Allow me to make three observations. In the first place, this is the first, and thus far, the only piece of evidence that there was a merchant among the disciples of Wang Yangming and Zou Shouyi. In the second place, it is highly significant that a Huizhou merchant was willing to take a long journey to study under Wang Yangming and Zou Shouyi. As we all know, during the Ming and Qing times, people in Huizhou, including merchants, generally held Zhu Xi in special veneration; after all, he was their most illustrious native "sage." Huang Shou's case is an unmistakable indication that by the sixteenth century, Wang Yangming's doctrine of "innate knowledge" had already become powerful enough to challenge the Neo-Confucian orthodoxy of Zhu Xi even in the latter's homeland. As *Records of Famous Clans in Xin-an* further shows, in addition to Huang Shou, there were also many others in Huizhou who admired or followed Wang Yangming and his leading disciples such as Zou Shouyi and Wang Gen.[88] In the third place, Huang Shou's adoption of the concept of *wei* (畏 fearfulness) as the name of his studio strongly suggests that he was probably more inspired by Zou Shouyi, who developed "innate knowledge" by way of a type of moral cultivation called *jing* (敬 reverence). The operation of "reverence," according to Zou, always requires the presence of "caution and dread" (*jieshen kongju* 戒慎恐懼).[89] I find it difficult to resist the temptation to associate Huang's "fearfulness" with "caution and dread. To the best of my judgment, there seems little doubt that Huang turned to Wang Yangming and Zou Shouyi out of a genuine pursuit for spiritual enlightenment.

Next, an early seventeenth-century case is also illuminating. According to an epitaph by Wu Weiye 吳偉業 (1609–1671), Zhuo Yu 卓禺 from Zhejiang Province was a scholar-turned-merchant who, before turning twenty, already grasped the essence of Wang Yangming's theory of "the unity of knowing and acting." He also followed the later development of Wang's Zhejiang disciples such as Wang Ji 王畿 (1498–1583), which pushed *liangzhi* closer to the sudden enlightenment of Chan Buddhism. What is particularly interesting about this case, however, is the suggestion in the epitaph, based on the testimony of a family member, that Zhuo Yu's business success may well have been helped by his immersion in Confucian learning in general and Wang Yangming's teaching in particular. As summarized by Wu Weiye:

> From fundamental principles to their application, Mr. Zhuo commanded a wide range of learning. . . . Even in business management, he could

apply himself to achieving the best results. With astuteness, energy, and shrewd reckoning, he was able to assign his assistants and servants to carry out works appropriate to their respective abilities. As a result, his annual earnings amounted to several times his capital, and he became, eventually, one of the wealthiest people in his hometown.[90]

There is plenty of evidence that from the sixteenth century on, a general belief tended to grow among merchants that Confucian learning could, one way or another, serve them well in their struggles in the business world.[91]

In this connection, it seems pertinent to introduce a general observation made by He Liangjun 何良俊 (1506–1573). In his *Siyou Zhai congshuo* 四友齋叢說 (Collected Talks from Four Friends Studio; preface dated 1569), he gave us a brief sketch of the rise and development of the popular "lecturing" movement in the Ming Period as follows:

> Among Neo-Confucian thinkers of our dynasty, Xue Xuan, Wu Yubi, and Chen Xianzhang all engaged in lecturing, but only to a few who shared the same sense of purpose. . . . Did they ever gather so many people? It was only Master Yangming who attracted the most followers! Yet the teachings of Wang Yangming certainly arouse people. . . . But mediocre Confucians of subsequent generations were ever so ready to follow suit. Alas! Rarely did they escape becoming a laughingstock of the world! Zhan Ruoshui, a contemporary of Yangming, also had many disciples when he was lecturing at the Imperial Academy in Nanjing. And later when he was appointed minister of rites in Nanjing (in 1533), even prominent salt merchants of Yangzhou and Yizhen went to study with him; he called them "disciples from salt families" (*xingwo zhong mensheng* 行窩中門生).[92]

I must hasten to point out that He was extremely biased against "popular lecturing," especially the kind of large gatherings organized by the Taizhou school. Nevertheless, his historical periodization of Ming Confucianism up to his own time is well grounded and I am inclined to believe that it lends considerable support to the central thesis in this study. Let me explain what I mean. First, as already shown in the first section, early Ming Confucians such as Xue Xuan, Wu Yubi, and Chen Xianzhang still subscribed to the traditional project, pinning their slender hopes of bringing *Dao* to the world on the support of the throne. Blocked by despotism, however, they could only pursue *Dao* on the personal level with self-edification as the main focus, thereby confining their private discussions to small circles of disciples and friends. Second, He Liangjun's identification of Wang Yangming as the person who first turned private "discussions" into public "lectures" with large gatherings corroborates my working hypothesis about Wang's revised Confucian project. As shown toward the end of the second section, late in life, he always emphasized the importance of "lecturing to the people of simple intelligence" because, in his revised project, the building of a public order guided by *Dao* must of necessity require the active participation of the masses. Third, by "mediocre Confucians of subsequent generations" He Liangjun specifically referred to the followers of the Taizhou school, whom he blamed for carrying the popular "lectures" to the non-elite masses too far. As he rightly observed, these people were following the example set by Wang Yangming. He was probably unaware, however, that these people of "subsequent generations," more often than not, lectured to the non-elite masses in response to the latter's requests. As we have seen in the above cases of Wang Gen and Han Zhen, merchants and farmers often came to them in large numbers for moral enlightenment. This new development should occasion no real surprise when viewed in the context of a rapidly changing society in sixteenth-century China in which social and cultural spaces were vastly expanded by the rising market.

Finally, He Liangjun's remark on the close relations between Zhan Ruoshui and salt merchants also merits a brief review. He did not believe that disciples from wealthy salt merchant families came to Zhan for philosophical instruction. Instead, he held, they came mainly for Zhan's considerable political influence, which could be fruitfully utilized in various ways. Here he definitely overstated his case even though his judgment was not groundless. For example, the above-discussed Ge Jian from a rich salt merchant family who studied under Zhan by his mother's order is reported by the credible scholar Tang Shunzhi as having become well acquainted with Zhan's central teaching: "realizing the principle of Heaven everywhere" (*suichu tiren tianli* 隨處體認天理).[93] There can be little doubt that Ge Jian's discipleship under Zhan was intellectually motivated. On the other hand, He Liangjun also underestimated the strong appeal of Zhan's philosophical ideas to various groups of people at the time, including merchants. A careful check of *Records of Famous Clans in Xin-an* reveals that there were as many followers of Zhan Ruoshui as those of Wang Yangming in Huizhou and among them, some can be identified as being from merchant families.[94] After all, it must be remembered that Zhan and Wang each created a major new school of thought in the middle of the Ming Period. Furthermore, the two schools competed as well as intermingled with each other in the same breath. As vividly described by Huang Zongxi, "While Zhan's disciples did not equal Wang's in number, many persons first studied under Zhan and finished under Wang or studied first under Wang and then went to Zhan, just as did the disciples of Zhu Xi and Lu Jiuyuan."[95] This description is also substantially borne out in Huizhou, where several individuals are reported as having studied under both Wang and Zhan.[96]

To bring the present section to an end, allow me to venture a speculative conjecture as to why both Wang's and Zhan's new ideas were so attractive to merchants as well. A possible clue may be traceable to a simplified view of the two schools that was widely in currency at the time. It goes as follows:

Wang's main focus was the extension of innate knowledge, while Zhan taught the realization of the principle of Heaven everywhere. Scholars regarded the two as having each started his own school of thought. Some tried to reconcile their teachings, saying that since "the principle of Heaven" is nothing but "innate knowledge" and "realizing" is the same as "extending," then what can one say about similarities and differences?[97]

Needless to say, the suggested reconciliation must not be taken seriously regarding the philosophical differences between the two Neo-Confucian systems.[98] Insofar as their social implications are concerned, however, Wang's "extending innate knowledge" and Zhan's "realizing the principle of Heaven everywhere" can indeed be understood, more or less, as conveying a similar message. As a matter of fact, this simplified view may well have started and grown among the non-elite masses, including merchants. It was Wang's unwavering faith that "extending innate knowledge" is achievable by every individual person irrespective of social status such as scholar, farmer, artisan, or merchant. He even went so far as to openly declare (as noted above) that as long as one is guided by "innate knowledge," "not even engagement in business transactions all day long will stand in one's way of becoming a sage." On the other hand, Zhan's famous formulation could be interpreted to serve the spiritual needs of merchants just as well. Since the principle of Heaven is to be realized "everywhere," it is inevitable that the marketplace also be included. Is it not, then, quite natural that merchants were to be found among the followers of the two most active Confucian schools of thought in sixteenth-century China?

REORIENTATION OF CONFUCIAN
SOCIAL THINKING

Finally, I shall conclude this study with a brief review of the reorientation of Confucian social thought in the age of Wang Yangming. The social intermingling of scholars with merchants and the interpenetration of the intellectual world and the business world in an ever-accelerating pace from the later fifteenth century on eventually led to important modifications as well as a significant shift of emphasis in many Confucian ideas and values. Taken together, it may not be too much to suggest that Confucianism as a whole underwent a gradual but fundamental transformation during the long period stretching from late Ming to early Qing. Due to space limitations, however, in what follows I can only give a few illustrative examples showing how some of the core Confucian ideas concerning state versus society as well as individual versus community came to be differently formulated from the sixteenth century onward.

To begin with, I propose to examine the idea of "protection of the rich" (baofu 保富) or "security of the rich" (anfu 安富). The idea had made an ephemeral appearance in Confucian discourse under the Song, but it received new emphasis and became generally accepted only in Ming and Qing times.[99] Toward the end of the fifteenth century, Qiu Jun (丘濬, 1418–1495) wrote:

> Rich and big families are not only what the common people depend on for livelihood but also where the country keeps its wealth in store among the people. But small people do not understand this and some even resent them as the source of their own miseries. The former kings . . . however, revealed their true feelings when they singled out the rich as the only category of people to be made secure (i.e., in *Zhouli* [Rites of Zhou]). It is thus clear that the rich are indispensable not only to the common people but to the entire country as well. Those who are narrow-minded often take pride in their ability to restrain the rich. Do they really understand the deep meanings of the *Rites of Zhou*?[100]

As far as I know, Qiu was the first major Ming scholar and high-ranking official who openly emphasized the economic importance of the rich to the imperial order. A few decades later, the idea was further developed by Huang Wan 黃綰 (1480–1554), an early student of Wang Yangming with a critical mind. In his last book, *Mingdao bian* 明道編 (On Illuminating the Dao), completed in 1550, he said:

> Seeing that common people are increasingly impoverished and the empire financially exhausted, when scholars discourse on governance nowadays, instead of inquiring into its fundamental causes, they invariably assume that it must have resulted from the encroachments of the rich and big families. Therefore, they all advocate that the rich be curbed to benefit the poor, the noble be curbed to benefit the lowly, and the big be curbed to benefit the small. They do not seem to know that all subjects of the king ought to be treated equally as [parts of] the same body. As far as the empire is concerned, what we ought to be worried about is that not too many people can get rich, noble, and big. How can we deliberately curb them in the name of "restraining the powerful in favor of the small people"? Such a policy, even based on a sense of ultimate justice, is nevertheless inconsistent with the Kingly Way (*wangdao* 王道).[101]

In this short passage, Huang made two very bold moves. First, he challenged the deeply seated bias against the rich in Confucian thinking since the Han dynasty. This was generally embodied in the proposal that the state must forcibly check the encroachments of the rich on the wealth in the world at the expense of the rest of the population. In theory, this traditional view was predicated on an implicit notion of distributive justice that most Confucians would, understandably, embrace with enthusiasm. More often than not in practice, however, it provided the state with the excuse to abuse the rich, especially rich merchants, without benefiting the poor at all. Second, in emphasizing that the rich as "subjects of the king" were equally entitled to the protection of the state, Huang was actually defending the "legal rights" of the rich in his own Confucian language. It was from this new point of departure that he denounced "restraining the rich to benefit the poor" on the part of the state as "inconsistent with the Kingly Way," which is tantamount to openly questioning the legitimacy of the long-established practice of the state playing Robin Hood. I may also add that Huang was not only a thinker originally from the Wang Yangming school but also a trusted official in the imperial court, rising eventually to minister of rites. Taking into consideration the unique combination of his intellectual orientation and political experience, the unconventional views about the rich that Huang developed seem to indicate that a significant change was taking place in Confucian social thought.

From the mid-sixteenth century on, Confucian scholars often spoke of "rich people" as the "primal vital force" of the empire (*fumin guo zhi yuanqi* 富民國之元氣);[102] when the "primal vital force" becomes wholly exhausted, they believed, the empire would surely be destined to decline. Therefore, like Qiu Jun and Huang Wan, they were also very much against excessive taxation of the rich. There was a general consensus among Confucian scholars during the late Ming and early Qing periods concerning the positive social function of the rich, namely, provision of reserves for large-scale relief work in times of emergency such as famine, flood, drought, etc. As clearly stated by Qi Biaojia 祁彪佳 (1602–1645): "For famine relief, it is important to make the rich secure. Rich people are the primal vital force of the country. . . . When the rich are completely wiped out, to whom can the poor turn for assistance?"[103] Wang Fuzhi 王夫之 (1619–1692) was even more appreciative of the contributions of the rich to society. As he saw it, when natural calamities such as flood or drought occurred, relief from the state was often slow and ineffectual, whereas quick help could always be expected from the rich in and around the disaster area. Moreover, in normal times, it was also the rich who offered opportunities of employment to the poor and the needy. "Big merchants and rich people," in his vivid metaphor, "are really the deity in charge of the life of a country" (*Dagu fumin zhe, guo zhi siming ye* 大賈富民者, 國之司命也). For this reason, therefore, he was most sharply critical of those corrupt and greedy officials who squeezed money out of them endlessly under the pretext of "uprooting the powerful."[104] His sympathy for the miseries of the "big merchants and rich people" was widely shared by others as well.[105]

Wang Fuzhi's point about the philanthropic spirit of the rich in times of crisis was well taken. As shown earlier, Wang Gen was able to help famine relief in his hometown twice, in 1523 and 1535, only with the huge contributions of a rich merchant and a wealthy local family. His brief reference to the employment of the poor by the rich deserves to be examined a little further, however. In this connection, allow me to begin with Lu Ji's 陸楫 (1515–1552) discussions of "luxury" (*she* 奢) as a social virtue. Though the son of distinguished scholar Lu Shen 陸深 (1477–1544), who once held the prestigious position of director of the Imperial Academy, Lu Ji himself never served in the government due to both his poor health and repeated failures in metropolitan examinations. For a succession of four generations, from Lu Shen's great-grandfather to his eldest brother, the Lus had been very much a merchant family. For his part, Lu Ji was also entrusted, for most of his short life, with the management of family business. Thus, his view of luxury to be briefly sketched below may very well have been growing out of the interpenetration of Confucian culture and business culture in the sixteenth century.

In his essay, Lu Ji challenged the long-established orthodox view that frugality (*jian* 儉) is an absolute virtue as opposed to luxury as an absolute vice. With an analytical and critical mind, he broke the problem into two different levels, public and private, and argued that luxury is a private vice but a public virtue, whereas frugality is a private virtue but a public vice. In support of his argument, he cited many examples to establish the following generalization: "In general, if a place is accustomed to extravagance, then the people there will find it easy to make a living, and if a place is accustomed to frugality, then the people there will find it difficult to make a living." His examples for "extravagance" were Suzhou and Hangzhou, and for "frugality," Ningbo, Shaoxing, Jinhua, and Quzhou—all the places familiar to him as a native of Shanghai. He then went on to explain why luxury must be considered as a public virtue: "But what is generally referred to as extravagance is merely the fact that rich merchants and powerful families spend much for their own houses, carts, horses, food, drink and clothing. When they are extravagant in meat and rice, farmers and cooks will share the profit; when they are extravagant in silk textiles, weavers and dealers will share the profit."[106] This explanation serves admirably well as a footnote to Wang Fuzhi's point about the employment of the poor by the rich.

It is very important to note that Lu Ji's new idea not only struck a sympathetic chord with scholars of his own time but also continued to circulate in subsequent centuries. For instance, a late sixteenth-century writer, Li Yuheng 李豫亨, gave a synopsis of the essay without the author's name, but with a note saying that he had heard it from his elders.[107] Li's synopsis was quoted in full by a Mongolian scholar named Fa-shi-shan 法式善 (1753–1813) with wholehearted endorsement.[108] The growing popularity of the idea of luxury as a way to provide employment was also enthusiastically embraced by another eighteenth-century writer from Suzhou, Gu Gongxie 顧公燮. In his notebook (preface dated 1785), Gu expressed the idea in a different way, saying: "The extravagance of thousands of people in one group (i.e., the rich) provides the job opportunities for thousands of people in another group (i.e., the poor). If you try to change the habit of extravagance of the former and force them to return to simplicity, then you will inevitably run the risk of eliminating the job opportunities of the latter."[109]

Gu was particularly known for his strong opposition to the prohibition of luxury as a state policy, which, he argued, would surely result in unemployment on a massive scale. By the middle of the eighteenth century, I must emphatically point out, these ideas were so widely spread that even the emperor had but to accept the validity of the argument. In his imperial tour to the south, the Qianlong Emperor (r. 1735–1799) was enormously impressed by the sumptuous lifestyle enjoyed by the great salt merchants of Yangzhou. He wrote a poem on the occasion, with a postscript that reads as follows:

> I often say that when wealthy merchants spend their surplus money to make up for the deficiency of the poor, people trained in various skills and crafts will all be able to make their livings. This is a great benefit to society as a whole. It is indeed easy to impose prohibitions on their lavish style of life involving all those singing and dancing entertainments. However, since the rich are generally parsimonious, should we then forcibly take away their personal wealth to feed the poor, which, after all, is inconsistent with the Kingly Way?[110]

Clearly, Qianlong not only appreciated the long-term contribution of rich merchants to social stability but also recognized luxury as a public virtue. What is even more amazing is that the ending phrase of the postscript with regard to the "Kingly Way" is completely identical to that of Huang Wan's passage quoted above. Thus, we see that two centuries later, even the emperor also came to the realization that, after all, it was wrong for the state to play Robin Hood.

The shift of emphasis in the polarity of "frugality versus luxury" was but one of the indications that Confucian social thought was undergoing a fundamental reorientation. A similar change also happened to other Confucian polarities such as "li (理, principle) versus qi (氣, material force)," "li (理) versus yu (欲, desire)," "ti (體, substance) versus yong (用, function)," "gong (公, common good) versus si (私, self-interest)," "yi (義, righteousness) versus li (利, profitableness)," etc. Since here we are concerned with only the social aspects of Confucian thinking, in what follows I shall briefly mention the last two polarities.

The problem of "common good vs. self-interest" has been much studied by modern scholars.[111] Generally speaking, it had long been established in the Confucian tradition that self-interest (si) must at all times be subordinate to common good (gong). However, this received view was being seriously questioned during the Ming-Qing transition. Various revisions were proposed by scholars such as Li Zhi, Chen Que 陳確 (1604–1677), Huang Zongxi, and Gu Yanwu (1613–1682).[112] Among them, Li Zhi's advocacy of "self-interest" as being inherent in the mind/heart (xin 心) of every individual person has been singled out by modern historians as the starting point of the new discourse.[113] Yet in my own research, I have discovered that the revision had its beginning in the first half of the sixteenth century and, moreover, the person who expressed it earlier than all the great names listed above happened to be a scholar-turned-merchant from Jiangxi named Yu Xie 喻燮 (1496–1583). Sometime during his middle life, Yu made a very interesting remark, as follows: "The common good can be established only if self-interest is realized in the first place. In this alone consists the benevolence of the sages."[114] This remark may well be taken as the beginning of a wholly new conception of "common good versus self-interest." Generally speaking, in trying to redefine the relationship between *gong* and *si*, all later scholars also took Yu's new line of thinking without necessarily knowing about his remark. Allow me to take the following formulation of Gu Yanwu as an example:

> It is natural and normal for everyone in the world to be concerned about his own family and cherish his own children. The Son of Heaven may care for his subjects, but he cannot possibly do better than they can for themselves. This has been the case even before the Three Dynasties (i.e., Xia, Shang, and Zhou). What the [ancient] sage [kings] did was to transform self-interest of every individual person into a common good for all, with his own person serving as the key link. In this way, a universal order was established. . . . Therefore, what is self-interest to every individual person in the world is common good to the Son of Heaven.[115]

A few words of clarification may be in order. First, the main gist of the argument is that "self-interest" (*si*) and "common good" (*gong*) are not opposed to each other as traditionally assumed. On the contrary, *gong* and *si* necessarily imply each other. Second, to show that this is the case, Gu Yanwu also broke the whole problem of "self-interest vs. common good" into two levels, public and private, exactly as Lu Ji did with that of "frugality vs. luxury." At the private level, it is very much human nature for every individual person to pursue his self-interest. Here he reminds us of Li Zhi, whom he otherwise bitterly denounced. At the public level, however, there must also be a common good above all individual self-interest. He established this point by appealing to his historical imagination concerning the origin of government. The earliest sage-kings created a public order through governmental institutions to make sure that self-interest of all people would be fulfilled. This is his definition of "common good," which must always remain the exclusive concern of the government and those who serve in it. Thus, his "Son of Heaven" must be understood as a reference to the state as a whole, not the individual person of an emperor. Third, in his famous *Rizhi lu* 日知錄 (Record of Daily Knowledge), he further sharpened his point, saying, "with all self-interest in the world combined, the common good is thus formed."[116] Taken together, it seems clear that in Gu's new formulation, the common good is conceived as but the sum total of all individual self-interest and therefore depends entirely on the latter for its very existence. In other words, the self-interests of all people are prior to the common good logically as well as temporally.

"Righteousness versus profitableness" is one of the oldest Confucian polarities traceable to Confucius and Mencius. In Song Confucianism, both Zhu Xi and Lu Xiangshan considered the former an absolutely positive value and the latter absolutely negative; the two were irreconcilable opposites. Over the centuries, a deep-rooted prejudice against merchants was also gradually formed among the educated elite, linking their occupation one-sidedly to "profitableness," as if they knew or cared nothing about "righteousness." From the early sixteenth century on, however, many a scholar-turned-merchant began to demolish this groundless assumption. Earlier in this section, we have noted Wang Xian's remark about "scholars and merchants pursuing different occupations but sharing the same mind" in Li Mengyang's epitaph dated 1523. With this remark, he actually meant to say that the moral sense of a merchant is exactly the same as that of a scholar. The Confucian moral principle of "righteousness versus profitableness" is therefore equally applicable to both occupational groups. In the marketplace, as he explicitly stated it, "profit is regulated by the principle of righteousness" (li yi yi zhi 利以義制) as well. Possibly influenced by Li's epitaph, Han Bangqi also expressed a very similar view. In an epitaph for his merchant-student, he first pointed out that all occupations, high or low, pure or turbid, stand between "righteousness" at one end and "profitableness" at the other. Then he went on to contrast the scholar class with the merchant class: When a scholar is thinking only of official career or fame, the notion of "profitableness" is already creeping into all of his studies. On the other hand, when a merchant is always honest in the market, the principle of righteousness is already pervading all of his business transactions. The distinction between profitableness and righteousness, he therefore concluded, lies not in the nature of one's occupation, but in the state of one's mind.[117]

The new intellectual interest of merchants and scholars in the polarity of righteousness versus profitableness eventually led to a revision of considerable importance. In this regard, allow me to introduce a cogent formulation given by Gu Xiancheng, leader of the Donglin school. In an epitaph he wrote for a merchant who died in 1604, Gu constructed two opposing views. One was that righteousness and profitableness are completely separated and always at war with each other. Needless to say, this is the traditional view that dominated the Confucian thinking since, especially, the Song dynasty. The other is that the two are united and mutually complimentary. In the latter case, "righteousness regulates profitableness while profitableness assists righteousness." This, of course, is a new conception that began to evolve since the early sixteenth century. He dismissed the first view as erroneous and praised the deceased merchant for his success in practicing the second one in his lifetime.[118] With his strong merchant background, it was only natural that he should take such a liberal interpretation of this polarity when applied specifically to a merchant. From this time on, Gu's second view gradually gained currency. Thus, in 1715, when Imperial Censor Zhang Degui 張德桂 wrote an essay to the stone monument in commemoration of the founding of the Cantonese merchant association in the capital, he went to considerable length to make the point that "righteousness" and "profitableness" are only "apparently opposite"; in reality, they often "depend on each other" for full realization and are therefore inseparable. Taking the merchant association as his living example, he argued that it kills two birds with the same stone: promoting the well-being of the merchant community as a whole through mutual support and at the same time helping every individual member of the association to conduct his business dealings in the local market of the capital. Insofar as communal well-being is concerned, the principle of righteousness is fulfilled, and insofar as each individual member's business is concerned, the principle of profitableness is also realized. This is how Zhang the imperial censor interpreted the mutual complementarity of "righteousness" and "profitableness."[119]

To sum up, as in cases of "frugality vs. luxury" and "common good vs. self-interest," the relationship between "righteousness" and "profitableness" was also transformed from antithetical to synthetical. This change, however, need not surprise us once we realize that Confucian social thinking during the Ming-Qing transition was by and large characterized by a tendency toward relaxation of moral absolutism.

As I have argued elsewhere, reorientation of Confucian social and political thinking since the sixteenth century eventually helped to create a frame of mind that made China more readily receptive to certain types of Western values and ideas.[120] The following three instances will, hopefully, suffice to bear my point out.

First, Chinese despotism did not meet any open, large-scale and systematic criticism until the final years of the Qing dynasty. As political reformists advocating the British type of constitutional monarchy, both Tan Sitong 譚嗣同 (1865–1898) and Liang Qichao 梁啟超 (1873–1929) denounced the despotic "sovereign" (jun 君) since the Qin unification in the worst possible terms. However, a careful reading of both men's texts shows right away that they were but elaborations of the views developed in the hitherto unpublished *Mingyi daifang lu* 明夷待訪錄 (A Plan for the Prince) by Huang Zongxi, a fine product of the Ming-Qing intellectual transition.[121] On the other hand, the revolutionist reader Sun Yat-sen, who took the American republic as his model, also presented a newly printed copy of *A Plan for the Prince* to a Japanese friend in 1895.[122] It seems safe to assume that Huang's powerful antidespotism must have prepared all of them intellectually as well as psychologically to look to the West for an alternative system of government.

Next, since its emergence in the sixteenth century, the idea of protection of the rich became firmly established and ever-increasingly deepened in Chinese social consciousness. During the nineteenth century, for example, the idea was enthusiastically advocated by famous scholars such as Bao Shichen 包世臣 (1775–1855), Wei Yuan 魏源 (1794–1856), Feng Guifen 馮桂芬 (1809–1874), and Wang Tao 王韜 (1828–1897).[123] It is interesting to note that it was through this Chinese idea that late Qing intellectuals came to appreciate Western capitalism. Following the new trend in the Ming-Qing Period, Tan Sitong praised "luxury" as a public virtue and condemned "frugality" as a public vice. He much admired the freer circulation of wealth in Western economies due to better monetary systems, which, he believed, made "luxury" affordable to more people.[124] As a Confucian, he was, of course, just as concerned about distributive justice. However, he explained, as things stood in his day, China was badly in need of rich merchants who alone were in a position to compete with foreign countries in commercial operations.[125] Obviously, he expected Chinese merchants to play the role of Western capitalists. By contrast, Liang Qichao described Western capitalists in comparison to Chinese merchants, saying that the former were more honored in the West (Taixi 泰西) as "the prime vital force of a country" (guo zhi yuanqi 國之元氣). He then went on to assure his readers that Western capitalists not only created jobs for the poor by establishing factories but also enriched the nation by developing the natural resources of the land. Moreover, these rich people often made donations in the millions to schools and hospitals, thereby giving rise to a new philanthropic wave in the West. All of this, he concluded, must be understood as resulting directly from the practice of "protection of the rich" (baofu).[126]

Last but not least, from the late Qing to the eve of the May Fourth Movement, the notion of the "autonomy of the individual self" (geren zizhu 個人自主) dominated the Chinese mind; leading intellectuals such as Zhang Binglin 章炳麟 (1869–1936), Tan Sitong, and Chen Duxiu 陳獨秀 (1879–1942) all took it as one of the ultimate goals to be realized through a total emancipation of thought.[127] In the final analysis, however, it actually evolved from the concept of "self-interest" (si) redefined vis-à-vis that of "common good" (gong), discussed above. The resultant priority of "self-interest" over the "common good" inevitably carries the focus of emphasis in the polarity to the individual self. In this connection, Liang Qichao's formulation of "rights" between the individual on the one hand and the nation as a whole on the other may serve as an illustrative example: "The combination of fractions of rights will make up the right of a totality. All the individual senses of right will add up to a collective sense of rights of the whole nation. Thus, cultivation of the sense of national right must start with the individual."[128] This formulation immediately reminds me of Gu Yanwu's statement quoted above: "With all self-interest combined, the common good is thus formed," which Liang must have known by heart all along. It also accords perfectly well with Yu Xie's saying: "common good can be established only if self-interest is realized in the first place." Clearly, Liang reached his understanding of the Western problem of "individual right versus national right" by way of his antecedent familiarity with the Chinese problem of "self-interest versus common good."

Viewed in this way, the new turn in Confucian social and political thinking in the age of Wang Yangming deserves to be most seriously considered as a major cultural and intellectual breakthrough in late imperial China.

NOTES

The first draft of this chapter was a keynote speech to the International Wang Yangming Conference, sponsored by the Third Global Future Generations Kyoto Forum, delivered on August 11, 1997, in Kyoto, Japan. I wrote a much-expanded second draft in September–November 2005 at the John W. Kluge Center, Library of Congress. A complete revision was finished on November 28, 2014.

1. Yü Ying-shih, "Xiandai ruxue de huigu yu zhanwang" 現代儒學的回顧與展望, *Zhong-guo wenhua* 11 (July 1995): 1–25; reprinted in Yü Ying-shih, *Xiandai ruxue lun* 現代儒學論 (Shanghai: Shanghai renmin, 1998), 1–57. Japanese translation in *Chûgoku: Shakai to Bunka* 10 (June 1995): 135–179.

2. For the Confucian idea of *dejun xingdao* 得君行道, see Yü Ying-shih 余英時, *Zhu Xi de lishi shijie* 朱熹的歷史世界, vol. 2 (Taipei: Yunchen, 2003), chap. 8, pp. 54–92.

3. The best general accounts of Ming despotism may be found in Frederick W. Mote, "The Growth of Chinese Despotism," *Oriens Extremus* 8, no. 1 (August 1961): 1–41, and F. W. Mote, *Imperial China, 900–1800* (Cambridge, Mass.: Harvard University Press, 1999), 579–582.

4. On the tension and conflict between Ming Taizu, the founding emperor, and the educated elites (*shi* 士) under his reign, see Qian Mu's 錢穆 1964 monograph, *Du Mingchu kaiguo zhuchen shiwenji* 讀明初開國諸臣詩文集, reprinted in *Qian Binsi xiansheng quanji* 錢賓四先生全集 (Taipei: Lianjing, 1998), 20:101–261. For a different view, see John W. Dardess, *Confucianism and Autocracy: Professional Elites in the Founding of the Ming Dynasty* (Berkeley: University of California Press, 1983), esp. pp. 9–10.

5. The above sketch of Song political culture is based on my *Zhu Xi de lishi shijie*, vol. 1, chaps. 2–6, pp. 271–387.

6. See Wu Han 吳晗, "Mingjiao yu Da Ming diguo" 明教與大明帝國, collected in his *Dushi zhaji* 讀史劄記 (Beijing: Sanlian, 1956), 235–270.

7. See Wu Han, "Hu Weiyong dang-an kao" 胡惟庸黨案考, *Yanjing xuebao* 15 (June 1934): 163–205.

8. See Kung-chuan Hsiao, "Legalism and Autocracy in Traditional China," *Tsing Hua Journal of Chinese Studies*, n.s., 4, no. 2 (February 1964), esp. p. 16, and Yü Ying-shih, *Song-Ming lixue yu zhengzhi wenhua* 宋明理學與政治文化 (Taipei: Yunchen, 2004), chap. 6, section 1, pp. 253–276.

9. Rong Zhaozu 容肇祖, "Ming Taizu de *Mengzi jiewen*" 明太祖的《孟子節文》, reprinted in *Rong Zhaozu ji* 容肇祖集 (Jinan: Qilu shushe, 1989), 170–183.

10. *Mingshi* (punctuated edition) (Beijing: Zhonghua, 1974), *juan* 139: 13.3988–3989.

11. Ibid., 3991–3992.

12. Ibid., *juan* 94: 8.2318.

13. In 1509, for instance, a certain Wang Yunfeng 王雲鳳 was forced to accept a court appointment against his will by the penal code of "refusal of *shi* to serve the emperor" (寰中士夫不為君用). See Gu Yingtai 谷應泰, *Mingshi jishi benmo* 明史紀事本末 (Shanghai: Shangwu, 1937), *juan* 43: 6.59.

14. *Mingshi, juan* 139: 13.3989 and 3991.

15. Ibid., *juan* 141: 13.4019–4021. Cf. F. W. Mote, "Fang Hsiao-ju," in *Dictionary of Ming Biography, 1368–1644*, ed. L. Carrington Goodrich and Chaoying Fang (hereafter *DMB*) (New York: Columbia University Press, 1976), 1:431–432.

16. Huang Zongxi 黃宗羲, *Mingru xue-an* 明儒學案 (hereafter *MRXA*) (Shanghai: Zhonghua, 1936); *SBBY*, vol. 1, *juan* 1: 1a–2a (Wu Yubi 吳與弼).

17. *MRXA, juan* 2: 1a (Hu Juren 胡居仁); *juan* 5: 1a (Chen Xianzhang 陳獻章); *Mingshi, juan* 282: 24.7241 (Xie Fu 謝復).

18. See my discussion in *Song-Ming lixue yu zhengzhi wenhua*, 274–276.

19. Wu Yubi, "Rilu" 日錄, in *Kangzhai ji* 康齋集, SKQS (Taipei: Shangwu, 1973), *juan* 11: 1a–42a. Cf. Wing-tsit Chan, "The Ch'eng-Chu School of Early Ming," in *Self and Society in Ming Thought*, ed. Wm. Theodore de Bary and the Conference on Ming Thought (New York: Columbia University Press, 1970), 29–51.

20. See Huang P'ei and Julia Ching, "Ch'en Hsien-chang," in *DMB*, 1:155; Julia Ching, "Hu Chü-jen," ibid., 626.

21. *MRXA, juan* 7: 3a.

22. See "Chenyan bianwushu" 陳言邊務疏, in *Wang Yangming quanji* 王陽明全集 (Shanghai: Shanghai guji, 1992), *juan* 9: 285–290.

23. Chen Rongjie 陳榮捷, *Wang Yangming chuanxilu xiangzhu jiping* 王陽明傳習錄詳註集評 (Taipei: Xuesheng shuju, 1983), 397.

24. Included in *Wang Yangming quanji, juan* 22: 841–842.

25. Meng Sen 孟森, *Mingdai shi* 明代史 (Taipei: Zhonghua congshu, 1957), 185–187; Chaoying Fang, "Chu Yu-t'ang," in *DMB*, 1:377–378.

26. Included in *Wang Yangming quanji, juan* 9: 291–292.

27. See "Wujing yishuo" 五經臆說, ibid., *juan* 26: 976–977.

28. "Longchangsheng wenda" 龍場生問答, ibid., *juan* 24: 912.

29. See *Nianpu* 年譜, ibid., *juan* 33: 1228.

30. See Wang Yangming's biography in *Mingshi, juan* 195: 17.5159.

31. "Jian ying Fo shu" 諫迎佛疏, *Wang Yangming quanji, juan* 9: 293–296.

32. See Wang Gen's *Nianpu* in *Wang Xinzhai xiansheng yiji* 王心齋先生遺集, ed. Yuan Chengye 袁承業 (Shanghai: Shenzhou Guoguang, 1912), *juan* 3: 3a–b. Cf. Wang Yangming's *Nianpu* in *Wang Xinzhai quanji* 王心齋全集, ed. Okada Takehiko 岡田武彥 and Araki Kengo 荒木見悟 (Taipei: Guangwen, 1987), *juan* 34: 1277–1278.

33. "Fu Tong Kegang" 復童克剛, *Wang Yangming quanji, juan* 21: 825–827.

34. *Nianpu* in *Wang Xinzhai xiansheng yiji, juan* 3: 4b.

35. Wm. Theodore de Bary, "Individualism and Humanitarianism in Late Ming Thought," in *Self and Society in Ming Thought*, 165.

36. This is his warning to a student/friend who wanted to test his ability in politics. See "Da Zong Shang-en" 答宗尚恩, in *Wang Xinzhai quanji* 王心齋全集, ed. Okada Takehiko 岡田

武彦 and Araki Kengo 荒木見悟 (Taipei: Zhongwen and Guangwen, n.d.), *juan* 5: 129–130.

37. See Qian Mu, *Yangmingxue shuyao* 陽明學述要, *Qian Binsi xiansheng quanji*, 10:82–92. The original text of the essay "Baben saiyuan" 拔本塞源 is included in *Chuanxilu* 傳習錄, part 2, *Wang Yangming quanji, juan* 2: 53–57. For a complete English translation, see *Instructions for Practical Living and Other Neo-Confucian Writings by Wang Yang-ming*, trans. with notes by Wing-tsit Chan (New York: Columbia University Press, 1963), 117–124.

38. Twice he emphasized the importance of the active participation of "farmer, artisans, and merchants" in his revised Confucian project. See *Instructions for Practical Living*, 119 and 120.

39. Ibid., 121.

40. Ibid., 230.

41. Ibid., 168.

42. Ibid., 124.

43. This memorial is included in *Wang Yangming quanji, juan* 39: 1494–1495. For the historical background of Geng Dingxiang's 耿定向 proposal, see Shen Defu 沈德符, *Wanli Yehuobian* 萬曆野獲編 (Beijing: Zhonghua, 1959), 2:362–364. For the controversy over his being honored in the Confucian temple, see Hung-lam Chu, "The Debate Over Recognition of Wang Yang-ming," *HJAS* 48, no. 1 (June 1988): 47–70.

44. Chen Rongjie, *Wang Yangming chuanxilu xiangzhu jiping*, 199.

45. Jiao Xun 焦循, "Liangzhilun" 良知論, in *Diaogulou ji* 雕菰樓集 (Suzhou: Wenxue shanfang, n.d.), *juan* 8: 20a.

46. *Wang Yangming quanji, juan* 32: 1172.

47. Wang Yangming, *Instructions for Practical Living*, 240.

48. "Yu Taihe Yang Mao" 諭泰和楊茂, in *Wang Yangming quanji, juan* 24: 919–920.

49. See Shimada Kenji 島田虔次, *Chūgoku ni okeru kindai shii no zasetsu* 中國における近代思惟の挫折 (Tokyo: Chikuma Shohō 筑摩書房, 1970), 101–110.

50. *MRXA, juan* 32: 9a.

51. Reprinted in Zhang Haipeng 張海鵬, Wang Tingyuan 王廷元, and Tang Lixing 唐力行, eds., *Ming-Qing Huishang ziliao xuanbian* 明清徽商資料選編 (Hefei: Huangshan, 1985), 251.

52. Wen Zhengming 文徵明, *Futian ji* 甫田集, SKQS, *juan* 25: 4b–5a.

53. For the problem of overpopulation of *shengyuan* 生員, see *Mingshi, juan* 69, 6:1686–1687, and Xu Shupi 徐樹丕, *Shixiao lu* 識小錄, *Hanfenlou miji* 涵芬樓秘笈 edition (Shanghai: Shangwu, 1924), *juan* 2: 15.

54. Han Bangqi 韓邦奇, *Yuanluo ji* 苑洛集, SKQS, *juan* 19: 4b–5b.

55. This general statement is in Ling Mengchu's 凌濛初 novel *Pai-an jingqi* 拍案驚奇, second edition, *juan* 37, quoted and discussed in Fujii Hiroshi 藤井宏, "Shinan shōnin no kenkyū" 新安商人の研究(4), *Tōyō gakuhō* 東洋學報 36, no. 4 (March 1954): 117.

56. Wang Daokun 汪道昆, "Jingyuan ji" 荊園記, in *Taihan ji* 太函集 (1591 edition in the Gest Library, Princeton University), *juan* 77: 9a.

57. Quoted and discussed in Terada Takanobu 寺田隆信, *Sansei shōnin no kenkyū* 山西商人の研究 (Kyoto: Tōyōshi kenkyūkai, 1972), 385–386.

58. *Wang Yangming quanji, juan* 25: 940–941.

59. Tang Shunzhi 唐順之, *Jingchuan xiansheng wenji* 荊川先生文集, SBCK suoben, *juan* 6: 119. It is interesting to note that about fifty years later, Li Le 李樂 (1532–1618) confirmed Tang's observation made in this letter as "a true fact" (*shishi* 實事). See Li Le, *Jianwen zaji* 見聞雜記 (Shanghai: Guji, 1986), 1:285.

60. Sang Yue 桑悅, *Sixuan ji* 思玄集 (Ming edition in the Gest Library, Princeton University), *juan* 7: 1a–b.

61. Kang Hai, *Duishan ji* 對山集 (1583 edition in the Library of Congress), *juan* 40: 3b–5a.

62. Ibid., *juan* 37: 9a–11b.

63. Chen Rongjie, *Wang Yangming chuanxilu xiangzhu jiping*, 398.

64. *Wang Yangming quanji, juan* 7: 256.

65. Li Mengyang 李夢陽, *Kongtong ji* 空同集, SKQS, *juan* 46: 4b. On Wang Xian 王現 and his family background, see Ono Kazuko 小野和子, *Minki tōsha kō* 明季黨社考 (Kyoto: Dohosha, 1996), 79–82.

66. Zhang Siwei 張四維, *Tiaolutang ji* 條麓堂集 (1592 edition in the Library of Congress), *juan* 23: 53b.

67. Reprinted in Zhang Haipeng and Wang Tingyuan, eds., *Ming-Qing Huishang ziliao xuanbian*, 440. For further discussions, see Zhang Haipeng and Tang Lixing 唐力行, "Lun Huishang 'gu er hao Ru' de tese" 論徽商'賈而好儒'的特色, *Zhongguoshi yanjiu* 4 (1984): 68.

68. Shen Yao 沈垚, *Luofanlou wenji* 落帆樓文集, *Wuxing congshu* (Beijing: Wenwu, 1987), *juan* 24: 12a–b.

69. Li Weizhen 李維楨, *Dabishanfang ji* 大泌山房集 (Wanli 萬曆 edition in the Gest Library, Princeton University), *juan* 87: 14b.

70. See Lü Miaofen 呂妙芬, *Yangmingxue shiren shequn* 陽明學士人社群 (Taipei: Institute of Modern History, Academia Sinica, 2003), 100–107; John Meskill, *Academies in Ming China: A Historical Essay* (Tucson: University of Arizona Press, 1982), 62–65.

71. Tang Shunzhi, *Jingchuan xiansheng wenji, juan* 16: 336–337.

72. See Cynthia J. Brokaw, *The Ledgers of Merit and Demerit: Social Change and Moral Order in Late Imperial China* (Princeton: Princeton University Press, 1991), 212–215.

73. See Li Chunfang 李春芳, "Chongrusi beiji" 崇儒祠碑記, in *Li Wending Gong Yi-antang ji* 李文定公貽安堂集 (Jinan: Qilu shushe, [1589] 1997), *juan* 9: 13a–b.

74. See a recorded statement in *Wang Yi-an xiansheng yiji* 王一菴先生遺集 (Shanghai: Shenzhou guoguang, 1912), *juan* 1: 15b; a slightly different version may be found in *MRXA, juan* 32: 24a.

75. See Wang Gen's *Nianpu* in *Wang Xinzhai xiansheng yiji, juan* 3: 3b–4a, 5a–b.

76. The above account is based on the recently discovered biographical data relating to Han Zhen in *Han Zhen ji*, included in *Yan Jun ji* 顏鈞集, ed. Huang Xuanmin 黃宣民 (Beijing: CASS Press, 1996), 189–190 and 201–203.

77. *MRXA, juan* 32: 12b and Geng Dingxiang 耿定向, "Taoren zhuan" 陶人傳, in *Han Zhen ji*, 188. English translation is based on Julia Ching, ed., *The Records of Ming Scholars* (Honolulu: University of Hawaii Press, 1987), 182.

78. Rong Zhaozu, ed., *He Xinyin ji* 何心隱集 (Beijing: Zhonghua, 1981), 53–54.

79. I have discussed the emergence of this new conception of *simin* in detail in my *Zhong-guo jinshi zongjiao lunli yu shangren jingshen* 中國近世宗教倫理與商人精神 (hereafter *Shangren jingshen*) (Taipei: Lianjing, 1987), esp. pp. 106–114. However, this point must not be mistaken to mean that the long-established idiomatic expression *shi nong gong shang* 士農工商 had ceased to circulate in written or spoken language since the sixteenth century. As a matter of fact, He Xinyin himself continued to use it. See *He Xin-yin ji*, 29.

80. Gu Xiancheng 顧憲成, *Xiaoxinzhai zhaji* 小心齋劄記 (Taipei: Guangwen, [1877] 1975), *juan* 14: 2b–3a.

81. Max Weber, *The Protestant Ethic and the Spirit of Capitalism*, trans. Talcott Parsons (London: George Allen and Unwin, 1930), 68.

82. On the merchant background of Gu's family, see my *Xiandai ruxue lun*, 82–83.

83. Li Zhi 李贄, *Fenshu* 焚書 (Beijing: Zhonghua, 1961), 47. See de Bary, *Self and Society in Ming Thought*, 206.

84. *Mingshi, juan* 81: 7.1978–1979.

85. *Ming shilu* 明實錄 (Taipei: Institute of History & Philology, Academia Sinica, 1966), 119.9927.

86. Quoted and discussed in my *Xiandai ruxue lun*, 94–95.

87. Dai Tingming 戴廷明, Cheng Shangkuan 程尚寬, and Zhu Wanshu 朱萬曙, eds., *Xin-an mingzu zhi* 新安名族志 (Hefei: Huangshan, 2004), 154.

88. Ibid., 231 (Wang Gen); p. 530 (Zou Shouyi).

89. *MRXA, juan* 16: 3b.

90. Wu Weiye 吳偉業, *Meicun jiacang gao* 梅村家藏稿, SBCK suoben, *juan* 50: 222.

91. See my *Shangren jingshen*, 124–136.

92. For the origin of the term *xingwo* 行窩 in relation to salt merchants, see Chaoying Fang, "Chan Jo-shui," in *DMB*, 1:38, and Wang Zhenzhong 王振忠, *Ming-Qing Huishang yu Huaiyang shehui bianqian* 明清徽商與淮揚社會變遷 (Beijing: Sanlian, 1996), 1–11.

93. Tang Shunzhi, *Jingchuan xiansheng wenji, juan* 16: 337.

94. *Xin-an mingzu zhi*, 124; 231; 325–326; 431; 481; 537. The last two, Bazi 巴鼐 and Xu Shi-run 許時潤, seem to have been from merchant families.

95. *MRXA, juan* 37: 1a. For English translation, see *The Records of Ming Scholars*, 202.

96. *Xin-an minzu zhi*, 217; 223; 516; 530.

97. *MRXA, juan* 37: 2b. English translation adapted from *The Records of Ming Scholars*, 203.

98. For a modern analysis, see Julia Ching, "A Contribution on Chan's Thought," in *DMB*, 1:41–42.

99. See Ye Tan 葉坦, *Fuguo fumin lun* 富國富民論 (Beijing: Beijing, 1991), 85–92.

100. Qiu Jun 丘濬, *Daxue Yanyi bu* 大學衍義補 (Taipei: Shangwu, [1605] 1972), 174. For a comprehensive study of Qiu Jun's thought, see Hung-lam Chu, *Ch'iu Chün (1421–1495) and the "Ta hsüeh yen i pu": Statecraft Thought in Fifteenth-Century China* (Ann Arbor, Mich.: University Microfilms International, 1983).

101. Huang Wan 黃綰, *Mingdao bian* 明道編 (Beijing: Zhonghua, 1959), 45. For a comprehensive study of Huang Wan, see *Rong Zhaozu ji*, 247–316.

102. This expression, *fumin guo zhi yuanqi* 富民國之元氣, was quoted by Li Yuheng 李豫亨 in his *Tuipeng wuyu* 推蓬寤語 as a common saying of the day (Lishi sijingtang 李氏思敬堂, 1571), *juan* 8: 18b.

103. *Qi Biaojia ji* 祁彪佳集 (Beijing: Zhonghua, 1960), 96.

104. Wang Fuzhi 王夫之, *Huang shu* 黃書 (Beijing: Guji, 1956), 28–29.

105. For examples, see Xu Zhenming 徐貞明 (d. 1590), *Lushui ketan* 潞水客談 (Taipei: Shangwu, 1966), 8; Tang Zhen 唐甄 (1630–1704), *Qianshu* 潛書 (Beijing: Zhonghua, 1963), 105–107 and 114.

106. Lu Ji 陸楫, *Jianjiatang zazhu zhechao* 蒹葭堂雜著摘抄, in Shen Jiefu 沈節甫 (1533–1601), *Guochao jilu huibian* 國朝紀錄彙編 (Taipei: Yiwen, 1971 [reprint]), *juan* 24: 214. For an English translation of Lu's essay, see Lien-sheng Yang, "A Sixteenth-Century Essay in Favor of Spending," appendix to "Economic Justification for Spending: An Uncommon Idea in Traditional China," in his *Studies in Chinese Institutional History* (Cambridge, Mass.: Harvard University Press, 1961), 72–74.

107. Li Yuheng, *Tuipeng wuyu*, *juan* 8: 18a.

108. Fa Shishan 法式善, *Taolu zalu* 陶廬雜錄 (Beijing: Zhonghua, 1959), 161.

109. Gu Gongxie 顧公燮, *Xiaoxia xianji zhechao* 消夏閑記摘抄 (Shanghai: Shangwu, 1917 [Hanfenlou miji 涵芬樓秘笈 edition]), *juan shang* 上, 27.

110. Zhang Shihuan 張世浣, *Chongxiu Yangzhoufu zhi* 重修揚州府志 (1810 edition), *juan* 3: 2b.

111. See the following important studies by Mizoguchi Yūzō 溝口雄三, "Chūgoku ni okeru ko-shi gainen no tenkai" 中國における公. 私概念の展開, *Shisô* 思想 669 (March 1980): 19–38, and "Chūgoku no ko-shi" 中國の公私, *Bungaku* 56 (September 1988): 88–102 and 56 (October 1988): 73–84.

112. See my *Shangren jingshen*, 102–104, and *Xiandai ruxue lun*, 20–25.

113. Li Zhi, *Cangshu* 藏書 (Beijing: Zhonghua, 1959), 3:544.

114. Li Weizhen, "Nanzhou gaoshi Yugong mubiao" 南州高士喻公墓表, *Dabishanfang ji*, *juan* 105: 28a.

115. Gu Yanwu 顧炎武, "Jun-xian lun, 5" 郡縣論五, *Gu Tinglin shiwen ji* 顧亭林詩文集 (Beijing: Zhonghua, 1959), 15.

116. Gu Yanwu, *Yuanchaoben Rizhilu* 原抄本日知錄 (Taipei: Minglun 明倫, 1970), 68.

117. Han Bangqi, *Yuanluo ji*, *juan* 7: 6a–b.

118. Gu Xiancheng, *Jinggao canggao* 涇皋藏稿, SKQS, *juan* 17: 11a.

119. Li Hua 李華, comp., *Ming-Qing yilai Beijing gongshang huiguan beike xuanbian* 明清以來北京工商會館碑刻選編 (Beijing: Wenwu, 1980), 16.

120. See *Xiandai ruxuelun*, 1–57.

121. Tan Sitong, "Renxue" 仁學, in *Tan Sitong quanji* 譚嗣同全集 (Beijing: Zhonghua, 1981), 2:338–342; Liang Qichao 梁啟超, "Lun zhuanzhi zhengti you baihai yu junzhu er wu yili" 論專制政體有百害於君主而無一利, *Yinbingshi heji* 飲冰室合集 9 文集九 (1989): 90–101. For Huang Zongxi's *Mingyi daifang lu* 明夷待訪錄, see the annotated translation of Wm. Theodore de Bary, *Waiting for the Dawn: A Plan for the Prince* (New York: Columbia University Press, 1993).

122. For the case of Sun Yat-sen, see Ying-shih Yü, "Democracy, Human Rights and Confucian Culture," in *The Fifth Huang Hsing Foundation Hsueh Chun-tu Distinguished Lecture in Asian Studies* (Oxford: Asian Studies Centre, St. Antony's College, University of Oxford, 2000), 12.

123. See Zhu Jiazhen 朱家楨, "Zhongguo fumin sixiang de lishi kaocha" 中國富民思想的歷史考察, *Pingzhun Xuekan* (Beijing: Zhongguo shangye, 1986), 3rd collection, 2:403.

124. *Tan Sitong quanji*, 2:326–327.

125. Ibid., 1:250.

126. Liang Qichao, "Shiji huozhi liezhuan jinyi" 《史記. 貨殖列傳》今義, *Yinbingshi heji* 2 (1989): 39–40.

127. For textual details, see my *Xiandai ruxue lun*, 5–6.

128. Liang Qichao, "Xinmin shuo" 新民說, *Yinbingshi heji* 4 專集四 (1989): 36. English translation by Hao Chang, *Liang Ch'i-ch'ao and the Intellectual Transition in China, 1890–1907* (Cambridge, Mass.: Harvard University Press, 1971), 195.

13. The Intellectual World of Jiao Hong Revisited

Jiao Hong 焦竑 (1540–1620) was an important figure in late Ming intellectual history. In his own day, he was praised for his accomplishments in prose writing as much as for his active interest in Neo-Confucian and Buddhist metaphysics. Since the eighteenth century, however, he has been remembered as a bibliophile and as a pioneer of "evidential research" (*kaozheng* 考證). He lived in an age of transition that witnessed many new developments in Chinese society, religion, and in elite as well as popular culture, but he was by no means merely a passive product of this transition. On the contrary, through his many-sided intellectual activities, he contributed significantly to the transition. On the one hand, his active participation in the movement known as "Oneness of the Three Teachings" (*Sanjiao heyi* 三教合一) precipitated the decline, if not demise, of Ming Neo-Confucianism as a philosophical enterprise. On the other hand, his promotion of a philological approach to ancient texts paved the way for the rise of classical and historical scholarship that dominated Qing intellectual history. There can be no question that a man holding such a strategic position in the Ming-Qing intellectual transition deserves to be studied thoroughly. Edward T. Ch'ien's *Chiao Hung and the Restructuring of Neo-Confucianism in the Late Ming* (New York: Columbia University Press, 1986) is therefore a welcome addition to the growing literature on Ming thought in the West.[1]

In this study, Ch'ien (hereafter "the author") has set for himself a goal far more ambitious than intellectual biography in the ordinary sense. As a matter of fact, the individual case of Jiao Hong merely provides the author with a convenient focus to play his own "game," to use the author's favorite expression, not only with Ming Neo-Confucianism but with the entire Chinese philosophical tradition. In this essay, however, I have confined myself to Ming-Qing intellectual history, focusing on the period in which Jiao Hong lived and wrote.

To read through this book requires a high degree of patience and concentration. This is the case primarily because most of its arguments, often tortuously labored, fly so high in metaphysical outer space that it is not always clear how to relate them to the realities of the intellectual world of late Ming China. To determine their precise meanings, I was compelled to examine, ever increasingly, the textual ground of these high-flying arguments. One thing led to another, and before I knew it, I found myself already deeply involved in a research project of my own. As a result, I have restudied practically all of Jiao Hong's basic writings as well as other related texts of the late Ming Period. The end product, as it now stands, is as much a revisit of the intellectual world of Jiao Hong as a review of the book about him. In my considered opinion, the subject matter itself alone merits this comprehensive reexamination. Moreover, the book also deserves to be taken most seriously and critically on account of, if nothing else, the author's seriousness of purpose in his heroic efforts to reconceptualize some of the central problems in Chinese intellectual history.

INTELLECTUAL HISTORY AS DIALOGUE WITH THE PAST

To be fair to the author, we must begin with a clear recognition of the nature and purpose of his new game. The name of this game is German phenomenology merged with French structuralism (and, of course, also poststructuralism). "Subjectivity," "objectivity," "discursive formation," "textuality," "restructuring," etc., are among the main conceptual pillars that support the structure of the castle built in this book. The author's basic building materials are, of course, Chinese ideas of the Confucian, Daoist, and Buddhist varieties. His Chinese materials are also of a particular brand, however, for he understands many of the pivotal ideas in the Chinese tradition as they have been interpreted by a few contemporary Chinese philosophers, notably the Kantian-oriented Mou Zongsan and the Hegelian-oriented Tang Junyi. Hence, in a general sense, his building materials are well suited to his structure, for, as is generally known, while seeking to transcend the limitations of the Kantian-Hegelian tradition, the contemporary phenomenological movement in the West with all of its ramifications is nonetheless continuous with it.

Playing a phenomenological-structuralist game with Chinese philosophical texts, the author's approach to intellectual history is predominantly "dialogical." In some phenomenological quarters today, a general distinction has been

drawn between intellectual history as a reconstruction of the past and as a dialogue with the past, with the emphasis placed on the latter.[2] This, of course, does
not imply that the author has taken a dialogical approach to the total exclusion of
reconstruction, which is practically impossible for any intellectual historian to
do. It seems reasonable to assume that each of the two approaches contains an
element of the other.[3] Even a strong advocate of the dialogical approach can
only say, "it is a hermeneutical necessity always to go beyond mere reconstruction," but not to do without it.[4] However, as will become crystal clear later, the
author's overwhelming enthusiasm in having a dialogue with the past has seriously impaired his reconstructive work.

The author's dialogical approach may be described in just a few words. He
first poses certain phenomenological-structuralist questions to Jiao Hong's texts
and then forces the texts to say what he is interested in knowing. Then, to show
what was "new" and "original" in Jiao Hong and late Ming Neo-Confucianism,
he carries his conversations back to pre-Ming times and puts the same kind
of questions to earlier (including ancient) philosophical texts. The author's
phenomenological-structuralist prejudice practically dominates the whole book.
Problems concerning language, mode of discourse, or structure are to be encountered everywhere. His repeated discussions of the relationship between
language and the *Dao* as reality, for instance, show particularly the profound
concern of contemporary continental philosophers such as Gadamer, Derrida,
and Foucault with the Western logocentric tradition.

Some methodological questions arise at this point. First, the idea of "dialogue with the past as intellectual history" can only be understood metaphor-
ically. There is really no exchange of questions and answers, as Paul Ricoeur says,
"between the writer and the reader. The writer does not respond to the reader."[5]
Second, even if we can speak analogously of the text as the "partner" in a dialogue, it is nevertheless only a silent "partner" who cannot supply the context
when the "dialogue" goes wrong.[6] This is a particularly serious problem with
Jiao Hong's philosophical remarks, which, being generally of a fragmentary
nature, are already out of context by themselves. Third, when phenomenologi-
cally oriented historians in the West speak of a "dialogue between the present
and the past," they naturally assume that it takes place within the same tradition, i.e., the Western philosophical tradition. The "dialogue" that, in Gadame-
rian terms, culminates in the "fusion of horizons" is possible primarily because
the horizon of the present is being continually formed in its encounter with the
horizon of the past in an ever-changing and ever-continuing tradition.[7] Now, in
the case of this book, the "dialogue" obviously takes place between two totally
different and historically unrelated traditions. The questions posed by the author to his silent "partner" are framed largely in terms of contemporary Western phenomenology and structuralism. They are generally questions of a formal and linguistic kind. It is of course not wholly impossible to force a silent
"partner" from a different tradition to answer questions of this kind. After all,

texts of all traditions have language and structure as their basic components. What is really at issue, however, is that questions central to one tradition at one historical time may only be peripheral to another tradition at another time. As far as I can judge, the "dialogue" between the Chinese past and the Western present in this book is very much dominated by the latter, with the result that Neo-Confucianism has been transformed into a "language game."

So much for the dialogical approach. Since this book is a study in intellectual history, it must be judged ultimately on historical grounds. In what follows, I propose to examine it primarily as a reconstruction of the past.

To begin with, the reader needs to know what sort of intellectual history the author intends his book to be. He tells us that Jiao Hong lived in a period corresponding to a crucial phase in Chinese social and intellectual history when Chinese society witnessed the activation of "new forces on several levels," and when Chinese thought experienced a "near revolution" (32). Except for this brief reference, however, he has made no effort to place the thought of Jiao Hong in the context of late Ming social and intellectual history. The author refers to himself as a "historian of ideas" (26), which seems to indicate that he is after the style of Arthur O. Lovejoy. At any rate, this study may well be characterized as a "search for shifting configurations of eternal ideas, as expressed by the most refined philosophical minds"[8] or, more likely, he has followed the "archaeological" method of Michel Foucault, especially in the latter's attempt to divorce discourse from its social setting and to discover the structural rules governing discourse alone.[9] Whatever the case may be, it seems fair to say that intellectual history for the author is a self-closed universe in which only abstract ideas interact with one another.

SOME FACTS ABOUT JIAO HONG'S LIFE

The author's failure to take intellectual history seriously as a reconstruction of the past comes from a chapter where it is least expected. In chapter 2, "The Man," he examines mainly three aspects of Jiao Hong's intellectual life together with a description of his "political involvement." To identify Jiao Hong as a member of the Taizhou school, a Wild-Chanist, a court official, and a critical scholar is, of course, not wrong, but fails to do full justice to "the man." In his lifetime, Jiao Hong was equally, if not better, known as a prose writer. All the "prefaces" to his *Danyuan ji* 澹園集 (Tranquil garden collection; *Collected Works of Jiao Hong*) and *Danyuan xuji* 澹園續集 (Tranquil garden second collection; *Collected Works of Jiao Hong*, vol. 2) by his friends and disciples, for example, stress emphatically his great achievement in literary art (*wen* 文 or *wenzhang* 文章). His best friend, Li Zhi 李贄 (1527–1602), even praised him as "The Su Shi 蘇軾 [1036–1101] of our day," referring specifically to his "immortality" as a literary artist.[10]

In reconstructing Jiao Hong's life, the author generally relies on the two biographical sketches in the *Mingshi* 明史 (History of the Ming Dynasty) and Huang Zongxi's 黃宗羲 (1610–1695) *Mingru xue-an* 明儒學案 (Scholarly Cases of Ming Classical Scholars), which often prove to be inadequate or inaccurate. No attempt seems to have been made by the author to search for contemporary sources. For example, Zhu Guozhen's 朱國楨 (1557–1632) *Yongchuang xiaopin* 湧幢小品 (Yongchuang Essays) contains a great deal of information about Jiao Hong's activities, including their conversations. Zhu and Jiao passed the *jinshi* examination in the same year and knew each other well, but the author does not seem to be aware of the existence of this important source. In his discussion of the case concerning Jiao Hong's *Yangzheng tujie* 養正圖解 (Historical exemplars with pictures on cultivating correct behavior), the author, following the *History of the Ming Dynasty*, mentions that this work aroused the jealousy and opposition of Jiao Hong's fellow lecturers, who felt that he compiled the book as a gimmick to "buy reputation" (52). In fact, the case was far more complicated than the brief account given in the *History of the Ming Dynasty*. According to Zhu Guozhen, under circumstances that were beyond Jiao Hong's control, printed copies of his book were presented to the throne through the intermediary of the powerful eunuch Chen Ju 陳矩 (1539–1608). This unexpected turn of events aroused the suspicion and resentment of some top-ranking officials at the court who thought that Jiao Hong was seeking an appointment in the Inner Cabinet (*neige* 內閣) by irregular means. Doubly unfortunate for Jiao Hong, the suspicion was deepened by a preface he had written earlier for Lü Kun's 呂坤 (1536–1618) "Guifan" (Regulations for women's quarters). It happened that Lü was also accused of trying to flatter the imperial consort Zheng with his compilation. As a result, Jiao Hong was immediately demoted and exiled to Fukien for a false and totally unrelated reason in 1597.[11] This setback practically ended his official career. It seems odd, to say the least, that an event of singular importance in Jiao Hong's otherwise uneventful public life is virtually ignored in a section dealing with his "political involvement." As a result, the author's account of Jiao Hong's demotion and retirement is also unsatisfactory (59).

The author twice appeals to the authority of Huang Zongxi for support when he discusses Jiao Hong's difficult personality (34) and his characterization of Li Zhi as a *kuang* 狂 person (41). Actually, in both cases, Huang Zongxi's source is the *Yongchuang Essays*. In the case of Li Zhi, the author says that Shen Defu's 沈德符 (1578–1642) remark that Jiao Hong "extolled him as a sage" was flatly contradicted by Huang Zongxi, who said otherwise (40–41). However, the original source runs as follows: "Jiao Ruohou (Hong) extolled Li Zhi to the utmost. Each time when he talked to me about him, I refused to respond. One day, Ruohou asked me, 'Are you not satisfied with him?' Even if he were not a sage, he may well be considered as a person who could bear on his shoulders the word *kuang* ('wild'), and who might sit next to a sage."[12] It seems clear that Jiao Hong probably did extol Li Zhi as a sage. It was only because of Zhu Guozhen's strong disapproval that he rather reluctantly moved from the level of "sage" to that of *kuang*. The author was obviously misled by Huang Zongxi's paraphrase in *Scholarly Cases of Ming Classical Scholars*. Being a junior contemporary, Shen Defu, after all, knew better. Methodologically, it is also not permissible for the historian to give greater weight to secondhand evidence than to a contemporaneous one. Moreover, in the case of Jiao Hong's personality, Huang Zongxi specifically named Zhu Guozhen as his source.

The author's interest in "reconstruction" goes only as far as it serves his "dialogue." He focuses on three aspects of Jiao Hong's intellectual life: as a philosopher of the Taizhou school, a Wild Chanist, and a critical scholar. These three aspects, it may be noted, correspond to the three broad issues in the late Ming with which this book is concerned: Neo-Confucian syncretism, the controversy between the Cheng-Zhu and Lu-Wang schools, and the emergence of "evidential research" (*kaozheng*) as a formation (1). When his "reconstruction" is out of step with his "dialogue," however, the author feels quite free to reshape the former to bring it into conformity with the latter. The following interesting example is worth examining. Discussing Jiao Hong's relationship with Buddhism, he writes:

> After he had obtained his *jinshi* as *zhuangyuan*, Chiao Hung wrote a letter to a monk named Lu-an in which he stated that he had "cultivated *karma*" (*xiuye* 修業) for twenty years, "more than half of which time he had spent at Lu-an's temple under Lu-an's care." The term *xiuye* as used in this letter can mean either "cultivation of *karma*" or "study for the civil service examination." I have chosen to render it as "cultivation of *karma*" because the twenty-year period indicated in the letter could not possibly have corresponded with the length of time which Jiao Hong spent preparing for the civil service examinations. He began his study for the examinations at least as early as 1555, and would have been engaged in such study for at least thirty-six years by the date of this letter, which was written in 1589. (42)

The term *xiuye* in this context can only mean "study for civil service examination," not "cultivation of karma." The latter is an impossible translation. Anyone who knows anything about the concept of karma knows that it is not something to be "cultivated." Nor can it be interpreted as "study of sûtras." This is an extreme case showing that the silent "partner" cannot supply the context when the "dialogue" goes wrong. The author has taken a sentence completely out of the context of the letter in which it was originally written. Jiao Hong wrote this letter to Lu-an with the sole and explicit purpose of expressing his deep gratitude for the monk's support during much of the twenty-year period of preparation—support that had, in his own words, "exceeded what could be expected from a family member."[13] The twenty-year period is a nonproblem because it refers to the period between 1564, when Jiao Hong passed his *juren* examination, and 1589, when he finally succeeded as a *zhuangyuan*. It was a common practice in traditional China to use round numbers in such informal writings. Elsewhere, Jiao Hong explicitly referred to the period of his repeated failures in *jinshi* examinations between 1564 and 1589 as "twenty years."[14] Moreover, one of Jiao Hong's texts clearly states that when he was in his twenties, he was staying at both Tianjie and Bao-en monasteries in Nanjing and pursuing his "metropolitan examinations studies" (*gongju ye* 公車業).[15] There cannot be the slightest doubt that the term *xiuye* is an abbreviated form of *xiu gongju ye*. It seems that the author is so uninterested in "reconstruction" that he did not even have the impulse to check his basic sources when he needed to determine the precise meaning of a key term used by Jiao Hong.

This is not a matter of simple misreading, however. On the contrary, the author has chosen the impossible interpretation to serve an important purpose in his "dialogue" with Jiao Hong. He has decided that Jiao Hong must have already been a confirmed Neo-Confucian for several years before he turned to Buddhism "not as an alternative, but as a further elaboration." The author further speculates, though without any basis in fact, that Jiao Hong made this move because "problems arising from his study of Confucianism compelled him to look into Buddhism, which, he said, could best clarify 'the cardinal meaning of the teachings of the sages and worthies'" (42). As we shall see below, this line of argument is of vital importance to the central thesis of this book that Jiao Hong successfully accomplished a creative synthesis from a Neo-Confucian base. According to the author, on the one hand, Jiao Hong's synthesis was "not indiscriminating lumping" (189), but, on the other hand, Jiao Hong remained "a good Confucian in spite of his deep involvements in the study of Buddhism and Daoism" (235). To support such an interpretation, the author obviously needs some evidence from Jiao Hong's intellectual life showing that this was indeed the case. The author makes this abundantly clear in the following passage:

> Jiao Hong's interest in Buddhism as a serious intellectual undertaking seems to have begun relatively late. There are in his writings a few fragmentary references to his studying at the various temples in Nanjing shortly after he came of age. However, we do not know whether he studied there to pursue his interest in Buddhism or to prepare for the civil service examinations. Moreover, these were the years before he "set his mind on learning." Therefore, whatever he might have read in Buddhism during this period was not likely to have produced a deep imprint on his mind; and he probably did not begin to study Buddhism seriously until he was in his late twenties or early thirties. (41–42)

In other words, Jiao Hong's early exposure to Buddhism must be explained away to make room for the point that he "came to Buddhism via Confucianism" (42). Thus, to interpret *xiuye* as "cultivation of karma" serves the author's thesis perfectly.

It is also very revealing that with regard to Jiao Hong's "references to his studying at the various temples in Nanjing," the author says, "we do not know whether he studied there to pursue his interest in Buddhism or to prepare for the civil service examinations." Here we have reason to believe that the author may not be telling the whole truth, for the very first of the texts cited in the footnote (295, n. 72) is the reference to Jiao Hong's pursuing "metropolitan examination studies," as mentioned earlier. The author is probably caught in a dilemma: on the one hand, to relate Jiao Hong's studying at the various monasteries to Buddhism would make the case too early for his "*via* Confucianism" theory. On the other hand, however, to relate it to examinations would directly contradict his interpretation of *xiuye* as "cultivation of karma." Whatever the case may be, one thing is quite certain: the author's inability to determine Jiao Hong's early relations with Buddhist monasteries reveals his lack of interest in historical "reconstruction." It does not seem to have ever occurred to the author that his case can be greatly helped by examining the secular functions of Buddhist monasteries in the late Ming.

It was a long-established practice since the Tang dynasty for examination candidates to study in monasteries, but the practice was particularly widespread in the late Ming. Travelers (such as the famous Xu Xiake 徐霞客, 1586–1641) visiting Buddhist monasteries could rarely find one without some candidates studying for examinations there.[16] The eminent monk Deqing 德清 (1546–1623), a friend of Jiao Hong's, was first attracted to Buddhism because he received his early Confucian education in a Buddhist monastery. As late as 1562, he was still pursuing Confucian studies for examinations at Bao-en 報恩 Monastery in Nanjing.[17] It is important to bear in mind that major Buddhist monasteries in both Beijing and Nanjing were placed under the direct control of the Board of Rites during the Ming Period. The abbot was to be appointed by the board on the basis of an examination in which knowledge of Buddhist sûtras was tested, but its very form was none other than the eight-legged essay.[18] As a result, monks in these monasteries (such as the above-mentioned Bao-en Monastery in Nanjing) studied the art of the eight-legged essay no less assiduously than candidates for civil service examinations.[19] The fact that Jiao Hong spent many years in his late twenties in the two major Buddhist monasteries of his native city—Bao-en and Tianjie 天界—can be easily understood in this light.

JIAO HONG'S SYNCRETISM IN HISTORICAL PERSPECTIVE

The problem of the "union of the Three Teachings in one" (*Sanjiao heyi*) figures prominently in the author's discussions of Jiao Hong's "syncretism," "synthesis," or "pluralism." Inspired by Judith Berling's observation that Lin Zhao-en 林兆恩 (1517–1598) refused to see the Three Teachings in terms of "compartmentalization" of the *Dao* or Way,[20] the author has made excessive use of the idea of "noncompartmentalization" to argue that "a notable change occurred in the syncretic situation of late Ming" (14). Based on the two isolated cases of Lin Zhao-en and Jiao Hong, he claims to have detected the emergence of "an expression in the altered structure of the syncretic logic" (14). Both Lin and Jiao, according to the author, no longer viewed Confucianism, Daoism, and Buddhism as three separate and different teachings, each confined to a compartment of the *Dao*. Instead, the Three Teachings were now conceived as "one" in the sense that "they had the fused integrity of a single entity and were mutually identified and indistinguishable" (119). The author is, of course, not wholly unaware of the difficulties of his theory. Lin Zhao-en's temple was segregated into three different chambers and Jiao Hong also, from time to time, "reverted to the compartmentalizing rhetoric of his syncretic predecessors" (120). However, the author obviously does not consider such difficulties to be so insurmountable as to prevent him from arguing for the "originality" and "systematicity" of Jiao Hong's "Neo-Confucian synthesis."

It is true that the syncretist movement of *Sanjiao heyi* reached its peak during the sixteenth and early seventeenth centuries at all levels of Chinese philosophical and religious imagination.[21] There is no evidence, however, that suggests a discernible trend from "compartmentalization" to "noncompartmentalization." At the level of popular religion, millenarian sects continued to follow the age-old logic of compartmentalization. The Hongyang jiao 弘陽教, for example, regarded Confucius, Buddha, and Laozi as the three sons of the Nonultimate Progenitor (*Wuji Laozu* 無極老祖) and the Eternal Mother (*Wusheng Laomu* 無生老母), each having established a reputation in his own area. This is clearly a vulgarized version of the traditional idea of "Three Teachings—One Source" (*Sanjiao yiyuan* 三教一源).[22] In the case of Luo jiao 羅教, an early text entitled *Wuwei zhengzong liaoyi baojuan* 無為正宗了義寶卷 distinguishes the Three Teachings from one another in two different compartmentalized ways. The first one is to see each teaching being based on a principle uniquely its own. Thus, Confucianism is identified with the principle of "uprightness" (*zheng* 正), Daoism with that of "honor" (*zun* 尊), and Buddhism with that of "greatness" (*da* 大). Here it is clear that the text follows the distinction first suggested by the Yuan syncretist Liu Mi.[23] With regard to the second one, the text says: "Buddhism can be compared to the sun, Confucianism to the moon, and Daoism to the five stars. Like the three lights in heaven, the world cannot afford to dispense with any [of the Three Teachings]."[24] As anyone familiar with the history of Chinese syncretism knows, this is the famous compartmentalizing metaphor of Li Shiqian 李士謙 (523–588) with the positions of Confucianism versus Daoism in the original formulation reversed. Thus, we see that at the popular level, the principle of compartmentalization continued to reign supreme in late Ming religious syncretism.

Since the author deals with the problem of *Sanjiao heyi* primarily at the philosophical level, we must now turn to Neo-Confucianism in the late Ming to see whether Jiao Hong's syncretism was something significantly new. To begin with, it may be noted that the author's lack of interest in historical reconstruction is nowhere more clearly shown than in his treatment of this problem. He has cited several pre-Ming religious syncretists, including the above-mentioned Li Shiqian and Liu Mi (5–14). His sole purpose, however, seems to be to establish a case of "compartmentalization" as a sharp contrast to what he takes to be Jiao Hong's new syncretic logic of "noncompartmentalization." He has made no attempt to trace Jiao Hong's syncretism to its Ming Neo-Confucian origins. Thus, Wang Yangming 王陽明 is lightly dismissed as still being on the opposite side of "the left-wing Neo-Confucians of the late Ming who tried, rather self-consciously, to unite The Three Teachings into one doctrine," (17) and the tremendous impact of Wang Ji's 王畿 (1498–1583) philosophical views of Sanjiao heyi on the so-called "left-wing Neo-Confucians of the late Ming" is nowhere even mentioned. It is common knowledge that the problem of Sanjiao heyi in Ming Neo-Confucianism began with Wang Yangming and received its most systematic, elaborate treatment in the hands of Wang Ji. When left-wing Neo-Confucians of the Taizhou school such as Li Zhi and Jiao Hong argued for the oneness of the Three Teachings at the philosophical level, they all followed Wang Yangming and, particularly, Wang Ji, in one way or another.

In 1524, when Wang Yangming was asked whether there was something to be learned from Daoism and Buddhism since each of the two teachings also enunciated the Dao in terms of xing 性 (Nature) and ming 命 (Destiny), he replied that both the Daoist and the Buddhist teachings in this particular respect originally had been integral parts of the Confucian learning. It was due to the fact that latter-day Confucians had failed to see the sagely learning holistically that both teachings were misunderstood as different from Confucianism. At the same time, however, Wang Yangming also admitted that since the primordial unity had been lost, the Dao was split into three parts, very much like a great hall partitioned into three chambers. Latter-day Confucians, he observed, vacated the right and left chambers to accommodate the Daoists and the Buddhists, respectively, while being content with reserving the central chamber for themselves.[25] Wang Yangming's emphasis on the original oneness of the Three Teachings with regard to the ultimate reality of the Dao was undoubtedly an important source of inspiration for the left-wing Neo-Confucians' advocacy of the idea of Sanjiao heyi. On the other hand, however, this new metaphor of the Three Chambers also exerted a lasting influence on the thinking of Neo-Confucian syncretists in the next one and a half centuries. In Lin Zhao-en's temple, we even see the Three-Chamber metaphor translated into reality.[26] Hence, compartmentalization and noncompartmentalization, if we are to use such terms at all, can only be understood as a pair of Siamese twins grown out of Ming Neo-Confucian syncretism from the very outset.

The most important single philosophical influence on Sanjiao heyi in the sixteenth century was, undoubtedly, Wang Ji, who developed his teacher's idea to its logical extremes. His famous essay written in commemoration of the founding of the Hall of Three Teachings begins by saying that Confucian learning cannot be clearly distinguished from Daoism or from Buddhism because it also speaks of the *Dao* in terms of "vacuity" (*xu* 虛) or "stillness" (*ji* 寂). The essay further questions the validity of the conventional view taking Daoism and Buddhism as "heresies" (*yiduan* 異端). As long as students of Daoism and Buddhism set the "restoration of nature" (*fuxing* 復性) as their central purpose, it argues, they ought to be regarded as "Daoist- or Buddhist-oriented Confucians" (*Dao-Shi zhi Ru* 道釋之儒). According to Wang Ji, with *liangzhi* 良知 (original-good-knowing) as the "axis," integration of the Three Teachings at the philosophical level is rather a matter of course.[27] By grounding his syncretism squarely in the doctrine of *liangzhi*, Wang Ji actually introduced a new strategy into the late Ming *Sanjiao heyi* movement, which was to be known as the "Three Teachings returning to Confucianism" (*Sanjiao gui Ru* 三教歸儒). Lin Zhao-en and Li Zhi, for example, each used this strategy to promote a syncretism uniquely his own.[28]

Wang Ji was more responsible than anyone else for the wide circulation of Wang Yangming's three-chamber metaphor in late Ming syncretist circles. He made constant references to it in his writings, as well as public lectures. What is even more significant is his translation of his teacher's metaphorical language into a kind of pseudo-historical language. He argued that "vacuity," "stillness," or "emptiness" constituted the "essence" of Confucian learning from the very beginning. It was unfortunate that in later ages, the Confucians ceded this "essence" to the Buddhists. In the time of Yao and Shun, when Buddhism nowhere existed, there were sages such as Chao Fu 巢父 and Xu You 許由 who held the type of otherworldly teaching comparable to Buddhism. Thus, in high antiquity, it was the likes of Chao Fu and Xu You who guarded the left and right chambers for sagely learning. He deplored very much that, as sagely learning declined over the centuries, the Confucians not only lost the two side chambers to Buddhism and Daoism but could not even hold their position firmly in the central chamber.[29]

Wang Ji also developed a "stage-of-life" argument for *Sanjiao heyi*. The Three Teachings are all centrally concerned with the "Mind" (*xin* 心), but each looks at the same "mind" from a different stage of life. Buddhism refers to the "mind" at the very moment of conception, and therefore speaks of "knowing the Mind and seeing the Nature" (*mingxin jianxing* 明心見性). Daoism refers to the Mind of the child, and therefore speaks of "preserving the Mind and Nurturing the Nature" (*cunxin yangxing* 存心養性). As a disciple of Wang Yangming, however, he identified the Mind with *liangzhi*, which, he argues, provides a focus of integration for all of the three stages.[30] This "stage-of-life" theory of *Sanjiao heyi* proved to be very influential. For example, Li Zhi's view on the fundamental oneness of the Three Teachings is established entirely on the basis of the stage-of-life argument.[31]

Scholars today generally associate late Ming *Sanjiao heyi* at the philosophical level with the Taizhou school. As the author rightly points out, however, Wang Gen, the founder of the school, "was not an advocate" of this syncretism (79).[32] In this connection, we must examine briefly Wang Ji's relationship with some of the leading members of the Taizhou school. Wang Bi 王襞 (1511–1187), Wang Gen's second son and Li Zhi's teacher, studied with Wang Ji for two decades beginning when he was a child.[33] According to Li Zhi, Wang Bi's thought was shaped more by Wang Ji than by his father.[34] Geng Dingxiang 耿定向 (1524–1596), Jiao Hong's teacher, was also intellectually indebted to Wang Ji.[35] For example, one of his basic views that *liangzhi* is always "present" (*xianzai* 現在) and "already realized" (*xiancheng* 現成) was obviously taken from Wang Ji.[36] Thus, in the debate between Wang Ji and the Jiangyou school concerning whether *liangzhi* is universally present in all men, therefore requiring no special effort of "cultivation," Geng Dingxiang clearly sided with the former.[37]

There can be no question that the rise of *Sanjiao heyi* as a type of syncretism within the Taizhou school was due largely to the influence of Wang Ji. In several of his essays and letters, Li Zhi expressed his unbounded admiration for Wang Ji on the one hand, and was critical of Wang Gen and Luo Rufang 羅汝芳 (1515–1588) on the other.[38] He was particularly overwhelmed by Wang Ji's philosophical synthesis of Confucianism, Buddhism, and Daoism and referred to him by the honorific title of "The Venerable Master of The Three Teachings" (*Sanjiao zongshi* 三教宗師).[39] There is also evidence that Jiao Hong shared Li Zhi's enthusiasm for Wang Ji. It was Jiao Hong who provided Li Zhi with the original edition of the *Complete Works of Wang Ji*.[40] Gu Yanwu 顧炎武 (1613–1682) is certainly well grounded when he identified Li Zhi as a "second-generation disciple" of Wang Ji instead of Wang Gen.[41]

Once it is established that Wang Ji was a major source for *Sanjiao heyi* at the philosophical level in the late Ming, we can readily see that there is nothing original in Jiao Hong's syncretism. The author's theory of an "altered structure of the syncretic logic" in Jiao Hong's "noncompartmentalization" is nowhere supported by evidence. When both Wang Yangming and Wang Ji spoke of the oneness of the Three Teachings, they referred only to that part in each of the Three Teachings that deals with the *Dao* as ultimate reality definable in terms of Nature, Mind, or Destiny. However, they continued to regard the Three Teachings in their totalities as different and, therefore, proposed that each be accommodated in a separate "chamber."

This was precisely the view followed by Jiao Hong. Thus, when he was asked to compare Confucianism and Buddhism, Jiao Hong said: "As far as the principles of Mind and Nature enunciated in the Buddhist sutras are concerned, how can Confucius and Mencius add anything to them? Buddhism as a teaching (*jiao* 教), however, consists of customs of a foreign land which must not be practiced in China."[42] Elsewhere, he also quoted with approval a contemporary statement that "the teachings [of Confucianism and Buddhism] are different, but their principles are the same" (*jiaoyi er litong* 教異而理同). By "principles," he again referred to the "principles of Nature" (*xingli* 性理).[43]

The author ascribes the following view to Jiao Hong: "As the Way is always one, the Three Teachings must also be always one" (121). This is not only highly misleading but also directly contradicted by Jiao Hong's own words, as quoted by the author two pages earlier: "The teachings of the sages are different, but they are one in regard to the cultivation of the Way for the purpose of restoring Nature. The sages in ancient times had different paths [which, however, all tended toward] the same ending" (119). Obviously, in adopting this "compartmentalizing logic" of "different path same ending" here, Jiao Hong must have had the "three-chamber" metaphor in mind.

To explain away the difficulty of Jiao Hong's continuing use of "the compartmentalizing logic," the author argues that Jiao Hong developed a new notion of "complementarity" of the Three Teachings that was no longer compartmentalizing as had been the case prior to Ming times. In his own words, "For [Jiao Hong], the Three Teachings were complementary not because they each explicated a part of the Way as the other two did not, but because they could be understood in terms of one another and were mutually explanatory and illuminating the Way as truth" (120). Unfortunately, the idea of "complementarity" so defined was, again, not original with Jiao Hong. When the lay Buddhist Zhang Shangying 張商英 (1043–1121) of the Northern Song stated, "I began to understand Confucianism only after I had studied Buddhism,"[44] what he meant to say is exactly that the two teachings "could be understood in terms of each other and were mutually explanatory and illuminating." As a matter of fact, Jiao Hong twice quoted Zhang Shangying's statement to support this syncretism.[45] In the late Ming, it was Wang Ji who advocated most vigorously this notion of complementarity. He emphatically pointed out, "the truths of the other two teachings can be fully confirmed only if Confucianism is clearly understood."[46] This is obviously the other side of the same coin.

By the twelfth century at the latest, the idea that the Three Teachings, though articulated differently, nevertheless shared the same Way as a whole, already enjoyed considerable popularity among syncretists. According to one Buddhist source, Emperor Xiaozong of the Southern Song had a discussion with the Chan Master Baoyin 寶印 on the problem of the Three Teachings in 1180. The Chan Master emphasized the point that Confucius's *Lunyu* (Analects) must be read, essentially, in the light of Chan Buddhist ideas. The emperor, on the other hand, reportedly replied, "This has been my understanding all along."[47] Whether this conversation actually took place is beside the point. It is nevertheless true that some Song scholars did begin to understand passages in the *Analects* in Chan Buddhist terms. According to one source, the poet Huang Tingjian 黃庭堅 (1045–1105) failed to grasp the meaning of the sentence "There is nothing that I hide from you" (*Analects*, 7.24) until he was enlightened by the famous monk Huitang 晦堂 (1025–1100) in a typical Chan Buddhist way.[48] In his *Hu-fa lun* 護法論 (Discourse on protecting the Dharma), Zhang Shangying also interpreted "hearing the way in the morning" (*Analects*, 4.8) as "the way of *Bodhi*."[49] It is little wonder, then, that Zhu Xi 朱熹 particularly singled out the following view for severe criticism: "There cannot be two Ways in the world. Nor can the sages possess two Minds. Though Confucianism and Buddhism are different, both of them nevertheless talk about the same Principle (*li*)."[50] This seems to be exactly the type of "noncompartmentalization" that the author says "had been inconceivable" before the late Ming (15).

In support of his argument for Jiao Hong's originality in syncretism, the author devotes several pages (110–113) to a discussion of two concepts in the *Analects* that were interpreted by Jiao Hong in Buddhist terms. The first concept is about birth and death based on the saying of Confucius already mentioned above in connection with Zhang Shangying's *Discourse on Protecting the Dharma*: "If a man in the morning hears the right way, he may die in the evening without regret." According to the author, Jiao Hong took this saying "as an example of the Confucian counterpart of the Buddhist doctrine of birth and death." The second concept is the term *kong* 空 (emptiness), which appears twice in the *Analects* (9.8, 40.19). Jiao Hong also gave it a Buddhist reading and considered "emptiness" to be a designation for the "original substance of Heaven's decree." Based on these two examples, the author then jumps to the conclusion that "Jiao Hong's practice of concept-matching is produced on the condition of a type of syncretic consciousness which is no longer constituted by the logic of compartmentalization." As has been shown earlier, however, Zhang Shangying of the Northern Song had already matched the concept of "morning Way" in the *Analects* with the Buddhist concept of *bodhi*—the "enlightenment" leading to "knowing the Mind and seeing the Nature" (*shixin jianxing* 識心見性). Here it is clear that Zhang Shangying was using this passage to argue for the case that the problem of "birth and death" was "a shared concern of Buddhism and classical Confucianism," exactly as the author says of Jiao Hong (112).

From the point of view of intellectual history, however, it is necessary to point out that in practicing this kind of concept-matching, Jiao Hong most certainly did not, as the author suggests, depart from any tradition (113). One may argue, though, without being very convincing, that Zhang Shangying was too early to bear significantly on Jiao Hong's practice of concept-matching. Yet the influence of Wang Ji cannot possibly be ignored. It so happened that the two concepts in the *Analects* were also Wang Ji's favorite examples when he argued for the oneness of Confucianism and Buddhism on the philosophical level. In his commentary on the *Analects* (4.8), Wang Ji says:

> The Way (*Dao* 道) has neither birth nor death. Having heard the Way, one
> can therefore sweep through the barrier between day and night as well as
> unify birth and death. [With one's mind] being vacuous, tranquil, and

full of light, one then leaves the world as if transcending it. There is neither birth nor death to be spoken of. Hence the saying, "he may die in the evening without regret," which means that he has experienced the state of neither birth nor death.[51]

This is indeed a Buddhist reading of the *Analects* to the highest degree. With regard to the concept of *kong* in the *Analects*, Wang Ji's Buddhist point of view is equally unconcealed. He insisted that when Confucius described himself as "empty-like" (*kongkong ruye* 空空如也) or spoke of Yan Hui as "often empty" (*lükong* 屢空), he was invariably defining "the substance of the Way" (*Daoti* 道體) in terms of "emptiness."[52] Thus, in both cases, we see Jiao Hong following Wang Ji very closely. The identification of his "original substance of Heaven's decree" with Wang Ji's "substance of the Way" is singularly unmistakable. Jiao Hong once argued for the oneness of the Way on the ground that "stillness" (*ji* 寂) and "vacuity" (*xu* 虛) are equally characteristic of the "wondrous principles" of Confucianism.[53] In this case, he was again following the paradigm of Wang Ji who, in his famous debate with Nie Bao 聶豹 (1487–1563), further identified Confucius's *kong* with "vacuity" and "stillness." "To be empty is to be vacuous and still," said he, "and here lie the vital arteries of [the Confucian] Learning."[54] Undoubtedly, Jiao Hong was an active participant in the philosophical movement of *Sanjiao heyi* in the late Ming. It is also evident, however, that most of his syncretic ideas were derivative, particularly from Wang Ji. Nevertheless, to say this is not to underrate his importance. Like any other thinker in history— great or ordinary—he can be truly understood only when the historian finds the exact place that he actually occupied in his intellectual world.

"EVIDENTIAL RESEARCH" WITHOUT EVIDENCE

Speculation on "evidential research" (*kaozheng* 考證) constitutes an important part of this study of Jiao Hong. The author is apparently unfamiliar with the actual practice of "evidential research," about which he nevertheless philosophizes a great deal. His dialogical interest in intellectual history is even more pronounced in this part than elsewhere in the book. It is particularly revealing that in his discussions on the relationship between Qing "evidential research" and Han classicism, the author relies wholly on the authority of Tang Junyi and ignores all the critical reflections on the subject by scholars since the nineteenth century. With all my respect for the erudition and originality of my former teacher, I must emphatically point out that the late philosopher is hardly the best guide for "evidential research." His general observations as summarized by the author (184–185) raise more questions than they can answer. In this section, however, I prefer not to discuss the philosophical implications of Qing "evidential research," which will be dealt with toward the end of this essay.

Instead, I shall focus on the problem of theoretical construction in relation to the textual basis of Chinese intellectual history. I have found it very disturbing that the author often resorts to an extreme procrustean method to make the evidence fit his theories.

A major thesis of this study, as we shall see later, is that Jiao Hong and "evidential" scholars actually belonged to the same "discursive" tradition. To show that the latter also shared Jiao Hung's "linguistic skepticism," which "implies the belief in the necessity of going beyond language to apprehend the *Dao* through experiential realization," the author cites Dai Zhen as evidence. He says:

> Even Dai Zhen, who was a towering figure in the Qing world of "evidential research" and who proclaimed that "when the language of the past is made clear, the old Classics will become clear," did not consider the "hearing of the Dao" to be simply a matter of mastering language. Rather, he said that one "must empty" one's "dependence" on language and "experientially comprehend" (*tihui* 體會) the Classics as texts. (192)

This alleged view of Dai Zhen's is based on Dai's "Letter to Someone."[55] It is a total distortion of the original message in the letter. The distortion is made through the following three steps. First, the sentence "one must empty one's dependence" is taken out of context. As the sentence that immediately follows makes abundantly clear, what Dai Zhen urged his fellow scholar to "empty" his "dependence" on are the authorities of latter-day commentators, including those of the Han, the Jin, and, particularly, the Song Confucians. Here, in his English translation, the author surreptitiously replaces "later commentaries" with the general term "language." As a result, Dai Zhen is misrepresented as if he held that one can study the classics without depending on language at all. In fact, the point Dai Zhen really wanted to make is that the true meaning of a classical text must be grasped through the language of its own age, not that of the later commentators. Hence, the sentence immediately preceding "the hearing of the Dao" says: "In the study of the Classics, one must first investigate the meaning of each and every word and then master the grammar." The author's quoting Dai Zhen out of context is thus complete, as he deliberately ignores the sentences both immediately preceding and following it.

Second, an undue emphasis is given to the compound verb *tihui* 體會, which is then literally translated as "to experientially comprehend." In the original letter, Dai Zhen only urged his friend "to comprehend the classical texts thoroughly and with an unbiased mind" (*pingxin tihui jingwen* 平心體會經文). By playing up the verb *tihui* and manipulating it in English translation, the author creates the impression that Dai Zhen was a religious mystic who believed that one must go beyond language to comprehend the *Dao* through some sort of intuition or pure experience.

Third, Dai Zhen's view is distorted not only through commission but through omission as well. The above-quoted phrase involving *tihui* is not a complete sentence in the original text; the second half of the sentence runs as follows: "for even a slight departure from the correct reading of a single word will inevitably pervert the meaning [of the entire text] and, consequently, the Dao will be lost." With these words, Dai Zhen made it perfectly clear what he meant by "comprehending the classical text thoroughly and with an unbiased mind." It is indeed a far cry from "linguistic skepticism."

Distortions of this kind are also often found in the author's treatment of Jiao Hong's writings. In the rest of this section, however, I shall focus on one particular document that the author has used as the textual basis to build a variety of theories about Jiao Hong's thought such as his criticism of Zhu Xi, his theory of language, and, above all, the philosophical background of his interest in "evidential research." This document is the long note entitled "Zhuzi" in the *Jiaoshi bicheng* 焦氏筆乘 (Miscellaneous essays of Jiao Hong).[56] In discussing Jiao Hong's conception of the relationship between language and the *Dao*, the author begins by summarizing a passage in this note as follows: "[Jiao Hong] said that the Dao as the Ancestor or *zong* 宗 is the source of speech. [A person who] establishes a doctrine without the Ancestor is like a blind man on a journey. He will run into obstacles wherever he turns (125)." Based on this paraphrase, the author then generously imputes the following grand theory of language to Jiao Hong: "This conception of language as a human activity to represent the Dao as reality means not only that *mimesis* has a share in the construction of language as a human creation, but that language as a human creation to render a mimetic representation of the Dao as reality, is not self-possessing." Unfortunately, however, when we check this beautiful theory against the original text, there is absolutely nothing that can give it even the slightest support. To substantiate this very serious charge against the author, I must give a full account of the passage in question.

The whole question of this passage arises out of Xunzi's criticism of Mencius. In Xunzi's view, Mencius "followed the early kings, in a general way, but did not know their fundamentals (*tong* 統)."[57] In defense of Mencius, the writer of this note on "Zhuzi" says:

> As regards the criticism that [Mencius] "did not know their fundamentals," I definitely would not dare to agree with Xunzi. Why? Because the so-called *tong* 統 (fundamentals) constitutes the central purpose (*zong* 宗) of the *Dao* as well as the source of all the doctrines (*yan* 言) [of the later thinkers]. To say that [someone] establishes a doctrine (*yan*) without a central purpose (*zong*) is to liken him to a blind man on a journey who will run into obstacles wherever he turns. How can this be the proper way of talking about Mencius? Clearly, the central purpose (*zong*) of Mencius's

[doctrine] consists in [what he spoke of as] "taking hold of the will and cultivating the *qi* 氣."[58]

Now we can proceed to see exactly how the author distorts this passage. To begin with, the entire passage says nothing about the relationship between "the Dao as reality" and "language as a human creation." It deals, generally, with the problem of the "fundamentals" (*tong* 統) established by the sage-kings in pre-Confucian antiquity vis-à-vis the various doctrines (*yan* 言) developed by later thinkers and, specifically, with the Mencian doctrine in relation to the "fundamentals" (*tong*) of the "early kings." The focus of the passage is clearly on the *tong*, not the *Dao*. Here the *tong* is the first-order concept from which the *Dao* derives its "purpose" (*zong*) and in which all the later "doctrines" (*yan*), if worthy to be so-called at all, are variously rooted. The author's one-sentence summary that "The Dao as Ancestor or *zong* is the source of speech" is but a garbled quotation combined with manipulations in translation. Allow me to show how this is done and why.

As we have seen, the original statement in the text on which the above quotation is based is this: "The *tong* constitutes the purpose (*zong*) of the *Dao* as well as the source of [all the later] doctrines (*yan*)." When the author uses the phrase "the Dao as Ancestor or *zong*," he has dropped the word *tong* altogether and put *Dao* in its place. Even if we follow his translation, we can only say "the *tong* as the Ancestor of the *Dao*" but definitely not "the Dao as Ancestor." Next, he manipulates the English translation by rendering *zong* 宗 as "Ancestor" and *yan* 言 as "speech" to justify "the Dao as reality" and "language as a human creation" in his theory. He is inconsistent in translation, however, for elsewhere he also renders *zong* and *yan* in the same text as "purpose" and "doctrine," respectively. For example, on page 69 he quotes the sentence "[they] each had a purpose (*zong* 宗) in their learning" from the same note on "Zhuzi" and identifies the translated word "purpose" explicitly with the original Chinese character *zong*. As for the Chinese character *yan* 言, it appears twice in the author's quotation. Without a word of explanation, he quietly renders the first *yan* as "speech" (in "source of speech") and the second one "doctrine" (in "a doctrine without Ancestor"). Since the two identical characters run continuously right in the middle of an argument, it is impossible to justify this inconsistency in translation on the ground that the meaning of *yan* takes a sudden change from "speech" to "doctrine" or vice versa.

Now the question is why must the author go to such a length to falsify this text and manipulate his translation? My conjecture is that it has resulted from the author's procrustean determination to make the evidence fit his theory, in this case, the theory about Jiao Hong's conception of language in relation to the *Dao*. First, the author cannot possibly follow the original statement and say that, in his translation, "the *tong* is the Ancestor (*zong*) of the Dao." In the original text, *tong* (fundamentals) is supposedly something created by the "early kings." If the *tong* turns out to be the Ancestor of the *Dao*, it would certainly make the *Dao* also a "human creation" and, even worse, a derivative one at that. Therefore, the word *tong* must go so that the *Dao* can take its place as "Ancestor." Second, *zong* must be rendered as "Ancestor" not only because it makes no sense to say that "the *Dao* as purpose is the source of speech," but because, more importantly, the *Dao* identified as Ancestor suggests something of an entity that is ultimate and self-generated. Finally, *yan* must also be translated as "speech" if a "theory of language" is to be attributed to Jiao Hong at all. On the other hand, the word "doctrine," though undoubtedly the closest English equivalent for *yan* in the present context, is nevertheless too confining to serve the author's dialogical purpose.

However, all the falsifications and manipulative translations done to the note on "Zhuzi" discussed above are nothing compared to what I am going to say below. The most shocking discovery I have made about this particular text is that it is not Jiao Hong's writing at all. With the exception of the two or three introductory sentences, it turns out that this lengthy note was authored by Zhao Zhenji 趙貞吉 (Mengjing 孟靜, 1508–1576), and Jiao Hong also stated the fact in no uncertain terms in his brief introduction. I have confirmed Jiao Hong's statement in a Ming edition of Zhao Zhenji's writings in the collection of the Gest Oriental Library at Princeton University. The entire note is practically a verbatim quotation from Zhao Zhenji's "Third Letter to Educational Intendant Wang" in *Zhao Wensu Gong wenji* 趙文肅公文集, compiled by none other than Li Zhi.[59] We are almost sure that Jiao Hong must have copied Zhao's letter from this edition.

It is common knowledge that Jiao Hong's *Bicheng*, like all the other *biji* 筆記 notebooks of its kind, consists mostly of quotations from works by earlier or contemporary scholars. Methodologically, it is not permissible for an intellectual historian to simply take these quotations as Jiao Hong's own writings. The author's attitude toward his sources is so uncritical, however, that he feels no need at all to distinguish Jiao Hong's own texts from texts merely quoted by him. On the contrary, he takes it for granted that a word quoted is also a word owned by Jiao Hong. Thus, throughout this study, we find that ideas of Yang Jian 楊簡 (1140–1226), Li Heng 李衡 (1100–1178), Su Shi, Geng Dingxiang, and many others are often presented directly as Jiao Hong's own.[60] As a result, we are unable to judge whether this book is a study of Jiao Hong's thoughts, or of ideas held by a variety of writers in different periods of Chinese intellectual history. The lengthy note on "Zhuzi" is also a case in point, but it is a case that deserves special attention because several important conclusions in this study are built on the basis of this single note.

Allow me to give two more examples. First, an amusing one:

Jiao Hong said that he had very much wanted to write a book to exonerate all the philosophers who had been attacked by Zhu Xi, and thereby to demonstrate that they "each had a purpose (*zong*) in their learning." After some consideration, however, he gave up on the idea, knowing that such a book "would involve a great deal" and that he "might not be able to get it done soon." Nevertheless, we may regard as a minor fulfillment of this wish the prefaces that he wrote to the "Philosophers" (*tzu* 子) section of his *Bibliographical Treatise*, where he discussed the reasons for all the seventeen schools of his classification and may therefore be said to have demonstrated that they "each had a purpose." (69)

This account is amusing because its textual basis is again the note on "Zhuzi." Needless to say, it was Zhao Zhenji, not Jiao Hong, who had wanted to write such a book.[61] It is really amazing that in this case, Jiao Hong is made not only to take possession of Zhao's unwritten book but even to have fulfilled a wish that he had never had in the first place.

However, a much more serious example concerns Jiao Hong and the origin of the "evidential research." The author writes:

Jiao Hong desired to thematize the intentionality of all the philosophers attacked by Zhu Xi so that he could demonstrate that they "each had a purpose in their learning." This concern for textuality accounts for his interest in philology and phonetics, which could help him overcome the technical multiplicity of language and thereby restore and reapprehend a text in its original materiality as a linguistic presence. (181)

I cannot pretend to understand all the foggy abstractions in this passage such as "intentionality," "textuality," "materiality," "linguistic presence," etc., which seem to be gaining currency in some circles of Chinese studies relating to philosophy and intellectual history as if they were credentials of philosophical competence and intellectual depth. If I may hazard a guess, however, I think what the passage is saying is, in plain English, that Jiao Hong's interest in "evidential research" grew out of his philosophical stance as a pluralist and syncretist who wanted to understand each and every text in terms of the language in which it had been originally written. Whether this interpretation is valid or not is a matter that I shall discuss at a later juncture. For the time being, let us just accept it as it stands. Nevertheless, by now it must be clear to the reader that the whole argument is once more based on Zhao Zhenji's "Third Letter to Educational Intendant Wang." Hence, if the author is right, then the intellectual history of Ming-Qing China must be thoroughly revised to reinstate Zhao Zhenji as a true founder of the school of "evidential research," for the kind of "concern for textuality," if indeed accountable for the rise of "evidential research" as the author has emphatically and repeatedly insisted in this book, is clearly Zhao Zhenji's, not Jiao Hong's.

"RAGE OF COHERENCE"

Throughout this study, Jiao Hong has been presented as a late Ming Neo-Confucian syncretist who was able, supposedly, "to integrate and hold in balance the divergent systems of Buddhism, Daoism, and Confucianism from which his own philosophy evolved as a synthesis" (46). The concept "synthesis" indeed holds the key to the author's interpretation of Jiao Hong. All of Jiao Hong's ideas and works, though apparently unrelated to or inconsistent with one another, are interpreted as systematic and consistent at a deeper structural level by reference to the alleged "synthesis." Jiao Hong's use of Buddhist and Daoist ideas, for example, is thus said to be "governed by a systematicity which coheres with the discursive regularity of his thought as a holistically monistic formation" (242). Even Jiao Hong's "evidential research" is also seen as an outgrowth of his philosophical "synthesis." True, sometimes an intellectual historian can be very enlightening when he is able to penetrate beyond surface inconsistencies to hidden connections, structural or otherwise. However, when he allows this "rage of coherence" to run wild in a state of methodological anarchy, he is surely heading for disaster, with the result that historical reconstruction becomes indistinguishable from fabrication.[62]

As the author repeatedly assures us, Jiao Hong's "synthesis was not indiscriminate jumping" (181, 189). If so, Jiao Hong could not possibly have developed a philosophical synthesis without being aware of it himself. We must therefore first determine what his attitude toward "synthesis" was. According to the author: "In his tombstone inscription for Guan [Zhidao 管志道, 1536–1608], Jiao Hong characterized Guan in terms that could well have applied to himself. He said that Guan 'attempted to encompass The Three Teachings and fuse the Nine Schools of thought in order to formulate a doctrine of his own'" (38–39). Here the author is actually following a suggestion originally made by Rong Zhaozu, though he does not acknowledge it.[63] To characterize Jiao Hong in this way is quite wide of the mark, however. It is directly contradicted by Jiao Hong's self-portrait sketched specifically as a contrast to Guan Zhidao. In his letter to Guan, Jiao Hong said: "What you have wanted to accomplish is a grand synthesis of Confucianism and Chan Buddhism that is broadly inclusive. On my part, however, I am rather troubled by the fact that I have not been thoroughly enlightened about Mind and Nature. What I am after is very limited in scope. The difference between the two of us is one of quantity."[64] This self-analysis practically leaves no room for any suggestion that Jiao Hong was interested in "synthesis," despite his great diversity of intellectual pursuits and enormous erudition.

What he said in the rest of the letter is no less interesting. He emphasized that what he really needed was some simple but true faith to help him overcome the ever-intensifying dread as death was drawing near. He asked if Guan could enlighten him on this matter in the simplest terms. What is particularly note-worthy is the following confessional sentence in the letter: "I now deeply regret that throughout my life, I have played games with empty ideas and doctrines." This letter explains a great deal about why at a deep emotional level, Jiao Hong was always committed to Buddhism. As he said elsewhere, what initially aroused a person's interest in Buddhism must always be the fear of death, which can be transcended only after he has acquired Buddha's wisdom. The fear of death, he further remarked, is actually the gateway to the *Dao*. To deny that one is concerned about death at all, as some Confucians have done, is simply self-deception.[65] We may therefore assume that it was his search for some simple, true faith to cope with deep personal concerns about life and death that drew Jiao Hong ever increasingly into Buddhism. As he explicitly stated, "The princi-ple of Nature and Destiny" is more fully elucidated in Buddhism than in either Confucianism or Daoism.[66]

His brief encounter with Luo Rufang in Nanjing, probably in 1586, also con-firms his mentality as revealed in the above-quoted letter to Guan Zhidao. After listening to Luo Rufang's lectures on the Confucian ethical teaching delivered at his residence, Jiao Hong expressed a mild disappointment, and asked Luo why he withheld the highest truth in Buddhist and Confucian teachings from his audience. By this, Jiao Hong referred specifically to the Buddhist doctrine concerning "Seeing Nature and Becoming Buddha" with which, we are now told, he was then deeply concerned.[67] Later, after Luo Rufang returned home, he wrote a letter to Jiao Hong in which he made the telling point that the realization of *ren*, or "humanity," consists in caring for the suffering of other people, not suiting one's personal spiritual needs.[68] Clearly, the letter was intended as a subtle criti-cism of Jiao Hong's preoccupation with personal concerns in his pursuit of the *Dao*. Thus, we see that Jiao Hong was indeed revealing his innermost thoughts to Guan Zhidao when he said that he was, ultimately, seeking to know the truth about Mind and Nature as a simple faith to live by. "Synthesis" does not seem to have been his name of the game.

As we all know, Jiao Hong's philosophical views are expressed, generally, in a highly fragmented form consisting mostly of isolated remarks on a wide range of specific quotations. To give them clear individual formulations is al-ready difficult, to determine their originality often unwarranted, and to see all of them as integral parts of a "synthesis" definitely absurd. However, the au-thor's claim concerning Jiao Hong's "synthesis" throughout this study is too strong to be passed over wholly unnoticed. Since it is practically impossible to argue with the author point by point, I shall select a few typical examples from chapter 5, "A Synthetic Neo-Confucianism as Restructured Neo-Confucianism," to illustrate some of the difficulties involved in the author's presentation of Jiao Hong's ideas as a "synthesis." In all of these cases, I have carefully checked the author's reconstructions against the original sources.

According to the author, Jiao Hong equated the concept of "impartiality" (*gong* 公) with "humanity" (*ren* 仁), which he then variously defined as: (a) "awareness" or "enlightenment" (*jue* 覺), (b) as "penetrating the beginning and end," (c) as "the mind of humane man . . . in being able to self-establish and self-penetrate," and (d) as "generation and regeneration" (207). However, it turns out that Jiao Hong neither equated "impartiality" with "humanity" nor defined "humanity" in terms of "awareness" or "enlightenment." In the case of (a), it was a questioner who asked Jiao Hong whether he would agree with defining "humanity" as "impartiality" or "awareness" as proposed by Song Neo-Confucians. In his reply, Jiao Hong rather dismissed them as "useless conjectures."[69] As for (c) and (d), "self-establish and self-penetrate" is a quote from the *Analects* (6.30), and "generation and regeneration" is a quote from a passage of Luo Rufang. In a word, this reconstruction not only distorts Jiao Hong's text but is actually based on a few terms taken out of context from disparate sources without either logical or historical connections between them. This fits admirably well with what the author calls "indiscriminate lumping."

In the section "Learning and the Sage," we are told that:

(a) Jiao Hong considered "learning" as "easy" and "difficult" at the same time (p. 231, nn. 253–255). The original text talks about the *Dao*, however, not "learning" itself. What it says is that to learn the *Dao* is difficult, whereas obtaining the *Dao* is easy.[70]

(b) The author attributes to Jiao Hong the view that gradual cultivation requires constant "effort" (*gongfu* 工夫), which is to be maintained in the midst of daily activity and not to be neglected, even "in moments of haste" or "in seasons of danger" (p. 319, n. 257). Again, the topic in the original discussion is not "cultivation" but "humanity." Moreover, Jiao Hong emphatically pointed out that "humanity" is inherent in human nature and therefore must not be mistaken as something acquired through "effort" (*gongfu*). The passage says nothing about "learning," and the idea that cultivation requires constant "effort" is nowhere to be found.[71]

(c) Jiao Hong is said to have considered "self-confidence" (*zixin* 自信) as necessary for a person to recover his "lost" mind (p. 231, n. 258). The text is Jiao Hong's comment on two passages in the "Zhongyong" (Doctrine of the Mean; chapters 11 and 12) concerning a person's inborn ability to understand and practice the virtue of the mean. Jiao's comment only says that this ability may be "lost" unless one has "self-confidence." There is definitely no "lost" mind to be recovered.[72]

(d) To underscore the importance of the idea of self-confidence to Jiao Hong's conception of "learning," the author cites two more texts to support his argument (p. 231, n. 259, and p. 232, nn. 260, 261). Unfortunately, neither text has anything to do with "self-confidence" (*zixin*). Instead, they discuss the Confucian concept of *xin* in the sense of "having faith" or "believing" in "humanity" (*ren*) or the *Dao*.[73]

In all of the above four cases, distortions may well have resulted from the author's misunderstanding of his texts at the linguistic level.

There is one more interesting case to be added. The author quotes Jiao Hong's reply to a student's question saying, "caution, care, dread and fear are manifestations of the vitality of Nature and Destiny" (p. 240, n. 320). Since the original text only says, "caution, care, dread and fear are Nature and Destiny," I was very puzzled by the phrase "manifestations of vitality." A further check revealed that it is a translation of the last three characters—*sheng yue ran* 生躍然—at the end of the paragraph. They are not part of Jiao Hong's reply but constitute another independent sentence meaning something like "comprehension suddenly dawned on the student."[74] The author obviously mistakes "student" (*sheng* 生) for "vitality." Misreading occurring at this level is indeed incongruous with the high-flown language of the book.

My last example concerns the logic of the author's argument. The author points out that Jiao Hong's concept of learning places emphasis on scholarship and culture as values (238). This is, of course, the generally accepted view. However, since this emphasis "would seem to make Jiao Hong a champion of 'comprehensive knowledge' (*boxue* 博學) in the tradition of the Song school" (239), and therefore contradicts the author's interpretation of Jiao Hong's thought as a radical "revolt against Cheng-Zhu Orthodoxy," he finds it necessary to explain it away. Thus, he writes: "On the other hand, Jiao Hong's 'extensive study of culture and intellectual inquiry' were meant to be carried in a conceptual framework of learning or cultivation which is markedly different from Zhu Xi" (239). I must hasten to call the reader's attention to the fact that the author almost stealthily slips in the word "cultivation" toward the end of the sentence, thereby suddenly shifting his ground from the "intellectual" to the "moral" aspect. He then goes on to speak of Jiao Hong's idea of "cultivation" as "deconditioning" and "as the self-functioning of the substance of the Mind." Jiao Hong's "identification of cultivation with the self-functioning of the substance of the Mind," the author concludes, "is part of the context for his thesis that cultivation requires no effort" (240). It may be recalled that only a few pages back (231), the author explicitly states that Jiao Hong's cultivation "requires constant effort (*gongfu*)." Which version are we going to follow? However, a far more serious problem here is: How can "extensive study" and "intellectual inquiry" possibly be carried out in a "conceptual framework of cultivation" that is "deconditioning" and "requires no effort"? Does this mean that Jiao Hong's "evidential research" resulted from "the self-functioning of the substance of the Mind" and that his "extensive study" in philology, phonetics, history, etc., required "no effort" on his part at all? I must confess that the author's line of reasoning eludes my understanding completely.

Such being the case, I am wholly unconvinced that the author has a case about Jiao Hong's "synthesis." As far as we can determine on the basis of Jiao Hong's writings, he neither intended nor accomplished anything that can be called a "synthesis." The most we can say is probably that the Chinese mind was at the crossroads in the late Ming and the intellectual tendencies of this period are more clearly shown in Jiao Hong's works than elsewhere. As was well put by George Herbert Palmer long ago: "the tendencies of an age appear more distinctly in its writers of inferior rank than in those of commanding genius. The latter tell of past and future, as well as of the age in which they live. They are for all time. But on the sensitive responsive souls, of less creative power, current ideals record themselves with clearness."[75] Jiao Hong seems to have been exactly such a "sensitive responsive soul."

The author does not seem to have a clear view of the intellectual world in which Jiao Hong lived and worked. Neo-Confucianism was only one of the several intellectual trends in the late Ming. The sixteenth century, in particular, witnessed the emergence of "evidential research" in the persons of Yang Shen 楊慎 (1488–1559), Chen Yaowen 陳耀文, Mei Zhuo 梅鷟, Zheng Xiao 鄭曉 (1499–1566), Chen Di 陳第 (1541–1617), and, of course, Jiao Hong. In his study of philology, etymology, and phonology, Jiao Hong was very much in Yang Shen's debt. This is clearly shown in the inclusion of Yang Shen's bibliographies on these subjects in the *Bicheng*.[76] Jiao Hong was also one of the compilers of Yang Shen's *Sheng-an waiji* 升庵外集 in 100 *juan*. As the author himself reports, this compilation "incorporates thirty-eight works by Yang Shen on Classics, history, philology, phonology, geography, calligraphy, painting, foods and utensils, etc" (286). It was apparently through Yang Shen that Jiao Hong traced philological and phonological studies all the way back to some of the Song predecessors. "Evidential research" as an intellectual undertaking in the late Ming not only had a life all its own but also was continuous with the Song-Yüan tradition. Take, for example, the so-called "ancient script text" of the *Guwen Shangshu* 古文尚書 (Book of History). There was a long line of scholars from Song to Ming who doubted the authenticity of this text, from Wu Yu 吳域 (d. 1154), Zhu Xi, and Wu Cheng 吳澄 (1247–1331) to Mei Zhuo. Jiao Hong's interest in this cause célèbre of "evidential research" was obviously aroused by his reading of Mei Zu's work, of which he apparently possessed a manuscript copy.[77] With this deep impression in mind, he made notes of whatever discussions he encountered on the matter in the writings of his contemporaries or earlier scholars. Thus, in the *Bicheng*, we find not only an essay by Gui Youguang 歸有光[78] but also a postscript by Zhao Mengfu 趙孟頫 (1254–1322), copied from the latter's calligraphy.[79] This is a concrete illustration showing clearly how Jiao Hong, as a scholar, got himself involved in an ongoing controversy in "evidential research." There is absolutely no evidence that his involvement in this case was philosophically oriented. Thus, Jiao Hong as a Neo-Confucian thinker, as an "evidential" scholar, and, also, as a man of letters, can best be understood in terms of the three parallel intellectual trends—philosophy, philology, and literature—in the Ming. Each of the three fields can be easily shown to have been autonomous, though not unrelated. Whether these three intellectual trends can be linked to the *Zeitgeist* of Ming-Qing China is too grand a synthesis to be built on a single case of Jiao Hong. There can be no question, however, that a variety of intellectual trends of Jiao Hong's day did, as Palmer says, "record themselves with clearness" on his "sensitive responsive soul."

STRUCTURALIST REDUCTION

This study of Jiao Hong ends with a structuralist reduction. The author, following some modern scholars, believes that a fundamental restructuring took place during the late Ming and the early Qing. As a result, "monism of *qi* 氣" of the Lu-Wang school prevailed over "dualism of *li* 理 and *qi* 氣" of the Cheng-Zhu school. In the author's words, "In terms of the situation since the mid-Ming, the significance of the restructured Neo-Confucianism as monism of *qi* lies not only in the reconceptualization of *li* as the *li* of *qi* but, even more importantly, in the identification of mind with Nature or *li* and the concomitant denial of *li* as an existence independent of mind" (270). The author's own thesis, however, lies elsewhere. He argues that the "evidential research" or Han Learning of the Qing Period must be understood as having directly developed out of this restructuring. As he announces early in the book, "This restructured Neo-Confucianism has significant implications for a number of developments that continued to pertain to the early Qing. Most notably, it constituted the context in which the Qing 'evidential research' operated" (30). Since this monistic restructuring, according to him, was a unique contribution of the Lu-Wang school, Qing "evidential" scholars must therefore be viewed as intellectual heirs of late Ming Lu-Wang Neo-Confucians, including, of course, Jiao Hong. Thus, in conclusion, he argues for his structuralist reduction on the basis of the three selected cases of Jiao Hong, Dai Zhen, and Zhang Xuecheng 章學誠, as follows:

> Nevertheless, different as they were as individuals, they all participated in a monistic discursive practice, the regularities of which as a Lu-Wang heritage informed their shared outlook as monists and actually governed their differences as the rules of their differentiation. For this reason, I have argued in this book for the placing in the Lu-Wang tradition of the obvious Jiao Hong, and not so obvious Dai Zhen and Zhang Xuecheng. To use the chess game as a metaphor, the tension between Jiao Hong as a "wild Chanist" and Dai Zhen as a spokesman for "evidential research" and between Dai Zhen as a reputed philological "fox" and Zhang Xuecheng as a philosophical "hedgehog" is like the rivalry in a chess game in which the two contenders play against one another, but nonetheless play the same game. (277–278)

At first it would seem very startling to learn that Dai Zhen was actually in the Lu-Wang tradition and played the same philosophical game with Jiao Hong, for such an interpretation runs counter to Dai Zhen's self-analysis. In his "Letter to Peng Shaosheng 彭紹升 (1740–1796)," a lay Buddhist with strong Lu-Wang inclinations, Dai Zhen said that since Peng advocated the *Dao* of the Lu-Wang school, "between the two of them, the philosophical differences are total and there is not even a similarity as slight as 'a single hair.'"[80] But evidence of this sort, I am afraid, may not be able to deter the author from holding fast to his own theory, for he could well argue that he has discovered some structural "regularity" in the "discursive formation" of Jiao Hong, Dai Zhen, and Zhang Xuecheng, whatever it may mean. On this ground, he could therefore claim that he actually knows Dai Zhen better than the spokesman for "evidential research" himself. He would say that when Dai Zhen insisted that there was absolutely nothing in common between the Lu-Wang school and himself, he was only talking about the differences with respect to the substance of thought. For the author's part, his "dialogical" approach provides him with a new focus on "structural regularity," something that Dai Zhen himself was never aware of. The kind of "dialogical" approach as exemplified in this book clearly suggests that in the study of intellectual history, the only methodological rule is that anything goes. As long as a common element, structural or otherwise, real or imaginary, is detected in two or more thinkers, it is always possible to assert that they "play the same game" or belong to the same "discursive" tradition, even though they are fundamentally different in every other aspect. Thus, according to the same logic, we may argue, perhaps more convincingly, that on account of their common concerns with problems of "knowledge and action," "investigation of things," etc., Wang Yangming must be placed in the Zhu Xi tradition. We may also argue equally well that on account of their common concern with "the overcoming of metaphysics," Heidegger and Carnap played the same game.

Now, let us return to the author's thesis that Qing "evidential research" operated in the context of the restructured Neo-Confucianism of the Lu-Wang school. The author never clearly defines the relationship between the Lu-Wang school of Neo-Confucianism in the Ming and "evidential research" in the Qing as any reasonable reader would expect of him (242–223). Nor does he show us exactly how the latter "operated in the context of" the former. At one point, he does argue that Jiao Hong's philosophical concern for "textuality" was accountable for his "evidential research." Unfortunately, as has been shown above, this "concern" was not Jiao Hong's own. Now in the last chapter, the author further suggests that some kind of inner logic also existed between the monistic restructuring of the Lu-Wang school on the one hand, and the rise of "evidential research" as a learned movement on the other. We must try to determine what the author means by this suggestion.

Strictly speaking, it is more appropriate to speak of a "monistic restructuring" of the Cheng-Zhu school in the Ming than of the Lu-Wang school. As we all know, the latter was monistic all along and needed no "restructuring" at all. It was rather the former that had been dualistic in structure until Luo Qinshun 羅欽順 (1465–1547) appeared on the scene, and then restructured the *li-qi* 理氣

duality into a monism of *qi*. This is exactly why Zhang Binglin 章炳麟 (1868–1936) insisted that Dai Zhen owed his *li-qi* theory to Luo Qinshun.[81] At any rate, it was an undeniable fact that monism of *qi* as a mode of thought in the Ming-Qing times cut across all doxographical lines. If "evidential research" must be interpreted as somehow related to "monistic restructuring," which is wholly without ground, is it not more logical to place it in the Cheng-Zhu rather than in the Lu-Wang school? After all, it has been well established that Zhu Xi was one of the true founders of "evidential research" in the Neo-Confucian tradition.[82] Moreover, as I have pointed out long ago, it was Luo Qinshun who insisted that philosophical controversies must be settled by resorting ultimately to textual evidence in the Confucian classics.[83]

However, the author is determined to place "evidential research" in the Lu-Wang tradition at any cost. To accomplish this, he finds it necessary first to dismiss Luo Qinshun's "monistic restructuring" as inconsequential on the ground that Luo still retained the dualistic distinction between Mind and Nature (270–273). Next, he cites Dai Zhen's case as his main argument because Dai was the spokesman for the entire "evidential research" school. Finally, since he cannot possibly establish any historical link between Dai Zhen and the Lu-Wang school in general, and Jiao Hong in particular, he has to build his case entirely on philosophical arguments. According to him, it was actually the Lu-Wang type of monism of *qi* that "prevailed not only in Jiao Hong in the late Ming, but also in Dai Zhen and Zhang Xuecheng in the Qing" (273). By this he means "a form of monism of *qi* which entailed the view of both *li* as *li* of *qi* and Nature as the Nature of mind" (272).

At this point, finally, the author's "dialogue with the past" turns to historical reconstruction, which gives us something tangible to work with. Now, we must determine whether all the three thinkers—Jiao Hong, Dai Zhen, and Zhang Xuecheng—were monists of *qi* answering precisely to the author's description. Of the three, Dai Zhen may indeed be characterized in such terms even though he defined *li*, *qi*, Mind, and Nature all differently from the Lu-Wang Neo-Confucian philosophy. How about Jiao Hong and Zhang Xuecheng? By the author's own admission, Zhang Xuecheng "did not engage in a sustained discourse on metaphysics of *li* and *qi* or the ontology of Nature and Mind" (273). In fact, Zhang Xuecheng never discussed the relationships between *li* and *qi* or Nature and Mind. No matter how hard the author tries to argue circuitously, as well as analogously, he nevertheless falls short of naming Zhang Xuecheng a "monist of *qi*."

Jiao Hong did not engage in a sustained discourse on *li* and *qi* either. The only reference to *qi* of any significance cited by the author is Jiao Hong's comment on the "nurturing of *qi*" in the *Mencius* (223). This is the famous "flood-like *qi*" (*haoran zhi qi* 浩然之氣), which Zhu Xi also characterized as "not the ordinary kind of *qi*."[84] But Jiao did not, as the author says, identify it with either Mind or Nature. On the contrary, he specifically distinguished Mind from *qi* in the following way: "Mind may be right or wrong, but *qi* makes no distinctions whatever."[85] Since this is an isolated remark on a technical term in the *Mencius* without even mentioning the concept of *li*, it is quite impossible to determine whether there is anything monistic in it. We are also not very sure about Jiao Hong's "identification of Mind with Nature." In one discussion, he expressed the view that the two imply each other like water and waves. However, he also showed some hesitancy in identifying Mind and Nature as one. Therefore, he said that the two are originally indistinguishable. Nevertheless, since they bear two different names, it is also permissible to distinguish the one from the other. In the end, he reached the following formulation: "Where Mind arises, Nature disappears; where Mind disappears, Nature emerges."[86] Yet to firmly establish the identification would entail a detailed knowledge of Jiao Hong's views of Mind and Nature, respectively, which are difficult to obtain, owing to the fragmentary nature of his philosophical remarks. The author does write a great deal about them. Unfortunately, as in the previous cases, his reconstructions are often vitiated by his uncritical use of sources. Take, for example, his treatment of Jiao Hong's idea of "Mind." The author attributes the following statements as characteristically Jiao Hong's: Mind "has neither a body nor location" and "is not a thing which can be held or pointed to." It is "without past or present." "The human mind is the *Dao* . . . the world calls it Mind because there is nothing of which it is not conscious" (214). But all of these quotes are from Yang Jian, a leading disciple of Lu Xiangshan.[87] The author also puts into Jiao Hong's mouth the following words: Mind "does not regard anything as external (*wuwai* 無外)" (214), which, again, turns out to be a sentence in an essay entitled "Xing Lun" 性論 (A Discourse on Nature) by another Song scholar, Fan Jun, whose essay on Mind was quoted by Zhu Xi.[88]

Confronted with such highly dubious reconstructions, I cannot possibly bring myself to share the author's confidence that Jiao Hong was a "monist of *qi*" according to his strict definition. Thus, out of the three cases of the author's own choosing, it is at least very doubtful whether two of them—Zhang Xuecheng and Jiao Hong—can be definitely established as having conceived *li* as *li* of *qi* and identified Mind with Nature. In that case, then, what evidence do we have to assert that all three of them "participated in a monistic discursive practice"? Moreover, even if we can establish the fact that most monists of *qi* in the late Ming were followers of the Lu-Wang school, there is still no basis either to identify Jiao Hong as one of them or to place Dai Zhen of the middle Qing in the Lu-Wang tradition. After all, not all that glitters is gold.

Suppose we accept the author's view that Jiao Hong, Dai Zhen, and Zhang Xuecheng were all monists of the Lu-Wang persuasion. We are still left with the thorny question of what connections to make between this monism of *qi* and "evidential research" as a learned movement. Logical connection? Historical connection? Or both? We cannot help asking the following questions: Why did a "restructuring" in Neo-Confucian metaphysics and ontology necessarily lead to the rise of philology? Precisely in what way did this particular kind of "monistic restructuring," as the author insists, constitute the "context" in which the Qing "evidential research" operated? Does this mean that in order to be able to conduct "evidential research," a scholar's mind must first be structurally reoriented in terms of not only monism of *qi* but also "identification of Mind with Nature or *li*"? If so, why, with the sole exception of Dai Zhen, did none of the mid-Qing "evidential" scholars show even the slightest interest in Neo-Confucian metaphysics and ontology? On questions like these, which are central to his thesis, the author is completely silent. Very recently, Irene Bloom has written:

> Many of the major Qing thinkers, including Wang Fuzhi (1619–1692) in the seventeenth century, and Dai Zhen in the eighteenth century, also espoused a philosophy of *qi*, and it may well be argued that the philosophy of *qi* was a necessary concomitant of, if not a precondition for, the new style of evidential research in the Qing. But, whereas the philosophy of *qi* was no doubt one of the underlying themes of Qing thought, and clearly a concern of several of the most prominent Qing thinkers, it appears not to have been the active focus of interest and debate throughout most of the period.[89]

Bloom has certainly put her finger on the right spot when she wonders why the philosophy of *qi* "appears not to have been the active focus of interest and debate" in Qing intellectual history. She also exemplifies the cautiousness and sensitivity of an intellectual historian in being able to rein her horse to a halt on the very edge of a precipice. The temptation to link philosophy of *qi* to "evidential research" is not easy to resist, but the fall from the precipice could be fatal.

NOTES

1.   Romanizations have been changed to Pinyin in quotes from Professor Ch'ien's book.—Eds.

2.   Dominick LaCapra, "Rethinking Intellectual History and Reading Texts," in *Modern European Intellectual History: Reappraisals and New Perspectives*, ed. Dominick LaCapra and Steven L. Kaplan (Ithaca, N.Y.: Cornell University Press, 1982), esp. pp. 78–85.

3.   Hayden White, "Method and Ideology in Intellectual History: The Case of Henry Adams," in LaCapra and Kaplan, *Modern European Intellectual History*, 283.

4.   Hans-Georg Gadamer, *Truth and Method* (London: Sheed & Ward, 1975), 337.

5.   Paul Ricoeur, *Hermeneutics and the Human Sciences*, ed. and trans. John B. Thompson (Cambridge: Cambridge University Press, 1981), 146.

6.   David Couzens Hoy, *The Critical Circle, Literature, History, and Philosophical Hermeneutics* (Berkeley: University of California Press, 1978), 77.

7. Gadamer, *Truth and Method*, 273.

8. Mark Poster, "The Future According to Foucault: *The Archaeology of Knowledge* and Intellectual History," in LaCapra and Kaplan, *Modern European Intellectual History*, 137.

9. Herbert L. Dreyfus and Paul Rabinow, *Michel Foucault: Beyond Structuralism and Hermeneutics*, 2nd ed. (Chicago: University of Chicago Press, 1983), 16–17.

10. Li Zhi, *Xu fenshu* 續焚書 (Beijing: Zhonghua, 1959), 68.

11. Zhu Guozhen, *Yongchuang xiaopin* 湧幢小品 (Shanghai: Zhonghua, 1959), *juan* 10: 216–217. See also Joanna F. Handlin, *Action in Late Ming Thought: The Reorientation of Lü K'un and Other Scholar-Officials* (Berkeley: University of California Press, 1983), 110.

12. *Yongchuang xiaopin*, *juan* 16: 369.

13. Jiao Hong, *Danyuan ji* 澹園集, *Jinling congshu*, 金陵叢書, 13:18b (Taipei: Lixing shuju, n.d.).

14. Ibid., 28:12a–b.

15. Ibid., 16:6b.

16. Chen Yuan 陳垣, *Mingji dianqian Fojiao kao* 明季滇黔佛教考 (Beijing: Zhonghua, 1962), 118–126.

17. *Han Shan dashi nianpu shushu* 憨山大師年譜疏注 (Taipei: Guangwen, 1967), 10–15.

18. Shen Defu 沈德符, *Wanli yehuo bian* 萬曆野獲編 (Beijing: Zhonghua, 1959), *juan* 27: 687–688.

19. Shen Zengzhi 沈曾植, *Hairi lou zhacong* 海日樓劄叢 (Shanghai: Zhonghua, 1962), 214.

20. Judith A. Berling, *The Syncretic Religion of Lin Chao-en* (New York: Columbia University Press, 1980), 216.

21. Ibid., 3.

22. Yu Songqing 喻松青, *Ming-Qing bailian jiao yanjiu* 明清白蓮教研究 (Chengdu: Sichuan renmin, 1987), 49.

23. For this text, see ibid., 242. Liu Mi's 劉謐 view may be found in his *Sanjiao pingxin lun* 三教平心論, in *Taishô shinshu daizôkyo* 大正新大藏經, vol. 52, no. 2117, 781. Lin Zhao-en also discussed this distinction. See Berling, *The Syncretic Religion of Lin Chao-en*, 201.

24. Quoted in Yu Songqing, *Ming-Qing bailian jiao yanjiu*, 242.

25. *Wang Wencheng Gong quanshu* 王文成公全書, SBCK, *juan* 34, *nianpu*, 959–960. For a slightly different version, see Liu Ts'un-yan, "Taoist Self-Cultivation in Ming Thought," in *Self and Society in Ming Thought*, ed. Wm. Theodore de Bary and the Conference on Ming Thought (New York: Columbia University Press, 1970), 316–317.

26. As late as the mid-seventeenth century, for instance, Fang Yizhi 方以智 (1610–1670) still more or less followed the Three-Chamber metaphor in his version of *Sanjiao heyi*. See Yü Ying-shih 余英時, *Fang Yizhi wanjie kao* 方以智晚節考, revised and expanded edition (Taipei: Yunchen, 1986), 66.

27. *Longxi Wang xiansheng quanji* 龍溪王先生全集 (hereafter *Longxi ji*), in *Jinshi hanji congkan* 近世漢籍叢刊, ed. Okada Takehiko 岡田武彥 and Araki Kengo 荒木見悟 (Taipei: Guangwen, 1972 [reprint]), *juan* 17: 1316–1318.

28. For Li Zhi, see his "Sanjiao guiru shuo" 三教歸儒說, in *Xu fenshu*, 77–78; for Lin Zhao-en, see Sakai Tadao 酒井忠夫, *Chûgoku zensho no kenkyu* 中國善書の研究 (Tokyo: Kôbundô, 1960), esp. pp. 266–276.

29. *Longxi ji, juan* 1: 133–135.

30. Ibid., *juan* 7: 508–510.

31. *Xu fenshu*, 1–2.

32. Wang Gen 王艮 was actually a radical anti-Buddhist. See his *nianpu* 年譜, in *Wang xinzhai quanji* 王心齋全集, *Jinshi hanji congkan*, 18.

33. Huang Zongxi 黃宗羲, *The Records of Ming Scholars*, ed. Julia Ching (Honolulu: University of Hawaii Press, 1987), 179.

34. *Xu fenshu*, 92.

35. *Longxi ji, juan* 10: 923–929; also *juan* 4: 360–369.

36. Julia Ching, "Keng Ting-hsiang," in *Dictionary of Ming Biography, 1368–1644*, ed. L. Carrington Goodrich and Chaoying Fang (New York: Columbia University Press, 1976), 719; Julia Ching, "Wang Chi," in ibid., 1353.

37. See Wang Ji's letter to Luo Hongxian 羅洪先 in *Longxi ji, juan* 10: 715, and Geng Dianxiang's view in Huang Zongxi, *MRXA, SBBY*, 35:6b.

38. *Fenshu* (Beijing: Zhonghua, 1961), 45, and 121–122; *Xu fenshu*, 28–29.

39. *Xu fenshu*, 26.

40. *Fenshu*, 45, and 118; *Xu fenshu*, 26.

41. *Yuan chaoben Rizhi lu* 原抄本日知録, punctuated by Xu Wenshan 徐文珊 (Taipei: Minglun, 1970), 538. For modern views, see Rong Zhaozu 容肇祖, *Mingdai sixiangshi* 明代思想史 (Taipei: Taiwan Kaiming, 1962 [reprint]), 235–237; Qian Mu 錢穆, "Lüelun Wangxue liubian" 略論王學流變, in his *Zhongguo xueshu sixiangshi luncong* 中國學術思想史論叢 (Taipei: Dongda, 1979), 7:161–162; Shimada Kenji 島田虔次, *Chugoku ni okeru kindai shii no zasetsu* 中國における近代思惟の挫折 (Tokyo: Hebonsha, 1949), 297–299.

42. *Danyuan ji*, 48:13a.

43. *Danyuan xuji*, 10:25a–b.

44. Zhipan 志磐, *Fozu tongji* 佛祖統記, in *Daizōkyo* 大正藏, vol. 49, no. 2035, 429.

45. *Danyuan ji*, 12:8a; Jiao Hong, *Jiaoshi bicheng xuji* (hereafter *Bicheng xu*), *GXJBCS*, 2:169.

46. *Longxi ji, juan* 7: 499; *juan* 17: 1318.

47. *Fozu tongji*, 429.

48. Luo Dajing 羅大經, *Helin yulu* 鶴林玉露 (Beijing: Zhonghua, 1983), 280.

49. Zhang Shangying, *Hufa lun, Daizōkyo*, vol. 52, no. 2114, 638.

50. *ZYL*, punctuated edition (Beijing: Zhonghua, 1986), 8:3015. The quoted words are from Zheng Xing's 鄭興 preface to Zhang Shangying's *Hufa lun*, dated 1171, 637.

51. *Longxi ji, juan* 3: 288–289.

52. Ibid., *juan* 3: 293; *juan* 6: 467–468.

53. *Danyuan ji*, 23:15a–b.

54. *Longxi ji, juan* 6: 467–468.

55. Dai Zhen 戴震, *MZS* (Beijing: Zhonghua, 1961), 173–174.

56. *Bicheng* 筆乘, 4:102–105.

57. Liang Qixiong 梁啟雄, *Xunzi jianshi* 荀子簡釋 (Hong Kong: Zhonghua, 1974), 62. I have followed the translation by Derk Bodde in Fung Yu-lan, *History of Chinese Philosophy* (Princeton: Princeton University Press, 1952), 1:281.

58. *Bicheng*, 4:103. "Taking hold of the will and cultivating the *qi*" may be found in *Mencius*, 2A.2.

59. This *wenji* is an undated Ming edition in two *juan* and the letter, entitled "Yu Wang Duxue disan shu" 與王督學第三書, i.e., "Fu Guangxi Duxue Wang Jing suo shu qi san" 復廣西督學王敬所書其三, may be found in *juan* 1: 51a–56b.

60. See, for example, 124n25; 234n280 and 282; 235n288; 236n291.

61. *Zhao Wensu Gong wenji*, *juan* 1: 56a.

62. I owe the term "rage of coherence" to Peter Gay, "The Social History of Ideas: Ernst Cassirer and After," in *The Critical Spirit: Essays in Honor of Herbert Marcuse*, ed. Kurt H. Wolff and Barrington Moore Jr. (Boston: Beacon Press, 1967), esp. pp. 114–117.

63. *Mingdai sixiangshi*, 264.

64. *Danyuan xu*, 5:11 a–b.

65. *Bicheng xu*, 2:187.

66. Ibid., 1:169.

67. *Xutan zhiquan* 盱壇直詮 (*Luo Jinxi yulu*) 羅近溪語錄 (Taipei: Guangwen, 1967), *juan*, *xu*, 10b–11a.

68. *Xutan zhiquan*, *juan*, *xu*, 11a–b.

69. *Danyuan ji*, 47:1b.

70. *Bicheng xu*, 2:185.

71. *Danyuan ji*, 49:2a–b.

72. Ibid., 47:9a.

73. Ibid., 49:2b, *Bicheng xu*, 1:151–152.

74. Ibid., 48:5b.

75. Quoted in Arthur O. Lovejoy, *The Great Chain of Being: A Study of the History of an Idea* (Cambridge, Mass.: Harvard University Press, 1957), 20.

76. *Bicheng*, 6:124–126; 6:127–128.

77. Ibid., 1:4. It seems inaccurate to say, as do Arthur W. Hummel and Chaoyang Fang, that Jiao Hong "was unable to consult the book himself." See *Dictionary of Ming Biography*, 11:1059.

78. *Bicheng xu*, 3:200. See also Gui Youguang, *Zhenchuan xiansheng ji* 震川先生集, SBCK, *juan* 1: 31. There are only a few minor discrepancies between Jiao Hong's quotation and the original text.

79. *Bicheng xu*, 3:210–211.

80. MZS, 161.

81. Zhang Binglin, *Guoxue lüeshuo* 國學略說, lectures edited by Sun Shiyang 孫世揚 (Hong Kong: Xianggang huanqiu wenhua fuwushe, 1972), 157.

82. Hu Shih, "The Scientific Spirit and Method in Chinese Philosophy," in *The Chinese Mind: Essentials of Chinese Philosophy and Culture*, ed. Charles A. Moore (Honolulu: University of Hawaii Press, 1967), 118–127; Qian Mu, *Zhuzi xin xue-an* (Taipei: Sanmin, 1971), 5:296–341.

83. Yü Ying-shih 余英時, *Lishi yu sixiang* 歷史與思想 (Taipei: Lianjing, 1987 [twelfth printing]), 101–102. For the original statement in English translation, see Irene Bloom, ed.

and trans., *Knowledge Painfully Acquired: The K'un-chih chi*, by Lo Ch'in-shun (New York: Columbia University Press, 1987), 143–145.

84. *ZYL*, 4:1259.

85. *Danyuan ji*, 48:8b.

86. Ibid., 49:3a; 6:4b and *Bicheng*, 1:15.

87. *Bicheng xu*, 1:156.

88. *Bicheng xu*, 4:213.

89. Bloom, *Knowledge Painfully Acquired*, 31–32.

14. Toward an Interpretation of the Intellectual Transition in Seventeenth-Century China

This is a review article of *The Unfolding of Neo-Confucianism* (New York: Columbia University Press, 1975), edited by William Theodore de Bary and the Conference on Seventeenth-Century Chinese Thought.

The Unfolding of Neo-Confucianism (hereafter *Unfolding*) is a product of a conference held at the Villa Serbelloni, Bellagio, Italy, in September 1970. This book consists of thirteen essays, as follows: Araki Kengo, "Confucianism and Buddhism in the Late Ming"; Pei-yi Wu, "The Spiritual Autobiography of Te-ch'ing (Deqing)"; Kristin Yü Greenblatt, "Chu-hung (Zhuhong) and Lay Buddhism in the Late Ming"; Wm. Theodore de Bary, "Neo-Confucian Cultivation and the Seventeenth-Century 'Enlightenment'"; Richard John Lynn, "Orthodoxy and Enlightenment: Wang Shih-chen's (Shizhen) Theory of Poetry and Its Antecedents"; Edward T. Ch'ien, "Chiao Hung (Jiao Hong) and the Revolt Against Ch'eng-Chu (Cheng-Zhu) Orthodoxy"; T'ang Chun-i (Tang Junyi), "Liu Tsung-chou's (Zongzhou) Doctrine of Moral Mind and Practice and His Critique of Wang Yang-ming"; William S. Atwell, "From Education to Politics: The Fu She"; Willard J. Peterson, "Fang I-chih (Yizhi): Western Learning and the 'Investigation of Things'"; Ian McMorran, "Wang Fu-chih (Fuzhi) and the Neo-Confucian Tradition"; Chung-ying Cheng, "Reason, Substance, and Human Desires in Seventeenth-Century Neo-Confucianism"; Wei-ming Tu, "Yen Yüan (Yan Yuan): From Inner Experience to Lived Concreteness"; and Wing-tsit Chan, "The *Hsing-li Ching-i* (*Xingli jingyi*) and the Ch'eng-Chu (Cheng-Zhu)

School of the Seventeenth Century." A long introduction by de Bary not only places the thirteen essays in proper historical perspective but also surveys the topography of the inner world of Neo-Confucianism.

All the essays are solidly based on original research. In terms of period, subject matter, and scholarly quality, this book makes an excellent sequel to the same editor's *Self and Society in Ming Thought* (hereafter *Self and Society*) published in 1970. Like *Self and Society*, *Unfolding* is also a work of international scholarly collaboration. The contributions by Araki Kengo and Tang Junyi are actually distillates of lifetime studies of the two leading scholars in their respective fields rather than conference papers in the ordinary sense. The reader is therefore referred to Araki's *Mindai Shisō kenkyū* 明代思想研究 (Research on Ming Dynasty Thought) (Tokyo: Sōbunsha, 1972; especially chap. 9) and Tang's *Zhongguo zhexue yuanlun, yuan jiao pian* 中國哲學原論—原教篇 (On The Essentials of Chinese Philosophy—On The Essentials of the Doctrine) (Taipei: Taiwan xuesheng shuju [1977] 1975; especially chap. 18) where the same topics are more fully treated. This book is dedicated to Tang Junyi in "recognition of a lifetime devoted to Neo-Confucian studies and in appreciation of the personal qualities of mind and spirit which he brought to our collaborative work." In hindsight, this dedication was timely and fitting, for Professor Tang passed away in Hong Kong in early 1978. It is particularly symbolic of a confirmed Confucianist that Professor Tang, having suffered from a long illness, died all of a sudden owing to his great emotional excitement over the news that Confucius was being restored to some grace in China through an article published in the historical journal *Lishi yanjiu* (Historical Research) (1978, no. 1).

Since the 1953 publication of "A Reappraisal of Neo-Confucianism" in Arthur F. Wright's *Studies in Chinese Thought* (Chicago: University of Chicago Press), Professor de Bary has been a leading scholar in promoting Neo-Confucian studies in the United States. Dissatisfied with the stereotyped modern characterization of Neo-Confucianism as a "rigid orthodoxy and ideological tool of an authoritarian system," he has not only written extensively to unfold the Neo-Confucian interiority but also provided opportunities for others to do the same by organizing a number of workshops as well as conferences, including the Regional Seminar in Neo-Confucian Studies at Columbia University. Without necessarily denying that the Neo-Confucian record was a mixed one (3), de Bary nevertheless urges us to see Neo-Confucianism as a spirituality of universal significance in its own right. According to him, "Neo-Confucian spirituality affords a degree of openness to new experience, and—especially in Ming thought—develops an enlarged, more expansive view of what it means to be human" (24). It is precisely this new approach that distinguishes the *Unfolding* (and of course the *Self and Society* as well) from other Neo-Confucian studies in the West.

As de Bary rightly points out, the seventeenth century represents a turning point in the development of Neo-Confucianism (4). While the nature of this turning is still, as it has always been, open to discussion, all the essays in the *Unfolding* have helped, each in its own way, to illuminate some of the fundamental changes in seventeenth-century Chinese thought. In what follows, I propose to discuss the various findings in the *Unfolding* in the historical context of this Ming-Qing intellectual transition, for in the opinion of the present reviewer, the total contribution of the volume lies precisely in this area.

Although the new developments in seventeenth-century Chinese thought have been variously interpreted, basically there are only two approaches to the problem. One is the internal interpretation, which sees these developments as germinating from the inner growth of the Song-Ming Neo-Confucian tradition. Another is the environmental interpretation, which takes them as responses to external changes in late Ming and early Qing society. Of the environmental interpretation, however, two schools may be further distinguished: a political school, represented by Liang Qichao and Zhang Binglin, stresses the tremendous impact of and fall of the Ming dynasty and, particularly, the Manchu conquest on the Chinese thinking world, and a socioeconomic school, represented by Hou Wailu, discerns in the Ming-Qing intellectual transition a class consciousness of a budding "civic bourgeoisie" (*shimin* 市民), which Hou characterizes as the "Enlightenment" in early modern China.

The internal and environmental interpretations are by no means mutually exclusive, however. On the contrary, any attempt at a balanced view of the transition must take into full account the various findings of both approaches, for it is a simple historical truth that there were two aspects to this transition. On the one hand, it evolved out of the Neo-Confucian tradition and, on the other hand, it also echoed with the deepening of the late Ming political and social crisis. Therefore, in actual practice, historians rarely deal with one aspect of the transition to the total exclusion of the other. Although the *Unfolding* as a whole falls into the category of internal approach, William S. Atwell's essay on the Fu She is par excellence a study of intellectual responses to the historical situation of the time. In his study on Neo-Confucian cultivation, de Bary has made a most comprehensive analysis of the Neo-Confucian roots of the seventeenth-century "Enlightenment." And yet this internal approach has not in the least affected the author's sensitivity to the environmental aspect of thought. As so well put by the author: "with the added shock of dynastic collapse and the damage to Chinese self-confidence of subjection to alien rule, the intellectual despair of the Confucian at mid-century was such as to generate both a deeper questioning of tradition and an effort to reestablish it on more solid foundations" (190). A most significant and obvious change in seventeenth-century thought took place in the domain of Neo-Confucian metaphysics. In his paper, Chung-ying Cheng examined *li–qi* 理一氣 (reason–substance, or principle–ether) and *li–yu* 理一欲 (reason–desire or principle–desire) relationships in Wang Fuzhi 王夫之 (1619–1692) and a number of other thinkers such as Huang Zongxi 黃宗羲 (1610–1695), Chen Que 陳確 (1604–1677), Li Yong 李顒 (1627–1705), Fang

Yizhi 方以智 (1611–1671), Yan Yuan 顏元 (1635–1704), and Li Gong 李塨 (1659–1733). He concludes:

> In our analysis, all these philosophers have demonstrated, with degrees of variation, opposition to Song-Ming Neo-Confucianism in a framework of anti-dualistic naturalism in both metaphysics and moral philosophy. The anti-dualistic naturalism in metaphysics consists in upholding the ontological primacy of indeterminate substance and the inherence of reason in the development of indeterminate substance. In morality it consists in asserting that the fulfillment of reason is inseparable from the fulfillment of desire, and of the intrinsic right and goodness of natural desire. (502)

Cheng is certainly right in pointing out a common tendency in seventeenth-century Neo-Confucianism toward antidualistic naturalism. This general observation of Cheng's is further confirmed in Ian McMorran's penetrating analysis of Wang Fuzhi's thought. I fully agree with his statement, "It was an ether-based monistic conception of the universe which provided the foundation on which Wang Fuzhi constructed his whole philosophical system, and which gave it its coherent structure" (437). He goes on to show that Wang's monistic view is by no means confined to li–qi and li–yu relationships, but extends to all other dualities in the Neo-Confucian tradition. Thus, in the realm of human nature, Wang takes the so-called universal nature (*tiandi zhi xing* 天地之性, or "moral nature" [*yili zhi xing* 義理之性]) and physical nature (*qizhi zhi xing* 氣質之性) as two aspects of the same thing, with the former being immanent in the latter. Discussing the origins and evolution of civilization, Wang insists that the Way (*Dao* 道) arises from and changes with concrete things (or "implements," *qi*). In Wang's philosophy of history, principle (*li* 理) and conditions (*shi* 勢) also form a unity similar to that of *li* and *qi*.[1]

This new trend of thought, however, did not begin in the seventeenth century. As de Bary has shown convincingly, Luo Qinshun 羅欽順 (1465–1547), the leading middle Ming philosopher of the Cheng-Zhu school, already turned Zhu Xi's *li*–*qi* dualism into a monism of *qi*. Moreover, Luo also challenged the orthodox view that physical desires are evil.[2] De Bary is well grounded when he says: "there is in fact a considerable development in the Cheng-Zhu school of the Ming which contributes to the philosophy of *qi* and reconverges with the Wang Yangming school's vitalistic emphasis on *qi* in the seventeenth century" (200). By the early seventeenth century, when "ideas circulated freely among thinkers and schools" (201), both Wang Yangming's revisionists and critics such as Liu Zongzhou 劉宗周 (1578–1645) and Gao Panlong 高攀龍 (1562–1626) further developed the monistic scheme of things, and therefore paved the way for the generation of Huang Zongxi, Gu Yanwu, and Wang Fuzhi to bring the intellectual transition to its final stage.

As the findings of Cheng, McMorran, and de Bary have conclusively shown, the new tendency in Neo-Confucian metaphysics not only originated in the middle Ming but also cut across the sectarian lines of the Cheng-Zhu and Lu-Wang schools. Now the problem that confronts us is how to explain its rise and great popularity. According to Cheng, "although there were many cultural and even political factors which occasioned this movement among Confucian scholars, the phenomenon can nevertheless be regarded as an internal dialectical development of Neo-Confucianism." By this, Cheng means that "the essentially Confucian mentality has arrived at a state of consistency and perfection and has therefore come to see the weakness of Neo-Confucianism under the conceptual influence of Buddhism" (471–472). There is indeed some truth in this observation, but as a historical explanation, it still falls short of precision.

I believe it is important to determine, first of all, what this metaphysical critique of Neo-Confucianism signifies in the historical context of the Ming-Qing transition. As far as I can see, it is a sure indication that Neo-Confucianism was undergoing a fundamental transformation from quietism to activism. Since the time of Zhu Xi, but especially during the Ming Period, Neo-Confucianists turned inwardly to spiritual cultivation of the self, owing, it must be noted, to the unfavorable external conditions for the realization of the Confucian *Dao*. Quiet-sitting and metaphysical speculation therefore became particularly characteristic of the life of Ming Neo-Confucianists from Chen Xianzhang 陳獻章 (1428–1500) onward. There can be no doubt that many of them must have reached a very high spiritual level of self-mastery and self-enjoyment. Nevertheless, it is also undeniable that Ming Neo-Confucianism on the whole was rather quietistically and inwardly oriented. The philosophy of Wang Yangming, with its emphasis on "the unity of knowledge and action," did set Neo-Confucianism in motion in an activistic direction, and it contributed to the growth of new trends in late Ming thought, including monism of *qi* and what de Bary calls "vitalism," which stressed the actualities of life and human nature (194–196). However, the immediate followers of Wang Yangming still developed the master's new ideas, especially the idea of *liangzhi* 良知 (innate knowledge), within the old quietist framework. As Huang Zongxi rightly observed, since Wang Yangming's emphasis on *liangzhi* had been more or less placed on its function to turn the mind inwardly (*shoulian* 收斂), his leading disciples such as Luo Hongxian 羅洪先 (1506–1564), Zou Shouyi 鄒守益 (1491–1562), and Wang Ji 王畿 (1498–1583) all tended to develop the idea of *liangzhi* in terms of "quiescence" or "stillness."[3]

It is highly significant that the Neo-Confucian movement to reformulate its metaphysical assumptions in the early seventeenth century went hand in hand with a shift in spiritual cultivation of the self from quietism to activism. For example, according to de Bary, Gao Panlong and Liu Zongzhou both incorporated into their philosophical systems "a monism of ether, a dynamic view of man's moral nature, and the effort to re-establish a bridge between subjective and objective morality." At the same time, "though both still practiced quiet-sitting, there was a subtle shift under way toward a more outward and outgoing view of the cultivation of one's nature, and away from the view of principle or nature as an immutable inner essence to be perceived in a quiescent state and expressed in exemplary conduct" (202). In this connection, perhaps the best illustration is provided by the case of Yan Yuan 顏元 (1635–1704) as analyzed in Wei-ming Tu's paper.[4] In early Qing intellectual history, Yan Yuan is particularly known as a vehement critic of the Cheng-Zhu school. In metaphysics and moral philosophy, he holds that principle (*li*) is inherent in ether (*qi*) and man's "moral nature" in "physical nature"; in spiritual cultivation, he rejects quiet-sitting and replaces it with what he calls "practicing reverential demeanor by sitting upright" (*duanzuo xigong* 端坐習恭). As Tu points out: "In the accounts of Yan Yuan's life it seems evident that he had never questioned the prominence of self-cultivation in the Confucian hierarchy of values. Even after he had become disillusioned with the Cheng-Zhu school, he still followed a rigorous plan of self-discipline. Ironically, his ritualized life style could have been praised by the Cheng-Zhu Confucianists as an excellent example of self-control" (523). At first sight, it is indeed difficult to distinguish Yan's kind of spiritual cultivation from that of his Song-Ming predecessors. Even in his own day, his disciples already questioned whether the master's "sitting upright" was the same as "quiet-sitting."[5] Now in the light of what de Bary has said about "a subtle shift" in the self-cultivation of Gao Panlong and Liu Zongzhou, it becomes clear that Yan's "sitting upright" can be better understood as activistically oriented. Tu undoubtedly hit the mark when he says, "activism in the form of moral practice" was Yan's "central concern" (519). Yan's activism is best expressed in his definition of sagehood. He says: "The Five Emperors, Three Kings, Duke of Zhou, and Confucius are all sages who taught the world how to move forward. They are all sages who shaped the Way (*Dao*) of the world through movement."[6] Hence, his sages, like Huang Zongxi's candidates for canonization, were, in de Bary's words, "men of action," "not sitting sages" (203). Unlike Wang Fuzhi, as Cheng says, Yan is not metaphysically inclined or interested in formulating his own metaphysics (491). Why, then, was it necessary for him to take a strong metaphysical position? A reasonable explanation, perhaps, would be that the transformation from quietism to activism in the metaphysically oriented Neo-Confucian tradition required a new metaphysical justification to begin with. Without limiting it to the original context of Wang Yangming's philosophy, we may say that "unity of knowledge and action" cannot be realized in a world in which principle and ether are bifurcated.

From the point of view of internal interpretation, however, a further question inevitably arises, namely, how is the transformation from quietism to activism in Neo-Confucianism itself to be accounted for? It would not do simply to refer it to external stimulation. For in the final analysis, it still takes some essence in Neo-Confucianism to respond to stimulation. I think the answer must be sought in the very nature of the Confucian *Dao* (including, of course, its Neo-Confucian variant). As we all know, from the very beginning, the Confucian *Dao* is supposed to function in two major areas of human activities, which have been traditionally identified as "sageness [or sageliness, as Professor Yü translates it elsewhere—Eds.] within and kingliness without." Or, as more clearly redefined by the seventeenth-century Neo-Confucian scholar Shao Tingcai 邵廷采 (1648–1711), the *Dao* functions "outwardly to put the world in order and inwardly to nourish man's nature and feelings."[7]

When the Neo-Confucian movement began in the tenth and eleventh centuries, it began with the high hope "to put the world in order." It was largely the frustrating experience of the failure of Wang Anshi's reforms that turned Neo-Confucianism inwardly toward the realm of "sageness within."[8] Yet the basic Confucian impulse to reorder the world was always there and waited for a better opportunity to reemerge. Marx once said, "Philosophers have only interpreted the world in various ways, but the real task is to alter it." Here, of course, Marx is referring to Western philosophers. In the case of Neo-Confucian philosophers, rather the opposite is true; they always considered it their real task to activate the *Dao* in order to alter the world. The profound political and social crisis at the end of Ming provided them with an opportunity to perform this task. Viewed in this light, it is only natural that a fundamental inner transformation from quietism to activism took place in seventeenth-century Neo-Confucianism.

By late Ming times, political and social decadence had reached such a degree that it was no longer possible to contain the Confucian impulse to reorder the world in the realm of ideas. As a result, it broke out in large-scale social actions, as exemplified by the Donglin and Fu She movements. In his study on the Fu She, Atwell shows clearly that the central purpose of this literary society was "to revive ancient teachings, so that future generations will be able to provide useful service [for the country]" (346). As Atwell rightly observes, "to revive the ancient teachings . . . was not a call for a blind, archconservative attempt to restore ancient institutions," but to "make creative use of the lessons of the past to solve contemporary problems." However, since the revival of "ancient teachings" centrally involved the Confucian classics, it must be noted that the Fu She was also genuinely concerned with the scholarly qualities of classical studies, which reached the lowest point at the end of Ming.[9] In this regard, the Fu She was actually following the example of the Donglin. Gu Xiancheng 顧憲成 (1550–1612), in a statement of purpose written for the Donglin group, listed "honoring the classics" (*zunjing* 尊經) as one of the four essentials.[10] In its own day, the Fu She 復社 was nicknamed "the Junior Donglin 東林" not only because many of its members were sons and grandsons of Donglin martyrs but also because the former was a spiritual heir to the latter.[11] The differences between the Donglin and the Fu She resulted mainly from the fact that the two groups were active in different times.

As Atwell's study shows, the Fu She, like many other Ming literary societies, including the original Ying She 應社, was able to attract a large number of followers because of the valuable services it rendered to the candidates in passing the provincial and metropolitan examinations. The literary societies not only selected and edited model *bagu* (eight-legged) essays for publication (in collaboration with bookstores) but also provided their members with expert *bagu* criticisms. The growth of the Fu She to a membership body of over three thousand apparently owed a great deal to its remarkable record of examination successes. However, it was not the purpose of the founders of the Fu She to promote examination success as such. On the contrary, their original purpose was to breathe new life into the then much degenerated *bagu* style, which had, in the course of time, become increasingly alienated from the teachings of the Confucian classics.[12] A central aspect of their effort to revive the "ancient teachings" was to combine genuine classical scholarship with the writing of the *bagu* essays.

Take the Ying She, the predecessor of Fu She, as an example. One of its projects related to studies in preparation for the examinations was to divide the members into five small groups, "each of which did detailed research on one of the Five Classics. They then held meetings, exchanged information, and ultimately published collections of essays based on their findings" (339). As Zhang Pu 張溥 (1602–1641), a founder of both the Ying She and the Fu She, explicitly stated, "When the Ying She was founded, it set as its ultimate goal to honor the classics and revive the ancient teachings."[13]As Atwell says, the Fu She leaders believed that "social and political reform depended upon improvements in education" (347). This is true enough, but it may be further concluded that they also believed that improvements in education depended on a creative combination of the examination system with what Zhang Pu calls "the wisdom embodied in the Classics" (345). Indeed, if we take Neo-Confucian metaphysics to be a high culture, then the *bagu* writings may very well be regarded as its popular counterpart. The fact that Neo-Confucianists now shifted their focus of attention from metaphysics to the *bagu* is a vivid illustration of a new tendency in late Ming thought, which stressed what de Bary calls "the actualities of life and the immediacy of the present" (196).[14]

Atwell's study further contributes to our understanding of the Ming-Qing intellectual transition by relating the Fu She to the new Neo-Confucian emphasis on "practical statesmanship" (*jingshi zhiyong* 經世致用). It is particularly important that our attention is called to the compilation of the monumental work entitled *Huang Ming jingshi wenbian* 皇明經世文編 (Illustrious Ming Dynasty Documents on Statecraft) by Chen Zilong 陳子龍 (1608–1647) and others in 1638 (348). The idea of *jingshi* (lit. "ordering the world") is so central to Confucianism that it is practically interchangeable with that of "kingliness without" in meaning. With the rise of Neo-Confucian activism since the late Ming, it had become a value shared by virtually all thinkers. In this sense, it would be very misleading to speak of *jingshi* as a school in the early Qing.[15] This new emphasis on *jingshi* or, rather, setting the world right, must also be understood as an integral part of the intellectual transition, because it arose directly from a new conception of *Dao*. Since Song times, the Confucian *Dao* has been generally defined in terms of a bifurcation between *ti* (substance) and *yong* (function). In Ming Neo-Confucianism, the substance of *Dao* was mainly conceived as a self-sufficient metaphysical reality of a moral character, which nevertheless generates a function of unlimited creativity. Therefore, it can be assumed that the function of *Dao* necessarily implies "ordering the world" (*jingshi*), at least in theory. However, since the central concern of Ming Neo-Confucianists was rather "how to become a sage," the function of *Dao* was in actual practice only confined to the realm of moral cultivation of the self and never reached into the external world. In the seventeenth century, there was a fundamental shift in emphasis from inwardness to outwardness with regard to the nature of *Dao*. When Gu Yanwu 顧炎武 (1613–1682), an outstanding member of the Fu She, spoke of "illuminating the *Dao*" (*ming Dao* 明道) and "saving the world" (*jiushi* 救世), he was clearly talking about the Confucian *Dao* that can set the world right, not a metaphysical reality to be perceived through introspection.[16] Elsewhere he further remarked, "I decided not to do any writing unless it had a relation to the actual affairs of the contemporary world as indicated in the Six Classics."[17] Thus, according to Gu, social utility or practicality was in the very nature of *Dao* as embodied in the Confucian classics. As a matter of fact, the Song-Ming bifurcation of *Dao* in terms of *ti* and *yong* was rejected outright as a Buddhist concept. It is interesting to note that Li Yong and Li Gong, though very different in intellectual orientations, arrived at the same conclusion that the *ti–yong* 體一用 duality was non-Confucian in origin.[18] Li Yong was in complete agreement with his friend Gu Yanwu when he said that if we must maintain the *tiyong* distinction, then the genuine Confucian *ti* consists in "illuminating the *Dao*," whereas the real Confucian *yong* consists in "putting the world in order" (*jingshi* 經世).[19]

This discussion, I believe, serves well to illustrate the above-quoted statement of the Fu She "to revive ancient teachings so that future generations will be able to provide useful service [for the country]." From the point of view of internal interpretation, the idea of *jingshi* may be shown to have been inherent in the Neo-Confucian transition from quietism to activism. Early in the sixteenth century, Zhao Zhenji 趙貞吉 (1508–1576), a member of the Taizhou school, already planned to compile a historical work entitled *Jingshi tong* 經世通 (A Comprehensive Study of Ordering the World).[20] Li Zhi 李贄 (1527–1602) of the same school also created a new biographical category of *jingshi* in his comprehensive history, the *Cangshu* 藏書 (A book to be hidden away).[21] Slightly later, Feng Yingjing 馮應京 (1555–1606), a friend of Matteo Ricci, edited an encyclopedia called *Huang Ming jingshi, shiyong bian* 皇明經世實用編 (Practical Ming Documents on Statecraft) in 28 *juan*. Feng's encyclopedia was highly influential in bringing the idea of *jingshi* to Neo-Confucian consciousness. Li

Gong particularly praised the work for its combination of ancient Confucian learning with contemporary practicality.[22] Judging by the title, it is more than probable that Chen Zilong's *Huang Ming jingshi wenbian* was compiled under its influence. These instances not only confirm a recent observation that the rise of classical studies in the early Qing may have been partially related to the *jingshi* trend of the late Ming but also enable us to date the beginning of the trend more precisely in the second half of the sixteenth century.[23]

Finally, in connection with the *jingshi* trend, mention must also be made of Wing-tsit Chan's careful analysis of the Cheng-Zhu school in the early Qing, an aspect that has been unjustly neglected in most modern studies of the intellectual developments of this period. Chan's detailed examinations of the contents and arrangements of Li Guangdi 李光地 (1642–1718)'s *Xingli jingyi* 性理精義 (Essential meaning of nature and principle) has led him to discover that, among other things, it "put matters of practical concern ahead of matters of abstract interest" (561). Li's treatment of the Great Ultimate has been cited as an illustration, which indicates a clear shift from abstract matters to the concrete. More important, Li Guangdi was by no means the only Cheng-Zhu scholar to show such a shift in intellectual orientation. On the contrary, the whole Cheng-Zhu school in the early Qing moved in the direction of "putting the world in order and practical application (*jingshi zhi yong*)." Lu Shiyi 陸世儀 (1611–1672), an eminent leader of the school, expressed the *jingshi* spirit most vividly when he said that, as quoted by Chan: "The Six Classics are not the only things people of today should study. They must study astronomy, geography, river works and irrigation, military craft, etc., which are all of practical use. Vulgar scholars who talk about nature and destiny with an air of superiority are of no help to the world." Chan is right in pointing out, "the spirit of practical application was in the air" (564). Chan's findings have firmly established the fact that, like the new emphasis on *qi* in Neo-Confucian metaphysics, the *jingshi* trend also cut across the sectarian lines of the Cheng-Zhu and Lu-Wang schools.

The intellectual transition of seventeenth-century Neo-Confucianism eventually landed in what is commonly called *kaozheng* 考證 (evidential investigation) of the Qing Period, which stressed, among other things, philological explications of classical texts. (For convenience, I shall simply follow David S. Nivison by referring to it as Qing philology.) At first glance, Ming metaphysics and Qing philology have almost nothing in common except that both share the same Confucian ancestry. It is precisely for this reason that the rise of Qing philology has been interpreted as a negative reaction against Ming metaphysics. I have dealt with this problem extensively elsewhere and come to see more continuities than discontinuities in terms of the "inner logic" of this Neo-Confucian development.[24] Now, the two case studies by Edward T. Ch'ien and Willard J. Peterson also throw new light on the problem.

Ch'ien's study is interesting because it sets as its central task to deal with "the apparent contradiction of Jiao Hong 焦竑 (1540–1620) as a left-winger and as a pioneer of Qing critical scholarship." More significantly, it suggests "the possibility of the left-wing Wang Yangming School of Mind being a positive source from which the early Qing development of Han Learning may properly be viewed as a logical outgrowth" (276). As a left-winger, Jiao Hong, as Ch'ien shows, was essentially a Neo-Confucianist with a strong tendency toward syncretism. His readiness to embrace Buddhist and Daoist ideas clearly indicates the great influence of both his teacher Luo Rufang 羅汝芳 (1515–1588), who was thoroughly versed in Buddhism and Daoism, and his friend Li Zhi, who figured centrally in the late Ming movement of the so-called "union of the Three Teachings in one" (*Sanjiao heyi* 三教合一). As a pioneer of Qing philology, Jiao Hong was among the earliest Neo-Confucianists of the late Ming to advocate a linguistic approach to the Confucian classics. Jiao Hong said, as quoted by Ch'ien, "The *Book of Odes* [Shijing] should be discussed in terms of its sound and the rest of the classics should be understood by way of their language" (292). Ch'ien concludes:

> Jiao Hong synthesized his Buddhist- and Daoist-tinged concept of the Way as ineffable truth with his basically Confucian valuation of learning, and established in his thought a philosophical pluralism which, together with his stress on the self's independence and the mind's autonomy, led logically to his rejection of the authority of Cheng-Zhu orthodoxy and to his advocacy of linguistic analysis as a method for the direct study of the classics. His pioneering in critical scholarship is thus deeply rooted in the philosophy of the Taizhou school. (296)

I am somewhat puzzled by this statement. If by "linguistic analysis" and "critical scholarship" the author is referring to Qing philology (the Han Learning), then I must confess that I fail to see its "logical" connectedness with Jiao Hong's "philosophical pluralism" or "the philosophy of the Taizhou school." In the first place, it was precisely on the ground that "the Buddhist- and Daoist-tinged concept of the Way" needed purification that Qing philologists urged people to return to the original sources of the classics. In the second place, none of the philosophers of the Taizhou school before Jiao Hong, from Wang Gen to Luo Rufang and Li Zhi, ever displayed any interest in *kaozheng* scholarship. Obviously, the source of Jiao Hong's philological approach to the classics lay elsewhere.

I also wish to take this opportunity to clarify my own view on the subject as twice quoted in Ch'ien's paper. First, in an earlier paper of mine, I did not simply identify "intellectualism" with the Cheng-Zhu school as Ch'ien seems to suggest (293–294). Nor did I equate the Lu-Wang school with "anti-intellectualism." All I said is that there was a tension between anti-intellectualism and intellectualism in the Neo-Confucian tradition, which resulted, respectively, from the Lu-Wang school's emphasis on *zun dexing* 尊德性 (honoring the moral nature) and the Cheng-Zhu school's emphasis on *dao wenxue* 道問學 (following the path of inquiry and study). In the original Neo-Confucian context, however, these two aspects are mutually complementary. *Zun dexing* implies, above all, the awakening of moral faith through the understanding of our true nature, which partakes of the moral quality of *Dao*. On the other hand, *dao wenxue* implies that every advancement in objective knowledge, which is supposed to possess a built-in moral quality, is a step further toward the awakening of moral faith. Hence, generally speaking, *zun dexing* and *dao wenxue* may be understood, respectively, as the moral and intellectual elements in Neo-Confucianism.

It is easy to understand why "following the path of inquiry and study" (*dao wenxue*) would give rise to intellectualism. The inner connection between "honoring the moral nature" (*zun dexing*) and anti-intellectualism needs a word of explanation, however. This is the case because there was a group of Neo-Confucianists, represented mainly by the Lu-Wang school, who held the view that recovery of the moral nature of man comes solely from cultivation of "moral knowledge" (*dexing zhi zhi* 德性之知), which deals with a higher realm beyond the reach of ordinary "intellectual knowledge" (*wenjian zhi zhi* 聞見之知, lit. "knowledge from hearing and seeing"). Developing this view to its extreme, one would even say that intellectual knowledge is a hindrance to moral cultivation of the self. It was mainly on this ground that many of the immediate followers of Wang Yangming became anti-intellectual.[25] In the history of Neo-Confucianism, however, the Ming Period is characteristically an age of *zun dexing* with a clear subordination of knowledge to moral cultivation. In the early Ming, even the Cheng-Zhu school also showed a tendency toward anti-intellectualism. Not until the late sixteenth and early seventeenth centuries did the Neo-Confucian pendulum gradually but steadily swing back to the intellectualistic side. So when I talked about "intellectualism" and "anti-intellectualism," I was not exactly thinking in sectarian terms of the Cheng-Zhu and the Lu-Wang. Rather, I was referring to a fundamental transformation in one of the Neo-Confucian assumptions that affected all its adherents irrespective of schools.

Second, I did not suggest, as Ch'ien says, that Jiao Hong's interest in philological scholarship is a "result" of his "intellectualism" (296). My original suggestion was that Jiao Hong may be fruitfully viewed as a transitional figure whose intellectual life is highly symbolic of the Neo-Confucian transition from *zun dexing* to *dao wenxue*, or, if properly understood, from "anti-intellectualism" to "intellectualism."[26] He was bringing the age of *zun dexing* to an end when he developed his "philosophical pluralism" in terms of "union of the Three Teachings in one," which was to be rejected by virtually all the leading Neo-Confucianists of the early Qing such as Gu Yanwu, Huang Zongxi, and Wang Fuzhi. But he was ushering in a new age of *dao wenxue* when he engaged in philological exercises that, from the point of view of the School of the Mind, would be totally unrelated to the recovery of one's moral nature. Whether Jiao

Hong's thought is self-consistent is a matter of interpretation. However, the undeniable fact remains that his intellectual life is not completely consistent with either Ming metaphysics or Qing philology.

In the same sense that Jiao Hong is a transitional figure, the thought and scholarship of Fang Yizhi 方以智 (1611–1671) also bears marks that are characteristically transitional. Before the fall of Beijing in 1644, he had already basically completed his *opus magnum* in *kaozheng* scholarship, the monumental *Tongya* 通雅 (Comprehensive Studies). However, in the last twenty years of his life as a Buddhist monk, due largely to changed circumstances, he turned to preach the gospels of "union of the Three Teachings in one" in his own way. Evidence clearly shows that this syncretist element in his thinking was a family inheritance. His maternal grandfather, Wu Yingbin 吳應賓, was a disciple of Lin Zhao-en 林兆恩 (1517–1598), the "Master of Three Teachings,"[27] but the simple fact that he was born seventy years later than Jiao Hong made an important difference: Jiao Hong lived in the beginning of the transition, whereas Fang Yizhi lived at the end of it. This explains, at least in part, why Fang's philology was enthusiastically received throughout the Qing Period while his philosophical ideas quickly fell into oblivion. By contrast, it was Jiao's lectures on Neo-Confucian metaphysics that attracted the audience, in Huang Zongxi's words, "like torrents flowing toward the bed."[28] It is also important to know that Fang Yizhi's interest in philology remained with him to the end of his life. As Peterson points out, "Fang as a monk had not repudiated his former endeavors even though he did not continue to pursue them" (376). It may be further noted, however, that it was lack of books rather than unwillingness on his part that had prevented Fang from continuing to pursue philological studies in his monastic life.[29] Moreover, Fang as a Buddhist monk was still so deeply concerned with Confucian scholarship that he formulated a thesis for the Neo-Confucian Academy at Qingyuan that says, "the study of *li* (principle) consists in the study of the classics" (*cang lixue yu jingxue* 藏理學於經學).[30] It is indeed amazing that Fang's formulation, apparently arrived at independently, bears a family resemblance to the famous thesis of Gu Yanwu's, "the study of *li* (principle) is the study of the classics" (*jingxue ji lixue* 經學即理學), almost as close as identical twins. This may be taken as a sure indication that the Neo-Confucian movement of "following the path of inquiry and study" (*dao wenxue*) was now well under way.

Peterson's study focuses on Fang's relationship with Western Learning as introduced to China by Jesuit missionaries. Nevertheless, it bears significantly on the Ming-Qing intellectual transition by relating Fang's approach to Western Learning to the problem of *gewu* 格物 (investigation of things). Peterson is on firm ground when he states, "Fang Yizhi was part of a movement under way in the seventeenth century which directed the attentions of scholars away from prevailing interpretations of *gewu* to what became known as Qing learning" (369). A careful comparison of Wang Yangming's theory of *gewu* with Fang's inclusive definition of *wu* has led Peterson to conclude that coming more than a century after Wang Yangming had dismissed "things of the world" as unworthy of investigation compared with what was to be found within our minds, Fang's definition of *wu* is part of his attempt to reinvest "things" with intellectual significance. (278) More important, through his case study of Fang Yizhi, Peterson has succeeded in establishing a historical link between Ming metaphysics and Qing philology. "In addition to redirecting the goal of *gewu*," Peterson says: "Fang was involved in the development of a new interpretation of the proper means of acquiring knowledge. His stress on accumulating items of knowledge and its opposition to introspection as a method anticipate two of the characteristics of the School of Evidential Research (*kaozheng xue* 考證學) which rose to prominence in Qing" (400). Viewed from this perspective, Fang Yizhi provides us with one of the best illustrations of the rise of Qing Confucian intellectualism.

Elsewhere I have suggested that "the intellectual transition from the Ming to the Qing is characterized mainly by a shift of emphasis in Neo-Confucianism from the moral element to the intellectual element."[31] Fang Yizhi's redirecting of *gewu* at that which is external to our minds is precisely such a shift of emphasis. In this connection, we may also cite Liu Zongzhou's view of "intellectual knowledge" as another example. Since Wang Yangming, the distinction between "moral knowledge" and "intellectual knowledge" had been stressed in such a way as to take "intellectual knowledge" to be at best morally irrelevant. Deeply dissatisfied with this extreme anti-intellectualism, Liu rejected the distinction as false. According to him, man's moral consciousness not only is inseparable from his intellectual nature but also depends on it for operation.[32] As the late Professor Tang Junyi rightly observed, Liu emphasized classical and historical studies much more than Wang Yangming and his direct disciples had. Therefore, the transition from Liu as a moral teacher to Huang Zongxi as a Confucian scholar is easily understandable (327).

From the point of view of internal interpretation, the growth of Qing classical and historical scholarship may be explained in a number of ways. The *jingshi* trend, discussed earlier, is one, and the introduction of textual evidence into metaphysical debates is another. However, in view of the cases of Fang Yizhi and Liu Zongzhou, perhaps none is more fundamental than the fact that the Confucian spirit of "inquiry and study" (*dao wenxue*), which had been suppressed all too long, was actively seeking ways for self-expression. As vividly exemplified by the new direction of Fang Yizhi's *gewu*, the transition from *zun dexing* to *dao wenxue* actually went hand in hand with the Neo-Confucian transformation from quietism to activism as well as from inwardness to outwardness.

Finally, the three valuable studies on late Ming Buddhism by Araki, Wu, and Greenblatt also deepen our understanding of the Neo-Confucian transition. As de Bary points out in the preface, Buddhist revival in the sixteenth and seventeenth centuries was largely a response to a strong stimulus of the Wang Yangming school, and therefore reflected Neo-Confucian tendencies. The complicated relationships between Buddhism and Neo-Confucianism since the time of Wang Yangming are clearly delineated in Araki's essay. The general situation is summed up admirably well in an interesting remark by the eminent monk Ouyi Zhixu 藕益智旭 (1599–1655) that "The rise or fall of the Buddha Dharma is contingent upon the rise or fall of Confucianism" (54). This completely confirms the keen observation of the great late Qing scholar Shen Zengzhi on this matter.[33] Araki's characterization of the Buddhist faith during this period as "closely linked to the everyday world" (56) shows that Buddhism, like Neo-Confucianism, was also undergoing a process of fundamental change from inward quietism to outward activism. As Greenblatt puts it so well, "The lay Buddhist movement at the end of the Ming was more activist than contemplative, more moralistic than theological, more world-affirming than world-rejecting." One concrete example is provided by the author's hero, Zhuhong 袾宏 (1535–1615), who placed a strong emphasis on moral action and relatively neglected doctrinal questions (131). Even the Neo-Confucian idea of *jingshi* also found its counterpart in late Ming Buddhism. This is particularly clear in Zibo Daguan's 紫柏達觀 (1544–1604) redefinition of the term *yong* 用 (function). For Daguan, *yong* was no longer a passive function of "response" as in Chan Buddhism. On the contrary, it "meant to work upon the world of historical reality by means of the enlightenment experience" (59). Thus, the Buddhist Dharma, like the Confucian *Dao*, was also activated to function in the external world in a positive way.

Most significant of all, we can even discern in late Ming Buddhism a movement toward intellectualism parallel to the Neo-Confucian development from *zun dexing* to *dao wenxue*. Wu points out the great popularity of the *Sûrangamasûtra* (Lengyan jing 楞嚴經) during Ming times and mentions Zhuhong and Zhixu among the well-known commentators of the sûtra. Deqing 德清 (1546–1623), the hero in Wu's study, we are told, also produced three exegetical works on it (80). As a matter of fact, this interest in the *Lengyan jing* shows only a small tip of an iceberg in view of the remarkable growth of Buddhist scholarship in this period. For example, Zhixu, perhaps the greatest Buddhist scholar of the Ming dynasty, wrote no less than fifty works with a total of about two hundred *juan*. His *Yuezang zhijin* 閱藏知津 (A guide to the study of the canon), a comprehensive annotated bibliography of Buddhist literature, has remained an important reference work to this day.

As we know, Chan Buddhism stresses direct transmission from mind to mind "without the use of written texts" (*buli wenzi* 不立文字). Now in late Ming times, just as Neo-Confucianists returned to their classical sources, Buddhist monks also began to develop a radically different view about "written texts." Zibo Daguan (also known as Zhenke 真可), for instance, believed that the truth can be obtained only if one knows how to "make use of written texts without being bound by them" (*zhi wenzi li wenzi* 執文字立文字).[34] However, fifty years later when Buddhist intellectualism was well under way, Zhixu came to the radical conclusion that "To stray from the scripture by a single word is to step into heresy." According to him, true teachings are contained in scriptural texts, and no one can obtain the truth through meditation without the help of teachings. It was for this reason that he turned to study the *Lengyan jing* and other important sûtras.[35]

The rise of Buddhist intellectualism may be further illustrated by the nationwide growth of Buddhist libraries at the end of Ming. According to Chen Yuan, an authority on Ming-Qing Buddhist history, there was a general movement in the Buddhist world to build up monastic libraries. In the late sixteenth and early seventeenth centuries, almost every good-sized monastery in Yunnan and Guizhou possessed a complete set of the Buddhist canon. Zibo Daguan also contributed importantly to this movement, for it was largely due to his promotion that the entire canon was published for the first time in the ordinary book form that greatly facilitated collection and reading.[36] Chen Yuan says:

> At the end of Ming, *kaozheng* studies developed as a result of the flourishing of the School of the Mind, whereas Buddhist scholarship arose as a result of the revival of Buddhism. Everybody was aware that it was no longer possible to persuade others simply by referring to introspection and without making use of written texts. Therefore, Confucianism and Buddhism began to take a drastic change at about the same time. Since then, the emphasis was equally placed on learning and moral nature, which, though apparently contradictory, nevertheless complemented each other.[37]

Terse and to the point, Chen Yuan has captured the spirit of the transition.

In conclusion, we must ask: What happened to the *jingshi* trend that had asserted itself so powerfully in the early stage of the transition? Why was it that the transition eventually ended in classical philology? Neither of these questions is answerable in terms of an internal approach to intellectual history alone. As I have said elsewhere: "The external functioning of *Dao* in terms of putting the world in order . . . transcended the realm of thought and depended for its final solution on external factors, which were by definition beyond the control of Confucian thinkers as individuals."[38] I believe the first question is closely related to what Thomas A. Metzger calls "the problem of linkage," an important idea worthy of further explorations.[39] To comment on the second question, I merely wish to call attention to the fate of the Yan-Li school in the early Qing. Unfortunately, with all his emphasis on "practicality" and "utility," Yan Yuan's enthusiasm to reorder the society led him nowhere because he failed to establish any "linkage" between his inner world of Confucian ideas and the external world of political reality. Ironically, with all his strong feelings against "the world of paper and ink," Yan Yuan was not even successful in preventing his leading disciple, Li Gong, from getting involved in philological controversies, for as long as Yan Yuan and Li Gong claimed that their ideas were derived from Confucius and Mencius, they could never get away from all sorts of philological problems inherent in the Confucian text. External forces apart, here we see that the Yan-Li school was also pushed by its own logic from the world of *jingshi* to the world of *kaozheng*.

Limited by the nature of my topic, I have not discussed Lynn's perceptive study of Wang Shizhen's theory of poetry, which certainly deserves the close attention of both literary and intellectual historians. Therefore, a brief note is in order. Free from modern "organic" bias, Lynn shows cultural sensitivity in his evaluation of the Chinese poetic tradition as a whole. In his attempt to establish a link between Chinese poetics and philosophy, his essay adds another dimension to the unfolding of Neo-Confucianism. He is undoubtedly right in suggesting that "enlightenment" (*wu* 悟) in either philosophy or poetics is essentially the same thing (256). Thirty years ago, Qian Zhongshu 錢鍾書 (1910–1998) also struck a similar note and quoted Gao Panlong and Lu Shiyi to support his argument in *Tanyi lu* 談藝録 (On the art of poetry), a modern classic of literary criticism apparently not consulted by Lynn.[40] In fact, *On the Art of Poetry* contains extensive discussions on Wang Shizhen's 王士禎 theory of poetry and its antecedents, including Lu Shiyong's 陸時雍 use of the term *shenyun* as noted in Lynn's essay (p. 264, n. 112).

Finally, it is interesting, as Lynn points out, that Yuan Hongdao 袁宏道 (1568–1610) wished to elevate drama and vernacular fiction to the same exalted position as Tang poetry (237). In this regard, attention may be called to the fact that a century later, Liu Jizhuang 劉繼莊 (1648–1695) even went further by comparing drama and fiction to the Six Classics.[41] Such a change in attitude toward drama and fiction, it seems to me, must also be understood against the background of the intellectual transition in seventeenth-century China.

NOTES

1. On Wang's philosophy of history, see articles by Yao Weiyuan 姚薇元 and Xiao Jiefu 5 蕭捷父 in *Wang Chuanshan xueshu taolun ji* 王船山學術討論集 (Beijing: Zhonghua, 1965), 285–331. [Romanization changed to Pinyin in quotations from Professor de Bary's book.—Eds.]

2. This point was first noted by Zhang Binglin 章炳麟 (Taiyan 太炎) in one of his lectures on Sinology. See his *Guoxue lüeshuo* 國學略說 (Hong Kong: Xianggang huanqiu wenhua fuwushe, 1972), 157.

3. Huang Zongxi 黃宗羲, *Mingru xue-an* 明儒學案 (hereafter *MRXA*), WYWK, 2:89.

4. Tu says that Liang Qichao's lecture on Yan Yuan in 1923 aroused the interest of Zhang Binglin (513). This is erroneous. Zhang's first essay on Yan Yuan entitled "Yanxue" 顏學 is included in his *Qiushu* 訄書, written before the end of the Qing in 1910.

5. *Yan Xizhai xiansheng yanxing lu* 顏習齋先生言行録, Yan-Li congshu 顏李叢書, *hsia*, 6a.

6. Ibid., *hsia*, 8b.

7. Shao Tingcai, "A Letter in Reply to Li Gong" (Da Lixian Li Shugu shu), in *Sifu Tang ji* 思復堂集, Shaoxing xianzheng yishu edition (1887–1893) 紹興先正遺書本, 7:1, 10b.

8. See Wm. Theodore de Bary, "A Reappraisal of Neo-Confucianism," in *Studies in Chinese Thought*, ed. Arthur Wright (Chicago: University of Chicago Press, 1953), 105–106.

9. Pi Xirui 皮錫瑞, *Jingxue lishi* 經學歷史, annotated by Zhou Yutong 周予同 (Hong Kong: Xianggang huanqiu wenhua fuwushe, 1973), 283–294. See also Edward Ch'ien's translation in *The Unfolding of Neo-Confucianism*, ed. William Theodore de Bary and the Conference on Seventeenth-Century Chinese Thought (New York and London: Columbia University Press, 1975), 293.

10. Rong Zhaozu 容肇祖, *Mingdai sixiangshi* 明代思想史 (Taipei: Kaiming, [1962] 1966), 291–292.

11. Xie Guozhen 謝國楨, *Ming-Qing zhi ji dangshe yundong kao* 明清之際黨社運動考 (Shanghai: Shangwu, 1934), 148.

12. See Shang Yanliu 商衍鎏, *Qingdai keju kaoshi shulue* 清代科舉考試述略 (Beijing: Sanlian, 1958), 238–241.

13. Quoted in Xie Guozhen, *Ming-Qing zhi ji dangshe yundong kao*, 159.

14. In early Qing, Lü Liuliang 呂留良 (1629–1683) also made a creative use of the *bagu* 八股 essay as a popular vehicle to preach his version of the Cheng-Zhu teachings. See Qian Mu 錢穆, *Zhongguo jin sanbainian xueshu shi* 中國近三百年學術史 (hereafter *ZJSNXS*) (Shanghai: Shangwu, 1937 [1948]), 1:177.

15. Liang Ch'i-ch'ao, *Intellectual Trends in the Ch'ing Period*, trans. Emmanuel C. Y. Hsü (Cambridge, Mass.: Harvard University Press, 1959), 84.

16. Gu Yanwu, *Gu Tinglin shiwen ji* 顧亭林詩文集 (Beijing: Zhonghua, 1959), 103.

17. Ibid., 95. English translation in Liang, *Intellectual Trends in the Ch'ing Period*, 32.

18. See Li Yong 李顒, *Erqu ji* 二曲集 (Beijing: Tianhuaguan daiyin,, 1930), 16:7a–9b. Li Gong 李塨, *Shugu houji* 恕谷後集, Yan-Li congshu, 13:5a–6a.

19. *Erqu ji*, 16:8a. Gu's reply is quoted on 9a.

20. *MRXA*, 6:100.

21. See chapters 13 and 14 in the *Cangshu*.

22. *Shugu houji*, 13:4a.

23. See Lu Baoqian 陸寶千, "Lun Qingdai jingxue" 論清代經學, in *Lishi xuebao* 歷史學報 3 (February 1975): 1–22.

24. "Some Preliminary Observations on the Rise of Qing Confucian Intellectualism," *Tsing Hua Journal of Chinese Studies*, n.s., 11, nos. 1 and 2 (December 1975): 105–146; *Lishi yu sixiang* 歷史與思想 (Taipei: Lianjing, 1976), 87–165; *Lun Dai Zhen yu Zhang Xuecheng* 論戴震與章學誠 (Hong Kong: Longmen, 1976).

25. On the anti-intellectualism of the Wang Yangming school, see Xiong Shili 熊十力, *Shili yuyao* 十力語要 (Taipei: Letian, 1971), 4:24a.

26. For further clarification of these two terms, see "Qing Intellectualism," 137–144.

27. See my *Fang Yizhi wanjie kao* 方以智晚節考 (Hong Kong: Xinya yanjiusuo, 1972), 64–65.

28. *MRXA*, 7:46.

29. See Yizhi's son Fang Zhonglu's proposal to build up a library at Qingyuan mountain in *Qingyuan shan zhilüe* 青原山志略 (1669 edition), 3:33a–35b.

30. Ibid., "fa-fan" section, 4b.

31. "Qing Intellectualism," 126.

32. Liu Zongzhou 劉宗周, *Lunyu xue-an* 論語學案, in *Liu Zi quanshu* 劉子全書 (1824 edition), 29:31a.

33. Shen Zengzhi 沈曾植, *Hairi Lou zhacong* 海日樓札叢 (Shanghai: Zhonghua, 1962), 214.

34. Quoted in *Qingyuan shan zhilue*, "fa-fan" 發凡 section, 5a.

35. Zhang Shengyan 張聖嚴, *Minmatsu Chûgoku bukkyo no kenkyu* 明末中國佛教の研究 (Tokyo: Sankibo busshorin, 1975), 283–286.

36. Chen Yuan 陳垣, *Mingji Dian Qian Fojiao kao* 明季滇黔佛教考 *juan* 2, esp. pp. 92–96 (Beijing: Zhonghua, 1962).

37. Ibid., 86.

38. "Qing Intellectualism," 120.

39. Thomas A. Metzger, *Escape from Predicament: Neo-Confucianism and China's Evolving Political Culture* (New York: Columbia University Press, 1975).

40. Qian Zhongshu, *Tanyi lu* (Shanghai: Kaiming shudian, 1948), 115–119.

41. *Guangyang Zaiji* 廣陽雜記 (Shanghai: Shangwu, 1941), 98.

ACKNOWLEDGMENTS

Chapter 1 originally appeared in Tu Weiming and Mary Evelyn Tucker, eds., *Confucian Spirituality* (New York: Crossroad Publishing, 2003), 62–80. This is volume 11A of *World Spirituality: An Encyclopedic History of the Religious Quest*.

Chapter 2 originally appeared in *Harvard Journal of Asiatic Studies* 25 (1964–1965): 80–122.

Chapter 3 originally appeared in *Harvard Journal of Asiatic Studies* 47, no. 2 (December 1987): 363–395. We have not reproduced the accompanying figures.—Eds.

Chapter 4 originally appeared in *Journal of Asian Studies* 41, no. 1 (November 1981): 81–85. Reprinted with the permission of Cambridge University Press. This is a review of Michael Loewe's *Ways to Paradise: The Chinese Quest for Immortality* (London: George Allen & Unwin, 1979).

Chapter 5 originally appeared in K. C. Chang, ed., *Food in Chinese Culture: Anthropological and Historical Perspectives* (New Haven: Yale University Press, 1977), 53–83.

Chapter 6 originally appeared in George Kao, ed., *The Translation of Things Past: Chinese History and Historiography* (Hong Kong: Chinese University of Hong Kong Press, 1982), 49–61. This article was translated by T. C. Tang and is from a Festschrift in honor of Professor Shen Gangbo 沈剛伯, *Shen Gangbo xiansheng bazhi rongqing lunwen ji* 沈剛伯先生八秩榮慶論文集 (Taipei: Lianjing, 1976). Figures have not been reproduced.—Eds.

Chapter 7 originally appeared in Donald Munro, ed., *Individualism and Holism: Studies in Confucian and Taoist Values* (Ann Arbor: University of Michigan Press, 1985), 121–155.

Chapter 8 originally appeared in Willard J. Peterson, Andrew H. Plaks, and Ying-shih Yü, eds., *The Power of Culture* (Hong Kong: Chinese University of Hong Kong Press, 1994), 158–171.

Chapter 9 originally appeared in Wing-tsit Chan, ed., *Chu Hsi and Neo-Confucianism* (Honolulu: University of Hawaii Press, 1986), 228–254.

Chapter 10 originally appeared in *The Challenge of the 21st Century: The Response of Eastern Ethics* (Seoul, South Korea: Asian Foundation International Symposium, 1998), 57–77.

Chapter 11 originally appeared in Wang Gungwu and Wong Siu-lun, eds., *Dynamic Hong Kong: Its Business and Culture* (Hong Kong: University of Hong Kong, Centre of Asian Studies, 1997), 1–84.

Chapter 13 originally appeared in *Ming Studies* 25 (Spring 1988): 24–66. The author would like to thank Professors F. W. Mote and Willard J. Peterson for their comments and suggestions on an earlier version of this article. For a rejoinder from Professor Ch'ien, see "Neither Structuralism nor Lovejoy's History of Ideas: A Disidentification with Professor Ying-Shih Yü's Review as a Discourse," *Ming Studies* 31 (1991): 42–86.

Chapter 14 originally appeared in *Journal of the American Oriental Society* 100, no. 2 (1980): 115–125, published by the American Oriental Society and reprinted with the permission of Cambridge University Press.

ADDRESS OF PROFESSOR YING-SHIH YÜ ON THE OCCASION OF RECEIVING THE JOHN W. KLUGE PRIZE AT THE LIBRARY OF CONGRESS

I feel enormously honored to be a corecipient of the John W. Kluge Prize in 2006, for which I am grateful. After much reflection, however, I have come to the realization that the main justification for my presence here today is that both the Chinese cultural tradition and Chinese intellectual history as a discipline are being honored through me. The former has been the subject of my lifetime scholarly pursuit, and the latter my chosen field of specialization.

When I first became seriously interested in the study of Chinese history and culture in the 1940s, the Chinese historical mind happened to be cast in a positivistic and antitraditionalistic mold. The whole Chinese past was viewed negatively, and whatever appeared to be uniquely Chinese was interpreted as a deviation from the universal norm of progress of civilization as exemplified in the historical development of the West. As a result, studies of aspects of the Chinese cultural tradition, from philosophy, law, and religion to literature and art, often amounted to condemnation and indictment. Needless to say, I was at a complete loss as to the Chinese cultural identity and, for that matter, also my personal identity. It was my good fortune that I was able to finish my college education in Hong Kong and pursued my graduate studies in the United States, now my adopted country.

As my intellectual horizon gradually widened over the years, the truth was beginning to dawn on me that Chinese culture must be clearly recognized as an indigenous tradition with characteristics distinctly its own. The crystallization of Chinese culture into its definitive shape took place in the time of Confucius (551–479 B.C.E.), a crucial moment in the ancient world better known in the West as the Axial Age. During this period, it has been observed, a spiritual awakening or "breakthrough" occurred in several highly developed cultures, including China, India, Persia, Israel, and Greece. It took the form of either philosophical reasoning or postmythical religious imagination, or, as in the case of China, a mixed type of moral-philosophic-religious consciousness. The awakening led directly to the emergence of the dichotomy between the actual world and the world beyond. The world beyond as a new vision provided the thinking individuals, be they philosophers, prophets, or sages, with the necessary transcending point from which the actual world could be examined and questioned, critically as well as reflectively. This is generally known as the original transcendence of the Axial Age, of which the exact shape, empirical content, and historical process varied from culture to culture. The transcendence is original in the sense that it would exert a long-lasting, shaping influence on the cultures involved.

As a result of the Chinese original transcendence in the time of Confucius, the all-important idea of *Dao* (Way) emerged as a symbol of the world beyond vis-à-vis the actual world of everyday life. But the Chinese transcendental world of *Dao* and the actual world of everyday life were conceived from the very beginning to be related to each other in a way that was different from other ancient cultures undergoing the Axial breakthrough. For example, there is nothing in the early Chinese philosophical visions that suggests Plato's conception of an unseen eternal world of which the actual world is only a pale copy. In the religious tradition, the sharp dichotomy of a Christian type between the world of God and the world of humans is also absent. Nor do we find in classical Chinese thought in all its varieties anything that closely resembles the radical negativity of early Buddhism, with its insistence on the unrealness and worthlessness of this world. By contrast, the world of *Dao* was not perceived as very far from the human world. As best expressed by Confucius: "The *Dao* is not far from man. When a man pursues the *Dao*, and remains away from man, his course cannot be considered the *Dao*." I must hasten to add, however, that the notion of *Dao* was not the monopoly of Confucius and his followers but was shared by all the major thinkers in the Chinese Axial Age, including Laozi, Mozi, and Zhuangzi. It was their common belief that *Dao* is hidden and yet functions everywhere in the human world; even men and women of simple intelligence can know and practice it in everyday life to a larger or lesser degree. Indeed, judging from the ever-growing and ever-deepening influences of the ideas originating in the Axial Age, especially Confucian and Daoist ideas, on all aspects of Chinese life down through the centuries, it may not be too much an exaggeration to suggest that *Dao* and history constitute the inside and the outside of Chinese civilization.

Taking the Chinese cultural tradition to be essentially one of indigenous origin and independent growth, I have tried over the decades to study Chinese history along two main lines. First, Chinese culture must be understood in its own terms, but at the same time, also in a comparative perspective. By "comparative perspective," I refer to both Indian Buddhism in the early imperial period and Western culture since the sixteenth century. Needless to say, China's second encounter with the West in the nineteenth century was a historical event of world-shaking magnitude. Since the beginning of the twentieth century, the Chinese mind has been largely preoccupied with the problematique of China-versus-the-West. To interpret the Chinese past solely in its own terms without a comparative perspective would surely run the risk of falling into the age-old trap of simple-minded Sinocentrism.

Second, in my study of Chinese intellectual, social, and cultural history, from classical antiquity to the twentieth century, my focus has always been placed on periods of change when one historical stage moved to the next. Compared to other civilizations, China's is particularly marked by its long historical continuity before, during, and since the Axial Age. But continuity and change went hand-in-hand in Chinese history. Therefore, the purpose I have set myself is twofold: first, to identify the major intellectual, social, and culture changes in the Chinese past and, second, to discern if at all possible the unique pattern of Chinese historical changes. More often than not, such broad and profound changes in Chinese history transcended the rise and fall of dynasties. Thus, the notion of "dynastic cycle," long held in traditional China but also briefly in vogue in the West, is highly misleading. In the early years of the twentieth century, Chinese historians, following the example of their Japanese colleagues, began to reconstruct and reinterpret the Chinese past according to the historical model of the West. Since then it has been generally assumed that China must have undergone similar stages of historical development as shown in European history. In the first half of the twentieth century, Chinese historians adopted the earlier European schemes of periodization by dividing Chinese history into ancient, medieval, and modern periods, which has been replaced since 1949 by the Marxist-Stalinist five-stage formulation. The latter remains the orthodoxy in China up to this day, at least in theory if not always in actual practice. This procrustean approach, whatever merits it may otherwise have, cannot possibly do full justice to Chinese culture as an indigenous tradition. Only by focusing on the unique course and shape of Chinese historical changes, I am convinced, can we hope to see more clearly how that great cultural tradition moved from stage to stage, driven mainly, if not entirely, by its internal dynamics.

Now let me turn to the question of how, as two different systems of values, does Chinese culture stand vis-à-vis Western culture in historical perspective? My earliest exposure to this question occurred in the late 1940s when the problematique of China-versus-the-West, mentioned earlier, dominated the Chinese intellectual world. It has not been out of my consciousness ever since. Living in the United States for half a century, the question has acquired a truly existential meaning for my life as I move between the two cultures from moment to moment. With some initial psychological readjustments, I have long been able to enjoy the American way of life while still retaining my Chinese cultural identity. However, the best guide with regard to whether Chinese culture is compatible with the core values of the West can only be provided by Chinese history.

China first encountered the modern West at the end of the sixteenth century when the Jesuits came to East Asia to do their missionary work. The culturally sensitive Matteo Ricci, who arrived in China in 1583, was very quick to discover that the Chinese religious atmosphere at that time was highly tolerant; Confucianism, Buddhism, and Daoism were generally regarded as one and the same thing. As a matter of fact, under the influence of Wang Yangming (1472–1529), late Ming Confucians firmly believed that each of the three religions in China captured a vision of the same *Dao* (Way). It was this spirit of religious tolerance that accounted for Ricci's extraordinary success in his conversion of many leading members of the Confucian elite, notably Xu Guangqi (1562–1633), Li Zhizao (1565–1630), and Yang Tingyun (1557–1627)—the "three pillars of evangelization." The Confucian faith in the sameness of human mind and the universal accessibility of *Dao* to every human person anywhere led some Chinese converts to promote a synthesis of Christianity with Confucianism. The Chinese *Dao* was now further expanded to include Christianity. This early relationship between China and the West at the religious level can by no means be described as a conflictual one.

In the late nineteenth century, it was also the open-minded Confucians who enthusiastically embraced values and ideas dominant in the modern West, such as democracy, liberty, equality, rule of law, autonomy of the individual person, and, above all, human rights. When some of them visited Europe or America for the first time and stayed there long enough to make firsthand observations, they were all deeply impressed, first of all, by the ideals and institutions of Western constitutional democracy. Wang Tao (1828–1897), who assisted James Legge in his English translation of Confucian classics, returned to Hong Kong from England in 1870 praising her political and legal systems to the sky. He was probably the first Confucian scholar to use the term "democracy" in Chinese (*minzhu*). Wang exerted a considerable influence on Confucian political thinking in the late Qing. At the turn of the century, there were two rival Confucian schools in China known as the New Text and Old Text, respectively. Both advocated democracy, though each in its own way. The former was in favor of constitutional monarchy, while the latter pushed for republicanism. Perhaps inspired by Wang Tao, who compared the British political and judicial systems favorably to China's Golden Age as described in Confucian classics, both Confucian schools began a systematic search for the origins and evolution of democratic ideas in early Confucian texts. In so doing, it is clear that they took the compatibility between Chinese culture and Western culture as two systems of values for granted.

Last but not least, I wish to say a word about "human rights." Like "democracy," "human rights" as a term is linguistically specific to the West and nonexistent in traditional Confucian discourse. However, if we agree that the concept of "human rights" as defined in the United Nations' Universal Declaration of 1948 is predicated on the double recognition of a common humanity and human dignity, then we are also justified to speak of a Confucian idea of "human rights" without the Western terminology. Recognition of a common humanity and respect for human dignity are both clearly articulated in the *Analects* of Confucius, the *Mencius*, and other early texts. It is remarkable that by the first century c.e. at the latest, the Confucian notion of human dignity was openly referred to in imperial decrees as sufficient grounds for the prohibition of the sale or killing of slaves. Both imperial decrees, dated 9 and 35 c.e., respectively, cited the same famous Confucian dictum: "Of all living things produced by Heaven and Earth, the human person is the noblest." Slavery as an institution was never accepted by Confucianism as legitimate. It was this Confucian humanism that predisposed late Qing Confucians to be so readily appreciative of the Western theory and practice of human rights.

If history is any guide, then there seems to be a great deal of overlapping consensus in basic values between Chinese culture and Western culture. After all, recognition of common humanity and human dignity is what the Chinese *Dao* has been about. I am more convinced than ever that once Chinese culture returns to the main flow of *Dao*, the problematique of China-versus-the-West will also come to an end.

Princeton University, December 1, 2006
(This talk was delivered on December 5, 2006, and published by the Library of Congress at http://www.loc.gov/today/pr/2006/06-A07.html)

ACCEPTANCE SPEECH ON THE OCCASION OF RECEIVING THE TANG PRIZE FOR SINOLOGY

To be awarded the inaugural Tang Prize in Sinology is the greatest honor I have received in my life. Needless to say, I feel grateful and elated even though deep in my heart, I must confess, lurks an indelible sense of undeservedness.

Sinology, my own field of research, writing, and teaching, calls for a comment. To begin with, I must pay tribute to the Tang Prize Foundation for its farsightedness in recognizing Sinology as one of its four prize categories. In my considered opinion, Sinology as a scholarly endeavor of ever-growing world importance is more in need of encouragement and support now than ever before. It is truly remarkable that the Tang Prize comes right in the nick of time.

In recent decades, Sinology as a field of study has been undergoing a gradual but very significant transformation. China has come to be viewed more and more as a civilization of indigenous origin and independent growth very much comparable to other long-lasting ancient civilizations such as India, Persia, Israel, and Greece. Unlike in the past, we begin to move away from the practice of reconstructing and interpreting the Chinese past according to the historical model of the West. Instead, Sinologists, in ever-growing numbers, tend to be interested in understanding the growth of Chinese civilization on its own terms. It is generally assumed that only by focusing on the unique course and shape of Chinese historical changes can we hope to see more clearly how that great cultural tradition moved from stage to stage, driven primarily by its internal dynamics. However, this must not be mistaken as advocacy of isolationism. On the contrary, the importance of a comparative perspective in Sinological studies is more emphasized today than ever before. The reason is not far to seek. The uniqueness of Chinese civilization and its developmental pattern cannot be firmly and fully established without comparisons with other civilizations, especially the Western one. On the other hand, to study Chinese history in total isolation would inevitably fall into the age-old trap of Sinocentrism.

As a result, Sinology today has become thoroughly globalized. Unlike in the first half of the twentieth century, we rarely, if ever, speak of Sinology along national lines such as Chinese, Japanese, French, or American. Sinology is one anywhere on the globe. At this very juncture, my memory naturally goes to my late mentor Yang Lien-sheng, who introduced me to world Sinology at Harvard in the late 1950s. In his 1967 introduction to Yang's path-breaking *Excursions in Sinology* [Cambridge, Mass.: Harvard University Press, 1969], Paul Demiéville, the dean of Sinology in Europe, characterizes the latter's scholarship as "international, truly *tianxia* (天下)." This clearly suggests that globalization of Sinology was already well underway at the time, and my mentor Yang was positively identified by Demiéville as one of its earliest practitioners.

In this age of rapid globalization of ours, this new development in Sinology urgently needs to be carried further on an ever-growing scale. It is therefore my earnest hope that the Tang Prize may serve to attract more young talents with vibrant minds that will bring fresh perspectives to the Sinological world.

This talk was delivered at the Academia Sinica in Taipei on September 18, 2014.

INDEX